G	growth	% CS_{mkt}	percent of common stock at market value to total value
GNP	gross national product		
IDB	Interamerican Development Bank	% D_{mkt}	percent of debt at market value to total value
IMF	International Monetary Fund	% PS_{mkt}	percent of preferred stock at market value to total value
K_e	cost of equity capital		
K_i	cost of debt	% RE	percent of retained earnings to net income after taxes
K_i(AT)	after-tax cost of debt		
K_i(BT)	before-tax cost of debt		
K_o	cost of capital	PI	profitability index
K_{ps}	cost of preferred stock	port	portfolio
LIFO	last-in, first-out	Prob	probability
MC	marginal contribution	PS_{mkt}	preferred stock at market value
MC$	marginal contribution in dollars		
MC%	marginal contribution as a percent	PV	present value
		r	correlation coefficient
MktPr or MP	market price	R or Rtn (tgt)	target return
NASD	National Association of Securities Dealers	RE	retained earnings
		ROE	return on equity
NCB	net cash benefit	ROI	return on investment
NCO	net cash outlay	Rtn	return
NIAT	net income after taxes	SEC	Securities and Exchange Commission
NIFO	next-in, first-out	SML	security market line
NP	net proceeds	SP	selling price
NPV	net present value	σ	sigma (standard deviation)
OL	operating leverage	TR	total revenues or tax rate
P	par value		
P/D	price-dividend ratio	V	coefficient of variation
P/E	price-earnings ratio	V(t)	value in period "t"
P/Enorm	normal price-earnings ratio	VC	variable costs
		V_{mkt}	value of the firm at market
%(n)	dollars invested in "n" as a percent of total dollars	V_{mkt} (max)	maximum value of the firm at market

Handbook For
FINANCIAL DECISION MAKERS

Handbook For
FINANCIAL DECISION MAKERS

JOHN J. HAMPTON
Seton Hall University

RESTON PUBLISHING COMPANY, INC.
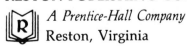
A Prentice-Hall Company
Reston, Virginia

658.15
H232

To Frances and Charles
God Bless you Both

Library of Congress Cataloging in Publication Data

Hampton, John J
  Handbook for financial decision makers.

  1. Corporation—Finance—Handbooks, manuals, etc. 2. Corporations—Finance—
Dictionaries. I. Title.

HG4011.H283	658.1'5	78-7440
ISBN 0-87909-353-6		

© 1979 by Reston Publishing Company, Inc.
A Prentice-Hall Company
Reston, Virginia 22090

1 3 5 7 9 10 8 6 4 2

PRINTED IN THE UNITED STATES OF AMERICA

CONTENTS

v

CONTENTS

PREFACE

A Handbook can be many things including:

1. *A Dictionary.* A collection of terms and definitions of a discipline.
2. *An Encyclopedia.* An authoritative examination of the major ideas and concepts in a field of inquiry.
3. *A Cookbook.* A listing of prominent "recipes" with step-by-step directions for success in applying techniques from an area of endeavor.

This *Handbook* serves all three purposes for the field of corporate finance. The alphabetical listing of over 700 terms and concepts serves as both a dictionary and encyclopedia of finance. The "How To" techniques provide "recipes" for managing working capital and capital investments and analyzing a broad range of decision areas in financial management.

This is meant to be a "no-nonsense" *Handbook.* Few words are wasted in getting to the point. All entries are clearly labeled and cross-referenced. Some techniques are relatively simple, some fairly sophisticated, all are straightforward. Certain people will find this a handy book to have, including:

Corporate Financial Decision Makers. Even the most sophisticated financial manager will find useful tools, techniques, and ideas in this book. Just as you will recognize some things, you will not have given much thought to others. In a busy corporation, who has the time for speculative financial thinking? Some of this has been done by the author.

Corporate Non-financial Decision Makers. All seasoned executives gain a working familiarity with finance, but not necessarily a complete grasp. This is a book to fill in some gaps. It provides terms, definitions, and explanations. Finance is the language of business, and this book will help you to speak and understand it better.

M.B.A. Candidates. Frequently, the graduate finance course is not all that clear or practical. This is a fact of life. How handy it would be to have some reference point for understanding the theories of Miller and Modigliani, Solomon, Gordon, Wlater, Markowitz, Graham and Dodd, Durand, Sharpe, and others. And how useful to read current concepts in capital structure management, capital budgeting, mergers, cost of capital, and the capital asset pricing model. This is a *Handbook* to be used in conjunction with an M.B.A. program.

You will find some extra features in this *Handbook* that help justify its price; like a section on International Finance; a collection of explanations of classic articles in the financial literature; some discussions on decision making under inflation; and a complete examination of the capital asset pricing model.

I think you will be pleased with this *Handbook*. I have done everything I possibly could to make it complete, relevant, and understandable. If you are pleased with it, great. If you have comments, suggestions, or criticisms, I invite you to write me at the W. Paul Stillman School of Business Administration, Seton Hall University, South Orange, New Jersey.

It takes time and energy and dedication to write a book like this. The project was made easier by Moira Juliano whose typing and editing went far beyond the call of duty. Thanks also to Weldon Rackley who conceived the project and contributed many of the ideas. We hope the final product meets your needs and expectations.

J.J.H.

Part One

"HOW TO" TECHNIQUES FOR FINANCIAL DECISION MAKERS

Chapter 1

CAPITAL BUDGETING

1. CASH-FLOW STREAM, HOW TO CALCULATE

The cash flow on a proposed **capital budgeting** project should be calculated using a step-by-step approach. This increases the chances that we will consider all factors resulting from a proposal which may affect the cash flow. Before beginning the step-by-step calculation, it is important to understand the kind of **cash-flow stream** we are seeking.

Differential After-Tax Stream

The differential stream results from taking the difference between a cash-flow stream without the new proposal and a stream with the new proposal. Several characteristics of a stream such as the one shown in Table 1-1 are the following:

1. *Normally Begins with an Outlay.* The decision to commit funds to a capital-budgeting project involves an initial outlay of funds. Reflecting this situation, the stream will begin with a **net cash outlay.** This is the amount of money that must be spent to get the project underway.
2. *Normally Has Inflows Downstream.* Once the money is invested, the firm expects a project to bring an additional return to the firm. This is shown in the form of inflows after the initial expenditure. The inflows may begin in year 1 or 2 or later, but they are normally sustained once the project begins to produce a return. These inflows are called **net cash benefits.**

3. *Some Actions Appear to Be Counted Twice.* Because the stream is based on the difference between two other cash-flow streams, it often appears that an item is being double-counted. As an example of this problem, we shall consider the cash value of the existing machinery when new machinery is being considered. As is shown in Table 1-2, the existing machinery can be sold immediately if the new project is accepted. Whatever cash is received becomes an inflow in year zero to the stream that shows cash effects as a result of the new purchase. If the new machinery were not purchased, the old machine would continue in operation and would be sold in the fifth year. This would then be a cash effect in the nonpurchase stream in year 5. Both effects would show up in the **differential after-tax cash-flow stream,** but it is because any one action can occur in each stream and it can occur at different times.

TABLE 1-1. Differential After-Tax Cash-Flow Stream.

Year	0	1	2	3	4
Cash Flow	−400,000	+70,000	+90,000	+110,000	+160,000

TABLE 1-2. Sale of Existing Machinery Appears Twice in the Differential Stream.

	Without Purchase	With Purchase	Differential
Sale of existing machinery immediately if not needed		Inflow	Inflow
Sale of existing machinery in year 5 if needed	Inflow		Outflow

4. *Nonpurchase Stream Inflows Are Differential Outflows and Vice Versa.* From Table 1-2, notice that the sale of existing machinery in 5 years is an inflow in the nonpurchase column but an outflow in the differential column. Let's try to understand why this happens. If the firm purchases the new machinery, it receives the inflow from the sale of the existing machinery immediately; this is an inflow in year zero. But it loses the inflow it would have received in year 5. Since this is a lost inflow, it is the same as an outflow in differential stream in year 5. Table 1-3 shows differential effects of inflows and outlays.

TABLE 1-3. Differential Effects of Cash Inflows and Outlays.

	Without Purchase	With Purchase	Differential
Situation with two inflows	+1,000	+1,200	+200
	+1,200	+1,000	−200
Situation with two outlays	−1,000	−1,200	−200
	−1,200	−1,000	+200

With these basic characteristics in mind, it is time to begin the step-by-step determination of a differential after-tax stream.

Financial Data for a Sample Problem

To illustrate the process of calculating a cash-flow stream, consider a firm that has an old machine and is considering the purchase of a new machine. The relevant data are as follows:

1. The new machine will cut operating expenses from $65,000 to $56,000 annually because one $9,000 operator can be transferred. Both machines involve the same approximate maintenance costs and have similar outputs.
2. The new machine costs $22,000 plus an additional $2,000 for transportation and installation.
3. Both the existing and new machines have service lives of 4 years beginning in year zero.
4. The new machine will require tying up $2,000 in additional inventories.
5. The **book salvage value** of the old machine is $8,000 and it is being depreciated at $2,000 per year to a zero book salvage value. If the existing machine were sold today, its **cash salvage value** would be $4,000. If it is held 4 years, it would have $1,000 cash salvage value.
6. In 4 years, the new machine will have a $4,000 book salvage value and a $3,000 cash salvage value. **Straight-line depreciation** is used for all the firm's equipment.

These data are presented in a tabular format in Figure 1-1.

Differential before-tax cash savings (65,000 − 56,000)	$ 9,000
Cost of the new machine	22,000
Transportation and installation of the new machine	2,000
Book salvage value of the new machine	4,000
Cash salvage value of the new machine	3,000
Working capital tied up during service life of new machine	2,000
Straight-line depreciation on the new machine	
Annual depreciation on the old machine, to zero book value	2,000
Current book salvage value of the old machine	8,000
Cash salvage value of the old machine today	4,000
Cash salvage value of the old machine in 4 years	1,000
Service lives of the old and new machines, 4 years each.	

Figure 1-1. Financial Data Affecting Cash Flow of Old and New Machines.

Step 1: Calculate the Net Cash Outlay

The net cash outlay is the differential amount of money that will be spent when the investment is made in year zero. Figure 1-2 shows the five major factors involved with this calculation.

Total Cost	= purchase price plus transportation and installation of the new machinery
Cash Salvage Value, Old Machine	= cash received for the old machine minus any costs associated with selling or removing it
Tax Savings	= tax rate times book loss, if any (book loss is the current book value minus the cash salvage value)
Additional Taxes To Be Paid	= opposite of tax savings; tax rate times gain on sale of old machinery (gain is the cash salvage value minus the book value)
Changes in Working Capital	= outlay of cash to be tied up or return of cash freed in inventories or receivables during service life of new machine

Figure 1-2. Factors Involved in Calculation of Net Cash Outlay.

The formula for calculating net cash outlay in our example is shown in Figure 1-3.

NCO = total cost ± changes in working capital + cash salvage value, old machine ± additional taxes or tax savings

NCO = − 24,000 − 2,000 + 4,000 + 2,000 = − 20,000 NCO

where

total cost = $22,000 purchase price plus $2,000 transportation and installation

changes in working capital = increase of $2,000 (an outlay)

cash salvage value, old machine = $4,000

tax savings =	Book value, old machine	$8,000
	Cash salvage value, today	4,000
	Book loss	$4,000
	50 percent tax rate	x .50
	Tax savings	$2,000

Figure 1-3. Calculation of Net Cash Outlay.

Step 2: Calculate the Depreciation on the New Machine

To keep the calculations simple, we shall always use straight-line depreciation. In a sense, this is unrealistic, since firms always accept the higher cash flow generated by **accelerated depreciation.** When performing actual calculations on the job, remember to always use the depreciation method employed by the firm for income tax purposes since only this method affects the actual tax shield and cash flow. Most firms use accelerated depreciation for tax purposes and straight line for reporting to stockholders. In these cases, the accelerated method is used.

In our example where the firm is using straight line for both income and tax reporting purposes, the depreciation on the new machine is given in Figure 1-4.

Depreciable cost = total cost of machine   − book salvage value
           = $24,000   − 4,000   = $20,000

Annual depreciation = $\frac{\text{depreciable cost}}{\text{years of life}}$ = $\frac{20,000}{4}$ = $5,000

Figure 1-4. Calculation of Depreciation on the New Machine.

With the straight-line method, the $5,000 depreciation is the same for each of the 4 years of the machine's estimated service life. With accelerated methods, the amount of depreciation differs each year and must be calculated separately for each year.

Step 3: Calculate Differential Depreciation

In this step, we compare the depreciation from the new machine with the depreciation from the old machine. Note that these are both inflows, but they are in different cash-flow columns—without the purchase and with the purchase. Thus, the differential means that we subtract the old machine's depreciation from the new machine's. Stated another way, since we shall not keep both machines, we shall gain the $5,000 depreciation tax shield and lose the $2,000 tax shield if we purchase the new machine, for a differential depreciation of $5,000 - 2,000 = $3,000. This figure is the same for all 4 years. If the old machine had depreciation for only 2 more years at $2,000 a year, the differential depreciation for years 3 and 4 would be $5,000 - 0 = $5,000.

Step 4: Calculate Annual Differential After-Tax Inflows

One technique for this calculation involves two columns, one for accounting effects and one for cash effects. This is illustrated in Table 1-4.
Note that the inflow is calculated in both columns. We add back depreciation in the accounting column or we can subtract the additional taxes from the cash savings in the cash-flow column.

If the differential figures are the same for each year (that is, if the cash flow is steady), we only perform this calculation once. If the cash flows are variable, a separate one must be calculated for each year.

TABLE 1-4. Calculating Annual Differential After-Tax Inflows.

		Accounting	Cash Flow
a.	Annual before-tax savings ($65,000 − $56,000) in both columns, since it is cash and accounting savings	$9,000	$9,000
b.	Less differential depreciation (affects accounting data only)	−3,000	
c.	Additional taxable income	$6,000	
d.	Additional tax to be paid (both columns since it must be paid in cash)	−3,000	−3,000
e.	Additional net income (NIAT)	$3,000	
f.	Add back differential depreciation to get cash flow	+3,000	
g.	Differential after-tax cash inflow	+$6,000	+$6,000

Step 5: Calculate Effects in Final Year

In the final year, two effects are of special importance to the cash-flow stream:

   1. *Working Capital Is Returned.* Any funds tied up at the beginning of the project are treated as inflows in the final year. In our example, the $2,000 **working capital** is an inflow in the differential column.

Net After-Tax Cash Salvage Value, New Machine	−	Net After-Tax Cash Salvage Value, Old Machine	=	Net Inflow (Outflow) in Final Year
$3,000 cash salvage value + 500 tax saving[1]		$1,000 cash salvage value −500 additional taxes[2]		
$3,500 net cash value		$ 500 net cash value	=	$3,000 net cash value (a differential inflow)

[1] For the new machine, the tax saving results because the firm would sell a $4,000 book value machine for $3,000, thereby incurring a $1,000 loss and a $500 tax saving.

[2] For the old machine, the additional taxes must be paid on the gain that results when the firm sells the zero book value machine for $1,000. The tax on the $1,000 gain would be $500.

Figure 1-5.   Net After-Tax Salvage-Value Effects in Final Year.

2. *Cash Salvage Value Effects Are Included.* The cash salvage values are difficult to handle but follow the general form of subtracting the after-tax cash salvage value of the old machine from the after-tax cash salvage value of the new machine to get a net inflow, as shown in Figure 1-5.

By combining the annual differential after-tax inflow (step 4) with the working capital and net salvage value effects, the firm has a final year inflow of $11,000, as follows:

Differential After-Tax Flows + Working Capital + Net Cash
Salvage Value $6,000 + $ 2,000
              + $ 3,000
              = $11,000 inflow in the final year

Step 6: Write the Differential After-Tax Cash-Flow Stream

The final cash-flow stream shows differential cash inflows and outlays as a result of the purchase of the new machine. It is written as follows:

Year	Differential Flows
0	− 20,000 _____Net cash outlay
1	+ 6,000
2	+ 6,000 _____Net cash benefits
3	+ 6,000
4	+11,000

This stream shows both the timing and amount of the net cash outlay and net cash benefits over the life of the new machine.

Step 7: Check To Be Sure All Effects Are Included

Any cash that is received, spent, or otherwise tied up during the life of the project must be included in the stream. All effects must be differential—the difference between having the project or machine and not having it. If the stream is inaccurate with respect to differential cash-flow effects, it cannot be used validly with techniques that consider the time value of money.

A Solved Problem

To illustrate the step-by-step approach to calculating a differential after-tax cash-flow stream, Figure 1-6 contains a solved problem.

Given:

1. Purchase price of the new machine $100,000
2. Transportation and installation   20,000
3. Increase in working capital in year zero   25,000
4. Book salvage value of the new machine   20,000
5. Cash salvage value of the new machine in 4 years   35.000
6. Annual differential cash savings before depreciation and taxes
   (also called differential EBDIT = earnings before depreciation,
   interest, and taxes)   40,000
7. Cash salvage value of the old machine today   50,000
8. Cash salvage value of the old machine in 4 years   10,000
9. Service life of both machines is 4 years.
10. Straight-line depreciation is used for the new machine.
11. The old machine will be depreciated at a rate of $10,000
    annually for 2 more years.
12. Current book value of the old machine   40,000

Step 1: Net Cash Outlay:

NCO =	Purchase price	− 100,000	*(a $40,000 machine will
	Transportation and installation	− 20,000	sell for $50,000, resulting
	Working capital tied up	− 25,000	in a $10,000 gain and
	Cash salvage value, old machine	+ 50,000	$5,000 taxes)
	Taxes on gain from sale of machinery	− 5,000*	
	Net Cash Outlay	− 100,000	

Step 2: Depreciation on New Machine:

$$\text{Annual depreciation} = \frac{\text{total cost} - \text{book salvage value}}{\text{years of service life}} = \frac{120,000 - 20,000}{4}$$

$$= \$25,000 \text{ per year}$$

Step 3: Differential Depreciation:

Year	Depreciation, New		Depreciation, Old		Differential Depreciation
1	$25,000	−	$10,000	=	$15,000
2	$25,000	−	$10,000	=	$15,000
3	$25,000	−	0	=	$25,000
4	$25,000	−	0	=	$25,000

Step 4: Annual Differential After-Tax Cash Flows:

Differential cash inflows = annual savings in cash before depreciation and taxes minus taxes to be paid on annual savings (cash-flow column)

or

Differential cash inflows = annual cash savings less differential depreciation less additional taxes plus differential depreciation (accounting column)

	Differential Cash Inflows (Years 1 and 2)		Differential Cash Inflows (Years 3 and 4)	
	Accounting	Cash Flow	Accounting	Cash Flow
a. EBDIT (annual cash savings)	$40,000	$40,000	$40,000	$40,000
b. Less differential depreciation	−15,000		−25,000	
c. Additional taxable income	$25,000		$15,000	
d. Additional tax	−12,500	−12,500	− 7,500	7,500
e. Additional NIAT	$12,500		$ 7,500	
f. Add back differential depreciation	+15,000		+25,000	
g. After-tax cash flow	$27,500	$27,500	$32,000	$32,500

Figure 1-6. Seven-Step Process for Calculating a Cash-Flow Stream.

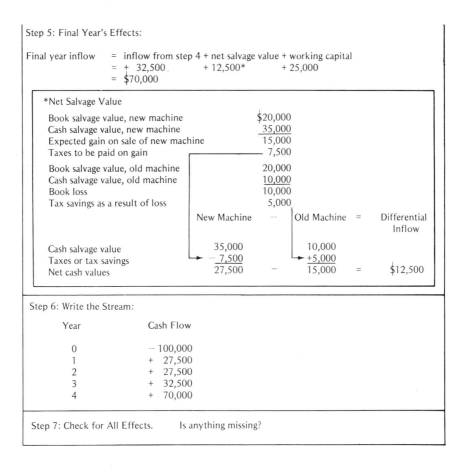

Step 5: Final Year's Effects:

Final year inflow = inflow from step 4 + net salvage value + working capital
                   = + 32,500   + 12,500*   + 25,000
                   = $70,000

*Net Salvage Value

Book salvage value, new machine	$20,000
Cash salvage value, new machine	35,000
Expected gain on sale of new machine	15,000
Taxes to be paid on gain	7,500
Book salvage value, old machine	20,000
Cash salvage value, old machine	10,000
Book loss	10,000
Tax savings as a result of loss	5,000

	New Machine	−	Old Machine	=	Differential Inflow
Cash salvage value	35,000		10,000		
Taxes or tax savings	− 7,500		+5,000		
Net cash values	27,500	−	15,000	=	$12,500

Step 6: Write the Stream:

Year	Cash Flow
0	− 100,000
1	+ 27,500
2	+ 27,500
3	+ 32,500
4	+ 70,000

Step 7: Check for All Effects.   Is anything missing?

Figure 1-6.   Continued.

2. INFLATION IN THE CAPITAL BUDGET, HOW TO ANALYZE

Because investment decisions involve long periods of time, a firm is usually concerned about the effects of **inflation** on its capital budget. When a firm invests in a **fixed asset**, the following items are most likely to be affected by inflation:

1. *Revenues.* When a firm purchases a fixed asset, it expects to generate revenues from that **asset**. These revenues may be in the form of output which can be sold, as in the case of a machine, or may be in the form of rentals on the use of the asset, as in the case of a truck purchased by a truck leasing company. Revenues are said to be responsive to inflationary pressures if the firm can raise the selling price of the output from the machine or the rental charge for the

truck. In some cases, however, revenues will not be responsive to inflation. This happens when market conditions or price controls restrict the ability of a firm to raise its selling prices. Or, in the case of the truck company, it could happen if the company entered into a long-term rental agreement at a fixed rate.

2. *Costs.* As a general rule, most of the costs associated with a fixed asset are responsive to inflation. Labor, raw materials, and maintenance are three major costs that rise with changes in a nation's cost of living. In a period of rising prices, it costs more to operate a machine and produce goods to sell; it costs more to operate and maintain a truck.

3. *Final Salvage Value.* In the capital budgeting process, the firm will estimate the final salvage value of the asset at the end of its service life. In a period of inflation, this salvage value will generally be higher than would be expected in a period of stable prices. The higher final salvage value represents a benefit that the firm realizes from inflation.

4. *Working Capital.* During the service life of a fixed asset, the firm will tie up working capital in support of the asset. During a period of inflation, the firm will periodically have to increase the level of working capital. This additional working capital will have a financing cost to the firm and is, in effect, an additional cost owed to inflation.

Two items will generally not be affected by inflation, as follows:

1. *Tax Savings from Depreciation.* The firm's depreciation schedule on a fixed asset does not change during periods of rising price levels. Thus, the tax savings from depreciation are not responsive to inflation.

2. *Fixed-Rate Financing Charges.* If a portion of the asset is financed with fixed-rate, long-term debt, the financing costs will not be responsive to inflationary pressure. On the other hand, as variable-rate financing becomes increasingly popular, high rates of inflation will produce increasingly high interest costs over the life of an asset. A firm that finances a fixed asset with variable-rate financing may therefore experience higher financing costs during periods of inflation.

Theoretical Adjustment for Inflation

Conceptually, it is possible to adjust for inflation in the capital budgeting calculation. To illustrate this process, let us consider a cash-flow stream that involves an outlay of $100,000 in year zero, a return of $30,000 a year for 3 years, and a $50,000 return in the 4th year. In the absence of any inflationary effects, the cash-flow stream and formula are as shown in Table 1-5.

TABLE 1-5. Present Value of Cash-Flow Stream and Formula, Inflation Not Considered.

Year	Cash Flow		10% Present- Value Factor		Present Value
0	−100,000	÷	1.00	=	−100,000
1	+ 30,000	÷	1.10	=	+ 27,273
2	+ 30,000	÷	1.10^2	=	+ 24,793
3	+ 30,000	÷	1.10^3	=	+ 22,539
4	+ 50,000	÷	1.10^4	=	+ 34,151
			Net Present Value		$ 8,756

$$\text{Profitability Index} = \frac{108,756}{100,000} = 1.09$$

Formula:

$$\text{Present Value} = \sum_{t=1}^{n} \frac{\text{Cash Flows}}{(1 + i)^n}$$

Now let us consider inflation. One assumption that we could make is that the cash inflows were not increased to keep up with inflation. Thus, inflation would erode the value of the inflows in the cash-flow stream. In this situation we must discount the cash flows both by the **time value** of money and by an **inflation factor,** as shown in Table 1-6.

TABLE 1-6. Present Value of Cash-Flow Stream and Formula, Inflows Do Not Increase to Keep up with Inflation.

Year	Cash Flow		10% Present Value Factor		8% Inflation Factor		Present Value
0	−100,000	÷	1.00	÷	1.00	=	−100,000
1	+ 30,000	÷	1.10	÷	1.08	=	+ 25,253
2	+ 30,000	÷	1.10^2	÷	1.08^2	=	+ 21,256
3	+ 30,000	÷	1.10^3	÷	1.08^3	=	+ 17,893
4	+ 50,000	÷	1.10^4	÷	1.08^4	=	+ 25,102
					Net Present Value		$−10,496

$$\text{Profitability Index} = \frac{89,504}{100,000} = .90$$

Formula:

$$\text{Present Value} = \sum_{t=1}^{n} \frac{\text{Cash Flows}}{(1 + i)^n \, (1 + \text{Inflation Rate})^n}$$

   As can be seen from Table 1-6, if the cash inflows do not increase to keep up with inflation, the capital budgeting project will be converted from an $8,756 positive to a $10,496 negative net present value. In fact, virtually all cash-flow streams in a firm's capital budget would keep up with inflation. Therefore, the forecasted cash inflows must be adjusted for inflation only when appropriate. Table 1-7 identifies elements of the cash-flow stream which should be adjusted to account for inflationary effects.

TABLE 1-7. Elements of Cash-Flow Stream to Be Adjusted for Inflation.

We Adjust	*We Do Not Adjust*
Revenues—if we can raise prices.	Revenues—if market conditions or price controls restrict ability to raise prices.
Costs—at forecasted rate of inflation.	Depreciation tax shields.
Estimated salvage value.	
Working capital required.	

   It is one matter to discuss the theory of inflation in capital budgets. It is another to incorporate it in the decision-making process. The following solved problem which varies slightly from the above format, illustrates a practical technique for dealing with inflation in a capital budgeting proposal.

   EXAMPLE: A company is evaluating an investment of $700,000 in an airplane that has a 5-year contract to carry mail from Toronto to a mining camp near Hudson Bay. The contract calls for revenues of $1,110,000 a year for 5 years on a fixed basis. To earn these revenues, the aircraft will have first-year expenses as follows: salary $120,000; maintenance $140,000; fuel $520,000; and miscellaneous $40,000. Costs are expected to rise at the following annual rates: salaries 10 percent, maintenance 15 percent, fuel 8 percent, and miscellaneous 5 percent. The firm's **cost of capital** *is 10 percent and the company pays no taxes. What is the* **net present value** *and* **profitability index** *on this investment without considering inflation? With inflation?*

   ANSWER: Without inflation, $399,080 is the net present value and the profitability index is 1.57.

Year	Cash Flow	10% Present Value Factor	Present Value	*Cash Profit
0	−700,000	1.00	−700,000	
1	+290,000*	.909	+263,610	1,110,000
2	+290,000	.826	+239,540	−120,000
3	+290,000	.751	+217,790	−140,000
4	+290,000	.683	+198,070	−520,000
5	+290,000	.621	+180,090	−40,000
		Net Present Value	+399,080	$290,000

$$\text{Profitability Index} = \frac{1,099,080}{700,000} = 1.57$$

With inflation, — 180,012 is the net present value and .74 is the profitability index.

	First Year	Second Year	Third Year	Fourth Year	Fifth Year
Revenues (fixed for 5 years)	1,110,000	1,110,000	1,110,000	1,110,000	1,110,000
Salaries (10% increase each year)	−120,000	−132,000	−145,200	−159,720	−175,692
Maintenance (15% increase each year)	−140,000	−161,000	−185,150	−212,923	−244,861
Fuel (8% increase each year)	−520,000	−561,600	−606,528	−655,050	−707,454
Miscellaneous (5% increase each year)	−40,000	−42,000	−44,100	−46,305	−48,620
Annual Cash Profit (Loss)	+290,000	+213,400	+129,022	+36,002	(−66,627)

Year	Cash-Flow Stream	10% Present Value Factor	Present Value
0	(700,000)	÷1.00	(700,000)
1	+290,000	÷1.10	+263,610
2	+213,400	÷1.10^2	+176,268
3	+129,022	÷1.10^3	96,896
4	+36,002	÷1.10^4	24,589
5	(66, 627)	÷1.10^5	(41,375)
		Net Present Value	(180,012)

$$\text{Profitability Index} = \frac{519,988}{700,000} = .74$$

As a result of inflation, a very profitable investment can be turned into a losing operation in a relatively short period of time. In our example, a 1.57 profitability index becomes .74 with only moderate inflation. A firm should exercise extreme care in handling inflation in its capital budgeting process.

3.   INTERNAL RATE OF RETURN, HOW TO CALCULATE

The **internal-rate-of-return** method calculates the actual rate of return provided by a specific stream of net cash benefits as compared to a specific net cash outlay. It uses a trial-and-error approach to find the **discount factor** (which is actually the rate of return) that equates the original investment to the net cash benefits. If we find that the 10-percent factor sets the benefits equal to the outlay, the internal rate of return for the investment is 10 percent.

As an example of this technique, we shall calculate a rate of return for a 4-year stream, as shown.

Year	Differential Flows	
0	−$18,000 − − − − − − − − − −	Net Cash Outlay
1	+ 6,000	
2	+ 6,000	Net Cash
3	+ 6,000	Benefits
4	+10,000	

We set the net cash outlay equal to the net cash benefits times the appropriate discount factors. The stream has an annuity of $6,000 for 3 years and a single payment in the year 4. The formula is

Net Cash
   Outlay   Net Cash Benefits
-$18,000 = ($6,000)(3-year annuity factor from Appendix B)
        + ($10,000)(4-year factor from Appendix A)

Given this formula, we must now estimate the rate of return and select a discount factor. This is essentially a trial-and-error process that is helped by experience. Try 10 percent as a factor. Using Appendices A and B, we get

10% factor
    -$18,000 = ($6,000)(2.487) + ($10,000)(.683)
            = $14,922 + 6,830 = $21,752

A net cash benefits of $21,752 is not very close to the net cash outlay of $18,000. We must now try another factor, and the question is *do we go up or down?* The rule is

In Using Present-Value Tables, Raising the Discount Factor Lowers the Present Value. Lowering the Discount Factor Raises the Present Value.

Thus, the discount factor of 10 percent is too low. Raise it to 18 percent to lower the present value of the benefits.

18% factor
    -$18,000 = ($6,000)(2.174) + ($10,000)(.516)
            = $13,044 + 5,160 = $18,204

This is much closer but still a little high. Try 20 percent to see if we can bracket the $18,000 net cash outlay.

20% factor
    − $18,000 = ($6,000)(2.106) + ($10,000)(.482) = $17,456

The answer is that the rate of return for the stream is between 18 and 20 percent, but closer to 18 percent because $18,204 is closer to $18,000 than is $17,456.

Alternative Technique

An alternative method of gaining this answer involves only the use of Appendix A. We can ignore the annuity of $6,000 for 3 years and treat the figures as individual payments. The formula is

$$\$18,000 = (\$6,000)(\text{year 1 factor}) + (\$6,000)(\text{year 2 factor}) + \\ (\$6,000)(\text{year 3 factor}) + (\$10,000)(\text{year 4 factor})$$

At 18 percent we would have

$$\$18,000 = (\$6,000)(.847) + (\$6,000)(.718) + (\$6,000)(.609) \\ + (\$10,000)(.516) \\ = \$5,082 + 4,308 + 3,654 + 5,160 = \underline{\$18,204}$$

A Solved Problem. What is the rate of return of the following stream?

Year	Diff. Cash Flow	Try 10%	Try 8%	Answer
0	−$15,000			Between 8 and 10%,
1	+ 5,000	(1.736) = $ 8,680	(1.783) = $ 8,915	almost in middle; so
2	+ 5,000			9%
3	+ 8,000	(.751) = 6,008	(.794) = 6,352	
		$14,688	$15,267	

4. NET PRESENT VALUE, HOW TO COMPARE PROPOSALS

The net-present-value method differs from the trial-and-error approach of the **discounted-cash-flow** method. It uses a fixed cost of capital, which may be defined as the rate of return the firm needs to realize from an investment to maintain or increase the value of the firm. In this sense of maximizing wealth, the cost of capital must be sufficiently high to cover the costs of raising money, paying expenses for fixed charges, plus an additional profit large enough to protect the value of the firm's stock and give the shareholder growth and dividends.

Because of the difficulty in calculating cost of capital, many firms use a **decision rule** for new investments. A firm might estimate its cost of capital to be 12 percent, and therefore it will make the decision rule that *this firm will not accept any projects that do not forecast a rate of return of 12 percent.* Stated differently, *this firm will accept only those projects which forecast a 12 percent or greater rate of return using present-value techniques.*

With the net-present-value method, all projects are discounted at the same rate. If the net present value of the benefits exceeds the outlay, the project is acceptable since it has a higher return than the firm's decision rule. If the present value of the benefits is less than the outlay, the project is rejected. The calculation of present value is the same as for discounted cash flow.

Profitability Index

A profitability index (PI) is a ratio of the present value of the net cash benefits to the present value of the net cash outlay. It is used in the net-present-value approach to compare projects. The higher the profitability index, the greater the return. Any project with a PI above 1 is acceptable since benefits exceed outlay. Projects with a PI below 1 are not acceptable. At a PI of exactly 1, the project has a return equal to the decision rule or cost of capital.

As an example of calculating a profitability index, consider the following cash-flow stream for a firm with a cost of capital of 12 percent.

Year	0	1	2	3	4
Diff. Cash Flow	−$18,000	+$6,000	+$6,000	+$6,000	+$10,000

The calculation of present value of net cash benefits at 12 percent is

$$- \ \$18,000 = (\$6,000)(2.402) + (\$10,000)(.636) = 20,772$$

Since the value of the benefits is greater than the outlay, the project is acceptable. Its profitability index is $20,772/18,000 or 1.154. This does not mean that the project has a return of 15.4 percent, only that the project has a high PI.

Comparing Projects with a Profitability Index

To illustrate the comparison of projects with a profitability index, let us assume a firm is faced with three possible investments but can only undertake one of them. It projects cash-flow streams and discounts each project at the 10 percent cost of capital, as shown in Table 1-8. The profitability indexes for each project are also computed in the table.

Project A is not acceptable because $13,186 is less than the $15,000 net cash outlay; thus, the rate of return is less than the cost of capital. This is also revealed by the profitability index, which is less than 1. Projects B and C are both acceptable, but the higher profitability index of B means it would be ranked higher than C on profit considerations. If only one can be accepted, B would be the choice.

TABLE 1-8. Computing Profitability Indexes for Three Proposals.

Year	Differential Cash-Flow Stream		Present Value Factor		Present Value	Profitability Index
Project A						
0	−15,000					$\dfrac{13,186}{15,000}$ = .88
1	+ 5,000					
2	+ 5,000	×	1.736	=	8,680	
3	+ 6,000	×	.751	=	4,506	
					13,186	
Project B						
0	−16,000					$\dfrac{17,926}{16,000}$ = 1.12
1	+ 6,000					
2	+ 6,000	×	1.736	=	10,416	
3	+10,000	×	.751	=	7,510	
					17,926	
Project C						
0	−16,000					$\dfrac{17,244}{16,000}$ = 1.08
1	+ 6,000	×	.909	=	5,454	
2	+ 7,000	×	.826	=	5,782	
3	+ 8,000	×	.751	=	6,008	
					17,244	

5. PRESENT VALUE OF MONEY, HOW TO CALCULATE

It becomes more difficult to decide between capital budgeting projects when we are dealing with different returns and different time periods. If a project offered $55,000 at the end of 3 years, how would it compare with a second project offering $50,000 at the end of 2 years? The answer is: We would adjust the dollar amount and express the future value of each project in terms of today's dollars. This is called discounting. We discount both dollar amounts to the present at an appropriate discount rate and compare the present value of each. The one with the higher present value is the better project.

The formula used to discount money to its present value is given in Figure 1-7.

$$PV = \frac{\$}{(1 + i)^n}$$

where
PV = present value in year zero
$ = dollar amount received in future
i = discount factor (interest rate)
n = number of years until dollar amount is received

Figure 1-7. Formula for the Present Value of a Single Future Payment.

If we use a 10 percent interest rate in our previous example, for the $50,000 to be received in 2 years, the present value would be $50,000/(1 + .10)^2 = \$41,322$. For the $55,000 in 3 years, the present value would be $\$55,000/(1 + .10)^3 = \$41,322$. At 10 percent, these two projects would be worth the same approximate amount. If the interest rate is less than 10 percent, the $55,000 project would have a higher present value. If the interest rate is greater than 10 percent, the $50,000 project would have the higher value. These effects are illustrated in Table 1-9.

TABLE 1-9. Bringing Back Future Dollar Amounts to Present Values.

Present Value	Year 1	Year 2	Year 3
Discounting by 5%			
$45,351	$47,619	$50,000	
47,511	49,887	52,381	$55,000
Discounting by 10%			
41,322	45,450	50,000	
41,322	45,450	50,000	55,000
Discounting by 15%			
37,807	43,478	50,000	
36,163	41,588	47,826	55,000

From the table, note the relationship between the discount factor and the present value of the future returns: the higher the discount factor, the lower the present value. Stated differently, with high interest rates less money is needed today to achieve a stated future goal. At 5 percent, we need $45,351 today to have $50,000 in 2 years. At 15 percent, only $37,807 is needed to have $50,000 in 2 years.

> *EXAMPLE: What is the present value of a $600,000 payment due in 7 years if interest rates are 9 percent?*
> *ANSWER: $328,228. The formula is $600,000/(1 + .09)^7 = 600,000/1.828 = \$328,228$.*

> *EXAMPLE: What is the present value of $4,500,000 due in 3 years if money has a time value of 14 percent?*
> *ANSWER: $3,036,437. 4,500,000/(1 + .14)^3 = 4,500,000/1.482 = \$3,036,437$.*

Present Value of Steady Streams

A difference occurs when projects are forecasted to provide a steady stream of annual returns. An **annuity** exists when a project offers a series of equal cash inflows that occur at the end of successive periods of equal duration. To calculate the present value of an annuity, we use the formula in Figure 1-8.

$$PV_a = (\$)\left(\frac{1}{i}\right)\left[1 - \frac{1}{(1+i)^n}\right]$$ where PV_a = present value of the annuity
$\$$ = dollar amount of each annual receipt
i = interest rate (discount factor)
n = number of years of successive receipts

Figure 1-8. Formula for the Present Value of an Annuity.

As an example of the use of this formula, a firm is considering two projects. Project A will return $50,000 annually for 2 years; project B will return $40,000 annually for 3 years. At a 10 percent discount factor, the present value of each project is

Project A

$$(\$50,000)\left(\frac{1}{.10}\right)\left(1 - \frac{1}{1.10^2}\right) = \$86,800$$

Project B

$$(\$40,000)\left(\frac{1}{.10}\right)\left(1 - \frac{1}{1.10^3}\right) = \$99,480$$

At a 10-percent time value of money, project B would be worth more to the firm because the present value of its future receipts is higher than the present value of the receipts from project A.

EXAMPLE: A project offers a $250,000 annual return for 4 years when money is worth 15 percent. What is the present value of the project?
ANSWER: $713,700.

The formula is ($250,000) $\left(\frac{1}{15}\right)\left(1 - \frac{1}{1.15^4}\right)$ = $713,700.

EXAMPLE: A proposal offers a $3,000,000 return annually for 3 years. Money has a time value of 5 percent. What is the present value of the proposal?
ANSWER: $8,172,000.

The formula is ($3,000,000) $\left(\frac{1}{.05}\right)\left(1 - \frac{1}{1.05^3}\right)$ = $8,172,000.

Using Present Value Tables

In practice, we do not use the actual formulas to calculate present value. Instead we use Appendix A to determine the present value of $1 received at the end of a future year. We locate the year in the left-hand column and read across to the appropriate interest rate. The number located where the year and percentage cross is the discount factor for the present value of a dollar. If we want the present value of $1,000, we multiply the factor by 1,000.

> *EXAMPLE: A firm is due to receive $10,000 at the end of 5 years when the interest rate is 6 percent. Using Appendix A, what is the present value of the $10,000? ANSWER: $7,470. At the juncture of the 5-year and 6 percent lines is the factor .747. This means that $1 would have a present value of 74.7 cents. For $10,000, we calculate ($10,000)(.747) = $7,470.*

Appendix B gives us the present value of an annuity, or $1 received each year for a number of years.

> *EXAMPLE: A firm is due to receive $2,000 annually for 6 years when money has a value of 8 percent. Using Appendix B, what is the present value of the annuity? ANSWER: $9,246. At the juncture of the 6-year and 8 percent lines is the factor 4.623. This means that receiving $1 every year for 6 years has a present value of $4.62. The present value of $2,000 annually for 6 years is ($2,000)(4.623) = $9,246.*

6. PRESENT VALUE TECHNIQUES, HOW TO SELECT THE CORRECT ONE

The internal rate-of-return and net-present-value methods can give different results because they make different assumptions on the reinvestment of proceeds. In effect, the internal rate-of-return method assumes that all proceeds are reinvested at the rate of return. The net-present-value method assumes that proceeds are reinvested at the cost of capital. This can make a difference as to which project would be ranked first between two competing projects, as is shown in Figure 1-9.

Ranking the Proposals

Using present value techniques, the financial manager will be better able to grasp the financial implications of different capital proposals. Before making proposals, several considerations should be noted.

> **1.** *Profitability Index of Less Than 1 Does Not Indicate a Loss.* If the PI is .98, it just missed achieving the firm's cost of capital as a rate of return. It does not mean the project loses money. If the cost of capital is 14 percent, the .98 PI probably indicates about a 13 percent return. This should be realized before the project is rejected, since other factors may make it sufficiently attractive to overcome the slight difference between 13 and 14 percent.

Project Data	Internal Rate of Return	Net Present Value (8% decision rule)
Project A Project B	(A) − $10,000 = ($12,000)(.833) = $9,996 at a 20% factor (B) − $10,000 = ($15,000)(.658) = $9,870 at a 15% factor	(A) − $10,000 = ($12,000)(.926) = $11,112 (the PI is 11,112/10,000 = 1.11) (B) − $10,000 = ($15,000)(.794) = $11,910 (the PI is 11,910/10,000 = 1.19)
0 − $10,000 − $10,000 1 + 12.000 0 2 0 0 3 0 + $15,000		

	Project A	Project B
Rate of return	20%	15%
Profitability index	1.11	1.19

Which project is better? It depends on whether the $12,000 from project A in the first year can be invested at 8 or 20 percent. If it can be invested at 20 percent, the internal rate of return method is more appropriate. If it can be invested at 8 percent, the PI method is more accurate.

Figure 1-9. Internal Rate of Return and Net Present Value Giving Different Results Based on Different Reinvestment Assumptions.

2. *Profitability Index Cannot Be Used to Determine Percent Return.* Sometimes people think that a 1.05 PI indicates a 5 percent rate of return, others think it means a rate of return 5 percent above the cost of capital. Neither is true. The PI is an index number and cannot be equated to the rate of return.

3. *Ignore Small Percentage Differences Between Projects.* If one proposal offers a rate of return of 18 percent and a second offers 18.5 percent, these are virtually identical in terms of **profits.** When we are forecasting cash flows years into the future, the results will not be extremely precise. It may be wise to round off your rate-of-return percents to the nearest whole percent to avoid making distinctions between very similar profit figures.

4. *Return Is a Single Input Only.* The use of rate-of-return techniques provides only one input into the final decision. In addition to profits and liquidity, the firm is interested in growth, diversification, company image, and other factors. These should be considered before ranking projects.

7. PRESENT VALUE TECHNIQUES, HOW TO AVOID BEING MANIPULATED BY

Although present value discounting of cash flow is one of the most powerful financial tools, the technique can be manipulated to produce a desired result. The selection of the discount factor is the key to this manipulation.

Consider, for example, a firm that is financing a $125,000 **capital asset** at a time when money costs 10 percent. It can make a $25,000 down payment and finance the balance over 10 years. The asset will have a $25,000 cash salvage value in 10 years. Taxes are omitted to simplify the analysis. The cash-flow stream is:

Year	Cash Flow	Present Value at 10%	
0	−25,000	−25,000	
1-10	−16,275[a]	−100,000	
10	+25,000	+9,639	
		−115,361	present value

[a] Payment to amortize $100,000 at 10 percent over 10-year period.

Now assume that the firm will buy the asset with 100 percent financing at 10 percent for 10 years. It will have to pay $20,343 a year to amortize its loan and its cash-flow stream would be:

Year	Cash Flow	Present Value at 10%	
0	0	0	
1-10	−20,343	−125,000	
10	+25,000	+9,639	
		−115,361	present value

In this analysis, the two cash-flow streams seem to have the same present value. This suggests the conclusion that owning the asset with a $25,000 down payment and annual finance charges of $16,275 is equivalent in cost to 100 percent financing of the asset at $20,343 per year. But the validity of this conclusion depends on the validity of the discount factor. Just because a firm can finance one asset at 10 percent does not mean that the firm's money is worth 10 percent. Overall, its money could be more or less costly. To see the results of these possibilities, consider the following table:

	With a Down Payment			With 100% Financing		
Year	Cash Flow	Present Value at 8%	Present Value at 12%	Cash Flow	Present Value at 8%	Present Value at 12%
0	−25,000	−25,000	−25,000	0	0	0
1-10	−16,275	−109,207	−91,957	−20,343	−136,503	−114,942
10	+25,000	+11,580	+8,049	+25,000	+11,580	+8,049
		−122,627	−108,908		−124,923	−106,893

The table shows the down-payment alternative to be less costly ($122,627 versus $124,923) in present value terms with an 8 percent factor. On the other hand, at 12 percent the 100 percent financing is less costly ($106,893 versus $108,908).

Only the financial manager can evaluate which factor best reflects the firm's cost of capital, but he should beware of manipulation. As an example of this danger, suppose a leasing company came to the firm and offered to purchase the asset and lease it to the firm for 10 years at an annual payment of $24,000. If this price were challenged, the lease company might discount it back at some assumed cost of capital, the higher the better. For example, at a 16 percent discount factor the present value of 10 payments of $24,000 is $115,997, an apparent bargain for an asset valued at $125,000.

The lease company could explain this value by claiming the ability to buy the asset at a lower price than the firm. But even at a cost of $125,000, the lease company makes money two ways:

1. *$24,000 is Greater than $20,343.* Assuming that the leasing company borrows at 10 percent and pays $20,343 to **amortize** the debt, it makes $3,657 annual profit from the transaction.
2. *Lease Company Gets Residual.* The $25,000 cash salvage value benefits the lessor under a lease agreement. This is a second source of profit to the leasing company.

Thus, if our assumptions are correct, the present value of the lease company's profit is $32,110, as follows:

Year	Cash Profit	Present Value at 10%
0	0	0
1-10	+3,657	+22,471
10	+25,000	+9,639
		+32,110

With a 16-percent discount factor, the lease firm appears to be losing money when it is actually profiting from the transaction. The knowledgeable firm will be wise to the importance of closely evaluating present-value calculations to avoid this kind of manipulation.

8.   RISK IN CAPITAL BUDGET, HOW TO MEASURE

Many techniques are available to measure **risk** in capital budgets. One makes use of the **standard deviation** and **coefficient of variation** in a probabilistic model. A **decision tree** is prepared for each possible future cash inflow and a **probability** is assigned to each **branch.** A standard deviation is then calculated as a measure of risk. To compare projects, the standard deviations are converted in coefficients of variation.

Five steps are used in this process, as follows:

1. *Calculate Cash-Flow Streams and Probabilities Annually for Each Branch.* We begin with the annual returns and the likelihood of their occurrence as forecasted by the analyst.
2. *Discount the Stream for Each Branch and Calculate Profitability Index.* Each possible return is multiplied by the appropriate present-value factor as well as by the probability of occurrence. The weighted averages are added to get the **expected value** for each year (present value actually). By adding the present values for each year, we get the present value of the net cash benefits.

EXAMPLE: A project branch has a 40 percent chance of returning $10,000 and a 60 percent chance of returning $15,000 in year 1. In the second and last year, the project has a 30 percent chance of returning $15,000 and a 70 percent chance of returning $20,000. What is the profitability index if the cost of capital is 10 percent and the net cash outlay is $25,000?

ANSWER: *Year 1*   *($10,000)(.40)(.909) = $ 3,636*
                              ($15,000)(.60)(.909) =   8,181
                                                $11,817

            Year 2   *($15,000)(.30)(.826) =   3,717*
                              ($20,000)(.70)(.826) = 11,564
                                                $15,281
                     Present Value NCB   *$27,098*
                     Profitability Index = 27,098/25,000 = 1.08

3. *Calculate Weighted Average Return for Each Year.* This calculation is needed for the calculation of the standard deviation. The **weighted-average return** is the sum of the likely returns times their probabilities. For the preceding example problem, the returns are

Year 1 ($10,000)(.40) + (15,000)(.60) = $4,000 + 9,000 = $13,000
Year 2 ($15,000)(.30) + (20,000)(.70) = $4,500 + 14,000 = $18,500

4. *Calculate the Standard Deviation for Each Year.* Because of the weighting of the likely returns for their probabilities, we can modify the standard formula for calculating standard deviation. We use the following:

$$\sigma \text{ each year} = \sqrt{\Sigma(\text{forecasted returns - weighted return})^2(\text{individual probability})}$$

where Σ = sum of
                      individual probability = probability of each forecasted
                                                        return
                      weighted return   = average return calculated in step 3
                                                        for the year

For our problem, we have

$$\sigma_1 = \sqrt{(10,000 - 13,000)^2 (.4) + (15,000 - 13,000)^2 (.6)}$$
$$= \sqrt{3,600,000 + 2,400,000} = \sqrt{6,000,000} = \underline{2,450}$$
$$\sigma_2 = \sqrt{(15,000 - 18,500)^2 (.3) + (20,000 - 18,500)^2 (.7)}$$
$$= \sqrt{3,675,000 + 1,575,000} = \sqrt{5,250,000} = \underline{2,290}$$

5. *Calculate the Standard Deviation for the Branch.* This is calculated by the formula

$$\sigma = \frac{\Sigma \, \sigma \text{ for each year}}{\text{no. of years}}$$

For our project, the calculation is

$$\sigma = \frac{2,450 + 2,290}{2} = \underline{2,370}$$

As with other uses of standard deviation, the branch with the highest deviation represents the decision with the largest risk. This must be used carefully in the context of the entire investment picture.

Expected Value and Standard Deviation for Comparing Projects

The approach described for using standard deviation to measure the risk of decision-tree alternatives may also be used to compare different projects. Following each decision point are two or more major branches. Stated differently, following a decision point may be a large, medium, and small project. Since these are three separate investment proposals (or two, or four), the technique just described will also work for separate proposals labeled A, B, C, and so on. The following solved problem will use the technique on separate proposals rather than separate branches of a decision tree.

Expected Value and Coefficient of Variation for Comparing Projects

Similarly, the coefficient of variation can be used as a measure of risk with the preceding technique. Step 3 gives us the weighted returns for each year.

To calculate a weighted return (R) for the project, use the following formula:

$$R = \frac{\Sigma \text{ annual weighted returns}}{\text{no. of years}}$$

In our problem, the weighted returns were $13,000 for year 1 and $18,500 for year 2. The return for the branch was

$$R = \frac{\$13,000 + 18,500}{2} = \$15,750$$

To calculate the coefficient of variation, we divide the σ of $2,370 by the return of $15,750 and get 2,370/15,750 = .15.

A Solved Problem

To illustrate the step-by-step approach to calculating the relative riskiness of various projects, a solved problem is given as Figure 1-10. For the solved problem, project B has the higher profitability index and lower coefficient of variation. Therefore, project B is more profitable and less risky than A.

Given: |
A firm is considering two proposals as part of its capital budget. Proposal A requires a net cash outlay of $12,000; B requires $15,000. Both projects will have an estimated life of 3 years. An analyst has estimated the returns after taxes. For project A: year 1, a 40 percent chance of $4,000 and a 60 percent chance of $5,000; year 2, a 30 percent chance of $8,000 and a 70 percent chance of $5,000; year 3, a 40 percent chance of $9,000 and a 60 percent chance of $5,000. For project B: year 1, a 50 percent chance of $4,000 and a 50 percent chance of $6,000; year 2, a 40 percent chance of $12,000 and a 60 percent chance of $8,000; year 3, a 30 percent chance of $7,000 and a 70 percent chance of $10,000. The firm's cost of capital is 10 percent.

Questions:
1. Which project has the higher weighted-average profitability index?
2. Which project has the larger standard deviation?
3. Which project has the larger coefficient of variation?

Step 1: Calculate Cash-Flow Streams and Probabilities:

Year	Project A After-Tax Return	Probability	Project B After-Tax Return	Probability
0	− 12,000	1.00	− 15,000	1.00
1	+ 4,000	.40	+ 4,000	.50
	+ 5,000	.60	+ 6,000	.50
2	+ 8,000	.30	+ 12,000	.40
	+ 5,000	.70	+ 8,000	.60
3	+ 9,000	.40	+ 7,000	.30
	+ 5,000	.60	+ 10,000	.70

Figure 1-10. Calculating the Relative Risk of Various Projects.

Step 2: Discount Stream and Calculate Profitability Index:

10% Cost of Capital = .909 year 1, .826 year 2, .751 year 3

Year	Project A	Project B
1	$(4,000)(.909)(.4)$ = 1,454 $(5,000)(.909)(.6)$ = 2,727 4,181	$(4,000)(.909)(.5)$ = 1,818 $(6,000)(.909)(.5)$ = 2,727 4,545
2	$(8,000)(.826)(.3)$ = 1,982 $(5,000)(.826)(.7)$ = 2,891 4,873	$(12,000)(.826)(.4)$ = 3,965 $(8,000)(.826)(.6)$ = 3,965 7,930
3	$(9,000)(.751)(.4)$ = 2,704 $(5,000)(.751)(.6)$ = 2,253 4,957 Present Value NCB 14,011	$(7,000)(.751)(.3)$ = 1,577 $(10,000)(.751)(.7)$ = 5,257 6,834 19,309
PI	14,011/12,000 = 1.17	19,309/15,000 $\doteq$ 1.29

Step 3: Calculate Weighted Return for Each Year:

Year	Project A	Project B
1	$(4,000)(.4) + (5,000)(.6) = 4,600$	$(4,000)(.5) + (6,000)$ $(.5) = 5,000$
2	$(8,000)(.3) + (5,000)(.7) = 5,900$	$(12,000)(.4) + (8,000)$ $(.6) = 9,600$
3	$(9,000)(.4) + (5,000)(.6) = 6,600$	$(7,000)(.3) + (10,000)(.7) = 9,100$

Step 4: Calculate Standard Deviation for Each Year (use σ^2 until last step):

Year	Project A	Project B
1	$\sigma^2 = (4,000 - 4,600)^2(.4)$ $+ (5,000 - 4,600)^2(.6)$ $= 144,000 + 96,000 = 240,000$ $\sigma = \sqrt{240,000} = 490$	$\sigma^2 = (4,000 - 5,000)^2(.5)$ $+ (6,000 - 5,000)^2(.5)$ $= 500,000 + 500,000 = 1,000,000$ $\sigma = \sqrt{1,000,000} = 1,000$
2	$\sigma^2 = (8,000 - 5,900)^2(.3)$ $+ (5,000 - 5,900)^2(.7)$ $= 1,323,000 + 567,000$ $= 1,890,000$ $\sigma = \sqrt{1,890,000} = 1,380$	$\sigma^2 = (12,000 - 9,600)^2(.4)$ $+ (8,000 - 9,600)^2(.6)$ $= 2,304,000 + 1,536,000$ $= 3,840,000$ $\sigma = \sqrt{3,840,000} = 1,960$
3	$\sigma^2 = (9,000 - 6,600)^2(.4)$ $+ (5,000 - 6,600)^2(.6)$ $= 2,304,000 + 1,536,000$ $= 3,840,000$ $\sigma = \sqrt{3,840,000} = 1,960$	$\sigma^2 = (7,000 - 9,100)^2(.3)$ $+ (10,000 - 9,100)^2(.7)$ $= 1,323,000 + 567,000$ $= 1,890,000$ $\sigma = \sqrt{1,890,000} = 1,380$

Figure 1-10. Continued.

Step 5: Calculate Standard Deviation for Each:

Project A	Project B
$\sigma_A = \dfrac{490 + 1,380 + 1,960}{3} = \underline{\underline{1,277}}$	$\sigma_B = \dfrac{1,000 + 1,960 + 1,380}{3} = \underline{\underline{1,447}}$

One Additional Step: Calculate Coefficient of Variation:

Project A	Project B
$R = \dfrac{4,600 + 5,900 + 6,600}{3} = 5,700$	$R = \dfrac{5,000 + 9,600 + 9,100}{3} = 7,900$
$V = \dfrac{1,277}{5,700} = \underline{\underline{.22}}$	$V = \dfrac{1,447}{7,900} = \underline{\underline{.18}}$

Answers to Questions
1. Profitability index: A = 1.17, B = 1.29;   B is higher.
2. Standard deviation: A = 1,277, B = 1,447;   B is larger.
3. Coefficient of variation: A = .22, B = .18;   A is larger.

Figure 1-10. Continued.

9. STANDARD DEVIATION, HOW TO ESTIMATE IN CAPITAL BUDGETING

The standard deviation is a useful and widely used measure of the variation or dispersion of a normal probability distribution. It is normally represented by the Greek letter sigma (σ). The standard deviation is also called the root-mean-square deviation since it basically solves for the square root of the mean of the squared deviations in a distribution.

In using the concept of standard deviation as a measure of the risk of investment proposals, we do not calculate the sigma value using the standard statistics approach. Rather, we estimate it using techniques similar to the following (see also Figure 1-11).

1. *Dispersion of Previous Investment Proposals.* For a firm that has invested in a variety of earlier investments, data can be developed on the closeness of the actual results to the original forecast. If our estimates were fairly close for investments similar to the current one, we would expect a small standard deviation. Larger dispersions on past projects would warrant a large estimated standard deviation.

2. *Two-Thirds Estimation Technique.* Approximately two-thirds of the time the project return will be within a range of one standard deviation (plus or minus) of the target value. This is by definition of the concept of standard deviation. Appendix E contains a standard normal distribution table, which can verify this fact. Between the target value

and the first standard deviation on either side of the **target value** is an area of return that will be realized 34.13 percent of the time. One standard deviation on either side will be achieved 68.26 percent (34.13 percent × 2) of the time. This is approximately two-thirds of the possibilities. With the two thirds estimation technique, a number of marketing and finance experts in the firm are asked to estimate the range of returns that are likely to happen two-thirds of the time. Once this range is forecasted as accurately as possible, we have a range of one standard deviation above and below the target value. Half this range will be a standard deviation.

3. *Ninety-Nine Percent Estimation Technique.* This method requires the company expert to estimate the entire likely range of returns from the proposal to a level of 99 percent accuracy. Once this range is determined, it represents six standard deviations by definition. One-sixth of the range is a standard deviation.

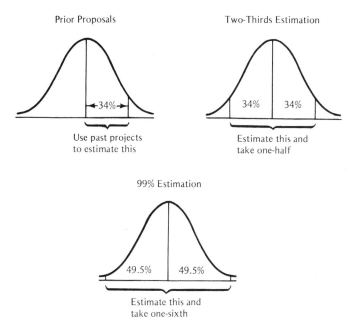

Figure 1-11. Three Techniques for Estimating the Standard Deviation on the Returns from an Investment Proposal.

Chapter 2

PROFIT PLANNING

10. BREAK-EVEN ANALYSIS, HOW TO USE

A fundamental profit planning tool involves the determination of the likely profits at different levels of production. To develop the necessary calculations, the financial manager builds on the basic tool of break-even analysis and expands it through **profit-volume analysis.**

Break-even analysis is used to determine the level of operations at which a firm will neither make a profit nor lose money. At this level, the firm operates at a zero profit level or **break-even point.** Break-even analysis makes use of **fixed costs, variable costs,** and revenues, and may be used graphically or mathematically.

Graphic Approach to Break-Even Analysis

The graphic approach to break-even analysis plots dollars on the vertical axis and units on the horizontal axis, as shown in Figure 2-1. The costs that are included in the analysis are:

1. *Fixed Costs* remain the same at all levels of production. An example would be the rent paid on a building. Graphically the fixed costs (FC) would be a horizontal line.
2. *Variable Costs* change directly with the number of units produced. At zero units of production, the firm incurs no variable costs. As production rises, the variable costs rise proportionally. Two aspects of variable costs are important and should be noted:

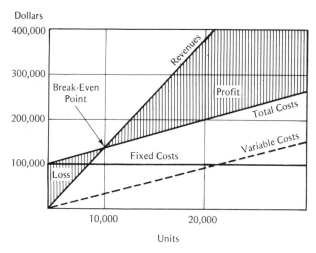

Figure 2-1. Break-Even Analysis.

a. *Variable Costs Plotted as Total Costs.* If the variable costs are plotted from the zero point on the graph, they reflect only the variable costs of production. It is more common, however, to plot them from the left-hand side of the fixed-costs line. When this is done, the line represents *total operating costs* and shows the slope of the variable costs. This is the total costs line in Figure 2-1.

b. *Variable Costs as Constant Costs.* It is traditional to plot variable costs using a straight line. This implies that variable costs are **constant costs;** that is, they are the same at all levels of production. If the first unit costs $3, the second also costs $3, and so on until the last. In fact, variable costs are not constant. The first units are very expensive until setup costs are absorbed. Then, the bulk of production is approximately constant until the production begins to bottleneck at some high level of production. At high levels, when overtime must be paid or machines must be run for excessively long periods without time for maintenance, variable costs rise and production is expensive on a per-unit basis.

For most purposes, variable costs may be treated as constant costs. This works when the analyst assumes that the firm is planning only for operations in the range where production is efficient; that is, efficient enough to overcome setup costs but not so much as to incur bottlenecks. Since production in this area involves relatively constant costs, our calculations will be fairly accurate and realistic.

Revenues, or sales, are needed to complete the picture of the break-even analysis. The total revenues (TR) are plotted diagonally beginning at unit zero and the slope of the line rises more quickly than total costs. This is true because the firm will receive more revenues per unit of production than the variable cost of producing each unit.

This completes the profit picture for the firm. The break-even point occurs at the crossing of the revenue and total cost lines. Above this production level, the firm will be profitable. Below it, the firm will incur a loss. Note that the profits ar measured in the triangle above the break-even point and losses below the break-even point, in each case in the areas defined by the revenue and total cost lines.

11. FINANCIAL LEVERAGE, HOW TO ANALYZE

Two types of **leverage** are commonly called by the term financial leverage. One is discussed under **fixed-charges leverage.** The second and more widely accepted usage of **financial leverage** refers to a situation in which both of the following exist:

1. *Limited-Return Securities.* A firm must be financing a portion of its assets by using debt, **preferred stock,** or some other security bearing a limited return.
2. *Return on Investment (ROI) Is Not Equal to Fixed Charges.* The firm's ROI must not be equal to the percentage of interest or dividend being paid on the limited-return security.

Three Possible Situations

The sole criterion for determining whether a firm has financial leverage involves a comparison of the firm's ROI with the interest rate on its debt. Three situations are possible:

1. *ROI Is Greater Than the Interest Rate.* If the ROI exceeds the interest rate, the firm is making money as a result of borrowing. It may be making 15 percent on its assets but is only paying 10 percent to its creditors. The extra 5 percent will be divided between the government (in the form of federal income taxes) and the shareholders. In this situation, it makes sense to borrow. When ROI exceeds interest rate, we say the firm has **favorable financial leverage.** Another common term to describe this situation is to say that the firm is **trading on the equity.**
2. *ROI Equal to Interest Rate.* In this situation, the firm is earning on the money exactly what it pays for the use of the money. It neither makes sense nor is totally objectionable to borrow in this position unless other factors are considered.

3. *ROI Is Less Than Interest Rate.* When this happens, the firm is borrowing and then losing money on the use of the funds. It does not make sense to borrow, conduct operations, and then make less than the cost of the borrowed money. This situation is called **unfavorable financial leverage.**

Importance of Financial Leverage

Many financial managers would argue that financial leverage is the most important of the leverage concepts. It finds particular application in **capital-structure management.** A firm's **capital structure** is the relation between the debt and **equity** securities that make up the firm's financing of its assets. A firm with no debt is said to have an all-equity capital structure. Since most firms have capital structures with both debt and equity elements, the financial manager is highly concerned with the effects of borrowing. If a firm is making money on its borrowing (has favorable financial leverage), the shareholders are realizing higher **earnings per share (EPS)** than would be the case in the absence of debt.

Capital-Structure Management—First Example

To demonstrate the effect of financial leverage in a firm's capital structure, consider four firms with $500,000 of assets. All four firms earn a 10 percent return on investment. Each firm has sold common stock for $10 a share. Firm A sold $500,000 of stock while firms B, C, and D sold $300,000 of stock. Firms B, C, and D borrowed the remaining $200,000 at different interest rates. Firm B borrowed at 5 percent and, with the 10 percent return on investment, has favorable financial leverage. Firm C borrowed at 10 percent and has neither favorable nor unfavorable leverage. Firm D borrowed at 15 percent and has unfavorable financial leverage. Financial data for each firm are given in Table 2-1.

Analyzing each situation in turn, we can see the effects of financial leverage. Even though the stock sold for $10 and a 10 percent ROI is present for each firm, the after-tax earnings and EPS varied. Firm A, with no debt, earns $.50 per share (a 5 percent, after-tax return). This is also the situation for Firm C, the firm that borrows at the same interest rate as its ROI. But firm B, the firm that borrows at less than its ROI, levers its profits to $.67 by paying only 5 percent to the creditors, who provide 40 percent of the assets ($200,000 of $500,000). Firm D has the reverse effect from firm B. Firm D is paying 15 percent interest, which is more than its ROI. This firm must use a portion of the profits otherwise designated for the shareholders to pay its creditors.

This example shows that it is logical for a firm to borrow, up to reasonable amounts, if it can earn a higher return on the borrowing than it pays for the money. Similarly, a firm should not borrow if it cannot earn more than the cost of the money.

TABLE 2-1. Four Firms with Identical Operating Incomes and Different Capital Structures, Illustrating the Effects of Financial Leverage.

	Firm A No Debt	Firm B	Firm C	Firm D
		Financial Leverage with Interest Rate of:		
		5% (Favorable)	10% (No Leverage)	15% (Unfavorable)
Equity	$500,000	$300,000	$300,000	$300,000
Debt	0	200,000	200,000	200,000
Total Assets	$500,000	$500,000	$500,000	$500,000
Earnings before interest and taxes (EBIT)	50,000	50,000	50,000	50,000
Interest	0	10,000	20,000	30,000
Earnings before taxes (EBT)	50,000	40,000	30,000	20,000
Taxes	25,000	20,000	15,000	10,000
Net income after taxes (NIAT)	$25,000	$20,000	$15,000	$10,000
Shares outstanding	50,000	30,000	30,000	30,000
EPS	$.50	$.67	$.50	$.33

Capital-Structure Management—Second Example

A second way to analyze financial leverage is to consider the effects of differing profit levels with each situation. A firm is not guaranteed a 10 percent ROI and management may consider the effects of achieving a lower or higher return. In the preceding situations with firms A, B, C, and D, we may evaluate how differing ROIs will affect EPS for each firm. Table 2-2 shows the EPS for each firm with four different ROIs.

TABLE 2-2. Measuring the Impact of Changes in ROI on Changes in EPS for Four Firms with Differing Capital Structures.

	Firm A EPS	Firm B EPS	Firm C EPS	Firm D EPS
$70,000 EBIT (14% ROI)	$.70	$1.00	$.83	$.67
$50,000 EBIT (10% ROI)	.50	.67	.50	.33
$30,000 EBIT (6% ROI)	.30	.33	.17	0
$10,000 EBIT (2% ROI)	.10	0	(.33)	(.67)

Table 2-2 illustrates the general pattern of effects for levered firms. When the ROI is high, the firms with favorable financial leverage report the highest earnings. Similarly, when ROI drops, the firms with the largest interest payments report the largest losses or smallest earnings. The firm with no debt has lower earnings in high-profit periods and higher earnings in low-profit periods than firms with debt. This can be seen more clearly by comparing only firms A and B. This is done graphically in Figure 2-2.

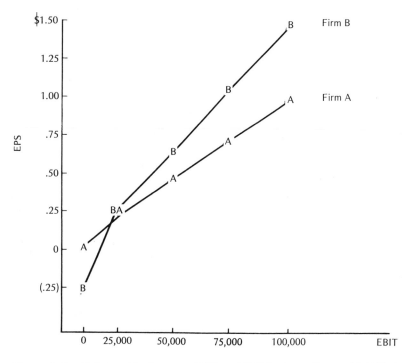

Figure 2-2. Relationship Between EBIT and EPS for Two Firms with Differing Capital Structures.

Financial Leverage with Preferred Stock

When calculating whether preferred stock offers a firm favorable financial leverage, a modification of the formula is necessary. The preferred **dividends** are declared after the payment of federal income taxes by the corporation. This means that the ROI must be greater than the combined taxes and dividends for the leverage to be favorable. The formula is

$$\text{ROI} > \frac{\textbf{dividend yield}}{1 - \text{tax rate}}$$

If, for example, the preferred stock carried a 5 percent **coupon rate** on $100 **par value,** the ROI must exceed .05/(1 - .5) = 10 percent (assumes 50 percent taxes) for the leverage to be favorable.

> *EXAMPLE: A firm is considering a 5 percent preferred-stock offering and has a 40 percent corporate tax rate. Above what ROI will the firm have favorable financial leverage?*
> *ANSWER: 8.33 percent. The calculation is .05/(1 -.4) = .0833.*

12. FLOW-OF-FUNDS STATEMENT, HOW TO DEVELOP FROM BALANCE SHEET AND INCOME STATEMENT

Most small businesses have accountants who prepare **balance sheets** and **income statements** at year-end. But in many cases these statements do not answer important questions concerning where the firm received and spent its funds. For example, it is common to hear a businessman state, "Our income statement shows a profit of $150,000 after taxes yet I have no money in the bank. How can that be?" The easiest way to answer that question is to take the firm's balance sheet and income statement and use them to prepare a **flow-of-funds statement.**

Several basic accounting techniques are needed to develop a flow-of-funds statement from other financial statements. These will be illustrated using the data on the Centurion Company. Note that our example provides a comparative balance sheet—the current and prior years' balances are displayed—and a current income statement. The major steps for developing a flow-of-funds statement are illustrated next.

CENTURION COMPANY Balance Sheet (December 31, 1974)

	1974	1973		1974	1973
Cash	$ 40,000	$ 100,000	Accts. payable	$ 90,000	$ 40,000
Mkt. secs.	20,000	70,000	Taxes payable	30,000	20,000
Accts. rec.	150,000	140,000	Mortgage (5%)	120,000	130,000
Inventories	300,000	250,000	Bonds (6%)	350,000	220,000
Plant and Equip.	900,000	600,000	Common Stock	200,000	150,000
Less acc. depr.	(250,000)	(200,000)	Premium	120,000	50,000
Misc. invest.	70,000	70,000	Retain. Earn.	630,000	730,000
Land	310,000	310,000		$1,540,000	$1,340,000
	$1,540,000	$1,340,000			

NOTE: The firm purchased $400,000 in equipment in 1974.

CENTURION COMPANY Income Statement (period ending December 31, 1974)

Sales	$750,000	
Misc. investments	2,000	$752,000
Production costs	$470,000	
Depreciation	80,000	
General expenses	234,000	
Interest	28,000	812,000
NIAT (loss)		$(60,000)

Funds from Operations

Funds from operations is the total of **net income after taxes (NIAT)** and noncash expenses. Centurion had a net loss, and this $60,000 is a **use of funds** rather than a **source.** The depreciation shielded a source of $80,000. Both figures are given on the income statement.

Changes in Plant and Equipment

The plant and equipment account can help identify both a source and use of funds, as follows:

1. *Purchases of Plant and Equipment Are Uses.* If the firm buys new plant or equipment, the expenditure is recorded as a use of funds. The new equipment will normally be recorded at cost. Since Centurion's plant and equipment balance rose from $600,000 to $900,000, the firm must have purchased a minimum of $300,000 of new equipment. The footnote reveals that it actually purchased $400,000, representing a $400,000 use of funds.
2. *Net Write-Offs Are Sources of Funds.* When a firm sells used equipment, the money it receives is a source of funds. To reflect this source, the firm has a **write-off** of the asset and its accumulated depreciation. A *net write-off* of a fixed asset is defined as the removal of the asset and associated accumulated depreciation from the firm's books, and may be calculated by the formula

$$\text{net write-off} = \frac{\text{fixed asset}}{\text{written off}} - \frac{\text{accumulated depreciation}}{\text{written off}}$$

The calculation of the net write-off for Centurion is:

Fixed Asset Written Off		Accumulated Depreciation Written Off	
1973 Plant and Equip.	$ 600,000	1973 accum. depr.	$200,000
1974 purchases	400,000	1974 depreciation	80,000
Total	$1,000,000	Total	$280,000
Less ending P&E	900,000	1974 ending depr.	250,000
Write-off	$ 100,000	Write-off	$ 30,000

Fixed asset written off — accum. depr. written off = net write-off
$100,000   —   30,000   = $70,000 source of funds

From the net write-off calculation and from the purchases on the balance sheet, we can determine that the plant and equipment account reveals a $400,000 use of funds and a $70,000 source of funds, both of which will appear on the flow-of-funds statement.

How Can We Be Sure That a Net Write-off Always Reflects a Source of Funds?

It is fairly easy to understand that a purchase involves a use of funds. More difficult to follow is why a net write-off is a source of funds. When a firm writes off equipment, three situations are possible:

1. *Selling Price Can Equal the Book Value.* A firm may have a machine that cost $50,000 with accumulated depreciation of $30,000, a **book value** of $20,000. If the firm receives $20,000 for the machine, the net write-off ($50,000-$30,000) is equal to the cash received; thus, a source of $20,000 is reflected in the write-off.
2. *Selling Price Can Exceed the Book Value.* When this happens, the firm receives more cash than the accounting value of the machine. If the firm had received $25,000 for the $20,000 book-value machine, the source would be $25,000. What happens to the extra $5,000? Since it is a gain on the sale of assets, it will be taxable and will be reflected as income on the income statement. Thus, the first $20,000 is reflected as a source in the equipment account, and the net gain is reflected after taxes on the income statement. The $20,000 may correctly be listed as a source of funds from the sale of assets; the excess is correctly shown as part of the net income after taxes (NIAT) on the income statement.
3. *Selling Price Can Be Less Than the Book Value.* When this happens, the firm receives less cash than the accounting value of the machine. If the firm had received only $15,000 for the $20,000 book-value machine, the source would be $15,000. What happens to the $5,000 difference between the cash received and the book value? It is a loss on the sale of assets and is picked up as a noncash expense on the income statement. It shields another $5,000 in addition to depreciation, and thus increases the total source to $20,000. The $20,000 may be correctly listed as a source of funds as long as the funds from operations does not include the noncash expense *loss on the sale of capital equipment.*

In all three situations, the firm's $20,000 net write-off can be validly and accurately used as a source of funds from the sale of fixed assets.

EXAMPLE: A firm's balance sheet shows the following:

	1979	1978
Machinery	700	500
Less acc. depr.	(300)	(280)

The footnotes tell us the firm bought $300,000 of new equipment and wrote off equipment with an accumulated depreciation of $50,000. How much machinery at cost did the firm write off? What is the firm's annual depreciation?

ANSWER: The firm wrote off $100,000 of equipment at cost. It bought $300,000, but its machinery account only went up by $200,000. The balance was written off. The firm had $70,000 in depreciation. If it had not written off any accumulated depreciation, the new total would be $280,000 + 70,000 = $350,000. Since 50,000 was written off, it is $350,000-50,000 or $300,000.

Machinery			Acc. Depr.	
500				280
300				70
	100		50	
―――	――――		――	――
700				300

EXAMPLE: A firm's balance sheet shows the following:

	1978	1977
Machinery	260	300
Less acc. depr.	(90)	(100)

The footnotes tell us the firm bought no new equipment and wrote off old equipment with an accumulated depreciation of $30,000. How much machinery at cost did the firm write off? What is the firm's annual depreciation?

ANSWER: The firm wrote off $40,000 of equipment ($300,000-$260,000). The firm's annual depreciation is $20,000. It wrote off $30,000, reducing accumulated depreciation from $100,000 to $70,000. Then the $20,000 annual depreciation increased the accumulated depreciation to $90,000.

Machinery			Acc. Depr.	
300				100
	40			20
			30	
―――	――――		――	――
260				90

EXAMPLE: A firm's balance sheet shows the following:

	1979	1978
Machinery	400	250
Less acc. depr.	(120)	(100)

The firm's NIAT for 1979 was $50,000. It wrote off $80,000 of machinery with accumulated depreciation of $10,000. What are the firm's funds from operations? uses of funds to purchase machinery?

ANSWER: The firm had $30,000 depreciation since it wrote off $10,000, but still increased accumulated depreciation by $20,000. This $30,000 plus $50,000 NIAT = $80,000 funds from operations. The firm wrote off $80,000 of machinery but still had an increase of $150,000 from $250,000 to 400,000. It must have purchased $150,000 + 80,000 or $230,000 of machinery.

	Machinery			Acc. Depr.	
250					100
230					30
		80		10	
—	—	—	—	—	—
400					120

Changes in Long-Term Liabilities

If the firm increases its liabilities, it has borrowed money and is provided with a source of funds. If it pays off debt, it is a use of funds. For the Centurion Company, $10,000 of funds were used to reduce the mortgage. Bonds increased from $220,000 to $350,000, indicating a source of funds of $130,000.

Changes in Contributed Capital

The **common-stock** and **premium** accounts represent capital contributed by the owners of the firm through purchases of stock. Their total increase of $120,000 indicates that the firm sold stock for this amount, thus realizing a source of funds.

EXAMPLE: If the Centurion Company has $5 par common stock, how many shares did it sell in 1974? How much did it receive per share?

ANSWER: 10,000 shares were issued. The $50,000 increase in the common-stock account is divided by the par value to get the number of shares issued. It received $12 per share. The total increase in common stock and premium of $120,000 is divided by 10,000 shares.

Changes in Retained Earnings

This account is affected by two major items:[1]

---

[1] Be sure to check the footnotes for possible accounting adjustments in retained earnings. Occasionally, auditors require the firm to make adjustments for past periods that affect this account.

1. *Net Income After Taxes or a Loss.* If the firm has a NIAT, the **retained-earnings** account will increase when the books are closed. A loss, on the other hand, decreases the retained-earnings account.
2. *Dividends.* If the firm declares cash dividends, the outflow of cash is a use of funds, which decreases the retained-earnings account.

In effect, the retained-earnings account reflects the sources of funds from net income after taxes or the uses of funds to cover a loss or pay dividends. The fundamental relationship may be expressed in a formula as follows:

$$\text{change in retained earnings} = \text{NIAT} - \text{dividends}$$

For the flow-of-funds statement, we do not need the retained-earnings account to calculate NIAT. This can be taken from the income statement and is already considered in the funds from operations. We can use the formula to calculate the dividends declared. For Centurion, the change in retained earnings is $630,000-$730,000 or a decrease of $100,000. The loss accounts for $60,000 of this drop. The remainder must be because the firm declared $40,000 in cash dividends during the year.

> *EXAMPLE: A firm has a 1978 retained-earnings balance of $600,000 and a 1979 balance of $550,000. It paid dividends of $20,000. What was its 1979 NIAT? ANSWER: A loss of $30,000. The decrease of $50,000 in retained earnings from 1978 to 1979 is accounted for by a $20,000 dividend and a $30,000 loss.*

Centurion Company Flow-of-Funds Statement

Since the flow-of-funds statement will measure the changes in net working capital (defined as current assets minus current liabilities), it is not necessary to record any movements of funds solely within the current accounts. The movements from current to noncurrent accounts and vice versa would result in the following statement for the Centurion Company:

CENTURION COMPANY Flow-of-Funds Statement (period ending December 31, 1974)

Sources of Funds		Uses of Funds		Changes in
Depreciation	$ 80,000	Net loss	$ 60,000	Net Working
Sale of bonds	130,000	Cash dividends	40,000	Capital
Sale of stock	120,000	Additions to		
Sale of equip.	70,000	Plant and Equip.	400,000	
		Mortgage reduc.	10,000	
	$400,000		$510,000	($110,000)

The Centurion Company experienced a $110,000 decrease in net working capital according to the statement we prepared. To check this figure, we can make use of the comparative balance sheet current accounts. First, we find the total net working capital for 1974. From this figure we subtract the net working capital for 1973. The difference is, in fact, $110,000.

Total Working Capital (Net), 1974		Total Working Capital (Net), 1973		Difference
Current assets	$510,000	Current assets	$560,000	
Current liabilities	120,000	Current liabilities	60,000	
Net working capital	$390,000	Net working capital	$500,000	−$110,000

13. LEVERAGE, HOW TO USE IN PROFIT PLANNING

Three kinds of leverage are identified with the **marginal-analysis** approach to **profit planning**. Each relates a profit measure to another aspect of the firm's operating or financial situation. We shall examine each in turn.

Operating Leverage

Operating leverage exists when changes in revenues produce greater changes in **earnings before interest and taxes (EBIT)**.Several important points should be noted about operating leverage:

1. *Related to Fixed Costs.* The degree of operating leverage is related to the fixed costs of the firm. If the firm has relatively large fixed costs, much of its **marginal contribution** (revenues minus variable costs) must be applied to cover fixed costs. Once the break-even point is reached (revenues = fixed + variable costs), all the marginal contribution becomes EBIT.
2. *Greatest Leverage near Break-Even Point.* As the firm reaches its break-even point, small-percentage increases in sales will cause larger-percentage increases in EBIT. In the same manner, a small drop in sales will erase the entire EBIT if the firm is near its break-even point.

    EXAMPLE: A firm has a marginal contribution (MC) of $5 and sells one unit of an item above the break-even point. EBIT is $5. If the firm sells a second unit, what happens to EBIT?
    ANSWER: It doubles to $10, a 100 percent rise in EBIT with a far smaller rise in revenues.

The degree of operating leverage at any single sales volume can be calculated from a ratio of marginal contribution to EBIT. If the marginal contribution is $90,000 and the EBIT is $45,000, the operating leverage is 90/45, or 2/1. Thus, any percentage increase in sales will result in twice that percentage increase in EBIT. Figure 2-3 shows two formulas for calculating operating leverage and gives an example of a calculation and check.

Formula 1 $OL = \dfrac{\text{Marginal Contribution}}{\text{EBIT}}$	Problem: A firm has sales of 100,000 units at $5, variable costs of $3, and fixed costs of $100,000. What is operating leverage? $OL = \dfrac{500,000 - 300,000}{500,000 - 300,000 - 100,000} = \dfrac{2}{1}$
Formula 2 $OL = \dfrac{\text{Revenue} - \text{VC}}{\text{Revenue} - \text{VC} - \text{FC}}$	Check: If sales rise 50% to 150,000 units, EBIT should rise 100% to $200,000 (EBIT is now $100,000). At the new sales level, we have
Why Two Formulas? They are the same. MC = Revenue − VC EBIT = Revenue − VC − FC	New OL = $\dfrac{750 - 450}{750 - 450 - 100} = \dfrac{300}{200} = \dfrac{3}{2}$ EBIT = 750 − 450 − 100 = 200,000

Figure 2-3. Calculation of Operating Leverage.

Note that the rise in sales in Figure 2-3 produces a new degree of operating leverage at 150,000 units. Another rise in sales will be accompanied by only one and a half times as large an increase in **operating income (EBIT)**. Operating leverage will decrease with each increase in sales above the break-even point, because fixed costs become relatively smaller compared to revenues and variable costs.

Significance of Operating Leverage

What does operating leverage tell the financial manager? It tells the impact of changes in sales on operating income. If a firm has a high degree of operating leverage, small changes in sales will have large effects on EBIT. If the change is a small rise in sales, profits will rise dramatically. But if the change is a small decline in forecasted sales, EBIT may be wiped out and a loss may be reported.

As a general rule, firms do not like to operate under conditions of a high degree of operating leverage. This is a high-risk situation in which a small drop in sales can be excessively damaging to the firm's efforts to achieve profitability. The firm prefers to operate sufficiently above break-even to avoid the danger of a fluctuation in sales and profits.

Fixed-Charges Leverage

Fixed-charges leverage (sometimes called financial leverage) exists whenever a firm has debt or other sources of funds that carry fixed charges. It gives us a measure of the degree to which changes in operating income will affect **earnings before taxes (EBT)**. It makes use of the same principle as operating leverage with a formula as follows:

$$\text{fixed-charges leverage} = \frac{\text{revenue - VC - FC}}{\text{revenue - VC - FC - I}} = \frac{\text{EBIT}}{\text{EBT}}$$

In our previous example, if the firm had annual interest payments of $25,000, its fixed-charges leverage at 100,000 units of sales would be

$$\text{fixed-charges leverage} = \frac{500 - 300 - 100}{500 - 300 - 100 - 25} = \frac{100}{75} = \frac{1.33}{1}$$

$$\text{or 1 1/3 times}$$

This means that any increase in EBIT would be accompanied by a 1-1/3 increase in EBT. If EBIT doubles to $200,000, EBT = 200 - 25 or 175,000, an increase of 100,000 from the original 75,000, or an increase of 133 percent. The new level of fixed-charges leverage would be 200/175, or 1.14/1. As with operating leverage, fixed-charges leverage also decreases with increases in EBIT.

Fixed-charges leverage is more commonly called financial leverage in the financial literature. This is confusing because there are two different leverage concepts identified by the term financial leverage. To avoid this confusion, an analyst should always check the meaning of "financial leverage" when the term is used by someone else.

Combined Leverage

Combined leverage is used to compare changes in revenues with changes in EBT. As the name implies, it combines the effects of operating and fixed-charges leverage. It may be calculated in two ways:

1. *A Ratio of Marginal Contribution to EBT.* This may be done with either the MC/EBT or (revenue − VC)/(revenue − VC −FC − I) formulas.
2. *Operating Leverage Times Fixed-Charges Leverage.*Thus, if the operating leverage is 2/1 and the fixed-charges leverage is 3/1, the combined leverage will be 6/1.

In the preceding example, at 100,000 units the combined leverage would be 2/1 times 1.33 (OL × FChL) = 2.66/1. This means that any change in sales will produce 2.66 times that percentage of change in EBT. The combined leverage for the example may also be calculated from the formula

$$\text{combined leverage} = \frac{MC}{EBT} = \frac{\text{revenue - VC}}{\text{revenue - VC - FC - I}}$$

$$= \frac{500 - 300}{500 - 300 - 100 - 25} = \frac{200,000}{75,000} = 2.66 \text{ times}$$

Table 2-3 gives the formulas and some of the important characteristics of each of the marginal-analysis leverages.

TABLE 2-3. Characteristics of the Three Kinds of Leverage in Profit Planning.

Operating Leverage

$\dfrac{\text{revenue - VC}}{\text{revenue - VC - FC}} = \dfrac{MC}{EBIT}$ Isolates fixed costs Compares changes in revenues to changes in EBIT by formula:

(O.L.) (% change in sales) = % change in EBIT

Fixed Charges Leverage

$\dfrac{\text{revenue - VC - FC}}{\text{revenue - VC - FC - I}} = \dfrac{EBIT}{EBT}$ Isolates interest Compares changes in EBIT to changes in EBT by formula:

(FChL) (% change in EBIT) = % change in EBT

Combined Leverage

$\dfrac{\text{revenue - VC}}{\text{revenue - VC - FC - I}} = \dfrac{MC}{EBT}$ Isolates both fixed costs and interest Compares changes in revenues to changes in EBT by formula:

(C.L.) (% change in sales) = % change in EBT

Two Questions on Profit Planning Leverage Concepts

1. *Why Can Changes in Revenues Be Measured Directly Even Though Operating Leverage and Combined Leverage Use Marginal Contribution, Not Sales?* With constant costs assumed in the range of operations, the relationship between revenues and variable costs does not change on a unit basis. Therefore, each additional unit of sales produces a unit of marginal contribution. With marginal contribution and sales locked in a fixed relationship, we can deal directly with changes in sales to see leverage effects.

2. *Does Leverage Work When Sales Are Decreasing As Well As Increasing?* Yes. If, for example, operating leverage were 2/1, a drop of 50 percent in sales will erase EBIT. Care should be exercised in dealing with decreases since losses involve negative numbers, but the leverage concepts apply.

EXAMPLE: A firm has sales of $2,000,000, variable costs of $1,400,000, fixed costs of $400,000, and debt of $1,000,000 at 10 percent. What are its operating, fixed charges, and combined leverages?

ANSWER:

$$\text{Operating leverage} = \frac{2,000 - 1,400}{2,000 - 1,400 - 400} = \frac{600}{200} = 3/1$$

$$\text{Fixed-charges leverage} = \frac{200}{200 - 100} = \frac{200}{100} = 2/1$$

$$\text{Combined leverage} = 600/100 = 6/1$$

EXAMPLE: If the preceding firm wants to double its EBIT, how much of a rise in sales would be needed on a percentage basis?

ANSWER: The formula is:

$$\left(\begin{array}{c}\text{operating}\\ \text{leverage}\end{array}\right) \left(\begin{array}{c}\text{percent change}\\ \text{in sales}\end{array}\right) = \begin{array}{c}\text{percent change}\\ \text{in EBIT}\end{array}$$

$$(3/1)(\% \text{ sales}) = 100\%$$

% sales = 100%/3 = 33 1/3 percent rise in sales to get a 100 percent rise in EBIT

EXAMPLE: If the preceding firm had a 20 percent rise in sales, what percentage rise would it have in EBIT? EBT?
ANSWER: 3/1 times 20 percent or a 60 percent rise in EBIT. 6/1 times 20 percent or a 120 percent rise in EBT.

EXAMPLE: If the preceding firm had a 50 percent decline in sales, what percentage drop would it have in EBIT? EBT?
ANSWER: 3/1 times 50 percent or a 150 percent drop in EBIT. The firm would show an operating loss. 6/1 times 50 percent or a 300 percent drop in EBT. The firm would show a loss.

EXAMPLE: Prepare income statements showing the effects of a 20 percent rise or 50 percent decline in sales. Do the answers above check with the income statements?
ANSWER: Yes. The income statements are:

	At Present	With 20% Rise in Sales		With 50% Decline in Sales	
Sales	2,000	2,400		1,000	
Variable costs	1,400	1,680		700	
Marginal contribution	600	720		300	
Fixed costs	400	400		400	
EBIT (loss)	200	320	[60% rise]	(100)	[150% drop]
Interest	100	100		100	
EBT	100	220	[120% rise]	(200)	[300% drop]
Federal income taxes	50	110		0	
NIAT (loss)	50	110		(200)	

14. LIQUIDITY, HOW TO ANALYZE WITH RATIOS

Cash, receivable, and **inventory ratios** should be used together to gain an overall grasp on the **liquidity** of the firm. We shall analyze each area and draw conclusions on the liquidity of Colorama, Inc., using the balance sheet and income statement provided.

The **current ratio** and **quick ratio** or **acid test** are as follows:

$$\text{current ratio} = \frac{\text{cash} + \text{marketable securities} + \text{accounts receivable} + \text{inventory}}{\text{accounts payable} + \text{miscellaneous payable}}$$

$$= \frac{7,000 + 21,000 + 60,000 + 75,000}{55,000 + 12,000} = \frac{163,000}{67,000}$$

$$= 2.4/1, \text{ for } 1975$$

$$\text{quick ratio} = \frac{\text{cash} + \text{marketable securities} + \text{accounts receivable}}{\text{accounts payable} + \text{miscellaneous payable}}$$

$$= \frac{7,000 + 21,000 + 60,000}{55,000 + 12,000} = \frac{88,000}{67,000} = 1.3/1, \text{ for } 1975$$

COLORAMA, INC., Balance Sheet (Year ending December 31, 1975)

	1975	1974		1975	1974
Current assets			Current liabilities		
Cash	$ 7,000	$ 10,000	Accts. payable	$ 55,000	$ 25,000
Mkt. securities	21,000	23,000	Misc. payable	12,000	7,000
Accts. receivable	60,000	45,000			
Inventories	75,000	62,000	Mortgage (5%)	70,000	75,000
			Bonds (7%)	80,000	90,000
Fixed assets			Equity		
Machinery (less acc. depr.)	80,000	75,000	Common stock	80,000	80,000
Plant (less acc. depr.)	166,000	110,000	Excess over par	25,000	25,000
Land	60,000	60,000	Retained earnings	147,000	83,000
Total Assets	$469,000	$385,000	Total	$469,000	$385,000

COLORAMA, INC., Income Statement (Year ending December 31, 1975)

	1975	1974
Net sales and other revenues	$495,000	$370,000
Cost of goods sold	225,000	165,000
Gross Margin	$270,000	$205,000
Administrative expenses	115,000	85,000
Operating Income	$155,000	$120,000
Interest paid	8,000	9,000
Earnings Before Taxes	$147,000	$111,000
Federal income taxes	67,000	52,000
Net Income After Taxes	$80,000	$59,000

Colorama, Inc., has a current ratio of 2.4/1, which exceeds a 2/1 guideline that is widely used as a norm. Its acid test is 1.3/1, which exceeds a 1/1 guideline that is also commonly used by analysts as a norm. Since both ratios are higher than the norms, the company appears to be sufficiently liquid. To check this conclusion, we can compare the 1975 ratios with 1974. In 1974, Colorama, Inc., had ratios of

$$\text{Current Ratio, 1974} \quad \frac{10 + 23 + 45 + 62}{25 + 7} = \frac{140}{32} = 4.4/1$$

$$\text{Quick Ratio, 1974} \quad \frac{10 + 23 + 45}{25 + 7} \qquad = \frac{78}{32} = 2.4/1$$

Between 1974 and 1975, the current ratio dropped from 4.4 to 2.4; the quick ratio dropped from 2.4 to 1.3. From this information, we can conclude that the firm is less liquid in 1975 than it was in 1974. Although the 1975 figures may still be adequate, the analyst may wish to investigate the reasons for the drop in both ratios.

To check the liquidity of accounts receivable, we can calculate the 1974 and 1975 turnover and collection period:

Accounts Receivable Turnover – Sales Receivables

$$\frac{495}{60} = 8.2 \text{ times} \quad 1975 \qquad \frac{370}{45} = 8.2 \text{ times} \quad 1974$$

Average Collection Period $= \dfrac{\text{Receivables}}{\text{Sales 1360 days}}$

$$\frac{60,000}{495,000/360 \text{ days}} = \frac{60}{1.38} = 44 \text{ days} \quad 1975$$

$$\frac{45,000}{370,000/360 \text{ days}} = \frac{45}{1.03} = 44 \text{ days} \quad 1974$$

Both ratios have remained steady at 8.2 and 44 days, respectively, indicating no deterioration in the receivables liquidity. (*Note:* To check the mathematics of our calculation, we can multiply the turnover times the collection period to see if we get approximately 360 days. 8.2 × 44 = 360.8 days. This reveals the relationship between the two ratios. A turnover of 8.2 is the same as waiting 44 days to collect the amount of accounts receivable shown on the balance sheet.)

To check the liquidity of the inventory, we can perform three calculations using the firm's sales and inventory:

$$\frac{\text{Inventory}}{\text{Turnover}} = \frac{\text{Sales}}{\text{Inventory}}$$

1975 **Inventory Turnover**   1974 Inventory Turnover

$$\frac{495,000}{75,000} = 6.6/1 \qquad\qquad\qquad \frac{370,000}{62,000} = 6.0/1$$

Turnover Using Average Inventory

$$\frac{495,000}{1/2(75,000 + 62,000)} = 7.4/1$$

From this overall liquidity analysis, we can conclude that the receivables and inventory ratios show little change in liquidity, and the current ratio and quick ratio show a possible deterioration. The analyst would make efforts to learn more about the company, but first he would examine the balance sheet to see why the ratios changed. The major cause of the change seems to be the large increase in accounts payable from 25,000 to 55,000. Although increases in receivables and inventories accompany the increase in payables, the analyst should inquire as to the cause of the payables rise.

15. OWNERSHIP FACTORS, HOW TO ANALYZE WITH RATIOS

Using the data from Colorama, Inc., an analyst has prepared a worksheet showing the **ownership ratios** for the company and the analyst's estimate of normal ratios for this kind of firm.

Worksheet of Ownership Ratios for Colorama, Inc.

Ratio	Colorama, 1975	Colorama, 1974	Norms
Earnings ratios			
Earnings per share[a]	80,000/40,000 = $2	59,000/40,000 = $1.47	None
Price-earnings[b]	17/2 = 8.5/1	15/1.47 = 10/1	12-15/1
Capitalization rate	2/17 = 12%	1.47/15 = 10%	7-8%
Capital structure			
Debt-equity	217,000/252,000 = .86/1	197,000/188,000 = 1.05/1	1/1
Debt-asset	217,000/469,000 = .46/1	197,000/385,000 = .51/1	.5/1
Book value	252/40 = $6.30 share	188/40 = $4.70 share	None
Dividend ratios[c]			
Dividends per share	16,000/40,000 = $.40	14,000/40,000 = $.35	None
Dividend payout	.40/2 = 20%	.35/1.47 = 24%	40%
Dividend yield	$.40/17 = 2.3%	$.35/15 = 2.3%	4%

[a] Colorama has 40,000 shares outstanding.
[b] Colorama's market price is $17 at the end of 1975 and $15 at the end of 1974.
[c] Colorama paid a $16,000 dividend in 1975 and a $14,000 dividend in 1974.

From the worksheet an analyst might draw the following conclusions about Colorama:

1. *It Offers a High Return.* The low **price-earnings** ratio results in a high **capitalization rate.** Since this is a measure of the profit earned by

the firm compared to the price of the stock, it indicates that the firm is above the expected return on a shareholder's investment. The price of the stock may be expected to increase until Colorama reaches its normal price-earnings range of 12-15/1.

2. *It Has a Reasonable Capital Structure.* The **debt-equity** and **debt-asset ratios** are close to the norm.

3. *It Does Not Offer Satisfactory Current Income.* The **dividend ratios** indicate that Colorama is retaining its earnings rather than paying expected cash dividends to its shareholders. The **dividend payout** is approximately half the norm, and the dividend yield is only slightly better.

From a potential owner's point of view, we might conclude that Colorama is a high-return, financially balanced firm that offers long-term prospects for increases in **market price** rather than payments of cash as current income. With a high profit and high retention of earnings, the firm may be expected to grow rapidly, with resulting increase in the price of its stock. Since the other ratios reveal that the firm is liquid and profitable, (see Section 14, "Liquidity, How to Analyze with Ratios" and Section 17, "Profitability, How to Analyze with Ratios.") our external analysis indicates it offers a good buy for the long-term investor who is not seeking current income.

COLORAMA, INC., Balance Sheet (Year ending December 31, 1975)

	1975	1974		1975	1974
Current assets			Current liabilities		
Cash	$ 7,000	$ 10,000	Accts. payable	$ 55,000	$ 25,000
Mkt. securities	21,000	23,000	Misc. payable	12,000	7,000
Accts. receivable	60,000	45,000			
Inventories	75,000	62,000	Mortgage (5%)	70,000	75,000
			Bonds (7%)	80,000	90,000
Fixed assets			Equity		
Machinery (less acc. depr.)	80,000	75,000	Common stock	80,000	80,000
Plant (less acc. depr.)	166,000	110,000	Excess over par	25,000	25,000
Land	60,000	60,000	Retained earnings	147,000	83,000
Total Assets	$469,000	$385,000	Total	$469,000	$385,000

COLORAMA, INC., Income Statement (Year ending December 31, 1975)

	1975	1974
Net sales and other revenues	$495,000	$370,000
Cost of goods sold	225,000	165,000
Gross Margin	$270,000	$205,000
Administrative expenses	115,000	85,000
Operating Income	$155,000	$120,000
Interest paid	8,000	9,000
Earnings Before Taxes	$147,000	$111,000
Federal income taxes	67,000	52,000
Net Income After Taxes	$80,000	$59,000

16. PROFIT PLANNING, HOW TO PRICE THE USE OF A CAPITAL ASSET

When a firm leases a capital asset for a given period of time, it must calculate the rental price to the user of the asset. Firms **leasing** computers or trucks, renting commercial real estate, or chartering ships face similar pricing decisions. If supporting services, such as operations, management, or maintenance are provided, these costs must be considered. Also, the firm must recover its capital, provide for inflation, evaluate the asset's **residual value**, and earn a profit. This section outlines an approach to consider these factors in pricing a capital asset.

Two Kinds of Costs

In the pricing decision, the firm must evaluate two distinct costs as follows:

1. *Services Costs.* If supporting services are provided, these must be included. If they will rise with inflation over the period of the contract, this inflation must be considered.
2. *Capital Recovery.* The firm must receive compensation for the decline in value of the fixed asset during the lease period. If, for example, a railroad car will decline from $2,000,000 to $800,000 during a 10-year lease, the firm must recover $1,200,000 plus a financing cost during the 10 years. Additionally, the lessor tied up another $800,000 during the asset's lease period. Even though this is returned in the form of a residual value, a financing charge must be added to pay for tying up the $800,000.

Crediting Back the Residual Value

A critical part of the pricing decision on a medium- to long-term lease is the forecast of the likely residual value (see Section 20, "Residual Values, How to Forecast"). The likely residual value should be credited back to the user in the form of lower annual payments. As an example, consider an automobile that cost $10,000, is leased for 3 years, and will have a **market value** of $4,000 at the end of the lease. Assume the leasing firm has a 10 percent cost of money. Using the compound interest table for an annuity, at the 3rd year, 10 percent crossing is the factor 3.310. Dividing this into the residual value of $4,000, we get $4,000/3.310 = $1,208.46. This means that an annual payment of $1,208.46 compounded at 10 percent will produce $4,000 in 3 years. Thus, if the leasing firm desired a $200 profit each year for arranging the lease and if no supporting services were provided, the pricing would be:

Cost of $10,000 amortized at 10%	
for 3 years ($10,000/2.487 from Table)	$4,021.15
Less credit for residual ($4,000/3.310)	−1,208.46
Plus desired profit each year	+200.00
Annual Lease Cost	$3,012.69

An alternative method of arriving at this value is commonly used. The difference between the original cost and the residual value is amortized directly. In our example, this would be $10,000 − 4,000 = $6,000. Then, a financing charge is added for tying up the residual for the period of the lease. Finally, profit is added. In our example, the calculation would be:

Cost of decline in asset value during	
3 year lease ($6,000/2.487 from Table)	$2,412.55
Cost of tying up $4,000 at 10%	400.00
Profit desired	200.00
Annual Lease Cost	$3,012.55

The effect of either calculation is to recognize the residual value in pricing the asset.

Effect of Inflation on Residual

In periods of forecasted high inflation, the residual should gain over the original estimate of its value. Assume in the example above that 10 percent annual inflation is expected during the 3-year lease period. If the market value of the car conservatively rises at half the rate of inflation, the residual value will be $4,000 \times (1.05)^3 = \$4,631$. The additional $631 can be credited to the user as follows:

Annual lease cost (calculated above)	$3,012.55
Less credit for inflationary increase on	
residual ($631/3.310 from Table)	190.63
Revised Annual Lease Cost	$2,821.92

Averaging Final Rate

Even though supporting services and residual values are subject to inflation, most users desire a fixed price for at least 3 to 5 years. To get such a rate, a simple arithmetic average is a good approximation of a fair rate. As an example, a lessor could quote a price of $2,250 per year if he needed the following each year on a 5-year lease:

Year	Appropriate Lease Rate
1	$ 2,100
2	2,165
3	2,230
4	2,320
5	2,435
	$11,250 ÷ 5 yrs. = $2,250 annual level rental

A Solved Problem

EXAMPLE: A computer services company is developing a quote for a 5-year full-service and operating lease on a $6,500,000 data processing center to be installed in a large manufacturing firm. The operating expenses (salaries, electricity, insurance, etc.) will cost $900,000 the first year and will increase by 10 percent each year thereafter. The residual value of the hardware is estimated at $3,000,000 but it will be higher than this amount by 5 percent a year due to inflation. The computer services company wants a $200,000 profit each year and the lessee wants a fixed rate. The firm's cost of capital is 12 percent. What should be the annual rental on the computer center?
ANSWER: $2,499,466 as follows:

Item	1st Year	2nd Year	3rd Year	4th Year	5th Year
Operating expenses (10% annual rise)	$ 900,000	$ 990,000	$1,089,000	$1,198,000	$1,318,000
Cost of $3,500,000 at 12% = (3,500,000/3.605 from table)	970,934	970,934	970,934	970,934	970,934
Cost of $3,000,000 residual tied up at 12% = ($3,000,000 × .12)	360,000	360,000	360,000	360,000	360,000
Credit for inflationary increase on residual [a] = (828,845/6.353 from table)	(130,468)	(130,468)	(130,468)	(130,468)	(130,468)
desired profit	200,000	200,000	200,000	200,000	200,000
Annual lease revenues	$2,300,466 +	$2,390,466 +	$2,489,466 +	$2,598,466 +	$2,718,466

Total revenues for 5 years = $12,497,330 ÷ 5 years

Average annual rental   = $2,499,466

[a] 3,000,000 × 1.05 ^{5} = 3,828,845 − 3,000,000 = $828,845 expected increase in residual value.

Conclusion

The above approach to pricing the use of a capital asset charges service costs, capital depletion, cost of tied up capital, and inflationary rises in costs to the user of an asset. It gives the user credit for the expected residual value and inflationary increases in that value. And it considers the desired profit as it reaches a fixed rate to quote to the user.

17. PROFITABILITY, HOW TO ANALYZE WITH RATIOS

As an example of **profitability analysis,** we shall use the Colorama, Inc., data. Colorama's **profit margins** are

$$\text{Profit Margin} = \frac{\text{Operating Income}}{\text{Sales}}$$

$$1975 \quad \frac{155,000}{495,000} = 31\% \qquad 1974 \quad \frac{120,000}{370,000} = 32\%$$

As a guideline, a profit margin of 15 to 25 percent is considered satisfactory. If firms similar to Colorama have profit margins in this range, Colorama is realizing a higher profit on sales than its competition.

Colorama's **gross profit margin** are

$$\text{Gross Profit Margin} = \frac{\text{Gross Margin}}{\text{Sales}}$$

$$1975 \quad \frac{270,000}{495,000} = 55\% \qquad 1974 \quad \frac{205,000}{370,000} = 55\%$$

This compares to a profit margin of 31 to 32 percent. Since the gross profit margin does not consider general and administrative expenses in the numerator of the fraction and hence covers fewer costs, the gross profit margin is always a larger percentage than the profit margin. As a general guideline, a gross profit margin of 35 to 50 percent is satisfactory.

The **asset turnovers** for Colorama are

$$\text{Asset Turnover} = \frac{\text{Sales}}{\text{Assets}}$$

$$1975 \quad \frac{495,000}{469,000} = 1.05 \text{ times} \quad 1974 \quad \frac{370,000}{385,000} = .96 \text{ times}$$

Note that these ratios do not mean that the firm is selling its operating assets. Rather, the dollar volume of Colorama's sales were 5 percent larger in 1975 and 4 percent smaller in 1974 than the dollar value of the firm's assets as shown on the balance sheet. A turnover of 1 to 2 times is considered satisfactory for most industrial firms.

The **returns on investment** (ROI) for Colorama are

$$\text{ROI} = \frac{\text{Operating Income}}{\text{Assets}}$$

1975 $\dfrac{155,000}{469,000} = 33\%$ 1974 $\dfrac{120,000}{385,000} = 31\%$

This may also be calculated by multiplying the profit margin by the asset turnover:

1975 (31%)(1.05) = 33%   1974 (32%)(.96) = 31%

As a guideline, we expect mature firms to have returns on investment in a range of 25 to 40 percent. Colorama is within this range.

Since Colorama has no preferred stock, we can use net income after taxes (NIAT) to calculate **return on equity (ROE)**:

$$\text{ROE} = \frac{\text{NIAT}}{\text{Equity}}$$

1975 $\dfrac{80,000}{80,000 + 25,000 + 147,000} = \dfrac{80,000}{252,000} = 32\%$

1974 $\dfrac{59,000}{80,000 + 25,000 + 83,000} = \dfrac{59,000}{188,000} = 31\%$

The return on equity will usually be considerably lower than the return on investment because ROE is an after-tax measure of profit, and corporate taxes take up approximately 40-50 percent of the firm's earnings before taxes. As a guideline, a satisfactory ROE is 60 to 80 percent of ROI. For example, if ROI is 20 percent, ROE should be 12 to 16 percent. Colorama has a very high ROE and appears to be very successful in converting operating income into earnings available to the common shareholder.

Colorama's **earning power (EP)** for each year is

$$\text{Earning Power} = \frac{\text{NIAT}}{\text{Assets}}$$

1975 $\dfrac{80,000}{469,000} = 17\%$ 1974 $\dfrac{59,000}{385,000} = 15\%$

A satisfactory earning power would be 10 to 15 percent. Colorama is at the top of this range and improved from 1974 to 1975.

Colorama's **times interest earned** ratios are

$$\text{Times Interest Earned} = \frac{\text{Operating Income}}{\text{Interest}}$$

$$1975 \quad \frac{155,000}{8,000} = 19 \text{ times} \qquad 1974 \quad \frac{120,000}{9,000} = 13 \text{ times}$$

These ratios far exceed the guideline of 5 to 7 times. In 1975, Colorama could experience a 95 percent drop in earnings before interest and taxes (a drop of $147,000) and still be able to cover its fixed charges on debt.

After calculating the profit ratios for Colorama, the analyst will prepare a matrix such as Table 2-4. This allows a comparison of the expected ratios and the actual figures for the company being examined. If any of the ratios fail to meet the guidelines, the analyst will consider the factors in Figure 2-4 and trace back the ratios to the causes of the inadequate performance. For example, the return on investment might be low and the cause may be a low selling price, idle assets, high production costs, inadequate sales, high administrative expenses, or a combination of these factors. Table 2-4 indicates that Colorama meets the profit guidelines established by the analyst.

TABLE 2-4. Comparison Matrix Showing Guidelines and Actual Ratios.

Profitability Ratio	Guideline	Colorama Actual	
		1975	1974
Gross profit margin	35-50%	55%	55%
Profit margin	15-25%	31%	32%
Asset turnover	1-2 times	1.05 times	.96 times
Return on investment	25-40%	33%	31%
Return on equity	60-80% of ROI	32% (97% of ROI)	31% (100% of ROI)
Earning power	10-15%	17%	15%
Times interest earned	5-7 times	19 times	13 times

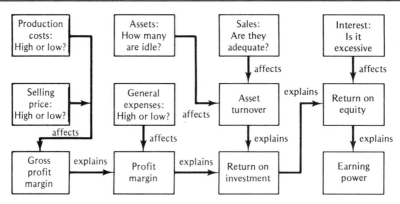

Figure 2-4. Factors Affecting Profit and the Interrelation of Profitability Ratios.

18. PROFITS, HOW TO MAINTAIN UNDER INFLATION

During periods of expected high inflation, the firm must include rising price levels in its profit planning for the short-term future. The failure to consider inflationary effects may cause cash shortages, a depletion of capital, and a liquidity crisis. The liquidity difficulties can usually be avoided if the firm properly plans to make adequate profits to keep pace with the inflation. In this section, we develop an inflation factor that can be used in a profit model to help the firm plan for appropriate profits under inflationary conditions.

Selecting the Inflation Factor

An inflation factor in profit planning is the annual percent rate of inflation that will apply to a firm's costs and capital needs during the next operating period. A firm usually selects an inflation factor from one of three sources:

1. *GNP Implicit Price Deflator.* This index number is prepared every month by the U.S. Department of Commerce and can be used by firms to measure the impact of inflation in the general economy. The **GNP implicit price deflator** has been accepted by the accounting profession (Accounting Principles Board, Statement Number 3, 1969) as the appropriate inflation measure to use in reporting price-level changes on financial statements. The major advantage and disadvantage to this index as a firm's inflation factor are as follows:
   a. Advantage: It is current and inexpensive since it is prepared and distributed by the government. It is a reasonable approximation of the price changes that occurred in previous periods and the effects of those changes on the firm's activities.
   b. Disadvantage: It cannot be used well as a measure of the next period's inflation because it is concerned only with historical price-level changes. For profit planning, the firm must forecast inflationary effects, not wait until they have already occurred.
2. *Industry Index.* The U.S. government or a trade association may identify the inflationary pressures on an entire industry. These pressures may be reported as expected price increases for labor, raw materials, or goods in the next period. For a representative firm in the industry, the industry index may be fairly accurate as an inflation factor.
3. *Specific Inflation Factor for the Firm.* The firm may gather data from a variety of sources and develop its own inflation factor that fits the firm's unique position in the economy. Although this may be costly, it will provide the most reliable estimate of the inflationary pressures on the firm in the next operating period.

Developing an Inflation Factor for a Specific Firm

A relatively simple approach to developing a specific inflation factor for a firm involves the use of a weighted-average technique. The firm's major cost categories are identified and weighted by their contribution to total costs. An analyst forecasts the inflationary impact on each item for the next year, and these impacts are weighted to get an overall effect. As an example of this technique, let us consider a firm that has six major cost categories to deal with during a period of rising prices. The categories and inflationary pressures are:

1. *Raw Materials.* The firm is in an industry that is dependent upon large amounts of copper and steel components. As a result of expected price rises in these materials, the firm forecasts a 12 percent rise in the cost of raw materials during the next year. Raw materials make up approximately 35 percent of the firm's total costs.

2. *Labor.* The firm should have no labor problems next year since employees are in the second year of a 4-year contract. The scheduled raise will occur at the start of the year and will be an average of 9.2 percent for all employees. Labor costs represent 30 percent of total costs.

3. *General and Administrative Expenses.* A strict budget has been imposed on these expenses and they will not be allowed to rise more than 3 percent. These comprise 10 percent of total expenses.

4. *Cash Overhead.* Because of heavy increases in municipal taxes, fuel oil, and utilities, these expenses are expected to rise by 11 percent even though the firm has been taking extreme economy measures. These costs make up 10 percent of total costs.

5. *Depreciation.* Although depreciation will not change, the firm's depreciation is not deemed adequate to allow replacement of the firm's plant and equipment when it wears out. Capital goods are rising at a 15 percent rate and the firm should plan to set aside this amount after taxes. Since the money set aside is not an expense and thus offers no tax shield, we must convert 15 percent to an after-tax rate. To do this, we use the following formula:

$$\frac{\text{rise in capital equipment prices}}{1 - \text{tax rate}} = \frac{15\%}{1 - 50\%} = 30\%$$

With a 50 percent tax rate, the firm must earn 30 percent to set aside 15 percent to replace machinery. The depreciation makes up 10 percent of total costs.

6. *Additional Working Capital Cost.* Because of the rising prices, the firm must generate funds to pay for additional inventory, receivables,

and cash. The firm should use its cost of capital as the cost and multiply the cost of capital times the additional money needed. For example, if a firm expected a $100,000 rise in working capital due to inflation and the cost of capital was 12 percent, the additional working capital cost would be ($100,000) (.12), or $12,000. For our firm, the cost of capital is 14 percent and the working capital as an additional cost will be 5 percent of total costs.

These effects are itemized and weighted in Table 2-5. The overall inflation factor for the firm for the next year is 12.06 percent. Stated another way, the firm will need to plan for a 12.06 rise in its costs during the next year if it is to finish the year with its forecasted profits and if it is to finish the year without suffering an erosion in its assets or in the ability to replace its assets as they wear out.

TABLE 2-5. Calculating an Inflation Factor.

	Inflation Factor	$\times$	Weighted Cost (%)	$=$	Weighted Average (%)
Raw materials	12.0%		35		4.20
Labor	9.2		30		2.76
General and Administrative	3.0		10		.30
Cash overhead	11.0		10		1.10
Depreciation	30.0		10		3.00
Cost of added working captial	14.0		5		.70
			100		12.06

Determining Selling Prices Under Inflation

When a firm sets its selling price for a product, it usually has a profit goal in mind. The profit goal is in **constant dollars**, which may be defined as a future dollar that has the same purchasing power as today's dollar. Under inflation, the profits may be realized in terms of **current dollars**, or dollars whose purchasing power fluctuates with inflation. As an example, a firm may set a $100,000 profit goal and may achieve it at a time when inflation is 10 percent. In current dollars, the firm has $100,000; in constant dollars the firm has $100,000/1.10, or $90,909. This means that the firm can use its $100,000 to purchase goods worth $90,909 today.

In order to reach a profit goal without a loss of purchasing power, the firm must consider inflation when it establishes its selling price for a product. A formula for determining selling price is given in Figure 2-5. The example in this figure involves a product that costs $4 per unit to produce. The firm desires a before-tax profit of $.60 per unit in constant dollars. To achieve this goal under inflation of 12 percent, the firm must sell the product for $5.15 and realize $.67 per unit in current dollars.

	Example of Model
Required selling price $= \dfrac{\left(\begin{array}{c}\text{Product}\\ \text{cost}\end{array}\right)\left(1 + \begin{array}{c}\text{inflation}\\ \text{factor}\end{array}\right)}{1 - \begin{array}{c}\text{desired profit}\\ \text{margin}\end{array}}$ where product cost = total costs involved in producing product $\begin{array}{c}\text{desired}\\ \text{profit}\\ \text{margin}\end{array} = \dfrac{\text{desired B-Tax profit}}{\begin{array}{c}\text{product}\\ \text{cost}\end{array} + \begin{array}{c}\text{desired}\\ \text{B} - \text{T profit}\end{array}}$	A product costs $4 to produce and the firm desires a $.60 profit on it before taxes. The inflation factor is 12%. What is the required selling price? ANS. selling price $= \dfrac{(\$4)(1.12)}{1 - (.60/4.60)} = \dfrac{\$4.48}{.87} = \$5.15$ $\$5.15 - \$4.48 = \$.67$ profit in current dollars

Figure 2-5. Determining Selling Price Under Inflation, a Model.

EXAMPLE: A firm expects its cost of goods sold to rise by 15 percent next year while general and administrative expenses rise by 5 percent. The cost of goods sold is 55 percent of total costs while general and administrative expenses are 25 percent. The firm's depreciation will be 10 percent less than the cash needed to replace fixed assets and depreciation makes up 15 percent of costs. The remaining 5 percent of total costs will be additional working capital needed as a result of inflation. The firm's cost of capital is 12 percent. The firm's major product costs $9 to manufacture and sell and the firm seeks a profit margin of 15 percent. What is the required selling price for the product? ANSWER: The inflation factor is 13.1 percent as follows:

	inflation factor (%) ×	weight (%) =	weighted average (%)
Cost of goods sold	15	55	8.25
General and admin.	5	25	1.25
Depreciation	20	15	3.00
Added working cap.	12	5	.60
		100	13.10

The required selling price is $11.98, as follows:

$$\frac{\$9(1.131)}{1 - 15\%} = \frac{10.179}{.85} = \$11.98$$

Why Are Interest Charges Omitted in Total Costs?

In the calculations above, the firm's interest on debt has been omitted in the calculations of total costs. In effect, we are dealing with total operating costs and are assuming that interest charges are not affected by inflation since they are fixed during the life of a loan. But a more important reason exists for omitting interest. When a firm selects a desired profit margin, the margin should be sufficiently high to cover interest and provide a profit for common shareholders. That is, a 15 percent profit margin results in an EBIT that can be used to make interest payments and dividend payments. If only interest were included in any calculations, it would imply that dividends are not a consideration. The firm with large amounts of debt would need more profit according to the formula than the equity-financed firm. Rather than give this impression, the formula requires the firm to set a desired profit margin sufficiently high to provide interest and dividend payments appropriate to the firm's situation.

As interest is omitted, the cost of additional working capital is included. This is an apparent contradiction. Still, it is correct to include the cost of additional working capital due to inflation. When the firm set its 15 percent profit margin, it planned to meet specific interest obligations and provide a certain profit to shareholders. If the additional financing cost from higher working capital is ignored, the firm will not meet its interest and dividend goals (profit goals also). To meet these goals, the firm must treat the cost of added working capital as an operating expense and include it in the calculation of required selling price.

When To Raise the Selling Price

Using the selling-price formula, we can calculate the final selling price for the next period. Since inflation is gradual over the period of a year, the selling price may be raised in several steps to reflect the inflationary pressures. In our example where the selling price must rise from $4.60 to $5.15 by year's end, we had costs rising from $4.00 to $4.48 over the year. Figure 2-6 shows the trend lines for the rises in costs and selling price. The figure also shows that the costs rise in several steps and the prices may rise in several steps. As long as the price rises approximate the trend line, the firm can carefully time the price changes to minimize any adverse effects that might occur on sales.

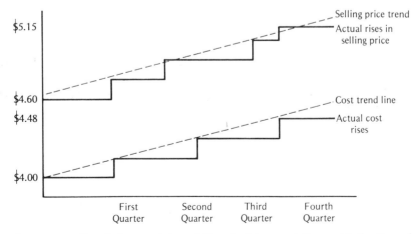

Figure 2-6. Trend Lines and Actual Rises in Prices and Costs with the Formula for Determining Selling Prices Under Inflation.

Conclusions on Profit Planning Under Inflation

This chapter focuses on the method of maintaining profits at desired levels during periods of inflation. As a conclusion, we might answer four questions raised by this method:

1. *If all firms use this approach, will it not cause additional inflationary pressures?* The answer is unquestionably yes. The techniques do not deal with ending inflation in any economy but rather are concerned with a firm maintaining its position under inflationary conditions.
2. *Is it not difficult to forecast the inflation factors used in the formula?* Yes, quite difficult. But the act of forecasting inflation will better prepare the firm for dealing in the next period.
3. *Is it not unfair to plan for a firm to maintain its capital base during inflation?* No. The firm begins a period with certain assets and these assets, notably inventory and fixed assets, should not be diminished during the period solely due to inflation.
4. *Is it not unfair to plan for additional working capital from the firm's profits?* The formula does not plan for additional working capital. It plans for paying the cost of additional working capital. It is fair to regain the costs of financing operations and the model considers the costs of financing additional inventory and receivables as a result of inflation.

Inflation has decided effects upon the firm's ability to maintain liquidity and profitability from its operations. These effects must be analyzed and methods must be developed to cope with adverse impacts. The firm that is prepared for the effects of inflation will be better prepared for operations in periods of rapidly rising price levels.

19. PROFIT-VOLUME ANALYSIS, HOW TO USE

A modification of the break-even formula results in a tool that relates profits to sales at different operating levels. By writing the break-even formulas so that fixed costs are replaced by both fixed costs and profits, the manager can solve for the sales volumes needed to produce desired profit levels. The general form of the formulas would be:

$$\$ \text{ sales} = \frac{FC + \text{profit}}{MC\%} = \begin{array}{l}\text{dollar sales needed to achieve} \\ \text{a desired profit}\end{array}$$

$$\text{Units} = \frac{FC + \text{profit}}{SP - VC} = \text{unit sales needed to achieve a desired profit}$$

Where SP = selling price
         VC = variable costs
         FC = fixed costs
       MC% = marginal contribution as a percent

These formulas recognize the fundamental relationship between sales and profits: *the excess of sales over costs, or marginal contribution, is the direct profit from operations.* This excess may be used to cover fixed costs that are not related to the volume of sales or operations. It is also available to cover any financing charges, such as interest on a mortgage, to pay federal income taxes, and to provide a profit to shareholders. Note that both formulas use marginal contribution, in the first case directly on a percentage basis and in the second case as the difference between selling price and variable costs.

The profit-volume formulas may be applied to different measures of profit. The basic meaning of profit in the formula is earnings before interest and taxes (EBIT). But EBIT may be broken out to reflect two other profit measures, as follows:

$$EBIT = interest + EBT \quad EBIT = interest + taxes + NIAT$$

Table 2-6 shows the breakout of the three profit measures and the formulas used to solve for each:

TABLE 2-6. Profit-Volume Formulas for Three Desired Profits.

Desired Profit	Dollar Sales Formula	Unit Sales Formula
EBIT	$\$ \text{sales} = \dfrac{FC + EBIT}{MC\%}$	$U = \dfrac{FC + EBIT}{SP - VC}$
EBT	$\$ \text{sales} = \dfrac{FC + interest + EBT}{MC\%}$	$U = \dfrac{FC + interest + EBT}{SP - VC}$
NIAT	$\$ \text{sales} = \dfrac{FC + interest + taxes + NIAT}{MC\%}$	$U = \dfrac{FC + interest + taxes + NIAT}{SP - VC}$

Although they solve for different profits, in effect the formulas in Table 2-6 represent break-even calculations at desired profit levels.

Profit-Volume Problems

To illustrate the use of these formulas, consider a firm that has a selling price of $6, variable costs of $4, fixed costs of $100,000, debt of $300,000 at 10 percent, and a 50 percent tax rate.

1. *Problem 1.* If the firm desires an EBIT of $200,000, what level of sales must it achieve?

$$\text{Answer: } \$ \text{ sales} = \frac{100,000 + 200,000}{(6 - 4)/6} = \frac{300,000}{33\ 1/3\%} = \underline{\$900,000}$$

$$U = \frac{100,000 + 200,000}{6 - 4} = \frac{300,000}{2} = \underline{150,000 \text{ units}}$$

2. *Problem 2.* If the firm desires an earnings before taxes (EBT) of $250,000, what level of sales must it achieve?

$$\text{Answer: } \$ \text{ sales} = \frac{100,000 + 30,000 + 250,000}{33\ 1/3\%} = \underline{\$1,140,000}$$

$$U = \frac{380,000}{6 - 4} = \underline{190,000 \text{ units}}$$

3. *Problem 3.* If the firm desires a net income after taxes (NIAT) of $300,000, what level of sales must be achieved?

$$\text{Answer: } \$ \text{ sales} = \frac{100,000 + 30,000 + 300,000 + 300,000}{33\ 1/3\%}$$

$$= \frac{730,000}{33\ 1/3\%} = \underline{\$2,190,000}$$

$$U = \frac{730,000}{6 - 4} = \underline{365,000 \text{ units}}$$

20. RESIDUAL VALUES, HOW TO FORECAST

In a lease or other long-term agreement to rent a fixed asset, the asset's residual value is a major consideration in arriving at the terms in the agreement. This section examines the considerations in forecasting residual values.

Rising-Value Assets

Real estate is an example of an asset that usually rises in value over the period of a long-term lease. The first step in forecasting a residual value is to estimate the long-term trend for inflation. Reviewing the forecasts of economists and past changes in price levels, a long-term inflationary trend is predicted. For illustrative purposes, let us assume a 10-year inflationary trend of 8 percent a year. A building valued at $100,000 today will be worth $100,000 $\times$ 1.08^{10} in 10 years if its value exactly matches inflation. From Appendix D, the residual would be $100,000 $\times$ 2.159 or $215,900 in 10 years.

Suppose, however, the asset is expected to rise at only half the rate of inflation. Or at twice the rate. Figure 2-7 shows the effects of these rises compared to the expected inflation.

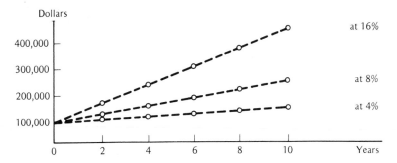

Figure 2-7. Changes in Residual Value on $100,000 Asset as a Function of Expected Rate of Inflation.

Year	If Asset Keeps up with 8% Inflation	If Asset Grows at Half of 8%	If Asset Grows at Twice 8%
0	$100,000	$100,000	$100,000
2	116,700	108,200	134,600
4	136,000	117,000	181,100
6	158,700	126,500	243,600
8	185,100	136,900	327,800
10	215,900	148,000	441,100

Declining-Value Assets

Most fixed assets will decline in value over the period of a long-term lease. As a general rule, the decline in value will exceed the rate of straight-line depreciation but lag the schedules of accelerated depreciation (**double-declining balance**), as shown in Figure 2-8.

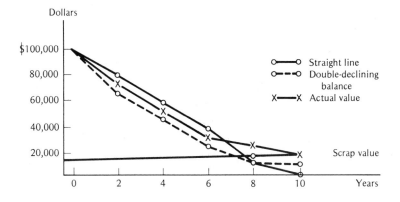

Figure 2-8. Declining Asset Value Compared to Depreciation Schedules.

Year	Straight Line	Double-Declining Balance	Actual Value
0	100,000	100,000	100,000
2	80,000	64,000	72,250
4	60,000	40,960	52,200
6	40,000	26,214	37,700
8	20,000	16,777	27,250
10	0	10,737	20,000

Effect of Inflation

The downward actual value line in Figure 2-8 will be pushed upward by the pressure of inflation, as is shown in Figure 2-9.

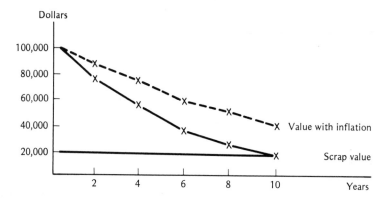

Figure 2-9.   Effect of Inflation on Asset Value.

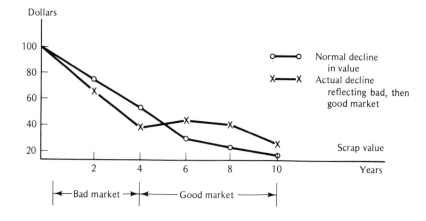

Figure 2-10.   Effect of Market Factors on Residual Values.

Effect of Market

Suppose a lease agreement is signed for a new asset. For the first 4 years of the lease it is expected that the market for this asset will weaken, then it will strengthen for the final 6 years. A 10-year lease will take advantage of this situation because the asset will decline more slowly in a good market and will make up for a rapid decline in a bad market. This effect is shown in Figure 2-10.

Conclusion

Many factors must be considered in evaluating the likely residual value of a fixed asset at the end of a long-term lease. The above technique considers some of the major issues and provides a framework for evaluating the effects of market and inflation factors on the residual value of a fixed asset.

21. RETURN ON INVESTMENT, HOW TO LEVER

Return on investment (ROI) is the prime indicator of management's efficiency in achieving a profit from operations. ROI is the product of two factors —asset turnover and profit margin. If either of these ratios can be increased, ROI will be increased to a greater degree, as shown below:

If Profit Margin = 6% and Asset Turnover = 3 times then ROI = 18%	By increasing Profit Margin by 1%, ROI increases by 3% (7% x 3 = 21%)	By increasing Asset Turnover by 1, ROI increases by 6% (6% x 4 = 24%)

Figure 2-11. Using Asset Turnover or Profit Margin to Produce ROI Leverage.

Asset-Turnover Side of ROI Leverage

The term **asset leverage** is frequently used to refer to the asset-turnover aspects of ROI leverage. It is the tool that links the firm's return on investment with its degree of efficiency in employing assets. It is important for two reasons:

1. *Similar Profit Margins Are Common.* When comparing firms producing similar products for similar markets, we might expect them to have the same approximate profit margins. This recognizes that their costs will be about the same and they will be forced by market factors to establish equal selling prices for the goods. In this situation, it is difficult to increase ROI by increasing profit margin, so the employment of assets becomes very important.

2. *Asset Turnover Reflects Efficiency.* The ability to generate a large volume of sales on a small asset base is a measure of a firm's operating efficiency. Firms with excessive idle assets tend to be poorly managed and are sluggish in their operating characteristics. Aggressive, profit-minded firms strive for a rapid turnover to gain the benefits of asset leverage on ROI.

Asset turnover is the tool we use to monitor the employment of assets on a comparative basis. If a firm has a relatively high asset turnover compared to other firms, we say it has a high degree of asset leverage. If low, it has a low degree of asset leverage. Note that a firm cannot have absolute high or low asset leverage; it has a relatively high or low leverage.

Examples of asset leverage are:

(a)				(b)
Company A has a higher ROI because of a higher degree of asset leverage.				Both companies increase their profit margins by 2% due to changes in their markets. Company A widens the difference in ROIs because of asset leverage.

	Profit margin	x	Asset turnover	= ROI
Co. A	5%		4	20%
Co. B	6%		3	18%

	PM	x	AT	= ROI
Co. A	7%		4	28%
Co. B	8%		3	24%

Profit-Margin Side of ROI Leverage

Although similar firms tend to have similar profit margins, careful cost control can increase profit margin with a levering effect on ROI. Some major areas where cost control is possible are the following:

1. *Production.* The process of producing goods involves a variety of costs, including manufacturing facilities and equipment, maintenance, labor, and losses due to equipment not properly operating.

2. *Selling Expenses.* In addition to salaries and salesmen's expenses, advertising and sales-support activities cost money. The firm makes efforts to identify essential items and minimize others as a part of cost control.

3. *Distribution.* The movement of goods from the factory to warehouses and on to the customer involves many handling and inspecting steps. These should be examined to see if all are necessary and if more streamlined distribution channels would reduce costs.

4. *Administrative Expenses.* The firm's miscellaneous and general expenses should be frequently reviewed to ensure that all are needed in the conduct of the daily business.

Levering ROI Through Tighter Management

Figure 2-12 shows an example of how the control costs can help a firm to lever its ROI. Small reductions in the size of operating assets combined with small decreases in operating costs can have significant effects. Careful planning can help the firm achieve the lower costs, which result in better use of assets and higher reported profits.

In Figure 2-12, the numbers above the boxes reflect the original estimates by the firm in its operating budget. The numbers below the boxes show the revised plan after efforts were made to find areas to economize. The change in ROI from 10 to 21 percent is significant.

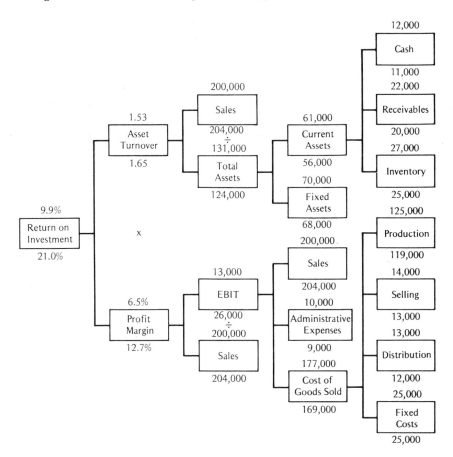

Note: Numbers above boxes indicate figures before tightening up.
         Numbers below boxes indicate results afterward.

Figure 2-12. Levering Return on Investment Through Tighter Management.

22. TAX FACTORS AFFECTING RETURN,
HOW TO EVALUATE

Tax consideration plays an important role in determining the final return to the firm's owners. Although the tax environment of American business is quite complex, several major tax factors should be identified as particularly significant to return. These are, in turn, corporate income taxes, capital-gains taxes, depreciation as a tax shield, and the difference between taxation on interest payments and dividends.

Corporate Income Taxes

Corporations are subject to different tax laws from individual taxpayers. Individual taxpayers pay personal income taxes using a scale graduated from 14 to 70 percent of taxable income.[2] Corporations are taxed at a 22 percent rate on taxable income up to $25,000. All taxable income above $25,000 is taxed at the 22 percent rate plus a 26 percent surtax, making a total tax rate of 48 percent. Table 2-7 shows the scales for individual unmarried taxpayers and for corporations.

TABLE 2-7. Tax Rates for Single Taxpayers and Corporations.

Taxable Income	Tax Due		Average Rate (%)	
	Individual	Corporation	Individual	Corporation
$500	$70	$110	14.0	22.0
1,000	145	220	14.5	22.0
2,000	310	440	15.5	22.0
10,000	2,090	2,200	20.9	22.0
25,000	7,190	5,500	28.8	22.0
50,000	20,190	17,500	40.3	35.0
100,000	53,090	41,500	53.1	41.5
$1,000,000	$683,090	$473,500	68.3	47.4

Several questions may be asked to provide further comparison of the tax rates for individuals and corporations:

1. *Is the Corporate Tax Rate Higher at the Low End and Lower at the High End of the Scale?* The answer is yes. For low incomes, the individual tax rate is 14 percent compared to 22 percent for corporations. Above $25,000, the individual rate rises to 70 percent; corporations are 48 percent.

2. *Would an Individual Save by Incorporating His Business?* The answer is no. The corporation involves a double taxation. An incorporated business first pays the corporate taxes; then the individual who receives

---

[2]See schedules X, Y, and Z of federal income tax form 1040.

dividends from the corporation must pay individual taxes. Thus, corporate profits are taxed once while in the corporation and once when distributed to the owners.

3. *To Get the Lower Tax Rates at Lower Income, Should Not Corporations with Large Profits Break up into Many Smaller Corporations with Less Than $25,000 Profit Each?* The answer is no. Although this once was possible, the law now provides that, for a group of firms with the same ownership, only one firm can elect to be taxed at the initial 22 percent rate on the first $25,000 of income. The remaining firms are taxed at 48 percent.

Capital-Gains Taxes

A capital asset is defined as any asset not bought and sold in the normal course of a firm's operations. For example, the sale of the firm's old warehouse when a new warehouse is opened would be the sale of a capital asset.

Gains or losses on the sale of capital assets are called **capital gains** and **losses,** and these may receive special tax treatment. The cutoff point is 12 months.[3] If a capital asset is held less than one year any gain is taxed as ordinary income. But if a capital asset is held more than one year, the gain becomes a **long-term capital gain,** which is taxed at a maximum rate of 30 percent. Thus, if the sale of the old warehouse brought a long-term capital gain of $100,000, the taxes would be $30,000, not the $48,000 due at the 48 percent rate. (The figure of $48,000 assumes that the firm already has ordinary income greater than $25,000. For gains when the total income is less than $25,000, the 22 percent rate applies.)

Depreciation as a Tax Shield

A firm's noncash expenses offer a tax shield on income and will reduce the amount of tax paid. The most important noncash expense is the depreciation on equipment. Depreciation is an accounting device that allows a firm to charge off a portion of the original cost of equipment as an expense each year over the service life of the equipment. This depreciation appears as an expense (but does not involve any cash) on the firm's income statement. Since expenses reduce reported profits, they also reduce taxable income.

Since depreciation acts as a tax shield and allows the firm to keep cash that would otherwise flow out to the Internal Revenue Service, depreciation increases the firm's cash flow. This effect is shown in Table 2-8. In this example, the firm with depreciation pays $2,000 less taxes than the firm without depreciation and is able to keep $7,000 in cash compared to $5,000 in cash.

---

[3] The Tax Reform Act of 1976 increased the holding period for long-term capital gains and losses from 6 months to 9 months for 1977.

The law allows a firm to use a number of methods of depreciating assets, including (1) straight line, (2) double-declining balance, and (3) **sum-of-the-years' digits.** The last two methods involve *accelerated depreciation,* a more rapid write-off of the assets than would be expected by the service life. The use of these methods of accelerated depreciation will increase the noncash expenses and therefore defer the payment of certain taxes until a future date. The effect is twofold:

TABLE 2-8. Effect of Depreciation on After-Tax Cash Flow.

	With $4,000 Depreciation	Without $4,000 Depreciation
Revenues	$16,000	$16,000
Less cash expenses	6,000	6,000
Less depreciation	4,000	0
Taxable revenues	6,000	10,000
Taxes at 50% rate	3,000	5,000
After-tax revenue	3,000	5,000
Plus revenue shielded	4,000	0
After-tax cash flow	$ 7,000	$ 5,000

1. *Cash Flow Is Speeded Up.* By reducing taxes in the early years of an asset's service life, accelerated depreciation methods speed up cash flow and make more cash available to the firm.
2. *Return Is Increased.* The more rapid cash inflows increase return when measured on a cash-flow basis. This is important when analyzing the investment of capital funds.

Different Tax Treatment of Interest and Dividends

When a firm borrows money, it pays interest on the debt. When it issues stock, it uses dividends to distribute the profits. Both debt and equity (stock) can be used as sources of funds for a firm. But the interest on debt can be paid before the tax rate is applied to corporate income. Dividends cannot be declared until the corporate income taxes are paid. The effect of the different treatment of interest and dividends has important effects on financial management.

23. VARYING SALES LEVELS OF COSTS, HOW TO ANALYZE THE EFFECT OF

Holding the selling price and variable costs constant, a financial analyst may wish to forecast profits at varying sales levels. In Table 2-9, the firm wants to know its profits if it sells 100,000, 150,000, or 200,000 units. If it has a selling price of $4, variable costs of $3, fixed costs of $120,000 and debt of $100,000 at 5 percent, marginal analysis provides three different net incomes after taxes (NIAT's): a loss of $25,000, an NIAT of $12,500, and an NIAT of $37,500. If the firm sells only 100,000 units, it will be operating below its break-even point and will incur a loss. Since it will make a profit at 150,000 units, the break-even point lies between 100,000 and 150,000 units. B/E = FC/(SP − VC), or B/E = 120,000/(4-3) = 120,000 units at break even.

TABLE 2-9. Marginal Analysis to Analyze the Effect of Varying Sales Level and Changes in Net Income.

	If We Sell:		
	100,000 units	*150,000 units*	*200,000 units*
Total revenues ($4 each)	$400,000	$600,000	$800,000
Variable costs ($3 each)	300,000	450,000	600,000
Marginal contribution	$100,000	$150,000	$200,000
Fixed costs	120,000	120,000	120,000
EBIT	$(20,000)	$ 30,000	$ 80,000
Interest Expense	5,000	5,000	5,000
EBT	$(25,000)	$ 25,000	$ 75,000
Taxes (50 percent)	0	12,500	37,500
NIAT or (loss)	$(25,000)	$ 12,500	$ 37,500

Varying Prices Resulting in Varying Sales

In most cases, a firm will consider several possible prices for a new product about to enter the marketplace. An established product also will frequently be evaluated with respect to the appropriateness of its selling price. Different prices will usually result in different levels of unit sales, with lower prices bringing more unit sales. The additional sales may or may not result in additional profits. In finance we want to determine whether a lower sales price is beneficial or not in terms of profits. To illustrate how marginal analysis helps in this determination, from our previous example in Table 2-9 assume that the firm believes it will sell only 100,000 units at $4. The marketing manager has predicted that it could sell 75,000 units if it raised the price to $5 or it could sell 125,000 units if it dropped the price to $3.50. Which price should the firm establish? Table 2-10 shows a profit only with the $5 price; the other two choices result in losses.

Using the language of economics, we could explain the differing profits in Table 2-10 in terms of elasticities of demand. From a financial point of view, it is sufficient to note that lowering the price to $3.50 lowers profits even though it increases sales. Increasing the price to $5 lowers sales, but the increased marginal contribution results in increased profits. If the firm is willing to accept a decline in sales, the $5 price should be established.

TABLE 2-10. Marginal Analysis to Analyze How Varying Prices Affect Net Income.

	If we sell:		
	100,000 units at $4	75,000 units at $5	125,000 units at $3.50
Total revenues	$400,000	$375,000	$437,500
Variable costs ($3 each)	300,000	225,000	375,000
Fixed costs	120,000	120,000	120,000
EBIT	$(20,000)	$ 30,000	$(57,500)
Interest	5,000	5,000	5,000
Taxes (50 percent)	0	12,500	0
NIAT or (loss)	$(25,000)	$12,500	$(62,500)

Varying Controllable Costs

In many cases, a firm will have some control over the relationship between fixed and variable costs. For example, a firm may be currently operating at a given level of fixed and variable costs. If the firm invests in more modern equipment it would incur increased fixed costs for such items as maintenance, depreciation, and insurance. But the greater efficiency of the new machinery might have the positive effect of lowering variable costs. If the firm has sufficient production so that the reduced variable costs provide greater savings than the costs which have increased, the firm would have higher profits by purchasing the equipment.

Using the preceding example in which the firm sells 75,000 units at $5, assume that the firm can lower its variable costs to $2.50 from $3 by accepting an increase in its fixed costs of $20,000. Comparing the two choices, we get the results shown in Table 2-11.

TABLE 2-11. Effect of Variable and Fixed Cost Changes.

	75,000 units at $5 with:	
	VC = $3 and FC = $120,000	VC = $2.50 and FC = $140,000
Total revenues	$375,000	$375,000
Variable costs	225,000	187,500
Fixed costs	120,000	140,000
Interest	5,000	5,000
EBT	$ 25,000	$ 42,500
Taxes (50 percent)	12,500	21,250
NIAT	$ 12,500	$ 21,250

From this use of marginal analysis, we can forecast higher profits as a result of purchasing the new equipment.

The major factor affecting the degree of profit with each choice is the forecasted level of sales. If the firm's sales fall short of the 75,000 predicted, the alternative with higher variable costs and lower fixed costs will result in the most profit or the least loss. In the preceding example, if the firm is able to sell only 30,000 units, the marginal analysis in Table 2-12 shows that the new equipment results in a $5,000 greater loss due to the additional fixed costs.

TABLE 2-12. Effect of Sales Shortages on Net Income.

	30,000 units at $5 with:	
	VC = $3 and FC = 120,000	VC = $2.50 and FC = 140,000
Total revenues	$150,000	$150,000
Variable costs	90,000	75,000
Fixed costs	120,000	140,000
Interest	5,000	5,000
(Loss)	$(65,000)	$ (70,000)

Chapter 3

MERGERS AND ACQUISITIONS

24. ACQUISITIONS, HOW TO ANALYZE

In making an acquisition, a firm must be aware of its own price-earnings (P/E) ratio, the ratio of the to-be-acquired firm, and the general condition of the stock market. Two factors are particularly important:

1. *Market Value Largely Determines the Exchange Ratio.* The **exchange ratio** is the factor that will determine how much common stock is issued or sold in making an acquisition. For example, a firm whose stock sells for $30 is planning to acquire a firm whose stock sells for $20. A logical exchange ratio might be 20/30 or two-thirds. This means the acquiring firm will have to give up two-thirds of a share of stock for every full share it acquires.

EXAMPLE: Firm X's stock sells for $75; Y's sells for $25. If X takes over Y, what might be the exchange ratio?
ANSWER: 1/3. X will have to exchange 1 share of stock for every 3 of Y.

In actual practice, the exchange ratio usually includes a premium to encourage the shareholders of the to-be-acquired firm to surrender their stock. The premium will normally range between 10 and 30 percent above the expected exchange ratio, which is normally based on market price. For example, in the preceding example, where X takes over Y whose stock sells for $25, if X decided to offer a 20 percent premium to encourage Y's shareholders to sell their stock, the Y stock would be revalued at ($25) (1.20) or $30. The new exchange ratio would be 30/75 or 40 percent rather than 33 1/3 percent.

EXAMPLE: Firm R's stock sells for $60; S's stock sells for $100. R wants to take over S and plans to offer a premium of 25 percent. What is the exchange ratio?
ANSWER: 125/60 or 208 percent. The premium is $100 times .25 or $25. The exchange price of the S stock is $100 + $25 or $125. The exchange ratio is 125/60 or 2.08 shares of R stock for every share of S stock.

EXAMPLE: Firm J's stock sells for $25; K's sells for $15. J wants to take over K and plans to offer a premium of 20 percent. What is the exchange ratio?
ANSWER: 18/25 or 72 percent. The premium is $15 times .20 or $3. The exchange price of the K stock is $15 + $3 or $18. The exchange ratio is 18/25 or .72 of a share of J stock for every share of K stock.

Note that the concept of the exchange ratio is valid even if the firm must sell its stock in the market and then use the proceeds to purchase another firm's stock. The acquiring firm must sell a block of shares at some price near the prevailing market price and then must pay a price at or above the current market price of the to-be-acquired firm. The transaction will involve cash in a manner similar to a direct exchange of stock.

2. *Price-Earnings Multiple Largely Determines Whether a Dilution of Earnings Will Occur.* A **dilution of earnings** is a decrease in earnings per share as a result of paying a high price for an acquisition. It will occur when a firm acquires another firm at a higher **P/E multiple** (after the premium is considered). To illustrate this concept, we shall make use of the data in Table 3-1. Three situations are shown. In each case, firm A is planning to take over B. In situation 1, the exchange ratio is based on the same P/E multiple. When this happens, firm A has a $2 earnings per share (EPS) before and after the acquisition—no dilution of earnings occurs.

TABLE 3-1. Sample Acquisition Illustrating the Concept of Dilution of Earnings.

NOTE: In the three situations, firm A is taking over firm B.

1. Exchange Ratio Based on Same P/E. No Dilution of Earnings Occurs.			*2. To-Be-Acquired Firm Has Higher P/E. A Dilution of Earnings Occurs.*			*3. To-Be-Acquired Firm Has Lower P/E. An Increase in Earnings Occurs.*		
	A	B		A	B		A	B
NIAT	$200	$100	NIAT	$200	$100	NIAT	$200	$100
Shares out.	100	100	Shares out.	100	100	Shares out.	100	100
EPS	$ 2	$ 1	EPS	$ 2	$ 1	EPS	$ 2	$ 1
Exch. P/E	20/1	20/1	Exch. P/E	10/1	20/1	Exch. P/E	20/1	10/1
Exch. price	$ 40	$ 20	Exch. price	$ 20	$ 20	Exch. price	$ 40	$ 10
Exch. ratio	1/2		Exch. ratio	1/1		Exch. ratio	1/4	

Firm A Issues 50 New Shares		*Firm A Issues 100 New Shares*		*Firm A Issues 25 New Shares*	
New Firm A		*New Firm A*		*New Firm A*	
NIAT	$300	NIAT	$300	NIAT	$300
Shares out.	150	Shares out.	200	Shares out.	125
EPS	$ 2	EPS	$1.50	EPS	$2.40

In situation 2, the exchange price is determined using different exchange P/E ratios. A's price reflects a 10/1 ratio; B's reflects 20/1. When this happens, the new firm A will experience a decrease in EPS to $1.50.

In situation 3, the exchange price reflects a 20/1 ratio for A but only a 10/1 ratio for B. In this case, B is a relative bargain in terms of its profits, and A will experience an increase in EPS after the acquisition.

Of the three situations, it should be obvious that 3 is preferred since it raises the reported earnings of the firm after the acquisition. As a minimum, the firm must achieve situation 1—the same P/E factor—if a dilution of earnings is to be avoided.

Postmerger Price-Earnings Multiple

After the two firms are merged, the stock market will have to establish a single P/E multiple to apply to the two firms. If the multiple will be low, the acquiring firm should avoid a **merger** and should operate the acquired firm as a **subsidiary** with its own common stock. If the multiple will be high, the two firms should probably be merged to gain the benefit of the high multiple on the combined earnings. Table 3-2 continues the examples in Table 3-1 and assumes that the market will probably give a merged firm a P/E multiple of the old firm A, the old firm B, or an average of the two.

TABLE 3-2. Different Common-Stock Prices Depending on Which Price-Earnings Multiple Is Given by the Stock Market.

NOTE: All data continued from the final EPS figures in Table 3-1.

1. Originally Firms A and B Had Same P/E		*2. Originally Firms A and B Had Different P/E's. New P/E Can Be High, Low, or Average of Old P/E's*				*3. Originally Firms A and B Had Different P/E's. New P/E Can Be High, Low, or Average of Old P/E's*			
			High	Avg.	Low		High	Avg.	Low
EPS	$ 2	EPS	$1.50			EPS	$2.40		
P/E	20/1	P/E	20/1	15/1	10/1	P/E	20/1	15/1	10/1
New mkt. price	$40	New mkt. price	$30	$22.50	$15	New mkt. price	$48	$36	$24
Old mkt. price	$40	Old mkt. price	$20	$20	$20	Old mkt. price	$40	$40	$40
Gain (loss)	0	Gain (loss)	$10	$ 2.50	($5)	Gain (loss)	$ 8	($4)	($16)

Note the importance of the new P/E multiple with respect to the price of the stock. Table 3-2 illustrates effects as follows:

a. When both firms have the same P/E, no gain or loss in market value occurs.

    b. When the acquiring firm has the lower P/E (the dilution of earnings situation), the acquiring firm can gain from either an average or high P/E multiple after the merger. The rise in P/E multiple offsets the dilution of earnings in these cases. But if the P/E multiple remains low (the acquiring firm's multiple), the dilution of earnings is translated into a reduction of market price of the stock.

    c. When the acquiring firm has the higher P/E (situation 3), any reduction in the P/E multiple can be very harmful. If the new firm takes the high P/E ratio, the stock value gains. But either an average or a low multiple causes a loss. In these cases, the lower P/E multiple offsets the higher earnings per share to reduce the price of the stock.

The different possibilities for EPS and P/E ratios and the effect on the future price of the stock are illustrated in Table 3-3.

TABLE 3-3. Changes in Earnings per Share and Price-Earnings and Their Effect on the Future Market Price of the Acquiring Firm's Stock.

Situation	Future EPS	Future P/E	Effect on Market Price of Stock
1	↑	↑	The stock will increase in value.
2	↓	↓	The stock will decrease in value.
3	↔	↔	The stock's value will not change.
4	↑	↔	Value will increase.
5	↓	↔	Value will decrease.
6	↔	↑	Value will increase.
7	↔	↓	Value will decrease.
8	↑	↓	Offsetting effects. Value may increase, decrease, or remain the same.
9	↓	↑	Offsetting effects. Value may increase, decrease, or remain the same.

It is one thing to recognize the different effects of possible dilutions of earnings and reduction of P/E multiples. It is another thing to predict exactly which P/E multiple will be given to the new company by investors in the stock market. As long as we know the preceding relationships, we can take steps to avoid diluting our earnings and encourage conditions and mergers that hold the prospect of increasing or maintaining our firm's P/E multiple.

25. ACQUISITIONS, HOW TO RESIST BEING ACQUIRED

In many cases, the management of a firm will decide that the firm should not be acquired by another firm. Many reasons may be given to explain the management's feelings:

    1. *Failure to Understand Target Firm's Problems.* The management may feel that the acquiring firm does not understand the real difficulties being faced by the existing management. This lack of understanding may cause even greater problems once the acquisition has been completed.

2. *Future Plans Not in the Interest of Target Firm's Shareholders.* The acquiring firm may be planning to operate the target firm as a subsidiary in a new or restricted role. The target firm's operations may be modified or partially eliminated to fit in with the parent firm's other activities. This reduction of growth in production and sales might be viewed as harmful to the remaining shareholders of the target firm.

3. *Tender Price or Exchange Ratio Is Too Low.* We have already noted that a firm that is about to be acquired is normally not realizing its full potential. If it were, the price of its stock would be too high for another firm to attempt a takeover. The target firm's management may feel that conditions will soon be improving and the target firm's stock will soon be rising rapidly. Thus, they may object to a takeover at the bargain price implied in the **tender** offer or exchange ratio.

4. *Acquiring Firm May Be Planning a New Management.* Perhaps the most common objection of the existing management is that a new management will be installed after the takeover. The acquiring firm usually makes a major effort to identify the deadwood in the old management and may even replace it entirely. If the old management were strong, the firm would be doing better. This reasoning is commonly used to replace the old management.

There are a number of tactics a firm may employ to avoid being taken over by another firm. Perhaps the classic defense against an attempted takeover occurred in the late 1960s when B. F. Goodrich successfully resisted the efforts of Northwest Industries. Some of the major features of that case were the following:

1. *Get Stockholders to Vote Against the Takeover.* The B. F. Goodrich management sent notices to all shareholders recommending that they refuse to sign proxies for the Northwest Industries group. This blocked the possibility that the takeover could be achieved through a merger approved by both companies' stockholders.

2. *Block Efforts to Solicit Tenders.* The B. F. Goodrich management refused to release the mailing list of its stockholders, thus making it difficult for Northwest to solicit tenders. This action forces the acquiring firm to use indirect means, such as advertisements in newspapers, to solicit tenders and reduces the effectiveness of the tender campaign.

3. *Get a Government Agency Involved.* If a government agency shows interest in the acquisition, it will make the effort more difficult. The Justice Department could investigate antitrust considerations or some other agency could step in. In the B. F. Goodrich case, Goodrich purchased a trucking company during the acquisition campaign. Since Northwest already owned a railroad and since the Interstate Commerce Commission normally objects to one company owning both a railroad and a trucking company, the action was designed to

get the ICC involved in the merger. To avoid this, Northwest was forced to go to court to try to block the purchase of the trucking company, an additional problem for Northwest.

4. *Get Controlling Stock into Friendly Hands.* The firm resisting the takeover may issue stock in return for assets to a corporation that will vote the stock on the side of management. The additional outstanding stock will make it more difficult for an unfriendly company to gain voting control. In the B. F. Goodrich case, stock was issued to the Gulf Oil Company in return for the assets of a chemical subsidiary of Gulf. The additional stock would be voted by Gulf on the side of management if the merger came to a vote.

5. *Begin an Unfavorable Publicity Campaign.* The very fact that management is openly willing to fight the acquisition in the newspapers will have a detrimental effect on the acquisition. The acquiring firm may feel that the unfavorable publicity is more harmful than the beneficial effects it expects from the successful takeover. Frequently, the publicity hurts the stock price of the acquiring firm, as it did the price of Northwest Industries stock. This drop in the stock price makes it difficult to raise additional money through the sale of stock, reduces the desirability of a stock for stock exchange, and generally is harmful to the management of the acquiring firm.

26. COMMON STOCK VALUE, HOW TO COMPARE TWO OR MORE STOCKS

In many cases a financial analyst will seek intrinsic value by comparing one firm with others. It can be argued that firms with similar operating characteristics will have similar intrinsic values. Three comparative approaches to determining intrinsic value are commonly used.

Price-Earnings (P/E) Value

In the **capitalization-of-earnings** approach to valuation, we base intrinsic value on a normal P/E ratio. But how do we determine the normal P/E ratio for a firm that is not publicly traded? One way is to use the P/E ratios of firms that are traded. For example, firm A is privately owned and has a $4 EPS. Firms B and C are in the same line of business and are **publicly traded** at a 20/1 P/E ratio. What is the value of firm A? An answer of $80 can be obtained by multiplying A's EPS times the P/E ratio of the similar firms.

> *EXAMPLE: Companies X, Y, and Z are similar firms. Company X is the strongest of the three and trades at 15/1 P/E multiple. Company Y is less strong and trades at 12/1. Company Z is least strong, is not publicly traded, but has an EPS of $2. What is the intrinsic value of company Z?*

ANSWER: If the strongest trades at 15/1 and the next strongest is 12/1, the least strong would trade at less than 12/1. At 10/1, company Z would have an intrinsic value of 10 × $2 = $20.

Comparative Dividend Growth Value

The comparative dividend growth value method employs the **dividend-growth model** with one significant change. It assumes that the market price of similar firms is also the intrinsic value of the firms. When this is done, the formula becomes

$$\text{market price} = \frac{\text{dividend}_{\text{curr}}}{CR_{\text{norm}} - (CR_{\text{act}})(\% RE)} \quad \text{or} \quad \frac{\text{dividend}}{CR_{\text{norm}} - G}$$

This formula has four components: market price, current dividend, growth rate, and the normal capitalization rate. For similar, publicly traded firms, the first three of these components are known. We can modify the formula to solve for the normal capitalization rate as follows:

$$CR_{\text{norm}} = \frac{\text{dividend}}{\text{market price}} + G$$

Once we have the normal capitalization rate for similar firms, we can apply it to the firm being valued. Since privately owned firms frequently pay dividends, we can use the dividend, growth rate, and normal capitalization rate to determine the probable market price if the stock were traded. Then we can assume that this would probably be close to the intrinsic value.

As an example of the use of this technique, a privately held firm has a 5 percent growth rate and pays a $6 dividend. A similar firm is publicly traded at $100 per share, pays a $4 dividend, and has an 8 percent growth rate. What is the value of the privately held firm? The normal capitalization rate is

$$CR_{\text{norm}} = \frac{\$4}{\$100} + .08, \qquad CR_{\text{norm}} = .12$$

The expected market price, and **intrinsic value,** of the privately held firm is

$$\text{market price} = \frac{\$6}{12\% - 5\%} = \frac{\$6}{.07} = \$85.71$$

EXAMPLE: Companies Q, R, and S are in the same basic industry. Company Q sells for $18 a share, pays a $1.50 dividend, and has a 5 percent growth rate. Company R sells for $36 a share, pays a $2.50 dividend, and has a 7 percent growth rate. Company S is privately owned, pays an $8 dividend, and has a 9 percent growth rate.

What is the value of the stock of company S?
ANSWER: The normal capitalization rates for Q and R can be calculated as

$$Q: \quad CR_{norm} = \frac{1.50}{18} + .05 = .13, \qquad R: \quad CR_{norm} = \frac{2.50}{36} + .07 = .14$$

Since company S is growing more rapidly, a higher P/E and lower capitalization rate should be used. Using .12, the intrinsic value of company S is $8/(.12- .09) = $8/.03 = $267.

Relationship of Market Price and Book Value

Although the book value of a firm cannot be used directly to determine the market or intrinsic value of a going concern, similar firms may have similar ratios of market price to book value. That is, if an industry has a 40 percent ratio of book to market value, this knowledge can be helpful in estimating the market value of a privately held firm. For example, a publicly traded firm has a book value of $30 per share and a market value of $120 per share. What is the intrinsic value of a similar firm with a $10 per share book value that is not publicly traded? Since the one firm has a 30/120 or 25 percent ratio of book to market value, the second firm might be worth $10/25 percent, or $40.

> *EXAMPLE: Companies A, B, and C are similar except that C is privately held. Company A has a market price of $100 and a book value of $55. Company B has a market price of $20 and a book value of $12. Company C has a book value of $40. What is the possible value of company C?*
> *ANSWER: For company A, the ratio of book to market value is 55/100 = 55 percent. For company B, the ratio of book to market value is 12/20 = 60 percent. For company C, dividing $40 book value by .55 and .60, we get a range of value from $67 to $73.*

27. MERGERS, HOW TO ANALYZE PROFITABILITY IN A TEN-STEP PROCESS

Many techniques can be used to measure the profitability of two or more firms after a merger has been completed. A measure of combined **future earnings per share** (EPS) is very useful for a publicly traded firm. The following technique projects future EPS and capital structure risk in a ten-step process using the merger of ITT and Canteen Corporation as an example.

The financial analysis of these firms requires a measurement of the effect of each possible acquisition on the growth rate of ITT. The corporate staff used the earnings per share and revenues trends to determine the following growth rates for each firm over the previous 5 years. These growth patterns were expected to continue into the future.

Miscellaneous Financial Data (m = million)

	ITT	Canteen
Market price, Dec. 31, 1968	$58.25	$31
Dividends per share	$.875	$.80
1968 Net income after taxes	192.4m	9.5m
1968 Preferred stock dividend	31.0m	
1968 Earn. available to common shareholders	161.4m	9.5m
1968 Shares outstanding	59m	6.955m
1968 Earnings per share	161.4/59	9.5/6.955
	= $2.74	= $1.37
1968 Debt	2,370m	63m
1968 Equity	1,652m	78m
1968 Debt-asset ratio	59%	45%
1968 Price-earnings ratio	21/1	23/1

INTERNATIONAL TELEPHONE AND TELEGRAPH CORP. Consolidated Balance Sheet

(December 31, 1968; 000s)

Cash	$ 296,839		Loans	$ 376,169	
Accts. and notes rec.	638,172		Accts. payable	563,215	
Inventories	705,851		Accrued taxes	149,180	
Other curr. assets	120,269		Curr. Liabs.	1,088,564	1,088,564
Total Curr. Assets		1,761,131			
			Deferred liabs.	202,641	
Investments, cost	166,817		Def. income taxes	69,340	
Rec. noncurrent	59,564		Long-term debt	931,772	
Other assets	199,095		Minor eq. subsids.	77,991	
Plant and equip.	2,882,438		Total Long-Term Debt	1,281,744	1,281,744
Less acc. deprc.	(1,046,645)				
Total Fixed Assets		2,261,269	Preferred stock	372,637	
			Common stock ($1 par)	59,059	
			Capital surplus	388,613	
			Ret. earnings	831,783	
			Total Equity		1,652,092
	$4,022,400				$4,022,400

CANTEEN CORPORATION Consolidated Balance Sheet

(December 31, 1968; 000s)

Cash	$ 11,393		Curr. maturities,		
Short-term invest.	23,932		long-term debt	$ 2,069	
Notes, accts. rec.	9,900		Accts. payable	12,564	
Inventories	13,768		Accrued liabs., taxes	10,925	
Prepd. expenses	451		Current Liabs.		25,558
Current Assets		59,444			

CANTEEN CORPORATION Consolidated Balance Sheet — continued

			Long-term debt	30,283	
Long-term receivables	24,813		Deferred credits	6,229	
Plant and equip.	124,945		Min. eq., subsids.	815	
Less acc. deprc.	(71,770)		Total Long-Term Debt		37,327
Deferred charges	3,455		Com. stk ($2.50 par)	17,938	
Total Fixed Assets		81,443	Addi. paid-in capital	38,881	
			Less treas. stk.		
			(219,526 shares)	(3,744)	
			Retained earnings	24,927	
			Total Equity		78,002
		$140,887			$140,887

	ITT	Canteen
EPS and revenues growth rates over the past 5 years	12.1%	10%

Analysis of Canteen Corporation

The office of the vice-president finance conducted a detailed analysis of the effect of a merger with the Canteen Corporation. Included in the financial analysis were the following elements:

1. *Growth Rate of ITT and Canteen Combined.* To calculate a combined growth rate of earnings, the analyst used a weighted-average approach. He figured the relative contribution of each firm to the new firm and multiplied each percentage times the growth rate of each firm. The 1968 earnings were used as follows:

Canteen 1968 earnings	$ 9,500,000	5.6%
ITT 1968 earnings	$161,400,000	94.4%
	$170,900,000	100.0%

Combined weighted-growth:

Canteen   ITT

$(5.6\%)(10\% \text{ growth}) + (94.4\%)(12.1\% \text{ growth}) = 12.0\%$ combined growth rate

2. *Exchange Ratio for Canteen.* If the merger were to be considered using an exchange of common stock for common stock, ITT would have to determine an exchange ratio for its offering price. At the present time, the firm uses a 10 percent premium above the current market

price of the acquired firm's stock. Since Canteen is selling at $31, the offering price would be $31 times 1.10 or $34.10. The exchange ratio would be

$$\frac{(31)(1.1)}{58.25} = .586$$

Thus, ITT would offer .586 of a share of its own stock for each share of Canteen's stock. Note that this is a preliminary figure used for other calculations. The actual offering price may be higher or lower depending on a variety of factors.

3. *New ITT Shares Needed for Exchange of Stock.* Canteen has 6,955,000 shares outstanding. At an exchange ratio of .586, ITT would have to issue shares as follows:

exchange ratio × Canteen's shares outstanding = new ITT shares
    .586   ×   6,955,000   = 4,075,600

4. *1969 Combined ITT and Canteen* **Earnings Available to the Common Shareholder (EACS)**. To forecast next year's earnings, we combine ITT's and Canteen's 1968 earnings and multiply times the combined growth rate factor (100 percent + growth rate).

1968 combined earnings × combined growth rate factor = 1969 earnings

Canteen	9.5			
ITT	161.4			
	170.9	×	1.12%	= $191,400,000

5. *1969 Earnings per Share with Exchange of Stock.* This is calculated by dividing the total number of ITT shares into the forecasted 1969 earnings as follows:

ITT shares = 59,000,000 old + 4,100,000 new = 63,100,000
1969 earnings divided by total shares = 1969 earnings per share
$191,400,000   ÷ 63,100,000   = $3.03

6. *Purchase Price of Canteen If Debt Financing Used.* If the exchange of stock proved unfeasible, the planning should include a purchase of Canteen Corporation. The 10 percent premium could still apply, so the purchase price would be $31 times 110 percent, or $34.10 for each

---

Figures are rounded to avoid the appearance of greater accuracy than is actually possible when making future forecasts.

share of Canteen's stock. With 6,955,000 shares outstanding, the purchase price for 100 percent ownership would be

total Canteen shares $\times$ price per share = purchase price for 100%
6,955,000 $\times$ $34.10 = $237,166,000

7. *1969 Combined Earnings with Debt Financing.* An investigation of the forecasted earnings with debt financing must rely heavily on two factors:
   a. *Interest Rate on the New Debt.* The treasurer of ITT checked with the firm's bankers and determined that new long-term debt would cost 5.25 percent for any or all of the acquisitions.
   b. *Tax Rate on Incremental Earnings.* Overall, ITT takes advantage of tax incentives and foreign operations to reduce its corporate taxes to less than 40 percent of its earnings before taxes. But incremental earnings from any one investment such as Canteen involve a tax rate closer to the 48 percent required by law. Thus, a borrowing decision will involve interest that provides a tax shield near the 48 percent figure. For ease of calculation, the corporate staff rounds this to a 50 percent tax rate.

Once the interest rate and tax rate are determined, ITT can use the 1969 combined earnings with the exchange-of-stock option as a base for calculating the 1969 EACS with debt financing. The calculation is as follows:

1969 Combined earnings (exchange of stock)	$191,400,000 (step 4)
1969 Combined earnings before taxes	382,800,000 (at 50 percent tax rate)
Less new interest ($237,166,000 purchase price times 5.25 percent interest)	12,451,215
1969 New earnings before taxes	$370,348,785
1969 Combined earnings with new debt	185,174,392[2]

8. *1969 Earnings per Share with Debt Financing.* Since ITT's shares will not change with debt financing, we simply divide the 1969 combined earnings (EACS) by the ITT shares outstanding. (Note that the preferred-stock dividends have been omitted since the beginning of the analysis and need not be considered here.)

---

[2]This calculation ignores the amortization of goodwill that would arise from the purchase of Canteen Corporation. Because of this amortization over some undetermined period, the actual EACS will be slightly lower than this figure.

1969 EACS with debt divided by ITT shares outstanding = 1969 EPS
$185,174,000   ÷   59,000,000   = $3.14

9. *New Capital Structure with Each Alternative.* As a measure of risk, the analyst should check the capital structure. The exchange of stock may result in either a **pooling of interests** or **purchase** balance sheet methods; the debt alternative can only qualify for the purchase method. The capital structures are as follows:

Exchange of Stock (000s omitted)

	Pooling of Interests					Purchase Method			
	ITT	Canteen	Combined			ITT	Canteen	Combined	
Debt	2,370	63	2,433	58%	Debt	2,370	63	2,433	56%
Equity	1,652	78	1,730	42%	Equity	1,652	237	1,889	44%
			4,163	100%				4,322	100%

Debt Financing, Purchase Method (000s omitted)

	ITT	New Debt	Canteen Debt	Combined	
Debt	2,370	237	63	2,670	62%
Equity	1,652			1,652	38%
				4,322	100%

10. *ITT's 1969 Earnings Without Any Acquisition.* To allow a comparison of the effect of acquiring Canteen, the analyst should calculate ITT's 1969 earnings without making an acquisition. This is a matter of multiplying its earnings by its growth rate (plus 100 percent) as follows:

1968 earnings per
      share   ×   ITT growth rate   =   1969 earnings per share
      $2.74   ×   112.1%   = $3.07

Recommendation:

At a 10 percent premium, Canteen seems to represent a reasonable merger candidate for the following reasons:

1. *Earnings per Share Are Reasonable.* Without the acquisition, ITT expects $3.07 EPS. Depending upon the financing, the combined EPS would be either $3.03 or $3.14 approximately. With or without the merger, ITT increases from its $2.74 of last year.

2. *Canteen Offers Diversification.* ITT is a **conglomerate** seeking external growth. Canteen offers a chance for diversification while earnings continue to grow.

3. *Increased Profits Possible.* In the past, Canteen's profits have been somewhat erratic. With ITT's management, Canteen offers the prospect of higher profits in the future.

In conclusion, the financial data seem to support further investigation of the possibility of a merger between ITT and Canteen.

28. POOLING AND PURCHASE METHODS, HOW TO USE IN MERGER ACCOUNTING

The prospects for a business combination may be affected by the accounting techniques used to record the merger. These techniques can have important effects on the balance sheet and reported earnings of the surviving firm. Two accounting techniques are generally accepted under the regulations of the **Securities and Exchange Commission.** These are the (1) pooling of interests and (2) purchase methods of accounting.

Pooling-of-Interests Versus Purchase Methods of Accounting

The pooling-of-interests method of accounting for a business combination assumes a continuity of both the asset values and the ownership of the combined firms. In effect, we combine the balance sheets of the merged firms and report their combined earnings to our shareholders. The purchase method assumes a new ownership and a need to reappraise the assets of the acquired firm in light of current market value. The balance sheet is restated to reflect the current values as the combination is completed. If a firm is acquired for a price in excess of its book value, the excess is recorded either as an increase in value on specific depreciable assets or in an account titled **goodwill.**

The pooling-of-interests method is generally preferred by corporations considering a business combination. To see why this is so, let us examine some of the differences between the two methods of accounting:

1. *Treatment of Goodwill.* Goodwill is the account used to report the excess paid for a firm over the book value of the depreciable assets. It is used only in the purchase method of accounting. Goodwill is an intangible-asset account carried on the balance sheet of the surviving or parent corporation. Two characteristics of goodwill are especially important in merger accounting:

a. *It must be written off* over some reasonable period not longer than 40 years. If the full 40 years is used, a write-off of 2.5 percent annually of the goodwill must be taken as a *reduction of reported profits.* This is not desirable, because it causes the combined firm to report lower profits than would be reported in the absence of goodwill.

b. *Goodwill is not deductible for tax purposes.* Whereas other write-offs such as depreciation are deductible, goodwill is not. Thus, goodwill has the disadvantage of reducing reported earnings while not allowing the benefit of lowered income taxes.

Goodwill is not recorded with the pooling-of-interests method of accounting; earnings are therefore not reduced by a required write-off.

2. *Sale of Assets Acquired at Depreciated Book Values.* Since pooling involves a combination of the balance sheets of the two firms, it does not provide for adjusting the value of undervalued depreciable assets. For example, a machine may have a market value of $100,000 and a book value of only $20,000. Under the purchase method, the machine would be revalued to $100,000 and a new depreciation schedule would be established. If the machine were sold for $100,000, no gain or loss would be reported. Under pooling, the machine would retain its $20,000 book value. If it were sold for $100,000, a profit of $80,000 could be recorded as a profit on the sale of assets on the combined income statement. When this is done, the combination could be used to create the appearance of a growth in profits. This, of course, would be misleading, but nonetheless is an advantage to pooling.

3. *Difference in the Asset Base.* When purchase accounting is used, the new balance sheet is increased by the amount of goodwill. For example, if a firm pays $50,000,000 for a company with a book value of $20,000,000, the $30,000,000 in goodwill is shown on the balance sheet. With pooling of interests, only the $20,000,000 in assets would be shown. This has the effect of reporting a lower asset base, which results in higher ratios, such as return on investment and return on equity. It also reduces the amount of equity for the debt-asset and debt-equity ratios.

Conditions Requiring the Pooling of Interests Method

Accounting Principles Board Opinion No. 16 specifies twelve conditions of which *all must* be met in order to classify the combination as a pooling of interests. In the event that one or more of these conditions are not met, the purchase method *must* be used for the purpose of combining the companies. These twelve specifications fall under these three categories:

1. *Attributes of the Combining Companies.* Each company must not have been a subsidiary of any corporation within the past 2 years, nor had

intercompany investments of voting common stock in excess of 10 percent.

2. *Manner of Combining Interests.* The combination must be the result of a single transaction or a plan that is completed within 1 year after the date that it is initiated. The corporation must issue only common stock with identical rights of the majority of its outstanding voting common stock, in exchange for at least 90 percent of the voting common stock of the other company. Each common stockholder who exchanges his stock must receive a voting common stock interest exactly in the same proportion to his relative voting common stock interest prior to the combination.

3. *Absence of Planned Transactions.* The combined corporation must not enter into other financial arrangements for the benefit of the former stockholders of a combining company, and must not agree, directly or indirectly, to retire or reacquire all or part of the common stock issued to effect the combination. Also, the combined corporation must not intend to dispose of a significant part of the assets of the combining companies within 2 years after the combination.

Merger Accounting with Purchase and Pooling

As an example of the differences in recording assets between the pooling and purchase methods of accounting, Table 3-4 shows a simplified balance sheet when firm X purchases firm Y and receives $1,200,000 in equity for $2,000,000. With respect to the purchase method, note the following:

1. *Goodwill Account.* This is the difference between the purchase price and the book value of the equity, as follows:

goodwill = purchase price − equity, $800,000 = $2,000,000 − $1,200,000

TABLE 3-4. Accounting Under the Pooling-of-Interests and Purchase Methods of Accounting (in millions of dollars).

Account	*X Alone*	*Y Alone*	*X + Y Purchase Method*[a]	*X + Y Pooling Method*[a]
Assets	14	1.6	15.6	15.6
Goodwill	0	0	.8	0
Total	14	1.6	16.4	15.6
Debt	6	.4	6.4	6.4
Equity	8	1.2	10.0[b]	9.2
Total	14	1.6	16.4	15.6

[a] Y is purchased for $2,000,000 and X receives 100 percent of stock.
[b] Includes the $800,000 difference between $1,200,000 book value and $2,000,000 purchase price.

2. *Increase in Accounting Value of Total Assets.* With increases in the goodwill account on the asset side and the equity account on the financing side, the balance sheet shows an increase of $800,000 on each side. Prior to the merger, the combined total assets had a book value of $14,000,000 and $1,600,000, or $15,600,000. Afterward, this increases by $800,000 to $16,400,000.

EXAMPLE: Company Q offers $12,000,000 for $4,000,000 of R's stock at book value. R has $1,000,000 debt. How much goodwill arises? If Q has $20,000,000 equity and $5,000,000 debt itself, what is the combined balance sheet using the purchase method? the pooling method?
ANSWER: $8,000,000 goodwill ($12,000,000 − 4,000,000). Balance sheets (in millions of dollars) are as follows:

	Purchase Method				Pooling-of-Interests Method		
Assets	30	Debt	6	Assets	30	Debt	6
Goodwill	8	Equity	32	Goodwill	0	Equity	24
Total	38	Total	38	Total	30	Total	30

Purchase and Pooling with Debt Used for Takeover

In Table 3-5, company X is taking over company Y by selling or exchanging X's own stock. The company may plan to issue shares of stock directly to the shareholders of Y, in which case it might qualify for pooling. Or it may sell the stock in the market to outside investors and use the cash to purchase Y, in which case the purchase method would be required. If company X had decided to borrow money to purchase Y, the final balance sheet would be changed as follows:

1. *Debt Would Increase.* The $2,000,000 raised through the sale of **debt securities** would be added to the debt of each individual firm on the new balance sheet.

TABLE 3-5. Accounting Using Purchase Method When Takeover Involves Borrowed Funds (in millions of dollars).

Account	X Alone	X After Borrowing	Y Alone	X + Y Purchase Method
Assets	14	16	1.6	15.6
Goodwill	0	0	0	.8
Total	14	16	1.6	16.4
Debt	6	8	.4	8.4
Equity	8	8	1.2	8.0
Total	14	16	1.6	16.4

2. *Equity Would Not Increase.* Company X would add the stock of company Y as an asset on the one side of the balance sheet, but no new equity would be created on the other side. In an exchange of stock, it is the issuance of new stock that causes an increase in the equity. When debt is used, no additional equity is created.

Table 3-5 shows the accounting for the takeover using the purchase method (since pooling is not allowed with a purchase for cash).

EXAMPLE: Company J offers $6,000,000 for $4,000,000 of K's stock at book value. K has $2,500,000 debt. How much goodwill arises? If J had $30,000,000 equity and $9,000,000 debt before it borrowed the $6,000,000 for the takeover, what would be the combined balance sheet?
ANSWER: $2,000,000 goodwill ($6,000,000 − 4,000,000). Balance sheets (in millions of dollars) are as follows:

	J Before	J After Borrowing	K Before	J + K Combined
Assets	39	45	6.5	45.5
Goodwill	0	0	0	2.0
Total	39	45	6.5	47.5
Debt	9	15	2.5	17.5
Equity	30	30	4.0	30.0
Total	39	45	6.5	47.5

29. TURN-AROUND CANDIDATE, HOW TO DETERMINE PURCHASE PRICE OF

The technique of estimating future earnings per share can be very useful in arriving at a purchase price for a company that is not performing up to its potential. To illustrate the use of this technique, we shall consider the possible acquisition of Lenox Products, Inc. The financial data are given in Table 3-6.

At the present time, the operating and financial characteristics indicate the following about Lenox:

1. Its P/E value is only $2 per share. Its current market price of $10 is thus based more on the value of its assets than on its profits.
2. It has excess cash. At present it could pay a $5 dividend per share ($10,000,000/2,000,000 shares). Half its assets are cash, an excessive amount for operations.
3. It has very small profits. Its EPS are only $.20. Its return on equity is 2.1 percent (400/19,000).

TABLE 3-6. Lenox Products, Inc. Financial Data at Present and After Being Acquired.

Present Balance Sheet		Projected Balance Sheet If Acquired	
Cash	$10,000,000	Cash	$ 2,000,000
Other assets	10,000,000	Other assets	28,000,000
Total	$20,000,000	Total	$30,000,000
Debt	$ 1,000,000	Debt	$11,000,000
Equity	19,000,000	Equity	19,000,000
Total	$20,000,000	Total	$30,000,000

Other Financial Data	Present	Future
Sales	$20,000,000	$60,000,000
Net income after taxes	400,000	6,000,000
Shares outstanding	2,000,000	2,000,000
Earnings per share	$ .20	$ 3.00
Market value of one share of stock at 10/1 P/E	$ 2.00	$ 30.00
Present market price of stock	$ 10.00	

If our firm acquires Lenox, we would take the following actions. The results of our actions are considered in the projected and future data in Table 3-6:

1. We would eliminate the excess cash and invest it in other assets. At the same time, we would take advantage of favorable financial leverage by borrowing $10,000,000 and increasing our debt-equity ratio to an acceptable .58/1.
2. We would use the additional capital to purchase new equipment, which could increase production and provide more units to sell.
3. We would use our own excellent marketing team to sell the products of Lenox, a step that would dramatically increase sales from $20,000,000 to $60,000,000.
4. The new equipment and larger sales volume would result in more acceptable profit levels, as reflected in the $3 EPS and the 32 percent return on equity ($6,000,000/$19,000,000).

In the case of Lenox, the current market price of $10 would make the stock seem overpriced on the basis of profits. But considering future earnings if the firm were acquired, we would be willing to pay $10 or more per share for the firm. How much to pay for one share? The answer is some price below $30, depending upon the degree of risk that we shall not be able to effect the **turn-around.** At $12 to $15 per share, the firm offers a chance for a sizable increase in the value of common stock if projected figures can be attained.

Chapter 4

WORKING CAPITAL

30. CASH-FLOW FORECAST, HOW TO PREPARE A

Two processes are required in managing current assets—forecasting the needed funds and acquiring the funds. To illustrate these processes with cash management, we shall use the example of the Mercury Printing Company.

Situation

The Mercury Printing Company is scheduled to open its doors for business on the first day of January. It will take over the accounts of Stafford's Print Shop, which is closing due to the retirement of Harry Stafford, its owner and operator. Mercury will begin with $4,000 in its checking account, and it has established a line of credit with Citizens Trust Bank that will allow it to borrow up to $12,000 at any time during the first year. As a safety measure, the firm's accountant has recommended that the cash balance should never go below 12 days of cash available; this figure has been set as a guide to calculate the firm's **safety level.** The firm has assumed a $7,000 short-term note previously owed by Stafford's in return for the accounts. It also assumed an $11,000 note as part of the purchasing of secondhand equipment for the new firm. The $7,000 note is due February 21 and the $11,000 note is due on April 7. The firm has scheduled a sale of stock to a group of private investors for June 15. The investors have agreed to purchase $12,000 worth of stock, but are waiting to see how business develops before deciding what percentage of the total stock will be represented by the $12,000.

Preparing Mercury's Cash-Flow Forecast

The financial manager begins with a sheet of accounting paper showing the months across the top and the categories of receipts and payments in the left-hand column. He begins with the $4,000 cash in the checking account. Since the firm will sell on terms of net 30, no collections on receivables are forecast for January. Cash sales of $1,000 are forecast for January and these are listed. Mercury will pay bills of $1,500 in January. By subtracting outlays ($1,500) from the available cash ($5,000), Mercury will have a cash balance of $3,500 at the end of January. This becomes the beginning balance for February. In February, the financial manager estimates that three fourths of January's sales will be collected, so $3,000 is shown as collections. Cash sales of $1,100 and outlays of $2,000 for operations are forecasted. The $7,000 note due on February 21 is shown. If nothing else is done, Mercury will have a $1,400 deficit in February. In March, the firm will be able to overcome the deficit and will end the month with a $1,300 surplus. A note payment of $11,000 on April 7 brings the firm back to a deficit position at the end of April and May. In June, the sale of stock will bring the firm back to a positive cash balance.

The forecast is shown in Table 4-1.

TABLE 4-1. Cash-Flow Forecast, 6-Month Period, Mercury Printing Company.

	Jan.	Feb.	Mar.	Apr.	May	June
Cash on hand, first of month	4,000	3,500	(1,400)	1,300	(9,200)	(6,700)
Collections on receivables	0	3,000	4,000	3,500	4,000	5,000
Cash sales	1,000	1,100	1,200	1,000	1,000	1,000
Sales of stock						12,000
Total Available Cash	5,000	7,600	3,800	5,800	(4,200)	11,300
Cash payments for operations	1,500	2,000	2,500	4,000	2,500	3,000
Payment of bank notes		7,000		11,000		
Total Cash Outlays	1,500	9,000	2,500	15,000	2,500	3,000
Cash on hand, end of month	3,500	(1,400)	1,300	(9,200)	(6,700)	8,300

Determining the Safety Level

The treasurer has decided that the firm should maintain 12 days of cash available. In calculating this ratio, he would not include the major payments on bank notes. These obligations are not variable as are cash payments for operations. Also, the financial manager must plan for major payments and must not rely on the day-to-day cash flow for these items.

Using cash payments for operations as the monthly outflow for safety-level purposes, the manager considers two alternatives:

1. *Use the Largest Monthly Outlay.* The April forecast of $4,000 cash payments is the largest for any month in the period. Using this month, the safety level would be

$$\text{safety level of cash} = (12 \text{ days}) \frac{\$4,000}{30} = (12)(\$133) = \$1,600$$

2. *Use an Average Outlay.* If the manager wanted to use an average figure, he could add the payments for each month and divide by 180 days. The calculation would be

$$\text{safety level} = (12 \text{ days}) \frac{\$1,500 + 2,000 + 2,500 + 4,000 + 2,500 + 3,000}{180 \text{ days}}$$

$$= (12) \frac{\$15,500}{180} = (12)(86.11) = \$1,033$$

Comparing these two figures, the financial manager may decide to select the added safety of the larger number and establish a $1,600 safety level. Or he may feel that the average of $1,033 would be better for the firm. In making his decision, he will consider the factors already discussed as affecting the size of the firm's cash balance.

To continue with our example, assume that the manager decides to average the two figures and set a safety level of available cash at $1,300.

Calculating the Cash Shortages

The financial manager is concerned with the cash on hand at the end of each month. Will the firm have adequate cash to meet the minimum requirements of the $1,300 safety level? Using the forecast in Table 4-1, he compares the cash on hand at the end of each month with the $1,300 safety level. In making this comparison, four conditions are possible:

1. *Surplus.* If the firm forecasts more cash than the safety level as being available, the firm has a surplus. No additional cash is needed and the manager may have the opportunity to invest excess cash when the time arrives.
2. *Optimum.* If the firm has approximately the same amount of cash forecasted as the safety level, no additional cash will be required. The term *approximately* will have different meanings to different analysts but might be defined as a cash balance within 5 to 10 percent of the safety level.
3. *Shortage.* If the firm has a positive cash balance (it is not forecasting running out) but the balance is below the safety level, the firm has a shortage. The manager will have to make plans to cover the shortage.
4. *Deficit.* If the firm forecasts a negative cash balance, it will not be able to make all its planned payments. The manager will need to make plans for cash to cover the deficit as well as the shortage below the safety level.

In comparing the ending cash on hand with the safety level, the manager can add lines to the worksheet for the safety level of cash and the surplus or shortage. The worksheet would then be as follows:

	Jan.	Feb.	Mar.	Apr.	May	June
Cash on hand, end of month	3,500	(1,400)	1,300	(9,200)	(6,700)	8,300
Safety level required	1,300	1,300	1,300	1,300	1,300	1,300
Surplus or shortage	+2,200	(2,700)	0	(10,500)	(8,000)	+7,000

The new worksheet reveals that the firm has surpluses forecasted for two months ($2,200 and $7,000), is at its optimum for one month (March), and has shortages for the remaining three months. Note that the three shortages include deficits as well. The February shortage is $2,700 including a deficit of $1,400; April is $10,500 including a $9,200 deficit; May is $8,000 including a $6,700 deficit.

Locating the Needed Funds

The three shortages in February, April, and May must be covered when they occur. Since the Citizens Trust Bank has allowed Mercury to establish a $12,000 backup line of credit, the treasurer can plan on short-term borrowing to cover the shortages until the firm sells its stock in June. In this example, the treasurer notifies the bank of the projected needs so that the bank will be ready to act quickly when the loan requests are made. The following needs are forecast:

1. *$3,000 from February 20 to June 20.* The $7,000 note is due February 21. A $3,000 loan on the preceding day will cover the February deficit and will be available in March. Note that the firm reaches its safety level at the end of March without the loan, but it would be below $1,300 cash on hand for most of the month. It begins with a $1,400 deficit and works its way to the safety level. On April 7, the firm must pay an $11,000 note. Rather than repay the $3,000 loan on April 1 only to borrow it again on April 7, the treasurer plans to keep the money through June 20 after the sale of stock.

2. *$8,000 from April 6 to June 20.* This money, combined with the $3,000 still outstanding, will allow the firm to repay the $11,000 note on April 7. Both loans will mature 5 days after the June sale of stock. The firm will have $11,000 to cover deficits in April and May.

The treasurer plans a little extra borrowing each time to avoid having to bother the bank if he should misjudge the firm's needs by a small margin. He also only plans for two loans, because the costs of arranging a series of smaller loans would be higher than any interest savings he would realize.

This example ties together the total scope of the cash-management function. With the aid of the cash-flow forecast, the financial manager is better able to identify future needs for cash. This does not mean that errors in projections will not be made. Rather, it means that the manager has attempted to determine the operating needs of the firm in the next period to allow him to prepare to deal with any likely cash shortages.

31. CASH SAFETY LEVEL, HOW TO CALCULATE

The financial manager may develop the firm's **cash safety level** with the aid of financial ratios. Many ratios are possible, including:

1. *During Normal Periods.* One ratio would compare the normal daily outflows of cash with the firm's cash on hand. The financial manager must provide the *desired days of cash available* in order to use the ratio. From the accounting department, he gets the average daily cash outflow. The ratio is cash safety level needed = desired days of cash × average daily outflows.

   For example, suppose a financial manager feels that a safety level should provide sufficient cash to cover cash payments for 7 days. The firm's average daily outflows of cash are $6,000. The safety level is 7 × $6,000 = $42,000.

2. *During Peak Periods.* This ratio measures the safety level as compared to the firm's busiest period. The highest daily outflows during the month are substituted in the preceding formula for average daily outflows. The financial manager may also be willing to get by with fewer days of cash during the busy period, so this factor may change. The formula is

$$\begin{array}{c} \text{cash safety} \\ \text{level needed} \end{array} = \begin{array}{c} \text{desired days of cash} \\ \text{at busiest period} \end{array} \times \begin{array}{c} \text{average of highest daily} \\ \text{cash outflows} \end{array}$$

As an example, during the 3 busiest days in June the firm's cash outflow was $7,500, $8,000, and $8,500. The average of highest daily cash outflows is calculated by ($7,500 + $8,000 + $8,500)/3 = $8,000. If the manager desired 5 days of cash available during the peak periods, the safety level would be $8,000 × 5 = $40,000.

Monitoring the Safety Level

The preceding ratios are also useful, in a rewritten form, to help the firm monitor the level of cash it maintains. As is shown in Table 4-2, the actual cash balance is compared with the outflows to give the days of cash available. This is then compared to the days of cash desired to see if the firm is above or below its safety level.

TABLE 4-2. Using Ratios to Determine and Monitor Safety Levels of Cash.

Period	Formula to Determine Safety Level of Cash		Formula to Calculate Days of Cash Available		Desired Days of Cash Available	Excess or Deficiency of Cash
Normal	Safety Level	= Desired Days of Cash × Average Daily Outflows	Days of Cash Available	= Average Cash Balance / Average Daily Outflows		
		= 6 × 30,000		= 100,000 / 30,000		
		= 180,000		= 3.3 days	6 days	Deficiency
Peak	Safety Level	= Desired Days at Peak × Highest Outflows	Days Available	= High Cash Balance / Peak Outflows		
		= 4 × 50,000		= 120,000 / 50,000		
		= 200,000		= 2.4 days	4 days	Deficiency

The data in Table 4-2 are for a firm that desires a 6-day safety level during normal periods but that actually has only a 3.3-day availability of cash. This is a deficiency. To see if you understand the other items, answer the following questions:

1. What is the firm's normal cash balance and its balance during the busiest period?
   Answer: $100,000 and 120,000, respectively.
2. What are the firm's normal daily outflows and its outflows during the peak period?
   Answer: $30,000 and 50,000, respectively.
3. How many days of cash available does the firm desire as a safety level during normal periods and at the peak period?
   Answer: 6 and 4 days, respectively.

Applying Cash-Management Ratios

As an example of the application of ratio analysis to the monitoring and determining of the safety level of cash on hand, consider a firm that has $150,000 cash balance on October 1 and $180,000 balance on October 31. Its total cash outlays during October came to $930,000; its three busiest days were October 3 through 5, when a total of $120,000 was spent. The financial manager has decided that a safety level of 6 days of cash is needed on the average, but a 4-day level is needed for the busiest period. He runs the following calculations:

$$\text{normal days of cash} = \frac{1/2(150,000 + 180,000)}{930,000/31}$$

$$= \frac{165,000}{30,000} = 5.5 \text{ days}$$

$$\text{peak days of cash} = \frac{165,000}{120,000/3 \text{ days}} = \frac{165,000}{40,000}$$

$$= 4.1 \text{ days}$$

$$\text{cash required at 6-day safety level} = (6 \text{ days})(\text{avg. daily outflow})$$

$$= (6 \text{ days}) \frac{930,000}{31} = \$180,000$$

$$\text{cash required at peak (4-day) level} = (4 \text{ days}) \frac{120,000}{3} = \$160,000$$

From these calculations, the financial manager learns at least two bits of information:

1. *Firm Is Below Safety Level.* In October the firm's 5.5 days of cash were below the 6-day safety level. Its 4.1 days of cash at the peak period were above the 4-day busiest period.
2. *$15,000 More Cash Is Needed.* To meet the deficiency, the firm needs to increase its cash balance from $165,000 to $180,000.

32. INVENTORY MANAGEMENT, HOW TO SET UP SYSTEM FOR

To effectively manage its inventories, a firm should utilize a systems approach to **inventory management.** A systems approach considers in a single model all the factors that affect the inventory. The model, called a system, may have any number of subsystems tied together to achieve a single goal. In the case of inventory systems, the goal is to minimize costs.

A system for effective inventory management involves three subsystems: **economic order quantity, reorder point,** and **stock level.** The computer brings these subsystems together to assist the financial manager in making inventory decisions. Each subsystem will be discussed in turn and then will be brought together into a single system.

Economic-Order-Quantity Subsystem

The economic order quantity refers to the size of order that will result in the lowest total of **order costs** and **carrying costs** for an item of inventory. If a firm places unnecessary orders, it will incur unneeded order costs. If it places too few orders, it will have to maintain large stocks of goods and will have excessive carrying costs. By calculating an economic order quantity, the firm identifies the number of units to order that results in the lowest total of these two costs.

A number of varying mathematical models are available to calculate the economic order quantity. Generally, they minimize a cost function. Without attempting to derive the formula, a simple calculation may be made when we assume the following:

1. *Demand Is Known.* Although it is difficult to accurately predict the firm's level of sales for individual items, the marketing manager must provide a sales forecast. Using past data and future plans, a reasonably accurate prediction of demand can often be made. This is expressed in units sold per year.
2. *Sales Occur at a Constant Rate.* This model may be used for goods that are sold in relatively constant amounts throughout the year. A more complicated model is needed for firms whose sales fluctuate in response to seasonal or other cyclical factors.
3. *Costs of Running Out of Goods Are Ignored.* Costs associated with shortages, delays, or lost sales are not considered. These costs are considered in the determination of safety level in the reorder-point subsystem.
4. *Safety Stock Level Is Not Considered.* The **safety stock level** is the minimum level of inventory that the firm wishes to hold as a protection against running out. Since the firm must always be above this level, the EOQ formula need not consider the costs of maintaining the safety stock level.

The formula for calculating the economic order quantity for an item of inventory is:

$$EOQ = \sqrt{\frac{(2)(U)(OC)}{(CC\%)(PP)}}$$

where 2 = mathematical factor that occurs during the deriving of the formula

U = units sold per year, a forecast provided by the marketing department

OC = cost of placing each individual order for more inventory, provided by cost accounting

CC% = inventory carrying costs expressed as a percentage of the average value of the inventory, an estimate usually provided by cost accounting

PP = purchase price for each unit of inventory, supplied by the purchasing department

As an example of the use of this formula, a firm anticipates 50,000 units of annual sales of a product that costs the firm $10. The cost of placing an order is $10, and the carrying costs have been estimated by cost accounting as 10 percent of the inventory value. The economic order quantity is

$$EOQ = \sqrt{\frac{(2)(50,000)(10)}{(10\%)(10)}} = \sqrt{\frac{1,000,000}{1}} = 1,000 \text{ units}$$

Thus, the firm should order 1,000 units if it places an order to minimize total order costs.

> *EXAMPLE: A firm has forecasted sales of 1,250,000 units of a product in the next 12 months. Each order would cost the firm $10. The firm pays $20 per unit for the product and estimates that inventory carrying costs are 20 percent of the inventory value. What is the economic order quantity for this product?*
> *ANSWER: 2,500 units. The formula is:*

$$EOQ = \sqrt{\frac{(2)(1,250,000)(10)}{(20\%)(20)}} = \sqrt{\frac{25,000,000}{4}} = 2,500 \text{ units}$$

Reorder-Point Subsystem

An important question in any inventory-management system is "When should an order be placed so that the firm does not run out of goods?" The answer, expressed in terms of units of inventory, is provided by the reorder-point subsystem.

The reorder point is the level of inventory at which the firm places an order in the amount of the economic order quantity. If the firm places the order when the inventory reaches the reorder point, the new goods will arrive before the firm runs out of goods to sell.

In designing a reorder-point subsystem, three items of information are needed as inputs to the subsystem:

1. *Usage Rate.* This is the rate per day at which the item is consumed in production or sold to customers. It is expressed in units. It may be calculated by dividing annual sales by 360 days. If the sales are 50,000 units, the **usage rate** is 50,000/360 or 140 units per day.
   A more complicated analysis may be used with computer-based reorder-point subsystems. The usage rate can be adjusted to reflect seasonal or cyclical factors and will result in differing reorder points at different times in the year.
2. *Lead Time.* This is the amount of time between placing an order and receiving the goods. This information is usually provided by the purchasing department. The **lead time** to allow for an order to arrive may be estimated from a check of the company's records and the time taken in the past for different suppliers to fill orders.
3. *Safety Stock Level.* This minimum level of inventory may be expressed in terms of a number of days sales. The level can be calculated by

multiplying the usage rate times the number of days the firm wants to hold as a protection against shortages. As an example, the firm may wish to hold sufficient inventory for 15 days of production in the event its order for raw materials does not arrive on time. In this case, the safety stock level is 15 days, and it is calculated in terms of units of inventory by multiplying 15 times the daily usage rate. Determining the number of days of safety stock to hold involves a complex number of variables. Some questions that must be answered are the following:

a. How much variation exists in the usage rate and how likely is it that the firm will run out of the goods?
b. How much does it cost in terms of lost revenues and profits if the firm runs out for 1 day? 2 days? 1 week?
c. At what point are the carrying costs higher than the lost revenues due to shortages?

Mathematical models exist to assist the inventory manager in dealing with these issues. These models are beyond the scope of this handbook. For most items of inventory, it is sufficient for the analyst to make a commonsense estimate of the number of days of safety stock needed for a product.

To calculate the reorder point, the following formula is used:

Reorder point = (UR)(LT) + (UR) (days of safety)
where UR = usage rate
LT = lead time
days of safety = days of safety stock desired by the firm

As an example of the use of this formula, consider a firm with a usage rate of 140 units per day, a lead time of 6 days, and a safety stock desired of 8 days of sales. The reorder point is

(140)(6) + (140)(8) = 840 + 1,120 = 1,960 units

In this case, the firm would place an order for the economic order quantity when the inventory gets down to 1,960 units.

EXAMPLE: A firm expects annual sales of 9,000 units, desires to maintain a 12-day safety stock level, and has an 8-day lead time for orders. What is the reorder point for the firm?
ANSWER: 500 units. The formula is 9,000/360 days = 25 units daily usage. (25)(8) + (25)(12) = 500 units.

Stock-Level Subsystem

This stock-level subsystem keeps track of the goods held by the firm, the issuing of goods, and the arrival of orders. It is made up of the records accounting for the goods in stock. Thus, the stock level subsystem maintains records of the current level of inventory. For any period of time, the current level is calculated by taking the beginning inventory, adding the inventory received, and subtracting the cost of goods sold. Whenever this subsystem reports that an item is at or below the reorder-point level, the firm will begin to place an order for the item.

Total System

The three subsystems are tied together in a single inventory-management system. This may be illustrated graphically by charting units of inventory on one axis and time on the other. Figure 4-1 shows a system for an item with a reorder point of 1,960 units, a safety stock level of 1,120 units, and an economic order quantity of 1,000 units. The firm reorders at 1,960 units, and continues to use its inventory until 1,120 units when the order of 1,000 arrives to return the inventory to 2,120 units.

The inventory-management system can also be illustrated in terms of the three subsystems that comprise it. Figure 4-2 ties each subsystem together and shows the three items of information needed for the decision to order additional inventory. The computer or analyst compares the level of the ending inventory with the reorder point for the item. If the ending inventory is less than the reorder point, an order should be placed for the economic order quantity.

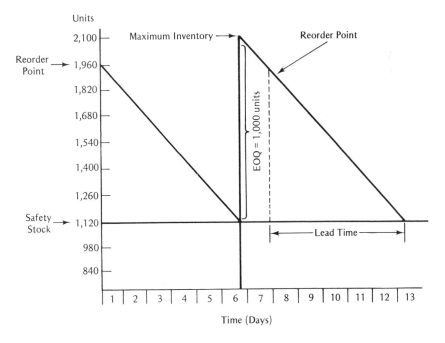

Figure 4-1. Inventory-Management System.

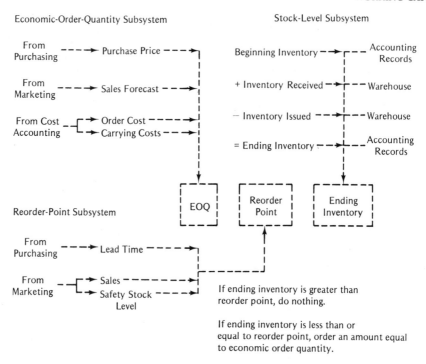

Economic-Order-Quantity Subsystem

Stock-Level Subsystem

Reorder-Point Subsystem

If ending inventory is greater than
reorder point, do nothing.

If ending inventory is less than or
equal to reorder point, order an amount equal
to economic order quantity.

Figure 4-2 Three Subsystems of the Inventory-Management System.

33. RECEIVABLES MANAGEMENT, HOW TO EVALUATE DIFFERING CREDIT POLICIES

In evaluating different proposals for credit or receivables policies, a major factor is the effect of each on the firm's profits. To analyze this effect, the firm prepares a pro forma or future income statement for each policy proposal. As an example of this technique, consider a firm that has a present policy of net 30 and is contemplating four possible policies: (1) no credit, (2) 2/10 net 30, (3) 2/10 net 60, and (4) net 60. A step-by-step approach will be used to analyze this decision.

Forecasting Sales with Each Alternative

The sales forecast is the first and perhaps most important step in preparing the income statement. If not reasonable, the forecast will distort all the following figures, including the final profit estimate.

The marketing department works closely with the finance department to forecast the likely level of sales with each alternative. In our example, the managers feel that the firm can achieve $300,000 in sales if 30-day credit is offered. If the terms are extended to 60 days, an additional $50,000 is expected in sales. Many of these sales will be made to customers experiencing liquidity problems, and a high level of bad-debt losses would be expected. If no credit were offered, the marketing manager estimates a drop in sales to $200,000. This is based on his detailed knowledge of the market, the prospective customers, and the fact that some of the firm's products are not available from other sources. Without credit, the marketing manager also feels that most customers would not be happy, because they are used to having time to receive and inspect the goods before preparing a check for payment.

Determining Cost of Goods Sold

The approximate percentage of **cost of goods sold** to the sales volume will be available from the cost-accounting department in most cases. At each sales level the percentage will drop because certain fixed costs such as depreciation will be already covered. In our example, the firm's cost of goods sold is estimated as follows:

1. *At $200,000 Sales Level.* Past data indicate that cost of goods sold will be approximately 60 percent of sales at this level.
2. *At $300,000 Sales Level.* The cost accountant estimates that this is the full production capacity for one shift. The efficient utilization of plant and equipment will drop cost of goods sold to 55 percent of sales.
3. *At $350,000 Sales Level.* This level will require overtime work and higher maintenance costs on the machinery. The cost accountant estimates that the cost of goods sold will return to a figure of 60 percent of sales.

Using cost of goods sold instead of variable costs is a modification of a break-even technique. If variable costs are readily obtainable, they may be used. The cost of goods sold and administrative cost breakdown is used because these figures are usually already known or more easily estimated by the cost accountant for different sales levels.

Forecasting Administrative Costs, Collection Costs, Bad-Debt Losses

The manager estimates that the firm will have $50,000 of administrative costs with any of the proposed credit policies. With the present policy, a part-time collection department is maintained. This costs approximately $10,000 per year, including the use of outside collectors at times. If the terms of trade are extended to 60 days, a full-time collection effort, costing approximately $22,000, will be needed. With no credit terms, no collection costs would be incurred.

Estimating bad-debt losses involves a judgment by the credit manager based on past data. With terms of 30 days, bad debts should be something less than 2 percent of sales, or $5,000. At 60-day terms of trade, bad debts may be as high as 4 percent of sales, or $12,000.

Forecasting Discounts Taken

Since two of the possible policies involve discounts for prompt payment (within 10 days), the firm must estimate the number of customers who will take the discount. Past data and the experience of other firms in the industry may be used. This is difficult to estimate, but at some point the credit manager forecasts a percentage of customers who will take the discount. The percentage is expressed in terms of the dollar value of sales, not the number of customers.

Once this percentage is forecast, the following formula is used to calculate discounts taken:

$$\text{discounts taken} = \begin{pmatrix} \% \text{ customers who will} \\ \text{pay in discount period} \end{pmatrix} (\% \text{ discount}) \begin{pmatrix} \text{annual} \\ \text{sales} \end{pmatrix}$$

If it is estimated that 70 percent of a firm's customers will take the discount and the terms are 2/10 net 30, a firm with $300,000 in sales will have discounts taken of $(.70)(.02)(\$300,000) = \$4,200$.

With terms of 2/10 net 60, it would be expected that a smaller percentage of customers would take the discount than at 2/10 net 30 because some customers would prefer the extra 30 days free use of the funds rather than the discount. If sales are $350,000 and 50 percent of the customers take the discount of 2 percent, the discounts taken will be $(.50)(.02)(\$350,000)$ or $3,500.

Forecasting the Average Collection Period

In calculating the average collection period, we recognize that a portion of the customers will take the discount and a portion will not. Those taking the discount will pay in the discount period. Of those not taking the discount, most will pay in the *net* period, but some will be late. Most firms include a factor for this late payment by some customers. In the following formula a 20 percent factor is used, because this will be realistic for a firm that is properly managing receivables. If the firm has a lax policy, a larger percentage should be used. For an extremely tight policy, a lower figure might be appropriate.

The formula for forecasting average collection period is

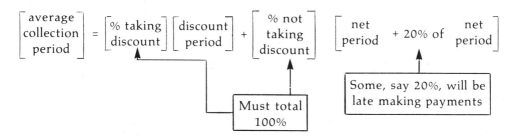

In our example of $300,000 sales with 70 percent taking a discount when terms are 2/10 net 30, the calculation is (.70)(10 days) + (.30)(30 days + .20 × 30 days) = 7 days + 10.8 days = 18 days average collection period. At 2/10 net 60 when sales are $350,000 and 50 percent take the discount, the calculation is (.50)(10 days) + (.50)(60 days + .20 × 60 days) = 5 days + 36 days = 41 days average collection period.

For the policies with no discount period, the percentage taking the discount is zero and the percentage paying after the net period is 100 percent. Only the second portion of the formula need be used. For terms of net 30, the average collection period is (.100)(30 + .20 × 30) = 36 days. For net 60, it is (.100)(60 + .20 × 60) = 72 days.

Forecasting Average Size of Accounts Receivable

If a firm has a steady level of sales throughout the year, we can forecast the average size of its receivables using a modification of a formula from ratio analysis. The modification is shown in Figure 4-3.

If	And	Then	So
$ART = \dfrac{sales}{AR}$	$ART = \dfrac{360\ days}{ACP}$	$AR = \dfrac{sales}{ART}$ or $\dfrac{sales}{360/ACP}$	$Est.\ AR = \dfrac{Est.\ sales}{360/ACP}$

Note: ART, accounts receivable turnover; AR, accounts receivable; ACP, average collection period; Est., estimated.

Figure 4-3. Modifying the Accounts-Receivable Turnover Formula to Estimate the Average Size of Accounts Receivable.

Using this formula for the firm in our example at each level of sales and credit policies, we obtain the following:

a. 2/10 net 30 $300,000 ÷ 360/18 = 300,000/20 = $15,000
average accounts receivable
b. net 30 $300,000 ÷ 360/36 = 300,000/10 = $30,000
average accounts receivable
c. 2/10 net 60 $350,000 ÷ 360/41 = 350,000/9 = $39,000
average accounts receivable
d. net 60 $350,000 ÷ 360/72 = 350,000/5 = $70,000
average accounts receivable

Calculating Marginal Cost of Funds Tied Up in Receivables

The firm's income statement already includes a certain level of receivables financed from the various sources of funds. The new level of receivables calculated in the previous step will involve greater or lesser costs of tying up funds in receivables. The firm presently has $75,000 in debt financed at 10 percent. This is part of the financing for the $30,000 receivables with the net 30 terms. The cost of changing the level of receivables can be added to the $7,500 in existing interest if receivables are increased; the savings from reducing receivables can be decreased from $7,500. Using the 10 percent cost of debt and assuming that it applies to new debt, the marginal cost of funds tied up in receivables with each credit policy would be as follows:

a. Zero receivables,
    no credit   (10%)(0–30,000)   = $3,000 savings
b. $15,000 receivables,
    2/10 net 30   (10%)(15,000–30,000) = $1,500 savings
c. $39,000 receivables,
    2/10 net 60   (10%)(39,000–30,000) = $900 added cost
d. $70,000 receivables,
    net 60   (10%)(70,000–30,000) = $4,000 added cost

Completing the Calculation Using Marginal Analysis

The final step involves arranging data in an income statement. Table 4-3 is the statement based on our example.

Profit Decision

The profits forecasted in Table 4-3 for the different credit policies indicate that the net 30 alternative will yield the most profit. It is closely followed by 2/10 net 30; the other alternatives are considerably less profitable. Based on profit aspects of receivables management, one of the two choices (net 30 or 2/10 net 30) is preferable to the others.

Before the final decision is made, the profit forecasts will be compared with the growth prospects and the likelihood of additional problems. It is only after taking this total viewpoint that a decision should be made.

TABLE 4-3. Profit Calculation for Five Credit Policies Using a Modified Marginal-Analysis Approach.

	Net 30	No Credit	2/10 Net 30	2/10 Net 60	Net 60
Forecasted sales	$300,000	$200,000	$300,000	$350,000	$350,000
Cost of goods sold (either 55% or 60%)	165,000	120,000	165,000	210,000	210,000
Gross margin	135,000	80,000	135,000	140,000	140,000
Administrative expenses (steady)	50,000	50,000	50,000	50,000	50,000
Collection costs	10,000	0	10,000	22,000	22,000
Bad-debt losses	5,000	0	5,000	12,000	12,000
Discounts taken	0	0	4,200	3,500	0
Forecasted operating income	70,000	30,000	65,800	52,500	56,000
Present interest on debt	7,500	7,500	7,500	7,500	7,500
Receivables cost or saving	0	(3,000)	(1,500)	900	4,000
Forecasted earnings before taxes	62,500	25,500	59,800	44,100	44,500
Taxes	31,500	12,750	29,900	22,050	22,250
Forecasted net income	$ 31,500	$ 12,750	$ 29,900	$ 22,050	$ 22,250

34. RECEIVABLES MANAGEMENT, HOW TO USE A RISK-CLASS APPROACH

To make routine the decision to extend credit, many firms use a **risk-class approach** to the approval of credit sales. The firm establishes a certain number of risk classes ranging from the strongest and most established customers to the weakest firms. A separate credit policy is developed for each class. When a customer first applies for credit, the customer will be investigated and placed into one of the classes. This eliminates the need to make a separate decision on extending credit each time the customer wants to make a purchase. Table 4-4 shows risk classes, a description of the type of firm in each class, and a brief statement of the applicable credit policy.

TABLE 4-4. Risk-Class Approach to Receivables Management.

Risk Class	Description of Firm	Credit Policy
1	Large firms whose financial position and past record indicate virtually no risk.	Open credit up to certain limit without approval required.
2	Financially sound firms not supported by a detailed past record.	Open credit with approval for purchases in excess of certain amounts up to a specified limit.
3	Solid firms with past records that indicate some risk.	Limited credit line with frequent checks.
4	Not-too-solid firms that require close watching.	Restricted credit.
5	High-risk, weak firms.	No credit.

As an example of the application of the risk-class approach, consider a firm in risk class 2 from Table 4-4. The firm is a relatively new customer and was placed in class 2 after a complete credit check. The credit limit for individual orders has been set at $70,000, and the outstanding balance has been limited to $225,000. The ledger card for receivables for this customer is as follows:

Acme Company—Accounts Receivable

Date	Item	Charges	Payments	Balance Due
Jan. 20	Invoice 963522	$45,000		$140,000
Jan. 23	Invoice 963641	50,000		190,000
Jan. 25	Invoice 963698	12,000		202,000
Jan. 25			$30,000	172,000
Jan. 28	Invoice 963811	40,000		212,000

On January 30, a purchase order is received from Acme for goods totaling $80,000. What does the firm do?

Answer: The accounting clerk will compare the order with the file on Acme and discover that the order exceeds the $70,000 single purchase limit authorized for the firm. A check of the ledger card reveals that the order will place the total receivables balance above the $225,000 limit. The order is brought to the financial manager who can take several possible actions:

1. *Raise the Limits.* The financial manager may decide that this firm deserves new credit limits. Since the original limits were imposed, the firm may have demonstrated that it pays promptly on its bills. The credit limits can be raised and the firm considered for possible movement to risk class 1.
2. *Investigate Further.* The manager may wish to call the Acme Company and inquire about the order. Did they know the order was larger than the limits? Do they want to be considered for higher limits? Will they supply information if needed to raise the limits? If the investigation reveals the credit should be extended, new credit limits may be set.
3. *Deny the Request.* If the financial manager has information that the request should not be granted, the purchase order will be returned with an explanation of why it was not filled. The manager may suggest that it be divided into two separate orders and be submitted after the balance is reduced.

35. RECEIVABLES MANAGEMENT, HOW TO ESTABLISH CREDIT LIMITS

A major decision area in working capital management is the establishment of credit limits for differing customers of the firm. In this section, we will examine techniques for dealing with two aspects of setting limits: (1) How to deal with numerous small accounts where credit information is limited or where the sales level is too low to justify detailed evaluation of the customer's credit, and (2) larger accounts where a balance sheet and income statement are available.

Handling Numerous Small Accounts

Many firms operate in industries where sales are divided among thousands of customers with average unit sales of $25 to $1,000. In this environment, the credit department will lack financial statements on most customers. An even greater problem is that it will lack the time to perform more than a cursory analysis of firms that are applying for credit. The credit manager may check with Dun and Bradstreet or a similar credit agency but, in most cases, the extension of credit will be almost automatic.

These accounts are probably best handled with an overall credit policy that strives for a good balance between cash at risk and first-year profit. The exact policy will vary with individual industries but a simple rule of thumb might be:

Credit Policy—First-Year Profit on an Account Should Equal or Exceed the Maximum Cash at Risk at Any One Time.

As an example of following this credit policy, let us consider a firm selling products with a 20 percent profit margin. The credit department has received an application for credit with a limit up to $5,000. The potential customer is expected to purchase goods worth $30,000 annually if the credit is approved. On the basis of this information, the credit department calculates the first-year profit and cash at risk as follows:

FIRST-YEAR PROFIT		CASH AT RISK	
Sales	$30,000	Credit limit	$5,000
Cost of sales (80%)	24,000	less profit (20% margin)	1,000
First-year profit	$6,000	Cash at risk	$4,000

In this example, the first-year profit exceeds the cash at risk and therefore the credit application falls within the established policy.

The above approach will not be acceptable to many credit departments. It makes no attempt to come to grips with the basic creditworthiness of the customer. As a practical matter, it is both difficult and expensive to monitor the creditworthiness of hundreds or thousands of small accounts. The firm must recognize that the price of doing business using the above policy will be moderate collection costs and bad debts. If, however, the collection costs and bad debts represent a dollar value of 5 to 10 percent of sales, the firm will earn a profit on these customers.

One additional guideline can be used in conjunction with the above policy to further reduce exposure. The firm can set a policy that no credit will be extended to firms that have not been in business a minimum period of time, say three years. Since a large portion of businesses fail in the first three years, the firm will avoid this high risk from sales to new and untested firms.

Credit Limits for Large Accounts

A totally different approach should be taken for establishing the credit limit for a large account. The first step is to require a credit application from the potential customer that contains a balance sheet and income statement for a recent period. In the discussion that follows, we shall use the financial data for Myron and Johnson, Inc. to illustrate the process of evaluating the application and establishing the credit limit.

Step 1. Maximum Credit Extended to Any One Customer

The first step in processing a credit application is to acknowledge the maximum credit that the firm is willing to extend to any one customer. The firm usually desires to limit its exposure to a single customer, no matter how creditworthy the customer may be. In our example, let us assume that our own firm will not grant credit in excess of $100,000 to any customer.

Step 2. Two Broad Guidelines—Net Worth and Net Working Capital

Before beginning a detailed financial analysis, the credit analyst should check the financial statements for adequacy of net worth and net working capital. **Net worth** is defined as the equity on the balance sheet. **Net working capital** is defined as the excess of current assets over current liabilities. The firm should establish broad guidelines for comparing credit limits to both items. For example, the firm might want to limit credit to 10 percent of net worth and 20 percent of net working capital. If these broad guidelines are used, the analyst can make a quick check to see the initial limits on Myron and Johnson's credit, as follows:

10% OF NET WORTH GUIDELINE		*20% OF NET WORKING CAPITAL GUIDELINE*	
Net worth from balance sheet	$1,900,000	Current assets	$1,150,000
		minus current liabilities	1,000,000
		Net working capital	150,000
times 10 percent factor	× .10	times 20 percent factor	× .20
Maximum credit	$ 190,000	maximum credit	$30,000

Using the lesser of the two broad guidelines, Myron and Johnson qualifies for a $30,000 maximum credit limit.

MYRON AND JOHNSON, INC. Balance Sheet (000s)

	1978		1977	
Cash	$ 100		$ 80	
Marketable securities	120		120	
Accounts receivable	350		200	
Inventories	580		300	
Total Current Assets		$1,150		$ 700
Plant and equipment (less acc. depr.)	1,500		1,400	
Land	750		750	
Total Fixed Assets		2,250		2,150
Total Assets		$3,400		$2,850
Accounts payable	300		60	
Notes payable	600		220	
Accrued liabilities	100		70	
Total Current Liabilities		1,000		350
First mortgage (6%)	200		300	
Second mortgage (9%)	-		200	
Bonds (6%)	300		300	
Total Long-Term Liabilities		500		800
Common stock ($1 par)	600		600	
Capital in excess of par	400		400	
Retained earnings	900		700	
Total Equity		1,900		1,700
Total Liabilities and Equity		$3,400		$2,850

MYRON AND JOHNSON, INC. Income Statement (000s)

	1978		1977	
Sales	$5,980		$5,780	
Income from investments	20		20	
Total Revenues		$6,000		$5,800
Beginning inventory	300		400	
Total manufacturing costs	4,200		3,200	
Less ending inventory	(580)		(300)	
Cost of Goods Sold		3,920		3,300
Gross profit		$2,080		$2,500
General and administrative expenses		950		750
Operating Income		$1,130		$1,750
Interest expenses		60		62
Earnings Before Taxes		$1,070		$1,688
Federal income taxes		480		674
Net Income After Taxes		$590		$1,014
Dividends declared and paid				250

Step 3. Stable Liquidity Test

Since we have a balance sheet with both 1977 and 1978 financial data, we can evaluate whether Myron and Johnson has sufficient liquidity to pay its bills on time. Four liquidity ratios can be used to overview the potential customer's cash and near-cash position:

LIQUIDITY OVERVIEW—MYRON AND JOHNSON, INC.

RATIO	CALCULATION OF RATIO	1978		1977	
Current Ratio	Current assets / Current liabilities	$\frac{1,150}{1,100}$	= 1.15	$\frac{700}{350}$	= 2.00
Acid Test	Current assets —Inventory / Current liabilities	$\frac{570}{1,000}$	= .57	$\frac{400}{350}$	= 1.14
Accounts Receivable Turnover	Sales / Receivables	$\frac{5,980}{350}$	= 17 times	$\frac{5,780}{200}$	= 29 times
Inventory Turnover	Sales / Inventory	$\frac{5,980}{580}$	= 10.3 times	$\frac{5,780}{300}$	= 19.3 times
	Cost of goods sold / Inventory	$\frac{3,920}{580}$	= 6.7 times	$\frac{3,300}{300}$	= 11 times

Two tests of the liquidity position can now be made. First, how does Myron and Johnson compare to average figures for the industry? Suppose the industry averages are:

CURRENT RATIO	1.8
ACID TEST	1.1
RECEIVABLES TURNOVER	10 times
INVENTORY TURNOVER	
With sales	11 times
With cost of goods sold	7 times

Myron and Johnson basically meets or exceeds the averages for 1977 but is below the current ratio and acid test averages in 1978.

Second, does the year-to-year comparison show that liquidity is strengthening, holding steady, or deteriorating? It appears that a major deterioration has occurred from 1977 to 1978.

At this point, the analyst should return to the original balance sheet to determine what has caused the liquidity decline in 1978. The major problem appears to be the rise in current liabilities from $350,000 to $1,000,000 during 1978. The analyst should make a note to ask the reason for this rise. The firm may have increased accounts payable to take advantage of low-cost trade credit and its current notes payable may have risen as a prelude to a long-term commercial bank financing which has not yet been completed. Or, the firm may be unable to obtain long-term financing and the heavy use of short-term financing may indicate that it is a serious credit risk.

Step 4. Stable Profitability Test

Combining the balance sheet and income statement, we can use ratios to check the profitability of Myron and Johnson, as follows:

PROFITABILITY OVERVIEW—MYRON AND JOHNSON, INC.

RATIO	CALCULATION OF RATIO	1978		1977	
Profit Margin	$\dfrac{\text{Operating income (EBIT)}}{\text{Sales}}$	$\dfrac{1{,}130}{5{,}980}$	= .19	$\dfrac{1{,}750}{5{,}780}$	= .30
Return on Investment	$\dfrac{\text{Operating income (EBIT)}}{\text{Assets}}$	$\dfrac{1{,}130}{3{,}400}$	= .33	$\dfrac{1{,}750}{2{,}850}$	= .61
Return on Equity	$\dfrac{\text{Net income after taxes}}{\text{Equity}}$	$\dfrac{590}{1{,}900}$	= .31	$\dfrac{1{,}014}{1{,}700}$	= .60

We now make the same two tests as for liquidity. First, if the industry averages are:

PROFIT MARGIN...................................... .15
RETURN ON INVESTMENT .... .20
RETURN ON EQUITY............................... .09

we can conclude that Myron and Johnson is relatively profitable compared to the industry average. Second, the year-to-year test indicates a declining profitability. Going back to the financial statements, two factors appear to account for much of the decline. There was a sharp rise in cost of goods sold from $3,300,000 to $3,920,000 on a sales rise of only $200,000. Also, general and administrative expenses rose sharply from $750,000 to $950,000. The firm should be asked about these cost rises.

Step 5. Liquidation Coverage

The next step is to determine whether Myron and Johnson has sufficient asset value to cover its liabilities in the event of forced liquidation. Even though we will extend credit only to firms that are likely to continue operations indefinitely, a liquidation coverage offers a view of the worst possible situation.

Assets can be sold at some fraction of their balance sheet value. In some cases, as with land, the assets may be grossly undervalued compared to actual market values. In other cases, as with inventory, the reported value may far exceed the liquidation value in the event of a distress liquidation. Each firm will determine its own liquidation percentages; let us use the following in our example:

CATEGORY OF ASSET	DOLLAR VALUE FOR MYRON AND JOHNSON, INC.	APPROPRIATE PERCENT	ASSUMED REALIZABLE VALUE
Cash	$100,000	100	$100,000
Marketable securities	120,000	100	120,000
Receivables	350,000	90	315,000
Inventory	580,000	60	348,000
Plant & equipment	1,500,000	40	600,000
Land	750,000	100	750,000
LIQUIDATION VALUE OF ASSETS		....	$2,233,000
less 100 percent of liabilities		....	1,500,000
NET LIQUIDATION VALUE		....	$733,000

It thus appears, given our percentages of assumed realizable value of the assets in a distress situation, that Myron and Johnson would be able to cover all its liabilities in the event of a liquidation.

Step 6. Gather the Additional Information

The credit analyst must now get answers to the questions raised in the liquidity and profitability analysis above. The analyst will also perform such tasks as checking the credit rating of the firm with the appropriate credit agencies and will call the references listed in the credit application. If all appears satisfactory when this process is completed, the final step must be taken.

Step 7. Establish the Credit Limit

In our analysis above, the restricting factor was the $30,000 which represents 20 percent of net working capital in step 2. This appears to be reasonable as an initial credit limit. If this limit is not acceptable to Myron and Johnson's needs, the credit analyst should work with the sales manager, the credit manager, and other interest persons to determine whether an exception to policy should be made and a larger limit established.

36. WORKING CAPITAL, HOW TO BALANCE SOURCES OF FUNDS

The firm's current assets are financed from a combination of short- and long-term sources. When inventory is purchased on terms of, say, net 30, the accounts payable is the source of funds. Similarly, a 20-year bond may be the source of funds for cash and receivables.

Matching an item of working capital to a single, specific source must be carefully done. It does not make sense, for example, to say a bond provided any single asset. A dollar is a dollar and all money goes into a pool of funds. From this pool, the firm draws money to pay for the resources it needs. It is not logical to say that accounts payable represents a source of cash (since buying on credit allowed the firm to hold on to its cash). It is more accurate to say that accounts payable is a source of the items of inventory purchased on credit. It is even more accurate to recognize that accounts payable is a source of funds that would otherwise have to be provided by other debt or equity financing.

Although we should not link a single debt or equity account with a single current asset, we do have guidelines for financing working capital.

TABLE 4-5. Three Sets of Guidelines for Sources of Funds to Finance Working Capital.

Permanent and Variable Working Capital		Major Current Asset Accounts		Total Current Assets	
Item	*Source*	*Item*	*Source*	*Item*	*Source*
Variable work. cap.	S-T	Cash and receivables	S-T	$\frac{1}{2}$ Current assets	S-T
$\frac{1}{3}$ Perm. work. cap.	S-T	Inventories	L-T	$\frac{1}{2}$ Current assets	L-T
$\frac{2}{3}$ Perm. work. cap.	L-T	Fixed assets	L-T	Fixed assets	L-T
Fixed assets	L-T				

These guidelines are shown in Table 4-5 and are mutually exclusive. That is, a firm will attempt to follow one norm, not all three. The rationales for each set of guidelines are as follows:

1. *Guidelines 1: Permanent and Variable Working Capital.* The sources of funds are compared against the firm's permanent and temporary working capital. A firm's variable needs for current assets should be financed from short-term sources and only for the periods needed. The permanent needs may be partially (perhaps one third) matched against short-term sources. The remainder of the permanent working capital

plus all the fixed assets should be financed from long-term sources.

2. *Guidelines 2: Major Current-Asset Accounts.* Cash and receivables are the most liquid assets and are or will soon be available to pay bills. These may be matched against current liabilities. Inventories and other assets are less liquid and should be financed from long-term sources.

3. *Guidelines 3: Total Current Assets.* A 2/1 normal current ratio means that one-half the current assets will be matched against short-term liabilities. The remaining current assets and all fixed assets will be financed by long-term sources of funds.

Why is it important to compare the current assets with the sources of funds on a short- and long-term basis? The problem involves liquidity. If the firm has a permanent need for certain levels of cash, receivables, and inventory, it cannot operate efficiently if it feels pressure to liquidate these assets to pay current liabilities. In the absence of adequate long-term financing, the financial manager will spend excessive time managing the liquidity aspects of current assets rather than focusing on the profits to be made from the assets. Thus, whatever the guidelines adopted, the firm must have long-term sources for a major portion of its working capital.

This rationale helps explain why a firm strives for a 2/1 current ratio and a 1/1 quick ratio. Both norms allow for a large part of current assets to be financed by long-term sources of funds. For the 2/1 current ratio, half the working capital is financed long term. For the 1/1 quick ratio, the entire inventory (which is usually approximately one-half the current assets) is financed long term. The norms for these ratios can apply to all three sets of guidelines.

Advantages of Long- and Short-Term Sources of Working Capital

By financing a portion of working capital with short-term sources of funds, the firms realizes several benefits:

1. *Lower Costs.* If variable working capital is financed on a short-term basis, the firm pays interest on funds only during the period of time they are needed. Also, the firm's accounts payable frequently do not carry any interest charges at all. By making credit purchases and waiting the full time to pay, the firm receives free use of a supplier's goods.

2. *Establishes Close Relations with Banks.* By borrowing money during peak periods and paying it back promptly when no longer needed, the financial managers work closely with the commercial loan officers at the firm's bank. These close relations can prove valuable in later, larger dealings with the bank.

By financing the remainder of its working capital and all its fixed assets with long-term sources of funds, the firm benefits as follows:

1. *Reduces Risk.* Long-term financing eliminates the need to repay loans at frequent intervals. This reduces the danger that a loan will be due and the firm will not have funds to pay it off.
2. *Provides Stability.* If assets are financed so that they will be available for a long period of time, they provide a certain stability to the firm's operations. The firm does not have to worry about not being able to purchase enough inventory for production because it has the cash to pay the account payable when it is due.
3. *Increases Liquidity.* Because the debt is not payable in the near future, the firm can tie up its working capital as needed to support business activities. Since the firm does not have to worry about these funds, the long-term sources have the effect of increasing liquidity.

Chapter 5

LONG-TERM FINANCING

37. BONDS, HOW TO CALCULATE VALUE OF

The value of secure **bonds** is commonly determined through the use of a capitalization technique. The stream of future interest payments and the principal repayment are discounted to the present with a selected capitalization rate. Table 5-1 illustrates this technique. A bond is due to mature in 5 years, has a 6 percent coupon, and the appropriate capitalization rate is 5 percent. The present value or **going-concern value** of the bond is $1,043.80.

TABLE 5-1. Present Value or Going-Concern Value of a 6 Percent Bond with 5 Years to Maturity Discounted at 5 Percent Capitalization Rate.

Year	Interest and Principal To Be Paid		5% Discount Factor		Present Value
1	60	×	.952	=	$ 57.12
2	60	×	.907	=	54.42
3	60	×	.864	=	51.84
4	60	×	.823	=	49.38
5	60 + 1,000	×	.784	=	831.04
					$1,043.80

Determining the Discount Factor

The capitalization rate or discount factor is usually the current market yield available on bonds that offer a similar degree of safety to the bond being valued. A bond will be issued with a fixed coupon rate. For example, a bond with a 6 percent coupon will pay $60 interest each year (assuming a $1,000 face value bond). But bond rates will change in the marketplace. When this happens, the current yield on the bond will change because the market value will change.

Identifying the appropriate current yield is made easier by investment services, such as Moody's and Standard and Poor's, who publish ratings of widely traded bonds. Bonds are rated from triple-A representing the most secure bonds to C, which indicates a bond in default on the payment of interest.

The greater the degree of safety for a bond, the lower the current yield and hence the lower the capitalization rate. This is reasonable. A safer bond should bring in a lower return than a riskier bond. Using the 6 percent coupon bond in Table 5-1 as an example, we can compare three bonds offering different degrees of safety. If the current market yields are 5 percent for an Aaa bond, 6 percent for an A bond, and 8 percent for a B bond, we shall have different values for the three 6 percent bonds. Table 5-1 showed how to calculate the present value for the Aaa bond. If we made the same calculations for all three bonds, we would have the present values shown in Table 5-2.

TABLE 5-2. Present Value of a 5-year, 6 Percent Bond with Different Safety Levels.

Bond Rating	Discount Factor	Present Value
Aaa	5%	$1,043.80
A	6%	$1,000.00
B	8%	$ 920.58

Note that the safest bond in Table 5-2, the triple-A bond, is worth $123 more than the less secure B-rated bond.

38. COST OF CAPITAL, HOW TO COMPARE THREE MAJOR THEORIES

Durand, Miller–Modigliani, and others have developed a number of techniques for looking at a firm's cost of capital. This section examines three major theories and focuses on the main contributions of each.

Simplifying Assumptions

In discussing the cost-of-capital theories, we shall make use of the following simplifying assumptions:

1. *No Change in Business Risk.* Business risk measures the ability of a corporation to operate successfully in the business community. The three theories assume that this risk does not change as the firm expands.

2. *Absence of Corporate Taxes.* The theories assume that the firm pays no corporate income taxes, thus removing the question of income tax leverage from the cost-of-capital calculations.

3. *Comparable Growth Rates.* Differing growth rates have a marked effect on the cutoff point for new proposals. To avoid dealing with the difficulties that are part of growth calculations, the theories assume that a firm will grow at a rate comparable to other firms.

4. *One Hundred Percent Dividend Payout.* To avoid becoming involved with the effect of dividends on cost of capital, the theories assume that all firms have a 100 percent dividend payout.

Unifying Elements

The different cost-of-capital theories make use of four important elements to provide a framework for analyzing a firm's cost of capital:

1. K_e *Is a Rate of Return, Not a Cost.* The cost of equity capital is measured as a rate of return in these theories, just as it is in the weighted-average calculation of cost of capital.

2. $K_e = EBT/CS_{mkt}$. The **weighted-average cost of capital** measures K_e with the formula $[EPS/(1 + G)^3]/MP$. If the growth rates are omitted as a factor, the formula would become EPS/MP. If the ratio were calculated in the aggregate instead of on a per share basis, the formula would become $NIAT/CS_{mkt}$. In a situation without taxes, NIAT equals EBT. Thus, the firm's cost of equity capital can be measured as a ratio of earnings before taxes to the value of the common stock in the market, or EBT/CS_{mkt}. All three theories measure K_e with this formula.

3. $K_o = EBIT/V_{mkt}$. The theories agree that the overall value of the firm is a function of the operating income (EBIT) and the cost of capital. A direct measure of cost of capital is given by a ratio of EBIT to V_{mkt}. This replaces the weighted calculation of K_o found in the weighted-average approach to cost of capital.

4. *Preferred Stock Is Omitted.* Since the theories are discussed in a framework without corporate taxes, preferred stock has basically the same characteristics as debt. If the analyst assumes that preferred-stock dividends must be declared (as most firms feel they must), the debt and preferred stock may be treated together. Because of the similarities between debt and preferred stock as fixed-return securities, the theories do not include any separate treatment of preferred stock.

Theory 1: Fixed K_e

A traditional approach to cost of capital begins with the position that the **cost of equity capital** (K_e) is fixed as a constant percentage for firms in a given risk class. The key to this position is the claim that EBT determines the value of the firm's common stock. Supporters of this theory would ask the following question. Why should two firms with similar risk and identical EBT's have a different value for their common stock? The argument continues that the investor is concerned about the earnings reported to the shareholders and will purchase stock at the best price for any given level of earnings. Thus, we should expect that similar-risk firms will have similar K_e values, since market pressures will establish a fixed K_e for a risk class of firms.

Solving for K_e if the K_o Is Fixed

If the cost-of-equity capital is fixed, we can solve for the overall cost of capital by using a single formula. We develop this formula using the following process:

1. *Begin with the Formula for K_o.* As given previously, the formula is

$$K_o = \frac{\text{EBIT}}{V_{\text{mkt}}}$$

2. *Modify the Formula with Respect to V_{mkt}.* The value of the firm in the market can be expressed as the sum of the values of the individual components of the capital structure. When this is done, the formula becomes

$$K_o = \frac{\text{EBIT}}{\text{CS}_{\text{mkt}} + \text{D}_{\text{mkt}}}$$

3. *Substitute EBT/K_e for CS_{mkt} in the Formula.* From the above unifying elements, we can substitute EBT/K_e for the CS_{mkt} to get

$$K_o = \frac{\text{EBIT}}{\text{EBT}/K_e + \text{D}_{\text{mkt}}}$$

This formula can be used to solve for the overall cost of capital since all the components are known. The debt can be treated at its face value. The common stock is valued as a function of the EBT to the fixed K_e.

As an example of using the fixed K_e theory, we can calculate the cost of capital for a firm with an EBIT of \$200,000, debt of \$400,000 at 5 percent, no preferred stock, and a K_e for its risk class of 10 percent. The calculation is

$$K_o = \frac{200,000}{180,000/.10 + 400,000} = \frac{200,000}{2,200,000} = 9.1\%$$

Contribution of Fixed K_e Theory

The strength of the **fixed K_e theory** is that it attempts to explain the effects of borrowing on the firm's overall cost of capital. Stated another way, it highlights favorable financial leverage. Using the formula, a firm can lower its overall cost of capital by increasing its debt with favorable financial leverage. To demonstrate this with the numbers just given, assume that the firm borrows $600,000 at 5 percent and earns 10 percent on the money. The EBIT will increase to $260,000 and the EBT to 210,000, leaving the formula as follows:

$$K_o = \frac{260,000}{210,000/.10 + 1,000,000} = \frac{260,000}{3,100,000} = 8.4\%$$

In this example, the additional borrowing with favorable financial leverage results in a decrease in the overall cost of capital. Even more important is the increase in the value of the common stock. Why does favorable financial leverage increase CS_{mkt}? The answer involves two steps:

1. *EBT Increases When Debt Is Added with Favorable Financial Leverage.* When we borrow at one rate and earn a return at a higher rate, the firm's EBT increases.
2. *Higher EBT Produces a Higher Common-Stock Value.* When a firm increases earnings, it can expect an increase in the value of common stock. With the formula $CS_{mkt} = EBT/K_e$, any increase in EBT will result in an increase in CS_{mkt} if the K_e is fixed.

In our example, the value of CS_{mkt} goes from 180,000/.10, or $1,800,000, to 210,000/.10, or $2,100,000, an increase of $300,000 due to the new debt with favorable financial leverage.

Weakness of Fixed K_e Theory

The major weakness of fixed K_e theory is that it fails to recognize the risks as the firm increases its debt. Under this theory, the firm should add debt indefinitely as long as the borrowing rate is less than the return on investment. The optimum capital structure would be all debt—or at least as much debt as can be borrowed with favorable financial leverage. This is unrealistic because it fails to consider the effects of extreme debt on the price of common stock. If debt is excessive, the investors will perceive the risk and sell the stock, causing a decline in CS_{mkt}. The fixed K_e theory cannot handle this possibility and is thus inadequate as a theory of capital-structure management.

The major points related to fixed K_e theory are found in Figure 5-1.

Major Claim of Theory	How to Solve for K_o
K_e is fixed in a relationship of EBT/CS_{mkt}.	$K_o = \dfrac{EBIT}{EBT/K_e + D_{mkt}}$
Contributions of Theory	Weaknesses of Theory
Points out that borrowing with favorable financial leverage can decrease K_o.	Unrealistic because it ignores the effects that extreme debt will have on CS_{mkt}.
Points out that borrowing with favorable financial leverage can increase CS_{mkt}.	Because it ignores effects on CS_{mkt}, it is inadequate as a theory of capital-structure management.

Figure 5-1.   Overview of Fixed K_e Theory.

Theory 2: Fixed K_o

A second traditional theory of cost of capital expresses K_o as a constant percentage for firms in a given risk class. It is expressed as a ratio of earnings to the overall value of the firm, as follows:

$$K_o = \frac{EBIT}{V_{mkt}}$$

The theory is supported by pointing out that the rate of return of similar firms is really the key determinant of value. At the same level of risk, we expect the same return. Thus, for any given level of EBIT, we would expect the same value of different firms. If two firms are able to earn $1,000,000 EBIT, and if the firms have similar characteristics, why should the two firms have different values? If the overall cost of capital is such that investors expect a 10 percent return, the values of the firms will be

$$V_{mkt} = \frac{EBIT}{K_o} = \frac{1,000,000}{10\%} = \$10,000,000$$

Under this theory, K_o is fixed for firms in a similar risk class; that is, K_o is given. Also, K_o does not change. It is independent of the capital structure and does not respond to changes in the firm's debt or equity.

Solving for K_e if the K_o Is Fixed

If the overall cost of capital is fixed for a group of similar firms, we do not need to calculate it. But we may want to calculate the cost of equity capital. We can develop our formula using the following process:

1. *Begin with the Formula for K_e.* The formula is

$$K_e = \frac{EBT}{CS_{mkt}}$$

2. *Substitute $V_{mkt} - D_{mkt}$ for CS_{mkt} in the Formula.* When this is done, the formula becomes

$$K_e = \frac{EBT}{V_{mkt} - D_{mkt}}$$

3. *Substitute $EBIT/K_o$ for V_{mkt} in the Formula.* This gives us

$$K_e = \frac{EBT}{EBIT/K_o - D_{mkt}}$$

In this formula, all the values including the fixed K_o are known. This allows us to solve for K_e. As an example of using the formula, assume that a firm has an EBIT of \$100,000, debt of \$300,000 at 6 percent, and is in a category of firms with a fixed K_o of 10 percent. The cost of equity capital would be

$$K_e = \frac{82,000}{100,000/.10 - 300,000} = \frac{82,000}{700,000} = 11.7\%$$

Contribution of Fixed K_o Theory

The major contribution of the early **fixed K_o theory** was the emphasis on the firm's operating income as a determinant of total value. Without earnings from its operations, the firm had only a liquidation value. The cutoff point for new projects should consider the relationship of EBIT to total value, not the relationship between the source of financing and the return from a single project. If the K_o is independent of the capital structure and is based on an expected return from the firm's operations, the issues of debt versus equity become less important than securing an adequate return.

Weakness of Fixed K_o Theory

The fixed K_o theory leads to the conclusion that all capital structures are the same; that is, there is no optimum capital structure. If the firm's cost of capital is indifferent to changes in the capital structure, the firm can ignore the changes for the most part. This would be a mistake. A firm must avoid the appearance of considerable risk in its financing mix. At the same time, a strong management attempts to make some use of favorable financial leverage. The fixed K_o theory does not help the firm understand these matters and make decisions with respect to them.

The major points related to fixed K_o theory are found in Figure 5-2.

Major Claim of Theory	How to Solve for K_e
K_o is fixed in a relationship of $EBIT/V_{mkt}$.	$K_e = \dfrac{EBT}{EBIT/K_o - D_{mkt}}$
Contributions of Theory	**Weaknesses of Theory**
Points out the importance of operating earnings (EBIT) as a determinant of V_{mkt}. Emphasizes EBIT in selecting the cutoff point for new projects.	Leads to a conclusion that all capital structures are basically alike. Erroneously encourages firm to overlook favorable financial leverage and risk from excessive debt.

Figure 5-2. Overview of Fixed K₀ Theory.

Theory 3: Varying K_e at Varying Debt Levels

A third traditional theory of cost of capital relates different costs of capital to the degree of risk in the firm's capital structure. The formula for K_o is identical to the formula in theory 1, a fixed K_e. The only difference is found in the value of K_e. Instead of being fixed for all firms in the risk category, K_e varies at differing levels of debt. As is shown in the following example, K_e increases as the level of debt increases:

Debt-Equity Ratio	Firm's K_e (%)
No debt	10
25%	11
50%	12
1/1	13

What does this changing K_e mean? It means that investors recognize the risk in the added debt and are willing to pay less for the firm's common stock. In the ratio EBT/CS_{mkt}, if the price of the stock drops, the K_e will rise. In effect, the investors are willing to pay less for the higher-risk stock, which is the same as requiring a higher return on their money.

Contribution of Varying K_e Theory

The varying K_e theory correctly ties in effects on the market price of common stock to the **cost of capital decision.** It encourages the firm to take advantage of favorable financial leverage but to avoid the rising K_e (drop in CS_{mkt}) at high debt levels.

Weakness of Varying K_e Theory

An underlying assumption of all three theories is the absence of corporate income taxes. In effect, this simplification is also a weakness of each theory. While the varying K_e theory does come to grips with favorable financial leverage and possible decreases in the market price of common stock, it is not complete without tax effects.

The major points related to a varying K_e theory are presented in Figure 5-3.

Major Claim of Theory	How to Solve For K_o
K_e varies with debt in the relationship EBT/CS_{mkt} because investors will pay less for common stock as debt increases.	$K_o = \dfrac{EBIT}{EBT/K_e + D_{mkt}}$ where K_e varies with debt level.
Contributions of Theory	Weakness of Theory
Points out the fact that adding debt to the capital structure will drop price of common stock. Ties favorable financial leverage and common-stock effects in single theory.	Does not include the impact of corporate taxes and their effects on cost of capital and capital structure.

Figure 5-3. Overview of Varying K_e Theory.

39. LEASE-BUY DECISION, HOW TO MAKE IT

Before a financial manager can calculate the costs of leasing versus the costs of ownership of assets, he must deal with a number of factors that will affect each alternative. In this section, we shall analyze these factors and then develop a step-by-step approach to be followed in making a lease-buy decision.

Cash-Flow Basis

The lease–buy comparison correctly uses cash outlays and inflows as a basis for decision making. The process is very similar to the technique used for making capital-budgeting decisions. The accounting effect with respect to earnings per share would be utilized only in cases when the market price of the firm's stock may be adversely affected by leasing the assets. In this case, both a cash-flow analysis and a future-earnings-per-share analysis should be used.

After-Tax Calculations

The full amount of the lease payments will be deductible for income tax purposes as operating expenses of the firm. If the firm purchases the assets, the interest portion of the borrowing is deductible, but the principal repayment is not. Since the tax payments are directly related to the lease–buy decision and affect the cash-flow stream, all calculations should be made on an after-tax basis.

Selecting the Discount Factor

Once cash-flow streams have been developed for the different alternatives, the streams should be discounted to reflect the time value of money. In lease-buy comparisons, frequently one alternative is more beneficial in the early years, whereas the other proves to be cheaper in the later years. Thus, for a long-term decision the discount factor can greatly affect the final decision.

In selecting the discount factor, the manager should consider the following possible rates:

1. *Overall Cost of Capital.* The firm's overall cost of capital (K_o) may be used for cash-flow items that contain approximately the same degree of risk as the firm's capital-budgeting projects. The most common example of a cash flow with this degree of risk is the residual value of the asset at the end of its service life. Will the firm actually receive cash equal to the estimated residual value of the asset? This is a risk the firm accepts, and it probably represents an average risk. Thus, consider a firm with a residual value of the asset forecasted at $50,000 and a 10 percent cost of capital. The present value of the residual value would be a 10 percent factor times the $50,000. If the asset had a 15-year service life, the present value would be ($50,000)(.239) = $11,950.

2. *After-Tax Cost of Debt.* The cash flows that arise in a lease–buy decision are more predictable than are cash flows from capital-budgeting projects. Thus, these cash flows should be discounted at a lower risk rate than the overall cost of capital. The after-tax cost of debt is usually lower than the cost of capital and is commonly used as the present-value factor for the cash flows other than cash salvage value.

In our calculations, we shall use the after-tax cost of debt as the discount factor for all cash flows with the exception of cash salvage value. The cost of capital, by definition, includes **business risk** as a component. In capital-budgeting decisions, business risk is a factor. This is not true for lease–buy decisions. In choosing the financing for fixed assets, only the **financial risk** should be included, because there is no risk to the firm from accepting the least expensive financing alternative. The after-tax cost of debt reflects only the financial risk and is appropriate for discounting most of the lease–buy cash flows.

Cash Salvage Value

When a firm purchases an asset, it will have full rights to the value of the asset at the end of its expected service life. In the case of assets with large ending cash salvage values, such as real estate or certain kinds of machinery, the cash salvage value affects the cost of purchasing versus leasing. For these fixed assets, the service life is usually much longer than the lease period and ending cash value is an important consideration.

In treating cash salvage value in the lease-buy decision, the following guidelines should be applied:

1. *Loss of Cash Salvage Value Affects Costs.* With the lease alternative, the firm loses the right to sell the asset at the end of the lease period. In our six-step process for lease-buy decisions, we shall treat the cash salvage value as an inflow in the purchase stream. It could also be treated as an outflow in the lease stream. The important consideration is that it only be included one time, to avoid double-counting the effect of cash salvage value.

2. *Cash Salvage Value Discounted at Overall Cost of Capital.* The exact cash salvage value will depend upon business conditions in the future. Since business risk is an important factor, the cash salvage value is discounted using the same factor found in capital budgeting, that is, the overall cost of capital.

Accelerated Depreciation

If the firm purchases the fixed asset, it will be allowed to gain the tax shield from depreciation. If it uses accelerated depreciation, the tax shield may exceed the amount of the lease payment, which is also a tax shield. Since the depreciation provides a tax shield with owning a fixed asset, the depreciation is used to reduce the after-tax cost of owning. In our examples, straight-line depreciation is used to simplify the calculations. In actual situations, accelerated depreciation is used.

Investment Tax Credits

For the purchase of certain assets, the Internal Revenue Service allows the owner to take an **investment tax credit** against the firm's federal income taxes. The credit is designed to encourage firms to invest in capital assets, thus expanding the level of economic activity.

To make full use of the investment tax credit, the firm must have to pay taxes at least equal to the credit. Sometimes, either when firms are rapidly purchasing fixed assets or when operating profits are low, the tax credit cannot be used. In these cases, a leasing firm can purchase the asset, thus taking advantage of the tax credit. This may allow the lessor to offer a lease on relatively favorable terms. In cases when the tax credit applies, it should be considered in calculating the cost of ownership of the assets. The tax credit is treated as an inflow in year zero in the cost-of-owning stream.

Rather than become involved with the mechanics of calculating an investment tax credit, the problems in this section either assume no tax credit or provide the final figure.

After-Tax Comparison

To calculate the cost of leasing versus buying, we prepare separate after-tax cash-flow streams for each financing alternative. The differences between the streams for the different years are discounted to the present value to provide either a present-value advantage to leasing or to buying.

The two formulas given in Table 5-3 are important to gain an overview of the lease-buy decision.

TABLE 5-3. Two Important Formulas in Lease—Buy Decisions.

After-tax Cost of Owning for Each Year

After-tax cost = loan payment − tax savings

Present-Value Advantage of Owning

Present-value advantage of owning = Σ(after-tax lease cost − after-tax cost of owning)
(present-value factor)   where Σ = sum of costs each year during life of lease

Building on the preceding considerations, the manager can employ a six-step process for analyzing the cash flow from the lease and purchase alternatives. We shall use sample data to develop this process.

Data

A firm desires to acquire the services of an $11,000 piece of machinery. The machine can be purchased with a $1,000 down payment and 10 annual payments at 6 percent, using the **steady-payment method.** If the firm owns the machine, it will receive an investment tax credit of $385 in year zero and will realize $2,000 from the sale of machine at the end of 10 years. The firm will use straight-line depreciation to a salvage value of zero over the 10 years. The firm has the option of leasing the machinery with no initial payment at annual payments of $1,500 for 10 years. Should the firm lease or buy? (*Note:* The firm's cost of capital is 10 percent.)

Step 1: Calculate the Loan-Payment Schedule.

With a $1,000 down payment on a $11,000 machine, the firm must finance $10,000 for 10 years at 6 percent. The annual payment will be

$$\frac{\text{amount borrowed}}{\text{present-value factor}} = \frac{\$10,000}{7.360} = \$1,358$$

where 7.360 is the 6 percent, 10-year factor in the annuity table. The annual interest is 6 percent on the outstanding balance. For the first year, it is ($10,000)(.06) = $600 interest. The principal reduction is $1,358 − 600 = $758. The outstanding balance at the end of the first year is $10,000 − 758 = $9,242. If we continue this process for 10 years, we obtain the figures in Table 5-4.

TABLE 5-4. Repayment Schedule for 6 Percent Loan for $10,000 Plus $1,000 Down Payment.

Year	6% Loan Payment	Annual Interest	Principal Repayment	Balance Outstanding
0	$ 1,000		$ 1,000	$10,000
1	1,358	$ 600	758	9,242
2	1,358	555	803	8,439
3	1,358	507	851	7,588
4	1,358	455	903	6,685
5	1,385	400	985	5,725
6	1,358	343	1,015	4,710
7	1,358	282	1,076	3,634
8	1,358	217	1,141	2,493
9	1,358	148	1,210	1,283
10	1,358	75	1,283	0
	$14,580	$3,580	$11,000	

Step 2: Calculate Savings from Investment Tax Credit.

If the purchase option allows the firm to realize a tax savings from an investment tax credit, the amount of the savings should be calculated in accordance with current tax law. In our example, the investment tax credit has already been determined by the firm's tax accountant and is given as $385 in year zero. This will be used as a tax savings to reduce the after-tax cost of owning in year zero.

Step 3: Calculate After-Tax Effect of Cash Salvage Value.

At the end of the 10 year service life, the machine will have a cash salvage value of $2,000. At the same time, the book value will be zero. The difference between the $2,000 cash salvage value and zero book value will represent a gain and will be taxable. The taxes will be $2,000 times 50 percent or $1,000. The after-tax net cash value is $2,000 − 1,000 = $1,000. This $1,000 is an inflow at the end of the final year and will reduce the after-tax cost of owning in year 10.

Step 4: Calculate the After-Tax Cost of Owning.

We have already seen that the after-tax cost of owning is calculated by subtracting the tax savings from the loan payment. This is done each year during the term of the loan to develop a cash-flow stream.

To get the tax savings, we add together the major tax shields that result from purchasing the machine and multiply them by the tax rate. In our example, the tax shields are the depreciation and interest. Other shields could be involved. For example, if the lease agreement included maintenance of the assets at no additional charge, the cost of maintenance would be added to the loan payment as a cost of owning. In this situation, the tax shield from the maintenance expense would be added to depreciation and interest in calculating the tax savings.

In our problem, the first-year depreciation using the straight-line method is $1,100 and the first-year interest is $600. The total tax shield is $1,700, and the tax saving is $1,700 times 50 percent or $850. We can subtract the $850 from the loan payment of $1,358 to get $508 as the first-year, after-tax cost of owning.

When steps 2, 3, and 4 are brought together in a single table showing the after-tax cost of owning, we get the streams in Table 5-5.

TABLE 5-5. After-Tax Cost of Owning for a Sample Problem.

Year	Loan Payment	Depreciation	Interest	Total Depreciation and Interest	Tax Savings (50%)(dep. + int.)	After-Tax Cost of Owning (loan payment − tax savings)
0	$1,000	$ 0	$ 0	$ 0	$385 [a]	$615
1	1,358	1,100	600	1,700	850	508
2	1,358	1,100	555	1,655	828	530
3	1,358	1,100	507	1,607	804	554
4	1,358	1,100	455	1,555	778	580
5	1,358	1,100	400	1,500	750	608
6	1,358	1,100	343	1,443	722	636
7	1,358	1,100	282	1,382	691	667
8	1,358	1,100	217	1,317	659	699
9	1,358	1,100	148	1,248	624	734
10	1,358	1,100	74	1,174	587	763
10						(1,000) [b]

[a] Investment tax credit.
[b] After-tax cash salvage value.

Step 5: Calculate After-Tax Lease Cost.

The entire lease payment each year may be used as an operating expense and therefore provides a tax shield. The after-tax cost of the payment is derived from the formula

$$\text{after-tax lease cost} = (\text{lease payment})(1 - \text{tax rate})$$

In our example, the annual lease payment is $1,500 for 10 years. The after-tax lease cost is $1,500 times (1 - 50 percent) = $750.

Step 6: Calculate Present-Value Advantage of Owning.

Once we have the annual after-tax costs of the lease and buy alternatives, we calculate the present-value advantage of owning for each year. The first calculation involves subtracting the ownership cost from the lease cost to get an advantage to owning. If the lease cost is greater than the owning cost, we get a positive figure; if the reverse is true, we get a negative figure, which represents an advantage to leasing.

TABLE 5-6. Calculating the Present-Value Advantage to Owning for a Sample Problem.

Year	After-Tax Lease Cost	After-Tax Cost Advantage of Owning to Owning		6% Present-Value Factor		Present-Value Advantage to Owning
0	$ 0	$615	$(615) ×	1.000	=	$(615)
1	750	508	242 ×	.943	=	228
2	750	530	220 ×	.890	=	196
3	750	554	196 ×	.840	=	165
4	750	580	170 ×	.792	=	135
5	750	608	142 ×	.747	=	106
6	750	636	114 ×	.705	=	80
7	750	667	83 ×	.665	=	55
8	750	699	51 ×	.627	=	32
9	750	734	16 ×	.592	=	9
10	750	763	(13) ×	.558	=	(7)
10	0	(1,000)	1,000 ×	.386[a]	=	386
						770

[a]10% cost-of-capital factor.

present-value advantage to owning

After calculating the advantage to owning for each year, we discount the value by the cost of debt. The cash salvage value is discounted at the cost of capital. This gives us a stream of the present-value advantage to owning each year. When we add together the present value advantages for all the year, we get one of the following:

1. *Advantage of Owning Indicated By a Positive Number.* If the final figure is positive, it indicates that owning is less costly than leasing.
2. *Advantage of Leasing Indicated By a Negative Number.* If the final figure is negative, leasing has a cost advantage over owning.
3. *No Advantage of Either Leasing or Owning Indicated by Zero or a Very Small Number.* If the final figure is zero, or if it is so small as to be insignificant, neither leasing nor owning can be said to have a cost advantage. The decision on the significance of the final figure must be made by the analyst. It is a highly subjective decision, which recognizes that we are making projections into an uncertain future.

In our example, the down payment and year 10 payments are advantages to leasing; all other payments provide an advantage to owning. This is shown by the parentheses in the advantage-to-owning column in Table 5-6. This table shows a calculation of the present-value advantage to owning with a final positive figure of $770. Based on the results of this table, owning offers a present-value advantage on a cost basis and should be selected as the financing means for the asset in the absence of other considerations.

40. LONG-TERM FINANCING, HOW TO COMPARE DIFFERENT ALTERNATIVES

The process for making comparisons of the different debt and equity sources of funds is best illustrated by using an actual example. We will consider the situation with respect to Acorn Industries, a firm that is evaluating a new venture that will cost $10,000,000. The venture will have a return on investment of 20 percent and the firm forecasts a 12 percent growth in earnings from the project. The proposal can be financed from a number of sources and the treasurer of Acorn Industries has specifically identified the following:

1. Common stock, to be sold at $42 per share which will net $40 per share.
2. Nonconvertible **debentures** with an 8 percent coupon to net $980 per bond.
3. **Convertible** bonds with a 6 percent coupon, $980 net, and convertible at $50 per share after 1978.
4. Debentures with **warrants** with a 6 percent coupon, to net $980, and with each bond having 10 warrants entitling the holder to buy one share of common stock at $50 after 1978.

The financing decision is being made in the fourth quarter of 1976. The 1976 pro forma balance sheet follows on the next page.

Over the past 10 years, Acorn Industries has been growing at a 10 percent rate of sales and earnings. The 1976 pro forma income statement follows the balance sheet.

The treasurer of Acorn expects the firm to continue to grow at a 10 percent rate even though the firm has traditionally paid 40 percent of its earnings as dividends. The dividend-payout ratio will continue into the future. The treasurer also expects Acorn's common stock to continue to rise in price. Using the price trend over the past 5 years, he has projected probable market price ranges for the next 3 years. The historical data and the projections of the treasurer are given in Table 5-7.

ACORN INDUSTRIES Pro Forma Balance Sheet (December 31, 1976; 000s)

	1976	1975		1976	1975
Cash	$ 2,200	$ 1,800	Accounts payable	$ 700	$ 600
Receivables	4,400	4,500	Other current liabs.	1,100	1,000
Inventories	6,400	6,200	Bonds (7%)	9,000	5,200
Other current assets	400	300	Mortgage (6%)	3,000	5,500
Plant and equipment	25,200	23,100	Common stock ($1 par)	1,000	1,000
(Less accumulated			Premium	4,000	4,000
depreciation)	(6,200)	(5,900)	Retained earnings	13,600	12,700
Total	$32,400	$30,000		$32,400	$30,000

ACORN INDUSTRIES Pro Forma Income Statement (000s)

	Sales	EBIT	Interest	EBT	NIAT	EPS
1976	$42,000	7,150	800	6,350	3,175	$3.18
1975	$38,000	6,500	700	5,800	2,900	$2.90

The management of Acorn was initially impressed by the fact that the new venture will increase sales by $12,000,000. Management is also interested in the expected 12 percent growth rate of the venture. But the Board has made it clear that it would probably not approve any financing method that raised the firm's debt-asset ratio above 40 percent.

TABLE 5-7. Historical and Forecasted Market Prices for Acorn Industries Common Stock.

HISTORICAL		FORECASTED		
Year	Market Price	Year	Probability	Market Price
1971	$22	1977	20%	$45
			60%	$50
1972	$25		20%	$60
1973	$33	1978	20%	$48
			60%	$55
1974	$27		20%	$62
1975	$38	1979	20%	$50
			60%	$60
Current	$45		20%	$70

With this information, we are ready to analyze the long-term sources of financing for the new proposal. This can be done using the following nine-step process.

Step 1: Determine Size of Offering with Each Financing Alternative.

As a firm considers differing financing alternatives, it must be aware of costs associated with raising the funds. To cover these costs, the face value of offerings must be higher than the amount of funds needed. Acorn Industries has identified four means of raising the $10,000,000 needed for the project. The formulas for the size of the offerings with each alternative are given in Table 5-8. From these calculations, we can see that Acorn must sell 250,000 shares of common stock or $10,200,000 of bonds to raise $10,000,000.

TABLE 5-8. Determining Size of Offerings for Acorn Industries.

Common-Stock Formula	Debt Formula
$\dfrac{\text{number of}}{\text{shares}} = \dfrac{\text{amount needed}}{\text{net proceeds per share}}$	$\dfrac{\text{number of}}{\text{bonds}} = \dfrac{\text{amount needed}}{\text{net proceeds per bond}}$
For Acorn—Common Stock $10,000,000/$40 = 250,000 shares	For Acorn—Bonds $10,000,000/$980 = 10,200 bonds

Step 2: Calculate Next Year's EBIT.

Although the financing method has no effect on next year's operating income, the firm must be aware of changes in sales and changes in EBIT. If the proposal does not generate sufficient profits, earnings per share could drop as could the price of the firm's common stock. As we can see from Table 5-9, the new proposal will increase Acorn Industries' EBIT by $2,000,000 in 1977.

TABLE 5-9. Calculating Next Year's EBIT.

Formula Without a New Project	Formula with a New Project
$\dfrac{\text{Next}}{\text{Year's}} = \left(\dfrac{\text{Current}}{\text{EBIT}}\right) \times \left(\dfrac{\text{Growth}}{\text{Factor}}\right)$ EBIT	$\dfrac{\text{Next}}{\text{Year's}} = \left(\dfrac{\text{Current}}{\text{EBIT}}\right) \times \left(\dfrac{\text{Growth}}{\text{Factor}}\right) + \left(\dfrac{\text{New}}{\text{Invest-}} \times \dfrac{\text{New}}{\text{ROI}}\right)$ EBIT $\quad\quad\quad\quad\quad\quad\quad\quad\quad\quad$ ment
where $(1+ G)$ = growth factor G = growth of firm without new project	where new investment = dollars $\quad\quad\quad\quad\quad\quad$ invested for new proposal new ROI $\quad$ = ROI forecasted for new $\quad\quad\quad\quad\quad\quad$ proposal
For Acorn—Without Project $7,150,000 × 1.10 = $7,865,000 new EBIT	For Acorn—With New Project ($7,150,000) (1.10) + (10,000,000) (20%) = $9,865,000 new EBIT

Step 3: Calculate EBIT at End of Planning Horizon.

For the purpose of selecting different financing alternatives, it may be argued that a 3- to 5-year planning horizon should be used. It is difficult to make valid forecasts of interest rates and stock prices beyond this time period. At the same time, a 3- to 5-year period is sufficiently long so as to allow the firm to consider the impact of convertibles and warrants in the financing decision. Table 5-10 shows the formulas for calculating EBIT 3 years into the future, the planning horizon that we will use for all our Acorn Industries calculations.

TABLE 5-10. Calculating EBIT 3 Years into the Future.

3-Year Formula Without Project	*3-Year Formula with Project*

$$\frac{\text{3-Year}}{\text{EBIT}} = \left(\frac{\text{Current}}{\text{EBIT}}\right) \times \left(\frac{\text{Growth}}{\text{Factor}}\right)^3$$

where growth factor = growth of firm without new project

$$\frac{\text{3-Year}}{\text{EBIT}} = \left(\frac{\text{Current}}{\text{EBIT}}\right) \times \left(\frac{\text{Growth}}{\text{Factor}}\right)^3 + \left(\frac{\text{New}}{\text{Investment}}\right)$$
$$\times \left(\frac{\text{New}}{\text{ROI}}\right) \times \left(\frac{\text{Project Growth}}{\text{Factor}}\right)^2$$

where project growth factor = growth of new proposal aside from growth of firm

For Acorn—Without Project
(7.150m) (1.10) ^{3} = \$9.520m EBIT

For Acorn—With New Project
(7.150m) (1.10) ^{3} + (\$10m) (20%)
(1.12) ^{2}
= \$12.030m EBIT

Step 4: Determine Likelihood of Conversion or Exercise of Warrants.

When the firm makes use of convertible or warrant financing, the firm normally expects the conversion or exercise of the warrant options in the 3- to 5-year planning horizon. If this were not likely, the **conversion feature** or warrant feature would have limited value to the investor and would not result in significantly lower interest costs on the debt.

TABLE 5-11. Calculating Expected Value of Acorn Industries Common Stock During 3-Year Planning Period.

Option or Conversion Price = \$50	Price with 20% Premium = \$60	
1977 Expected Price	*1978 Expected Price*	*1979 Expected Price*
\$45 × 20% = 9	\$48 × 20% = 9.6	\$50 × 20% = 10
50 × 60% = 30	55 × 60% = 33	60 × 60% = 36
60 × 20% = 12	62 × 20% = 12.4	70 × 20% = 14
\$51	\$55	\$60

As a general guideline, the firm's stock must rise 10 to 20 percent above the conversion or option price before investors will begin converting their bonds or exercising the warrant options. Table 5-11 shows the expected value of the Acorn Industries common stock during each year of the 3-year planning period. Since the **conversion price** and option price are $50 per share, we would conclude that it is likely that some equity will be created by 1979 as a result of conversions or the exercise of warrants, if one of these financing methods is used.

Step 5: Calculate Effects of Conversion and Exercise of Warrants.

Although the firm cannot be certain that bonds will be converted or warrants exercised, it should be aware of the effects of such actions. The **convertible bonds** will be replaced by shares of common stock after the conversion. With the warrant financing, the debt is not replaced. Instead, new shares are sold at the option price and the firm realizes additional common shares and additional equity. The formulas and calculations for Acorn Industries are given in Table 5-12.

TABLE 5-12. New Shares of Common Stock and Equity Calculations from Conversion or Exercise of Warrants.

Common Stock from Conversion	*Common Stock from Exercise of Warrants*
$\left(\begin{matrix}\text{(Bonds)}\\\text{(Issued)}\end{matrix}\right) \times \left(\begin{matrix}\text{(Shares pe)r}\\\text{(Bond)}\end{matrix}\right) = \begin{matrix}\text{Number of}\\\text{New Shares}\end{matrix}$	$\left(\begin{matrix}\text{(Bonds)}\\\text{(Issued)}\end{matrix}\right) \times \left(\begin{matrix}\text{(Shares per)}\\\text{(Bond)}\end{matrix}\right) = \begin{matrix}\text{Number of}\\\text{New Shares}\end{matrix}$
For Arcorn Industries	For Acorn Industries
10,200 × 20 = 204,000 new shares	10,200 × 10 = 102,000 new shares

New Equity Created by Conversion or Exercise of Warrants
New Shares × Option or Conversion Price = New Equity
Conversion 204,000 × $50 = $10,200,000 new equity for Acorn
Warrants   102,000 × $50 = $5,100,000 new equity for Acorn

Although warrants and convertibles are similar in the creation of equity, one important distinction must be noted. With convertible bonds, no additional capital is provided at conversion. Instead, the bonds are exchanged for common stock. When warrants are exercised, the holder of the warrant must pay for additional stock. The bonds are not retired and thus the firm has additional capital to invest.

In forecasting future earnings per share, the firm must consider a likely profit on the additional capital provided by the exercise of the warrants. This can be forecasted separately and the likely return on investment can be included in earnings calculations. In the absence of sufficient data to make a separate forecast, or as a shorthand method, the firm can follow the rule stated in Table 5-13. By using the lower figure between average return for the firm and the return on the new proposal, the firm is being conservative in its profit projections from the warrant capital.

TABLE 5-13. Calculating Return on Investment from Capital Provided by the Exercise of Warrants.

Rule:	AVERAGE RETURN ON MARKET VALUE OF FIRM $[EBIT/(D_{mkt} + CS_{mkt})]$
Use lower of	or
	RETURN ON INVESTMENT FROM NEW PROPOSAL

For Acorn Industries

Average Return on Market Value for Firm	ROI from new Proposal	EBIT if Warrants are Exercised
1976 EBIT = $7,150 1976 Debt = $13,800		$5,100 new equity
1976 CS_{mkt} = 1,000 shares × $45 = $45,000		× 12.2%
7,150/(13,800 + 45,000) = 12.2%	20%	622 new EBIT

Step 6: Calculate Next Year's Earnings per Share.

The firm is interested in the short-term effects of new proposals. If the firm experiences a sharp dilution of earnings from a proposal, it may cause a drop in the price of the firm's common stock. To analyze this possibility, the firm can calculate next year's earnings per share, as is done for Acorn Industries in Table 5-14.

TABLE 5-14. Calculating Next Year's Earnings per Share for Acorn Industries.

	No New Projects	Straight Debt	Convert- ible Debt	Warrant Debt	Common Stock
EBIT (Table 5-9)	$7,865	$9,865	$9,865	$9,865	$9,865
Interest (old)	800	800	800	800	800
Interest (new)	—	816	612	612	—
EBT	7,065	8,249	8,453	8,453	9,065
NIAT	3,533	4,125	4,227	4,227	4,533
Shares outstanding	1,000	1,000	1,000	1,000	1,250
1977 Earnings per Share	$3.53	$4.13	$4.23	$4.23	$3.63

TABLE 5-15. Calculating 1979 Earnings per Share for Acorn Industries.

	No New Projects	Straight Debt	Convert- ible Debt	Warrant Debt	Common Stock
EBIT (Table 5-10)	$9,520	$12,030	$12,030	$12,030	$12,030
plus EBIT from warrants	—	—	—	622	—
less interest (old)	800	800	800	800	800
less interest (new)	—	816	—	612	—
EBT	8,720	10,414	11,230	11,240	11,230
NIAT	4,360	5,207	5,615	5,620	5,615
Shares outstanding	1,000	1,000	1,204	1,102	1,250
1979 Earnings per Share	$4.36	$5.21	$4.66	$5.09	$4.49

Step 7: Calculate Earnings per Share at End of Planning Horizon.

The firm is also interested in the long-term effects on earnings per share. In these calculations, we assume that all bonds were converted and all warrants were exercised. This gives us the fully diluted earnings per share for each of the financing alternatives. Table 5-15 projects Acorn Industries' earnings per share for 1979.

Step 8: Determine Increase in Retained Earnings.

The firm should assess the impact of each financing alternative on its capital structure. The calculations should reflect the immediate effect (before any new profits arise) as well as the effect at the end of the planning horizon.

    The first step in this process involves calculating the increase in retained earnings over the 3- to 5-year planning period. A shorthand formula is given in Table 5-16. This formula averages the first and last year's NIAT's to get an average NIAT for the 3- to 5-year period. This average NIAT is multiplied by a dividend retention factor and by the number of years in the planning horizon to get the increase in retained earnings. The increase in retained earnings with each financing alternative will be used in the capital structure analysis in step 9.

TABLE 5-16. Shorthand Formula for Determining Increases in Retained Earnings.

$$\left(Formula:\ \frac{1st\ Yr\ NIAT + Last\ Yr\ NIAT}{2}\right)\ (1-Payout)\ \frac{Number\ of}{Years}\ =\ \frac{Increase\ in\ Retained}{Earnings}$$

For Acorn Industries Figures show total increases over 3-year planning period.

1979	Increase with Straight Debt	$\dfrac{4{,}125 + 5{,}207}{2} \times (1 - 40\%) \times 3 = \$8{,}400$
1979	Increase with Warrants	$\dfrac{4{,}227 + 5{,}620}{2} \times 60\% \times 3 = \$8{,}862$
1979	Increase in Retailed Earnings Without New Project	$\dfrac{3{,}533 + 4{,}360}{2} \times 60\% \times 3 = \$7{,}100$
1979	Increase with Convertibles	$\dfrac{4{,}227 + 5{,}615}{2} \times 60\% \times 3 = \$8{,}860$
1979	Increase with Common Stock	$\dfrac{4{,}533 + 5{,}615}{2} \times 60\% \times 3 = \$9{,}130$

Step 9: Analyze the Degree of Risk in the Capital Structure.

The firm is now prepared to measure the degree of risk in its capital structure as a result of each financing alternative. The relationship between debt and equity can be measured through either the debt-equity or debt-asset ratios. The capital structure should be analyzed immediately after the funds are raised. An analysis should also be forecasted for the 3- to 5-year planning period. Table 5-17 performs the calculations for Acorn Industries immediately after financing and at the end of 1979.

Acorn Industries has a guideline of 40 percent as the maximum debt-asset ratio. In the immediate future, all the debt-financing methods will raise Acorn to a 56 percent ratio, a figure that will be unacceptable to the firm if it holds to its guideline. By 1979, the **convertible alternative** and debt with warrants become more acceptable if conversion occurs and the warrants are exercised. The final decision would probably be referred to top management or perhaps even the Board of Directors of Acorn Industries.

TABLE 5-17. Measuring Debt-Asset Ratios for Acorn Industries.

Immediate Effects (end of 1976)	Without Project	Straight Debt	Convert-ibles	Warrants	Common Stock
Old debt	13.8m	13.8m	13.8m	13.8m	13.8m
New debt	—	10.2m	10.2m	10.2m	—
Debt	13.8m	24.0m	24.0m	24.0m	13.8m
Old equity	18.6m	18.6m	18.6m	18.6m	18.6m
New equity	—	—	—	—	10.0m
Equity	18.6m	18.6m	18.6m	18.6m	28.6m
Total assets	32.4m	42.6m	42.6m	42.6m	42.4m
Debt-asset ratio	43%	56%	56%	56%	33%
1979 Effects					
Old Debt	13.8m	13.8m	13.8m	13.8m	13.8m
New debt	—	10.2m	—	10.2m	—
Debt	13.8m	24.0m	13.8m	24.0m	13.8m
Old equity	18.6m	18.6m	18.6m	18.6m	18.6m
New equity	—	—	10.2m	5.1m	10.0m
Increase in retained earnings	7.1m	8.4m	8.9m	8.9m	9.1m
Equity	25.7m	27.0m	37.7m	32.6m	37.7m
Total assets	39.5m	51.0m	51.5m	56.6m	51.5m
Debt-asset ratio	35%	47%	27%	42%	27%

Conclusion to Acorn Industries

An overview of the relevant factors for comparing debt and equity financing for Acorn Industries is provided in Table 5-18.

From these data we might draw the following tentative conclusions to be presented to top management for further consideration:

1. *Straight Debt*. Offers high earnings per share but exceeds the 40 percent debt-asset guideline immediately and after 1979.
2. *Convertibles*. Offers high earnings and exceeds debt-asset guideline immediately. Offers possibility of being within guideline by 1979.
3. *Warrants*. High earnings but exceeds guideline for debt-asset ratio. Will still exceed ratio slightly after warrants are exercised.
4. *Common Stock*. Offers high earnings and is well within guideline.

TABLE 5-18. Summary of Earnings and Capital-Structure Data for Acorn Industries.

	Without Project	Straight Debt	Convert- ibles	Warrants	Common Stock
1977 earnings	$3.53	$4.13	$4.23	$4.23	$3.63
1979 earnings	$4.36	$5.21	$4.66	$5.09	$4.49
Immediate debt-asset ratio	43%	56%	56%	56%	33%
1979 debt-asset ratio	35%	47%	27%	42%	27%

In conclusion, the firm probably should consider financing the project to gain the large rise in earnings. The common stock, or a mixture of common stock and debt financing, represents the most attractive financing alternative. With mixed financing, the firm can achieve a significant rise in earnings without incurring the risk of exceeding the 40 percent debt-asset guideline.

41. OPTIMAL CAPITAL STRUCTURE, HOW TO DETERMINE

Four theories are useful for evaluating the optimal capital structure of a firm. These are:

1. *Fixed K_e*. Although largely discarded by the mid- to late-1950's, this theory isolates the role of favorable financial leverage.
2. *Fixed K_o*. As given in the Miller–Modigliani proof, no optimum can be said to exist under this theory.
3. *Varying K_e*. Building upon the work of Durand, Solomon, and others, this theory ties together leverage and market factors.
4. *Empirical Approach*. This offers a less rigorous but practical approach to managing the firm's capital structure and striving for the optimal.

The four theories lead to different conclusions with respect to the optimal capital structure for the firm. This section examines each theory in turn.

Fixed K_e—Optimum Capital Structure

Under the **fixed K_e theory,** the *optimum capital structure* for the firm occurs at the point where the firm can no longer take advantage of favorable financial leverage. The firm should continue to borrow until the interest rate on its debt would equal or exceed the return from its projects. Each borrowing with favorable financial leverage increases the EBT, and, since K_e is fixed in a relationship of EBT/CS$_{mkt}$, each increase in EBT also increases the value of the firm's common stock.

Figure 5-4 shows the optimum capital structure under fixed K_e theory in a graphic format.

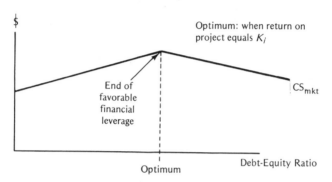

Figure 5-4.   Firm's Optimal Capital Structure with Fixed K$_e$ Theory.

Fixed K_o—Optimum Capital Structure

Under the fixed K_o theory, no capital structure is considered to be optimum. The overall cost of capital does not vary with changes in debt or equity. The value of common stock will change, but these changes are offset by the changes in risk in the capital structure, as follows:

1. *Increasing Debt, Decreasing CS$_{mkt}$.* When the firm increases the debt in its capital structure with favorable financial leverage, the firm's common stock will drop in price. The drop reflects the added risk and increases K_e. The rise in K_e offsets the inexpensive borrowing and maintains a steady overall cost of capital.

2. *Decreasing Debt, Increasing CS$_{mkt}$.* When a firm pays off a portion of its debt, the common stock will rise in the market. This has the effect of lowering K_e. The drop in K_e offsets the loss of inexpensive borrowing and maintains the steady K_o.

Because the changes in the value of the common stock are offset by changes in risk, no one capital structure is said to be the optimum. Under a fixed K_o theory, we measure the capital structure as shown in Figure 5-5.

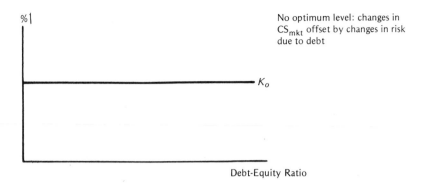

Figure 5-5. Optimal Capital Structure Under Fixed K_o Theory.

Varying K_e—Optimal Capital Structure

Under the theory in which K_e varies with changes in the level of debt, the optimum capital structure is a function of two factors:

1. *Favorable Financial Leverage.* With this theory, the firm is encouraged to borrow to take advantage of favorable financial leverage. This factor pushes the firm to higher debt levels.
2. *Added Risk Lowers CS_{mkt}.* Adding debt decreases the value of the common stock and thus increases the cost of equity capital.

As an example of how these two factors influence the value of the common stock, consider the firm in Table 5-19. When the firm considers borrowing the first $250,000, it has favorable financial leverage, but must overcome a 1 percent rise in K_e. The leverage overcomes the rise in K_e and the value of the common stock rises by $22,000. When it considers the second borrowing, the degree of financial leverage is less because the interest rate is higher. The leverage cannot overcome another 1 percent rise in K_e, and the value of the common stock would drop to $979,000. The optimum structure is closer to the level where the firm has $250,000 in debt rather than no debt or $500,000 in debt. This situation is shown graphically in Figure 5-6.

The major conceptual discussions among cost-of-capital theorists focused on theories 2 and 3. Theory 3 became the favorite of financial managers, and by the late 1950s it was generally accepted that favorable financial leverage effectively lowers a firm's cost of capital, increases the value of its common stock, and helps determine an optimum capital structure. It was reasoned that firms do not normally borrow in excess of the optimum debt level; thus, additional debt, when added below the optimum, increased CS_{mkt} even though K_e increased.

TABLE 5-19. Optimal Capital Structure with Varying K_e Theory.

Assume that a firm has a $100,000 EBIT and no debt. Should it borrow $250,000 at 5 percent on which it can earn 10 percent? If it does, K_e will rise from 10 to 11 percent. Should it borrow another $250,000 at 8 percent if the first borrowing makes sense? If it does, K_e will rise to 12 percent.

	$100,000 EBIT *No Debt*	*Borrow $250,000* *at 5%, Earn 10%* *on the Money*	*Borrow Another* *$250,000 at 8%* *Earn 10%*
EBIT	100,000	125,000	150,000
Interest	0	12,500	32,500
EBT	100,000	112,500	117,500
K_e	10%	11%	12%
EBT/K_e = CS$_{mkt}$	1,000,000	1,022,000	979,000

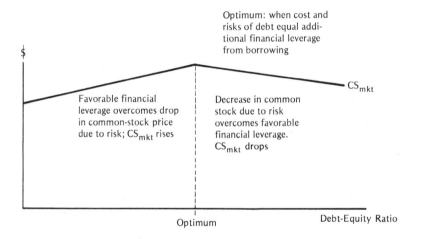

Figure 5-6. Optimal Capital Structure Under Varying K_e Theory.

A review of the major cost-of-capital theories has revealed several methods of approaching the issue of the optimal capital structure of a firm. One theory concludes that the optimal structure occurs at the point where additional borrowing cannot take place with favorable financial leverage. Another theory ties in the risk of high debt to the degree of financial leverage. The optimum occurs when favorable financial leverage can no longer overcome the drop in the price of the common stock due to the risk of high debt. Our review of the third model indicates that no single capital structure may be said to be the optimum.

Building from these three theories, we might conclude that any approach to an optimal capital structure must bring together three variables:

1. *Favorable Financial Leverage.*
2. *Income Tax Leverage.*
3. *Market Conditions.* The reaction of investors to changes in the capital structure is an important part of any decision to use debt or equity financing. Market conditions must be considered in any search for an optimal capital structure.

Empirical Approach to Managing the Capital Structure

To develop an approach to capital-structure management that incorporates both financial leverage and market conditions, we must go beyond theory. A totally theoretical model cannot be developed to adequately handle both factors. Market factors are highly psychological, very complex, and do not always follow accepted theory, since capital markets are, after all, not perfect. As an example, a firm may borrow money and the price of its stock may go up because of investors' speculations on future profits. The higher degree of leverage may, in many people's minds, indicate an aggressive management that will bring in high profits in the future. This would be a contradiction to normal expectations.

One way to deal with market conditions is through an empirical approach to measuring capital structure. For example, a firm may be in an industry that has an average debt-equity ratio of 1/1. It may be empirically demonstrated that the investing public does not discount the value of the firm's stock as long as the firm stays within a 40 percent range of the industry average. If we view the optimum capital structure as a range instead of a point, we can develop an optimum range based on our observation. The optimum range begins 40 percent below 1/1 and continues to 40 percent above it, or a debt-equity range from .6/1 to 1.4/1.

If a firm maintains a capital structure within the empirically optimum range, the common stock will not experience a decline in value due to excessive perceived risk by investors. As a management technique, the firm can seek to maintain a position near the top of the range, thus allowing the firm to take maximum advantage of financial leverage and the benefits of the income tax effect on interest. At the same time, the price of the common stock will not drop because of risk. Indeed, if investors discover the strategy, they may react by increasing the price-earnings multiple on the premise that the company is exceptionally well managed to make such good use of financial and income tax leverage.

Analysis of the Empirical Model

Although this model is weakened by a reliance on empirical data, it offers several advantages over current approaches to locating the optimal capital structure:

1. *Recognizes a Slow-Reacting Market.* The theory recognizes that the stock market is not totally and immediately responsive to changes in capital structure. In fact, the firm can operate in a capital-structure range without much effect on the price of common stock.
2. *Different Optimal Structures.* The theory allows individual industries and groups of firms to have different optimal capital structures. Empirical data suggest that this is correct.
3. *Ties Together Leverage and Stock Prices.* The theory includes the effects of financial leverage, income tax leverage, and market factors affecting common stock in a single, after-tax model.

What Is the Optimal Capital Structure?

The optimum mix of debt and equity securities is found at a point near the top of the empirically located debt-equity range. At this point, the firm makes maximum use of financial and income tax leverage while not experiencing a drop in the common-stock price due to excessive risk.

Figure 5-7 contains an overview of the after-tax empirical model of managing capital structure.

Considers	Advantages	Concludes
Financial leverage Income tax leverage Market conditions	Recognizes that the stock market is slow to react to capital structure changes. Allows for different optimum structures. Ties together leverage and stock prices.	The optimum capital structure occurs at a point near the top of an empirically located debt-equity range.

Figure 5-7.   Empirical, After-Tax Model for Managing Capital Structure.

42. REFUNDING A BOND ISSUE, HOW TO MAKE THE DECISION

A specific long-term financing decision occurs with the refunding of outstanding debt. **Refunding** is the replacement of maturing or outstanding long-term debt with new long-term debt. Most firms use a modified capital budgeting technique to analyze the refunding decision.[1] This procedure is outlined below.

---

[1]O. D. Bowlin, "The Refunding Decision," *Journal of Finance,* March 1966.

Reasons for Refunding

The refunding decision arises to allow the firm to take advantage of one or more of the following goals:

1. *Extend the Due Date of Maturing Debt.* When a firm lacks the cash to retire outstanding debt that is about to mature, the firm must replace the debt with new debt. In many cases the firm has the cash but management desires to refund the debt to continue taking advantage of favorable financial leverage. In this situation, the refunding allows the firm to use the cash for expansion or for the payment of dividends to shareholders.

2. *Take Advantage of Lower Interest Rates.* Many firms refund following a period of marked decline in long-term interest rates. The firm will save money by retiring a costly bond offering and replacing it with a lower-cost issue. In many cases, firms borrow during periods of high interest rates with the intention of refunding when interest rates decline.

3. *Remove Restrictions or Burdensome Clauses in Outstanding Bonds.* If a firm wants to borrow when it is experiencing difficulty, it may have to agree to certain restrictions on its actions. For example, as a price for the borrowing, the firm may agree to reduce the size of its regular dividend to common shareholders. When the difficulties have passed, the firm may wish to increase the dividend. By refunding the outstanding debt, the original restriction can be removed.

Costs Involved with Refunding

The decision to refund outstanding debt will involve two basic costs:

1. *Call Premium.* When a firm calls or retires debt prior to maturity, the **indenture** will normally require the firm to pay a premium over the face value of the debt. It is common to have a $1,050 call price for a $1,000 bond. The difference between the call price and face value is the **call premium** and this premium is a cost to the firm. A $1,000 bond with a $50 call premium involves a 50/1,000, or 5 percent, cost to the firm.

2. *Flotation Cost of New Issue.* The underwriting commission, registration fees, and other costs of floating a new debt issue are costs of refunding and are treated as such in the analysis. The total flotation costs are a cash outlay at the time of refunding. They are also an expense that may be amortized over the life of the bond. Both the flotation costs and the tax savings from these costs are included in the analysis.

Differential After-Tax Annual Savings

The difference in interest payments between the old and new bond issue will be the major savings from a refunding decision. The differential annual savings is calculated by the formula:

$$\text{old interest} - \text{new interest} = \genfrac{}{}{0pt}{}{\text{differential}}{\text{interest}} \times (1 - \genfrac{}{}{0pt}{}{\text{tax}}{\text{rate}}) = \genfrac{}{}{0pt}{}{\text{differential}}{\substack{\text{annual} \\ \text{savings}}}$$

The lower interest payments will result in savings over the entire life of the outstanding bonds. To compare these savings with the costs of refunding, we must calculate the present value of the savings. As a discount factor, we can use the after-tax cost of debt.[2] The formula is

$$\left(\genfrac{}{}{0pt}{}{\text{annuity factor for}}{\text{after-tax cost of debt}} \right) \times \left(\genfrac{}{}{0pt}{}{\text{differential}}{\text{annual savings}} \right) = \genfrac{}{}{0pt}{}{\text{present value}}{\text{of savings}}$$

The present value of savings is included in the net savings formula given below.

Tax Savings from Amortization of Old Issue

In order to receive a tax credit for flotation costs, the firm must amortize such costs over the life of the bond issue. This is similar to the treatment of depreciation when the firm purchases fixed assets.

At the time of refunding, the firm will be amortizing the flotation costs associated with the outstanding bond issue. By calling the bond issue, the firm may take an immediate tax credit for the costs that have not yet been amortized. This tax credit will give the firm a present value savings as a result of the refunding.

This savings may be calculated in three steps. To illustrate this calculation, consider a firm that is refunding a $10,000,000 bond issue with flotation costs of $200,000 being amortized over 10 years. The bond is being refunded at the end of the fourth year. The firm's after-tax cost of debt is 6 percent. The steps in the calculation are

---

[2]The cash flows arising from a saving in fixed interest payments are highly predictable. Therefore, they should be discounted at a factor with a lower risk rate than capital budgeting proposals. The after-tax cost of debt is a low-risk factor and is used instead of the after-tax cost of capital as a discount factor.

Step 1: Present Value of Immediate Tax Savings.

The annual amortization expense is 200,000/10 years or $20,000. Six years are remaining on the issue. The tax rate is 50 percent. The tax savings is

$20,000 × 6 years × 50% = $60,000

Step 2: Present Value of Tax Savings from Amortization Schedule.

If the firm does not refund, it will receive a tax savings over the remaining six years of the issue. Using the 6 percent after-tax debt factor for 6 years, the tax savings is

$20,000 × 4.917 × 50% = $49,170

Step 3: Differential Tax Savings.

Subtracting the value calculated in step 2 from the value in step 1 gives the differential tax savings as follows:

$60,000 - 49,170 = $10,830

Tax Savings from Amortizing Flotation Costs of New Issue

When the firm refunds the bond issue, it will incur flotation costs for the new issue. These costs will be amortized over the life of the issue and will provide a tax savings to the firm. The present value of this tax saving is correctly included in the refunding analysis.

As an example of this calculation, consider a firm that is refunding a $20,000,000 bond with a new, 15-year offering. The flotation costs for the new issue are $750,000. The after-tax cost of debt is 4 percent. The steps in the calculation are

Step 1: Annual Amortization Expense.

We divide the flotation costs by the number of years to get

$750,000/15 years = $50,000

Step 2: Tax Savings.

This is calculated by multiplying the annual amortization expense by the tax rate to get

$50,000 × 50% = $25,000

Step 3: Present Value of Tax Savings.

This is calculated by multiplying the tax saving by the annuity factor. In this example, a 4-percent, 15-year factor is appropriate.

$25,000 $\times$ 11.12 = $278,000

Net Savings from Refunding

The net savings from refunding will be the difference between the total of the savings and the total of the costs of the refunding. It may be calculated from the following formula.

$$\begin{matrix} \text{net} \\ \text{savings} \end{matrix} = \begin{pmatrix} \text{differential} \\ \text{after-tax} \\ \text{annual} \\ \text{savings} \end{pmatrix} - \begin{pmatrix} \text{call} \\ \text{premium} \end{pmatrix} - \begin{pmatrix} \text{flotation} \\ \text{costs} \end{pmatrix} + \begin{pmatrix} \text{tax sav-} \\ \text{ings on} \\ \text{flotation} \\ \text{costs of} \\ \text{new issue} \end{pmatrix}$$

$$+ \begin{pmatrix} \text{differential} \\ \text{tax savings} \\ \text{from} \\ \text{amortization} \\ \text{of old issue} \end{pmatrix}$$

Example of Refunding Decision

As an example of the decision to refund a bond offering, consider a firm with a $30,000,000 issue outstanding. The bond has 12 years remaining until maturity, has an 8.75 percent coupon, and is callable at $1,050 per bond. It had flotation costs of $420,000 which are being amortized at a $30,000 annual rate. The flotation costs for the new issue will be $900,000 and the new interest rate would be 6.25 percent. The after-tax cost of debt is 4 percent. Should the firm refund the outstanding debt?

The calculations are:

Step 1: Present Value of Differential Annual Savings. (after-tax)

Old Interest   = $30,000,000 $\times$ .0875 $\times$ 50% = $1,312,500
New Interest   =   30,000,000 $\times$ .0625 $\times$ 50% =   937,500
    ANNUAL AFTER-TAX SAVINGS $ 375,000

Present Value of Savings
(12-year, 4% annuity factor) = $375,000 $\times$ 9.385 = $3,519,375

Step 2: Call Premium.

The call premium is $1,050 - 1,000 = $50 or 50/1,000 = 5%. (5%) (30,000,000) = $1,500,000 call premium before taxes. Since the call premium can be written off as an expense in the year the call is made, the after-tax call premium is $1,500,000 - (1,500,000 × 50%) = $750,000.

Step 3: Flotation Costs.

The total flotation costs of $900,000 will be a cash outlay at the time of the new offering.

Step 4: Tax Savings from Amortization of Flotation Costs.

The flotation costs are an expense of the bond offering and may be amortized over the life of the bond. The steps are:

Annual Amortization Expense   = $900,000/12 years = $75,000
Tax Savings = $75,000 × 50%   = $37,500
Present Value of Tax Savings   = $37,500 × 12-year, 4% annuity
                                         factor
                                         37,500 × 9.385 = $351,938

Step 5: Differential Tax Savings from Amortization of Old Issue.

The old issue had flotation costs which are being amortized at a rate of $30,000 annually for 12 years. If the bond issue is called, these costs may be taken as an immediate tax credit. The present value difference between the immediate credit and the amortization credit is a benefit from refunding. The calculations are:

Present Value of Immediate Tax
Savings   = 30,000 × 12 years × 50%
                                                   = $180,000

Present Value of Amortization Using
12-year, 4% annuity factor   = 30,000 × 50% × 9.385
                                                   = $140,775

Present Value of Savings   = 180,000 - 140,775
                                                   = $39,225

Step 6: Net After-Tax Savings.

Using the formula given above,

$$\text{net savings} = \begin{pmatrix} \text{differential} \\ \text{after-tax} \\ \text{annual} \\ \text{savings} \end{pmatrix} - \begin{pmatrix} \text{call} \\ \text{premium} \end{pmatrix} - \begin{pmatrix} \text{flotation} \\ \text{costs} \end{pmatrix} + \begin{pmatrix} \text{tax savings} \\ \text{on flotation} \\ \text{costs of new} \\ \text{issue} \end{pmatrix} + \begin{pmatrix} \text{differential tax} \\ \text{savings from} \\ \text{amortization of} \\ \text{old issue} \end{pmatrix}$$

$$3{,}519{,}375 \quad - \quad 750{,}000 \quad - \quad 900{,}000 \quad + \quad 351{,}938 \quad + \quad 39{,}225$$

$$= \$2{,}260{,}538$$

In this example, the net savings of $2,260,538 appears to be a major benefit from refunding a $30,000,000 bond issue.

Final Note—Only Incremental Costs Are Included

In comparing the new and old issues in refunding decisions, the analyst must ensure that only incremental data are included. As an example, suppose that a firm wants to replace an issue with 7 remaining years to maturity with a new bond that will have 20 years to maturity. Only the effects of the first 7 years will be included in the analysis. Similarly, suppose that a $10,000,000 offering is to be replaced with a $16,000,000 bond. Only the effects on the first $10,000,000 will be considered in the refunding analysis.

43. WEIGHTED-AVERAGE COST OF CAPITAL, HOW TO CALCULATE

To calculate the overall weighted-average cost of capital, we use a three-step process:

1. *Calculate the Cost of Each Individual Component.* Using the preceding formulas, we determine the cost of existing debt, new debt, preferred stock, existing common stock, and new common stock.
2. *Multiply Each After-Tax Cost by the Percentage of the Component in the Capital Structure.* First we calculate the percentage of the total capital structure comprised by each source of funds—debt, preferred stock, and common stock. Then we multiply this percentage by the after-tax cost of the component.
3. *Add the After-Tax Costs of Each Component to Get a Weighted Average K_0.* The weighted cost of each component can be added together to get an overall weighted-average cost of capital.

Figure 5-8 provides an overview of the calculation of the weighted-average cost of capital.

As an example of the complete calculation of a firm's weighted-average cost of capital, consider a firm with the following capital structure:

1. Accounts payable, $100,000 with no interest charges.
2. Existing debt, $500,000 at 8 percent for 6 years.
3. New debt, $300,000 at 6 percent for 10 years with a net proceeds of $280,000.
4. Preferred stock, $100,000 with a 5 percent coupon (1,000 shares).
5. Existing common stock, 40,000 shares with a current market price of $15. The firm's EPS are $2, its growth rate is 6 percent, and its dividend payout is 60 percent.
6. Proposed common stock, 10,000 shares to be sold at $13 share. The offering would involve $10,000 in flotation costs.

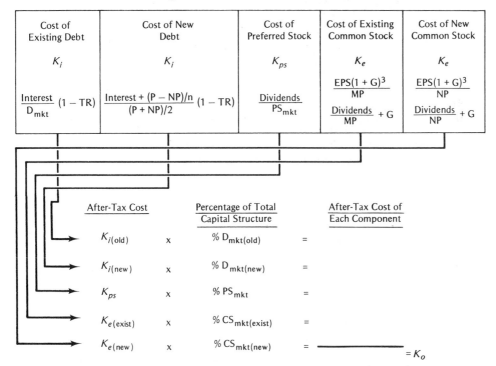

Figure 5-8.   Overview of the Weighted-Average Cost of Capital.

The calculation of the weighted-average cost of capital can be developed in a seven-step process as shown in Figure 5-9.

1. Existing Debt.   Interest = $40,000($500,000 x 8%), D_{mkt} =   100,000 Accts. pay.
+ 500,000 exist. debt
$600,000
$\dfrac{40,000}{600,000}$ (1 − 50%) = (6.67)(.50) = 3.33%

Figure 5-9.   Seven-Step Process for Calculating the Weighted-Average Cost of Capital.

2. <u>New Debt.</u> Interest = $18,000(300,000 x 6%).

$$\frac{18,000 + (300,000 - 280,000)/10}{(300,000 + 280,000)/2} \ (1 - 50\%) = \frac{18,000 + 2,000}{290,000} \ (.50) = \underline{3.45\%}$$

3. <u>Preferred Stock.</u> Dividend = $5,000 divided by 1,000 shares or $5 share.
   Par value = $100,000/1,000 shares or $100.

$$\frac{\$5}{\$100} = \underline{5\%}$$

4. Existing Common Stock

	Dividend Method	Average

$$\frac{\$2(1.06)^3}{\$15} = \frac{2.38}{15} = \underline{15.88\%}, \qquad \frac{\$1.20}{15} + 6\% = \underline{14.00\%}, \qquad \frac{15.88\% + 14\%}{2} = \underline{14.94\%}$$

5. <u>New Common Stock.</u> Net proceeds = $13 − 1 = $12 ($10,000 ÷ 10,000 shares = $1).

$$\frac{\$2(1.06)^3}{12} = \underline{19.83\%}, \qquad \frac{\$1.20}{12} + 6\% = \underline{16\%}, \qquad \text{Average} = \frac{19.83\% + 16\%}{2} = \underline{17.92\%}$$

6. <u>Percentage of Total Capital Structure Comprised by Each Component</u>

   a. Total capital structure at market

(1)	Existing debt	$ 600,000	
(2)	New debt	300,000	at face value, not net proceeds
(3)	Preferred stock	100,000	
(4)	Existing common stock	600,000	(40,000 shares x $15)
(5)	New common stock	150,000	(10,000 shares x $15; firm is issuing
	Total Structure	$1,750,000	shares below market price but does
			not expect drop in MP)

   b. Percentage of each component at market

(1)	Existing debt	34
(2)	New debt	17
(3)	Preferred stock	6
(4)	Existing common stock	34
(5)	New common stock	9
		100%

7. Weighted-Average Cost of Capital

	After-Tax Cost		% of Total Structure	=	After-Tax Cost
$K_{i(old)}$	.0333	x	.34	=	.0113
$K_{i(new)}$	.0345	x	.17	=	.0059
K_{ps}	.05	x	.06	=	.0030
$K_{e(exist)}$	.1494	x	.34	=	.0508
$K_{e(new)}$	.1792	x	.09	=	.0161
					.0871 = $\underline{8.71\% \ K_o}$

Figure 5-9. Continued.

Chapter 6

INTERNATIONAL FINANCE

44. ARBITRAGE IN FOREIGN EXCHANGE MARKETS, HOW TO ANALYZE

Arbitrage may be defined as a situation where a guaranteed and riskless profit can be made by simultaneously purchasing and selling a currency in one or more foreign exchange markets. Two types of arbitrage are common:

1. *Space Arbitrage.* This term refers to the fact that physical distance (space) separates the two transactions from which the arbitrage originates. Space arbitrage occurs when a speculator executes two or more simultaneous contracts to buy and sell currencies in two or more different capital centers for delivery on the same day. The contracts can be executed in the **spot market or forward market**, but delivery must be identical for all contracts.
2. *Time Arbitrage.* This occurs when an investor or speculator makes a riskless profit by executing a spot and forward contract to buy and sell a single currency. The arbitrage arises because the speculator invests the purchased currency at higher interest rates than would have been available with the currency that was sold. The forward contract guarantees that the investor can return to his original currency without risk of loss. The riskless higher interest provides the arbitrage profit in this kind of transaction.

EXAMPLE OF SPACE ARBITRAGE: A foreign exchange dealer in Paris is in telephonic contact with banks and dealers all over the world. While talking to Zurich and Montreal, he receives the following quotes:

	Zurich	Montreal
Sterling/Dollar Spot rate	£1/$1.9695	1/$1.9694
Sterling/Dollar 30-day delivery	£1/$1.9615	1/$1.9612
Sterling/Dollar 90-day delivery	£1/$1.9477	1/$1.9512

The dealer executes two simultaneous 90-day contracts to buy and sell sterling. He buys £100,000 in Zurich and sells £100,000 in Montreal. On the delivery date in 90 days, the following will happen:

Sell £100,000 × 1.9512 = $195,120
Buy £100,000 × 1.9477 =   194,770
$ 350 profit before costs
    -35 cost of cables and other
       direct expenses
$ 315 arbitrage (riskless) profit

EXAMPLE OF TIME ARBITRAGE: A dealer can borrow or invest dollars or Deutschmarks at an 8 percent annual yield for a period of 90 days. He notes the following rates quoted by a London bank:

Dollar/Mark Spot rate	$.3897/1DM
Dollar/Mark 30-day delivery	$.3904/1DM
Dollar/Mark 90-day delivery	$.4061/1DM

The dealer executes two simultaneous contracts: (1) to buy $100,000 worth of Deutschmarks in the spot market and (2) sell 261,740 marks for delivery in 90 days. The effects of these transactions are:

1. On the spot transaction he borrows $100,000 at 8 percent for 90 days so he will repay $100,000 + (100,000)(8%)(90/360) = $102,000
2. He converts to 256,608 DM (100,000 ÷ .3897), invests them at 8 percent for 90 days so he has 256,608 + (256,608)(8%)(90/360) = 261,740 marks which are delivered in 90 days for $106,293 (261,740 × .4061)
3. Results $106,293
                    −102,000
                    4,293 arbitrage profit

Why Do Arbitrage Profits Occur?

Arbitrage opportunities exist when the forward markets and interest differentials for two currencies are in a state of **disequilibrium.** Table 6-1 shows the trade-off between interest differentials and discounts or premiums in the forward market.

TABLE 6-1. Equilibrium and Disequilibrium Conditions Between Dollars and Francs.

Interest Rates (U.S.)	Interest Rates (France)	Differential in Favor of Dollar	Forward Exchange Discount or Premium on Dollar Expressed as a Percent per Annum						
			−3%	−2%	−1%	0	+1%	+2%	+3%
11%	8%	+3%	EQ.	$	$	$	$	$	$
10%	8%	+2%	fr.	EQ.	$	$	$	$	$
9%	8%	+1%	fr.	fr.	EQ.	$	$	$	$
8%	8%	0	fr.	fr.	fr.	EQ.	$	$	$
7%	8%	−1%	fr.	fr.	fr.	fr.	EQ.	$	$
6%	8%	−2%	fr.	fr.	fr.	fr.	fr.	EQ.	$
5%	8%	−3%	fr.	fr.	fr.	fr.	fr.	fr.	EQ.

EQ. = equilibrium between dollars and francs
fr. = conditions where individuals will convert dollars to francs to take advantage of arbitrage profit.
$ = conditions where individuals will convert francs to dollars to take arbitrage profit.

In Table 6-1 the **equilibrium** points occur where interest rate differential between the two currencies is offset by the forward discount or premium. For example, when the dollar can earn 11 percent compared to the franc's 8 percent, the equilibrium point occurs when the dollar trades at a 3 percent discount in the forward market. If the discount were only 2 percent, individuals would sell francs in the spot market for dollars and invest the dollars at 11 percent. They would purchase a forward contract losing two percent when they returned to francs. But the 3 percent interest differential would provide an arbitrage profit.

In practice, currencies are generally close to the equilibrium points and only limited arbitrage opportunities exist. But exist they do. Because of inadequate communications or actions by governments to support currencies, fast-moving traders can earn a living on the arbitrage from foreign-exchange transactions.

45. CAPITAL BUDGETING INTERNATIONAL, HOW TO CALCULATE CAPITAL COST

When the World Bank, a development bank, or a multinational firm evaluates the viability of the financing on a project, the analysis must recognize factors unique to the international environment. If a project is to be financed with a mixture of "**hard**" and "**soft**" currencies, **currency**strength must be considered in the analysis. This section presents a technique for calculating the capital cost of a project financed by two or more currencies in a high inflation environment.

Capital Cost of a Project

The **capital cost** for an economic development project or capital budgeting proposal is defined as the "hard" currency equivalent of all monies committed or expended in order to complete the project. During the planning stage, a project will have a **proposed capital cost;** upon completion it will have an **actual capital cost.** Due to the uncertainties of the international environment, the two costs may differ significantly.

The following steps may be used to calculate the capital cost for a project:

1. *Determine "Hard" Currency Needed.* A strong currency will normally be needed for the purchase of capital equipment from manufacturers in the industrialized nations. In addition, raw materials or supplies which must be imported will generally be paid for using a "hard" currency. Foreign technical advisers may also require payment in a strong currency.
2. *Determine "Soft" Currency Needed.* Host country labor, raw materials, and supplies will be paid in the national currency of the local or developing nation.
3. *Develop Two Cash-Flow Streams Considering Inflation.* The timing and amounts of all "hard" currency expenditures should be developed into a cash-flow stream. A separate stream is developed for the "soft" currency disbursements. The effects of inflation on the cost of labor, raw materials, and capital equipment should be considered in the calculation of each cash-flow stream. The following formula can be used to measure these effects.

$$\frac{\text{Total}}{\text{Cost}} = \sum_{t=1}^{n} \frac{\text{Forecasted}}{\text{Annual}}_{\text{Expenditures}} \times \left(1 + \frac{\text{Inflation}}{\text{Factor}}\right)^n$$

EXAMPLE: A project has been budgeted to cost 12,000,000 lira annually for 5 years. An economist at the World Bank is forecasting 9 percent annual inflation for Italy for the next 5 years. What is the cash-flow stream for this project?

Year	Forecasted Annual Expenditure		Inflation Factor	Expected Cost with Inflation
1	12,000,000	×	1.09	13,080.000
2	12,000,000	×	1.09^2	14,257,200
3	12,000,000	×	1.09^3	15,540,348
4	12,000,000	×	1.09^4	16,938,979
5	12,000,000	×	1.09^5	18,463,487
		Total Cost of Project with Inflation		78,280,014

4. *Capitalize the Costs for Each Stream.* In addition to rising costs due to inflation, the analyst must consider the financing cost of the capital employed in the project. During the construction stage on a project, money spent during the first year will be more costly than money spent during the final year. By capitalizing the costs for each stream, we calculate a single capital cost in each currency for the project as of the day of completion. This differs from domestic approaches to capital budgeting where the cash flows are returned to a present value. This is done by the following formula:

$$\text{Capitalized Cost} = \sum_{t=1}^{n} \frac{\text{Annual Cost with Inflation}}{} \times \left(1 + \frac{\text{Financing}}{\text{Factor}}\right)^{n^{*1}}$$

EXAMPLE: For the project given above, the lira can be borrowed at 12 percent annual interest. What is the capitalized cost of the project considering both inflation and the cost of funds?
ANSWER:

Year	Expected Cost with Inflation	Financing Factor	Capitalized Cash-Flow Stream
1	13,080,000	1.12^5	23,051,429
2	14,257,200	1.12^4	22,433,980
3	15,540,348	1.12^3	21,833,070
4	16,938,979	1.12^2	21,248,255
5	18,463,487	1.12	20,679,105
	Total Capitalized Cost of Project		109,245,839

---

[1] n^* is reverse sum of years (1st year is n; 2nd year is n-1; final year is 1).

5. *Calculate "Hard" Currency Equivalent of Total Costs.* To get a single capital cost, we must total the expenditures in the "hard" and "soft" currencies. Because of its greater stability, the "hard" currency is normally used to express the capital cost of a project. This equivalent recognizes the inflationary impact of a changing **exchange rate** on the two currencies. One method of calculating the "hard" currency equivalent follows.

Forecasting "Hard" Currency Equivalent

Converting the **weak currency** expenditures into a strong currency equivalent involves forecasting differential rates of inflation in the country of each currency. This technique is based on the research of Professor Rolf Treuherz who examined the statistical relationship between changes in the cost of living and changes in exchange rates for 5 Latin American nations. His findings are presented in Table 6-2.

TABLE 6-2. Comparison of Changes in Price Levels and Exchange Rates for Selected Latin American Countries.

	For a Percentage Annual Increase in the Cost of Living of	There was a Percentage Annual Increase in the Dollar Rate of
Argentina		
4-year average (1964-67)	28%	28%
7-year average (1961-67)	25%	25%
14-year average (1954-67)	31%	29%
Brazil		
4-year average (1964-67)	60%	58%
7-year average (1961-67)	54%	55%
14-year average (1954-67)	39%	39%
Chile		
4-year average (1964-67)	28%	28%
7-year average (1961-67)	28%	26%
14-year average (1954-67)	29%	35%
Colombia		
4-year average (1964-67)	15%	12%
7-year average (1961-67)	14%	13%
14-year average (1954-67)	14%	11%
Peru		
4-year average (1964-67)	12%	12%
7-year average (1961-67)	7%	11%
14-year average (1954-67)	6%	8%

Rolf M. Treuherz, "Forecasting Foreign Exchange Rates in Inflationary Economies," *Financial Executive,* February 1969, page 57.

Table 6-2 compares changes in the cost of living for each country with changes in the exchange rate between the local currency and the U.S. dollar. For example, between 1964 and 1967 in Argentina the cost of living rose 28 percent annually while the Argentine peso declined in value by 28 percent compared to the dollar. The data in the Table supports a conclusion that, over a period of time, a nation's rate of inflation is closely correlated to changes in the value of its currency.

To be correct theoretically, Table 6-2 should identify differential changes in the cost of living between each Latin American nation and the United States. Professor Treuherz omitted a differential calculation, probably because the United States had minimal inflation during most of the period 1954-1967. This means that, in effect, the changes in the cost of living shown in Table 6-2 are very close to the differential changes in cost of living for the periods indicated.

The following formula can be used to forecast a future exchange rate between 2 currencies when given rates of inflation are assumed:

$$\begin{array}{c}\text{Forecasted}\\\text{Exchange}\\\text{Rate}\\\text{A/B}\end{array} = \begin{array}{c}\text{Spot}\\\text{Units A}\\\hline\text{Spot}\\\text{Units B}\end{array} \times \left[1 + \left(\begin{array}{c}\text{Inflation}\\\text{Rate in}\\\text{Country}\\\text{A}\end{array} - \begin{array}{c}\text{Inflation}\\\text{Rate in}\\\text{Country}\\\text{B}\end{array} \right) \right]^{\begin{array}{c}\text{Number}\\\text{of}\\\text{Years}\end{array}}$$

As an example, assume that the current exchange rate is two units of currency A for one unit of currency B. Further, assume that annual domestic inflation is 25 percent in country A and 10 percent in country B. The forecasted exchange rate in four years is:

$$\frac{2A}{1B} \times \left[1 + (25\% - 16\%) \right]^4 = 2/1 \times 1.75 = 3.5A/1B$$

Example of Calculating Capital Cost

The World Bank is evaluating a project in a small Latin American nation. A detailed analysis indicates that $22,000,000 of foreign exchange will be required for the capital equipment portion of the project. Forty percent of this amount will be spent in the first year with the balance in the second year. Labor and raw materials will cost 65,000,000 pesos to be expended at a rate of 30 percent the first year, 40 percent the second year, and 30 percent in the third year. The financing cost is 6 percent for the dollars and 14 percent for the pesos. The spot rate between dollars and pesos is $1/8.2P. During the life of the project, an economist has projected the U.S. rate of inflation at 8 percent and the local inflation at 16 percent annually. What is the total capital cost of the project?

1. *"Hard" Currency Needed:* $22,000,000
2. *"Soft" Currency Needed:* 65,000,000 pesos
3. *Cash-Flow Stream in Each Currency:* (000's)

Year	For Dollars	
1	$22{,}000 \times .40 \times \left(1 + \dfrac{.08}{2}\right)^a$	= 9,152
2	$22{,}000 \times .60 \times 1.08 \times \left(1 + \dfrac{.08}{2}\right)$	= 14,826
3	-0-	

Year	For Pesos	
1	$65{,}000 \times .3 \times \left(1 + \dfrac{16}{2}\right)$	= 21,060
2	$65{,}000 \times .4 \times 1.16 \times 1.08$	= 32,573
3	$65{,}000 \times .3 \times (1.16)^2 \times 1.08$	= 28,338
		81,971 total pesos with inflation

[a] Average inflation is ½ annual inflation.

4. *Capitalized Cost of the Project:* (000's)

Dollars

$$\$ \, 9{,}152 \times 1.06^3 = \$ \, 10{,}900$$
$$14{,}826 \times 1.06^2 = \underline{16{,}659}$$
$$\$ \, 27{,}559 \text{ Capitalized Cost of Dollars}$$

Pesos

$$21{,}060 \times 1.14^3 = 31{,}201$$
$$32{,}573 \times 1.14^2 = 42{,}332$$
$$28{,}338 \times 1.14 = \underline{32{,}306}$$
$$105{,}839 \text{ Capitalized Cost of Pesos}$$

5. *"Hard" Currency Equivalent.* Assuming that the $/peso exchange rate keeps pace with inflation, the capital cost of the project is calculated using the following:

The difference between a 16 percent rate of local and an 8 percent rate of U.S. inflation represents an 8 percent drop in the value of the peso against the dollar. The following formula considers the effective inflation on the capitalized cost of the weak currency:

$$
\begin{array}{l}
\text{Forecasted} \\
\text{Exchange} \\
\text{Rate}
\end{array}
= \frac{\text{Spot Rate}}{\text{Peso}/\$} \times \left[1 + \left(\begin{array}{c} \text{Local} \\ \text{Inflation} \\ \text{Rate} \end{array} - \begin{array}{c} \text{U.S.} \\ \text{Inflation} \\ \text{Rate} \end{array} \right) \right]^n
$$

$$
\text{Peso}/\$ = 8.2\text{P}/\$1 \quad \times \quad \left[1 + (.16 - .08) \right]^3
$$

$$
= 8.2\text{P}/\$1 \quad \times \quad 1.26 = 10.332\text{P}/\$1 \text{ forecasted exchange}
$$
rate in 3 years

In our example, the "hard" currency equivalent of the capital cost of the pesos would be:

$$
\text{Total Pesos} \div \frac{\text{Future}}{\text{Exchange Rate}} = \frac{\text{Capital}}{\text{Cost}}
$$

$$
105,839,000 \div \quad 10.332\text{P}/\$1 \quad = \$10,243,806
$$
(say) $10,244,000

The total capital cost of the project in terms of the "hard" currency will be $27,559,000 + 10,244,000 = $37,803,000.

   The significance of inflation and financing costs becomes apparent when we compare the $37,803,000 "hard" currency equivalent with the original $22,000,000 and 65,000,000 pesos being budgeted. At 8.2P/$1, the dollar equivalent of the pesos is 65,000,000/8.2 = $7,926,829 and the total capital would be $7,926,829 + 22,000,000 = $29,926,829. The actual capital cost of $37,803,000 is some $7,876,000 higher as a result of the costs of financing and inflation.

46. EQUILIBRIUM EXCHANGE RATES, HOW TO CALCULATE

Under a system where the values of currencies are fixed in terms of gold, we may use the following formula to calculate the *equilibrium* exchange rate between two currencies:

where ER_{ab} = exchange rate between currencies A and B

Gold Equiv. A = the equivalent amount of gold equal to one
                unit of currency A

Gold Equiv. B = the equivalent amount of gold equal to one
unit of currency B

As an example of the use of this formula, consider a situation where currency
A is worth .05 ounces of gold and currency B is worth .03 ounces. The
exchange rate between currencies A and B would be

$$ER_{ab} = .03/.05 \qquad ER_{ab} = .6A/1B$$

One unit of currency B would be worth six-tenths of a unit of currency A.
One unit of A would be worth $1/.6 = 1.67$ units of currency B. At any other
exchange rate, the currencies would be in disequilibrium.

> PROBLEM: One dollar can be converted into .04 ounces of gold. One peso can be
> converted into .008 ounces of gold. The exchange rate between dollars and pesos is
> $1/6P. Are the currencies in equilibrium? If not, at what exchange rate would they
> be in equilibrium?

> ANSWER: No. The equilibrium exchange rate would be $ER_{\$p} = .008/.04$. $ER_{\$p}$
> $= \$.2/1P$. One peso is worth $.20, 5 pesos = $1. The equilibrium exchange rate
> is $1/5P.

Equilibrium Following Period of Inflation

When currencies experience changes in purchasing power and when
they were previously in equilibrium at the existing exchange rate, the new
equilibrium exchange rate may be calculated by the following formula:

Index Factor		Existing Exchange Rate		New Exchange Rate
$\dfrac{PP\%_{curr.\ A.}}{PP\%_{curr.\ B}}$	$\times$	$\dfrac{\text{Units of B}}{\text{Units of A}}$	$=$	$\dfrac{\text{Units of B}}{\text{Units of A}}$

where $PP\%_{curr.\ A}$ = current purchasing power of currency A as a
percent of the original purchasing power
(example: when purchasing power increases 10
percent, factor = 110%)

> EXAMPLE: Currencies A and B were in equilibrium at 20A/1B which is also
> .05B/1A. A's purchasing power has declined 20 percent while B's has risen 10
> percent. The new equilibrium exchange rate is:

$$(80\%/110\%)(1B/20A) = .0364B/1A \quad \text{or}$$
$$(110\%/80\%)(20A/1B) = 27.5A/1B$$

47. FORWARD MARKET, HOW TO CALCULATE BID AND ASK QUOTES

Forward exchange contracts are available from the international departments of large commercial banks. The bank itself may write the contract or it may be written with the bank acting as a representative for a monetary speculator. If the bank is willing to buy *the currency,* a **bid** price will be quoted. If the bank is willing to sell the currency, an **ask** price will be quoted. If the bank is willing to issue a forward contract either to buy or sell the currency, both a bid and ask price may be quoted. As an example,

Barclay's Bank, 90-day Contracts on U.S. Dollars		
	Bid	*Ask*
Dollar/Sterling rate	£1/$2.10	£1/$2.07
Dollar/Franc	$1/3.7413Fr	$1/3.7722Fr
Dollar/Peso		9.5P/$1
Dollar/Krona	$1/5.438Kr	

From these quotes, we can see that the bank (or the speculator that it is representing) is willing to make a market for sterling or francs against the dollar, but the bank is only willing to sell dollars for pesos or buy dollars for krona in the future market. Two factors normally account for an unwillingness to provide both bid and ask prices:

1. *Weak Currencies May Not Be Quoted.* The bank would not want to agree to make a future purchase of a weak currency if it is not sure that it will profit from the transaction. In the example of krona, the bank is willing to buy dollars with its own krona but is not willing to sell dollars at a stipulated rate for a future delivery of krona. This may indicate that krona is either weak or wildly fluctuating in foreign exchange markets and the bank does not want to undertake the risk of a forward contract to buy it.

2. *Bank's Position in Currency May Be Exposed.* An **exposed foreign exchange position** means that a bank or corporation has greater obligations in one currency with respect to borrowing or holding than it has balancing obligations. As an example, suppose a firm holds $3,300,000 and owes $5,300,000. This firm has a borrowing **exposure** of the difference between the two figures, or $2,000,000. If the dollar was revalued, the debt would increase more than the cash held and thus the firm would lose money when it had to repay its debt.

EXAMPLE: A bank is writing 90-day contracts to buy or sell francs. It has contracts totalling 394,000,000 francs to be purchased and 146,000,000 to be sold on March 1st. What is the bank's exposure?
ANSWER: 248,000,000 francs. (394,000,000 minus 146,000,000)

To reduce its exposure, a bank may halt quotations in a currency on the bid or ask side until the exposure is reduced to an acceptable level.

Establishing the Premium or Discount

When a bank or monetary speculator quotes forward exchange rates, it must reflect both interest rate differentials and relative currency strengths. The following formula may be used:

$$
\begin{array}{ccc}
\text{Future} & & \text{Forward Contract} \\
\text{Exchange Rate} \quad \times & \text{Interest Rate Differential} \quad = & \text{Forward Rate} \\
& & \text{A to B}
\end{array}
$$

$$
\frac{\text{Future Units A}}{\text{Future Units B}} \times \left[1 - \left(\begin{array}{c} \text{Annual} \\ \text{Interest} \\ \text{Rate B} \end{array} - \begin{array}{c} \text{Annual} \\ \text{Interest} \\ \text{Rate A} \end{array} \right) \left(\frac{\text{No. of days}}{360 \text{ days}} \right) \right]
$$

The two major components of the formula may be obtained as follows:

1. *Future Exchange Rate.* The future exchange rate between currencies A and B is the analyst's best estimate of the rate that will exist in the spot market at the maturity date of the contract. To forecast this rate, the analyst must consider economic factors that will affect both currencies during the time period of the forward contract. Factors such as inflation, economic problems, and balance of payments deficits are particularly important in this analysis.
2. *Calculating Interest Rate Differentials.* This step requires the analyst to make a determination of the difference in the yields available from debt securities in the capital markets of the two nations A and B. Because of the variety of yields available from different securities in a sophisticated capital market, this analysis requires considerable knowledge and skills on the part of the analyst. As a general rule, government bond rates, institutional rates (London Inter-bank rate), or yields on corporate bonds may be appropriate in making the comparison. From the different alternatives, the analyst will identify an annual interest rate for each currency and will place these rates in the formula.

EXAMPLE: The spot rate between francs and pesetas is 2.4fr/1.0p. A First National City economist is forecasting a 2.5fr/1.0p spot rate in 90 days. The franc can be invested for 90 days at an annual yield of 14 percent; the peseta at 9 percent. What is the expected exchange rate that the bank should use in writing forward contracts for 90 days?

ANSWER:
2.53fr/1p or .3950p/1fr

$$\frac{2.5fr}{1.0p} \times 1 - [.09 - .14] \left(\frac{90}{360}\right) = 2.53fr/1p$$

$$\frac{1.0p}{2.5fr} \times 1 - [(.14 - .09] \left(\frac{90}{360}\right) = .3950p/1fr$$

Bank's Profit on Foreign Exchange Contracts

The bank can cover its costs of writing foreign exchange contracts by adding a service charge to the price of the contract. As a general rule, this service charge is reflected as a differential between the bid and the ask price of the contract. The rate calculated by the above formula will be bracketed; that is the bid and ask rates will be quoted so that the bank receives a service charge on any forward contract it writes. The bank will buy currencies at slightly less than the formula rate; the bank will sell currencies at slightly higher than the formula rate.

48. HEDGING FOREIGN EXCHANGE TRANSACTIONS, HOW TO EVALUATE ALTERNATIVES

The decision on how to deal with foreign exchange risk should be made after considering the costs of full exposure versus **hedging.** An overview of this procedure is given in Figure 6-1.

Alternative	Measuring the Cost
1. Full Exposure	a. Estimate high, most likely, and low exchange rate on delivery date.
	b. Compare amount received at each rate. Use weighted average technique to gain value of alternative.
2. Forward Contract	Calculate amount to be received or paid under terms of contract.
3. Borrowing	Use the following formula.

Amount Received = or Paid	Funds from Conversion at Spot Rate	Interest − to be Paid	Interest + to be Earned

Figure 6-1. Comparing Costs of Hedging.

The amount of the desired currency to be received or paid is calculated with each alternative in Figure 6-1. The firm then selects the largest figure if money is to be received or the smallest figure if it is to be paid.

Note that it does not matter whether the firm will actually pay or earn interest on the borrowing method. Borrowing is used to imput a cost to money that is tied up or a return from money that is freed. Some cost or benefit must be included for a correct analysis; we shall use borrowing rates for simplicity sake. In actual situations, other costs of capital may be used by firms.

Calculations in the Hedging Decision

Two types of transactions require a decision to hedge or not to hedge:

1. *Future Receipt of Foreign Currency.* In this example, an exporter is due to receive 300,000 pesos in 90 days. The spot market is 1p/$.2234 and the 90-day rate is 1p/$.2230. A bank has estimated a 50 percent chance of the same spot rate in 90 days and a 50 percent chance of 1p/$.2350. The exporter can borrow dollars at 12 percent or pesos at 16 percent; he can lend dollars at 9 percent or pesos at 11 percent; all annual rates on 90 day funds. Should the exporter hedge this transaction?

   a. Fully exposed

$$50\% \times .2234 = .1117$$
$$50\% \times .2350 = \underline{.1175}$$
$$.2292 \text{ weighted rate}$$

   .2292 × 300,000 pesos = $68,760 weighted value

   b. Forward market

   .2230 × 300,000 = $66,900 fully hedged

   c. Borrowing

   (1) Borrow 300,000/(1 + .04*) = 288,462 pesos. *16% × 90/360 = 4%. Exporter will owe 300,000 in 90 days and can deliver them to pay off loan.
   (2) Convert in spot market 288,462 × .2234 = $64,442.
   (3) Invest at .0225* and earn $1,450 interest ($64,442 × .0225). *9% × 90/360 = 2.25.
   (4) Total dollars = 64,442 + 1,450 = $65,892

ANSWER: The highest value comes from the fully exposed position. If the exporter is not willing to take this risk, the borrowing alternative produces a higher dollar amount than the forward market so the exporter should borrow to hedge.

2. *Future Payment of Foreign Currency.* Using the same data as the first example, assume that the exporter had to make a payment of 500,000 pesos in 90 days. Should he hedge this transaction?
   a. Fully exposed

   .2292 × 500,000 pesos = $114,600

b. Forward market

.2230 $\times$ 500,000 pesos = $\underline{\$111,500}$

c. Borrowing

(1) He will need 500,000 pesos. If he borrows dollars today, converts to pesos and invests them at 2.75 percent (11% $\times$ 90/360), he will need 486,618 pesos today [500,000/(1 + .0275)].

(2) 486,618 $\times$ .2234 spot = $108,711 needed to get the pesos.

(3) To borrow $108,711 at 3 percent (12% $\times$ 90/360), he will pay $3,261 interest and have total costs of $108,711 + 3,261 = $\underline{\$111,972}$.

ANSWER: The lowest cost occurs with the forward market alternative and since this is even better than the fully exposed position, he should hedge in the forward market.

The Hedging Decision—Hemley Shipping Case

As an example of making the decision to hedge foreign exchange, let us consider the case of Hemley Shipping Company. This firm specializes in exporting and importing for a select list of clients including specialty shops and several major department stores. Located in Norfolk, Virginia, the firm receives shipments from abroad and distributes them to its U.S. customers. The firm also arranges for exporting a variety of U.S. goods to customers primarily in Europe and North Africa.

One of Hemley's customers has signed an agreement to ship finished textiles to Austria with 250,000 Austrian shillings as payment to be delivered in 90 days. The shillings will be paid with a draft on an Austrian bank in Vienna. The current exchange rate is $.0541/Sh 1. A Richmond bank has indicated that Hemley could hedge the transaction by executing a forward contract to sell shillings in 90 days at $.05435/Sh 1.

A second hedging alternative would be to borrow 250,000 shillings in Vienna for 90 days at 8 percent. This could be arranged through Chase Manhattan at no cost to Hemley. After converting to dollars, the money could be invested in New York to net 6 percent annually for 90 days.

Hemley knew that its customer could also decide to accept full exposure on the money. Hemley's Richmond banker felt that a $.054/Sh 1 rate was likely in 90 days (a 60-percent chance). He indicated a 10-percent chance of a $.055/Sh 1 rate but a 30-percent chance of $.0525/Sh 1 rate.

Hemley knew that its customer would want a recommendation on how to handle the expected inflow of shillings. The firm analyzed the situation and forwarded the following letter to the customer.

HEMLEY SHIPPING COMPANY
12 Orient Way
Norfolk, Va.   23506

Cable: HEMCO

Larkin Brothers
2304 Pulaski Road
Baltimore, Maryland 21223

Sirs:

We have evaluated the 250,000 shillings due you in 90 days from Burtschafen A. G. as follows:

FULL EXPOSURE: Using likely exchange rates quoted by our banker, we estimate you will
                    receive $13,425 upon delivery:

                    10% x $.055/Sh 1 = .0055
                    60% x .054/Sh 1 = .0324
                    30% x .0525/Sh 1 = .0158
                                         .0537 weighted exchange rate

                    .0537 x 250,000 shillings = $13,425

FORWARD MARKET: At the rate quoted by our bank you will be guaranteed $13,588.

                    .05435 x 250,000 schillings = $13,588

BORROWING: We can arrange to immediately borrow shillings in Vienna which can be converted
                    immediately to dollars. When the loan matures in 90 days, we will repay it with the
                    250,000 shillings. The dollars must be left on deposit in New York at 6 percent
                    as collateral for the loan. The shillings would cost 8 percent. This alternative
                    provides you with $13,459.

                    (1) 8 percent annually is 2 percent over 90 days. We should borrow 250,000/1.02
                         or 245,098 shillings. In 90 days, we will owe 250,000 and can repay it.
                         (245,098 principal + 4,902 interest = 250,000)
                    (2) Convert 245,098 at spot rate

                             245,098 x 0.541 = $13,260

                    (3) Invest $13,260 at 6 percent for 90 days = $199 interest
                    (4) Total received = $13,260 + 199 = $13,459.

We recommend that you authorize us to arrange a forward contract since the $13,588 from this alternative
is the highest value and it is fully protected against foreign exchange loss. Please advise.

HEMLEY SHIPPING CO.

49. PREMIUM OR DISCOUNT ON FOREIGN EXCHANGE, HOW TO CALCULATE

The percent of premium or discount may be calculated for a single unit of a currency by using the formula given in Figure 6-2. Basically, the differential between the forward and the spot rate is divided by the spot rate. We then annualize percentage by multiplying it times 360 days divided by the number of days in the forward contract.

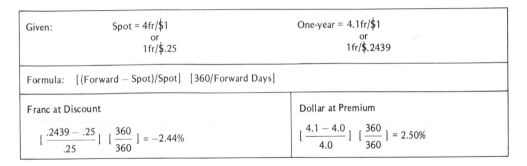

Given:	Spot = 4fr/$1	One-year = 4.1fr/$1
	or	or
	1fr/$.25	1fr/$.2439

Formula: [(Forward − Spot)/Spot]   [360/Forward Days]

Franc at Discount	Dollar at Premium
$[\dfrac{.2439 - .25}{.25}] \ [\dfrac{360}{360}] = -2.44\%$	$[\dfrac{4.1 - 4.0}{4.0}] \ [\dfrac{360}{360}] = 2.50\%$

Figure 6-2.   Calculation of Premium or Discount.

In Figure 6-2 the percent of the discount is less than the percent of the premium. This effect is similar to what happens when we discount a domestic bond as compared with paying interest on it. For example, suppose we have a 6 percent $1,000 bond and we have a choice of paying interest for one year or discount the interest immediately. In the first case, the yield is 60/1,000 or 6 percent; in the second case, the yield is 60/940 or 6.38 percent. The difference in the two yields is due to discounting in one case and adding interest in the second. This same effect occurs in calculating premiums and discounts for currencies.

50. PROTECTING LOCAL ASSETS IN HIGH-INFLATION COUNTRY, HOW TO

In a high-inflation economy with a currency that is likely to suffer a continuing decline in its value, the multinational firm must be concerned with protecting the value of its local assets. Some general rules are:

1. *Borrow Weak, Hold Strong.* A weak currency is defined as a currency that is likely to decline in value compared to other currencies in the near future, normally the next year or two. A strong currency is likely to maintain or increase its value compared to other currencies. A firm should borrow the weak currency since a devaluation or decline in value means the firm will pay back a loan with a lower future value than the present value. If the firm borrowed a strong currency, it might owe more in the future than at present. Similarly, the firm should hold as much cash as possible in strong currencies. When devaluations occur, these currencies are likely to hold their value. The axiom to borrow weak and hold strong is illustrated in Table 6-3.

TABLE 6-3. An Illustration of the Principle "Borrow Weak, Hold Strong".

SITUATION: A firm needs the equivalent of $1,000,000 of working capital for a foreign operation. The firm can borrow either currency A, B, or C. The working capital can be held for one year in any of the three currencies and can be paid back at the end of the year. The currencies are freely convertible into dollars at the rates given below. The exchange rates that are expected at the end of one year are also given. Which currency should be borrowed? Which currency should be held?

	Currency A,	Currency B,	Currency C,
Beginning exchange rate	10A/$1	5B/$1	2c/$1
Units to borrow to have equivalent of $1,000,000	10,000,000A	5,000,000B	2,000,000C
Forecasted ending exchange rate	8A/$1	5B/$1	3C/$1
Value of cash if held in each currency	$1,250,000	$1,000,000	$666,667
Amount owed if each currency borrowed	$1,250,000	$1,000,000	$666,667

SOLUTION: Borrow C and hold A. If C is borrowed and converted into A, the firm will finish with a holding of $1,250,000 and a debt of $666,667. The difference of $583,333 is a profit from foreign exchange transactions. In this example, A was revalued and C devalued. Borrow the weak C and hold the strong A.

2. *Hold Inventories, Not Cash or Receivables.* The fixed local currency value of cash and receivables will be eroded by inflation. Holding cash and allowing large outstanding balances of accounts receivable is similar to holding the weak currency and violates the rule to hold the strong currency. In many cases, though, the firm will be unable to convert the weak currency into a strong currency due to exchange restrictions. In this situation, the firm is advised to convert its cash into inventories. The reasoning is that inventories will appreciate in value in a high-inflation economy and will afford some protection against inflation. Table 6-4 shows an example of how inventories offer some protection against inflation.

3. *Invest Excess Cash in Fixed Assets.* In many cases, firms will accumulate far more cash than can be converted to inventories. Rather than hold the cash, the firm should seek investment opportunities through the purchase of fixed assets. A fixed asset will generally rise in value to keep up with inflation. Some fixed assets, such as real estate, may rise more quickly than inflation. In addition to maintaining their value, fixed assets may offer the firm opportunities to convert their cash to foreign currencies. For example, if a firm purchases a mining operation, it may be able to export and receive foreign currencies for

the country. The fact that the firm is helping the nation with its balance-of-payments difficulties may qualify the firm to make larger remittances to its parent than would be the case without the earning of foreign exchange.

TABLE 6-4. An Illustration of the Principle "Hold Inventories, Not Cash or Receivables.

SITUATION: Companies A and B each hold 200,000 francs in an economy where inflation will be 10 percent next period. Company B has converted its cash into inventories whose value will rise 8 percent next period. What will be the purchasing power in constant units for each currency next period?

	Company A	Company B
Cash at beginning of period	200,000 francs	200,000 francs
Convert cash to inventories	0	200,000
Inventory value with 8% rise	0	216,000
Cash value, end of period	200,000 francs	216,000 francs
Approximate purchasing power in		
Constant units, end of period (francs/110%)	181,818	196,364

---

51. THIRD-COUNTRY INVOICING, HOW TO USE TO AVOID CURRENCY CONTROLS

Third-country invoicing is a specific example of using **transfer pricing** to avoid controls on foreign exchange. Figure 6-3 shows how it works. In the figure, a subsidiary in country A ships goods worth $100 or 600 pesos to a customer in country B. A bill for 300 pesos or $50 is sent to a second subsidiary in country C. The subsidiary in country C invoices the customer in country B for the full $100. The customer pays $100 and the subsidiary in country C pays $50, a situation that results in $50 excess cash in country C. Since country C was selected because it has no controls on foreign exchange, the 50 dollar overage can be used at the parent's discretion and the exchange controls of country A have been avoided.

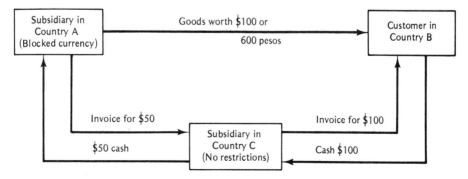

Figure 6-3. Example of Third-Country Invoicing.

Conflicts with Host Government

Attempts to avoid paying local taxes or complying with restrictions on foreign exchange transactions frequently bring the multinational firm into conflict with the host government. Officials in foreign governments are becoming increasingly sophisticated in dealing with the actions of multinational firms and may take steps to change company policies on transfer pricing and other techniques to avoid taxes and restrictions. When an aggressively managed multinational firm meets the competent government of a nation with balance of payments difficulties, conflicts can be expected.

52. TRANSFER PRICING, HOW TO USE TO AVOID CURRENCY CONTROLS

Transfer pricing is a term that refers to the price established for goods or services transferred between corporate subsidiaries in different countries.

TABLE 6-5. Example of Transfer Pricing to Reduce Level of Taxes.

SITUATION: Subsidiary A has sold machine components to subsidiary B and has asked the parent corporation to determine the selling price of the components. Country A will probably allow a minimum selling price of 60,000 pesos and a maximum selling price of 120,000 without investigating the tax implications of the sale. If the components were transferred at no charge, subsidiary A would have an earnings before taxes (EBT) of 300,000 pesos and subsidiary B would have an EBT of 500,000 shillings. The exchange rates are 6P/$1 and 5S/$1. Should the transfer price be 60,000 or 120,000 pesos if the income tax rates are 40 percent in country A and 20 percent in country B?

	60,000 PESOS = $10,000		120,000 PESOS = $20,000	
	A	B	A	B
EBT in local currency	300,000P	500,000S	300,000P	500,000S
EBT expressed in dollars	$50,000	$100,000	$50,000	$100,000
+ or − transfer price	+10,000	− 10,000	+20,000	− 20,000
New EBT with transfer price	$60,000	$ 90,000	$70,000	$ 80,000
Taxes at 40 percent	−24,000		−28,000	
at 20 percent		− 18,000		− 16,000
Net Income After Taxes	$36,000	$ 72,000	$42,000	$ 64,000

SOLUTION: With a 60,000 peso transfer price, the total taxes are 24,000+18,000= 42,000 dollar equivalent compared to 28,000+ 16,000= 44,000. The lower transfer price results in less taxes because of the higher tax rate in country A. The transfer price should be 60,000 pesos which gives a total net income after taxes (NIAT) of 36,000+ 72,000=108,000 dollar equivalent compared to 42,000+ 64,000= 106,000 with the higher transfer price.

When goods or services are exchanged between divisions or subsidiaries of a multinational firm, market factors are not important in establishing the price of such goods and services. Rather, the parent will encourage pricing that achieves corporate goals including the following:

1. *Avoid Taxes.* Different countries have varying taxes on the income of corporations. Transfer pricing can be used to decrease the taxable income of a subsidiary in a country with a high income-tax rate and to increase the taxable income in a country with a low income-tax rate. Table 6-5 illustrates how transfer pricing can affect the level of taxes and profits of a firm.

2. *Reduce Tariffs.* An **ad valorem tariff** is a duty levied on imports according to their invoiced value. A low transfer price will result in a lower invoice price and lower duties to be paid.

3. *Avoid Controls on Exchange Transactions.* A firm may be operating in a country where the local currency is blocked or is otherwise inconvertible into the currency of the parent country. By setting low transfer prices on goods shipped out of the country, the subsidiary will accumulate goods of higher value in another country. When these goods are resold at the higher value, the profit can be transferred to the parent company. Transfer pricing can be used in this manner to minimize the effects of restrictions on foreign exchange transactions.

Chapter 7

MISCELLANY

53. BOND VALUES, HOW TO MEASURE INTEREST RATE RISKS ON

A major risk to the holders of bonds is possible changes in the capitalization rate due to changes in the current yields of similar bonds. The **interest-rate risk** is the loss of principal of a fixed-return security due to increases in the general level of interest rates. Two aspects of the interest-rate risk are particularly important:

1. *Market Value Fluctuates in Opposite Direction of Interest Rates.* The market value of outstanding bonds will fluctuate in the opposite direction of the interest rates offered on new securities entering the marketplace. When interest rates rise, the value of outstanding bonds drops, and vice-versa.
2. *Time to Maturity Is Key Factor.* The degree of interest-rate risk is directly related to the length of time to maturity for a bond. If the bond is held to maturity, there is no loss of principal from market yield fluctuations. Thus, if the term to maturity is fairly short, bond value will fluctuate within a relatively narrow range. If the term to maturity is long, market value may fluctuate widely. Table 7-1 shows the difference in market value for 1- and 5-year 6 percent bonds when current yields change from 5 to 8 percent.

Table 7-1 shows why treasurers prefer treasury bills and other short-term securities to corporate bonds for investing excess cash. There is a greater degree of risk for bonds with longer maturities, even though the risk of default may be the same as a bond with a short maturity. The interest-rate risk offsets the fact that long-term bonds can be readily sold and provide higher yields than short-term bonds. The interest-rate risk is one factor to help explain why short-term bonds usually have lower yields than long-term bonds.

TABLE 7-1. Effect of Time to Maturity on the Degree of Interest-Rate Risk.

Bond	Discount Factor	Present Value	Change in Current Market Value Because of Interest-Rate Change
6%, 1 yr	5%	$1,009.12	
	8%	$ 981.56	− $27.56
6%, 5 yr	5%	$1,043.80	
	8%	$ 920.80	−$123.00

The fluctuations of bonds due to the interest-rate risk are shown graphically in Figure 7-1. The Aaa bonds have higher present values than the A bonds (and thus a lower yield if they are purchased at the higher price). But note that the difference in the degree of safety has no effect with respect to interest-rate changes. The length of time to maturity causes large fluctuations in the present value of the 5-year bonds. The 1-year bonds show little fluctuation in present value.

One final point with respect to interest-rate risk is that it only affects the present value of the bond. It has no effect on the value of the bond in the future when the bond reaches maturity. At the maturity date, the bond will be redeemed for $1,000. It is the danger of a large drop in principal value if the security must be sold on short notice that comprises the interest-rate risk.

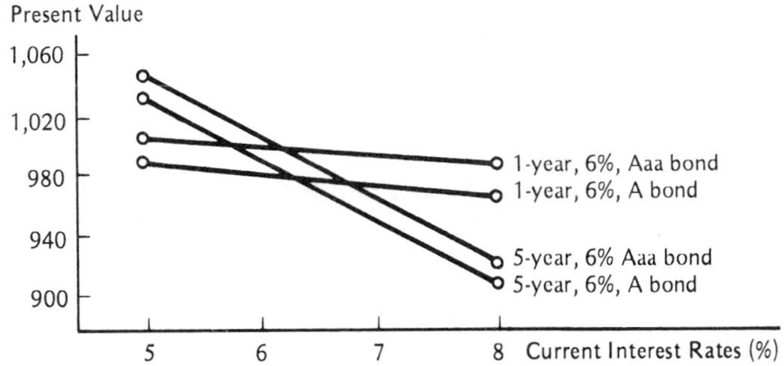

Figure 7-1. Effect of Time to Maturity on the Present Value of Bonds with Different Discount Factors.

EXAMPLE: A treasurer is considering the purchase of marketable securities to hold for a period of 18 months to 2 years. He is particularly interested in two General Electric bonds: GE 6¼ percent coupon, 1981 maturity, and GE 3½ percent coupon, 1978 maturity. On January 1, 1975, the yield on 3-year similar bonds was 4 percent; on 6-year bonds it was 5 percent. What is the present value of each bond?
ANSWER: $986 for the 1978 bond. $1,063 for the 1981 bond.

1978 Issue at 4 Percent Capitalization
Rate
1976-1978 interest $35 × 2.775 = $ 97 where 2.775 = 3-year, 4% factor
in annuity table

1978 principal $1,000 × .889   =   889 where .889 = 3-year, 4% factor
Present Value $986   in single-payment
table

1981 Issue at 5 Percent Capitalization Rate
1976-1981 interest $62.50 × 5.076 = $ 317 where 5.076 = 6-year, 5%
factor

1981 principal $1,000 × .746   =   746 where .746 = 6-year, 5%
Present Value $1,063   factor

EXAMPLE: If interest rates rise by 1 percent, what will be the change in value of the two bonds (assume an immediate drop on January 1, 1976)?
ANSWER: A rise in interest rates causes bond values to drop. We would expect the longer-term bond to experience the largest drop, because long-term bonds fluctuate in a wider price range in the market. The new values would be

1978 Issue at a New 5% = $ 35 × 2.723 = $ 95
$1,000 × .864   = 864
$959 new value
1981 Issue at a New 6% = $62.50 × 4.917 = $ 307
= $1,000 × .705 = 705
$1,012 new value

The 1978 issue dropped from $986 to $959, or $27.
The 1981 issue dropped from $1,063 to $1,012, or $51.

54. COMPOUND INTEREST, HOW TO CALCULATE

Compounding occurs when the interest earned on a sum of money becomes part of the principal at the end of each period. Annual compounding refers to interest which is paid once a year and is calculated by the formula

$$\text{Compounded Sum} = \text{Principal} \times (1 + i)^n$$

where Principal = initial principal
i = the annual rate of interest expressed as a percent
n = the number of years the interest is paid

As an example of the use of this formula, consider $1,000 invested at 8 percent for 6 years. The calculation is:

Compounded
Sum $= \$1,000(1 + .08)^6 = \$1,000(1.587) = \$1,587$

An alternative way to calculate **compound interest** involves using a compound interest table, such as those in Appendices C and D. For the compound sum of a single dollar in the previous example, we locate the value where 6 years and 8 percent meet in the table in Appendix C. The factor is 1.587 which means that each dollar invested will yield $1.587 in 6 years. $1,000 times 1.587 will produce $1,587 in 6 years.

An annuity is a stream of equal annual payments. Interest can be compounded on an annuity in a manner similar to the single dollar above. Appendix D provides a table for compounding a dollar received at the end of future years for a number of consecutive future years. For example, if a person begins one year from today investing $1,000 a year for 5 years at 8 percent interest, the factor from Appendix D is 5.867 and the compound value of the annuity is $1,000 times 5.867 equals $5,867.

EXAMPLE: A woman invests $17,000 in a 4-year certificate of deposit to yield 8 percent compounded semiannually. How much will she have in 4 years?
ANSWER: $23,273, as follows: Eight percent compounded semiannually for 4 years is identical to 4 percent compounded for 8 periods in Appendix C. The factor is 1.369 and the compound sum is $17,000 times 1.369 = $23,273.

EXAMPLE: A woman plans to invest $2,000 a year beginning now in a savings account that pays 6 percent annually. She will make 10 successive deposits. How much will she have at the end of 10 years?
ANSWER: $27,942, as follows: By investing in year zero, she will earn interest during the first year. This means we must adjust the table in Appendix D since it shows no interest in year one. (The table is designed for the first payment to occur in one year, not today.) We can take the 11-year factor at 6 percent, 14.971, and multiply it times $2,000 to get $29,942. If we subtract one $2,000 installment at zero interest, we have $29,942 − 2,000 = $27,942.

55. DECISION TREE, HOW TO BUILD ONE

A decision tree is a graphic display of the relationship between a present decision and possible future events, future decisions, and their consequences. The sequence of events is mapped out over time in a format resembling branches of a tree. Because the events are linked chronologically with forecasted probabilities where appropriate, the decision tree allows a systematic look at decisions and their forecasted outcomes.

Building a Decision Tree

The important steps in constructing and using a decision tree may be outlined as follows:

1. *Define a Proposal.* Capital-budgeting projects may be proposed by marketing, production, or other management departments. Examples of proposals would be to enter a new market or to design and produce a new product line.

2. *Identify Decision Alternatives.* Every proposal will have at least two possible decisions—accept or reject. Additional alternatives may be available. For example, a firm may be considering building a new factory to produce a new product. The firm might believe that it has four choices—build a large plant, a medium-sized plant, a small plant, or no plant. Each possibility will have different consequences for the firm.

3. *Graph the Decision Tree.* The decision tree is laid out showing the decision points, alternatives, and other data.

4. *Gather Data and Forecast Cash Flows on Each Branch.* The decision tree is completed by locating estimates of results on each branch and calculating the value of each decision.

5. *Evaluate Results and Reconsider Alternatives.* Once the projected cash flows for each branch are calculated, the results must be analyzed. Some alternatives may appear to be highly desirable; others may be based on weak or incomplete data. The results may indicate that the firm can proceed, or they may point to the need for reconsideration of the alternatives.

Components of Decision Trees

The development of a decision tree requires the recognition of five distinct components:

1. *Decision Point.* Decision trees begin with an investment choice that defines the net cash outlay for two or more decision branches. If the investment has different stages, additional decision points may appear along each branch.

2. *Branching Probabilities.* The branches are defined by forecasted future conditions that will result in different returns from the investment decision. Each possibility is assigned a probability so that the probabilities for each decision total 100 percent (or 1).

3. *Branching Present Values of Cash Flows.* The cash-flow stream for each future probability is calculated and brought back to the present value, using the firm's cost of capital. Each present value is linked to the probability of its occurrence.

4. *Expected Values of Future Returns.* Each branch resulting from an investment choice has an expected value; this is calculated and the total expected value for the decision is determined.

5. *Profitability Index for Each Decision.* The expected value of the net cash benefits is divided by the net cash outlay to determine a profitability index for each investment decision.

Sample Decision Tree

Figure 7-2 is a sample decision tree for an investment under consideration by a firm. The firm must choose between constructing a large or small factory to produce a new line of products. The large plant would be needed if the future brings a high demand for the new products. But the large plant would have net cash benefits less than the $10,000,000 net cash outlay if demand is medium or light. The smaller plant produces a lower return if future demand is high, but will also be acceptable if the demand is medium. Only a low future demand would make the proposal unacceptable.

The profitability index for the two choices indicates that the small factory is a better investment at the present time. This decision would not necessarily preclude a future expansion should the high demand materialize for the firm's products. To analyze this possibility, we can use a decision tree with multiple decision points. To do this, another decision tree begins at the end of the high-demand branch for the small factory.

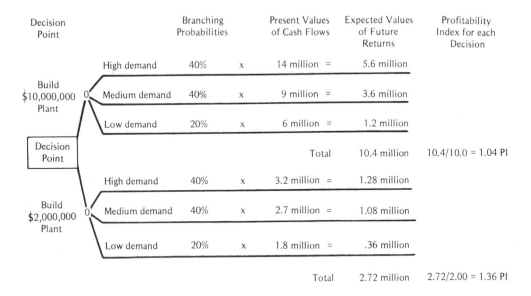

Figure 7-2. Decision Tree for an Investment Decision To Invest in a Large or Small Factory.

56. DEPRECIATION, HOW TO CALCULATE

Accelerated methods of depreciation recognize that many fixed assets are more valuable when they are new compared to later years. This is true because, with age, a machine's efficiency declines, maintenance costs increase, and newer equipment may become available that makes a machine obsolete. Since the firm benefits more from a machine during its early years, a larger portion of the machine's cost should be taken as an expense in the early years. This is the rationale for accelerated methods of depreciation.

The Internal Revenue Act of 1954 identified 2 accelerated methods of depreciation which could be used as alternatives to the straight-line method. These are the double-declining balance method and the sum-of-the-years' digits method. The effect of either accelerated method is to write off approximately two-thirds of the cost of an asset in the first half of the asset's estimated life. This contrasts with the straight-line method under which half the cost is written off in each half of the asset's service life. The 3 methods may be contrasted, as follows:

1. *Straight-Line Method.* Using this method, the cost of a fixed asset is spread equally over its expected service life. For example, a machine costing $5,000 and having a life expectancy of 10 years would be depreciated at a 10-percent rate of $500 a year. The machine is expected to have a salvage value at the end of its service life. This salvage value must be deducted from the total cost before the depreciation is calculated. Thus, if the $5,000 machine had an estimated final salvage value of $600, the depreciable cost would be $4,400 (5,000 — 600) and the annual depreciation would be $440 (4,400/10). Two formulas related to straight-line depreciation are:

   a)
   $$\frac{\text{Annual}}{\text{Depreciation}} = \frac{\text{Depreciable Cost}}{\text{Years of Service Life}}$$

   b)
   $$\frac{\text{Percent Allowed Each Year}}{} = \frac{100\%}{\text{Years of Service Life}}$$

   where Depreciable Cost = Total Cost — Salvage Value

2. *Declining Balance Method.* Under this method, the company can deduct up to double the straight-line rate on the "undepreciated" balance each year. The original total cost is used only in the first year. Applying the double-declining balance method to a $5,000 machine with a $600 salvage value and a 10-year service life, the first year's depreciation would be 20 percent of $5,000 or $1,000. The second

year's depreciation would be 20 percent of the remaining $4,000 book value, and would be $800. The third year's depreciation would be 20 percent of the remaining $3,200 or $640; and so on. This method can never result in a 100 percent depreciation of the asset nor can the asset be depreciated below its estimated salvage value. The following formula applies to the declining balance method:

$$\frac{\text{Annual}}{\text{Depreciation}} = \frac{\text{Book Value}}{\text{Each Year}} \times \frac{100\%}{\substack{\text{Years of} \\ \text{Service Life}}} \times \frac{\text{Acceleration}^*}{\text{Factor}}$$

3. *Sum-of-the-Years' Digits Method.* This method, which is actually a variation of the declining balance method, is developed as follows:

  a. The years of the estimated service life of the asset are summed and the resulting figure becomes the denominator of a ratio. For a machine with a 10-year service life, the total of the digits 1, 2, 3 . . . 10 is 55, and this 55 is the denominator in the fraction.

  b. The numerator each year is the number of years of remaining service life of the fixed asset. In our example, the numerator would be 10 in the first year since the machine has 10 years of remaining service life. It becomes 9 in the second year and so on down to 1 in the final year.

  c. The ratio is multiplied by the depreciable cost (Total Cost − Salvage Value) of the asset to get the annual depreciation. The depreciable cost does not change with each annual calculation; only the ratio changes. In our example of a $5,000 machine with a 10-year service life and $600 salvage value, the first year's depreciation would be 10/55 of $4,400 or $800 in the first year. In the second year, the depreciation would be 9/55 times $4,400 = $720. This method is continued until the asset is depreciated down to its book salvage value. The following formula may be used in calculating sum-of-the-years' digits depreciation:

$$\frac{\text{Annual}}{\text{Depreciation}} = \frac{\text{Depreciable}}{\text{Cost}} \times \frac{\text{Years of Remaining Life}}{\text{Sum of Years of Service Life}}$$

The three methods of calculating depreciation are given in Table 7-2 for an asset that costs $110,000 with a $10,000 estimated salvage value in 10 years.

---

* The acceleration factor is prescribed by the Internal Revenue Service and will vary with different fixed assets. There will always be more than one but cannot, under the present law, exceed two.

TABLE 7-2. Comparison of Three Depreciation Methods For $110,000 Asset, 10 Years, $10,000 Salvage Value.

Year	Straight Line	Double-Declining Balance	Sum-of-Years' Digits	(Rate)
1	$ 10,000	$22,000	$ 18,182	(10/55)
2	10,000	17,600	16,364	(9/55)
3	10,000	14,080	14,545	(8/55)
4	10,000	11,264	12,727	(7/55)
5	10,000	9,011	10,909	(6/55)
6	10,000	7,209	9,091	(5/55)
7	10,000	5,767	7,273	(4/55)
8	10,000	4,614	5,455	(3/55)
9	10,000	3,691	3,636	(2/55)
10	10,000	2,953	1,818	(1/55)
TOTAL	$100,000	$98,189	$100,000	

57. FIELDS OF FINANCE, HOW TO DISTINGUISH

The academic discipline of financial management may be viewed in terms of five specialized fields. In each field, the financial manager is dealing with the management of money and claims against money. Distinctions arise because different organizations pursue different objectives and do not face the same basic set of problems. There are five generally recognized areas of finance:

Public Finance	Securities and Investment Analysis
Used in federal, state, and local government. Examines taxes and other revenues. Pursues nonprofit goals.	Used by individual and institutional investors. Measures risk in securities transactions. Measures likely return.
Institutional Finance	International Finance
Examines banks, insurance companies, and pension funds. Studies saving and capital formation.	Studies economic transactions among nations and individuals internationally. Concerned with flows among countries.

Financial Management		
Studies financial problems in individual firms.	Seeks sources of low-cost funds.	Seeks profitable business activities.

1. *Public Finance.* Federal, state, and local governments handle large sums of money, which are received from many sources and must be utilized in accordance with detailed policies and procedures. Govern-

ments have the authority to tax and otherwise raise funds, and must dispense funds according to legislative and other limitations. Also, governments do not conduct their activities to achieve the same goals as do private organizations. Businesses try to make profits, whereas a government will attempt to accomplish social or economic objectives. As a result of these and other differences, a specialized field of public finance has emerged to deal with governmental financial matters.

2. *Securities and Investment Analysis.* Purchases of stocks, bonds, and other securities involve analysis and techniques that are highly specialized. An investor must study the legal and investment characteristics of each type of security, measure the degree of risk involved with each investment, and forecast probable performance in the market. Usually this analysis occurs without the investor having any direct control over the firm or institution represented by the form of security. The field of investment analysis deals with these matters and attempts to develop techniques to help the investor reduce the risk and increase the likely return from the purchase of selected securities.

3. *International Finance.* When money crosses international boundaries, individuals, businesses, and governments must deal with special kinds of problems. Each country has its own national currency; thus a citizen of the United States must convert dollars to French francs before being able to purchase goods or services in Paris. Most governments have imposed restrictions on the exchange of currencies, and these may affect business transactions. Governments may be facing financial difficulties, such as balance-of-payments deficits, or may be dealing with economic problems, such as inflation or high levels of unemployment. In these cases, they may require detailed accounting for the flows of funds or may allow only certain types of international transactions. The study of flows of funds between individuals and organizations across national borders and the development of methods of handling the flows more efficiently are properly within the scope of international finance.

4. *Institutional Finance.* A nation's economic structure contains a number of financial institutions, such as banks, insurance companies, pension funds, and credit unions. These institutions gather money from individual savers and accumulate sufficient amounts for efficient investment. Without these institutions, funds would not be readily available to finance business transactions, the purchase of private homes and commercial facilities, and the variety of other activities that require substantial amounts of capital. Institutional finance deals with issues of capital formation and the organizations that perform the financing function of the economy.

5. *Financial Management.* Individual businesses face problems dealing with the acquisition of funds to carry on their activities and with the determination of optimum methods of employing the funds. In a competitive marketplace, businesses must actively manage their funds to achieve their goals. Many tools and techniques have been developed to assist financial managers to recommend proper courses of action. These tools help the manager determine which sources offer the lowest cost of funds and which activities will provide the greatest return on invested capital. Financial management is the field of greatest 'concern to the corporate financial officers.

58. RISK-RETURN ANALYSIS, HOW TO USE A SYSTEMS APPROACH

Considerable analysis is needed and many questions must be answered before a firm can make certain decisions. Bringing together all relevant information into a problem-solving process makes use of a systems approach to decision making.

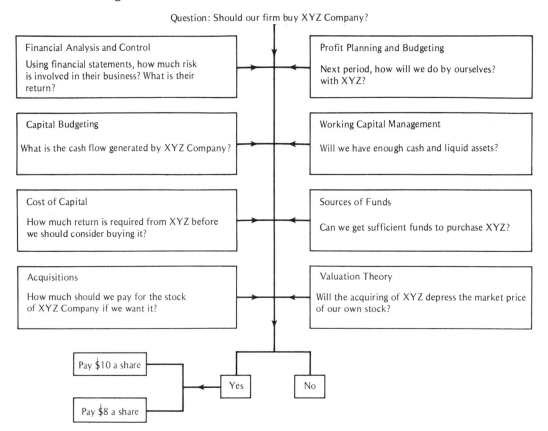

Figure 7-3. Systems View of the Analysis of Risk and Return in a Decision to Acquire a Firm.

A typical problem suited to a systems approach is the decision to purchase another company. A large volume of data must be collected. A considerable amount of analysis is needed, generally making use of the computer. The final decision—a simple *yes* or *no*—cannot be made without many accurate and timely inputs. A systems approach brings together all the necessary data and processes them so that a valid decision can be made. Figure 7-3 illustrates how the eight risk-return areas can provide inputs to the decision to acquire a company.

59. SENSITIVITY ANALYSIS, HOW TO USE

When changes in one variable are measured for their impact on another variable, the analyst is employing **sensitivity analysis.** As an example, suppose a shipping firm is evaluating the purchase of a ship that will probably cost $25,000,000 to build. The ship will be financed over 20 years and the firm's cost of capital[1] is 10 percent. The ship can be chartered for 20 years at $4,800,000 per year and the shipping firm must pay $1,300,000 of operating costs. If costs rise above this level, the charter will rise by the same amount since the firm has a fully escalated charter. The first question is "What is the rate of return on the ship?" The annual profit is:

Revenues from charter	$4,800,000
Operating Costs	−1,300,000
Operating Profit	$3,500,000

Dividing $25,000,000 by 3,500,000, we get 7.143. Reading Appendix B (present value of annuity of one dollar) on the 20-year line, the rate of return is just below 13 percent (12.7 percent actually). Since the firm's cost of capital is 10 percent, this is an acceptable investment.

But what happens if the ship actually costs $30,000,000 when it is completed? Or $35,000,000? Or $20,000,000? This is where sensitivity analysis is useful. Table 7-3 shows the effects of the varying capital amounts.

TABLE 7-3. Sensitivity Analysis of Capital Costs and Rate of Return on a Proposed Vessel.

Capital Cost	÷	Operating Profit	=	20-Year Factor in Appendix B	Rate of Return
$15,000,000	÷	$3,500,000	=	4.286	23.0%
20,000,000	÷	3,500,000	=	5.714	16.7
25,000,000	÷	3,500,000	=	7.143	12.7
30,000,000	÷	3,500,000	=	8.571	9.9
35,000,000	÷	3,500,000	=	10.000	7.8
40,000,000	÷	3,500,000	=	11.429	6.0

[1] Taxes are omitted to simplify this analysis.

From Table 7-3, a graph could be prepared to illustrate the sensitivity of capital, as is done in Figure 7-4.

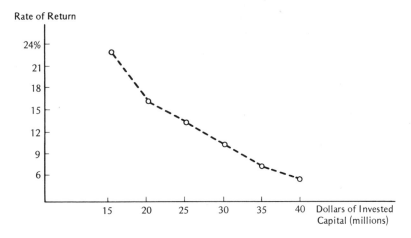

Figure 7-4. Sensitivity Analysis of Capital Costs and Rate of Return.

A second approach to sensitivity analysis would be to measure how each increment of capital affects the annual profit. For example, assume the shipping company plans to borrow the $25,000,000 at 10 percent amortized over 20 years. The annual cash profit after debt service would be:

Revenues	$4,800,000
Operating Costs	-1,300,000
Debt Service (20 years, 10%, $25,000,000)	
= $25,000,000/8.514 =	-2,936,340
Profit after Debt Service	$ 563,660

Each million dollars of capital would require $1,000,000/8.514 or $117,454 of debt service and each $5,000,000 of capital would cost $587,268 annually. Therefore, a profile could be prepared showing the sensitivity of differing levels of capital. This situation is shown graphically in Figure 7-5.

Many other approaches can be used to measure the sensitivity of one variable to another. Some common examples relate profits or return to such variables as inflation, changes in selling price, changes in wages, and changes in units of sales. These and other comparisons are useful in helping the analyst evaluate the soundness and stability of profit projections, budget forecasts, or similar financial plans.

TABLE 7-4. Sensitivity Analysis, Capital Costs and Profit.

Capital Cost	Profit After Debt Service
$15,000,000	$1,738,196
20,000,000	1,150,928
25,000,000	563,660
30,000,000	(23,608)
35,000,000	(610,876)
40,000,000	(1,198,144)

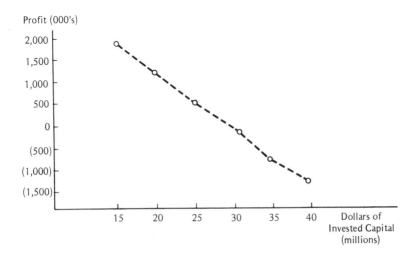

Figure 7-5. Sensitivity Analysis, Capital Costs and Profit.

60. STANDARD DEVIATION, HOW TO MEASURE RISK WITH

Three of the most common uses of the standard deviation as a measure of risk are the following:

1. *Comparing Projects with Different Standard Deviations.* As an example of this use, we shall compare proposals A, B, and C, which are being evaluated by a firm. Project A has an expected return of 15 percent with a standard deviation (σ) of 2 percent; project B has a return of 18 percent with a σ of 3 percent; and project C has a return of 20 percent with a σ of 4 percent. Figure 7-6 shows the range of possible

returns for each project. Proposal C has the highest target value but also the widest dispersion of returns. On this basis, it would be considered the riskiest project.

2. *Risk That Minimum Level Will Not Be Achieved.* A second use of standard deviation is to predict the probability that some minimum level of return will be achieved. The standard normal distribution table in Appendix E can be used for this purpose. Being a one-tailed table, we can find the percentage of occurrences between the target value and any standard deviation value. Some sample problems can help explain the use of the table (refer to Figure 7-6).

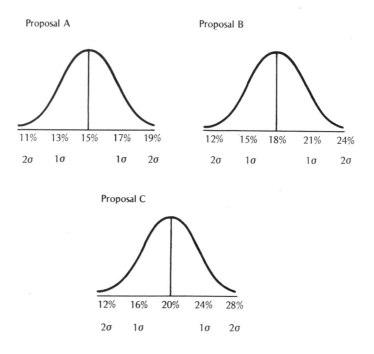

Figure 7-6. Comparing Riskiness of Projects with Different Standard Deviations.

EXAMPLE: For proposal A, what is the probability that the firm will realize a return of at least 17 percent?

ANSWER: Approximately 16 percent. There is a 50 percent chance of being above the target return. From the table, there is a 34.13 percent chance of being between the target value and one σ (which is 17 percent). Subtracting 34 percent from 50 percent, there is a 16 percent chance of being above one σ or 17 percent return.

EXAMPLE: For proposal B, what is the probability that at least 12 percent will be realized?

ANSWER: Approximately 98 percent. Twelve percent is two σ from the target value. The table gives this value as 47.72 percent. By adding this to the 50 percent that is above the target value, we get a 98 percent probability of attaining 12 percent.

EXAMPLE: For proposal C, what is the probability that at least 18 percent will be realized?
ANSWER: Approximately 69 percent. Eighteen percent is one-half σ from the target value. The table gives 19.15 percent as the value to add to the 50 percent above the target value, or a total chance of 69 percent of being above 18 percent return.

3. *Probability of Achieving a Desired Range of Returns.* A third use of the standard deviation is to forecast the likelihood of achieving some range of returns. Some sample problems can explain this (refer to Figure 7-6):

EXAMPLE: For proposal A, what is the chance that our return will be 13 to 17 percent?
ANSWER: 68 percent. One σ above and below the target value is 34 percent on each side, or 68 percent.

EXAMPLE: For proposal C, what is the chance of a return between 18 and 22 percent?
ANSWER: 38 percent. One-half σ above and below the target value is 19.15 percent on each side, or 38 percent.

61. WEIGHTED-AVERAGE APPROACH TO RISK AND RETURN, HOW TO USE

Through the use of a weighted-average technique, we can combine the risk and return factors into a single numerical value. A weighted average is a mathematical value that expresses the likelihood of different risks and their effect on the return from a proposal. Five steps are involved in calculating a weighted average:

1. *Identify Possible Future Conditions.* The first step in calculating a weighted average is to forecast future conditions that would affect the return from a proposal. As an example, a firm is considering a proposal to market air-conditioning units in its retail outlets next summer. The firm can anticipate three possible future conditions important to this project:
   a. Very hot summer.
   b. Normal summer.
   c. Very cool summer.
2. *Estimate the Likelihood of Each Possible Future Condition.* The firm assumes that there is a 100-percent chance that next summer will either be

very hot, normal, or very cool. The problem now is to determine the likelihood of each of the three conditions. The financial manager may consult with the firm's marketing and production personnel, economists, or other specialists. In our example, the weather bureau may have helpful data and advice. At some point, the manager must subjectively assign a probability to each possible occurrence. In our example, he has assigned probabilities as follows:

a. Very hot summer   20%
b. Normal summer   55%
c. Very cool summer   25%
   Total   100%

3. *Estimate the Return with Each Future Condition.* The different future conditions may have a profound effect on the expected return. After discussing the matter with marketing personnel, we expect the following returns from the sale of air conditioners next summer (parentheses indicate a loss):

a. Very hot summer $60,000
b. Normal summer $40,000
c. Very cool summer   ($10,000)

4. *Multiply Probabilities Times Estimated Returns.* To get a weighted value for each possible future condition in terms of its expected return, we multiply each probability times the return:

a. Very hot summer $60,000 × 20%   = $12,000
b. Normal summer $40,000 × 55%   = $22,000
c. Very cool summer   ($10,000) × 25%   = ($2,500)

5. *Add Individual Weighted Values to Get Expected Return.* The expected value or weighted average for the entire proposal may be calculated by adding the individual weighted values:

$12,000 + 22,000 - 2,500 = $31,500 weighted average

Even though the decision to sell air conditioners involves different returns under different conditions, we can use the $31,500 weighted average to compare this proposal with other proposals. For example, suppose that we also had a chance to sell raincoats next summer, and we estimated the following:

a. Very wet summer   20% chance $80,000 expected return
b. Normal summer   60% chance $30,000
c. Dry summer   20% chance $20,000

The expected value of this project is

a.   Very wet summer   20% × $80,000   = $16,000
b.   Normal summer   60% × $30,000   = 18,000
c.   Dry summer   20% × $20,000   =   4,000
                                           $38,000 expected
                                           value

If we only had the space available in our stores for one of the items—air conditioners or raincoats—we would choose the raincoats, because they offer a higher weighted-average return.

> *EXAMPLE: A firm is considering a proposal with three possible returns. A pessimistic estimate is that the firm will lose $10,000. The most probable return, which we estimate to be 40 percent, is an inflow of $20,000. Optimistically, we can expect $40,000 and we have a 50:50 chance of getting it. What is the expected value of this proposal?*
>
> *ANSWER: $27,000.*   *Low*   *10% × ($10,000) = − 1,000*
> *Likely*   *40% × $20,000 = + 8,000*
> *High*   *50% × $40,000 = + 20,000*
>   *+ 27,000 expected*
>   *value or weighted*
>   *average*

Part Two

"CLASSICS"
IN FINANCIAL THEORY

C 1. DURAND ON THE COST OF CAPITAL

In 1952, David Durand published "Cost of Debt and Equity Funds for Business: Trends and Problems of Measurement." The article established an important part of the foundation for cost of capital theory. This section outlines that article. *

BASIC CONSIDERATIONS

Durand refutes the classical economic position that businesses should invest where marginal cost equals marginal return. In doing this, he points out that maximizing wealth is not the same as maximizing income. The short-term concept that a firm should maximize its earnings per share is not an adequate criterion as a goal of the firm. Rather, the firm should seek to maximize **wealth** which is defined as the present value of its future income stream. Maximizing income and maximizing wealth are identical only in situations of constant returns and absolute certainty. Most firms do not face such situations.

Under a marginal return theory, business would invest in a project if the profit on the project exceeds the financing costs on an incremental basis. As an example, if a firm can borrow at 7 percent and earn 9 percent on the money, the project would be acceptable. Durand rejects this concept. Instead of marginal return, the firm needs to determine its *required return* which is defined as the level of return from a new project that will maintain or increase the wealth of the firm. Thus, in order to be acceptable an investment must, on a per-share basis, increase the present value of all future income to the firm.

---

*SOURCE: David Durand, "Cost of Debt and Equity Funds for Business: Trends and Problems of Measurement," reprinted in Archer and D'Ambrosio, *The Theory of Business Finance* (New York: Macmillan Publishing Company, Inc., 1976).

FORMULA FOR REQUIRED RETURN

Durand's concept of required return is identical to our present concept of the firm's overall cost of capital. He proposed the following formula to calculate required return:

$$K_o = \text{New Int}_{atax} + CS_{mkt} \left[\frac{\Delta \text{ Caprate}}{\text{New D}_{mkt}} \right]$$

where K_o = Required return from a new investment.

New Int$_{atax}$ = After-tax cost of the debt used to finance the new project expressed as a percent and calculated by multiplying the before-tax effective cost times one minus the firm's tax rate $[(\text{Int})(1 - t_r)]$.

CS$_{mkt}$ = Total dollar value of the firm's outstanding common stock in the market calculated by multiplying the firm's price-earnings multiple times its earnings per share times the number of outstanding shares.

Δ Caprate   = Change in the firm's capitalization rate on its common stock where capitalization rate is defined as the reciprocal of the price earnings multiple and the change is the difference between the existing capitalization rate and the new capitalization rate.

New D$_{mkt}$ = Face value in dollars of the additional debt needed to finance the investment.

This formula is important to the financial literature because of 3 characteristics, as follows:

1. *After-Tax Cost of Capital.* In evaluating an investment, a firm can choose to make the evaluation on a before-tax or after-tax basis. An after-tax approach is generally preferred in capital budgeting and cost of capital analyses, and Durand's formula can be applied directly because it is expressed on an after-tax basis.
2. *Incorporates Financing Risk.* The factor of a changing capitalization rate is a reflection of a financing risk. With additional debt in the capital structure shareholders will perceive greater risk on their investment. Some shareholders will sell their common stock causing a decline in the market price. This selling pressure will also cause a decline in the price-earnings multiple and this decline is reflected in Durand's formula by the change in capitalization rate.
3. *Employs a Weighted Financial Risk.* By in effect multiplying the change in the firm's capitalization rate times a fraction comprised of the value of common stock divided by the value of the new debt, Du-

rand in effect "weights" the effect of the changing capitalization rate. This can be seen by rewriting the last element in the formula as [CS_{mkt}/New D_{mkt}] [Δ Caprate]. This weighted effect becomes a premium that must be earned in addition to the interest costs (the direct financing costs) on the investment. This differs significantly from the concept of weighted-average cost of capital. In the weighted-average cost of capital no change is allowed in the firm's price-earnings multiple. Instead, it is assumed that the additional earnings per share resulting from favorable financial leverage will offset the decline in the price-earnings multiple, thus maintaining the value of the common stock in the market. Durand's formula and the weighted-average approach both consider financing risk; Durand's formula may be more difficult to use because it requires a subjective forecast of the decline in the P/E multiple (change in the capitalization rate). The weighted-average approach eliminates the need to make this forecast.

4. *Ties Together Financial Leverage and Common Stock Prices.* Durand's formula recognizes the direct relationship between debt financing of an investment and the additional risk posed to common shareholders. The degree of favorable financial leverage, expressed as a premium above the after-tax interest costs, must be sufficient to offset the declining price-earnings multiple and thus maintain the current value of the firm's common stock. If a firm accepts projects with a likely return in excess of the required return using Durand's formula, the value of the firm's common stock should increase on a per-share basis.

APPLICATION OF DURAND'S FORMULA

As an example of the use of the Durand formula, let us consider a firm that has 1,000,000 shares of common stock outstanding and $12,000,000 of debt at a 6 percent before-tax cost. The firm's earnings per share are $2.50 and it is capitalized at an 8/1 price-earnings multiple. The firm is considering borrowing $10,000,000 at an 8 percent before-tax rate, an action that will cause its price-earnings multiple to drop to 6 2/3rds due to the risk from the additional debt. The firm's tax rate is 50 percent. Using Durand's formula, what is the required return from the new investment?

$$K_o = (8\%)(1 - .50) + (8/1)(\$2.50)(1,000,000)\left[\frac{+.025}{10,000,000}\right] = 4\% + 5\% = 9\%$$

where .025 in the formula = .15 − .125 reflecting change from 8/1 to 6 2/3rds price-earnings multiple. (Capitalization rate is the reciprocal of the price-earnings multiple.)

PROOF OF DURAND'S FORMULA

If the Durand formula is correct, the market value of a share of the firm's common stock in the example will not change as a result of the new investment. This can be demonstrated by a proof, as follows:

1. *Current Market Value.* The current market value of the stock must be $20 since (8/1) ($2.50) = $20. This value of $20 is achieved at present earnings per share of $2.50.
2. *Earnings per Share Required.* Accepting the new investment will mean a drop in the price-earnings multiple from 8/1 to 6 2/3rds/1 or stated differently, a rise in the capitalization rate from .125 to .15. Multiplying the new capitalization rate by the current market value we get $20 × .15 = $3 per share. The firm's new overall earnings per share must be $3 to maintain a $20 market price.
3. *Additional NIAT.* In order to achieve a $3 earnings per share, an additional $.50 per share is needed. Since the firm has 1,000,000 outstanding shares of common stock, an increase of $500,000 is needed in net income after taxes. ($.50 × 1,000,000)
4. *Additional Operating Income Needed.* In order to raise $500,000 in net income after taxes with a 50 percent tax rate, the firm must have a $1,000,000 increase in earnings before taxes. Since the firm needs $800,000 to cover its new debt, it must have $1,800,000 as a total rise in operating income (EBIT).
5. *Required Rate of Return.* To raise $1,800,000 on an investment of $10,000,000, the firm must have a before-tax return of 18 percent. At a 50-percent tax rate, this is a 9 percent after-tax return.

Since both methods give a 9 percent after-tax return, the Durand formula is valid. With the information given in the example, the income statements before and after the investment are given as follows:

	Before $10,000,000 Investment	After $10,000,000 Investment
EBIT	$ 5,720,000	$ 7,520,000
Interest at 6%	720,000	720,000
Interest at 8%	0	800,000
EBT	$ 5,000,000	$ 6,000,000
Federal Income Taxes	2,500,000	3,000,000
Net Income After Taxes (NIAT)	$ 2,500,000	$ 3,000,000
Times P/E Multiple	X 8	X 6.67
Market Value of Common Stock	$20,000,000	$20,000,000
÷ Total Shares Outstanding	1,000,000	1,000,000
Market Price Per Share	$20	$20

THREE THEORIES ON COST OF CAPITAL

Durand identifies two overall approaches to cost of capital and divides one of the approaches into two major theories. Overall, the result is three major theories as follows:

1. *Net Operating Income (NOI) Approach.* Under this theory, operating income (EBIT) is the fundamental determinant of the value of the firm's securities in the market place. Thus, the firm's cost of capital is calculated by the formula $K_o = \text{EBIT}/V_{mkt}$. This formula can be changed to express the value of the firm as $V_{mkt} = \text{EBIT}/K_o$. This formula reflects the fact that the total investment or value of the firm's securities will be the same at all debt levels and therefore is not dependent upon capital structure. The NOI approach also argues that the totality of risk confronting the firm cannot be altered by merely changing capitalization proportions. The NOI approach is identical to **fixed K_o theory.**

2. *Net Income (NI) Approach.* This approach focuses on the value of the firm's common stock and expresses such value by the formula $CS_{mkt} = \text{EBT}/K_e$. Under this concept, the total investment value of the firm will increase as the firm adds debt with favorable financial leverage; then the market value of the firm will level off before risk comes into play. Durand presents two major theories under the net income approach:

   a. *Fixed K_e.* Under this theory, conservative increases in debt do not increase risk. Therefore, the firm's K_e is fixed in the relationship of EBT/CS_{mkt}. Durand rejects this theory.

   b. *Varying K_e.* Under this theory, a conservative proportion of debt reflecting favorable financial leverage will increase the overall value of the firm. The degree of favorable financial leverage must produce sufficient profits to offset the decline in the price-earnings ratio at higher levels of debt. Durand accepts this theory.

OPTIMAL CAPITAL STRUCTURE

Under Durand's concept of required return or cost of capital, the optimal capital structure is measured in terms of the value of the firm's common stock on a per-share basis. With a going-concern method of valuation, the market price of the firm's common stock will reflect the present value of all future income discounted at an appropriate rate for the firm's risk class. Thus, the capital structure that maximizes future income will also maximize the per-share price of the common stock. Such a maximization will occur as the firm accepts new projects until the required return and the marginal return are identical. Once this level is achieved, no further projects should be accepted.

If additional projects are accepted, the additional income will not have a sufficient effect on earnings per share to offset the drop in the price-earnings multiple and the value of the common stock will decline on a per-share basis. This situation is shown in Figure C1-1.

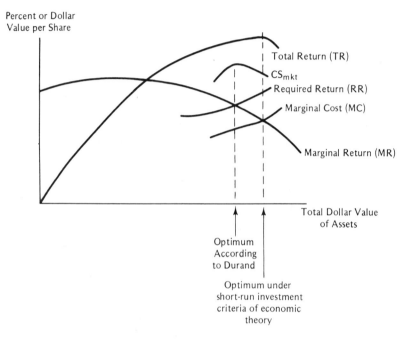

Figure C1-1.   Optimal Capital Structure under Durand Theory Occurs at Crossing of RR and MR Curves.

CALCULATING K_e FOR
NET OPERATING INCOME (NOI) METHOD

In the article on common stock, Durand presents a formula for calculating the capitalization rate (K_e) under the net operating income theory. Taxes are omitted in the formula. The following analysis presents data for a firm and compares 3 formulas calculating the cost of equity capital. The 3 formulas are:

1. *Durand Formula.* This is a restating of the formula contained in the Durand article.

$$K_e = \frac{1 - \text{Int/EBIT}}{1/K_o - (\text{Int/EBIT})(1/K_i)} = \frac{1 - 40,000/200,000}{1/.10 - (40,000/200,000)(1/.06)}$$

$$= \frac{.80}{6.667} = 12\%$$

2. *Miller-Modigliani Formula.* Since Miller and Modigliani argue for a fixed overall cost of capital, the analyst must calculate the cost of equity capital. This is developed from the relationship EBT/CS_{mkt}.

$$K_e = K_o + (K_o - K_i)(D_{mkt}/CS_{mkt}) = 10\% + (10\% - 6\%)\ (666,667/1,333,333)$$

$$= 12\%$$

3. *Weighted-Average Formula.* Ezra Solomon's formula for solving for cost of capital in a world without income taxes is reworked to isolate K_e.

$$K_o = (K_i)(\%\ D_{mkt}) + (K_e)(\%\ CS_{mkt})$$

$$K_e = \frac{K_o - (K_i)(\%\ D_{mkt})}{\%\ CS_{mkt}} = \frac{.10 - (.06)(.33)}{.67} = \frac{.08}{.67} = 12\%$$

As can be seen, all 3 formulas give the same 12 percent cost of equity capital for the firm in the example. We may therefore conclude that the formula in the Durand article is consistent with the more widely used formulas of Miller and Modigliani and Ezra Solomon.

CONCEPT OF THE SUPERPREMIUM

Durand defines **superpremium** as the difference between the interest rate demanded by creditors of the firm and the actual interest that must be paid on the bonds if they are issued during a period of relatively low interest rates. For example, suppose that investors demand a 7-percent return on the bonds of a firm but the firm is able to float bonds at 5 percent during a period of easy money. A 2 percent superpremium will exist in this situation.

Durand argues that a superpremium will increase the total value of the firm. The larger the superpremium, the higher will be the value of the total firm as a result of favorable financial leverage.

THE DURAND THEORETICAL COMPROMISE

Durand developed a theoretical compromise on the calculation of cost of capital (required return) between positions advocated by the NOI and NI methods (fixed K_o, fixed K_e, and varying K_e theories).

1. *Totality of Risk Does Not Change.* Durand agrees with the fixed K_o theory that the totality of risk inherent in all the securities of a single firm will always remain the same regardless of the capital structure. This is basically a recognition that the operating risks in the market place do not change as a result of the capitalization.

2. *Capitalization Can Increase V_{mkt}.* Durand agrees with the fixed K_e theory that the market will pay more for the same totality of risk if the company is properly capitalized with bonds and stocks. This is a recognition that a firm with a conservative proportion of bonds in its capital structure will command a higher market price than a firm with common stock alone. Durand explains that this is proper because restrictions actually exist in the investment market which limit the ability of arbitragers to equalize risks on all investments. The arbitrage action is the key element of the rigorous Miller-Modigliani defense of fixed K_o theory and Durand is saying that, in practice, the economic theory is not fully realized in the market.

Example Supporting Durand Compromise

Durand develops his compromise on the cost of capital through the mechanism of the superpremium. He takes a hypothetical company that is expected by the market to earn 10 percent on its investments. He then supposes that it could be determined that well-protected bonds of this company should be properly valued at 5 percent; that is, a 5 percent differential between bonds at 5 percent and common stock at 10 percent would just compensate for the difference in risk accepted by the creditors and shareholders. He further supposes that restrictions on banks, insurance companies, and other investors create an increased demand for these relatively safe bonds and the result of this increased demand is that the firm is able to float the bonds at 4 percent instead of 5 percent. A 1-percent superpremium is thus created.

Durand argues that the common shareholders of the company have no need to pay this premium and are justified in writing down the value of the firm's bonds to a 5-percent basis. That is, a $5,000,000 offering of 4-percent bonds would be valued at $4,000,000 in estimating the value of the common stock because a 4 percent $1,000 bond is only worth $800 at 5 percent.[1]   To illustrate this process, consider a firm with the above characteristics and a $2,000,000 operating income. The total value of the firm would be:

Operating income	$ 2,000,000
Capitalization rate (10 percent $= 10/1$ P/E ratio)	$\times$ 10
Total value if 100 percent common stock	$20,000,000
Shareholders' valuation of bonds (5 percent basis)	4,000,000
Value of common stock	$16,000,000
Restricted investors' valuation of bonds (4 percent basis)	5,000,000
Total value of the firm	$21,000,000

---

[1] This assumes that bonds are issued in perpetuity, a simplifying assumption that does not weaken the analysis.

Building on the above discussion, Durand spends considerable time showing the effects of capital structure on the value of the firm and cost of equity capital under three assumptions. These are shown in Figure C1-2 and are:

1. *Under NOI (Fixed K_o) Theory.* Leverage has no effect on V_{mkt} because it is a function of EBIT solely. Increasing debt does require a rising K_e to offset financing risk.

2. *Under NI (Fixed or Varying K_e) Theory.* Leverage raises V_{mkt} up to some optimum level of debt. K_e is fixed at low levels of debt but then begins to rise.

3. *With a Super premium.* Adding debt with a superpremium will increase V_{mkt} and will also cause a rise in K_e. Note from Figure C1-2 that this is a middle ground in each case between the NOI and NI theories.

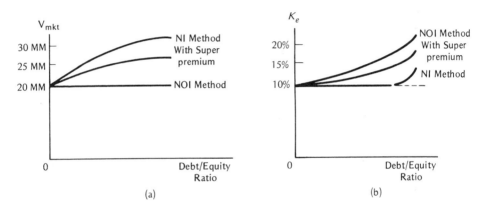

Figure C1-2   Effects of NOI Theory, NI Theory, and Superpremiums on Value of the Firm and Cost of Equity Capital.

INTEREST RATES AND BUSINESS CYCLE THEORY

Durand examines the role of interest rates in the macroeconomic context of aggregate investment. He notes that some theorists feel that interest-rate levels can play strategic roles in encouraging or discouraging capital expenditures. This role is theoretically questionable in light of the net operating income theory where the required rate of return determines investment and the inclusion or omission of debt in the capital structure does not affect the decision. In light of Miller-Modigliani's later rigorous proof of their proposition 1, which supports NOI or fixed K_o theory, much of the theoretical base for interest rates affecting investment has been eroded.

INTEREST RATES AND KEYNES' POSITION

Durand also examines the role of interest rates in light of classical Keynesian economics. Keynes said that easy money, and hence low interest rates, would not stimulate investment during depressions because of the low marginal efficiency of capital. That is, even if interest rates were as low as 3 percent, investment opportunities might offer less than a 3 percent return. Durand supports the Keynesian conclusion but not the effect. He points out that low stock prices during a depression produce a high cost of equity capital. To show this situation, consider a company with a $1 earnings per share and a $10 market price per share of common stock. The after-tax K_e is 1/10 or 10 percent. After the start of a depression when the firm's earnings drop to 50 cents and its stock price drops to $2, the K_e is .50/2 or 25 percent. The rise in K_e means that new investment proposals must earn a higher return during the depression than would have been required earlier. Durand's conclusion is that interest rates are not a factor; rather, that businessmen will not incur obligations during a depression unless they can expect a higher return than would be expected during a period of prosperity.

C 2. MILLER AND MODIGLIANI ON COST OF CAPITAL

By the mid-1950s, it was generally accepted that favorable financial leverage effectively lowers a firm's cost of capital, increases the value of its common stock, and helps determine an optimum capital structure. In "The Cost of Capital, Corporate Finance and the Theory of Investment," Miller and Modigliani revived the theory that cost of capital is fixed for firms in a similar risk class by rigorously supporting the Fixed K_0 Theory. This was presented in the absence of taxes. In the 1963 article cited above, Miller and Modigliani modified their position and agreed that the differing tax treatments of interest and dividends could affect the cost of capital for a firm. This section examines both Miller and Modigliani positions and develops techniques for using the Miller and Modigliani theory to determine a firm's cost of capital. Since this section builds upon the cost of capital literature up to the mid-1960s, the reader is asked to review "Three Important Cost-of-Capital Theories" prior to working through this section.*

SIMPLIFYING ASSUMPTIONS

The Miller-Modigliani position makes use of four simplifying assumptions:

1. *Perfect Capital Markets.* All financial securities are traded in perfect capital markets by completely knowledgeable and rational investors. All information and changes in conditions are known immediately by all investors.
2. *No Transaction Costs.* The purchase and sale of securities involve no fees such as broker's commissions.
3. *No Corporate Taxes.* Firms are not required to pay corporate taxes.
4. *Borrowing Against Stock.* Investors are able to borrow against common stock. The common stock is still owned by the investor but may be pledged as collateral for a loan.

Although these are major simplifications, they do not materially affect the conclusions drawn by Miller and Modigliani. By simplifying the environment, they allow the analyst to focus on the real contribution of the Miller-Modigliani position.

---

*SOURCES: Merton H. Miller and Franco Modigliani, "The Cost of Capital, Corporate Finance and the Theory of Investment," *American Economic Review,* June, 1958.

————"Taxes and the Cost of Capital: A Correction," *American Economic Review,* June, 1963.

Proposition 1

The Miller-Modigliani position is expressed with the help of three distinct yet related propositions. Proposition 1 may be expressed two ways:

1. *In Words.* The market value of any firm is independent of its capital structure and is given by capitalizing its expected return at the rate appropriate to its class.
2. *In a Formula.* The formula is: $V_{mkt} = EBIT/K_0$.

Alternatively, proposition 1 may be expressed as follows:

1. *In Words.* The average cost of capital to any firm is completely independent of its capital structure and is equal to the capitalization rate of a pure equity stream of its class.
2. *In a Formula.* The formula is $K_0 = EBIT/V_{mkt}$.

In effect, proposition 1 is a statement of the formula relating the EBIT, V_{mkt}, and K_0.

Proof of the Correctness of Proposition 1

The central feature of the Miller-Modigliani theory is the rigorous and conceptually correct proof supporting proposition 1. To demonstrate their point, the theorists compare two firms and assume that their proposition is incorrect. The incorrect data are given in Table C2-1.

TABLE C2-1. Data to Support the Proof of Proposition 1 of Miller-Modigliani

Given	*Company X*	*Company Y*
Identical EBITs	$100,000	$100,000
Different shares outstanding	100,000	60,000
Co. Y has debt, Co. X does not	0	$400,000 (at 5%)
K_e is different for each firm[a]	10%	11%

[a] Since company X has no debt and thus a lower degree of risk, we would expect that it would have a lower K_e than company Y. In this example, the K_e values are given but have been carefully selected to give a different V_{mkt} for the two firms. This will produce a different V_{mkt} for each firm, a situation that is not possible according to Miller and Modigliani.

Miller and Modigliani argue that companies X and Y cannot have different total values (V_{mkt}) if they have the same basic characteristics with the exception of the capital structure. Yet the data in Table C2-1 lead to a different total value, as is seen in Table C2-2.

TABLE C2-2. Calculating the Total Value of the Firm Using Miller-Modigliani Proof of Proposition 1.

CALCULATIONS	Company X	Company Y
EBIT	100,000	100,000
Less interest	0	20,000
EBT and NIAT (no taxes)	100,000	80,000
Divided by K_e to get CS_{mkt}	$\div 10\%$	$\div 11\%$
Market value of common stock (CS_{mkt})	1,000,000	730,000
Market value of debt (D_{mkt})	0	400,000
Total Value of Firm (V_{mkt})	1,000,000	1,130,000

Three additional items of information are needed before beginning the proof. These are given in Table C2-3.

TABLE C2-3. Additional Information Needed for Miller-Modigliani Proof.

ADDITIONAL ITEMS	Company X	Company Y
Market price per share (CS_{mkt} divided by shares outstanding)	$10	$12.20
Dividends per share (assume 100% dividend payout)	$ 1	$ 1.33
Debt-equity ratio	0	.548/1

To prove that companies X and Y cannot have different V_{mkt} values, consider the actions of a rational investor who owns 100 shares of common stock in firm Y. At $12.20 each, these shares would be overvalued according to Miller-Modigliani. The investor would take the following actions:

1 *Sell the Shares in Company Y.* The 100 shares would bring $1,220.
2. *Invest the Money in Company X.* The $1,220 would buy 122 shares of company X common stock at $10 per share.
3. *Gain Leverage in the Personal Portfolio.* The debt-equity ratio for company Y was .55/1. If the investor was willing to accept this risk in company Y, he probably is willing to accept the same degree of risk in his personal portfolio. To gain this leverage with company X, he could borrow 55 percent of $1,220, or $670, and pledge his stock in company X as collateral. With the $670, he would buy 67 shares of company X, giving him a total of 189 shares. With the same degree of risk he was accepting in company Y, he now owns 189 shares of company X.

Why did the investor bother to take these steps? The reason can be seen if we compare the return on each investment as follows:

1. *With 100 Shares of Company Y Stock.* The investor would receive 100 times $1.33 dividends, or $133.
2. *With 189 Shares of Company X Stock.* The investor would receive dividends of 189 times $1, or $189. From this he must deduct the 5 percent interest on the $670 borrowed, or $34. The net return is $189 - 34 = $155.

With the same degree of risk, the investor received $22 more from the investment in company X than in company Y.

Conclusion from Miller-Modigliani's Proposition 1

Since the investor can profit from the preceding transactions, the market prices of the stocks will be forced together. The K_e values for each firm may be different, but they will adjust so that the K_o for each firm is identical. In the example given, company Y would have a K_e of 13.3 percent since $80,000 NIAT divided by .133 gives a CS_{mkt} of $600,000 and a V_{mkt} of $1,000,000, the same as firm X.

When the two values of the total firm are identical, note that the investors in company Y would receive more dividends than investors in company X. The difference is $1.33 versus $1.00. This difference in return recognizes the higher risk of owning stock in a firm with a debt-equity ratio of .55/1 and is compensation for the higher degree of risk.

Proposition 2

Related to their initial proposition, Miller-Modigliani provide a formula for determining the cost of equity capital. Proposition 2 may be expressed two ways:

1. *In Words.* The expected yield of a share of stock is equal to the appropriate capitalization rate K_o for a pure equity stream in the class, plus a premium related to financial risk and equal to the debt-equity ratio times the spread between K_o and the interest rate, K_i.
2. *In a Formula.* The formula is $K_e = K_o + (K_o - K_i)(D_{mkt}/CS_{mkt})$.

As an example of calculating K_e from proposition 2, consider a firm with a K_o of 10 percent, an interest charge on its debt of 6 percent, and a debt-equity ratio of 1/1. The K_e will be

$$K_e = 10\% + (10\% - 6\%)(\tfrac{1}{1}) = 14\%$$

If the debt-equity ratio goes up to 5/1, the K_e will become

$$K_e = 10\% + (10\% - 6\%)\left(\frac{5}{1}\right) = 30\%$$

The rise in K_e occurs because of a drop in CS_{mkt} to compensate for the degree of risk inherent in a 5/1 debt-equity ratio.

Purpose of Proposition 2

In this proposition, Miller-Modigliani illustrate the effects of financial leverage. The variable $K_o - K_i$ is a measure of the degree of financial leverage. The same is true for the debt-equity ratio. When a firm increases its financial leverage, the total value of the firm does not increase. Rather, K_e increases because shareholders in a levered firm will demand a higher return than in an unlevered firm. Proposition 2 focuses on the effect of financial leverage —to increase return—rather than to increase the value of the firm (V_{mkt}).

Proposition 3

The logical conclusion to the Miller-Modigliani position is found in proposition 3, which states that the cutoff point for investment in the firm will, in all cases, be K_o and will be completely unaffected by the type of security used to finance the investment. In other words, the gain from being able to borrow cheap funds is offset by the market's discounting the common stock to reflect the added risk.

Criticisms of the Miller-Modigliani Theory

The Miller-Modigliani defense of the fixed K_o theory has been criticized on several grounds:

1. *Perfect Markets Do Not Exist.* One criticism points out that perfect markets do not exist. Investors are not always rational and do not always have the needed information to make the correct decisions on value.
2. *Oversimplified Model.* By omitting taxes and transactions costs, the model is too simple to reflect actual conditions in the securities markets.
3. *Investors May Not Be Willing to Borrow.* The proof of proposition 1 assumes that investors are willing to pledge their stock as collateral to borrow money. Investors may not be willing to accept such a personal risk. The borrowing will increase the total amount of money they have invested and will increase the degree of risk, even though the debt-equity ratios of the firm and individual are the

same. Also, it is one thing for a corporation to accept the risk of leverage; it is quite another thing for an investor to accept the risk individually. This may result in an investor's unwillingness to borrow.

4. *Investors May Not Be Able to Borrow at Low Corporate Rate.* Even if investors were willing to borrow, they probably would not be able to borrow at the same low rate as the firm. The higher individual borrowing rate would reduce the effect of the proof of proposition 1.

Analysis of Criticisms of Miller-Modigliani Theory

The simplifying assumptions of the Miller-Modigliani theory do not destroy the validity of its conclusions. It is true that securities markets do not function in the relatively simple, orderly fashion of the Miller-Modigliani proof of proposition 1. At the same time, individuals and institutions do seek to identify overvalued and undervalued securities and will buy and sell to take advantage of perceived discrepancies between intrinsic and actual value. The Miller-Modigliani theory does point out factors that are operating in the actual securities markets.

The major weakness of the Miller-Modigliani position deals with the absence of corporate income taxes. We shall deal with this weakness in the next section.

Conclusions from Miller-Modigliani Theory

Three conclusions, each related to a proposition in the theory, may be drawn from this examination of Miller and Modigliani's discussion on cost of capital:

1. *EBIT Is Major Determinant of K_o and V_{mkt}.* The proof of proposition 1 shows that the cost of capital and value of the firm are linked closely with EBIT.
2. *Financial Leverage Affects K_e, not V_{mkt}.* Proposition 2 shows how K_e rises with favorable financial leverage; proposition 1 shows that V_{mkt} is not affected.
3. *Cutoff Point for Capital-Budgeting Proposals Is K_o.* Proposition 3 states that the firm must use its overall cost of capital as a cutoff point for new investment. This is a natural conclusion based on proposition 1.

An overview of the Miller-Modigliani theory is presented in Table C2-4.

TABLE C2-4. Overview of the Miller-Modigliani Theory of Cost of Capital.

Assumes	Three Propositions	Significance of Propositions
1. Perfect capital markets.	1. $K_o = \text{EBIT}/V_{mkt}$ or $V_{mkt} = \text{EBIT}/K_o.$	EBIT is major determinant of value of a firm and the cost of capital.
2. No transaction costs.	2. $K_e = K_o + (K_o - K_i)\,(D_{mkt}/CS_{mkt}).$	K_e increases with favorable financial leverage.
3. No corporate taxes.	3. K_o is cutoff point for new proposals.	Firm cannot increase V_{mkt}
4. Borrowing against stock possible.		by using financial leverage.

Major Contribution	Major Criticism	Conclusion on Criticism
The rigorous conceptual proof of proposition 1.	The model is oversimplified.	Except for omission of taxes, model is conceptually valid.

MILLER-MODIGLIANI AFTER-TAXES

A number of theorists, including Ezra Solomon, have pointed out that the tax laws which allow the deduction of interest payments before taxes can result in a higher total value of a company that makes use of favorable financial leverage. This is equivalent to saying that favorable financial leverage can lower the overall cost of capital for a firm. Miller and Modigliani agreed with this statement in a 1963 article.

To measure the effect of corporate taxes on the firm's cost of capital, we must examine the Miller-Modigliani proposition 1 in a world of corporate taxes. We shall begin this examination by separately reviewing each of the three components of proposition 1: EBIT, V_{mkt}, and K_o.

Significance of EBIT in a World of Corporate Taxes

The firm's EBIT remains the major determinant of value in a world of corporate taxes. We will see that going-concern methods of valuation rely largely on the firm's prospects for future profits. All profits are eventually reflected in the firm's operating income, or EBIT.

Although the firm's creditors and owners are interested in EBIT, they are especially concerned with the portion of EBIT that can be claimed by them. There are three major claims on EBIT (assuming no preferred stock):

1. *Interest.* This is the portion claimed by the creditors of the firm.
2. *Taxes.* This is the portion claimed by the federal government.
3. *NIAT.* This is the portion claimed by the owners of the firm.

For purposes of determining value, only two of these components of EBIT are useful—interest and NIAT. The portion representing taxes is lost to the firm and will not affect the firm's value in a direct way. We might then conclude that the determinants of value in a world of corporate taxes are interest and NIAT. Or, stated another way, the return to creditors and owners is the EBIT minus taxes.

Significance of V_{mkt} in a World of Corporate Taxes

Miller-Modigliani defined V_{mkt} as being equal to EBIT/K_o. In a setting with corporate taxes, both EBIT and K_o should be converted to an after-tax basis. We have already seen that EBIT should be converted to the sum of interest and NIAT. The K_o should also be converted to an after-tax capitalization rate ($CR_{A\text{-}TAX}$).

What is the after-tax capitalization rate? It is probably closely related to the reciprocal of the normal price-earnings multiple for the firm, or

$$CR_{A\text{-}TAX} = \frac{1}{PE_{norm}}$$

The criterion for selecting the after-tax capitalization rate is that it must be appropriate to capitalize both interest and NIAT at this rate. This presents a most difficult conceptual problem for two reasons:

1. *Interest and After-Tax Profits Are Not Alike.* The creditors of a firm have invested to achieve a stable, secure return. The owners have accepted higher risk and less security in order to have a chance for higher returns. No one capitalization rate can easily reflect the different goals of the creditors and owners.
2. *$2 of Interest Equals $1 of NIAT.* With a 50-percent corporate tax rate, we must earn $2 to have $1 after taxes. With respect to our financing of projects, it is conceptually correct to recognize that from every $2 of EBIT we can pay $2 of financing costs when we use debt and only $1 when we use equity. This is very important when we are capitalizing interest and NIAT together. If we use more debt, we are increasing the total value of the firm in accordance with the formula

$$V_{mkt} = \frac{NIAT + interest}{CR_{A\text{-}TAX}}$$

In spite of the conceptual problem of capitalizing both NIAT and interest with a single capitalization rate, as a practical matter a firm's total value is a function of both NIAT and interest. Capitalizing them together at an appropriate rate will give an approximation of value that reflects corporate income taxes. Thus, we shall use (NIAT + interest)/$CR_{A\text{-}TAX}$ as a measure of V_{mkt}.

Significance of K_o in a World of Corporate Taxes

The firm's overall cost of capital is as valid a concept in an environment of taxes as it is in the theoretical models discussed earlier. The firm must still select a cutoff point for new projects that will allow the firm to increase in value. The formula for K_o can remain $EBIT/V_{mkt}$ if we incorporate the tax factors in the V_{mkt} component of the formula. On an after-tax basis, the formula for K_o becomes

$$K_o = \frac{EBIT}{V_{mkt}} = \frac{EBIT}{(NIAT + interest)/CR_{A\text{-}TAX}} = \frac{(EBIT)(CR_{A\text{-}TAX})}{NIAT + interest}$$

Solving for K_o Using Miller-Modigliani After-Taxes

To illustrate the Miller-Modigliani after-tax solution for K_o, consider the two firms in Table C2-5. Firm J has no debt and firm K has $1,000,000 debt at 5 percent. The after-tax capitalization rate that applies to their class of firms is 6%.

TABLE C2-5. Solving for K_o Using Miller-Modigliani After-Taxes.

	Firm J	Firm K
EBIT	200,000	200,000
Interest (K has $1,000,000 debt at 5%)	0	50,000
EBT	200,000	150,000
NIAT	100,000	75,000
(NIAT + interest)/$CR_{A\text{-}TAX}$	(100,000 + 0)/6%	(75,000 + 50,000)/6%
Equals V_{MKT}	= 1,667,000	= 2,083,000
$K_o = EBIT/V_{MKT}$	200,000/1,667,000	200,000/2,083,000
	= 12%	= 9.6%

We can use the alternative formula $K_o = (EBIT)(CR_{A\text{-}TAX})/(NIAT + interest)$ to check the 12 and 9.6 percent figures obtained in Table C2-5. The calculations are

$$\text{For firm J:} \quad K_o = \frac{(200)(.06)}{100 + 0} = \frac{12}{100} = 12\%;$$

$$\text{For firm K:} \quad K_o = \frac{(200)(.06)}{75 + 50} = 9.6\%$$

C 3.   WESTON'S TEST ON (COST OF CAPITAL RELATIONSHIPS)

The following discussion outlines Professor Weston's classic, "A Test of Cost of Capital Propositions" which tests the Miller-Modigliani proposition that cost of capital is fixed for firms in similar risk classes.* The discussion requires a reader background as follows:

1. Understanding of Miller-Modigliani Position. Since the discussion builds on the original rationale for fixed K_o theory, the section on "Miller-Modigliani on Cost of Capital" should be read first;

2. Understanding of Regression Analysis. A regression equation describes a line or a plane fitted to data. A basic knowledge of linear and multiple regression concepts is needed to understand the Weston empirical tests.

MILLER AND MODIGLIANI PROPOSITIONS AND TRADITIONAL THEORY

Durand's net operating income (NOI) and Miller-Modigliani's proposition 1 are logically equivalent and may be expressed by the following formulas:

$$V_{mkt} = EBIT/K_o = (D_{mkt} + CS_{mkt}) \qquad (1)$$

or

$$K_o = EBIT/V_{mkt} = EBIT/(D_{mkt} + CS_{mkt}) \qquad (2)$$

To get to Miller-Modigliani's proposition 2, we start with the generally accepted formula for the cost of equity capital (in the absence of corporate taxes) and expand it as follows:

$$K_e = \frac{EBT}{CS_{mkt}} = \frac{EBIT - (K_i)(D_{mkt})}{CS_{mkt}} \qquad (3)$$

From formula 1 we know that $EBIT = (K_o) (V_{mkt})$, which equals $(K_o) (D_{mkt} + CS_{mkt})$. Substituting this in formula 3, we get

$$K_e = \frac{(K_o)(D_{mkt} + CS_{mkt}) - (K_i)(D_{mkt})}{CS_{mkt}}$$

$$= \frac{(K_o)(D_{mkt}) + (K_o)(CS_{mkt}) - (K_i)(D_{mkt})}{CS_{mkt}}$$

---

* SOURCE: J. Fred Weston, "A Test of Cost of Capital Propositions," *Southern Economic Journal,* October 1963.

222

$$= \frac{(K_o)(D_{mkt}) + K_o - (K_i)(D_{mkt})}{CS_{mkt}} \qquad \frac{}{CS_{mkt}}$$

$$= K_o + (K_o - K_i)(D_{mkt}/CS_{mkt}) \qquad (4)$$

which is proposition 2.

The implications of propositions 1 and 2 are repeated directly from the original Miller-Modigliani article. Proposition 1 implies that cost of capital is determined by a relationship of EBIT to the overall value of the firm and is not affected by leverage. Proposition 2 implies that K_e is a linear function of leverage in the formula A + B(X), the slope of the line being the difference between K_o and K_i.

EMPIRICAL TESTS OF THE INFLUENCE OF LEVERAGE ON THE COST OF CAPITAL

The concept of "risk class" poses many problems for developing valid empirical tests on cost of capital. In a test of 1947–48 data, Miller-Modigliani used the oil industry to avoid problems of defending the selection of firms in given risk classes. Weston used the electrical utility industry and tested 1959 data.

Table C3-1 correlates cost of capital with capital structure using linear regression equations fitted by the method of least squares. Two equations are used:

1. *For Cost of Equity Capital*

$$K_e = A + B \left(\frac{D_{mkt} + PS_{mkt}}{CS_{mkt}} \right)$$

2. *For Overall Cost of Capital*

$$K_o = A + B \left(\frac{D_{mkt} + PS_{mkt}}{V_{mkt}} \right)$$

Table C3-1 has three columns, as follows:

1. *Capital Structure Situation.* The first column identifies the dependent variable, either K_e or K_o, and the independent variable that is a measure of capital structure.
2. *Miller-Modigliani Findings.* The second column gives the regression equation fitted by Miller-Modigliani from their 1947–48 data. The coefficient of determination (r^2) shows the percent of variations in K_e or K_o that may be explained by the relationship with the leverage factor [$(D_{mkt} + PS_{mkt})/CS_{mkt}$ or $(D_{mkt} + PS_{mkt})/V_{mkt}$ respectively for K_e and K_o].

3. *Weston Findings.* The third column gives the regression equation and r^2 values when Weston replicated the study using 1959 data.

Table C3-1. Cost of Capital Comparisons, Weston Versus Miller-Modigliani, Using Empirical Tests.

Situation	Findings of M-M Using 1947-1948 Data for Oil Industry	Findings of Weston Using 1959 Data for Electrical Utilities
A. Comparing K_e with Debt-Equity Ratio at Market. (Preferred Stock Treated as Debt)	$K_e = A + (B) \left(\dfrac{D_{mkt} + PS_{mkt}}{CS_{mkt}} \right)$	
	$K_e = 6.6$ $+ .017 \left(\dfrac{D_{mkt} + PS_{mkt}}{CS_{mkt}} \right)$	$K_e = 4.9$ $+ .014 \left(\dfrac{D_{mkt} + PS_{mkt}}{CS_{mkt}} \right)$
	$r = .53\ (\pm .004)$	$r = .43\ (\pm .004)$
	$r^2 = 28\%$	$r^2 = 18\%$
B. Comparing K_o with Debt-Asset Ratio at Market. (Preferred Stock Treated as Debt)	$K_o = A + B \left(\dfrac{D_{mkt} + PS_{mkt}}{V_{mkt}} \right)$	
	$K_o = 5.3$ $+ .006 \left(\dfrac{D_{mkt} + PS_{mkt}}{V_{mkt}} \right)$	$K_o = 4.27$ $+ .027 \left(\dfrac{D_{mkt} + PS_{mkt}}{V_{mkt}} \right)$
	$r = .12\ (\pm .008)$	$r = .46\ (\pm .007)$
	$r^2 = 1\%$	$r^2 = 21\%$

NOTES:

1. Formulas are expressed as $A + B(X)$ in a linear regression format. A is the crossing of the X axis and B is the slope of the line.
2. r equals the correlation coefficient where +1 is a good fit and zero is a poor fit. The figure in brackets next to "r" with a + sign is the regression coefficient confidence interval for 95 percent and is not related to the "r" value.
3. r^2 is the coefficient of determination and shows the percent of variations of K_e or K_o that are explained by the linear regression equation.

Table C3-1 produces tentative conclusions that:

1. K_e *is Correlated to Capital Structure.* Both studies reveal a strong positive correlation between K_e and the leverage factor. For Miller-Modigliani's data, 28 percent of the variation in K_e could be explained by variations in the capital structure. For Weston's data, the r^2 is 18 percent. Both are significant.

2. *Findings on K_o are Mixed.* Miller-Modigliani's data produced an r^2 of 1 percent which would justify a conclusion that K_o is not correlated to capital structure. Weston's r^2 was 21 percent which justifies the opposite conclusion.

To shed further light on the relationship between K_o and capital structure, Weston ran two additional tests varying the leverage factor. In one test, he calculated debt on an after-tax basis; in the second test, he omitted preferred stock as a fixed charge. His findings, shown in Table C3-2, support tentative conclusions as follows:

1. K_o *Shows Correlation to Capital Structure.* Even though the degrees of correlation are lower than the 21 percent in Table C3-1, Weston produced r^2 values of 3.7 and 8.0 percent. This supports a finding of some correlation between K_o and the leverage factor.

Table C3-2. Additional Empirical Tests on Cost of Capital and Capital Structure.

Situation	Weston 1959 Findings
C. Comparing K_o with Debt-Asset Ratio (as in Table 3-1, situation B) with after-tax treatment of debt used in computing K_o.	$K_o = A + B\left(\dfrac{D_{mkt} + PS_{mkt}}{V_{mkt}}\right)$
	$K_o = 5.07 - .010\left(\dfrac{D_{mkt} + PS_{mkt}}{V_{mkt}}\right)$
	$r = -.193\ (\pm .007)$
	$r^2 = 3.7\%$
D. Comparing K_o with Debt-Asset ratio (as in Table 3-1, situation B) but preferred stock not included as a fixed charge.	$K_o = A + B\left(\dfrac{D_{mkt}}{V_{mkt}}\right)$
	$K_o = 5.25 - 0.17\left(\dfrac{D_{mkt}}{V_{mkt}}\right)$
	$r = -.283\ (\pm .008)$
	$r^2 = 8.0\%$

2. *Correlation is Negative.* An interesting finding in Table C3-2 is the negative correlation coefficients. In Table C3-1, a positive correlation indicates K_o rising with additional debt or preferred stock. The negative correlations indicate that K_o drops with additional debt. The two situations are shown in Figure C3-1.

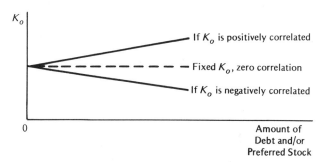

Figure C3-1.   The Effect of Positive and Negative Correlation Coefficients on K_o and Leverage.

Influence of Growth on the Cost of Capital

In the article, Weston used quantitative techniques to examine the possible reasons for the mixed findings on K_o. One logical explanation would be the presence of some other variable to which K_o was strongly correlated. He added growth and asset size as independent variables in his formula and used a multiple regression test on his data. Table C 3-3 displays his findings which can be summarized as follows:

1. *Asset Size Produced No Correlation.* The quantity of assets held by the firm was not correlated to the firm's K_o or K_e.

2. *Growth of EPS Has High Negative Correlation.* Growth was shown to be highly and negatively correlated to both K_e and K_o. Table C3-3 shows higher beta coefficients for the growth variable than for the capital structure variable. When growth is added to the formula, the coefficient of determination R^2 is 16.3 percent for K_e and 27.8 percent for K_o.

3. *Capital Structure Correlated to K_o, not K_e.* The high beta of .4333 and minus sign in front of .0265 show a high negative correlation between capital structure and K_o. The low beta of .0253 shows minimal correlation between capital structure and K_e.

Weston performed one additional test to examine the correlation between capital structure (dependent variable) and growth (independent variable). The results are shown in Table C 3-4 and may be summarized by noting that capital structure is highly and negatively correlated to growth.

Table C3-3. Multiple Regression Analysis of K_e and K_o Incorporating Growth of Earnings) for Electrical Utilities, 1959 Data.

Situation	*Weston 1959 Findings*
A. Comparing K_e with Debt-Equity ratio at market (Preferred stock treated as debt) plus total assets at book value plus growth of earnings per share.	$K_e = A + B\left(\dfrac{D_{mkt} + PS_{mkt}}{CS_{mkt}}\right) + C\,(\text{Assets}) + D\left(\dfrac{\text{Growth}}{\text{of EPS}}\right)$ $K_e = 6.75 \quad -.0029\left(\dfrac{D_{mkt} + PS_{mkt}}{CS_{mkt}}\right)$ $\qquad\quad + 0.0\,(\text{Assets}) - .1352\left(\dfrac{\text{Growth}}{\text{of EPS}}\right)$ $\quad R = .4032 \quad B = .0253 \text{ for } \dfrac{D_{mkt} + PS_{mkt}}{CS_{mkt}}$ $\quad R^2 = 16.3\% \quad B = .4110 \text{ for Growth}$ $\qquad\qquad\qquad\qquad\qquad \text{of EPS}$
B. Comparing K_o with Debt-Asset ratio at market (Preferred stock treated as debt) plus total assets at book value plus growth of earnings per share.	$K_o = A + B\left(\dfrac{D_{mkt} + PS_{mkt}}{V_{mkt}}\right) + C\,(\text{Assets}) + D\left(\dfrac{\text{Growth}}{\text{of EPS}}\right)$ $K_o = 5.91 -.0265\left(\dfrac{D_{mkt} + PS_{mkt}}{V_{mkt}}\right)$ $\qquad\quad + 0.0\,(\text{Assets}) -.0822\left(\dfrac{\text{Growth}}{\text{of EPS}}\right)$ $\quad R = .5268 \quad B = .4333 \text{ for } \dfrac{D_{mkt} + PS_{mkt}}{V_{mkt}}$ $\quad R^2 = 27.8\% \quad B = .4702 \text{ for growth}$ $\qquad\qquad\qquad\qquad\qquad \text{of EPS}$

NOTES:
1. Multiple regression defines a plane instead of a straight line as was the case with linear regression.
2. A beta coefficient "B" is used to measure the relative strength of each independent variable.
3. The capital letter "R" is the multiple correlation coefficient with the same basic role as the small letter "r" in linear regression.
4. R^2 is the coefficient of determination and shows the percent of variations in K_e or K_o that are explained by the multiple correlation equation.

Table C3-4. Linear Regression Analysis Comparing Capital Structure to Growth of Earnings for Electrical Utilities, 1959 Data.

Situation	*Weston 1959 Findings*
A. Comparing capital structure (Preferred stock treated as debt) with growth of earnings.	$\dfrac{D_{mkt} + PS_{mkt}}{V_{mkt}} = A + B\left(\dfrac{Growth}{of\ EPS}\right)$
	$\dfrac{D_{mkt} + PS_{mkt}}{V_{mkt}} = 51.66 - \underset{(\pm .34)}{1.78}\left(\dfrac{Growth}{of\ EPS}\right)$
	$r = -0.58$ $\qquad$ $r^2 = 33.6\%$
B. Comparing capital structure with growth of earnings.	$\dfrac{D_{mkt}}{V_{mkt}} = A + B\left(\dfrac{Growth}{of\ EPS}\right)$
	$\dfrac{D_{mkt}}{V_{mkt}} = 39.59 - \underset{(\pm .29)}{1.16}\left(\dfrac{Growth}{of\ EPS}\right)$
	$r = -0.48$ $\qquad$ $r^2 = 23.0\%$

NOTE: The figure in brackets with the $\pm$ sign is a measure of the dispersion of values beside the regression line.

The correlations in Tables C3-3 and C3-4 are shown graphically in Figure C3-2.

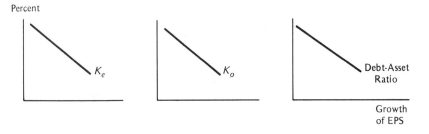

Figure C3-2. Relationship of Growth to K_e, K_o, and Capital Structure. (High, Negative Correlation in Each Case)

MEASUREMENT OF THE COST OF (EQUITY FUNDS WITH GROWTH)

In the article, Weston discusses briefly the relationship between growth and K_e. A traditional statement for a firm's cost of equity capital is the reciprocal of the price-earnings multiple; that is, $K_e = (EPS/Mkt\ Pr)$ or $NIAT/CS_{mkt}$.

This is inadequate, according to Weston, for firms accepting new investments in a growth situation. To avoid understating K_e, and hence K_o, a firm with a growing EPS must add a growth factor in the calculation of K_e. As an example of how this is done, consider the Gordon model where K_e is calculated by EPS $[(1 + G)/\text{Mkt Pr}]$.

Conclusion

The Weston article draws the overall conclusion that leverage does influence a firm's cost of capital and therefore the Miller-Modigliani approach is not correct. Weston's data produced mixed results on the slope of the regression line. One set of data resulted in a positive correlation; a second in a negative correlation. In further empirical tests, the growth of EPS was found to have a significant impact with a high negative correlation to K_o, K_e, and the debt-asset ratio. Asset size was found to have no correlation.

C 4.   SCHWARTZ ON CAPITAL-STRUCTURE THEORY

In the article "Theory of the Capital Structure of the Firm," Eli Schwartz outlined a theory of optimal capital structure that switched the emphasis away from favorable financial leverage and earnings per share maximization. The new focus was the value of the firm's common stock in the marketplace. This section outlines that article and then goes beyond it with an example of the Schwartz theory.*

TWO TYPES OF RISK

A business firm operating in a competitive market environment faces two types of basic risk, as follows:

1. *External Risk (Business Risk).* This refers to the firm's ability to operate successfully in the marketplace. Factors affecting the degree of external risk would include the stability of earnings, degree of liquidity and safety with respect to the prompt payment of bills, and the marketability of the firm's products as compared with similar products.
2. *Internal Risk (Financial Risk).* This refers to the firm's ability to meet the obligations and expectations of its investors. It includes the firm's ability to generate a sufficient operating profit so as to cover the interest payments on its debt and provide dividends and earnings for its common shareholders.

GOAL OF CAPITAL STRUCTURE MANAGEMENT

The firm should manage its capital structure so as to maximize the long-run value per share of the firm's common stock in the marketplace. Owing to volatility and irrational pressures, financial managers should not be guided solely by immediate market prices. Nevertheless, the prevailing prices in security markets are an important guide to security value. Knowledgeable investors will base their purchases on future expectations; thus, future earnings, dividends, and growth will have already been discounted in today's prices. The financial manager works for long-term value but recognizes the importance of current price levels of common stock.

---

*SOURCE: Eli Schwartz, "Theory of the Capital Structure of the Firm," *Journal of Finance,* March, 1959.

A TRADITIONAL APPROACH TO (OPTIMAL CAPITAL STRUCTURE)

For many years it was assumed that a firm should borrow until it no longer could take advantage of favorable financial leverage. For example, if the firm could borrow at 7 percent and could earn 8 percent on the money, the firm's earnings per share (EPS) would rise and the borrowing was appropriate.

To illustrate this concept, Schwartz prepared a diagram such as is shown in Figure C4-1. The key terms in this figure are:

1. *MRE Curve.* The Marginal Return on Equity curve is actually the return on any capital (debt or equity) employed by the firm. In the absence of debt, the entire area under the curve up to the amount of capital employed would be profit. The MRE curve slopes downward on the premise that a rational firm would always choose the highest-return projects first. As it makes the decision to employ more capital, it would be financing increasingly less attractive projects.

2. *SEF Line.* The Supply of External Funds line begins at the point where interest-bearing debt is added to the capital structure (after equity and trade credit). It is defined as the average cost of debt to the firm.

3. *E Line.* The External Funds line represents the marginal cost of borrowing. As the firm increases its debt, the interest cost is assumed to rise to reflect the increased financial risk. Under this theory, the optimal capital structure occurs at the crossing of the MRE and E lines.

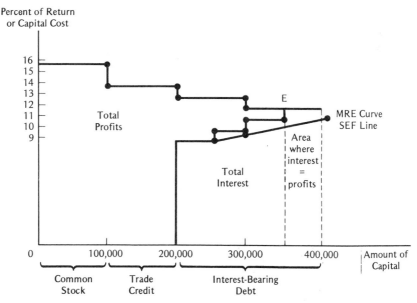

Figure C4-1. Optimal Capital Structure Under Traditional Favorable Financial Leverage Position.

Figure C4-1 is developed based on the data in Table C4-1. In this example, a firm raises $100,000 by selling 10,000 shares of common stock and gains another $100,000 by taking advantage of non-interest-bearing trade credit. The firm can issue up to $200,000 of long-term bonds. If it issues only $50,000 of the bonds, its cost will be 9 percent. Issuing another $50,000 will not change the cost of the first increment but, because of different maturities on the second increment, the cost will be 10 percent. A third increment of $50,000 would cost 11 percent and the final $50,000 would cost 12 percent. These marginal costs are shown in Figure C4-1 as the E line.

In the example, the firm has earnings capabilities at decreasing rates as additional capital is employed. The first $100,000 can return 16 percent, the second $100,000 can return 14 percent, the third $100,000 can return 13 percent, and the fourth $100,000 can return 12 percent.

The firm's optimal capital structure under the traditional view occurs at $350,000 total capital where the E line crosses the MRE line. This is the end of favorable financial leverage. There is no reason to increase capital to $400,000 since the marginal cost of debt at 12 percent is equal to the marginal return and no additional profits are realized. Earnings per share are maximized at $1.70 at the $350,000 level of capital employed. The firm would not add debt to reach a $400,000 level because this would increase its financing risk with no gain in earnings per share.

TABLE C4-1. EARNINGS PER SHARE AT INCREASING LEVELS OF DEBT IN THE FIRM'S CAPITAL STRUCTURE.

CAPITAL	AMOUNT OF ADDITIONAL FINANCING	MARGINAL COST (E LINE)	AVERAGE COST (SEF LINE)	MARGINAL RETURN MRE LINE	INCREMENTAL PROFIT %	INCREMENTAL PROFIT $	TOTAL PROFIT	AFTER-TAX PROFIT	EPS
10,000 SHARES OF COMMON STOCK	$100,000	-0-	-0-	16%	16	16,000	$16,000	$ 8,000	$ .80
TRADE CREDIT	100,000	-0-	-0-	14%	14	14,000	30,000	15,000	1.50
¼ Bond	50,000	9%	9%	13%	4	2,000	32,000	16,000	1.60
½ Bond	50,000	10%	9.5%	13%	3	1,500	33,500	16,750	1.68
¾ Bond	50,000	11%	10%	12%	1	500	34,000	17,000	1.70
Full Bond	50,000	12%	10.5%	12%	0	-0-	34,000	17,000	1.70

MRE CURVE

A firm with stable revenues and earnings will have a relatively elastic supply of external debt and a lower slope of its SEF curve. This reflects the fact that the cost of funds rises slowly with small incremental amounts of financing. On the other hand, firms with less stable revenues or earnings offer a greater degree of risk to the creditor and these firms will have a higher slope to their SEF curve. These two effects are shown in Figure C4-2.

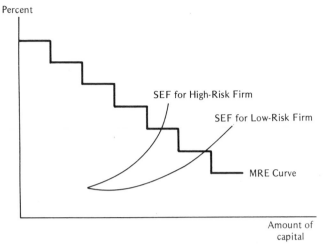

Figure C4-2.   Slope of SEF Curve for Low-Risk and High-Risk Firms.

SINGLE- AND MULTIPLE-SOURCE FINANCING

Schwartz points out that many firms can choose from multiple sources of financing for debt funds. The different sources will have varying maturities and costs. The basic decision in selecting these funds revolves around achieving the lowest total financing costs. Figure C4-3 shows the discrimination between a single source and multiple sources of funds. The firm can raise money through a single large financing under which it will incur the total interest cost Ti. Or, it can raise its funds in two steps from sources A and B in which case it will incur interest costs of Ai and Bi. If Ti is greater than the sum of Ai and Bi, the firm should discriminate in favor of two financings with the lower total cost. In practice, this process is more complicated because of a large number of alternatives with varying maturities. Still, the principle is the same.

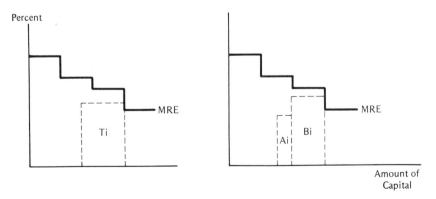

Figure C4-3.   Comparison of Single Source and Multiple Source Financing.

GROWTH

Figure C4-4 shows that there are two ways for the firm to experience growth:

1. *Shift in SEF Line.* Due to conditions in the capital or money markets, the cost of external financing will vary. During periods of loose money or when interest rates are declining because of economic factors, the firm will experience a shift in its SEF curve. This is shown in Figure C4-4a by the movement from SEF to SEF'. When this happens, the amount of capital employed by the firm will expand from line EC (point E represents the crossing of the MRE curve and the marginal cost of borrowing curve) to line E' C' (point E' represents the new marginal cost of borrowing curve). This increase in capital represents growth.

2. *Shift in MRE Function.* During periods of relative prosperity and expanding economic activity, the firm may be able to take advantage of higher return investments. This is shown in Figure C4-4b by the shift of the MRE function from MRE to MRE'. Growth occurs because the firm increases its employed capital from EC to E'C'.

Growth from shifting SEF or MRE functions is important to the firm because either situation gives management the opportunity to recast its capital structure. The lower cost of debt financing which results with a shifting SEF curve gives the firm an opportunity to increase the use of favorable financial leverage. The higher profits which result from a shifting MRE function may offer an opportunity for the firm to issue new common stock. Growth opportunities are important in the timing of changes in debt and equity relationships as the firm pursues an optimal capital structure.

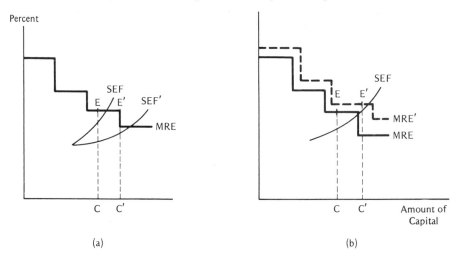

Figure C4-4. Two Ways for Growth to Occur.

ASSUMPTIONS IN THE SCHWARTZ MODEL

Schwartz develops his approach to determining the optimal capital structure for a firm building upon the following assumptions:

1. *Debt and Equity Are Variable and Substitutable.* The model assumes that, over time, the firm will be able to vary the proportions of its debt and equity capital. This means that each form of capital can be substituted for the other.

2. *Constant Debt, Varying Equity.* In the majority of articles in the finance literature, capital structure effects are measured by holding the equity constant and varying the level of debt. Schwartz reverses this procedure. His model assumes a constant level of debt (D1) and varying levels of equity (C1, C2, . . . , C5).

3. *Adding Equity Raises K_o.* As the firm sells additional shares of common stock, two effects occur:

   a. *Rise in higher-cost component.* The new shares of common stock increase equity (CS_{mkt}) as a percentage of the overall capital structure. Since equity has a higher cost than debt (K_e is greater than K_i), the higher percentage of equity tends to push up the firm's cost of capital (K_o).

   b. *Changes in K_e and K_i.* As new shares are issued, a lower issuing price will be required in order to sell the larger volume of equity. That is, if the stock is presently selling for $20, additional stock could be issued at $18. To issue further stock, the price may have to drop to $16. The lower net proceeds as more stock is issued raises the firm's cost of equity capital. At the same time, the firm's cost of debt (K_i) will decrease with the additional equity. Creditors will perceive less financial risk as the firm's debt-equity ratio improves and, eventually, an interest savings will result.

   The rise in the higher-cost component ($K_e \times \% \ CS_{mkt}$) and the decline in the lower-cost component ($K_i \times \% \ D_{mkt}$) are offsetting effects but the net result in most cases will be a rise in the overall cost of capital (K_o). This is true because the decline in K_i caused by reduced financial risk is relatively small compared to the changes in K_e and equity needed to produce it. In other words, the lower K_i will have a minor impact compared to the additional common stock outstanding and increased K_e.

4. *Adding Equity Raises Price–Earnings Ratio.* Although the additional common stock causes a rise in K_o, it also should result in a higher price-earnings multiple in the stock market. The larger proportion of equity in the firm's capital structure decreases financial risk. Although the firm may suffer a dilution of earnings as a result of the additional common stock, once the earnings per share (EPS) have

been reported, the stock can be expected to trade at a higher P/E multiple.

OPTIMAL CAPITAL STRUCTURE (ACCORDING TO SCHWARTZ)

Building upon these assumptions, Schwartz proposes that the optimal capital structure occurs at that mixture of debt and equity securities that optimizes the market price of an individual share of common stock. His model modifies two elements of the traditional approach to optimal capital structure as follows:

1. *Role of Favorable Financial Leverage.* In the traditional theory, the firm seeks to take maximum advantage of the beneficial effects of favorable financial leverage. Schwartz plays this down. Under the Schwartz approach, the increase in earnings per share as a result of favorable financial leverage must exceed any decrease in the P/E multiple which would cause a decline in the market price of the firm's stock. That is, both EPS and market price must rise in order for the firm to take advantage of trading on the equity.
2. *Maximizing Earnings per Share.* A major focus of the traditional theory is on the rising level of profits under the MRE curve. This emphasis is diminished under Schwartz. Once again, the rising EPS must also produce a rising market price of the common stock. If this is not the case, the firm should not seek to borrow in order to raise its earnings per share.

EXAMPLE OF THE SCHWARTZ MODEL

The following example differs slightly from the presentation in the original article but allows the reader to see the effect of focusing on the value of the firm's common stock as opposed to focusing on the firm's cost of capital or earnings.

As an example of the Schwartz model, let us consider a firm that has $270,000 in total assets at market (not book) value. The firm's equity is $70,000 representing 10,000 shares at a $7 market price per share. The firm's debt is $200,000 and this is held constant in the example. The firm is considering expanding by adding equity to its capital structure so that stock will be issued in increments of $100,000 depending upon the level of total assets chosen. At the current $270,000 level of assets, the firm's marginal return on all assets (MRE) will be 11.1 percent. The first additional $100,000 of stock will produce a 40-percent incremental return; then 30 percent, 20 percent, and 10 percent with each additional $100,000. Figure C4-5 shows the MRE curve for this firm at the different capital levels. Note that this figure changes the positioning of debt as compared to Figure C4-1.

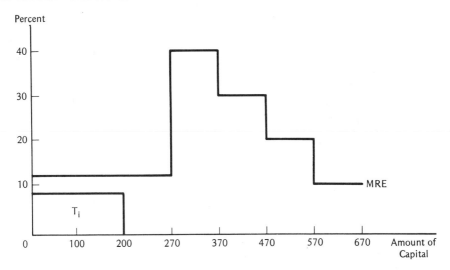

Figure C4-5.   MRE Curve for Firm in Example.

In order to raise capital to finance the additional investments, the firm plans to sell common stock at $10 per share. This is higher than the existing market price of $7 per share because the new projects are more profitable than the existing investments and, as soon as the firm commits to them, the existing market price will rise.

The firm's planning department has been estimating the impact of the new proposals on the firm's price-earnings ratio in the market. The stock presently trades at a 10/1 multiple and the first $100,000 of investment will probably not change it. But a second $100,000 of new common stock should cause investors to perceive less risk in the capital structure and the P/E ratio should rise to 11/1. Still another increment of $100,000 should raise it to 12/1 and the final increment will probably raise it to 13/1.

The financial data based on these facts and assumptions, including operating income, net income after taxes, earnings per share, and market price at each capital level, are shown in Table C4-2.

TABLE C4-2. Calculation of Market Price of Common Stock for Firm in Example.

Level	Marginal MRE	Marginal EBIT	Total EBIT	Interest	EBT	NIAT	EPS	P/E	Market Price
C_1	11.1%	30,000	30,000	16,000	14,000	7,000	.70	10/1	$ 7.00
C_2	40.0%	40,000	70,000	16,000	54,000	27,000	1.35	10/1	13.50
C_3	30.0%	30,000	100,000	16,000	84,000	42,000	1.40	11/1	15.40
C_4	20.0%	20,000	120,000	16,000	104,000	52,000	1.30	12/1	15.60
C_5	10.0%	10,000	130,000	16,000	114,000	57,000	1.14	13/1	14.82

The rising P/E multiple and changing EPS will produce differing financial data than that shown in Figure C4-5. The major change will occur in V_{mkt}. When we add $100,000 of equity to the $270,000 value at C_1, we should get $370,000 as shown in Figure C4-5. But the rising EPS will produce $476,000 V_{mkt}, the sum $200,000 of debt and 20,000 shares at $13.80. The new V_{mkt} values at each capital level as well as the new overall cost of capital after taxes are given in Table C4-3.

TABLE C4-3. Calculation of After-Tax Cost of Capital for Firm in Example.

Formula $= K_o$ (after taxes) $= \dfrac{EBIT\ (1-\ tr)}{D\ mkt+ (mkt\ Price)\ (\#\ shares)}$

Level

C_1	$\dfrac{30{,}000\ (1-.50)}{200{,}000\ +\ (7)\ (10{,}000)}$	$=$	$\dfrac{15{,}000}{270{,}000}$	$=$	5.6%
C_2	$\dfrac{70{,}000\ (1-.50)}{200{,}000\ +\ (13.50)\ (20{,}000)}$	$=$	$\dfrac{35{,}000}{470{,}000}$	$=$	7.4%
C_3	$\dfrac{100{,}000\ (1-.50)}{200{,}000\ +\ (15.40)\ (30{,}000)}$	$=$	$\dfrac{50{,}000}{662{,}000}$	$=$	7.6%
C_4	$\dfrac{120{,}000\ (1-.50)}{200{,}000\ +\ (15.60)\ (40{,}000)}$	$=$	$\dfrac{60{,}000}{824{,}000}$	$=$	7.3%
C_5	$\dfrac{130{,}000\ (1-.50)}{200{,}000\ +\ (14.82)\ (50{,}000)}$	$=$	$\dfrac{65{,}000}{941{,}000}$	$=$	6.9%

Tables C4-2 and C4-3 can be used to plot the relationship of earnings per share, market price of the firm's common stock, and after-tax cost of capital, as is done in Figure C4-6.

CONCLUSIONS FROM SCHWARTZ EXAMPLE

The firm in the above example leads us to several conclusions, as follows:

1. *K_o is not always downward sloping.* It is traditional to depict a firm's cost of capital as decreasing up to some level of capital and then rising after reaching some minimum point. This model only applies when the firm is considering debt capital. For equity capital, as shown in Figure C4-6, the K_o function may take a different slope.
2. *Maximum CS_{mkt} may not be identical to maximum EPS.* Figure C4-6 shows the highest value of common stock at $600,000 of total assets while

the maximum earnings per share occur at $500,000. The difference, as Schwartz correctly notes, is due to the rising price-earnings multiple with less financing risk at the $600,000 asset level. According to Schwartz, this is also the optimum capital structure level.

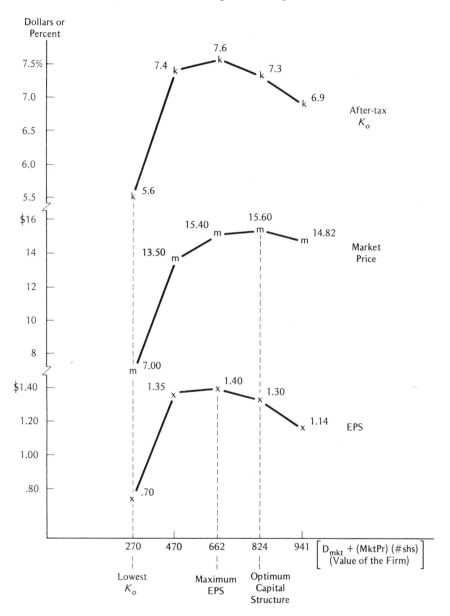

Figure C4-6. Graph of Earnings Per Share, Market Price, and Cost of Capital for Firm in Example.

C 5. SOLOMON ON FUTURE EARNINGS PER SHARE

In financial planning, it is important that the firm consider the effect of different courses of action on the value of its common stock. If the firm takes actions that cause a decline in earnings per share and lead to a decline in common stock prices, management may be criticized by angry shareholders. A valuable tool for analyzing the future market price of the stock was put forth in "Measuring a Company's Cost of Capital" by Ezra Solomon. This section develops Solomon's idea and illustrates a technique for applying it.*

WHY FUTURE EARNINGS PER SHARE ARE CRITICAL

In profit planning, two measures of corporate profits are especially important:

1. *Return on Investment (ROI).* This is an operating indicator of profits and a key measure of the success of the firm's management. If this ratio is high, the firm is generating sufficient sales on its asset base and is making sufficient profit margins on its sales. The use of ROI allows a financial manager to make comparisons of the operating profits of different firms or of the same firm in different time periods.

2. *Earnings per Share (EPS).* This is a market indicator of profits and the most important profit measure for stockholders and other individuals outside the firm. If the earnings continue to increase on a per-share basis, the firm is judged to be increasingly successful. On the other hand, a drop in earnings per share is viewed as a symptom of problems.

Given the important role of earnings per share in the eyes of shareholders and the investing public, the firm must be particularly conscious of actions that will affect the reported earnings. For this reason, profit planning focuses on how different alternatives will affect the future earnings per share reported by the firm.

---

* SOURCE: Ezra Solomon, "Measuring a Company's Cost of Capital," *The Journal of Business,* October, 1955.

COMPARING FUTURE EVENTS AT THE MARGIN

The technique of forecasting future earnings per share measures the effect of each decision at the margin. That is, the technique recognizes that the firm will have some future earnings per share without any decisions being required. The firm is presently operating and, should it continue its operations without major changes, it will achieve some level of earnings. When the firm considers new investments, the revenues and expenses associated with the investments will change the projected earnings. To determine the effect of each project, the firm will do the following:

1. *Project EPS with No New Projects.* The analyst estimates the sales and expenses for the next period in the absence of any new investment.
2. *Project Each Separate Proposal's Effect on EPS.* The analyst begins with the first proposal and forecasts future EPS on a combined basis. If the EPS are higher with the proposal than without it, the analyst knows that the proposal will help increase EPS. If the EPS are lower with the proposal, the analyst knows the proposal weakens future profitability.

Comparing future events at the margin means that each proposed investment is evaluated separately to see how it will affect the firm's sales and profits. If, for example, two projects were combined, the undesirable effects of one project might be obscured by the desirable effects of the other. This is avoided by individually combining each new proposal with the existing operations.

NORMAL PRICE-EARNINGS MULTIPLE

A **normal price-earnings ratio** is the ratio expected when a firm is realizing a satisfactory return on its capital and the stock market is not disturbed by unusual psychological or economic factors. It may be determined by analyzing historical data, similar firms, industry norms, or by common sense. If, for example, a firm's stock sells at a 12/1 multiple this year, we may expect it to continue to sell at this multiple in the future. If the firm maintains this norm and its EPS rises from $2 to $3, the market price of the stock will rise from $24 to $36. To analyze likely future market prices, we forecast future earnings per share and multiply EPS by normal P/E.

EXAMPLE: A firm is considering accepting project A. Without the project, its EPS next year will be $2.15. With the project, EPS will be $2.35. Its normal P/E is 10/1. What will be its market value next year with and without the project?

ANSWER: ($2.35)(10) = $23.50 with the project. ($2.15)(10) = $21.50 without the project.

FORECASTING SALES AND EBIT

To use the future-earnings-per-share approach to profit planning, we begin with a forecast of sales next period without any new investments. Marginal analysis is then used to calculate the EBIT. Next, each separate investment possibility is analyzed with respect to future sales and EBIT. A separate income statement is prepared showing the combined results of the firm's planned activities plus the project. Thus, in Table C5-1, the second column shows the combined sales of the firm if it accepts project A. If the Property Management Corporation accepts no new projects, it will have sales of $10, 000,000. If it accepts project A, sales will be $15,000,000 ($10,000,000 by itself and $5,000,000 contributed by A). If it accepts B and rejects A, the combined sales will be $50,000,000 ($40,000,000 of which will be contributed by B).

CALCULATING THE FINANCING CHARGES

For a firm to invest in new major projects, it must have the capital available. The method it uses to raise funds may or may not affect the calculation of earnings per share. Four major financing choices are possible:

1. *Internal Funds.* If the firm has an adequate cash flow, it may retain a large sum of funds from operations. These can be used to finance new investments. If this means is used, future EPS should rise because internal funds have no financing charge nor do they require the issuance of additional shares of stock.

2. *Debt Financing.* If a firm borrows to raise money to finance the project, it will have interest payments to make. These are shown on the income statement and will affect the EPS. If the firm earns more on the project than it pays in financing charges, EPS will increase. If it earns less, EPS will decrease.

3. *Preferred-Stock Financing.* If this method is used to raise funds, the dividends payable to preferred shareholders will affect EPS. With a 50 percent tax rate, the firm must earn at least 2 percent on the project for every 1 percent of dividends in order to increase EPS. If it makes less than this 2/1 ratio, EPS will decrease, because the firm must pay taxes on earnings before taxes before declaring dividends to preferred shareholders.

4. *Common-Stock Financing.* This method involves no additional charges for the new project, but it does mean that NIAT must be divided among a larger number of shares than previously. If the new project is not as profitable as the firm's existing projects, EPS will decrease. This drop resulting from the acceptance of less profitable projects than current is called dilution of earnings, and generally is not viewed favorably by shareholders, who expect EPS to increase. If the

new project is more profitable than existing operations, EPS will increase.

CALCULATING FUTURE MARKET PRICE

Once all the financing charges are calculated, the income statement is completed down to the NIAT or earnings available to the common shareholder (EACS) if the firm has preferred stock. The NIAT or EACS is then divided by the shares outstanding to get future EPS. This is multiplied by the normal P/E ratio and the expected future market price is obtained. Needless to say, the firm will normally prefer the projects and financing method that offer the highest future value to the firm.

OTHER FACTORS RELATED TO FUTURE EPS

It should be noted that the firm does not limit its decision solely to the future EPS, since such factors as the following will affect future market price:

1. *Risk from High Levels of Debt.* Borrowing is less costly than preferred-stock financing and avoids the dilution of earnings associated with common-stock financing. But debt involves more risk than equity financing. If interest payments are not made, the firm may face unpleasant consequences, including bankruptcy. The market value of the stock will drop if the firm makes excessive use of debt funds and incurs a high level of risk as a result.

2. *Growth.* The future-EPS technique makes a projection only 1 year into the future. Long-term growth will be a different factor than next year's earnings, and the expected growth characteristics of a proposal will affect the firm's future market value aside from the likely profits.

3. *Difficulties in Implementing Proposals.* In some cases, a firm will not want to accept a profitable project that may cause complications for its other operations. The proposal may be highly complicated and may require extensive time from key operating personnel, time that will be taken from other areas. Or the project may cause the firm to receive adverse publicity or to experience other difficulties that make it undesirable. These difficulties can affect the market price of the firm's stock and will influence acceptance of a project.

4. *Risk from Uncertain Ventures or Unstable Returns.* Any proposal contains the risk that the firm will be unable to achieve the projected returns. This risk may arise from changes in the general level of economic activity, the entry of strong competitors into a firm's primary market, or other factors. The degree of business risk and the expected stability of returns are factors which affect the decision to accept or reject proposals.

PROPERTY MANAGEMENT CORPORATION— (A SOLVED CASE USING FUTURE EPS)

To illustrate the calculation of future earnings per share and future market price, we shall consider the situation of Property Management Corporation (PMC). This firm forecasts sales next year of $10,000,000 and an EBIT of $4,600,000. It currently has $10,000,000 in debt at 6 percent interest. It has 1,000,000 shares of outstanding common stock and is in an industry with a 12/1 normal P/E ratio. The firm is considering investing in a new real estate venture tentatively identified in the corporate planning department as project A. This project will generate sales of $5,000,000 next year and will produce an EBIT of $4,000,000. To invest in this project, the firm must raise $10,000,000. PMC is also considering project B, a larger and more comprehensive activity that will generate sales of $40,000,000 and an EBIT of $6,000,000. The cost of project B is $50,000,000. Both projects A and B will continue to generate sales well into the future.

Property Management Corporation can raise funds several ways. Bonds can be floated at a cost of 5 percent. Preferred stock can be sold with a 4 percent dividend. Common stock can be sold to yield $20 per share. In each case, the cost includes the commissions paid to the investment banker; the commissions need not be included in the calculations.

TABLE C5-1. Property Management Corporation Example of the Calculation of Future Earnings per Share and Future Market Price.

	PMC	PMC + A			PMC + B		
	Alone	Debt 5%	P.S. 4%	C.S.	Debt 5%	P.S. 4%	C.S.
Est. sales next yr.	10,000	15,000	15,000	15,000	50,000	50,000	50,000
Est. EBIT next yr.	4,600	8,600	8,600	8,600	10,600	10,600	10,600
Current debt (6%)	10,000	10,000	10,000	10,000	10,000	10,000	10,000
Current interest	600	600	600	600	600	600	600
New debt (5%)	0	10,000	0	0	50,000	0	0
New interest	0	500	0	0	2,500	0	0
EBT	4,000	7,500	8,000	8,000	7,500	10,000	10,000
NIAT	2,000	3,750	4,000	4,000	3,750	5,000	5,000
Current pref. stock	0	0	0	0	0	0	0
New pref. stock 4% div.	0	0	10,000	0	0	50,000	0
Pref. stock dividend	0	0	400	0	0	2,000	0
Earn. avail. comm. share	2,000	3,750	3,600	4,000	3,750	3,000	5,000
Current common stock	1,000	1,000	1,000	1,000	1,000	1,000	1,000
New C.S. $20 share	0	0	0	500	0	0	2,500
Total common stock	1,000	1,000	1,000	1,500	1,000	1,000	3,500
Earnings per share	$2	$3.75	$3.60	$2.67	$3.75	$3	$1.43
Normal P/E ratio	12/1	12/1	12/1	12/1	12/1	12/1	12/1
Approx. mkt. price	$24	$45	$43	$32	$45	$36	$17

(all data in 000s except EPS and market price)

Table C5-1 shows the calculation of future earnings per share and market price. The table reveals significant differences in the kind of financing used for each project. The borrowing alternatives produce a forecasted $3.75 future EPS for each project when combined with PMC's existing operations. The preferred-stock financing will give $3.60 with project A and $3 with B. The common stock is least attractive, but is an improvement upon not accepting project A.

The financial manager may conclude that both projects offer high prospects for profits. Still, borrowing $50,000,000 to finance project B would involve considerable risk for the firm. Borrowing $10,000,000 for A involves less risk. The large growth in sales with B is also appealing. The manager may want to recommend mixed financing—some debt and some equity—to reduce the risk but allow the firm to gain the profits from both projects.

C 6. GRAHAM AND DODD APPROACHES TO COMMON STOCK VALUE

Graham and Dodd in the 1930s developed some of the lasting practical techniques for the valuation of common stock. Graham and Dodd specialized in the determination of fundamental or intrinsic value. If we have some idea of the real value of a firm's stock, we can begin to deal with the problems of acquiring it, holding it, or disposing of it. Without a benchmark of fundamental value, these decisions are difficult to make.

In Security Analysis, *Graham and Dodd developed a number of capitalization approaches to determine intrinsic value. Following are two definitions of the term capitalize: 1. To calculate the present value of future returns from a business; 2. To convert future earnings, dividends, and/or growth into one sum equivalent to the firm's present value.*

Capitalization techniques are methods of determining intrinsic value by converting a firm's earnings, dividends, and/or growth rate into a present value. This section identifies a number of formulas which employ capitalization techniques.*

CAPITALIZATION OF EARNINGS

The **capitalization-of-earnings** method of stock valuation is the most important single technique used by investors and analysts to calculate intrinsic value. It is based simply on a calculation using earnings per share and a price-earnings ratio. The technique may be used to calculate today's intrinsic value or it may be used to determine a future intrinsic value (what will be the present value at a future moment in time). To capitalize earnings, we simply multiply earnings per share times a normal or expected price-earnings ratio. Four variations of the formula are shown in Figure C6-1.

In Figure C6-1, the analyst would be building upon different assumptions to consider possible changes in the stock's intrinsic value. What would happen if earnings stabilized? Figure C6-1c shows future intrinsic value with stable earnings. What happens if the normal P/E ratio changes? Figures C6-1b and c handle this kind of change.

---

* **SOURCE:** Benjamin Graham, D.L. Dodd, and S. Cottle, *Security Analysis* (New York: McGraw-Hill Book Company, 1962).

(a) Intrinsic Value Today	(b) Intrinsic Value in Future
current normal P/E x current EPS	future normal P/E x future EPS
(c) Future Intrinsic Value If EPS Does Not Increase (zero growth)	(d) Future Intrinsic Value If Normal P/E Does Not Change
future normal P/E x current EPS	current normal P/E x future EPS

Figure C6-1. Four Methods of Using the Capitalization-of-Earnings Formula.

An alternative method of capitalizing earnings is to divide a capitalization rate (the reciprocal of the P/E ratio) into the earnings per share. A normal P/E ratio of 12/1 means that the market demands a rate of return of 1/12 or 8.33 percent. For a stock with $2 EPS, the intrinsic value would be the same for each method of calculating it:

$$\text{intrinsic value} = \frac{\text{EPS}}{\text{capitalization rate}} = \frac{\$2}{.0833} = \underline{\underline{\$24}}$$

$$\text{intrinsic value} = (\text{EPS})(\text{P/E}) = (2)(12) = \underline{\underline{\$24}}$$

EXAMPLE: A firm presently has $2 EPS but expects $2.50 EPS in 3 years. A normal P/E multiple is 15/1. What is the current intrinsic value and what will be the future value if the P/E multiple does not change? if the normal P/E rises to 20/1? ANSWER: $30 currently ($2 × 15). $37.50 in 3 years with same P/E ($2.50 × 15). $50 in 3 years with new P/E ($2.50 × 20).

CAPITALIZATION OF DIVIDENDS

The **capitalization-of-dividends** method of stock valuation is similar to the capitalization of earnings. This formula recognizes that dividends are the major source of income to shareholders of stock in mature corporations. The calculation makes use of dividends per share and either (1) a dividends capitalization rate, or (2) a **normal price-dividends (P/D) ratio,** as follows:

$$\text{intrinsic value} = \frac{\text{dividends/share}}{\text{dividend capitalization rate}}$$

$$\text{intrinsic value} = (\text{dividends/share})(\text{normal P/D ratio})$$

The appropriate normal P/D ratio will be larger than the normal P/E ratio in the capitalization-of-earnings formula. The appropriate ratio will depend on what we consider to be the normal dividend payout and the normal P/E ratio. For mature corporations, a **normal dividend payout** is the payout expected by the stockholders and investing public so they will purchase and hold the stock. If the actual payout is higher than normal, the stock rises in value because income-conscious investors will purchase it for the dividends. If the actual payout is lower than normal, these same investors will seek other stocks.

The formula for the normal P/D ratio is

$$\text{normal P/D ratio} = \frac{\text{normal P/E ratio}}{\text{normal dividend payout}}$$

The capitalization-of-earnings and capitalization-of-dividends formulas are set up to give the same intrinsic value if the firm's actual and normal dividend payouts are identical. A higher actual payout than the norm raises the value using the dividend formula but does not affect the earnings formula value. The reverse is true for a lower actual payout than the norm. This relationship is expressed in Figure C6-2.

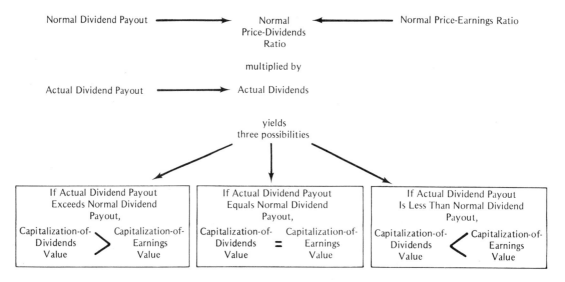

Figure C6-2. *Comparing the Capitalization-of-Earnings and Capitalization-of-Dividends Methods of Determining Intrinsic Value.*

Table C6-1 gives an example of the effect explained in Figure C6-2. It compares the value of a firm using the capitalization-of-earnings formula and makes three different assumptions on actual dividend payout. Note the intrinsic value yielded by capitalization of earnings and capitalization of dividends is the same only when the actual and normal dividend payouts are identical.

Capitalization of dividends is useful as a supplemental indicator of value. It can be used with present or future dividends, similar to the uses of earnings in Figure C6-1. Its major shortcoming is that it cannot handle firms that do not pay cash dividends or that pay very small dividends. If these firms are retaining their earnings for future growth or some other valid reason, the value from capitalization of dividends will be too low. As a general rule, capitalization of dividends is useful only when a firm consistently pays out 40 percent or more of its net income after taxes as dividends.

TABLE C6-1. Comparing Intrinsic Values at Different Dividend Payouts.

Problem: A firm has EPS of $3, a normal dividend payout of 50%, and a normal P/E ratio of 10/1. The firm is considering a 40%, 50%, or 60% dividend payout. What is its intrinsic value using capitalization of earnings and capitalization of dividends at each dividend payout?

Value Using Capitalization of Earnings	Value with 40% Actual and 50% Normal Dividend Payout	Value with 50% Actual and 50% Normal Dividend Payout	Value with 60% Actual and 50% Normal Dividend Payout
(P/E)(EPS)	(P/D[a])(dividends/share)	(P/D[a])(dividends/share)	(P/D[a])(dividends/share)
10/1 × $3 = $30	20/1 × $1.20 = $24	20/1 × $1.50 = $30	20/1 × $1.80 = $36

[a] The normal P/D ratio is 10/1 ÷ 50% normal dividend payout = 20/1.

CAPITALIZATION OF EARNINGS AND DIVIDENDS

Benjamin Graham and David Dodd, two pioneers of security analysis, have suggested an intrinsic-value approach that capitalizes both earnings and dividends in a single formula. The formula multiplies the dividends and a portion of the earnings by the normal price-earnings ratio as follows:

$$\text{intrinsic value} = P/E_{norm} \left(\text{dividends/share} + \frac{1}{3} \text{ EPS}\right)$$

If a firm is in an industry with a normal P/E multiple of 20/1, has dividends per share of $.50, and EPS of $1, the value is $(20/1)(\$.50 + 1/3 \times 1)$ or $(20)(\$.83) = \$16.60$.

Graham and Dodd apply the formula to only a certain category of stocks —those considered below-average compared to other available securities. For these stocks, the assumption is made that below-average firms should pay out two-thirds of their earnings as dividends. If this were done, the dividends per share plus one-third earnings per share would be equal to earnings per share by itself. Thus, when a firm has a dividend payout of two-thirds, the capitalization-of-earnings and the capitalization-of-earnings-and-dividends formulas will yield the same intrinsic value for the firm.

To apply the Graham and Dodd model to a wide range of mature companies, the financial analyst can modify the formula for each situation. For example, if the analyst believes that a firm should pay out one-half of its earnings as dividends, the formula would be rewritten:

$$\text{intrinsic value} = \text{P/E}_{norm}(\text{dividends/share} + \tfrac{1}{2}\text{ EPS})$$

This formula would be applicable to stocks in the 50 percent normal dividend payout category. For stocks that would have a normal 40 percent payout, the formula would include .60 $\times$ EPS. If the normal payout were 75 percent, the formula would have .25 $\times$ EPS. As you can see, the EPS factor is calculated by subtracting the percentage of payout from 100 percent.

At the present time, a dividend payout of 50 percent is widely accepted as a norm for large corporations. Table C6-2 shows how the intrinsic value of a security would be affected at different dividend payouts with a 50 percent normal payout.

Table C6-2 shows that the dividend payout and assumptions of the amount of the normal dividend payout will both affect the value of the firm's stock. As the dividends increase, the intrinsic value increases. Or, if the normal dividend payout was greater or less than 50 percent, the values would have been different.

The capitalization-of-earnings-and-dividends model is useful in conjunction with other estimates of intrinsic value. It correctly reflects the fact that earnings and dividends are both elements in determining the intrinsic value of mature corporations. Its major weakness is that it cannot handle intrinsic value at high dividend payouts. Table C6-2 gives the impression that a 100 percent dividend payout produces a higher intrinsic value than the normal 50 percent payout. If this is true, it is only for the short run. The reason for the 50 percent norm is that we expect the firm to retain one half its earnings to finance its operations. A 100 percent payout when only 50 percent is expected should lower intrinsic value. The correct relationship between intrinsic value and earnings and dividends is given in Figure C6-3.

TABLE C6-2. Intrinsic Value from Capitalization of Earnings and Dividends at Different Dividend Payouts.

EPS = \$3	*P/E$_{norm}$= 15/1*	*Dividend Payout$_{norm}$= 50%*
Dividend Payout(%)	*Dividends/Share (\$)*	*Intrinsic Value = (P/E)(Dividends/Share + ½ EPS)*
20	.60	(15/1)(\$.60 + 1.50) = \$31.50
33	1.00	(15/1)(\$1.00 + 1.50) = \$37.50
50	1.50	(15/1)(\$1.50 + 1.50) = \$45.00[a]
67	2.00	(15/1)(\$2.00 + 1.50) = \$52.50
100	3.00	(15/1)(\$3.00 + 1.50) = \$67.50

[a] Value yielded by the capitalization-of-earnings method.

EXAMPLE: An analyst believes that a firm should pay out 60 percent of its earnings as dividends. What is the formula this analyst will use for capitalizing earnings and dividends?
ANSWER: (P/E)(dividends/share + 40% EPS).

EXAMPLE: An analyst believes that a firm should pay out 25 percent of its earnings as dividends. The firm under consideration is in an industry with a 17/1 P/E ratio. The firm has a $1.20 EPS and a dividend payout of 60 percent. What is the intrinsic value using capitalization of earnings and dividends?
ANSWER: $27.54. The formula is (P/E)(dividends/share + 75% EPS) = (17)(.72 + .90) = $27.54.

(a) Earnings: as EPS increases, so does intrinsic value, indefinitely

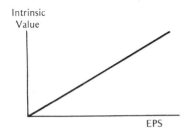

(b) Dividend Payout: intrinsic value rises to some point just above normal dividend payout, then decreases.

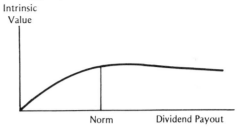

Figure C6-3. *Relationship Between Intrinsic Value and Earnings and Dividends.*

CAPITALIZATION OF GROWTH RATE

The **capitalization-of-growth-rate** method is used to give value to a growth factor in a firm's activities. Graham and Dodd proposed that a stock's intrinsic value can incorporate a growth factor by using the formula

$$\text{intrinsic value} = EPS_7(8.5 + 2G)$$

where EPS_7 = average estimated EPS for the next 7 years[1]

G = average annual growth rate expected over the next 7 years for EPS where G is expressed without a percent (example: 4% becomes 4)

8.5 = normal P/E ratio for a firm with a zero growth rate

---

[1]Graham and Dodd use the fourth year as the average of 7 years. Thus, EPS_7 may be calculated by multiplying current EPS times 1 plus a growth factor compounded to the fourth year, or $(EPS_{curr})(1 + G)^4$.

As an example of the use of this formula, a firm with a $3 current EPS and a 3 percent growth rate would have an EPS_7 of $(\$3)(1 + .03)^4 = \$3.38$ and an intrinsic value of $\$3.38[8.5 + (2)(3)] = \$49.00$.

The Graham and Dodd growth model correctly recognizes that a firm has some value in the absence of growth, specifically a value equal to an 8.5 P/E multiple, which is approximately a 12 percent capitalization rate. If the firm does not grow, but is yielding 12 percent, this will be acceptable to investors. At zero growth, the formula becomes $(EPS_{curr})(8.5 + 0)$, which is the same as $(EPS)(P/E_{norm})$ where 8.5 is the norm. At zero growth, the current EPS is also the average for the next 7 years.

This model for growth rate presents certain problems to the analyst:

1. Although it is theoretically logical at the lower growth rates, it results in extremely high P/E multiples when the growth rate exceeds 15 to 20%.
2. It requires an estimate of the average EPS for the next 7 years. This is a difficult estimate to make.
3. Growth is measured in terms of earnings. In most cases, it is easier to forecast growth in terms of a firm's sales.
4. The 8.5 P/E factor is slightly low in most markets. If a firm is not growing, it must be paying out approximately 100 percent of its earnings as dividends. A 10 percent dividend yield, or 10/1 P/E factor, is more realistic in most cases than the 8.5 factor.

To overcome some of these weaknesses and to provide an alternative model for capitalizing growth rate, we can modify the formula to the following:

$$\text{intrinsic value} = EPS_{curr}(10 + 1.5G)$$

where EPS_{curr} = current earnings per share
  G = growth rate in sales for the next 3 to 5 years (omit %)
  10 = the normal P/E ratio at zero growth rate

This model makes use of current EPS instead of an average of future EPS, a more realistic P/E norm, and sales growth over the near future (3 to 5 years). If this model does not seem to reflect current market conditions, the analyst can devise still another formula to examine the effect of a growth factor on the intrinsic value of a stock.

EXAMPLE: An analyst is viewing a stock with EPS of $4 this year, a 5 percent per year growth in EPS is forecasted for the next 7 years, and a 6 percent growth rate of sales for the next 5 years. What is the intrinsic value of the stock using the two growth models?

ANSWER: $89.90 using Graham and Dodd. $EPS_7 = (\$4)(1.05)^4 = \$4.86$. The formula is $\$4.86(8.5 + 2 \times 5) = \$4.86(18.5) = \$89.90$. $76 using the modified formula. The calculation is $\$4(1 + 1.5 \times 6) = \$4(19) = \$76$.

CAPITALIZATION TECHNIQUES—A SOLVED PROBLEM

The determination of a stock's intrinsic value should include a variety of approaches. The analyst attempts to gain a complete picture of the different components of value: earnings, dividends, and growth. With the aid of a small computer, it is possible to develop the basic data, enter it into the computer, and receive a table of intrinsic values by each of the different methods. Figure C6-4 is an example of evaluating a stock using all the capitalization techniques described previously.

From the values in Figure C6-4, the analyst might conclude that the stock had a current intrinsic value of $30 to $35 with an upward tendency due to the higher values using the growth factor methods. Projecting ahead, the intrinsic value in 4 years should be near $40, with a higher value if the growth is continuing. No attempt is made to capitalize the growth rate to get a value in 4 years.

The final step in the valuation process is to compare the intrinsic value with the current market price, or, in the case of an acquisition, the possible offering price. If the market price or asking price were $26, the stock would appear to be a good buy. If it were $35, the stock would be fairly priced in relation to its intrinsic value. If it were $48, it would be overpriced.

Input Data	1974	1975	1976	1977	1978	1979	1980	1981	1982
Earnings per share $	3.00	3.10	3.25	3.40	3.60	3.85	4.15	4.40	4.70

Growth rate of sales	8%	Growth rate of EPS	5%
Actual Dividend payout	50%	Normal P/E ratio	12/1
Normal P/D multiple	20/1	Normal dividend payout	60%

1. Capitalization of Earnings

    a. Current value   = EPS x P/E = $3 x 12/1 = $36

    b. Value in 4 years = EPS_4 x P/E = $3.60 x 12/1 = $43.20

2. Capitalization of Dividends

    a. Current value   = D/S x P/D = $1.50 x 20/1 = $30

    b. Value in 4 years = $D/S_{yr\,4}$ x P/D = $1.80 x 20/1 = $36

3. Capitalization of Earnings and Dividends

    a. Current value = P/E(D/S + 40% EPS) = 12(1.50 + .40 x $3) = 12 x 2.70 = $32.40

    b. Value in 4 years = 12(1.80 + .40 x 3.60) = 12 x 3.24 = $38.88

Figure C6-4. *Solved Problem Using Capitalization Techniques.*

4. Capitalization of Growth Rate

   a. Graham and Dodd. Value = $EPS_7 (8.5 + 2G) = \$3.68(8.5 + 2 \times 5) = \$3.68 \times 18.5 = \$68.08$

   b. Modified. Value = $EPS(10 + 1.5G) = \$3(10 + 1.5 \times 8) = (\$3)(22) = \$66.00$

5. Table of Values Generated By Using the Capitalization Techniques

	Current Value	Value in 4 Years
a. Capitalization of earnings	$36	$43
b. Capitalization of dividends	$30	$36
c. Capitalization of earnings and dividends	$32	$39
d. Capitalization of growth rate	$68	
Growth modified	$66	

Note: All values rounded to nearest dollar to avoid the appearance of excessive accuracy with values to nearest cent.

Figure C6-4. *continued*

C 7. GORDON ON COMMON STOCK VALUE

A mathematical model must deal with the ways that investors receive returns from the purchase of common stock. Basically, there are three methods of estimating the return:

1. Use Future Earnings Per Share. A model can estimate the future EPS from a common-stock investment and assume that the stockholders will eventually claim the earnings. This is done in the capitalization-of-earnings method of valuation (see "Graham and Dodd Approaches to Common Stock Value");

2. Use Future Dividends Per Share. A model can assume that only the future dividends will be a real return to the investor. If the investor plans to hold the stock indefinitely, the level of dividends represents the real value;

3. Use Future Dividends Plus a Final Selling Price. With this approach, the value of the stock is a combination of the present value of future dividends plus any premium or loss that will occur when the stock is sold at some future date.

The dividend-growth model developed in "The Investment, Financing and Valuation of the Corporation" by Myron J. Gordon assumes that future dividends per share determine the intrinsic value of a common stock. This section examines that model.*

FACTORS INCORPORATED IN THE GORDON MODEL

A number of factors have been considered by Gordon to improve upon the limitations and weaknesses of capitalization techniques. Some of these are:

1. *Restriction of the Shareholder's Return to a Single Variable.* In many capitalization formulas, the return to the shareholder involves a combination of earnings and dividends linked through the dividend payout. In the Gordon model, the income factor is limited to the current dividend. Earnings retained in the firm are part of the growth factor that will operate to increase the current dividend, but only the dividend and its expected increases are considered as a return.

---

* **SOURCE:** Myron J. Gordon, *The Investment, Financing and Valuation of the Corporation* (Homewood, Ill: Richard D. Irwin, Inc., 1962).

2. *Inclusion of Two Capitalization Rates.* The dividend-growth model makes use of two capitalization rates:

    a. *Normal Capitalization Rate* (CR_{norm}). The market will demand a certain rate of return from the investment in a firm's common stock. This may be expressed by a normal reciprocal of the P/E ratio. If the firm is not able to achieve such a return at the existing market price, shareholders will sell their shares, thus depressing the market price and raising the rate of return. The normal capitalization rate is the reciprocal of the normal P/E multiple for a firm.

    b. *Actual Capitalization Rate* (CR_{act}). The firm's actual capitalization rate is the relationship of its actual EPS to the market price of its stock. This is an important factor influencing growth. A firm with higher profits will have more funds to retain and hence more money to finance growth than will a firm with lower profits. The actual capitalization rate is an important element in a growth factor.

3. *Inclusion of a Growth Factor.* In common-stock valuation, we are primarily concerned with a firm's growth financed from retained earnings. We eliminate the following sources of funds for growth for the reasons indicated:

    a. *Use of Debt or Other Limited-Return Securities.* It is true that a firm may be able to borrow and use the financial leverage to increase the growth rate of its dividends. But these securities will increase the risk that the firm will not be able to declare dividends on its common stock. The increased risk is considered an offsetting factor to the increased growth, with the result being no increase in the value of the common stock. Only the most complicated valuation models attempt to deal with this factor.

    b. *Floating Additional Common Stock.* When a firm issues common stock to finance growth, the benefits of growing must be shared with the new shareholders. This means that the benefits of growth will not increase the growth rate of dividends to the existing shareholders. The additional shares will not increase the value of the firm, so this source of growth can be omitted.

The important growth factor to an intrinsic-value model is the increases in the current dividend because the firm retains a portion of its after-tax profits and uses the funds to finance growth. One useful way to express this growth factor is to combine the actual capitalization rate with the percentage of retained earnings (RE) as follows:

$$\text{growth factor} = (CR_{act})(\%\ RE)$$

Table C7-1 shows how growth is affected by changes in the actual capitalization rate or in the percentage of retained earnings.

TABLE C7-1. Growth Factor in the Dividend-Growth-Model.

Capitalization Rate, Actual		Retained Earnings, Percent	Amount of Growth	Explanation
0		0	None	No profits to retain.
5%		0	None	All profits paid out as dividends.
5%	×	50%	= 2.5%	
10%	×	50%	= 5.0%	Growth increases owing to higher profits.
10%	×	60%	= 6.0%	Growth increases owing to higher level of retained earnings.

Dividend-Growth Model

Building on the features just discussed, Gordon and others developed and refined a mathematically rigorous model that assumes that future dividends are the sole determinant of the intrinsic value of common stock. The model may be written:

$$\text{intrinsic value} = \frac{\text{Div}_{curr}}{\text{CR}_{norm} - (\text{CR}_{act})(\% \text{ RE})}$$

where Div_{curr} = current dividend in dollars (annual basis)
CR_{norm} = capitalization rate demanded by the market for a stock of this type
CR_{act} = actual capitalization rate based on the firm's current earnings (provided they are relatively normal) and current market price
$\% \text{ RE}$ = percentage of future earnings the corporation is likely to retain

The dividend-growth model shows the value of a share of stock as the stock's current dividend divided by the amount that the demanded profit exceeds the rate of growth in the dividend. Stated graphically, the model shows value as

$$\text{intrinsic value} = \frac{\text{current dividend}}{\text{demanded after-tax profit} > \text{dividend growth}}$$

EXAMPLE: Multiplying the actual capitalization rate by the percentage of retained earnings gives the growth rate in dividends per share, assuming no change in dividend payout. If a firm has a 10 percent actual capitalization rate, a dividend payout of 40 percent, and declares a $1 dividend in 1974, what is the growth rate? the likely stream of dividends through 1978?

ANSWER: The firm is retaining 60 percent of the 10 percent after-tax profits for a 6 percent growth rate. The stream of dividend payments at a 6 percent growth rate is as follows:

Year	1974	1975	1976	1977	1978
Dividend Factor		1.06	$(1.06)^2$	$(1.06)^3$	$(1.06)^4$
Dividend	$1.00	$1.06	$1.12	$1.19	$1.26

EXAMPLE: If the firm in the preceding example is in an industry with a 12 percent normal capitalization rate, what is the intrinsic value using the dividend-growth formula?

ANSWER: $16.67. The formula is $1 ÷ [12% − (10%)(60%)] = $1/.06 = $16.67.

ANALYZING THE DIVIDEND-GROWTH MODEL

To see the utility of the dividend-growth model, we must examine the effect of changing the dividend payout under different situations with respect to the capitalization rates. To do this, consider a company with an EPS of $2 and an actual capitalization rate of 10 percent. There are three possible situations:

1. *Normal Capitalization Rate Less Than Actual Capitalization Rate.* If this is the case, the stockholder is gaining more earnings by investing in the company than he expects as a norm. For example, he may be expecting an 8 percent rate and the firm is actually achieving 10 percent. The shareholder would want the firm to retain the earnings and achieve a 10 percent return on them. If dividends are paid, the investor can probably only earn 8 percent or so from similar investments. Thus, we would expect that raising the dividend payout would lower the intrinsic value, since it lowers the growth rate of a highly profitable firm. Table C7-2 shows that intrinsic value drops from $60 at a 30 percent dividend payout to $25 at 100 percent payout, confirming our expectation.

2. *Normal CapitalizationRate Equal to Actual Capitalization Rate.* In this case, the firm is doing about as well as expected and the shareholder probably does not care about the level of dividends. If they are declared, they will be reinvested in the firm or in a similar firm. We would expect that intrinsic value would be unaffected by the level of dividend payouts. Table C7-2 shows an intrinsic value of $20 at all payouts when the firm earns what is expected as a norm.

3. *Normal Capitalization Rate More Than Actual Capitalization Rate.* In this case the firm is not doing as well as expected. Overall, the intrinsic value will be less than a firm that is doing as well as expected. But we would expect the intrinsic value to rise if the firm increased its dividend payout, since the shareholders would like to have cash to invest at a higher return elsewhere. Table C7-2 shows that the intrinsic value increases from $12 to $16.67 when the dividend payout is raised from 30 to 100 percent.

The validity of the dividend-growth model is supported by the data in Table C7-2. Changing the dividend payout has different results, depending upon the relationship between the normal and actual capitalization rates. A firm that is doing better than the norm has a higher intrinsic value than a firm doing worse. The dividend-growth model thus provides an additional measure of the intrinsic value of common stock and may be used to supplement other valuation methods.

TABLE C7-2. Comparing Intrinsic Value with the Dividend-Growth Model Under Different Capitalization Rates and Dividend Payouts.

NOTE: All data are for a firm with $2 EPS and a 10 percent actual capitalization rate.

	Capitalization Rate Normal		
	8%	10%	12%
30% Dividend Payout	$\dfrac{\$.60}{8\% - (10\% \times 70\%)} = \$60.00$	$\dfrac{\$.60}{10\% - (10\% \times 70\%)} = \$20.00$	$\dfrac{\$.60}{12\% - (10\% \times 70\%)} = \$12.00$
50% Dividend Payout	$\dfrac{\$1.00}{8\% - (10\% \times 50\%)} = \$33.33$	$\dfrac{\$1.00}{10\% - (10\% \times 50\%)} = \$20.00$	$\dfrac{\$1.00}{12\% - (10\% \times 50\%)} = \$14.29$
70% Dividend Payout	$\dfrac{\$1.40}{8\% - (10\% \times 30\%)} = \$28.00$	$\dfrac{\$1.40}{10\% - (10\% \times 30\%)} = \$20.00$	$\dfrac{\$1.40}{12\% - (10\% \times 30\%)} = \$15.56$
100% Dividend Payout	$\dfrac{\$2.00}{8\% - (10\% \times 0\%)} = \$25.00$	$\dfrac{\$2.00}{10\% - (10\% \times 0\%)} = \$20.00$	$\dfrac{\$2.00}{12\% - (10\% \times 0\%)} = \$16.67$

C 8. WALTER AND GORDON ON DIVIDEND DECISIONS

Although the dividend decision lends itself to many qualitative considerations, it is possible to use mathematical tools to assist in decision making. In this section we will work with the Gordon model (see "Gordon on Common Stock Value") and the Walter model (see "Dividend Policies and Common Stock Price") to examine how the level of dividends affects the value of the firm's common stock.*

DIVIDEND GROWTH MODEL

The dividend growth model of Myron Gordon is reviewed in detail in "Gordon on Common Stock Value." It can be used to measure the effect of different dividend policies on the intrinsic value of a firm's common stock. When used in this way, it would be written:

$$\text{Value} = \frac{\text{Div}_{\text{curr}}}{\text{CR}_{\text{norm}} - (\text{CR}_{\text{act}})(\%\text{RE})}$$

where Div_{curr} = the current dividend declared by the firm

CR_{norm} = capitalization rate demanded by the market for a stock of this type

CR_{act} = actual capitalization rate based on the firm's current earnings (provided they are relatively normal) and current market price

$\%\text{RE}$ = percentage of future earnings the corporation is likely to retain

WALTER FORMULA

The Walter formula has virtually the same effect as the Gordon formula. It measures the effect of dividends on common stock value by using a comparison of the actual and normal capitalization rates. The formula may be expressed as follows:

---

* **SOURCE:** James Walter, "Dividend Policies and Common Stock Price," *Journal of Finance,* March, 1956. Myron J. Gordon, *The Investment, Financing and Valuation of the Corporation* (Homewood, Ill: Richard D. Irwin, Inc., 1962).

$$\text{Value} = \frac{\text{Div}_{\text{curr}} + \left(\dfrac{\text{CR}_{\text{act}}}{\text{CR}_{\text{norm}}} \right) (\$ \text{ RE})}{\text{CR}_{\text{norm}}}$$

where CR_{act} & CR_{norm} = actual and normal capitalization rates

$\quad\quad\quad \text{Div}_{\text{curr}}$ = current dividend in dollars per share

$\quad\quad\quad \$ \text{ RE}$ = retained earnings in dollars per share

Analyzing the Walter Formula

In order to understand the workings of the Walter formula, we might begin with the formula for capitalizing earnings. This formula divides the earnings per share by the normal capitalization rate. Another way to write the formula is to divide earnings per share into the dividend and retained earnings. These two formulas are given below.

$$\text{Value} = \frac{\text{EPS}}{\text{CR}_{\text{norm}}} \quad\quad\quad \text{Value} = \frac{\text{Div}_{\text{curr}} + \$\text{RE}}{\text{CR}_{\text{norm}}}$$

The Walter formula gives an added or reduced weight to the retained earnings portion of the capitalization of earnings formula. The factor $\text{CR}_{\text{act}}/\text{CR}_{\text{norm}}$ is placed in front of retained earnings to change its weighted value under three different situations as follows:

1. *CR_{act}/CR_{norm} Greater Than 1.* This factor is greater than 1 when the firm is earning more than the norm. In this situation, we want the firm to retain its earnings since our alternative investments offer a lower return than the firm is able to secure. Each dollar of retained earnings will have a higher weighting in the Walter formula than a comparable dollar of dividends. Thus, the more the firm retains, the higher the value of the firm.

EXAMPLE: A firm has $5 EPS and pays a $2 dividend. Its actual capitalization rate is 15 percent and its normal capitalization rate is 10 percent. What is the value of the firm using the capitalization-of-earnings and Walter formula methods?
ANSWER: Since it is more profitable than the norm, the higher weight of the retained earnings will result in greater value with the Walter formula than with the capitalization-of-earnings formula. The two calculations are:

Capitalization of Earnings	The Walter Formula
Value = $5/10% = $50	$\text{Value} = \dfrac{\$2 + [15\%/10\%]\,[\$3]}{10\%} = \$65$

2. CR_{act}/CR_{norm} *Equals 1.* The factor equals 1 when the actual and normal capitalization rates are identical. In this case, the retained earnings has the same weighted value as dividends and the Walter formula gives the same value as the capitalization-of-earnings formula.

3. CR_{act}/CR_{norm} *Less Than 1.* The factor is less than 1 when the firm is earning less than the norm. In this situation, we want the firm to declare dividends so we can invest the dividends in more profitable companies. Each dollar of retained earnings will have a lower weighting than dividends. Thus, the less the firm retains, the higher its value.

An example of the three different situations and the effect of different dividend payouts on value is given in Table C8-1.

Table C8-1. Comparing Value with the Walter Formula Under Different Capitalization Rates and Dividend Payouts.

Note: All data for a firm with a $2 EPS and 10% normal capitalization rate.

CR_{act}	Cap. of Earnings	Dividend Payout 20%	Dividend Payout 50%	Dividend Payout 80%
5%	$\dfrac{\$2}{10\%}$ = $20	$\dfrac{.40 + \left(\dfrac{05}{10}\right)(1.60)}{10\%}$ = $12	$\dfrac{1.00 + \left(\dfrac{05}{10}\right)(1.00)}{10\%}$ = $15	$\dfrac{1.60 + \left(\dfrac{05}{10}\right)(.40)}{10\%}$ = $18
10%	$\dfrac{\$2}{10\%}$ = $20	$\dfrac{.40 + \left(\dfrac{10}{10}\right)(1.60)}{10\%}$ = $20	$\dfrac{1.00 + \left(\dfrac{10}{10}\right)(1.00)}{10\%}$ = $20	$\dfrac{1.60 + \left(\dfrac{10}{10}\right)(.40)}{10\%}$ = $20
15%	$\dfrac{\$2}{10\%}$ = $20	$\dfrac{.40 + \left(\dfrac{15}{10}\right)(1.60)}{10\%}$ = $28	$\dfrac{1.00 + \left(\dfrac{15}{10}\right)(1.00)}{10\%}$ = $25	$\dfrac{1.60 + \left(\dfrac{15}{10}\right)(.40)}{10\%}$ = $22

Example of Using Mathematical Approaches to Dividend Decisions

As an example of the use of the dividend-growth formula and the Walter formula to assist in a dividend decision, let us consider a firm with a $4 earnings per share and a $3 current dividend. The firm is currently selling for $22 per share and thus has an actual capitalization rate of 4/22, or 18 percent. The normal capitalization rate for the industry is 12 percent. The firm has a need for cash and is considering lowering the dividend to $2 per share. What effect would this have on the value of the common stock?

Since the firm is earning more than the norm, both formulas would support lowering the dividend. The calculations are:

Dividend-Growth Model		Walter Formula	
Value with $3 Dividend	Value with $2 Dividend	Value with $3 Dividend	Value with $2 Dividend
$\dfrac{\$3}{.12 - (.18)(.25)}$	$\dfrac{\$2}{.12 - (.18)(.50)}$	$3 + \left(\dfrac{18}{12}\right)(1)$	$2 + \left(\dfrac{18}{12}\right)(2)$
$= \underline{\$40}$	$= \underline{\$67}$	$= \underline{\$37.50}$	$= \underline{\$41.67}$

Using the capitalization-of-earnings method, the value of the stock is $4/.12, or $33. Since the firm is presently selling for only $22 per share, the market may not be aware of its real value. It is not likely that the lowering of the dividend would depress the price even further. As a matter of fact, the change in dividend may draw attention to the stock and cause investor interest, which could result in a rise in stock price. The mathematical approaches to dividend decisions support the lowering of the dividend in this example.

C 9. MILLER AND MODIGLIANI ON DIVIDEND POLICY

In a complex and highly mathematical article "Dividend Policy, Growth, and the Valuation of Shares," Miller and Modigliani demonstrate the relationship between dividend and investment policy and conclude that the value of common stock is independent of the firm's dividend policy. This contrasts directly with the findings of Gordon (see Gordon on Common Stock Value, p. 255) and Walter (see Walter and Gordon on Dividend Decisions, p. 260). The Miller-Modigliani article also draws some conclusions on the role of growth rates in common stock value.

The formulas in this section are numbered to correspond to the numbering of formulas in the cited article.*

EFFECT OF DIVIDEND POLICY UNDER CERTAINTY

Miller-Modigliani begin their analysis with the assumption of perfect capital markets, rational behavior on the part of investors, and perfect certainty to preclude the possibility of default or bankruptcy. Under these circumstances, common stock is as safe and secure and its return is as predictable as the debt securities issued by a firm. Therefore, we can ignore leverage and focus in solely on the firm's cost of equity capital as follows:

$$K_e = \frac{\text{Div} + \text{Cap. gains}}{\text{CS}_{mkt}} \quad \frac{\text{Div} + (\text{CS}_{fut} - \text{CS}_{mkt})}{\text{CS}_{mkt}} \qquad (1)$$

where Div = next year's cash dividends, assuming they are representative of all future annual dividends[1]

Cap gains = likely rise in stock's total market value during next year $(\text{CS}_{fut} - \text{CS}_{mkt})$

CS_{fut} = likely market value of all common stock at the end of one year determined by multiplying the number of shares outstanding next year by the likely market price per share next year

---

* SOURCE: Merton H. Miller and Franco Modigliani, "Dividend Policy, Growth, and the Valuation of Shares," *Journal of Business,* October, 1961.

[1]All data, where possible, has been treated over a period of one year to simplify the concepts in this explanation. The analysis is applicable with present-value techniques for any future periods.

CS_{mkt} = market value of all common stock today determined by multiplying the number of shares outstanding by the current market price per share

EXAMPLE: A firm has 2,000,000 shares of common stock outstanding selling at $20 per share. The stock should rise to $22 by next year. The firm expects to declare dividends of $1,500,000 in the next year. What is the cost of equity capital (K_e)? ANSWER: 13.75 percent, as follows:

$$K_e = \frac{1,500 + (44,000 - 40,000)}{40,000} = \frac{5,500}{40,000} = 13.75 \ percent$$

To solve equation (1) for CS_{mkt}, we cross multiply and transpose,

$(K_e)(CS_{mkt}) = Div + CS_{fut} - CS_{mkt}$ or,

$(K_e)(CS_{mkt}) + CS_{mkt} = Div + CS_{fut}$ or,

$CS_{mkt}(1 + K_e) = Div + CS_{fut}$ or,

$$CS_{mkt} = \frac{1}{1 + K_e}(Div + CS_{fut}) \tag{2}$$

EXAMPLE: The cost of equity capital is 13.75 percent for a firm with 2,000,000 shares of common stock outstanding that will trade for $22 in one year. The next year's dividends will be $1,500,000. What is the current market value of the common stock? ANSWER: $40,000,000 or $20 per share.

$$CS_{mkt} = \frac{1}{1 + .1375}(1,500 + 44,000) = \frac{45,500}{1.1375} = \$40,000$$

DIVIDEND POLICY AND EXTERNAL CAPITAL

Miller and Modigliani next add a new element to the analysis. They retain the assumptions of perfect and riskless markets and hence debt is still omitted since common stock is as safe as debt. The new element is that the firm can raise new capital externally; that is, it can issue new shares of common stock. When this happens, equation (2) changes. Since

$$CS_{fut} = \frac{1}{1 + K_e}[Div + (\#Sh_{fut})(MktPr_{fut})]$$

where $\#Sh_{fut}$ = total of shares of stock outstanding at the end of one year

$MktPr_{fut}$ = market price of one share of stock next year then

$$CS_{mkt} = \frac{1}{1 + K_e} [Div + CS_{fut} - (\#Sh_{new})(MktPr_{fut})] \qquad (3)$$

where $\#Sh_{new}$ = number of new shares to be issued.

EXAMPLE: A firm has the same characteristics as the previous example but will issue 500,000 new shares at $18 net proceeds per share during the next year. The return on the investments financed with these shares will allow dividends to be raised from $1,500,000 to $2,000,000. What is the firm's K_e? its new CS_{mkt}?
ANSWER: K_e = 14 percent, as follows: The future value of common stock is

$$CS_{fut} = (2,000,000)(\$22) + (500,000)(\$22) = \$55,000,000$$

The current CS_{mkt} to use to find K_e in equation 1 should consider the existing and new shares in terms of the current market price of $20. This is true because, even though the new shares will be issued at $18, the firm's management must protect the $20 per share value of the existing common stock. At $20 each, the 2,500,000 shares that will be outstanding in the future have a CS_{mkt} of $50,000,000. Therefore, K_e is:

$$K_e = \frac{Div + (CS_{fut} - CS_{mkt})}{CS_{mkt}} = \frac{2,000 + (55,000 - 50,000)}{50,000} = 14 \; percent$$

And the value of common stock at market will then be:

$$CS_{mkt} = \frac{1}{1 + K_e} [Div + CS_{fut} - (\#Sh_{new})(MktPr_{fut})]$$

$$= \frac{1}{1.14} [2,000 + 55,000 - (500)(22)] = \frac{46,000}{1.14} = \$40,350,877$$

Therefore, the issuing of new shares helps to raise the current market price for the firm's common stock to $20.18 (40,350,877 divided by 2,000,000 shares).

TWO EFFECTS OF DIVIDEND POLICY

Equation 3 gives the value of common stock as the sum of (1) dividends, and (2) future value of common stock less any new shares times their future value. The equation focuses on the two effects of dividend policy that Miller and Modigliani are highlighting in this article, namely:

1. *Role of Dividends on Value.* Most analysts would acknowledge that raising or lowering dividends paid by a firm contributes directly to raising or lowering the value of common stock. The equation me-

chanically supports this argument. In the next section, Miller and Modigliani take exception to this role of dividends on value for a growing firm.

2. *Effect of Dividends on Growth.* The declaration and payment of dividends mean less earnings are retained to finance growth. In equation 3 the higher the level of dividends, the higher will be the level of new common stock to finance growth. In the equation, these appear to be offsetting effects. This is also covered in the next section.

HOW SHOULD THE FIRM FINANCE GROWTH?

The firm faces the choice of raising dividends and floating new shares or lowering dividends and financing with retained earnings. Miller and Modigliani argue that, in an ideal world, it does not matter. They demonstrate this by showing, first, the amount of actual outside financing will be

$$(\#Sh_{new})(MktPr_{new}) = Cap_{growth(act)} - (NIAT - Div)$$

where $MktPr_{new}$ = net proceeds per share from the issue of new common stock

$Cap_{growth(act)}$ = actual capital needed to finance growth

$(NIAT - Div)$ = net income after taxes minus dividends, or retained earnings, for next period

Once the new shares have been issued and the net proceeds have been invested, the net proceeds are no longer relevant. Instead, the future market price of the shares will determine the value of the outside financing so that

$$(\#Sh_{new})(MktPr_{fut}) = Cap_{growth(fut)} - (NIAT - Div) \qquad (4)$$

where $Cap_{growth(fut)}$ = next year's market value of the capital needed to finance this year's growth.

We begin with equation (3)

$$CS_{mkt} = \frac{1}{1 + K_e} [Div + CS_{fut} - (\#Sh_{new})(MktPr_{fut})] \qquad (3)$$

and substitute the market value of the external financing to produce

$$CS_{mkt} = \frac{1}{1 + K_e} [Div + CS_{fut} - Cap_{growth(fut)} + NIAT - Div]$$

Since the dividends cancel, the value of the common stock must be independent of the dividend policy in an ideal world and the formula is:

$$CS_{mkt} = \frac{1}{1 + K_e} [CS_{fut} - Cap_{growth(fut)} + NIAT] \qquad (5)$$

REAL-WORLD FACTORS AFFECTING DIVIDEND RELEVANCE

Although the Miller and Modigliani article does not cover them, two factors affect the concept of the relevance of dividends in real-world situations:

1. *Tax Effects.* Investors must pay personal income taxes on dividends when received and may prefer a policy of retaining earnings to finance growth. The absence of such a policy may cause investors to sell the stock and depress its market value.
2. *Net Proceeds Lower than Market Value.* When the firm must issue stock at a discount from current market value, a penalty is imposed by external financing as opposed to retaining earnings. This penalty is not reflected in our example above where we had a $22 future market price and an $18 net proceeds. If the net proceeds had been higher, fewer shares would have been needed to finance growth and the market price would have been more than $22 in the future.

EXAMPLE: Two identical firms are planning to use different approaches to financing growth. Both firms have 300,000 shares of common stock outstanding at a market price of $10 per share. Both firms have previously paid $200,000 in dividends and Firm A plans to continue this policy. Firm B, however, will skip its dividend and use the $200,000 to finance growth. Firm A plans to sell 22,222 shares of new common stock at $9 net proceeds to finance its growth. Both firms should have a value in one year of $3,500,000 based upon a capitalization of earnings method using a K_e of 10 percent. What is the current market value of each firm's common stock?
ANSWER: $3,141,000 for Firm A compared to $3,182,000 for Firm B, as follows:

$$CS_{mkt} = \frac{1}{1 + K_e} [Div + CS_{fut} - (\#Sh_{new})(MktPr_{fut})]$$

$$CS_{mkt}(A) = \frac{1}{1.10} [200 + 3,500 - (22.222)(11)] = \frac{3456}{1.10} = \$3,141 \text{ for A}$$

$$CS_{mkt}(B) = \frac{1}{1.10} \quad [0 + 3,500 - (0)(11)] = \frac{3500}{1.10} = \$3,182 \text{ for B}$$

The higher value for firm B is because of the fact that the net proceeds from the stock offering are less than the future market value of the stock. If the net proceeds were $11, the value of A's stock would be the same as for B, as follows:

$$CS_{mkt} = \frac{1}{1.10}[200 + 3,500 - (18.182)(11)] = \frac{3500}{1.10} = \$3,182$$

The lower value for firm A in the above example is true also on a per share basis for both the current and future value, as follows:

	Current Value Per Share	Future Value Per Share
Firm A, 22,222 new shares (Dividends counted in future value to shareholders)	3,141/300 = $10.47	(3,500 + 200)/322 = $11.48
Firm B, $200,000 retained to finance growth	3,182/300 = 10.61	3500/300 = 11.67

In equation 5, it does not matter whether a firm finances its growth with retained earnings or external financing when $Cap_{growth(Mkt)}$ has no penalty for the net proceeds and NIAT is added to reflect earnings. If we apply equation 5 to the firms in the example and assume a 100 percent dividend payout (Div = NIAT), we would get

Situation

$$CS_{mkt} = \frac{1}{1 + K_e}[CS_{fut} - Cap_{growth(mkt)} + NIAT] \qquad (5)$$

Firm A, net proceeds
= $9 per share

$$CS_{mkt}(A) = \frac{1}{1.10}[3,500 - 244 + 200] = \frac{3456}{1.10} = \$3,141$$

Firm A, net proceeds
= $11 per share

$$CS_{mkt}(A) = \frac{1}{1.10}[3,500 - 200 + 200] = \frac{3500}{1.10} = \$3,182$$

Firm B, dividends to
finance growth

$$CS_{mkt}(B) = \frac{1}{1.10}[3,500 - 200 + 200] = \frac{3500}{1.10} = \$3,182$$

which are identical to the results with equation 3.

WHAT DOES THE MARKET REALLY CAPITALIZE?

Miller and Modigliani are arguing that dividends are irrelevant in perfect capital markets. This raises the question of what the market actually capitalizes. Their answer is that the market capitalizes the future return on a cash or earnings basis. To demonstrate this, they rewrite equation 5 from

$$CS_{mkt} = \frac{1}{1 + K_e} [CS_{fut} - Cap_{growth(fut)} + NIAT] \tag{5}$$

to

$$CS_{mkt} = \frac{1}{1 + K_e} [CS_{fut} - (NIAT - Cap_{growth(fut)})]$$

Assume that growth is financed by retained earnings (RE) so that $Cap_{growth(mkt)}$ equals RE and we have

$$CS_{mkt} = \frac{1}{1 + K_e} [CS_{fut} + (NIAT - RE)] \tag{7}$$

Next we assume that will operate indefinitely so that CS_{fut} is replaced by an infinite stream of dividends [NIAT − RE] and we get

$$CS_{mkt} = \sum_{t=0}^{\infty} \frac{1}{1 + K_e} [Div] \tag{9}$$

where $\sum_{t=0}^{\infty}$ = sum of element following the sign (in this case, dividends) for a period from year zero to year infinity

Equation 9 assumes that the steady level of dividends is the only cash returned to the investors and, while the formula uses dividends, the market is really capitalizing return. Miller and Modigliani continue on to demonstrate that this is identical to the internal rate of return method from capital budgeting. Consider the firm to be a single project and determine the value of common stock by

$$CS_{mkt} = \sum_{t=0}^{\infty} \frac{1}{1 + K_e} [inflows - outlays] \tag{11}$$

Thus, Miller and Modigliani's answer is that the market really capitalizes return to the investor. In equation 5, the return is the sum of dividends plus increases (decreases) in stock value. In equations 9 and 11, the return is cash to the investor.

Investment Opportunities Approach

Miller and Modigliani next consider the dividend decision compared to the investment opportunities for shareholders outside the firm. Key concepts are:

1. *Normal Capitalization Rate* (CR_{norm}). This is the K_e for other investments outside the firm that have similar risk to investment in the firm's stock.

2. *Actual Capitalization Rate* (CR_{act}). This is the K_e for the firm itself. If the CR_{act} is greater than the CR_{norm}, the firm is more profitable than comparable investments and earnings should be retained. If the reverse is true, earnings should be paid out as dividends.

3. *Walter Formula.* Cited at the start of this section, the Walter Formula relates dividends and retained earnings to the actual and normal capitalization rates and gives a value of common stock. The formula is

$$CS_{mkt} = \frac{Div + \dfrac{CR_{act}}{CR_{norm}}(RE)}{CR_{norm}}$$

To evaluate the effect of growth, we can compare the results in three situations as is shown in Table C9-1.

TABLE C9-1. The Value of Common Stock Using the Water Formula with the Actual Capitalization Rate Being Less Than, Equal to, and Greater Than the Normal Capitalization Rate.

Situation	CS_{mkt}	$= \dfrac{Div + \dfrac{CR_{act}}{CR_{norm}}(\$RE)}{CR_{norm}}$		
$CR_{act} < CR_{norm}$	CS_{mkt}	$= \dfrac{100 + \dfrac{.08}{.10}(100)}{.10}$	$= \dfrac{180}{.10}$	$= \$1,800$
$CR_{act} = CR_{norm}$	CS_{mkt}	$= \dfrac{100 + \dfrac{.10}{.10}(100)}{.10}$	$= \dfrac{200}{.10}$	$= \$2,000$
$CR_{act} > CR_{norm}$	CS_{mkt}	$= \dfrac{100 + \dfrac{.12}{.10}(100)}{.10}$	$= \dfrac{220}{.10}$	$= \$2,200$

NOTE: NIAT = $200 with 50 percent dividend payout; CR_{norm} is held constant at 10 percent; CR_{act} varies at 8, 10, and 12 percent.

When the CR_{act} equals the CR_{norm}, the value is \$2,000. This is identica.
to simply capitalizing the \$200 NIAT (200/.10). From this situation, Miller
and Modigliani draw two conclusions:

1. *Growth Is Defined as CR_{act} Greater than CR_{norm}.* If they are the same, all
   that is being capitalized is the return. Only when profits are "increasing" rather than "expanding" is the firm experiencing growth.
2. *If CR_{act} Is Less than CR_{norm}, CS_{mkt} Will Drop.* This is a proof of the
   Miller-Modigliani proposition 3, which states that the cutoff point
   for new investments is the firm's cost of capital.

Miller and Modigliani then point out that the investment-opportunities
approach is the same as the earlier capitalization of return equations. They
also demonstrate the same situation for the stream-of-dividends approach to
value

$$CS_{mkt} = \sum_{t=0}^{\infty} \frac{1}{1 + K_e} [Div] \qquad (14)$$

and stream of earnings approach

$$CS_{mkt} = \sum_{t=0}^{\infty} \frac{1}{1 + K_e} [NIAT]$$

VALUE OF MILLER AND MODIGLIANI PROOFS

The rigorous proofs in this article demonstrate that the market capitalizes
return to the investor whether measured by earnings, cash flow, dividends,
or a combination thereof. They also demonstrate that all these equations have
a common base in a perfect and riskless market.

EARNINGS, DIVIDENDS, AND GROWTH

The next section of the Miller and Modigliani article examines whether
dividend policies can affect the return to the investor during a period if the
firm is a "growth" firm; that is, if CR_{act} is greater than CR_{norm}. The conclusion is no.

Miller and Modigliani begin by pointing out that a firm's earnings will
be the sum of two components:

1. *Last Period's NIAT.* This is shown by the symbol $NIAT_{(t-1)}$.

2. *Return on New Capital.* The new capital ($Cap_{growth(act)}$) can be from retained earnings or from the issuance of common stock. The earnings will be at a rate of the actual capitalization rate.

The formula that gives the firm's earnings is:

$$NIAT = NIAT_{(t-1)} + (CR_{act})(Cap_{growth(act)}) \tag{21}$$

Miller and Modigliani then employ the Gordon model cited at the start of this section which gives a value of common stock as follows:

$$CS_{mkt} = \frac{NIAT\ (1 - \%\ RE)}{CR_{norm} - (CR_{act})(\%\ RE)} \tag{24}$$

Miller and Modigliani incorporate external financing into the model by replacingNIAT$(1 - \%\ RE)$, or dividends, with NIAT $[1 - \%\ Cap_{growth(act)}]$ so that the formula is:

$$CS_{mkt} = \frac{NIAT\ [1 - \%\ Cap_{growth(act)}]}{\left[CR_{norm}\ CR_{act} \right] - \left[\%\ Cap_{growth(act)} \right]} \tag{23}$$

Miller and Modigliani then work the formulas to draw some interesting conclusions. Without repeating the steps they used, the major conclusions are:

1. *For Growth, CR_{act} Must be Greater than CR_{norm}.* If a firm is reinvesting a portion of its earnings or if it is issuing new common stock, it is not really growing unless its CR_{act} exceeds investors' opportunities elsewhere. The investor can have dividends today or in the future; retaining them when CR_{act} is less than or equal to CR_{norm} does not make them "grow." Also, issuing new shares and sharing profits with new shareholders is not "growth" since it does not benefit existing shareholders unless CR_{act} exceeds CR_{norm}.
2. *Growth Is Possible at a 100 Percent Dividend Payout.* The logical corollary to the preceding conclusion is that the firm will grow when CR_{act} exceeds CR_{norm} even at a 100 percent dividend payout. The high future return compared to other investments will produce a "growth" in the investment.
3. *Growth of Dividends Is Not Same as Growth of Firm.* As the firm increases in size or earnings, the position of the individual shareholder may decline compared to other investment opportunities. Growth is an increase in the rate of capital accumulation over the normal expectation; it is not the normal or less than normal return from a capital investment. Or, in simpler terms, the firm may expand, but the investor may be able to do better elsewhere.

DIVIDEND POLICY UNDER UNCERTAINTY

In this section, Miller and Modigliani drop the assumption of certainty. Three effects are then given:

1. *Random Dividends and Future Stock Value.* In the absence of certainty, events in the market will produce random movements of stock prices. Also, business conditions may affect dividend levels and policies. This means that, from the point of view of the investor, dividends and future stock value become subject to random fluctuations.

2. *Difficulties in Determining K_e.* The discount factor $1/(1 + K_e)$ applies now to a probable distribution of returns, not a given return. Miller and Modigliani conclude that the discount factor has limited value under uncertainty because of the difficulties in determining K_e.

3. *Dividends Are Still Irrelevant.* Under conditions of uncertainty, Miller and Modigliani switch the emphasis from solving for CS_{mkt} (which is known by empirical observation) to solving for K_e which is probabilistic. Dividends continue to be irrelevant because the market capitalizes future return in uncertain as well as certain markets. Thus, the conceptual proofs already presented will still apply.

The formula for calculating the probabilistic K_e begins with

$$CS_{mkt} = \frac{1}{1 + K_e} \, (CS_{fut} - Cap_{growth(mkt)} + NIAT) \qquad (5)$$

and solves for K_e as follows:

$$K_e = \frac{CS_{fut} - Cap_{growth(mkt)} + NIAT}{CS_{mkt}} - 1 \qquad (30)$$

with tildes ($\sim$) used in the original article to indicate that values are drawn from a probability distribution.

INFORMATIONAL CONTENT OF DIVIDENDS

In this section, Miller and Modigliani address the fact that dividend announcements tend to affect the price of the common stock. They conclude that changes in dividends reflect future earnings and growth opportunities. The dividend changes thus provide the *occasion* for price changes; they are not the *cause* of price changes. This is what Miller and Modigliani call the **informational content of dividends**.

DIVIDEND POLICY AND MARKET IMPERFECTIONS

Miller and Modigliani point out the difficulty of abandoning the assumption of perfect markets in developing dividend theory. The real problem is that no unique set of circumstances can be said to constitute imperfection. One exception would be the case of **systematic imperfections** which might lead an investor to prefer dividends to capital gains or vice-versa.

Miller and Modigliani identify only one market imperfection that could systematically affect value in terms of dividends. This is the advantage accorded capital gains as compared with dividends under the personal income tax.

A second factor affecting value is the **clientele effect** that occurs when a firm attracts a body of investors who agree with its individual dividend policies. This effect can influence the value of common stock.

Miller and Modigliani comment on empirical differences in value because of dividend policies. They conclude that it can only be accounted for by **systematic irrationality** on the part of the investing public.

PART THREE

CAPITAL ASSET
PRICING MODEL

CAPITAL ASSET PRICING MODEL

To many financial theorists and practitioners, the foundation of financial management is a clear understanding of the Capital Asset Pricing Model (CAPM). The CAPM is a financial theory relating risk and return, and is widely used by analysts dealing with a portfolio of securities or assets. It employs a **capital market line** (CML) and the concept of **efficient portfolios** to recognize that higher-risk securities will require higher rates of return than lower-risk securities. The CAPM builds upon the pioneering work of Markowitz and Sharpe and the refinements of a number of people including Jensen, Fama, and Lintner. It can be used to calculate a firm's cost of capital and to assist in capital budgeting decisions. Because of its importance as a current topic in finance, this *Handbook* highlights the capital asset pricing model as a self-contained unit.

PORTFOLIO THEORY

A **portfolio** is defined as a combination of assets which are owned by an individual or firm for the purpose of earning a return. **Portfolio theory** is the body of knowledge that deals with the relationships between risk and return in portfolios. The goal of portfolio theory is to select optimal combinations of financial or capital assets in terms of achieving the highest possible expected return for any degree of risk or the lowest possible degree of risk for any expected return. A number of techniques have been developed to assist the analyst in selecting the securities or assets to be included in an optimal portfolio.

Kinds of Assets

A portfolio may contain three kinds of assets:

1. *Financial Assets.* The common stock, preferred stock, and bonds issued by corporations or governments. Financial assets are easily identified with specific returns, are easily purchased and sold in capital markets, and are available from a wide variety of sources. As a result, considerable data is available on such assets.

2. *Capital Assets.* These are the factories, warehouses, vessels, vehicles, pipelines, and other plant, equipment, or real estate representing fixed or capital investments. Capital assets are usually not easily identified with specific returns and do not have the liquidity of financial assets. Even so, a group of capital assets may be treated as a portfolio using the techniques in this chapter.

3. *Intangible Assets.* These are items such as leases, royalties, patents, trademarks, and contracts that can be used to earn profits. **Intangible assets** frequently share the characteristics of either financial or capital assets in that they may or may not be easily identified with specific returns, and they may or may not be liquid. These too, may be analyzed using the techniques in this chapter.

Risk as Variability of Return

The amount of risk in a portfolio is determined by the likely variability of its future returns. As an example, if an investor purchases short-term United States government bonds expected to yield 7 percent, little fluctuation would be expected in the 7-percent return. The investment would be viewed as possessing very low risk. On the other hand, if the investor purchases shares of common stock in an oil exploration venture, the return will be highly variable. If no oil is discovered, the capital invested may not be returned so a total loss is possible. Or, if a large oil deposit is discovered, a small investment will produce great returns. The common stock of this company has a potential for high returns but is said to be very risky.

Probability Distributions

A decision to invest in financial or capital assets generally involves the forecast of an expected return, which is defined as the "most likely" or "best" estimate of the return from the portfolio. As an example, a portfolio with $100,000 in assets may be forecasted to return $6,000 over a one-year period so that it is worth $106,000 next year. The $6,000 or 6 percent (6,000/100,000) is the expected return.

To measure risk, we develop a **probability distribution** which is defined as the probability estimates associated with differing future outcomes. To illustrate this concept in our example, suppose the $6,000 target return has a 40 percent probability, returns of $4,000 or $8,000 have 20 percent probabilities respectively, and returns of $2,000 or $10,000 have probabilities of 10 percent each. A **discrete probability distribution,** defined as having a limited number of identifiable values, can be formed as shown in Figure T-1.

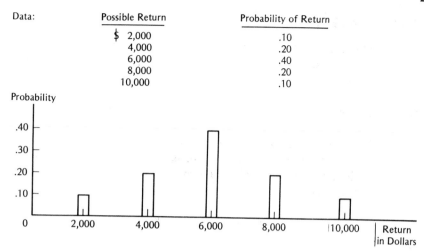

Data:

Possible Return	Probability of Return
$ 2,000	.10
4,000	.20
6,000	.40
8,000	.20
10,000	.10

Figure T-1. A Discrete Probability Distribution Formed From Data in Example.

A **continuous probability distribution** is defined as a distribution that can take on all possible numerical values over the range between the highest and lowest values. The normal or "bell-shaped" distribution is continuous and has been found to describe many types of frequency data quite accurately. Two normal probability distributions are given in Figure T-2.

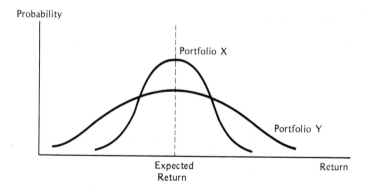

Figure T-2 Probability Distributions for Two Portfolios.

Portfolios X and Y have the same expected returns but have markedly different forecasted dispersions. Portfolio X has less variability of return and hence is said to be less risky than portfolio Y. Both portfolio returns are shown as normal, continuous probability distributions.

RETURN CONCEPTS

The rate of return on the investment in an asset is developed in detail in the capital asset pricing model. This section discusses some of the return concepts.

Expected Return

The likely or **expected return** from a portfolio of securities or capital assets is the sum of the individual returns weighted by the percent of each security in the total portfolio. The expected return may be calculated from the following formula:

$$E(Rtn)_{port} = Rtn_1 \times \%_1 + Rtn_2 \times \%_2 \ldots + Rtn_n \times \%_n$$

where $E(Rtn)_{port}$ = expected or likely return on the portfolio expressed as a percent
Rtn_1 = likely return on the first security
Rtn_n = likely return on the nth security
$\%_1$ = dollars invested in the first security as a percent of the dollars invested in the portfolio of n securities; ($ in 1)/($ in portfolio)
$\%_n$ = dollars invested in the nth security as a percent of total dollars in portfolio

A shorthand expression of the formula for the expected return on a portfolio is:

$$E(Rtn)_{port} = \sum_{j=1}^{n} Rtn_j \times \%_j$$

where $\sum_{j=1}^{n}$ = sum of the values for a portfolio with n securities beginning with security j (the first security) and ending with security n.
Rtn_j = expected return on the jth security
$\%_j$ = ratio of j/n in dollars similar to $\%_1$

EXAMPLE: A portfolio of three securities has $100,000 invested in common stock A which has an expected return of 9 percent; $200,000 in B with E(Rtn)$_B$ equals 6 percent; $300,000 in C with E(Rtn)$_C$ equals 8 percent. What is the expected return for the portfolio?

ANSWER: 7.5 percent, as follows:

$$E(Rtn)_{port} = Rtn_1 \times \%_1 + Rtn_2 \times \%_2 + Rtn_3 \times \%_3$$

$$= [9\% \times 100/600] + [6\% \times 200/600] + [8\% \times 300/600]$$

$$= 1.5\% + 2\% + 4\% = 7.5\%$$

Market Rate of Return [E(Rtn)Mkt]

The **market rate of return** is the expected return on the market portfolio; that is, on a portfolio consisting of all securities weighted at their respective market values. For example, assume that the market is defined as all common stocks listed on a regional stock exchange. Further, assume these stocks were worth 900 million dollars today, that they rose from 850 million dollars one year ago, and that they declared and paid cash dividends of 60 million dollars in the past year. The market rate of return could be calculated by the formula:

$$E(Rtn)_{Mkt} = \frac{V_1 - V_0 + Div}{V_0}$$

where $E(Rtn)_{Mkt}$ = market rate of return
V_1 = value of securities at market at end of year one
V_0 = value of securities at market at year zero
Div = dividends paid during period

In our example, the market rate of return would be (000's):

$$E(Rtn)_{Mkt} = \frac{900,000 - 850,000}{850,000} + 60,000 = \frac{110,000}{850,000} = 12.9 \text{ percent}$$

Forecasting Expected Rate of Return

In developing the expected rate of return E(Rtn) or market rate of return $E(Rtn)_{Mkt}$, two approaches are commonly used:

1. *Use Past Market Returns.* This method assumes that investors will require future returns similar to past returns. Therefore, to solve for expected rate of return, we calculate prior market returns and use them as an estimate of future return. As an example, suppose we had five years of data as follows:

Year	Beginning Market Value[a]	Gain (Loss) in Market Value	+ Cash Dividends	Total = Return	Return Divided by Beginning Market Value	Actual Market Rate of Return = $E(Rtn)_{mkt}$
1	550	50	40	90	90/550	16.4%
2	600	140	50	190	190/600	31.7
3	740	(30)	40	10	10/740	1.4
4	710	110	60	170	170/710	23.9
5	820	80	65	145	145/820	17.7

[a] Hundreds of millions of dollars   Average $E(Rtn)_{Mkt}$ = 18.2 percent

Over the 5-year period, the market had differing returns each year with an average annual market rate of return of 18.2 percent. This could be used as an estimate of expected rate of return.

2. *Forecast Next Period's E(Rtn)*. The second, and conceptually more sound, method of determining the expected return is to prepare a forecast of likely future returns. Historical data is only valid to the extent that current and future conditions reflect past conditions. If, for example, a nation is experiencing an economic recovery following a period of stagnation or recession, past returns will not provide valid estimates of future expected returns. A better approach to estimating E(Rtn) would be to forecast interest rate levels, money supply, corporate profits, government spending, and similar variables which affect the expected rate of return. By incorporating these variables in a simulation model along with current security price levels, price-earnings multiples, and dividend policies, an analyst can forecast the expected rate of return for an investment in a portfolio of financial or capital assets.

RISK CONCEPTS

A number of risk concepts and measurements are used in the capital asset pricing model. This section deals with the nature and characteristics of the differing kinds of risk facing the investor.

Security and Portfolio Risk

Security risk is defined as the degree of uncertainty of return inherent in the investment in a single financial asset such as common stock or bonds. It differs from **portfolio risk** which is defined as the degree of uncertainty inherent in the investment in a portfolio of financial or capital assets.

The security risk of two or more assets can be offsetting when viewed in the context of portfolio risk. As an example, let us consider securities A and B that have different expected returns depending upon the level of economic activity. The likely returns are forecasted as follows:

	Security A Return	Security B Return
In the event of a recession	5%	8%
In the event of normal activity	8	6
In the event of high economic growth	10	5

The security risk of A ranges from 5 to 10 percent; for B it is 5 to 8 percent. But what happens if we have a portfolio with 50 percent of each stock. The new expected returns are

	Portfolio of 50 Percent Each Security A and B
Recession	(5 + 8)/2 = 6.5%
Normal	(8 + 6)/2 = 7.0
High	(10 + 5)/2 = 7.5

The portfolio risk ranges from 6.5 to 7.5 percent return, a much smaller range than the individual security risks.

Systematic and Unsystematic Risk

Portfolio risk is divided into two components under the theory of the capital asset pricing model. They are:

1. *Systematic Risk.* This is the market-related component of portfolio risk. It is commonly measured by the regression coefficient "beta," or the beta coefficient. **Systematic risk** *cannot* be eliminated through diversification. As an example, consider a portfolio with a beta coefficient[1] of 0.60, at a time when investments in the market overall should yield a 10 percent return and investment in the portfolio should yield 8 percent. Now assume that the market return drops to 5 percent, a 50-percent decline. The portfolio will drop by 60 percent of the market decline or 60% × 8% = 4.8 percent. A 30

---

[1]Beta is a measure of risk that will be covered in detail in the next section. It correlates the movement of a security to the movement of the market. A .60 beta means that any change in market return will be accompanied by a 60-percent change in the security's return.

percent drop from 8 percent would produce a return of 3.2 percent on the portfolio. The drop in return from 8 percent to 3.2 percent represents the portfolio's systematic risk which was not eliminated through diversification. Thus, the larger the beta coefficient for a portfolio, the greater is the portfolio's systematic or nondiversifiable risk.

2. *Unsystematic Risk.* This is the component of portfolio risk that can be eliminated through diversification. **Unsystematic risk** differs from systematic or market-related risk which cannot be eliminated through diversification. As an example, consider a portfolio with a beta coefficient of 0.55. This means that a decline of "x" percent in the return of the overall market will be accompanied by a .55 decline in the return on the portfolio. The 1 − .55 or 45 percent that the portfolio's return will not decline represents the unsystematic risk that has been eliminated through diversification. In effect, diversification is eliminating the random movements in the return of individual securities. The random pluses for some securities are offset by random minuses for others and, with a sufficiently large portfolio, the net effect of random movements will approach zero.

Measuring Risk—Single Asset

Three measures of risk are commonly used to compare the likely variability of return from an investment. These are:

1. *Standard Deviation (σ).* This is expressed by the symbol σ, or "sigma," and is a measure of dispersion of returns that approximate a normal probability distribution. A small standard deviation indicates a tight probability distribution and identifies a portfolio with less risk than similar portfolios with a larger standard deviation. The standard deviation is calculated by the following formula:

$$\sigma = \sum_{s=1}^{n} [E(Rtn)_s - E(Rtn)_{mean}]^2 \times Prob_s$$

where $\sum_{s=1}^{n}$ = the sum of probable future conditions where condition s is the first future state and n is the last state

$E(Rtn)_s$ = expected return in future state s

$E(Rtn)_{mean}$ = the mean value or average value of the n possible returns

$Prob_s$ = the probability of occurrence of the s state of the economy

2. *Variance(σ^2).* This is simply the standard deviation squared. The

variance plays the same basic role as a measure of dispersion as the standard deviation.

3. *Coefficient of Variation [σ/E(Rtn)].* This is the ratio of the standard deviation to the likely or expected return from an asset. This is an improvement over the standard deviation or variance by themselves because the coefficient of variation relates the amount of the dispersion to the magnitude of the returns. As an example, consider projects X and Y, both of which have a standard deviation of 2 percent. Project X has an expected return of 8 percent; Y has 22 percent. On a percentage basis, the deviation from the mean value is much greater for project X than Y.

For X σ/E(Rtn)X = 2%/8% = .25 coefficient of variation
For Y σ/E(Rtn)Y = 2%/22% = .09

Measuring Risk—Multiple Assets

When comparing the degree of risk of a single asset in a portfolio of assets, two additional risk measures are used:

1. *Covariance(Cov).* A statistical value that measures the risk between two variables. **Covariance** is calculated from a formula with two elements:

   a. *Correlation Coefficient (r).* This is a measure of the degree of relationship between two variables. The **correlation coefficient** is calculated by a formula that measures goodness of fit of data to the regression line and is symbolized by the letter r. If the r is close to zero, the fit is poor and the relationship is said to be weak or nonexistent. If r is close to plus or minus one, a strong correlation or linear relationship exists. In calculating a covariance for two securities, the forecasted return for each security is the variable that is correlated.

   b. *Standard Deviations (σ's).* The standard deviation, as a measure of the expected dispersion of the return, is needed for each variable.

The covariance is calculated by multiplying the correlation coefficient by the standard deviation of each variable as follows:

$$\text{Cov}_{XY} = (r_{XY})(\sigma_X)(\sigma_Y)$$

where Cov_{XY} = covariance of security X to security Y
r_{xy} = correlation coefficient of security X to security Y
σ_x = standard deviation of security X

EXAMPLE: A portfolio has 3 stocks. The standard deviation for R is .2; S is .4; and T is .6. The correlation coefficient of return for the securities is — .5 for R to S; zero for R to T; + .5 for S to T. What are the covariances for each pair of securities?

ANSWER:

Cov_{XY}	=	$(r_{xy})(\sigma_x)(\sigma_y)$
Cov_{RS}	=	$(-.5)(.2)(.4) = -.04$
Cov_{RT}	=	$(0)(.2)(.6) = 0$
Cov_{ST}	=	$(+.5)(.4)(.6) = +.12$

2. *Beta Coefficient (Beta).* This is a regression coefficient identified in a procedure developed by William Sharpe[2] to separate the standard deviation of returns from individual securities into systematic and unsystematic components. The beta coefficient Beta shows the degree of systematic or market-related risk inherent in an investment in a security. It is calculated using the formula

$$Beta_X = \frac{(r_{X, mkt})(\sigma_X)}{\sigma_{mkt}}$$

where $Beta_X$ = Beta coefficient for asset x

    $r_{x,mkt}$ = correlation coefficient between asset x and the market for all assets

    σ_x = standard deviation of asset x

    σ_{mkt} = standard deviation of portfolio of all market assets

The beta coefficient converts the correlation coefficient into a precise measure of how market changes will affect the expected or likely return from the security. To do this, it "proportions" the correlation coefficient by the standard deviations of the security and the market.

EXAMPLE: Securities R and S each have a standard deviation of 1.2 percent on a likely return of 9.5 percent at a time when the total market's likely return is 8.0 percent with a standard deviation of .7 percent. The correlation between R and the market is — .8 and the correlation between S and the market is + .5. What is the Beta for each security? Which security has the highest level of risk?
ANSWER: R has a higher level of risk because it has the higher beta coefficient, as follows:

$$Beta = \frac{[r_{X,mkt}][\sigma_X]}{\sigma_{mkt}}$$

---

[2]William F. Sharpe, *Portfolio Theory and Capital Markets.* (New York, McGraw-Hill Book Company, 1970.)

$$\text{Beta}_R = \frac{(-.8)(1.2)}{.7} = -1.37 \text{ Beta}_R$$

$$\text{Beta}_S = \frac{(.5)(1.2)}{.7} = .86 \text{ Beta}_S$$

CAPITAL ASSET PRICING MODEL (CAPM)

The capital asset pricing model is a financial theory that ties together the risk and return concepts discussed thus far. This section examines the model in detail.

Assumptions of Capital Asset Pricing Model

The following assumptions provide the conceptual framework for examining risk and return using the capital asset pricing model:[3]

1. *Competitive Market.* Financial securities or capital assets are bought and sold in a highly competitive market where information on the likely risks and returns on the assets is freely available and is known to all participants. In effect, the assets are traded in perfect markets.
2. *No Taxes or Costs.* Securities can be exchanged without the payment of brokerage commissions, fees, or taxes and without any other transaction costs.
3. *Riskless Borrowing Rate.* Investors, both large and small, are able to borrow freely at a riskless rate of interest; that is, at a rate of interest equal to the return that can be obtained by investing in a riskless security such as government bonds.
4. *Rational Investment Goals.* Investors are rational and strive to receive the highest return from an acceptable level of risk or the lowest risk from a target level of return. These goals are pursued by trading or selling short perfectly divisible and liquid assets in a program designed to maximize individual wealth.

Diversification

The capital asset pricing model recognizes an important role for **diversification** which is defined as the strategy of investing in more than one financial or capital asset. When risk is measured through variations in expected return, the level of risk can be lowered through a diversification strategy. Portfolio theory recognizes several characteristics of broadly-diversified portfolios, including:

---

[3]M. C. Jensen, "Capital Markets: Theory and Evidence," *Bell Journal of Economics and Management Science,* Autumn, 1972.

1. *Correlation with Market.* The return from a portfolio of 20 or more properly selected assets will, in most cases, approximate the return from the market for all assets. Stated in the language of portfolio theory, the expected rate of return on a diversified portfolio will approximate the market rate of return.

2. *Elimination of Unsystematic Risk.* Unsystematic or diversifiable risk can be eliminated through diversification which is, in effect, eliminating the random movements in the return of individual securities. The random pluses for some securities are offset by random minuses for others and, with a sufficiently large portfolio, the net effect of random movements will approach zero.

3. *No Effect on Systematic Risk.* Diversification cannot eliminate the systematic or market-related risk. This is commonly measured by the beta coefficient. The larger the beta coefficient for a portfolio or security, the greater is the portfolio's systematic risk.

Capital Market Line (CML)

The capital market line shows the relationship between risk and return in a portfolio and can be diagrammed as follows:

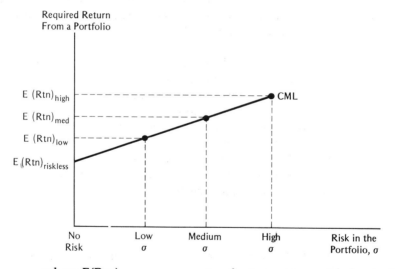

where $E(Rtn)_{riskless}$ = rate of return at zero risk (generally the return on U.S. Treasury securities)

$E(Rtn)_{low}$ = rate of return required on a low-risk portfolio

$E(Rtn)_{med}$ = rate of return required on a medium-risk portfolio

$E(Rtn)_{high}$ = rate of return required on a high-risk portfolio

Security Market Line (SML)

The **security market line** is used by some theorists in the capital asset pricing model to measure the relationship between risk and return. It is diagrammed in the same manner as the capital market line but differs from it in two respects:

1. *Covariance Is Risk Measure.* In computing the CML, risk is measured using the standard deviation of the expected returns from the individual securities or assets. In computing the SML, risk is measured using the covariance of the individual security with the overall portfolio. This is a key difference because, by using the covariance, the SML recognizes the risk of a single security in terms of its effect on the risk of the portfolio as a whole.
2. *Variance (σ^2) Replaces Standard Deviation (σ).* The second difference is that the market variance (σ^2_{mkt}) replaces the market standard deviation (σ_{mkt}) in the formula (given in the next section). This has the effect of changing the position of the SML as compared to the CML.

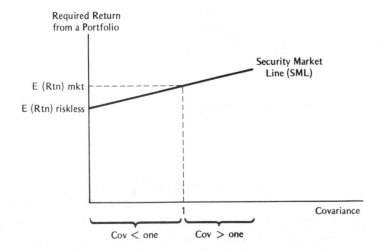

Efficient Frontier

The foundation for the capital asset pricing model (and for modern portfolio theory as well) is the original work of Harry Markowitz.[4] He analyzed the relationship between risk and return and drew a graphic representation showing rising levels of risk accompanying rising levels of return:

---

4 Harry Markowitz, "Portfolio Selection," *Journal of Finance,* March 1952.

He developed this pattern into the concept of the **efficient frontier** which is defined as the outer edge of a set of portfolios, where each portfolio on the frontier provides the highest possible expected return for any degree of risk or the lowest possible degree of risk for any expected return. In the diagram, the line ABCDEFA defines the possible portfolios with the shaded area showing all portfolios. Portfolios A through F are specifically identified and, of these six, only B, C, and D are efficient portfolios. The line BCD defines the efficient frontier.

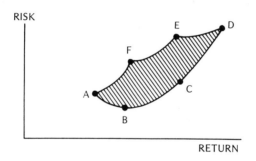

Sharpe Model

Developed by William F. Sharpe,[5] the **Sharpe model** outlines a method of separating the systematic (market-related) and unsystematic (random-fluctuation) risk components of overall portfolio risk. The model is widely used to calculate the expected return from an individual security or portfolio. It requires fewer calculations and less computer capacity than other formulas for expected return and hence can be used to select portfolios from a large collection of individual assets. It is, therefore, an integral part of most approaches to using the capital asset pricing model.

The Sharpe model can be expressed by the following formula:

$$E(Rtn) = Alpha + [Beta] [E(Rtn)Mkt] + E(Random)$$

---

[5]W.F. Sharpe, "Capital Asset Prices: A Theory of Market Equilibrium Under Conditions of Risk," *Journal of Finance,* September 1964.

where E(Rtn)   = the expected return on an individual
                        security or portfolio

Alpha   = the expected return if the market neither
                        rises nor declines. This is an intercept of the
                        horizontal axis that shows the return
                        based on the fundamental or intrinsic
                        value of the security

Beta   = a regression coefficient that correlates the
                        movement of a security to the movement
                        of the market for all securities. This
                        coefficient is generally positive indicating
                        that most securities tend to move with the
                        market. If the coefficient is greater than
                        one, the security is more volatile than the
                        market. A coefficient less than one
                        indicates a security that is less volatile
                        than the market

E(Rtn)Mkt   = market rate of return which is the ex-
                        pected or actual return on the market
                        portfolio; that is, on all the securities
                        in the market weighted at their respective
                        market values

E(Random)   = a random error variable. The regression
                        line calculated by the formula will be
                        fitted to a security's past performance but
                        few observations will actually be directly
                        on the line. The error variable explains
                        random movements, leads and lags for a
                        single observation

The Sharpe model produces a linear relationship that is expressed as the security's **characteristic line.** Figure T-3 shows two such lines for stocks X and Y which have an expected return calculated by the given formulas.

With respect to the characteristic line in the Sharpe model, two effects are important:

1. *Linear Relationships.* Empirical evidence from the financial literature supports the linear nature of the characteristic line. Therefore, only two points are needed to plot it. One point can be the Alpha value at zero market return. The second point can be any assumed level of market return.

2. *Beta Is Slope of Line.* The Beta Coefficient is the slope of the line. Thus, the larger the Beta, the greater the return in a rising market or the greater the loss in a declining market.

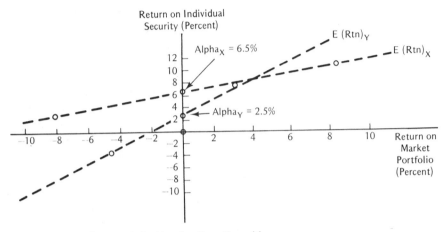

Data, 1968 to 1978 $E(Rtn)_X = 6.5\% + [.50] [E(Rtn)_{Mkt}] + E(Random)$

$E(Rtn)_Y = 2.5\% + [1.4] [E(Rtn)_{Mkt}] + E(Random)$

Figure T-3.   Characteristic Line for Two Securities.

> *EXAMPLE: From Figure 1-3, at what E(Rtn)_Mkt does each security provide neither a return nor a loss?*
> *ANSWER: At minus 13.5 percent for X and minus 1.8 percent for Y, both where the Alpha factor divided by the negative Beta factor equals the answer:*

$E(Rtn)_{Mkt}$ = Alpha/−Beta
                   = 6.5%/−.50 for X to have zero return = 13.5 percent
                   = 2.5%/−1.4 for Y to have zero return = 1.8 percent

Three Formulas for Measuring Risk and Return

In calculating the risk and return tradeoffs on the capital market line or security market line, three formulas are commonly used:

1. *CML with Standard Deviations.* The capital market line is formed by linking the expected return on a risk-free asset [$E(Rtn)_{riskless}$] with the point where the expected return on the market portfolio [$E(Rtn)_{Mkt}$] and the standard deviation of the market portfolio (σ mkt) cross, as follows:

To determine the expected return from any portfolio on the capital market line, we use the following formula:

$$E(Rtn)_{port} = E(Rtn)_{riskless} + \frac{E(Rtn)_{Mkt} - E(Rtn)_{riskless}}{\sigma_{mkt}} [\sigma_{port}]$$

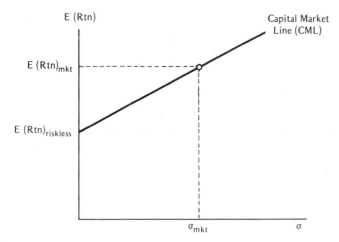

EXAMPLE: An investor is seeking an efficient portfolio with a standard deviation of 2.0 percent. The standard deviation for the market portfolio is 1.5 percent. The expected return from a risk-free asset is 4 percent and from the market portfolio is 9 percent. What is the expected return on the portfolio sought by the investor?
ANSWER: 10.67 percent, as follows:

$$E(Rtn)_{port} = 4\% + \frac{9\% - 4\%}{1.5} \, (2) = 4\% + 6.67\% = 10.67 \text{ percent}$$

2. *Security Market Line.* The expected return on an individual security will be related to the degree of risk offered by that security as compared to the market for all securities. The security market line is formed in a fashion similar to the capital market line but its slope is not identical to the CML. The difference in slope reflects the fact that risk is measured by comparing the individual security to the market using the covariance which is calculated

$$\text{Cov}_{X, mkt} = r_{X, mkt}(\sigma_X)(\sigma_{mkt})$$

where $\text{Cov}_{X, mkt}$ = the covariance between security or asset X and the market for all assets

$r_{X, mkt}$ = the correlation coefficient for asset X and the market

The formula for calculating expected return on any portfolio or security on the security market line is:

$$E(Rtn)_{port} = E(Rtn)_{riskless} + \frac{E(Rtn)_{Mkt} - E(Rtn)_{riskless}}{\sigma^2_{mkt}} [\text{Cov}_{sec, mkt}]$$

where $Cov_{sec,mkt}$ $\quad$ = the covariance between the security and the market

$O^2{}_{mkt}$ $\quad$ = the variance (standard deviation squared) of the market portfolio

EXAMPLE: An investor is seeking the price to pay for a security whose standard deviation is 2.0. The correlation coefficient for the security with the market is .8 and the market standard deviation is 1.5 percent. The expected return from a risk-free security is 4 percent and from the market portfolio is 9 percent. What is the expected return on the security? (Note: This assumes that, by calculating expected return, the investor can then calculate the price to pay for the security.)
ANSWER: 9.33 percent, as follows:

$$E(Rtn)_{sec} = 4\% + \frac{9\% - 4\%}{1.5^2} (.8)(1.5)(2.0) = 4\% + 5.33\% = 9.33 \text{ percent}$$

3. **CML with Beta Coefficient.** The third formula for calculating expected return applies to the capital market line. The beta coefficient, which is used as a measure of risk, follows a procedure developed by William Sharpe (and is, in effect, an extension of the Sharpe model already discussed). The formula for the beta coefficient is

$$Beta_X = \frac{(r_{X,mkt})(\sigma_X)}{\sigma_{mkt}}$$

and the formula for expected return is

$$E(Rtn)_{port} = E(Rtn)_{riskless} + Beta_{port} [E(Rtn)_{Mkt} - E(Rtn)_{riskless}]$$

EXAMPLE: An investor is seeking an efficient portfolio with a standard deviation of .5 percent at a time when the standard deviation for the market portfolio is 1.5 percent. The portfolio should correlate with the market at approximately + .5 correlation coefficient. The expected return from a risk-free asset is 4 percent and from the market return is 9 percent. What is the expected return on the portfolio sought by the investor?
ANSWER: 4.9 percent, as follows

$$Beta_{port} = \frac{(r_{port,mkt})(\sigma_{port})}{\sigma_{mkt}} = \frac{(+.5)(.5)}{1.5} = +.17$$

$$E(Rtn)_{port} = .04 + .17 (.09 - .04) = .049$$

Selecting the Optimal Portfolio

The conclusion to the capital asset pricing model is the selection of a portfolio where the investor can maximize return for any given risk level or minimize risk for any given level of return. The optimal is expressed in terms of utility theory as shown in Figure T-4.

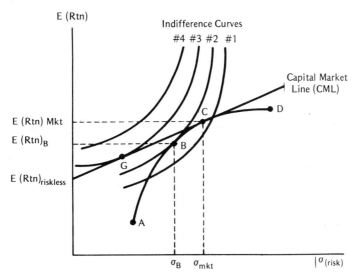

Figure T-4. Optimal Portfolio Selection.

The following are the key points to understanding the figure.

1. *Risk Is Independent Variable.* Since the standard deviation (σ) is placed on the horizontal axis, it is treated as the independent variable. In the CAPM, return is viewed as being dependent upon risk in a portfolio. This differs from our earlier discussion of the Markowitz efficient frontier where the risk and return axis were reversed.

2. *Point C Is Market.* The point where the capital market line is tangent to the efficient frontier is the market portfolio; that is, point C represents a portfolio containing every asset in exact proportion to that asset's percentage of the total market.

3. *Point B Is Optimum Portfolio of Risk-Bearing Assets.* The line ABCD shows the efficient frontier of portfolios containing risk-bearing assets. The investor selects a portfolio on the frontier that places him on the highest possible indifference curve showing his view towards the trade-off between risk and return. This means that indifference curve 2 is preferable to curve 1, and so on. At point B, the investor has a tangency solution with the efficient frontier and this is an optimum portfolio of risk-bearing assets.

4. *Point G Is the Overall Optimum.* The investor can improve upon his choices on the efficient frontier by including in his portfolio that risk-free asset that yields $E(Rtn)_{riskless}$. If this is done, he can move to the CML and can hold portfolio G which places him on a higher indifference curve. This is the optimum portfolio overall.

Overview of the Capital Asset Pricing Model

To tie together the elements of portfolio theory and the capital asset pricing model, Figure T-5 presents an overview of the major concepts discussed in this section.

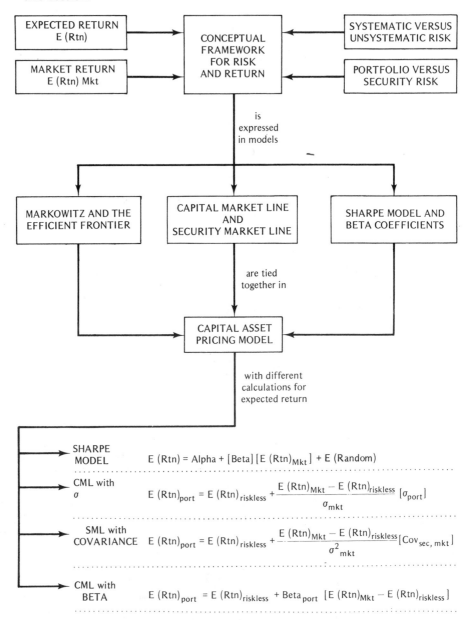

Figure T-5. An Overview of the Capital Asset Pricing Model.

Conclusion

Although the theoretical foundation for the capital asset pricing model is complex and highly quantitative, it is a key concept in modern thinking concerning the relationship between risk and return. In this section, we have built from basic concepts of risk and return and have developed a comprehensive model for measuring the expected return from a security, portfolio, or capital asset. The capital asset pricing model is finding increasing application in the areas of cost of capital, capital structure management, and capital budgeting. Thus, an understanding of the basic components and structure of the CAPM is fundamental to an understanding of corporate and investment finance.

Part Four

GLOSSARY
OF FINANCIAL TERMS
AND
CONCEPTS

ABC system for inventory control. A management system that divides a firm's inventory into 3 groups according to the value of the individual item. "A" items are the most valuable and will be managed most closely. As a general guideline, these items make up approximately 20 percent of the inventory in terms of units and 80 to 90 percent in terms of dollar value. Because of their value, these items are generally managed using Economic Order Quantity (EOQ) and similar techniques. "B" items should normally make up 25 to 35 percent of the inventory in terms of items and 8 to 10 percent of the dollar value. "C" items make up only a few percent of the dollar investment but nearly half of the average inventory.

CROSS-REFERENCES:
inventory, p. 441
economic order quantity, p. 393

accelerated depreciation. Methods of depreciation that write off the value of a firm's fixed assets at a faster rate than straight line depreciation. The two most common approaches under the guidelines of the Internal Revenue Service are Double-Declining Balance and Sum-of-the-Years' Digits Methods. The effect of accelerated depreciation is to provide the firm with a larger noncash expense in the early years of a fixed asset's life. This provides a larger tax shield for the firm and increases the firm's cash flow by deferring taxes to future periods.

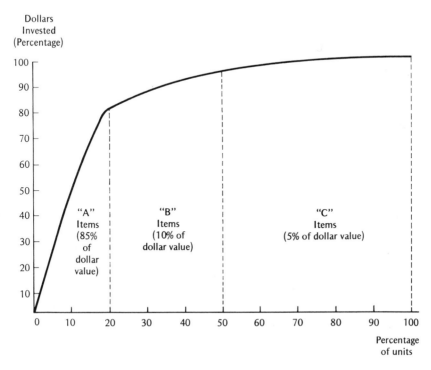

Inventory Item Distribution in Dollars and Units.

acceptance. With a negotiable instrument, agreement by the drawee of a draft to make payment on the instrument. A draft is an instrument drawn by one person (drawer) ordering a second person (drawee) to pay a specified sum of money to a third person. Upon acceptance, the drawee is viewed as being primarily liable for payment of the draft. An acceptance must be in writing and must be signed by the accepting party. The drawee's signature and date of signing on the face of the draft is an effective acceptance.

CROSS–REFERENCE:

draft, p. 391

acceptance criterion. A guideline established by a firm to assist it in evaluating proposals. The following are examples of acceptance criteria:

1. *Accept Minimum-Risk Proposals.* With this acceptance criterion, all projects above a certain minimum return (say 10 percent) are ranked according to risk. The least risky (proposal *A* in the figure) is accepted. If the firm is interested in two projects, proposal *B* would also be accepted.
2. *Assign Varying Hurdle Rates for Varying Risk Levels.* A hurdle rate is the level of return a proposal must reach before it

can be accepted. A firm may decide that all proposals must offer an expected return of at least 20 percent. By assigning different hurdle rates at different risk levels, the firm recognizes that higher risk should result in higher potential returns. An example of a hurdle-rate schedule is given in the table. With this schedule, a firm may be considering two proposals. Proposal *X* has a high risk and promises a 22 percent return. Proposal *Y* has medium risk and a 17 percent return. Project *X* would not be acceptable because it does not hurdle the 24 percent required of high-risk projects, whereas *Y* is acceptable since it hurdles the 16 percent required of medium-risk projects.

Relationship Between Risk and Return

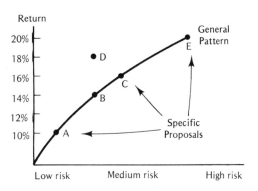

Relationship Between Risk and Return.

3. *Avoid Widely Fluctuating Proposals.* Some proposals offer wide fluctuations in possible returns. As an example, we may expect a return of 25 percent on a project, a figure that exceeds our hurdle rate for high-risk projects. But the project involves a chance—a

Hurdle-Rate Schedule.

Degree of Risk in Proposal	High	Medium-high	Medium	Medium-low	Low
Required Rate of Return (%)	24	20	16	14	12

small chance, perhaps 5 percent—of disaster. If this small chance is realized, the firm will be forced into bankruptcy. Since firms are seeking a long-term maximization of wealth, this proposal is in conflict with that goal and will probably be rejected even though it promises a high return.

4. *Use a Weighted-Average Approach.* This acceptance-criterion approach is discussed in the section "How to Use a Weighted Average Approach to Risk and Return."

EXAMPLE: Using the proposals *A* through *E* and the hurdle-rate schedule above, which of the projects are acceptable?

ANSWER: Proposals *B, C,* and *D.* The other proposals do not meet the required rate of return for the degree of risk involved.

CROSS-REFERENCES:
hurdle rate, p. 427
risk, p. 512
weighted average, p. 548

accounting rate of return. This rate matches Net Income After Taxes (NIAT) with the investment required for a project. It attempts to devise a rate of return similar to return on investment. The calculation may be performed using several formulas, giving highly varied results:

1. *NIAT/Total Investment.* With this formula, the full dollar amount of the investment is compared to the reported after-tax profit from the project. A $1,000,000 project that yields a NIAT of $50,000 has a 50,000/1,000,000 or 5 percent accounting rate of return.

2. *NIAT/One Half Total Investment.* With this formula, we recognize that the investment will be depreciated over its service life and will have an average value only half its original total

value. In the preceding example, the accounting rate of return would rise to 10 percent [50/(1/2)(1,000)] with this formula.

3. *NIAT/One Half Total Investment Plus All Working Capital Tied Up.* This method considers it appropriate to use only half the investment, as in formula 2, but to include also the working capital tied up in the project. If, in our example, $200,000 of additional working capital was needed, the accounting rate of return would be 50/[(1/2)($1,000) + 200] = 7.14 percent.

The accounting rate of return should not be used in capital-budgeting decisions. It has three major weaknesses:

1. *Accounting Information, Not Cash Flow.* Accounting information is not suitable for investment decisions because it does not precisely distinguish between cash flowing in and out of the firm and bookkeeping transactions.

2. *Ignores Time Value of Money.* The ability to use the time value of money in investment decisions has greatly strengthened the technique of cash-flow analysis. This is not true for accounting rate of return, which ignores the timing of receipts and expenditures.

3. *Several Concepts of Investment.* There is no full agreement on the proper measure of the term *investment.* Thus, different managers have different meanings when they refer to accounting rate of return.

CROSS-REFERENCE:
net income after taxes, p. 466

accounts payable. A *current liability* account on a balance sheet that is created when a firm makes a purchase on credit and which remains until the cash is paid for the goods. It reflects the fact that the firm has incurred an obligation to pay for the goods according to the terms given by the seller.

CROSS-REFERENCES:

liquidity, how to analyze with ratios, p. 49
working capital, how to balance sources of funds, p. 121
liabilities, p. 452

accounts receivable. A *balance sheet* account that reflects the amount of money owed to a firm as a result of credit sales that have not yet been collected.

CROSS-REFERENCES:

liquidity, how to analyze with ratios, p. 49
receivables management, how to evaluate differing credit policies, p. 108
balance sheet accounts, p. 318
aging of accounts receivable, p. 309
aging schedule, p. 309
current assets, p. 369
pledging of accounts receivable, p. 481

accounts receivable, factors affecting size of. The firm's receivables are a major component of its *current assets.* The approximate size of the receivables is determined by a number of factors. Three primary factors are the level of credit sales, the credit policies established by the firm, and the terms of trade.

Level of Sales   The most important factor in determining the volume of receivables is the level of the firm's credit sales. Since the terms of trade are similar in most industries, one firm in the industry with a large volume of sales will have a larger level of receivables than a firm with a small volume of sales.

Sales levels can be used to forecast changes in receivables. If a firm predicts an increase of 20 percent in its credit sales for the next period, it will proba-

bly also experience a 20 percent increase in receivables.

Credit Policies   The philosophy behind the firm's policies on extending credit will determine the amount of risk it is willing to undertake in its sales activities. If the firm has a relatively lax credit policy, it will experience a higher level of receivables than a firm with a more rigid policy. This is true for two reasons:

1. *Strong Customers Will Be Less Careful.* A lax credit policy encourages firms to settle their accounts without haste. Companies which otherwise pay their bills on time will not be overly concerned if they are a few days late in paying bills to a firm that seems to accept slow payments as normal.
2. *Weak Customers Will Default.* With pressure to pay, weak firms are more prompt in payment. In the absence of this pressure, defaults on payments will be more common. A number of firms will delay for long periods and then declare bankruptcy, resulting in bad-debt losses.

In establishing its credit policies, the firm tries to find a satisfactory middle ground between incurring the excessive collection costs that accompany a highly aggressive policy and the excessive defaults and bad debts that accompany a lax policy.

Terms of Trade   The size of the receivables balance is closely related to the firm's credit terms. If, for example, a firm changes its credit terms from net 15 to net 30—a 100 percent increase—it could expect a 100 percent increase in the size of its receivables. Customers who previously had waited 15 days to pay their bills would take advantage of the new situation and wait an additional 15 days. Similarly, if the firm changed from net 30 to 2/10 net 30, many customers would take advantage of the 2 percent discount for prompt payment and would pay in 10 instead of 30 days. This would cost the firm the 2 percent discount but would reduce the volume of receivables.

CROSS-REFERENCE:
assets, p. 313

accounts receivable turnover. A ratio that compares the size of a firm's sales with the size of its uncollected bills. If the firm is having difficulty collecting its money, it will have a large receivables balance and a low ratio. If it has a strict credit policy and aggressive collection procedures, it will have a low receivables balance and a high ratio.

CROSS-REFERENCES:
liquidity, how to analyze with ratios, p. 49
receivables ratios, p. 506

accruals. A current liability account commonly found on balance sheets. This account reflects expenses for which payment has not yet been made. Common accrual accounts are accrued wages and accrued taxes.

CROSS-REFERENCE:
accrual system, p. 307

accrual system. A method of accounting that allocates revenues and expenses to the time period in which they are incurred. According to standardized and generally accepted principles of accounting, revenues are recognized (accrue) at the point of sale even though cash may be received at a later time. Similarly, expenses are recognized when the obligations are created, not necessarily when they are paid. Revenues resulting from credit sales which have not yet been paid will appear on the balance sheet as an account receivable, a temporary asset account. Expenses which have been incurred but

not paid will appear on the balance sheet as accounts payable.

CROSS-REFERENCE:
accruals, p. 307

acid-test ratio. Also called quick ratio, a measure of liquidity that is calculated by dividing the firm's current assets minus its inventory by its current liabilities. The higher the ratio, the higher the level of liquidity in the firm.

CROSS-REFERENCES:
liquidity, how to analyze with ratios, p. 49
liquidity, p. 453
current ratio and acid test, p. 371
quick ratio, p. 500

acquisition. A form of external growth for a firm where the firm purchases or otherwise takes over the assets of another firm and uses such assets to continue the business operations of the other firm.

CROSS-REFERENCES:
acquisitions, how to analyze, p. 78
holding company, p. 427
mergers, p. 460

acquisitions, three approaches. Once management selects a firm to become the target of a takeover, it must decide how the takeover will occur. Basically, there are three major choices:

1. *Negotiations.* Frequently, management can approach the management or large shareholders of the target firm and discuss a possible merger or purchase. If they are interested, the accounting and legal departments with their counterparts in the to-be-acquired firm can work out details and develop the data needed to determine a purchase price or exchange ratio. With approval of both companies, the combination can take place.

2. *Solicit Tenders.* A *tender* is an offer to sell a definite number of shares at a specific price. When a firm selects this method of obtaining voting control, it will solicit tenders from the stockholders. This is done by placing a public notice or by sending letters to all shareholders announcing that the acquiring firm will pay a certain price for shares of stock tendered by the shareholders of the target firm. Normally, a limit is placed on the number of shares and a deadline is specified. For example, the notice may state that:

Roberts, Inc., will pay $14 per share for up to 1,200,000 shares of Lenox Products, Inc., common stock. Tenders should be sent to Roberts, Inc., in care of the Chase Manhattan Bank postmarked not later than April 1st.

If enough shares are tendered, the acquiring firm will be able to purchase voting control.

3. *Solicit Proxies.* A *proxy* is a written power of attorney allowing one person to vote the specific shares of a corporation's stock held by another person. Normally, proxies are sent out prior to stockholders' meetings to allow stockholders to have their interest represented without their personal presence at the annual meeting. Most companies routinely mail proxies to shareholders asking permission for management to vote the shares of stock at the meeting. If the stockholders return enough proxies, management can decide to accept or reject a takeover. If an outside company solicits proxies for the purpose of voting for a takeover, a *proxy fight* can result between the management and the acquiring firm. If the acquiring firm receives sufficient proxies, it will have enough votes to effect the takeover.

CROSS-REFERENCES:

acquisitions, how to analyze, p. 78

act of bankruptcy. Six conditions under the Chandler Act of 1938 allow a creditor to file an involuntary petition of bankruptcy against a firm. The acts are:

1. *Fraudulent Conveyance.* Permitting a debtor's assets to be concealed or removed with a goal of hindering, delaying, or defrauding creditors.
2. *Preference.* Transferring property to one or more of a firm's creditors in order to favor those creditors over the others.
3. *Allowing a Creditor to Obtain a Lien.* The action of an insolvent firm in permitting a creditor to obtain a lien on the firm's property.
4. *General Assignment.* Assigning or passing title on a firm's assets for the benefit of specific creditors.
5. *Appointing a Receiver.* Allowing a receiver or trustee to take charge of the property of an insolvent firm.
6. *Admission of Bankruptcy.* The admission by a firm in writing that it is unable to pay its debts and is willing to be judged bankrupt.

CROSS-REFERENCE:

bankruptcy, p. 320

agency. A relationship that exists when one person (the principal) authorizes a second person (the agent) to deal for him with third parties. An agency may be created by a specific act of the two parties or its existence may be implied under the law. The agency agreement can authorize actions with respect to specific transactions only (a special agent) or it can allow a broad authority on all matters (a general agent).

CROSS-REFERENCE

assignment, p. 314

aging of accounts receivable. A technique for evaluating the composition of a firm's receivables to determine whether the firm is using efficient collection policies. An aging schedule is prepared that breaks down each receivable into groups based on the time of sale. Although less common, a similar aging schedule can be prepared for accounts payable if the firm is seeking to pinpoint payment problems.

CROSS-REFERENCES:
accounts receivable, p. 306
aging schedule, p. 309

aging schedule. A tabular classification of receivables showing the length of time the accounts have been outstanding. The schedule may present the accounts by dollar amount, percentage breakdown, or both.

The table shows a firm that has a $600,000 balance of receivables on January 1. By checking the ledger cards for the accounts receivable, the financial manager discovered that $300,000 represented sales made in December, $150,000 sales in November, $100,000 in October, $20,000 in September, and $30,000 earlier than September. Using $600,000 as 100 percent, the aging schedule displays the dollar amounts outstanding by month of sale and the percentage outstanding.

To properly use the aging schedule in the table, we must know the credit terms of the firm. If the terms for the firm were 2/10 net 30, 50 percent of the receivables would be current, 25 percent would be up to 1 month overdue, 17 percent up to 2 months overdue, and 8 percent more than 2 months overdue. With 50 percent of its receivables overdue, it would appear that the firm was lax in collecting its receivables. If, on the other hand, the terms of trade were net 60, only 25 percent would be overdue—those from October and earlier. A 25 percent overdue figure still indicates problems. In either of these cases, the firm should make a review of its credit and collection policies.

CROSS-REFERENCE:
aging of accounts receivable, p. 309

alpha. In the *Sharpe Model,* an expected return from the investment in a security or portfolio when such return will be likely in the absence of market factors. In an efficient market, the alpha value will be equal to the rate of return on riskless securities times one minus the beta coefficient, or Alpha = $[1 - \text{beta}]$ $[E(\text{Rtn})$ riskless.]

CROSS-REFERENCES:
beta, p. 321
capital asset pricing model, p. 279
Sharpe Model, p. 521

American Stock Exchange. The second largest exchange in the country. It is located near the New York Stock Ex-

Aging Schedule of Accounts Receivable.

	Receivables Balance on January 1	Representing Sales Made in				
		Dec.	*Nov.*	*Oct.*	*Sept.*	*Pre-Sept.*
Dollar amount (000s)	600	300	150	100	20	30
Percentage of total	100	50	25	17	3	5
		Current with terms of net 30	Overdue with terms of net 30			

change in New York City. Firms may not list their securities on both the New York and American exchanges, but may list securities on one of these as well as on other exchanges outside New York City.

The American Stock Exchange is smaller in size than the New York Stock Exchange with approximately 500 seats. Unlike the New York Stock Exchange, the American Stock Exchange allows trading in both listed and unlisted securities. The companies represented in the trading are generally smaller than those on the New York Stock Exchange and usually trade at lower prices, with most shares in the range of $30 or less.

amortization. The process of allocating a capital investment, expense, or loan payment to a certain period of time. For example, if a firm purchases a fixed asset with a 20-year service life, it will want to receive sufficient income from that asset so as to amortize its capital investment within a 20-year period. As another example, if a bank makes a 7-year loan to a firm, the loan payment will be sufficiently large to pay the interest and to amortize the principal in a 7-year period.

CROSS-REFERENCES:
present-value techniques, how to avoid being manipulated by, p. 23
refunding a bond issue, how to make the decision, p. 152
fully amortizing, p. 416

annual cleanup. A provision in a line of credit agreement that requires the borrower to "cleanup" its loans during 1 or more periods a year. A line of credit is normally extended to assist the firm in meeting its short-term or cyclical needs for working capital. If the needs are really short term or cyclical in nature, at some point in the year the firm should have a zero loan balance against the line

of credit. The annual cleanup is a way of ensuring that such needs really are short term.

CROSS-REFERENCE:
line of credit, p. 453

annuity. A series of equal annual cash flows, commonly used to refer to the inflows from a capital investment. For example, when an investor purchases a 20-year $1,000 bond with a 10 percent coupon, the interest from the bond will provide the investor with an annuity of $100 a year for 20 years.

CROSS-REFERENCES:
present value of money, how to calculate, p. 19
profit planning, how to price the use of a capital asset, p. 53

anticipation approach to common stock value. This approach involves purchasing stocks whose market price is expected to rise in the immediate future. The analyst identifies the reasons for the expected rise and plans to hold the stock during the rise, then sell it once the rise is completed. The real value of the stock may be considered, but the emphasis is on short-term factors that will cause the rise. The fact that the stock may later decline is not important since the stock will have been sold after the rise. This method is commonly used by managers of performance-oriented mutual funds and by speculators in the market.

EXAMPLE: An analyst has discovered a firm whose main item of production is an electronic component for cable television. The investor learns that Congress will probably pass a bill allowing cable television in large urban areas where it is presently banned. This will greatly increase sales for firms in this industry. The analyst recommends buying the stock of the electronics firm. This represents which approach to valuation?

ANSWER: Anticipation approach. The growth approach should be ruled out because no long-term sales projections are indicated.

CROSS-REFERENCES:

Graham and Dodd approaches to common stock valuation, p. 246
growth approach to common stock value, p. 422

antitrust factors affecting mergers. The United States has laws forbidding business combinations that have the effect of substantially lessening competition or that tend to create a monopoly. Three statutes provide the framework for antitrust legislation:

1. *Sherman Act (1890).* The stated goal of the Sherman Act is to protect trade and commerce against unlawful restraints and monopolies. Two sections are noteworthy with respect to business combinations:

SECTION 1. Every contract, combination in the form of trust or otherwise, or conspiracy, in restraint of trade or commerce among the several States, or with foreign nations, is hereby declared to be illegal. . . .

SECTION 2. Every person who shall monopolize, or attempt to monopolize, or combine or conspire . . . to monopolize any part of the trade or commerce among the several States, or with foreign nations, shall be deemed guilty of a misdemeanor.
. . .

2. *Clayton Act (1914).* The Clayton Act forbids restrictive or monopolistic practices whose effect may be *to substantially lessen competition.* With respect to business combinations, the major restrictions were the following:
   a. Section 7 prohibited stock acquisitions that lessened competition between competitors. It did not forbid acquisitions of suppliers, customers, or others in the production or distribution channels of a single market.
   b. Section 8 forbid interlocking di-

rectorates that had the effect of lessening competition.

3. *Celler–Kefauver Amendment (1950).* This amendment to the Clayton Act resulted in a major change in government antitrust policy. It has three major impacts:
   a. Section 7 of the Clayton Act forbade the acquisition of *stock* when competition was lessened. The amendment broadens the prohibition to *stock or assets.* This prevents a monopoly created when one firm sells the assets of an operating division without selling any corporate stock.
   b. The amendment applies the Clayton Act to *individual markets,* a narrower scope than the previous lessening of competition between competitors. It does this by amending Section 7 so that it applies *in any line of commerce in any section of the country.* This allows government intervention to prevent monopolistic practices in major metropolitan areas or regional markets. It also prevents many combinations whereby one firm can control the supply and distribution channels and thereby make it difficult for its competitors to operate successfully.
   c. The amendment authorizes *divestment of assets or stock* acquired in violation of section 7 of the Clayton Act. This is highly significant because it allows the government to apply an after-the-fact remedy to business combinations that tend to lessen competition.

The antitrust laws are enforced through the combined efforts of the Department of Justice, Antitrust Division, and the Federal Trade Commission. Their major responsibilities are as follows:

1. *Federal Trade Commission (FTC).* Created by the Federal Trade Commission

Act (1914), the FTC is

a. Empowered and directed to prevent unfair methods of competition in commerce (within the scope of the laws).

b. Authorized to enforce compliance with the provisions of the Clayton Act.

c. Authorized to order divestment of assets and stock acquired in violation of the Clayton Act.

2. *Antitrust Division, Department of Justice.*

a. Enforcement of the Sherman Act, which allows criminal penalties for violation. The act provides for fines up to $50,000, prison terms up to 1 year, or both.

b. Instituting civil proceedings to prevent and restrain violations of the law. In recent years, this has been a highly significant power since it allows the Justice Department to seek injunctions against future combinations that would violate antitrust laws.

The enforcement measures used by the Antitrust Division of the Justice Department and the Federal Trade Commission have major impacts on firms that are considering external growth. For this reason, firms considering combinations with other firms must hire expert legal counsel and must be aware of any antitrust aspects of the proposed combinations. If a firm has questions on possible government intervention in a combination, it may deal directly with the Justice Department and Federal Trade Commission to receive advice and even formal opinions on combinations under the scope of the Clayton Act.

If favorable opinions are received on a proposed combination, the firm may proceed with some confidence. It is still possible, but not likely, that the government will attempt to block or divest a combination that has been favorably re-

viewed in advance. If a negative opinion is received, the firm may still proceed, but it must be prepared for lengthy and costly legal battles to resist the civil proceedings of the Justice Department or to overturn the orders of the Federal Trade Commission.

CROSS-REFERENCES:

Sherman Act, p. 522
Clayton Act, p. 349
Celler–Kefauver Amendment, p. 346

arbitrage. The buying of securities, foreign exchange, or commodities in one market and simultaneously selling the same in another market to take advantage of a difference in price quotations between the two markets, thus earning a riskless profit.

CROSS-REFERENCE:

arbitrage in foreign exchange markets, how to analyze, p. 161

arbitration. The submission of a dispute to a third party, often after agreeing that the decision of the third party will settle the dispute (binding arbitration). The third party is often a three-person board with one member selected by one party to the disagreement, a second member selected by the other party, and the final member selected by the first two members.

arrangement. In *voluntary settlements* or *bankruptcy* situations, a form of reorganization that protects the bankrupt firm in the near term and allows it time to get back on its feet. An arrangement must be agreed to by creditors. The management of the firm can be placed in the hands of a *receiver* or can be continued by existing officers. Normally, an arrangement is proposed by the debtor as part of a plan for discharging creditors' claims.

CROSS-REFERENCES:

bankruptcy, p. 320
composition, p. 355
extension, p. 400
reorganization, p. 508

Asian Development Bank. Headquartered in Manila, this bank was established in the mid-1960s by a number of countries including several European nations and the United States. It makes loans using criteria similar to those of the World Bank, while seeking to increase its capability to make "soft" loans.

CROSS-REFERENCE:
World Bank, p. 556

ask. The price that a seller is willing to accept for a particular security or commodity at a given time.

CROSS-REFERENCES:
forward market, how to calculate bid and ask quotes, p. 171
over-the-counter market, p. 475

asset. A resource that allows a firm to conduct its business. Assets may be identified as tangible versus intangible, current versus fixed, or liquid versus illiquid.

CROSS-REFERENCES:
present-value techniques, how to avoid being manipulated by, p. 23
flow-of-funds statement, how to develop from balance sheet and income statement, p. 38
pooling and purchase methods, how to use in merger accounting, p. 91
protecting local assets in high-inflation country, p. 177
circulating assets, p. 349

asset leverage. A term frequently used to refer to the asset turnover aspects of levering return on investment. If a firm has a relatively high asset turnover compared to similar firms, it is said to have a high degree of asset leverage.

CROSS-REFERENCES:
return on investment, how to lever, p. 69
asset turnover, p. 313

asset turnover. Highlights the amount of assets the firm used to produce its total sales. The ability to produce a large volume of sales on a small asset base is an important part of the firm's profit picture. Idle or improperly used assets increase the firm's need for costly financing and the expenses for maintenance and upkeep. By achieving a high asset turnover, a firm reduces costs and increases the eventual profit to its owners.

The asset turnover is calculated by dividing sales by the firm's assets.

Asset Turnover

$$\frac{\text{sales}}{\text{total assets}} \quad \text{or} \quad \frac{\text{sales}}{\text{operating assets}}$$

In the calculation of asset turnover, assets may be defined three ways:

1. *Total Assets.* The most common usage of assets involves the total assets reported on the balance sheet. This is basically the book value of current and fixed assets. It is the most common asset measure since it is the most readily available, appearing annually in the firm's annual report.

2. *Operating Assets.* A more accurate measure of the assets used to generate a given volume of sales is the actual operating assets. The analyst might eliminate excess current assets, capital tied up in expansion activities, or other assets not used in the firm's operations to produce the reported EBIT. The difficulty in using operating assets is identifying them. If the firm is constructing a $25,000,-000 factory, this may be noted in the

annual report. Since it is not operating yet, it can be eliminated from the total assets. But there may be other, unused assets, and this may not be known.

3. *Total Assets Plus Estimated Value of Leased Assets.* When a firm leases plant or equipment, it is earning a return on an asset that is not shown on the balance sheet. When comparing different firms, the approximate value of each firm's assets should be reflected. If an airline is leasing a $20,000,000 jet plane, it should be included as a portion of the assets in the calculation of asset turnover.

CROSS-REFERENCES:
profitability, how to analyze with ratios, p. 56
return on investment, how to lever, p. 69
asset leverage, p. 313
assets, managing, p. 314

assets, kinds of. A portfolio may contain three kinds of assets:
1. *Financial Assets.* The common stock, preferred stock, and bonds issued by corporations or governments. Financial assets are easily identified with specific returns, are easily purchased and sold in capital markets, and are available from a wide variety of sources.
2. *Capital Assets.* The factories, warehouses, vessels, vehicles, pipelines, and other plant, equipment, or real estate representing fixed or capital investments. Capital assets are usually not easily identified with specific returns and do not have the liquidity of financial assets.
3. *Intangible Assets.* Items such as leases, royalties, patents, trademarks, and contracts that can be used to earn profits. Intangible assets frequently share the characteristics of either financial or capital assets in that they

may or may not be easily identified with specific returns and they may or may not be liquid.

CROSS-REFERENCE:
capital asset pricing model, p. 279

assets, managing. Finance personnel meet with other officers of the firm and participate in making decisions affecting the current and future utilization of the firm's resources. As an example, these managers may discuss the total amount of assets needed by the firm to carry out its operations. They will determine the composition or mix of assets that will help the firm best achieve its goals. They will identify ways to more effectively use existing assets and reduce waste and unneeded expenses.

This decision-making role crosses liquidity and profitability lines. Converting idle equipment to cash improves liquidity. Reducing costs improves profitability.

CROSS-REFERENCE:
asset turnover, p. 313

assignment. A transfer of a person's or organization's rights to another person or organization. A typical assignment would be the case of the creditor who assigns his right to collect on a note to a collection agency.

CROSS-REFERENCE:
agency, p. 308

audit. A formal procedure of evaluating a firm's financial transactions during a given period of time normally resulting in a verification of a firm's assets, liabilities, and equity as of a given date (balance sheet) and a verification of the transactions that occurred during the period (income statement and/or flow-of-funds statement).

CROSS-REFERENCES:
income statement, p. 429
flow-of-funds statement, p. 410

authorized capital. The total par or stated value of the shares of common stock that a corporation is empowered to issue. This amount is generally stipulated in the corporate charter.

CROSS-REFERENCE:
par value, p. 477

average collection period. A ratio that compares the receivables balance with the daily sales required to produce the balance. If the firm has $1,000 of sales each day and a receivables balance of $30,000, it took 30 days to accumulate the receivables if sales are relatively constant. More important, if collections are relatively constant, it will take the firm 30 days to collect the $30,000 currently held as receivables. Although this reasoning is highly simplified, the average collection period does provide a useful measure of the firm's liquidity.

CROSS-REFERENCES:
liquidity, how to analyze with ratios, p. 49
receivables, changing collection costs and bad-debt losses, p. 503
receivables ratio, p. 506

average rate of return. A ratio, now largely discarded, for evaluating proposed capital expenditures. Calculated by dividing the average earnings after taxes forecasted from a project by the average investment required by the project. For most firms, present value cash flow techniques have replaced the average rate of return as an evaluation tool.

CROSS-REFERENCES:
internal rate of return, how to calculate p. 15
net present value, how to compare proposals, p. 17

B

bad-debt loss. A loss that results when a firm makes sales on credit and then is unable to collect the receivable. Bad-debt losses are taken as an expense on the firm's income statement. This expense is calculated as the percentage of credit sales for which payment has not been received or is not expected. The expense is generally estimated as a percentage of sales and a reserve account is established to cover it.

CROSS-REFERENCE:
receivables management, how to evaluate different credit policies, p. 108

balance of payments. A record of economic transactions between one nation's citizens and those of other nations. A balance of payments is calculated very systematically over a designated period of time, usually one year, with interim calculations for months or quarters. Some of the major characteristics of balance-of-payments accounting are:

1. *Double-Entry Bookkeeping System.* Every financial transaction involves both a debit and credit, as is customary in double-entry bookkeeping. When all entries have been recorded, the debits and credits will balance. This means that special techniques must be used to calculate any imbalances in a nation's payments. Such imbalances will not be obvious from the double-entry accounting for balance of payments.

2. *Transactions, not Payments.* Traditionally, the phrase balance of payments is used when it would be more correct to use balance of international *transactions.* A transaction is a business agreement or activity that is followed at some point by a payment. For example, goods may be shipped abroad under the terms of a binding contract and payment will follow in 60 days. The balance of payments effect is recorded when the transaction occurs rather than at the time of payment.

3. *Transactions are Actual or Expertly Estimated.* At times it is difficult to determine when a transaction has taken place. Experts at the Department of Commerce record the actual transactions and estimate other transactions as best they can. A rather sizable *errors and omissions* account is frequently needed to balance the U.S. balance of payments.

4. *Foreigners Included in Host Country Figures.* A person living abroad is treated just like the residents in his host country. If an Italian living in England receives money from France, the transaction is an outflow from France and an inflow to England.

CROSS-REFERENCES:
international finance, "how to" sections, p. 161
balance of payments, analyzing, p. 316
capital controls for dealing with balance-of-payments deficits, p. 333
monetary policy, effect on balance of payments, p. 463

balance of payments, analyzing. In analyzing the significance of a deficit or surplus in a nation's balance of payments, a number of factors must be considered including:

1. *Techniques of Calculation Vary from Nation to Nation.* Although nations are becoming increasingly sophisticated in measuring the effects of economic transactions, the analyst should recognize that national differences exist in balance-of-payment accounting. The complexities of identifying transactions and estimating

their effects can bring errors or delays into the figures for a nation. This factor is more important in dealing with recent figures and is less important in evaluating a nation's long-term figures.

2. *Important Distinction between Stocks and Changes.* A nation's *stock of reserves* is the total of the monetary reserves supporting its currency. The balance of payments measures *changes in reserves* when deficits or surpluses are discussed. With large stocks, deficits are less serious than with small stocks. A nation with limited monetary reserves will have difficulties with relatively small deficits. A nation with large stocks of monetary reserves can finance small deficits over an extended period of time.

3. *Important Distinction Between Long- and Short-Term.* As a general rule, deficits become important only as a long-run situation. A nation can finance occasional deficits without serious difficulty. The most damaging short-run deficit occurs when confidence has been lost in a nation's currency. In this situation, individuals and businesses are not willing to hold the currency and intense pressures develop. Even though the long-term situation is not critical, the short-term pressures can force a devaluation.

4. *High Interdependence Exists among Accounts.* In dealing with difficulties, nations must realize that there is a high interdependence among the differing accounts that comprise a nation's balance of payments. For example, the United States has frequently discussed reductions of troop concentrations in Europe as a means of reducing its balance of payments deficits. It is reasoned that fewer goods and services would be purchased from foreigners if fewer dollars were in the hands of military personnel and families abroad. While this is undoubtedly true, a troop reduction might also result in a reduction of U.S. exports since foreigners would have fewer dollars to buy U.S. goods. Any discussion of balance-of-payments effects should recognize this high interdependence among accounts.

CROSS-REFERENCES:
balance of payments, p. 316
international finance, "how to" sections, p. 161
monetary policy, effect on balance of payments, p. 463

balance sheet. Shows the assets, liabilities, and equity for the firm as of a specific date, usually at the close of the last day in a month or fiscal year. It shows how the resources of the firm (assets) are provided by capital from creditors (liabilities) and owners (equity). It provides a snapshot, if you will, of the firm's financial position at the close of an accounting period.

A balance sheet is usually written in two columns that illustrate the relationship between the assets and the sources of assets. The assets or resources of the firm are displayed in the left-hand column, and the sources of those assets in the right-hand column. In this sense, the assets are balanced by the sources (debt and equity) of the assets. It should be carefully noted that no resources are contained in the equity accounts such as common stock or retained earnings. These are balancing accounts, showing sources of assets, and do not represent bank balances.

Each of the major categories on the balance sheet is divided into subsections on most balance sheets. Many different accounts can be listed depending upon such factors as the nature of the firm's business, the kind of assets it owns, and the sources of its assets.

balance sheet, a quick quiz. The following questions on the Morgan Company offer a quick quiz on proficiency in reading a balance sheet. The table provides the necessary data.

1. What are the total liabilities of the Morgan Company at the end of 1974?
2. What is the net value of the firm's equipment at the end of 1973?
3. What is the minimum amount of new equipment purchased by the firm in 1974?
4. What percentage of the firm's assets are fixed assets at the end of 1974?
5. How much did current liabilities increase during 1974?
6. How many shares of stock are outstanding at the end of 1974?
7. What percentage of the firm's assets are financed by borrowing at the end of 1974?
8. (*Tough bonus question*) How many shares of stock were sold during 1974 and how much did the company receive for each share?

ANSWERS:

1. $110,000	5. $8,000
2. $75,000	6. $6,000
3. $40,000	7. 33%
4. 44%	8. 2,400 at $29.16

MORGAN COMPANY, INC., Balance Sheet (December 31, 1974)

Assets	1974	1973	Liabilities and Equity	1974	1973
Current assets			Current liabilities		
Cash	$ 45,000	$ 30,000	Accts. payable	$ 60,000	$ 52,000
Accts. receivable	60,000	50,000			
Inventories	81,000	63,000	Long-term debt		
			Mortgage (7%)	50,000	60,000
Equipment	155,000	115,000			
Less Accum. depre.	(55,000)	(40,000)	Common stock ($25 par)	150,000	90,000
			Premium on stock	10,000	—
Land	45,000	30,000	Retained earnings	61,000	46,000
Total Assets	$331,000	$248,000	Total	$331,000	$248,000

balance sheet accounts, titles and arrangement. Individual balance sheets vary considerably and may or may not show accounts with the titles listed in this handbook. For example, contributed capital in excess of par may be called *surplus* or *premium on common stock.* Whatever the title, the analyst should be thoroughly acquainted with the kinds of accounts appearing on the balance sheet.

An important characteristic of the balance sheet is that the items are recorded in a certain order. Assets, for example, are listed in order of liquidity or nearness to cash. Cash, the most liquid asset, comes first; marketable securities, slightly less liquid, comes second, and so on through the highly illiquid plant and equipment. Liabilities, on the other hand, are listed in the approximate order of repayment. The most urgent debts (those to be paid first) are listed first. The long-term debt, a low-urgency obligation, is listed near the end of the liabilities section. In the equity section, the common stock that was issued to start the business is listed first. The retained earnings, which accrued after the business was in operation, are listed last.

```
Order of Balance-Sheet Accounts

Assets — In order of nearness to
cash
Liabilities — In order of nearness to
repayment
Equity — Contributed capital before
retained earnings
```

Order of Accounts.

CROSS-REFERENCE:
current liabilities, p. 370

balance sheet, limitations. Although it provides useful information, the balance sheet has its limitations. It does not show the events or activities that resulted in the balances in each of the accounts, nor the accounting techniques used to prepare them. Many accounting methods are standard, but some variance is permitted, which could greatly change the amounts reported in certain accounts. Another weakness is that the analyst preparing the balance sheet may make improper assumptions either mistakenly or to distort the picture shown on the balance sheet. Assumptions as to when obligations have been incurred or when revenues have accrued can have marked effects on the final figures on the balance sheet.

```
Limitations on Balance-Sheet Uses

No explanation of how balances occurred.

Accounting techniques may vary.

Not all assumptions are known.
```

Limitations on the Use of the Balance Sheet.

balance sheet, uses of. The major use of the balance sheet as a financial tool is as a statement of a firm's financial condition at a given point in time. It shows balances in permanent accounts and the result of all the accounting transactions since the first day of operation. It lists the accounting (not market) value of the firm's assets and shows the portion of the assets financed by debt and equity.

When used in conjunction with an income statement and other financial data, the balance sheet provides valuable information on the firm. Financial ratios can be developed to gain an insight into the liquidity and profitability aspects of the business. This is particularly true because most balance sheets are comparative. A comparative balance sheet displays the current balances and the prior year's balances for each account in two columns. This allows the analyst to compare the beginning and end of year positions and to measure the changes in each account during the course of the year.

If properly prepared and certified by a certified public accountant, the balance sheet can be used as a reasonably accurate picture of a firm's financial position at a moment in time.

CROSS-REFERENCE:
deferred charges, p. 375

balloon payment in loan. Fixed-asset financing may be designed to allow the

Payment Schedule with a Balloon Payment.

$125,000 Asset with $25,000 Down Payment, 5-Year Loan Schedule at 9%
with a Balloon Payment in the Final Year

Year	Interest at 9%	Principal Repayment	Total Payment
0		$ 25,000	$ 25,000
1	$ 9,000	0	9,000
2	9,000	0	9,000
3	9,000	20,000	29,000
4	7,200	20,000	27,200
5	5,400	60,000	65,400
	$39,600 +	$125,000 =	$164,600

firm to pay smaller amounts at first and larger amounts, or *balloon payments,* in the later stages of the loan period. The loan contract may stipulate that only interest payments will be made for the first few years, interest plus a portion of the principal will be paid for a few more years, and a large principal repayment will accompany the interest in the final year.

The interest rate for balloon-payment financing is usually higher than the rates for steady-principal-reduction or steady-payment plans. The later principal payments involve greater risk for the lender, and hence the lender must be compensated for bearing such risk. A balloon-payment schedule can help a firm that needs time to establish the sales from the use of the fixed assets before it will be able to make payments on the principal.

The table gives an example of a steady-principal-reduction   schedule modified with a balloon payment.

CROSS-REFERENCE:
steady-principal-reduction loan,
p. 526

bank acceptance. A draft accepted by a commercial bank or similar entity. The acceptance is used in short-term financing in both domestic and foreign trade to facilitate a transaction without the requirement for an immediate money investment. Basically, the bank is guaranteeing payment of the purchase, commonly in situations when the two parties do not have regular dealings.

CROSS-REFERENCE:
draft, p. 391

bankruptcy. A legal state which can only occur when a firm's liabilities exceed the fair value of its assets. The *Chandler Act of 1938* is the primary statute applying to bankruptcy situations. Two basic types of bankruptcy can be identified:
1. *Voluntary.* A firm may file a petition of bankruptcy in a Federal District Court admitting its inability to pay its debts and its willingness to be judged bankrupt. This can be done because the owners desire an orderly liquidation that protects the value of their equity investment. Or, it can be done as a first step in reorganizing the firm for continued operations when it can once again pay its bills.
2. *Involuntary.* An outside party, normally a creditor, can file an involuntary petition of bankruptcy against a firm that is behind in paying its bills or if the firm has committed an *act of bankruptcy.* This can be the first step in a liquidation or reorganization.

Bayesian statistics. In statistics, a probability is defined as the relative frequency with which an event takes place in the long run. If we say a proposal has a .37 probability of making at least $100,000, we mean that it will be profitable at or above this figure 37 percent of the time.

In capital budgeting, we are not faced with the problem of measuring the relative frequency of known events. Rather, we must forecast the likelihood of future events that will affect different proposals. To do this, we make use of subjective probabilities.

It is important to distinguish between objective and subjective probabilities. An objective probability is supported by rigorous theory, past experience, and the laws of chance. For example, it is an objective probability that, over the long run, flipping a coin will produce an equal number of heads and tails. Stated another way, the probability of a head on one toss of a coin is .50. It is quite a different matter to predict the likelihood of a depression in the next 5 years. There is no formal body of theory that explains the relative frequency of economic depressions in a changing economy. In this case, a subjective interpretation of political and economic data is the only approach to estimating the likelihood of the event. This method of forecasting probabilities is widely used in business decision making and is called Bayesian statistics.

bear market. In the trading of securities, a market in which price levels are declining in a well-defined downward trend.

bearer bond. A highly negotiable bond issued by a corporation or government that is owned by the person who has physical possession of it, just as a dollar bill is owned by its bearer. It differs from a registered bond that requires that the owner's name be listed on the books of the corporation or its agent.

benefit-cost ratio. See Profitability Index, p. 494.

best-efforts basis. A situation where a group of underwriters agree to sell a security offering at an established price without accepting the risk for unsold securities. This differs from the normal underwriting where the investment banker and its partners accept the risk that they will not be able to sell the entire offering.

beta coefficient. In the capital asset pricing model, the regression coefficient used to measure the degree of systematic or market-related risk from investing in a security. Beta may be calculated by the formula

$$Beta_x = \frac{[\,r_{x,mkt}\,][\sigma_x\,]}{\sigma_{mkt}}$$

where $Beta_x$ = the beta coefficient for security x

$r_{x,mkt}$ = the correlation coefficient showing the degree of correlation between security x and the total market for all securities.

σ_x = standard deviation of the likely return from security x

σ_{mkt} = standard deviation of the likely return from the entire market

The correlation coefficient r can range between minus one and plus one and has significance as follows:

1. *Minus One (— 1.0).* A correlation coefficient of — 1.0 indicates a perfect negative correlation with the market. If the market rises, the security will decline. A security with a high negative correlation will rise in declining markets and decline in rising markets.
2. *Zero.* A zero correlation coefficient indicates no relationship between movements in the returns of the security and the market.
3. *Plus One (+ 1.0).* A correlation coefficient of + 1.0 indicates a perfect positive correlation with the market. If the market rises, the security will also rise.

CROSS–REFERENCE:
capital asset pricing model, p. 279.

bid. The price that a buyer is willing to pay for a particular security or commodity at a given time.

CROSS–REFERENCE:
over-the-counter market, p. 475

bill of exchange. An instrument drawn by one person (drawer) ordering a second person (drawee) to pay a specified sum of money to a third person either on sight (a sight draft) or at some future time (a time draft). Also called a draft.

CROSS–REFERENCE:
draft, p. 391

bill of lading. A contract for the transportation of goods between the shipper and the carrier, that serves as the principal transit document and title for the goods. A straight bill of lading gives title to the person designated to receive the shipment (consignee), is not negotiable, and may not be used as collateral for a loan.

An order bill of lading is negotiable, may be endorsed to a third party, and may be used as collateral for a loan.

black market. A term applied to the illegal purchase and sale of commodities or foreign exchange at prices above those fixed by government regulations or restrictions.

CROSS–REFERENCE:
foreign exchange, p. 414

blocked currency. Money held by a person or firm that may not be converted into a foreign currency because of restrictions imposed by the issuing government.

CROSS–REFERENCE:
foreign exchange, p. 414

blue sky laws. State laws regulating the sale of securities, and providing for the disclosure of specific information and accurate representation of securities traded. So-called because the laws prevent the sale of securities that promise nothing but "blue sky".

CROSS–REFERENCE:
security, financial, p. 519

board of directors. A group of individuals elected by the common shareholders of a corporation who meet as a body to conduct the ordinary business activities of the company.

CROSS-REFERENCE:
corporation, p. 364

bond. A long-term debt security of a firm. A bond issue allows the firm to raise large sums of money for a long period of time. The issue will contain many bonds, usually divided into $1,000 units. Maturities of 10 to 25 years are common with semiannual interest payments.

CROSS-REFERENCES:
bonds, how to calculate value of, p. 124
refunding a bond issue, how to make the decision, p. 152
bearer bond, p. 321
call feature, p. 328
conversion feature, p. 358
corporate bonds, characteristics of, p. 361
debenture, p. 373
income bonds, p. 429

bond discount. When a firm issues a bond for less than the face or par value of the bond, it is sold at a discount. Since the firm must repay the face value at maturity of the bond, the discount must be amortized over the life of the bond. The discount will be divided into equal units and each will be taken as a noncash expense during the life of the bond. For example, if a $1,000 bond with a 10-year maturity sells for $970, the $30 discount will be amortized over 10 years with a noncash expense of $3 per year.

bond premium. If a firm sells a bond for more than its face or par value, it is sold at a premium. The premium is divided into equal units over the life of the bond and each unit is considered as noncash income. For example, if a $1,000, 10-year bond sells for $1,050, the $50 premium is amortized at $5 noncash income per year.

bond rating. An assessment by a financial service, such as Moody's or Standard and Poor's, of the riskiness of publicly traded bonds. The rating is based on the overall quality of the issuing corporation and measures the safety of principal and interest. Moody's has 9 ratings, from least risky to most risk; Aaa, Aa, A, Baa, Ba, B, Caa, Ca, and C. Standard and Poor's uses a similar rating system.

bond value. The current market worth of a bond, normally estimated by calculating the present value of its future interest payments and principal repayment.

CROSS-REFERENCE:
bond value, how to measure interest rate risks on, p. 182

book salvage value. The estimated value of a fixed asset at the completion of its service life that is used in the calculation of a depreciation schedule. When the asset reaches its book salvage value, it is said to be fully depreciated. Cash salvage value will be the actual amount of money received when the asset is finally sold. In most cases, the book and cash salvage values will differ.

CROSS-REFERENCES:
cash-flow stream, how to calculate, p. 3
cash salvage value, p. 346
salvage-value effects in capital budgeting, p. 517

book value. The accounting value of an asset or equity. The book value of an asset is its original cost less any accumulated depreciation charged to it.

The book value of a share of common stock is the firm's equity divided by the number of shares outstanding.

book value per share. The value of a firm's common stock calculated by dividing the stockholders' equity by the number of shares outstanding. This ownership ratio is somewhat related to capital-structure ratios, since it measures the accounting value of a portion of the firm's assets–the portion financed by the owners.

It is important to note that the book value of a share of stock involves a claim against the common stock, contributed capital in excess of par, and retained earnings accounts. That is, a portion of the retained earnings must be considered in addition to the contributed capital accounts. If a firm has $50,000,000 in the common-stock account, $25,000,000 in contributed capital in excess of par, and $25,000,000 in retained earnings, each of its 1,000,000 shares has a book value of $100 [($50,-000,000 + $25,000,000 + 25,000,000) /1,000,000 = $100]. In effect, this book value indicates that each share of common stock should be credited with contributing $100 to finance the firm's assets.

Book value is the reflection of the accounting records of the firm rather than a strong measure of the real value of the firm's assets. If two otherwise identical firms used different depreciation schedules, the book value of their assets would be different. As a general rule, the book value results from the use of conservative accounting techniques and is considerably lower than the market value of the stock. For this reason, it is of limited value as an ownership ratio. Three valid uses of book value may be identified:

1. *Liquidation Value.* When a firm is experiencing liquidity or profitability problems, it may consider selling its assets, paying off its debt, and distributing the remaining money, if any, to its shareholders. In cases of possible liquidation, the book value will give an indication of the amount that can be distributed to shareholders. If the firm can sell its assets for, say, 80 percent of the recorded asset value, and it pays its debt at 100 percent of value, the remainder is available for common stockholders. Normally, a firm with a high book value per share will have more remaining for shareholders than a firm with a low book value per share.

2. *Market Price Near Book Value.* In many cases, an interesting phenomenon occurs when a firm's market price nears its book value. Investors will note that the firm's assets support a certain price (book value) and will not allow the market price to drop below that price. In effect, the book value becomes a support level for the price of the common stock. In some cases, it may become a rallying point, and investor demand will begin to push up the price of the stock. Analysts and investors take notice of the low market price in relation to book value and begin to purchase the apparently undervalued stock.

3. *Legal Proceedings.* In certain legal or tax proceedings, book value may have a use. It may become the taxable base for taxes on securities.

borrowing capacity and leasing. Defined as the additional long-term debt that could be added to its capital structure without seriously damaging the credit rating of the firm and the market price of its common stock. As the firm adds debt without corresponding increases in equity, borrowing capacity is reduced. Conversely, the paying off of debt tends to increase borrowing capacity.

It may be argued that leasing increases a firm's borrowing capacity. The rationale is that the lease obligation does not appear as debt on a firm's balance sheet and thus does not adversely affect the firm's debt-equity ratio. If a firm has borrowing capacity when it leases, it will still be able to borrow after the lease is signed.

Although financial leasing imposes basically the same obligations and risks as debt financing, research indicates that investors and the financial community are more conscious of debt obligations than leasing commitments. Because this is the case, we may conclude that, in many cases, one advantage to leasing is that it provides a firm with more assets than its borrowing capacity might otherwise allow.

As an example of this point, consider a firm with $5,000,000 in debt and $7,000,000 in equity on its balance sheet. The firm is in an industry with a normal 1/1 debt-equity ratio. If the firm needs $4,000,000 to finance an expansion, a bond issue for this amount would result in a debt-equity ratio of $9,000,000/$7,000,000 or 1.3/1. This exceeds the industry norm and may have harmful effects on the firm's stock price in the market. Rather than risk such a lowering of the price of the stock, the firm might choose leasing and the lower debt-equity ratio. If the firm leases for its $4,000,000, its debt-equity ratio remains $5,000,000/$7,000,000 or .71/1. The firm has $2,000,000 of unused borrowing capacity at this point. The firm would still be able to borrow another $2,000,000 before reaching the 1/1 industry debt-equity norm.

As leasing becomes more common, this advantage will tend to be reduced. Large financial institutions are already becoming increasingly aware of the risk in leased assets. As more firms include leaseholds in their financial statements, the investing public will also become more critical of increasing borrowing capacity through the use of leaseholds.

CROSS-REFERENCES:
debt-equity ratio, p. 373
hedging, foreign exchange transactions, how to evaluate alternatives, p. 173

bottleneck item. A unit of inventory which can close down a firm's production if it is not available. An example would be a single transistor required for many components produced by an electronics firm.

CROSS-REFERENCE:
inventory management, how to set up system for, p. 103

branch. In a decision tree, a branch is a line representing one of the possible future alternatives.

CROSS-REFERENCES:
risk in capital budget, how to measure, p. 25
decision tree, how to build one, p. 185

break-even analysis. A technique for evaluating the relationship between sales, fixed and variable costs, and profits. The break-even point is the volume of sales at which the firm's revenues equal its total operating costs so that there is neither a profit nor a loss to the firm.

break-even point. In break-even analysis, the volume of sales in units or dollars at which the firm's revenues are identical to its total operating costs.

Bretton Woods, 1944. In 1944, representatives of the Allied Powers met at Bretton Woods, New Hampshire, to develop the post-war structure of financial transactions among nations. Under the strong influence of the United States and Great Britain, these nations sought to end the disastrous restrictions and practices of the depression years and replace them with a rational system for international finance.

While the nations agreed on many factors, three major issues had to be resolved. Lord Keynes, the British representative, was arguing for a totally new approach to an international monetary system. The issues which embodied his proposed system were:

1. *World Central Bank versus Stabilization Fund.* The British proposed the creation of a world central bank with functions similar to those of the differing national central banks. The bank would be empowered to control the world's money supply and be the major clearinghouse for international transactions. The opposing position, supported by the United States, recognized that nations were not willing, for the most part, to surrender national sovereignty over their currencies and monetary policies. Instead of a world central bank, these nations proposed a stabilization fund with a "bag" full of world currencies. The fund would use its currencies and influence to promote order in international finance.

2. *Size of Monetary Reserves.* The British proposed a large increase in the liquid reserves supporting the currencies of the individual nations. An increase in reserves would be needed so that the world's money supply could be large enough to finance trade and the reconstruction of the war-torn economies of Western Europe. The United States, possessing some two-thirds of the world's gold, opposed such an increase in reserves. The U.S. representatives felt that this would amount to a giveaway of the U.S. gold and financial power and might weaken the dollar.

3. *Responsibility for Correcting Imbalances.* Prior to Bretton Woods, deficits in a nation's balance of payments were the problem of the deficit nation. The creditor nations were not considered part of the solution to payments imbalances. The British proposed that imbalances were the problem of both nations and mutual efforts should be required to correct them. The United States, believing that it would never be faced with balance of payments deficits, disagreed. Instead, a scarce currency clause was proposed. Under this clause, a debtor nation could declare the currency of a creditor nation to be a scarce currency. This allowed the debtor nation to restrict transactions with that creditor nation until the imbalance was corrected.

At the end of World War II, the United States held the bulk of the

Issues Raised at Bretton Woods and the Outcome.

British Position	U.S. Position	Outcome
A world central bank with power to control world money supply.	A stabilization fund with "bag" full of world currencies.	Stabilization fund
A large increase in the world's liquid reserves.	Gold and foreign exchange to continue their role as monetary reserves.	Gold and foreign exchange remained as monetary reserves
Mutual efforts by debtors and creditors to correct imbalances.	Scarce currency clause to be used by debtors to correct imbalances.	Scarce currency clause to correct imbalances.

world's gold reserves, had a largely intact and high-production economy, and was economically the dominant nation among the Allied Powers. As a result of these factors, the will of the United States prevailed for the most part at Bretton Woods. The table outlines the issues raised and the final result.

broker. A person or firm who trades securities by acting as an agent for others and receiving a commission for assisting in a transaction.

CROSS-REFERENCE:
secondary markets, p. 519

budget. A formal plan expressed in dollars. The process of financial planning is frequently called budgeting, and makes use of pro forma, or future, financial statements. Balance sheets, income statements, fund-flow statements, and other formal statements may be incorporated in the firm's budget.

bull market. In securities trading, a market in which prices are advancing in a well-defined upward trend.

CROSS-REFERENCES:
bear market, p. 321
securities, financial, p. 519

business cycle. The alternating periods of expansion and contraction in overall economic activity. Economists generally refer to these alternating periods as economic fluctuations and reject the term "cycle" as misleading because it implies regularity of the changes.

business risk. The likelihood that a firm will not have the ability to successfully operate in the business community. Some causes of business risk are that a firm's products may not sell, its machinery may not operate properly, or it may face disruptions to its normal business conditions.

CROSS-REFERENCE:
lease-buy decision, how to make it, p. 132

C

call feature. An option in most bond offerings that allows the issuer to repurchase the bonds under stated conditions prior to the maturity of the bond. The call price will be higher than the face value of the bond and it may vary at different points in time. The call feature is frequently used with convertible securities in order to force their conversion into common stock. Preferred stock may also be callable.

CROSS-REFERENCES:
bond, p. 323
convertible securities, p. 359
preferred stock, p. 481
preferred stock, value of, p. 483

call premium. Callable bonds or preferred stock contain a provision that allows the corporation to retire the issue at a fixed price prior to maturity. The difference between face value of the debt and the call price is the call premium. For example, if a $1,000 bond is callable at $1,050, a $50 call premium exists.

CROSS-REFERENCES:
refunding a bond issue, how to make the decision, p. 152
bond, p. 323
preferred stock, p. 481

capital. In accounting, the equity of a firm. In economics, one of the three "factors of production." The other two are land and labor. In corporate law, the portion of the consideration received by the corporation upon the issuance of stock that has been recorded as capital in accordance with the laws of the incorporating state. In business, the total assets of the firm.

CROSS-REFERENCE:
equity, p. 396

capital asset. An item of value owned by a business or an individual that has been acquired for long use and will assist the firm or individual in generating earnings.

CROSS-REFERENCES:
present-value techniques, how to avoid being manipulated by, p. 23
profit planning, how to price the use of a capital asset, p. 53
tax factors affecting return, how to evaluate, p. 72
capital asset pricing model, p. 279

capital asset pricing model. A financial theory relating risk and return that is widely used by theorists to measure the risk in a portfolio of securities. The model employs a capital market line (CML) to recognize that higher risk securities will require higher rates of return than lower risk securities. The model can be used to calculate a firm's cost of capital and to assist in capital budgeting decisions.

CROSS-REFERENCE:
capital market line, p. 279

capital asset pricing model, assumptions of. The following assumptions provide the conceptual framework for examining risk and return using the capital asset pricing model: [1]
1. *Competitive Market.* Financial securities or capital assets are bought and sold in a highly competitive market where information on the likely risks and returns on the assets is freely available and is known to all participants. In effect, the assets are traded in perfect markets.

---

[1] M. C. Jensen, "Capital Markets: Theory and Evidence," *Bell Journal of Economics and Management Science,* Autumn, 1972.

2. *No Taxes Costs.* Securities can be exchanged without the payment of brokerage commissions, fees, or taxes and without any other transaction costs.

3. *Riskless Borrowing Rate.* Both large and small investors are able to borrow freely at a riskless rate of interest; that is, at a rate of interest equal to the return that can be obtained by investing in a riskless security such as government bonds.

4. *Rational Investment Goals.* Investors are rational and strive to receive the highest return from an acceptable level of risk or the lowest risk from a target level of return. These goals are pursued by trading or selling short perfectly divisible and liquid assets in a program designed to maximize individual wealth.

CROSS-REFERENCE:
capital asset pricing model, p. 279

capital budgeting. The decision-making process by which firms evaluate the purchase of major fixed assets, including buildings, machinery, and equipment. It is part of the firm's formal planning process for the acquisition and investment of capital. It results in a capital budget, the firm's formal plan for the expenditure of money to purchase fixed assets.

Operating Versus Capital Budget Most large firms prepare two different budgets each year. The operating budget is prepared for the short term, normally 1 year, and is concerned with the revenues and expenses related to the firm's daily operations. The capital budget deals exclusively with major investment proposals and is prepared to help the firm deal with the long term. For most firms, there is only a limited overlap between the two budgets.

CROSS-REFERENCES:
capital budgeting, "how to" section, p. 3
lease-buy decision, how to make it, p. 132
operating budget, p. 471

capital budget cash inflow, two sides. To be a worthwhile investment, a firm must receive differential after-tax cash inflows from a proposed project. This inflow can occur by two means:

1. *Additional Revenues.* If a firm is entering a market that will increase sales, the excess of cash revenues over cash expenses provides a net cash inflow. As an example, a firm forecasting $120,000 in additional sales and $90,000 in additional cash expenditures will have a $30,000 net cash inflow.

2. *Cash Savings on Operations.* Sometimes a proposal is intended to reduce operating costs. A firm may be currently expending $50,000 for the operation of a large machine. A new machine would cost $80,000 but would reduce the need for one operator, thus reducing costs to $40,000. This is a net cash inflow of $50,000 minus $40,000, or $10,000.

In either case, the inflow is shown in the stream preceded by a plus sign. In the first case, the inflow is additional revenue; in the second, a reduction of a cash outflow.

CROSS-REFERENCES:
operating budget, p.471
payback, p. 477

capital budget, significance of. The preparation of the firm's capital budget is highly significant for a number of reasons:

1. *Substantial Expenditures.* Capital expenditures may range from pieces of equipment costing thousands of dollars to complete factories and other physical facilities costing millions of

dollars. A $25,000,000 factory or ocean-going vessel has become commonplace and a $300,000,000 oil refinery is an occasional investment. The very size of these items in terms of dollars underlies their importance to the firm.

2. *Long Time Periods.* The effects of capital-spending decisions will be felt by the firm over extended periods of time. Once a multimillion dollar building is begun, the firm cannot easily withdraw from continuing the construction. When a firm forecasts the need for additional manufacturing space, it may begin constructing a factory. If changes in the marketplace eliminate the need for the extra capacity, the firm faces a serious problem. Does it keep the facility, incurring heavy fixed costs with no revenues, in the hope that conditions will improve and the capacity will be needed? Or does it sell the plant at a potentially large loss? The long-term commitment adds considerable risk to the firm's capital-budgeting decisions.

3. *Implied Sales Forecasts.* The spending of funds for fixed assets represents an implied forecast of future sales. If machinery or a building is not purchased, the firm may not be able to meet demand in the future. If too much is purchased, the firm is stuck with unneeded capacity. An important part of the capital-budgeting process is forecasting sales, possibly 10 or 15 years into the future.

4. *Over- and Undercapacity.* If the budget is carefully drawn, it will usually improve the timing and quality of asset acquisition. If done poorly, it will cost the firm large sums of money because of overcapacity or undercapacity—sometimes at the same time. The firm may have idle assets to produce a product that is not in demand while it has a shortage of the machinery and facilities to produce a much-demanded, high-profit product.

capital-budgeting policies. Because of the importance of capital-budgeting decisions, firms usually have detailed policies for administering the budget. Several major issues facing firms are:

1. *Estimating Needs.* The amount of funds needed for a project should be estimated by using a combination of past performance and historical data, future expectations, and the recommendations of all interested departments in the firm. By including all three sources of information, the firm reduces the possibility of omitting a major factor. It takes a special skill to bring together the estimates and data, check the different items for accuracy, and resolve the differences. This is an important part of the financial manager's ability to develop a realistic and accurate capital budget.

2. *Approval for Proposals.* Approvals for expenditures are usually linked to the size of the investment proposal. Larger dollar amounts normally must be approved at higher levels in the corporation than smaller dollar amounts. The purchase of a small piece of machinery may be approved by a plant manager without further discussion. A major purchase, such as would be involved in the installation of a new computer system, may be discussed by top management and may require the approval of the board of directors.

3. *Planning Horizon.* The capital budget is prepared at least one year in advance and may extend 5, 10, or even 15 years into the future. Five to 7 years is common. The most important factor affecting the planning horizon is the rate of change in technology in the industry. If a firm is in an indus-

try with relatively few advancements in technology, a capital investment will be useful for many years. The firm can plan for 10, 15, or even more years of service life from an asset. This is not the case for a firm facing rapid technological change. In this situation, the firm must plan for an early return on investments so that funds will be available to replace obsolete equipment. Firms dealing with costly or complex technologies may establish two planning horizons. First, a specific set of proposals will be considered for the next 5 to 7 years. Second, a different set of expectations will be prepared for the long-term period beyond 7 years. Although the long-term predictions will be subject to continuous review, the long-term plan helps the firm analyze its needs and direction into the distant future and encourages management to prepare for technological changes.

capital budgeting, problems with ranking proposals. Once the capital budget is nearing completion and a variety of alternative projects has been identified, the firm must select the projects it will finance. Among problems that arise are the following:

1. *Mutually Exclusive Projects.* If the firm accepts one project, it may rule out the need for another. These are called mutually exclusive projects. An example of this kind of project would be the need to transport supplies from a loading dock to the warehouse. The firm may be considering two proposals—forklifts to pick up the goods and move them, or a conveyor belt connecting the dock and warehouse. If the firm accepts one proposal, it eliminates the need for the other.

2. *Contingent Projects.* The utility of some proposals is contingent upon the ac-

ceptance of others. For example, a firm may be considering the construction of a new headquarters building and a new employee parking lot. If it decides not to build the headquarters, the need for the lot is gone. At the same time, if the firm builds the headquarters and not the lot, the employees will have no place to park. These are contingent projects.

3. *Capital Rationing.* Firms will normally have more proposals than can be funded properly. In this case, only the most desirable projects will receive approval. Capital rationing occurs when the firm has more acceptable proposals than it can finance. In this situation, the firm should rank the projects from highest to lowest priority. Then a cutoff point is selected. Proposals above the cutoff will be funded; those below will be rejected or delayed. The cutoff point is selected after carefully considering the number of projects, the goals of the firm, and the availability of capital to finance the capital budget.

CROSS-REFERENCES:
capital rationing, p. 335
contingent projects, p. 357
mutually exclusive projects, p. 465

capital-budgeting proposals, kinds of. A firm may include several different kinds of proposals in its capital-budgeting process. One classification identifies five kinds of proposals:

1. *Replacements.* As fixed assets are used, they wear out or become outdated by new technology. Money may be budgeted to replace worn-out or obsolete equipment.

2. *Expansion.* Successful firms tend to experience growth in the sales of primary products. If a firm is experiencing shortages or delays in high-demand products because of

inadequate production facilities, it will consider proposals to add capacity to existing product lines.

3. *Diversification.* A business can reduce the risk of failure by operating in several markets rather than a single market. Diversification allows the firm to protect itself against the collapse of sales in a single product. Firms seeking the facilities to enter new markets will consider proposals for the purchase of new machinery and facilities to handle the new products.

4. *Research and Development.* Firms in industries where technology is rapidly changing will expend large sums of money for researching and developing new products. If large sums of money are needed for equipment, these proposals will normally be included in the capital budget.

5. *Miscellaneous.* A firm will frequently have proposals that do not directly help achieve profit-oriented goals. The proposal to install pollution-control equipment on a factory's smokestacks is an example. Safety items, such as automatic sprinkling systems to protect against fire, may involve considerable expenditures. These types of proposals may be included in the firm's capital-budgeting process.

capital-budgeting stream, funds tied up.
In capital budgeting, the timing of cash movements is the prime concern. Cash flowing out in one year and returning in a later year is recorded as an outlay initially and an inflow later. It does not matter that the money was not actually spent. It only matters that it was tied up and not available to the firm.

Working capital is an example of funds tied up during the life of a capital-budgeting proposal. A firm may be considering the purchase of a machine that is capable of faster production than the old machine. This will allow the firm to process more inventory and to sell more items, thus increasing receivables. The cash tied up in year zero to increase inventories and receivables is treated as an outflow. After the new machine ends its production in a number of years, the inventories may be liquidated and the receivables collected. The funds tied up in working capital would be treated as an inflow in the final year of the cash-flow stream.

It may be argued that the working capital does not return to cash at the end of the machine's service life. Rather, a new machine will be purchased and the funds remain tied up. This does not matter. By handling working capital as an outflow in year zero and inflow in the final year, we make a mathematical adjustment that will be important when we consider the time value of money. The outflow will have a higher present value than the inflow, and the tying up of funds will reduce the rate of return from the project. This is correct, since the more we expend or tie up, the lower the return.

Sometimes a proposal will free working capital. For example, a new machine may be so efficient that we do not have to store large volumes of inventory of finished goods; the machine can produce them as needed. If a proposal frees working capital, it is treated as an in-

Effect of Tying Up Funds or Freeing Them.

If Working Capital Increases	*If Working Capital Decreases*
an outlay in year zero.	an inflow in year zero.
an inflow in final year.	an outflow in final year.

flow in year zero and an outlay in the final year. This recognizes that the freed working capital is not really a revenue, but does mathematically adjust the value of freeing the funds when the time value of money is considered.

CROSS-REFERENCES:
cash-flow stream in capital budgeting, p. 344

capital controls for dealing with balance-of-payments deficits. For nations' balance-of-payments difficulties, direct government or central bank actions can be taken to restrict the outflows of capital or accelerate the inflows. These include:
1. *Restrictions on Profit Remittances.* Many nations have policies that restrict multinational firms from returning their local profits to the foreign parent corporation. In effect, the local currency is blocked from freely transferring in response to corporate needs. Viewed from the multinational's point of view, a blockage represents a risk to conducting business in a nation with chronic balance-of-payments difficulties.
2. *Controls on Convertibility.* A nation can suspend the convertibility of its currency for a short period of time. This may be done selectively so the controls only apply to certain transactions. One technique is to distinguish between essential and nonessential needs for foreign currency. By documenting that it has a need for foreign currency to support economically essential activities, a firm can receive permission to convert its local currency into other currencies. Nonessential conversions would be denied.
3. *Multiple Exchange Rates.* A government can establish different exchange rates for different categories of transactions. For example, a rate of 4 pesos to the dollar can be established for

essential transactions; 8 to 1 can be the rate for nonessential transactions. In this situation, a citizen seeking to buy a luxury foreign car (nonessential) would have to pay twice as much for each dollar as the firm seeking to buy a foreign truck (essential).

CROSS-REFERENCE:
balance of payments, p. 316

capital depletion. A decline in the value of a firm's fixed assets that occurs when the firm fails to modernize its asset base. This is a problem particularly during inflationary periods, because depreciation is not sufficient to replace the firm's fixed assets when they wear out. To return to its original asset position, the firm must use a portion of its reported profits or must seek outside financing. The need to use profits to replace depleted capital produces an argument that the firm overstated the profits during the period of inflation.

CROSS-REFERENCE:
fixed assets, p. 407

capital gain. When a firm sells a fixed asset for more than the asset's original purchase price, the difference between the sale price and the purchase price is called a capital gain. A short-term capital gain occurs when an asset is held for less than a minimum period of time (12 months in 1978); a long-term capital gain occurs when the asset is held for more than the minimum period of time. Only long-term capital gains, as defined by the Internal Revenue Service, receive special tax treatment. Short-term gains are taxed as ordinary income, which is 48 percent for a firm's earnings over $25,000 per year. Long-term capital gains may be taxed at a rate of 30 percent or the normal tax rate, whichever is lower. By definition, a capital gain does not occur when a firm sells an asset for more than its book value but less than its original cost. Such a gain is taxed as normal income.

CROSS-REFERENCES:
tax factors affecting return, how to evaluate, p. 72
dividends, why investors want them, p. 387
mergers, tax factors affecting, p. 462

capital loss. When a firm sells an asset not used in business or trade (for example, a marketable security) for less than its original purchase price, a capital loss is realized. A capital loss can be used to offset past, present, or future capital gains but may not be used as an ordinary business expense.

CROSS-REFERENCE:
tax factors affecting return, how to evaluate, p. 72

capital market. A linkage of institutions between the suppliers and users of long-term funds. Prominent institutions in the capital market include the organized security exchanges, the over-the-counter market, and financial intermediaries such as commercial banks and insurance companies.

CROSS-REFERENCES:
Miller and Modigliani on cost of capital, p. 213
money market, p. 464

capital market line (CML). In the capital asset pricing model, the line showing the relationship between risk and return in a portfolio of securities or capital assets.

CROSS-REFERENCE:
capital asset pricing model, p. 279

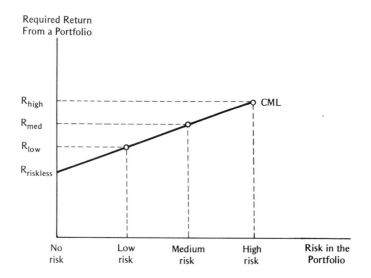

$R_{riskless}$ = rate of return at zero risk (generally the return on U.S. Treasury securities)
R_{low} = rate of return required on a low-risk portfolio
R_{med} = rate of return required on a medium-risk portfolio
R_{high} = rate of return required on a high-risk portfolio

capital rationing. A situation that occurs when a firm has a limited amount of funds that must be allocated to a number of competing capital-budgeting projects. The firm must rank the project and ration its funds to those proposals with the highest priority.

CROSS-REFERENCE:
capital budgeting, problems with ranking proposals, p. 331

capital structure. Capital structure is the composition of debt and equity securities that comprise a firm's asset financing. Both debt and equity securities are used in most large corporations. The choice of the amount of debt and equity is made after making a comparison of certain characteristics of each kind of security, of internal factors related to the firm's operations, and of external factors that can affect the firm.

CROSS-REFERENCES:
ownership factors, how to analyze with ratios, p. 51
mergers, how to analyze profitability in a ten-step process, p. 85
Durand on cost of capital, p. 203
cost of capital, factors affecting, p. 365
cost of capital, importance of, p. 366
Schwartz on capital structure theory, p. 230
optimal capital structure, how to determine, p. 147

capital structure, external factors affecting. Those considerations outside the firm that have a bearing on the composition of debt and equity securities, such as the following:
1. *General Level of Business Activity.* If the overall level of business activity is rising, most firms will need money to expand their operations. The need for additional long-term funds will bring a firm to the money markets for either debt or equity funds. On the other hand, a decline in business activity may allow a firm to cut back its operations and use its cash to retire debt or equity securities.
2. *Level of Interest Rates.* Interest rates on bonds fluctuate in the market in response to supply and demand factors. If interest rates become excessive, firms will delay debt financing, will switch to short-term financing until long-term debt can be offered at lower rates, or will switch to equity securities.
3. *Level of Stock Prices.* When firms issue new common stock, they hope to receive as much money as possible from each share. When stock prices are depressed, the firm will not offer common stock. If stock prices are high, the firm can raise relatively large amounts of money by issuing relatively few new shares.
4. *Availability of Funds in the Money Markets.* Money markets in the United States are a constantly changing, complex phenomenon. At times money is plentiful and any reasonably priced debt or equity offering will be sold. At other times, money is scarce and offerings will fail to sell out. The availability of funds affects the firm's ability to offer debt and equity securities.
5. *Tax Policy on Interest and Dividends.* At the present time, interest is paid on debt prior to the calculation of the corporate income tax. Dividends are declared after the tax calculation. This tax policy makes the payment of dividends more costly than the payment of interest, and has severely reduced the number of issues of preferred stock in recent years.

CROSS-REFERENCE:
Schwartz on capital structure theory, p. 230

capital structure, internal factors affecting. Those considerations within the firm that have a bearing on the kinds and amounts of securities in the capital structure, such as the following:

1. *Matching Fluctuating Needs Against Short-Term Sources.* A firm may have a busy season just before Christmas and may need extra money during October, November, and December to conduct its business. Since the need is only for 3 months each year, it would be expensive to use long-term financing that requires interest or dividends on an annual basis. For fluctuating needs, the firm would probably reject debt and equity securities and prefer a short-term loan from a bank.

2. *Degree of Risk.* The more debt a firm has, the larger the interest payments and the greater the chance of inability to make the payments, with consequent bankruptcy. Equity securities need not be repaid and dividends need not be declared. Thus, equity securities reduce risk; debt securities increase risk.

3. *Increasing Owners' Profits.* If the firm can borrow at 6 percent and earn 12 percent with the money, all profits above the 6 percent interest will be distributed to the owners (after taxes are paid, of course). The ability to increase the owners' return without increasing their investment is an argument for using debt financing.

4. *Surrendering Operational Control.* In some cases, a firm will not be able to sell bonds without agreeing to allow the bondholders to exercise certain operational controls, such as selecting a member of the board of directors if interest payments are not made on time. At the same time, the sale of common stock brings new voting investors into the firm and dilutes the control of the existing shareholders. The possible loss of operational control is a factor influencing the financing mix.

5. *Future Flexibility.* A firm is expected to maintain a balanced mixture of debt and equity securities. Excessive debt reduces the firm's ability to borrow in the future and hence reduces flexibility. The need to maintain a balance to ensure future flexibility of

Internal Factors That Affect Capital Structure.

	Bonds	*Preferred Stock*	*Common Stock*
Matching fluctuating needs against short-term sources		Not useful, a long-term security.	Not useful, a long-term security.
Degree of risk	Payments required, risk increased.	Payments not required, low risk.	Payments not required, low risk.
Increasing owners' profits	All profits above interest go to owners.	All profits above fixed dividends go to owners.	All profits shared equally by existing and new shareholders.
Surrendering operational control	No control, except restrictions or default.	Control only if voting rights granted.	New shareholders gain voice, except Class A nonvoting stock.
Future flexibility	Excessive debt restricts future borrowing.	Increases flexibility	Increases flexibility

financing alternatives affects the capital structure.

CROSS-REFERENCES:

risk and return, major decision areas, p. 513
profitability function, p. 493
Schwartz on capital structure theory, p. 230
optimal capital structure, how to determine, p. 147

capital structure management, goals of. In managing the firm's capital structure, the financial analyst is attempting to determine the mix of debt and equity securities that maximizes the value of the common stock on a per share basis. In achieving this single, overall goal, the analyst must be concerned with the attainment of related goals as follows:

1. *Taking Advantage of Favorable Financial Leverage.* A small amount of debt offers minimal risk to the operations of the firm. At the same time, favorable financial leverage will increase the return to the common shareholders. Within the limits of acceptable risk, most investors and analysts expect that firms will take advantage of the higher return possible through the use of favorable financial leverage.

2. *Taking Advantage of Leverage Offered by Corporate Taxes.* A high corporate income tax provides a form of leverage with respect to capital-structure management. The leverage occurs because interest is deducted before the tax calculation, whereas dividends are declared after taxes. As an example of this leverage, consider a firm that can finance a project with either a 6 percent bond or a 6 percent preferred stock. Assuming a 50 percent tax rate, the firm must earn twice as much to meet the dividend payment for the stock alternative as

is needed to meet the interest payment for the bond alternative. The higher expense of equity financing can be avoided by the use of debt, which, in effect, provides a form of income tax leverage to the common shareholders.

EXAMPLE: A firm can finance a proposal with an 8 percent bond or a 9 percent preferred-stock issue. The total project costs $300,000. How much additional earnings will accrue to the common shareholders if the bond alternative is used? How much of the earnings accrue solely as a result of the income tax leverage? (Assume the project has a 20 percent return.)
ANSWER:

	With 8% Debt	With 9% Preferred Stock
EBIT (20% × 300,000)	60,000	60,000
Interest (8% × 300,000)	24,000	0
EBT	36,000	60,000
Taxes	18,000	30,000
NIAT	18,000	30,000
Preferred dividend (9% × 300,000)	0	27,000
EACS	18,000	3,000

The common shareholders receive $15,000 additional earnings ($18,000 − 3,000) with the bond alternative. $3,000 of this difference is owed to the higher cost of preferred stock (9 percent versus 8 percent). Had both rates been the same (8 percent), the EACS would have been $18,000 versus $6,000. The difference of $12,-000 ($18,000 − 6,000) is solely because of the income tax leverage.

3. *Avoiding a Perceived High-Risk Capital Structure.* If common-stock investors perceive an excessive amount of debt in a firm's capital structure, the price of the common stock will drop.

Avoiding this perception is a primary goal of capital-structure management. When a firm is considering debt financing, it may decide that the debt does not add significant risk to the capital structure. If the investing community agrees, the firm may float the offering. But if the firm's bankers or brokers disagree, the firm must reconsider the offering. The firm does not want to issue debt, whether risky or not, if the creditors and investors will perceive an excessive risk and depress common-stock prices.

CROSS-REFERENCES:
financial leverage, how to analyze, p. 34
financial leverage, p. 405

capital-structure ratios. Two ratios are important in analyzing the relationship between the debt and equity components of the firm's capital structure:

1. *Debt-Equity Ratio.* This is calculated by dividing the total debt by the total equity.
2. *Debt-Asset Ratio.* This is calculated by dividing the total debt by the total assets.

These ratios show how much of the firm's assets are financed by debt and equity and give important information about prospects for future financing. If a firm has excessive debt, it will experience difficulty in locating additional debt financing. The firm will be able to borrow only at high interest rates, if at all. On the other hand, if the ratio is low (virtually no debt), it may indicate a failure to use cheap borrowed funds to raise the return earned on the common stock.

Analysts differ on whether short-term debt should be included in the capital-structure ratios. One group reasons that accounts payable and similar short-term items allow a temporary use of assets (notably inventory), but are not really a form of borrowing to finance the firm's resources. In other words, current liabilities are not a permanent part of the capital employed by the firm. Another group includes current liabilities in the debt-equity and debt-asset ratios. The reasoning is that careful management of the short-term debt accounts allows the firm to take advantage of inexpensive (and frequently free) funds that it would otherwise have to borrow at higher rates. Also, short-term debt represents obligations of the firm. If capital-structure ratios measure a degree of financial risk by showing how much the firm owes, they should reflect all debt owed by the firm.

There are three major uses of capital-structure ratios:

1. *To Identify Sources of Funds.* The firm finances all its resources from debt or equity sources. The amount of resources from each source is shown by these ratios.
2. *To Measure Financing Risk.* One measure of the degree of risk resulting from debt financing is provided by these ratios. If the firm has been increasing the percentage of debt in its capital structure over a period of time, this may indicate an increase in risk for its shareholders.
3. *To Forecast Future Borrowing Prospects.* If the firm is considering expansion and needs to raise additional money, the capital-structure ratios offer an indication of whether debt funds will be available. If the ratios are too high, the firm may not be able to borrow.

As a general guideline, the debt should not exceed 60 percent of the total sources of funds. Thus, a debt-equity ratio of 1.5/1 or a debt-asset ratio of .6/1 should be maximum for industrial firms.

CROSS-REFERENCES:
debt-equity ratio, p. 373
debt-asset ratio, p. 373
ownership ratios, p. 475

Comparison of Capital-Structure Ratios.

If the Debt-Equity Ratio is:	Then the Debt-Asset Ratio is:	And the Percentage of Total Assets Financed by Debt Are:
0	0	0
.2/1	.167/1	16.7
.4/1	.286/1	28.6
.6/1	.375/1	37.5
.8/1	.444/1	44.4
1.0/1	.50/1	50.0
1.5/1	.60/1	60.0
2.0/1	.67/1	66.7
5.0/1	.83/1	83.3

capital structure, security characteristics affecting. Security characteristics that affect the firm's capital structure fall under four classifications:

1. *Ownership Rights.* The issuance of new securities involves the question of extending the ownership rights to the new security holders. Creditors exercise no ownership control during routine periods of operation. In some cases, the debt agreement might place restrictions on management activities, such as the prohibition of paying dividends, should cash fall below a certain level. The holders of preferred stock may or may not have any ownership rights, depending on whether the stock is voting or non-voting. New holders of common stock, except for nonvoting stock, receive immediate and full ownership rights.

   If the shareholders do not wish to share their ownership rights with new investors, the firm will attempt to use debt or preferred-stock financing rather than common-stock financing. The firm's ability to use these financing means may be limited by other factors; but, as a general rule, ownership rights accompany the residual owners—common shareholders—rather than the preferred owners or creditors.

2. *Repayment Requirements.* Debt matures and must be repaid according to the conditions in the bond indenture or other agreement. Preferred stock ordinarily has no maturity date, although it usually has a call feature that allows its retirement. Common stock involves no repayment requirements.

   If the firm does not wish to face specific repayment requirements, preferred or common stock will be preferable to debt.

3. *Claim on Assets.* The bondholders have the first claim on assets in the event of liquidation, the preferred shareholders the next claim, and the common shareholders have the residual claim. If the firm does not want to give new investors a priority claim on assets, common stock will be desirable.

4. *Claim on Profits.* Interest must be paid on bonds regardless of the level of profits. Although bondholders have no right to share in profits, they have a legally enforceable right to the payment of the stipulated interest. The preferred shareholders have the first right to share in the profits, but only up to a specified limit. The common shareholders have the absolute right to share in the profits of the firm.

   If the firm wants to restrict the right of new investors to share in the

Security Characteristics That Affect Capital Structure.

	Bonds	*Preferred Stock*	*Common Stock*
Ownership rights	None, in most cases.	None, unless voting.	Full rights.
Repayment requirements	Full requirement; must be repaid.	None, but may be callable.	None.
Claim on assets	A senior security, first claim.	Senior to common stock, a second claim.	A junior security, last claim.
Claim on profits	None, but interest must be paid first.	First claim, but only up to specified amount.	Full claim on residual profits.

firm's profits, debt or preferred stock will be desirable.

capitalization. The total value of ownership capital and borrowed capital used by the firm to finance its total assets.

CROSS-REFERENCES:

capital, p. 328
Gordon on common stock value, p. 255

capitalization of dividends. A method of stock value similar to the *capitalization of earnings* that recognizes that dividends are the major source of income to shareholders of stock in mature corporations.

CROSS-REFERENCES:

Graham and Dodd approaches to common stock value, p. 246
capitalization, p. 340
Gordon on common stock value, p. 255

capitalization of earnings. A method of stock valuation based on a comparison of earnings per share and the price-earnings ratio. It is the most important single technique used by investors and analysts to calculate common stocks' intrinsic value.

CROSS-REFERENCES:

common stock value, how to compare two or more stocks, p. 83

Graham and Dodd approaches to common stock value, p. 246
Gordon on common stock value, p. 255

capitalization of growth rate. A method of determining the intrinsic value of a firm's common stock by considering how a growth factor increases the present worth from a future earnings stream. The general formula is:

$$\text{Intrinsic Value} = [\text{EPS}][\text{P/E}_{zero} + \text{coefficient (Growth)}]$$

where EPS = current or average earnings per share

P/E_{zero} = a normal price-earnings multiple for a firm with a zero growth rate

coefficient = a numerical value that is multiplied times the growth rate to properly weight the effect of growth. This normally ranges from 1 to 2.

Growth = growth rate in sales or profits and is expressed without the percent (Example: 4 percent becomes 4)

CROSS-REFERENCE:

Graham and Dodd approaches to common stock value, p. 246

capitalization rate. A measure of the rate of return investors demand before they will purchase a stock, calculated by dividing the firm's earnings per share by its market price. This is the reciprocal of the price-earnings ratio. As an example a stock with a $2.00 EPS and a $20.00 selling price has a capitalization rate of 2/20 or 10 percent. This 10 percent capitalization rate means that the firm earns 10 percent on the value of its common stock. If investors did not require this return, they would pay more for the stock and the rate of return or capitalization rate would drop.

CROSS-REFERENCES:
ownership factors, how to analyze with ratios, p. 51
common stock value, how to compare two or more stocks, p. 83
bonds, how to calculate value of, p. 124
bond values, how to measure interest rate risks on, p. 182
Graham and Dodd approaches to common stock value, p. 246

capitalization techniques. Methods of determining the real or intrinsic value of common stock that convert a firm's earnings, dividends, and/or growth rate into a present value.

CROSS-REFERENCES:
Graham and Dodd approaches to common stock value, p. 246
present value, p. 486

capitalize. To calculate the present value of future returns from a business. Also, to convert future earnings, dividends, and/or growth into one sum equivalent to the firm's present value.

CROSS-REFERENCES:
Graham and Dodd approaches to common stock value, p. 246
present value, p. 486

carry-back. A privilege in the tax law that allows a firm to apply an ordinary operating loss against profits from an earlier period to reduce those reported profits and thus receive a tax refund.

CROSS-REFERENCE:
mergers, tax factors affecting, p. 462

carry-forward. A privilege under the tax law that allows a corporation that sustains an ordinary operating loss to apply such loss against the income in future periods. This has the effect of reducing future taxes.

CROSS-REFERENCE:
mergers, tax factors affecting, p. 462

carrying costs. The expenses involved in maintaining inventories, including storage costs, insurance, obsolescence or spoilage, and damage or theft.

CROSS-REFERENCES:
inventory management, how to set up system for, p. 103
inventories, p. 441

cash. In a financial sense, all money items and sources that are immediately available to help pay a firm's bills. On the balance sheet, a firm will normally list cash assets in two categories:

1. *Cash.* Included in this category are coin and currency held by the firm in cash registers and petty cash, and balances in checking accounts. This money is immediately usable to pay bills.

2. *Marketable Securities.* If the firm has excess cash, it may decide to convert it to short-term investments. The financial manager will purchase low-risk, high-liquidity money-market instruments that can be converted back to cash without delay if the need arises. These securities provide a small profit on cash that may not be

needed immediately for the firm's operations.

cash accounting. A method of keeping a firm's books that recognizes only cash receipts and disbursements. Income is not considered earned unless it has been received; expenses are recognized only when paid. This method of accounting, normally used by small firms, differs from the more widely accepted method of accrual accounting.

cash balance, factors affecting. Several important factors may be identified as affecting the size of the cash balance maintained by a firm:

1. *Availability of Short-Term Credit.* To avoid holding unnecessarily large balances of cash for contingency or opportunity needs, most firms attempt to make arrangements to borrow money in case of unexpected needs. One useful agreement between the firm and its bank is the *line of credit,* a formal or informal agreement that obligates the bank to provide future credit if it is requested. The bank may agree, for example, to supply up to $100,000 on 72-hour notice for maturities of 30 days to 1 year. The loan would be charged at the prevailing interest rate for its corporate customers whenever the request is made. With such an arrangement, the firm will pay a slightly higher rate of interest than on long-term debt, but will have to pay interest only during the period the money is actually needed. Because a line of credit allows a firm to rely upon a guaranteed loan for unexpected needs, it reduces the size of the balance needed in the cash account.

2. *Money-Market Rates.* The money market consists of the institutions and individuals who lend or borrow money as part of the normal course of business activity. The interest charged on any loan will be affected by a number of factors, including the size of the loan and the credit rating of the borrower. Perhaps the most important factor in the overall level of interest rates is the availability of money to lend. If money is plentiful, interest rates will be low. If money is scarce, interest rates will be high.

   How does the level of interest rates —high or low—affect the size of the cash balance maintained by a firm? If money will bring only a low return in the money markets, a firm may choose not to invest it. Since the loss of profit is small, it may not be worth the trouble to make the loan. Thus, the firm will keep excess cash in its checking account, and this has the effect of increasing cash balances. On the other hand, if interest rates are very high, every extra dollar will be invested. High money-market rates will attract funds from firms that otherwise would not invest for the short term.

3. *Variations in Cash Flows.* In addition to contingency needs, some firms experience wide fluctuations in cash flows as a routine matter. If a firm requires its customers to pay their bills on the tenth day of the month, it will receive a much larger cash inflow at that time than at other times during the month. This firm will have a larger average cash balance than will a firm that collects its re-

ceivables throughout the month. If the city experiences a storm that delays mail for several days near the tenth of the month, the firm may be unable to meet its own obligations due at the same time. Another example is a firm whose main customers are small businesses with cash problems. This firm will experience many delays in payment. Some months the cash will arrive as expected. Other months, the firms will be slow to pay.

As a general rule, a firm with steady inflows and outflows will be able to maintain a fairly uniform cash balance. The balance will also be lower than for firms with widely fluctuating flows. The firm will be able to more accurately predict its future cash balances and will have fewer difficulties with cash management.

4. *Compensating Balances.* If a firm has borrowed money from a bank, the loan agreement may require the firm to maintain a minimum balance of cash in its checking account. This is called a compensating balance. In effect, this requires the firm to use the services of the bank making the loan and gives the bank a guaranteed deposit of money on which it pays no interest. Another reason for a compensating balance is when the bank is expected to provide certain free services for the firm. The interest-free deposit is the bank's compensation for its advice and assistance.

A requirement to maintain a minimum cash balance will increase the amount of cash the firm must hold. It may be argued that this does not, in fact, increase the firm's liquidity. Since the firm cannot write checks on the compensating balance, it does not really have liquidity from the funds.

CROSS-REFERENCES:

cash-flow forecast, how to prepare a, p. 97
cash safety level, how to calculate, p. 101
compensating balance, p. 354

cash budget. A detailed statement of the cash receipts and disbursements forecasted by the firm for the coming year, generally on a month to month basis. It is a short-term planning tool used by the firm to determine the future periods of cash shortages or surpluses.

CROSS-REFERENCE:

cash-flow forecast, how to prepare a, p. 97

cash flow. The movement of cash through a firm. A firm's cash flow may be measured through a cash budget, a cash-flow forecast, or a flow-of-funds statement.

cash-flow forecast. The forecasting of cash flows is designed to help the firm achieve its twin goals of liquidity and profitability.

1. *Liquidity.* By predicting cash surpluses or shortages, the firm achieves liquidity—sufficient money in the bank to pay debts as they come due.
2. *Profitability.* Accurate cash forecasting achieves profits by allowing the firm to take profitable discounts on purchases, invest surplus funds, or reduce the costs of maintaining idle cash balances.

A useful tool to deal with the forecasting aspect of cash-flow management is the cash-flow forecast. This is a schedule over time of cash inflows and outlays. Several characteristics of this tool are important.

1. *Focuses on Receipts and Payments.* The cash-flow forecast ignores profits or losses, sales, and costs as such. It concentrates on the cash receipts, regardless of when the sales were

made. Thus, cash sales would be included as would the collections on the accounts receivable, which were created by credit sales. With respect to debts of the firm, only the cash payments are included. The creation of liabilities does not involve a flow of cash and is omitted.

2. *Noncash Expenses Are Exluded.* It should be obvious that, since noncash expenses such as depreciation involve no payments, they are not considered in a cash-flow forecast. Cash payments to purchase machinery would be included.

3. *Joint Effort of Several Departments.* Although the cash-flow forecast is prepared under the direction of the financial manager, it represents a joint effort of several operating departments. The sales prediction, and indirectly the collections on receivables, is provided by the marketing personnel. The production expenses are calculated with production-department managers and cost accountants. Other departments will be involved to the degree that they are responsible for receiving or disbursing cash.

Cash-flow forecasting is characterized by lags, which are delays between an action and the cash flow that results from the action. To illustrate the lags with respect to inflows and outlays, consider the following:

	June 26	July 2	July 9	July 16	July 19	Aug 2
Action	Sale, 30,000 net 20	Purchase, 16,000 net 30	Purchase, 24,000 net 10			
Cash Flow				+30,000	−24,000	−16,000

In this example, the credit sale on June 26 with trade terms of net 20 brings an inflow (indicated by the plus sign) on July 16. The two purchases result in outflows (indicated by the minus signs) on future dates that are appropriate to the credit terms.

In preparing cash-flow forecasts, it is particularly important to check the timing of flows and to identify all the lags. If, for example, the firm knows that a certain percentage of receivables is not collected on time, it should not expect the cash from 100 percent of receivables within the period specified by the terms of trade. If it does not consider lags properly, cash shortages may needlessly occur.

CROSS-REFERENCES:

cash-flow forecast, how to prepare a, p. 97

lease-buy decision, p. 132

liquidity, p. 453

lag, p. 449

cash-flow stream in capital budgeting. A series of cash expenditures or receipts written so that their timing can be seen. The cash-flow stream in the Table will be used to illustrate the differential after-tax flow for a proposed project. In the first column, the years are listed beginning with year zero. As a matter of standard form, cash-flow streams begin with the investment decision that occurs in *year zero.* This is normally a cash outlay on the new proposal, which is indicated by a minus sign in front of the dollar amount. The outlay in the Table is $100,000. Since the firm incurs no outlay if it does not invest in the project, the differential column shows the difference between zero and $100,000.

In year 1, the firm forecasts that its cash inflows will exceed its cash outlays on existing operations by $40,000. The net inflow is indicated by a plus sign. If the firm accepts the new proposal, inflows will increase from $40,000 to $60,000, a differential of $20,000, which is recorded in the differential column. This process continues for the life of the new proposal.

CROSS-REFERENCES:

Differential After-Tax Cash-Flow Stream.

Year	Without Proposal	With Proposal	Differential After-Tax Flow
0	0	−100,000	− 100,000
1	+40,000	+ 60,000	+ 20,000
2	+45,000	+ 67,000	+ 22,000
3	+51,000	+ 74,000	+ 23,000
4	+58,000	+ 82,000	+ 24,000
5	+66,000	+122,000	+ 56,000

cash, needs for. The size of a firm's cash balance will depend basically upon the three major reasons for liquidity. The firm's major needs for cash are the following:

1. *Transaction Needs.* A firm needs cash to carry out the day-to-day functions of the business. Just as the firm's level of operations affects working-capital requirements, it affects the need for cash. If the volume of sales increases, cash will be received from customers and will be expended for materials and wages in larger amounts. Adequate cash to cover these and other transactions allows the firm to pay its bills on time.

2. *Contingency Needs.* If the firm could perfectly forecast its needs for cash, it would not have to be concerned with unexpected occurrences or emergencies that require cash. Because this is not possible, the firm must be prepared for contingencies.

If suddenly a major customer does not pay his bill, the cash inflows will be reduced below the forecasted level. The firm must have money to pay its own bills until the customer's check arrives. Or a supplier may be having difficulties and may be forced to eliminate the firm's credit purchases. The unanticipated elimination of credit may mean the firm has to pay cash to buy raw materials, a contingency need related to cash outflows.

3. *Opportunity Needs.* These involve the chance to profit from having cash available. For example, a supplier may have had several cancellations of orders and may wish to move a large unwanted inventory of raw materials from his warehouse. If the supplier offers a large discount for cash purchasing of the materials, the firm will have the opportunity to realize a substantial savings on its

purchases and, hence, additional profits from the sale of the finished goods.

CROSS-REFERENCE:

liquidity, p. 453

cash safety level. An important factor in determining the size of the firm's cash balance is the safety level established by the treasurer. In setting policies for the firm's cash management, the treasurer considers the differing needs and other factors that affect the amount of cash needed. Then he must establish the minimum available cash (not tied up in compensating balances) the firm needs to protect itself against the risks associated with cash-balance errors. A firm that maintains a $2,000 minimum cash balance—a $2,000 safety level—believes that this amount is sufficient to avoid the risks or costs of running out of funds.

Three examples of risks or costs of errors in cash management are the following:

1. *Default.* The failure to pay interest or principal payments on a firm's fixed obligations is a default and may result in liquidation or legal action by the firm's creditors.
2. *Overdue Bills.* The failure to pay short-term obligations, such as payables, is less serious than default on long-term debts, but may result in a lowering of the firm's credit rating in the business community. This may be accompanied by higher interest rates when the firm applies for future loans, or may cause creditors to refuse to ship supplies on credit.
3. *Lost Savings on Purchases.* Inadequate cash may cause the firm to lose opportunities to make special cash purchases or to take generous trade discounts on purchases of goods.

CROSS-REFERENCES:

cash safety level, how to calculate, p. 101
safety level, p. 517
default, p. 375

cash salvage value. The amount of money received by a firm when a fixed asset is sold at the end of its service life. This will normally differ from the book salvage value which was estimated at the start of the asset's service life for depreciation calculations.

CROSS-REFERENCES:

cash-flow stream, how to calculate, p. 3
present-value techniques, how to avoid being manipulated, p. 23
lease-buy decision, how to make it, p. 132
book salvage value, p. 323
salvage value effects in capital budgeting, p. 517

Celler–Kefauver amendment (1950). An amendment to the Clayton Act that broadened the government's power to deal with restrictive or monopolistic practices that substantially lessen competition.

CROSS-REFERENCES:

antitrust factors affecting mergers, p. 311
Clayton Act, p. 349

certificates of deposit. A receipt for a time deposit at a bank. The bank agrees to pay the bearer the amount of the deposit plus a stipulated amount of interest at maturity. The certificates of prime banks (the nation's largest and strongest banks) have been very popular with financial managers for two reasons:

1. *Secure, High Yields.* Certificates of deposit are very secure investments

with slightly higher yields than treasury bills, yields that are competitive with those on commercial and finance paper.

2. *Highly Liquid.* Unlike commercial paper, there is a large and active secondary market for certificates of deposit; they can be quickly sold before maturity, if desired.

In recent years, there have been many developments in the markets for certificates of deposit. The kinds and characteristics of certificates of deposits may be expected to change as banks compete with increasing sophistication for their share of funds in the nation's capital markets.

CROSS-REFERENCE:

negotiable certificate of deposit, p. 466

Chandler Act of 1938. The primary bankruptcy legislation, based largely on the earlier Bankruptcy Act of 1898, which provides procedures to follow by individuals and firms unable to pay their bills. The Chandler Act has two major objectives. First, it provides for procedures to allow an equitable distribution of the assets of the bankrupt firm or individual. Second, it discharges the debts of the bankrupt individual, thus allowing the debtor to make a fresh start. The Act has fifteen separate chapters of which the two most commonly cited are Chapters X and XI. Chapter X deals with corporate reorganizations and describes legal procedures to be followed in a *reorganization* of a bankrupt corporation. Chapter XI deals with *arrangements* that protect the bankrupt firm

in the near term and allow it the opportunity to get back on its feet.

CROSS-REFERENCES:

bankruptcy, p. 320
arrangement, p. 312
Chapter X reorganization, p. 348
Chapter XI reorganization, p. 348
reorganization, p. 508

changing role of the financial manager. Not too many years ago, the financial manager had a very limited role in an American firm. He kept accurate financial records, prepared reports on the firm's status and performance, and managed cash so the firm could always pay its bills on time. As a specialized staff officer in the company, he was called upon only when his specialty was needed. For example, when the firm ran short of cash, the financial manager was responsible for locating and obtaining additional funds.

The role of the financial manager has changed considerably during the past 20 or so years. As businesses became larger and more complex, the financial manager transcended his traditional role of raising external funds for the firm. He became involved in the problems and decisions related to the management of the firm's assets. He dealt with the total amount of capital employed by the firm, with the allocation of funds to differing projects and activities, and with the measurement of the results of each allocation. In this context, he needed a much broader outlook of the firm and a much stronger grasp of the nature and scope of the finance function.

Difference Between Traditional and Modern Financial Manager.

Traditional Financial Manager	Modern Financial Manager
Concerned with raising funds.	Concerned with all aspects of the employment of capital.

To handle new responsibilities the modern financial manager needs a variety of qualitative and quantitative skills. He must be able to provide financial inputs in order to help the firm deal with developments such as the following:

1. Decentralization of decision making, which has resulted from increases in the size and complexity of business operations.
2. Diversification by firms into differing product lines.
3. Diversification by firms into a variety of markets, both domestic and foreign.
4. Emphasis on growth, with its requirements for new sources of funds and better use of existing funds.
5. Rapid changes in technology in major industries, a product of major spending on research and development by firms and the federal government.
6. Speedy dissemination of information, which accompanied the advent of third-generation computers and new transportation and communication systems.

Chapter X reorganization. Under the Chandler Act of 1938, a reorganization of a bankrupt corporation that must follow the legal procedures outlined in Chapter X of the Act. A Chapter X reorganization may be initiated by the debtor corporation which is a *voluntary bankruptcy* or by three or more creditors having total claims of $500 or more, an *involuntary bankruptcy*. The reorganization petition is submitted in Federal District Court. If it is approved by the judge, a trustee may be appointed or, in situations where the liabilities are less than $250,000, the assets may remain in the hands of the debtor. The trustee or firm must submit a reorganization plan to the court. The court will determine whether the plan is fair and equitable, which means that it must maintain the priorities of the creditors, preferred shareholders, and common shareholders. The plan must also be feasible, which means that it must allow the corporation to have adequate working capital, credit, and ability to operate efficiently while paying its obligations. If the plan meets the fair and equitable, and feasible standards, the reorganization may be approved.

CROSS-REFERENCES:
bankruptcy, p. 320
Chandler Act of 1938, p. 347
voluntary settlement, p. 545

Chapter XI reorganization. Under the Chandler Act of 1938, a reorganization of a bankrupt firm after developing arrangements to protect the firm in the near term. A firm initiates a Chapter XI reorganization by petitioning in Federal District Court for an arrangement on settling unsecured debts. A plan is submitted that must be accepted by creditors and be approved by the court. This is similar to a *voluntary settlement* because a Chapter XI arrangement or reorganization is less complicated than a Chapter X reorganization.

CROSS-REFERENCES:
arrangement, p. 312
bankruptcy, p. 320
Chandler Act of 1938, p. 347
Chapter X reorganization, p. 348
reorganization, p. 508
voluntary settlement, p. 545

chattel mortgage. Used less frequently to finance fixed assets than is the conditional sales contract, the chattel mortgage is similar to the conditional sales contract with only two important distinctions:

1. *Immediate Transfer of Title.* The title to the fixed assets is transferred from

the manufacturer to the purchaser when the equipment is sold. With the conditional sales contract, the title is held by the manufacturer until after the last installment payment is received.

2. *All Money Flows Through Financing Insti-*

tution. The bank or finance company is involved in all flows of money. The purchaser gives the down payment to the bank and the bank sends the full purchase price to the manufacturer. An example of a chattel mortgage is shown in the figure.

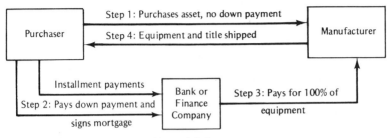

Chattel Mortage.

circulating assets. A firm's current assets, so-called because the assets circulate among several balance-sheet accounts. Cash is used to purchase inventories which are sold to produce accounts receivables which bring cash when collected which is then used to purchase inventories.

CROSS-REFERENCE:
asset, p. 313

Clayton Act (1914). A federal statute that forbids restrictive or monopolistic practices whose effect may be to substantially lessen competition.

CROSS-REFERENCES:
anti-trust factors affecting mergers, p. 311
Celler–Kefauver Amendment, p. 346

clientele effect. The phenomenon whereby the value of a firm's stock is increased because the firm attracts stockholders who agree with the firm's dividend policy. The effect is to increase the market price of a firm's stock to a higher level than would otherwise be

expected. The clientele effect is identified by Modigliani and Miller as an example of a systematic irrationality in the capital market.

CROSS-REFERENCE:
Miller and Modigliani on cost of capital, p. 213

coefficient of variation. The coefficient of variation is calculated by dividing the standard deviation for a project by the target or forecasted return on a project. It is used to compare the degree of dispersion with the dollar value of the likely returns. This is an improvement over the use of the standard deviation by itself. To see why this is so, consider projects X and Y, both of which have a standard deviation of 2 percent return. Project X forecasts an expected value of 8 percent; Y forecasts 22 percent. On a percentage basis, the deviation from the expected value is much greater for project X than Y. To get a relative measure of the degree of risk compared to the likely return, we divide the standard deviation (σ) by the expected return E (Rtn) and get the coefficient of variation (V) as follows:

Proposal A

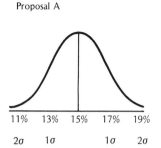

| 11% | 13% | 15% | 17% | 19% |
| 2σ | 1σ | | 1σ | 2σ |

Proposal B

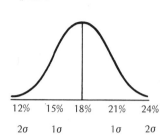

| 12% | 15% | 18% | 21% | 24% |
| 2σ | 1σ | | 1σ | 2σ |

Proposal C

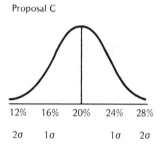

| 12% | 16% | 20% | 24% | 28% |
| 2σ | 1σ | | 1σ | 2σ |

Comparing Riskiness of Projects with Different Standard Deviations.

For proposal X   For proposal Y

$$V = \frac{\sigma}{R} \qquad V = \frac{2\%}{8\%} = .25 \qquad V = \frac{2\%}{22\%} = .09$$

The larger coefficient of variation for project X indicates a larger dispersion compared to the likely return and, therefore, a higher degree of risk than for project Y.

Making the same comparison with proposals A, B, and C in the Figure we get

For proposal A   For proposal B

$$V = \frac{2\%}{15\%} = .13 \qquad V = \frac{3\%}{18\%} = .17$$

For proposal C

$$V = \frac{4\%}{20\%} = .20$$

Proposal C has the largest dispersion compared to the likely return and, therefore, is riskiest compared to the other projects, according to the coefficient of variation. But be sure to note the *importance of common sense.* Project C has a larger dispersion compared to the target return, but the higher expected return means that C is really a better proposal than A or B.

CROSS–REFERENCES:

capital asset pricing model, p. 279
risk in capital budget, how to measure, p. 25

collateral. Any asset with a market value that can be pledged with a creditor as security for a debt. Because collateral provides additional security for the liability, finance charges will normally be lower than for unsecured loans.

collateral trust bond. A bond that is secured by a physical asset, such as common stock or bonds, held by a trustee.

CROSS-REFERENCE:
collateral, p. 350

collection costs. The expenses required by a firm to follow up on overdue bills. Examples are the preparation and mailing of reminders that the payment is overdue and the hiring of personnel or collection agencies to visit delinquent customers and demand payment.

CROSS-REFERENCES:
receivables, changing collection costs and bad-debt losses, p: 503
receivables, cost of, p. 504

combined leverage. A ratio of the marginal contribution to the earnings before taxes that is used in profit planning to compare changes in revenues with changes in earnings before taxes. It is the product of operating leverage times fixed-charges leverage.

CROSS-REFERENCE:
leverage, how to use in profit planning, p. 44

commercial bank. A bank chartered by a state or by the Controller of the Currency whose primary functions are the acceptance of demand deposits and the granting of short-term credit. Commercial banks also perform other functions, such as accepting time deposits, making mortgage loans or personal loans, and administering personal trusts.

commercial finance company. A nonbank institution that makes business loans at higher-than-bank rates, normally to medium-risk companies. Generally the loans will be secured with some collateral such as a pledge of accounts receivable, inventory, or other assets.

commercial paper. Short-term, unsecured promissory notes of large nonfinancial corporations. Finance paper refers to similar notes from finance companies. These notes are issued by firms needing cash for periods of 30 days to 1 year. They are purchased by other firms with excess cash who have a desire to earn a higher yield than is available from treasury bills. In return for the higher yield the firm accepts slightly greater risk and less liquidity.

Commercial paper is normally purchased through a bank or securities dealer, while the bulk of finance paper is purchased directly from finance companies. In both cases, the paper is usually held to maturity, since no active secondary market exists to transfer paper. In some cases, finance companies will honor requests to buy back their paper, usually charging a fee for this service.

Commercial and finance paper have been growing in importance over the years. At one time, conservative managements insisted that treasurers limit their short-term investments to treasury securities. The excellent repayment record and higher yields of paper from large, stable companies has encouraged firms to become more active in the paper market.

CROSS-REFERENCE:
finance paper, p. 403

commodity exchange. An organization of dealers and brokers whose members meet to transact business under the rules and regulations laid down by the exchange. Commodity exchanges exist to trade products such as grains, livestock, metals, farm products, and currencies.

common stock. A security representing the residual ownership of a corporation. It guarantees only the right to participate in sharing the earnings of the firm if the firm is profitable. Common shareholders usually have the additional right to vote at stockholder's meetings on issues affecting fundamental policies of the corporation. Also, the shareholders have the right to elect the members of the board of directors, the right to inspect the firm's books (only for the legitimate purpose of evaluating the performance of management), and the right to obtain a list of the names and addresses of other shareholders.

An exception to the above-stated rights may occur if the firm issues more than one class of common stock. In this situation, the firm is said to have classified common stock, which is often divided into two classes normally designated as class A and class B. The holders of one class will not have the right to vote on corporate matters except in specified situations. In return for giving up this right, the shareholders will receive first rights to common dividends. The other class will have all the rights of common shareholders, unless somehow restricted by provisions in the stock certificate.

The firm's common shareholders are entitled to receive dividends, if and when they are declared by the board of directors. Dividends are a share of the profits, which are distributed among all the outstanding shares of common stock. The dividend will vary with the performance of the company and the amount of cash available. If the firm needs the cash for expansion or if business is poor, the dividend may be omitted or a noncash dividend may be declared.

Common stockholders have other rights. They may transfer their ownership by selling their stock without the consent of the corporation. They are entitled to share in the proceeds of a liquidation, but they have the last claim on assets after the liabilities, bondholders, and preferred stockholders have been paid. And they have the right to maintain their share of earnings and assets by purchasing proportionate amounts of future stock offerings. This is called a preemptive right.

CROSS-REFERENCES:

common stock, cost of. Determining the cost of common stock presents greater difficulties than the known costs associated with bonds and preferred stock. The common shareholder does not expect to receive any fixed, predetermined return on his purchase of common stock. Rather, he receives the right to participate in sharing future earnings of the firm and the right to receive future dividends. To recognize these rights, the cost of equity capital makes use of a relationship between either earnings or dividends and the market value of the common stock. The formulas are as follows:

1. *Earnings Formula.* The earnings formula considers the current earnings, adds a growth factor, and divides the value by the current market price. The formula is

$$K_e = \frac{\text{EPS}(1 + G)^3}{\text{MP}}$$

where K_e = cost of equity capital
$(1 + G)^3$ = growth factor, where G is the growth rate of EPS as a percentage
MP = current market price per share

As an example of the use of this formula, consider a firm with $2 EPS, a 10 percent growth rate of earnings, and a $40 market price. The cost of capital for this firm's common stock is $K_e = \$2(1.10)^3/\$40 = \$2.67/\$40$

= 6.67 percent. Two elements of the earnings formula deserve particular notice:

a. *The formula is actually the capitalization rate or P/E reciprocal.* The cost of equity capital formula using earnings projects an EPS over a market price. The formula could be rewritten EPS_3/MP, where the EPS_3 represented future EPS.

b. *Different financial analysts may prefer different growth factors.* A 3-year growth factor is somewhat arbitrary. It reflects an analyst's view that future proposals accepted by the firm must hurdle a cost of capital that considers growth. To see the meaning of this growth factor, consider the preceding example with a cost of equity of 6.67 percent. Without a growth factor, the cost of equity capital would be $2/$40 or 5 percent. If the firm had no debt or preferred stock, this would be the hurdle rate for new proposals. The question then is *should new proposals have to hurdle 5 or 6.67 percent?* Since the shareholders desire the higher return of 6.67 percent, and in fact expect to achieve this return in 3 years, it should also be expected of new proposals. We might conclude that some growth factor should be included. The 3-year time span might be modified by the analyst if it was not appropriate in a given situation.

2. *Dividends Formula.* A second approach to the cost of equity capital employs the Gordon formula as follows:

$$K_e = \frac{dividend}{MP} + G$$

where dividend = current dividend per share

G   = growth rate of dividends per share

This model has the advantage of reflecting the direct return to the shareholder—the dividends on the stock. An analyst would be wise to use both formulas in calculating the cost of equity capital. Since the cost of equity will be similar with each formula, the analyst will have to select one or use an average.

Cost of Newly Issued Common Stock   When a firm is considering the financing of a new proposal, it may require more funds than are currently available. If it is considering floating new common stock, the firm will have to calculate a cost of the new shares. This is done by using the earnings or dividends formula modified to reflect the flotation costs. The formulas are

$$K_e = \frac{EPS(1+G)^3}{NP} \quad \text{or} \quad K_e = \frac{dividend}{NP} + G$$

where NP = net proceeds (market price minus flotation costs) from the new common-stock offering

As an example of the use of net proceeds, assume that a firm has $5 EPS, a 5 percent growth rate, and is considering a public offering for $80 on which it will have flotation costs of $5 per share. The cost of equity would be (a 50 percent dividend payout)

$$K_e = \frac{\$5(1.05)^3}{\$80 - \$5} = \frac{\$5.79}{\$75} = 7.72\%$$

$$K_e = \frac{\$2.50}{\$75} + 5\% = 3.33\% + 5\% = 8.33\%$$

Cost of Retained Earnings and Depreciation   It is not necessary to calculate a separate cost of retained earnings from the firm's previous profits. This cost is included in the cost of the existing common stock. Note that our formula used the existing market price per share to determine the

Key Characteristics of the Five Broad Approaches to the Valuation of Common Stock.

Valuation Method	Goal of Method	Applied To	Used By	Value Defined By
Intrinsic value	Find "real" value	All stocks	All investors	Fundamental factors
Current market value	Find low prices	Actively traded stocks	All investors	Market factors
Diversification	Reduce risk	All stocks	Portfolio managers	Low risk
Anticipation	Quick gains	Actively traded stocks	Speculators	Market factors
Growth	Long-term gains	High-growth stocks	All investors	Future prospects

cost of capital of the outstanding shares. Since these shares have claims against both the stock value and retained earnings (against the assets really), a separate cost of retained earnings does not exist. The cost of all equity is considered in the preceding earnings or dividends formula.

A final source of funds is provided by the cash flow shielded by depreciation and other noncash expenses. Do these have a separate cost? The answer is no. Since these funds were originally supplied by a mixture of the sources already discussed, it would be reasonable to assume that the cost of capital for depreciation funds is the same as the overall cost of capital. Therefore, no separate calculation is needed to handle the cost of funds shielded by depreciation or noncash expenses.

CROSS-REFERENCES:
optimal capital structure, how to determine, p. 147
Durand on cost of capital, p. 203

common stock valuation, five approaches. The Table identifies the five broad approaches to the valuation of common stocks and a number of key characteristics that help to define and distinguish them.

CROSS-REFERENCES:
common stock value, how to compare two or more stocks, p. 83
Gordon on common stock value, p. 255
Graham and Dodd approaches to common stock value, p. 246
anticipation approach to common stock value, p. 310
current-market-value approach to common stock, p. 370

compensating balance. A requirement commonly found in a line of credit or other short-term unsecured loan whereby the borrower is required to maintain a certain minimum balance in his checking account. Compensating balances of 10 to 20 percent are commonly required. Since the borrower earns no interest on this balance, it has the effect of raising the effective cost of borrowing.

CROSS-REFERENCE:
cash balance, factors affecting, p. 342

composition. In voluntary settlements or bankruptcy situations, an arrangement whereby creditors agree to accept a partial cash settlement in lieu of full payment of a debt. The settlement is usually pro rated so that all creditors receive the same fixed percentage of the original obligation. A composition differs from an extension where full payment is received on a delayed basis. A composition will result only in situations where creditors feel that this alternative yields more money to them than other alternatives, such as liquidation of the firm. A majority of creditors must agree to a composition. If most do not agree, the agreeing creditors can allow full payment to dissenting creditors or the firm can be liquidated.

CROSS-REFERENCES:
act of bankruptcy, p. 308
bankruptcy, p. 320
Chandler Act, p. 347
Chapter X reorganization, p. 348
Chapter XI reorganization, p. 348
extension, p. 400
voluntary settlement, p. 545

compound interest. Interest that is paid both on the original principal and on interest earned in early periods. The interest earned in one period becomes, in effect, part of the principal in following periods. Interest is normally compounded on bank deposits and fixed-term securities when the interest is not withdrawn at regular intervals.

CROSS-REFERENCES:
compound interest, how to calculate, p. 184
interest, p. 436

compound value of annuity. The future value of an equal annual deposit of money into a savings account or other investment medium where interest is paid at a fixed and specified rate.

CROSS-REFERENCE:
compound interest, how to calculate, p. 184

compounding. A situation that exists when the interest earned on a sum of money becomes part of the principal at the end of each period and future interest is earned on the new and larger principal. The formula for calculating a compounded sum is:

$$\text{Compounded Sum} = \text{Principal} \times (1+i)^n$$

where
Principal = the initial principal

i = the annual rate of interest as a percent

n = the number of years the interest is to be paid

CROSS-REFERENCE:
compound interest, how to calculate, p. 184

concentration banking. A technique whereby geographically disbursed collection centers are used to speed up the collection of receivables. A firm with geographically distributed sales outlets will designate regional collection centers and customers will remit their payments directly to these centers. Checks will be deposited in local banks and a policy will be established for transferring the funds by wire to a concentration or disbursing bank, where funds are centrally managed. A major benefit of concentration banking is to reduce the mailing time on check payments. The time required for the customer's check to "clear" will also be reduced if the customer's bank is in the same Federal Reserve district as the collecting bank. This reduction in clearing time speeds up the availability of funds to the firm.

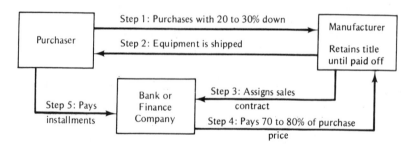

Conditional Sales Contract.

conditional sales contract. One of the most common secured financing forms. Under this method, the firm purchasing the equipment is required to make a 20 to 30 percent down payment. The purchaser signs a sales contract that allows the manufacturer to retain the title to the assets until all the payments are made. After shipping the equipment, the manufacturer will assign the sales contract to a bank or finance company in return for the remaining 70 to 80 percent of the purchase price. The purchaser will make periodic payments to the financing institution. When all installment payments have been made, the finance company will notify the manufacturer to transfer the title for the equipment to the purchaser.

A purchase under a conditional sales contract is diagrammed in the Figure.

The conditional sales contract can be written with a steady-principal-reduction or steady-payment method of installment payments. It is not likely that a balloon-payment method would be allowed. Banks require a down payment and installments sufficiently large so that the outstanding debt is less than the net resale value of the assets if repossession were necessary due to default.

conglomerate. A firm that has grown externally through a number of mergers or acquisitions of companies whose businesses are not related either vertically or horizontally.

CROSS–REFERENCES:

mergers, how to analyze profitability in a ten-step process, p. 85
mergers, p. 460

consideration. The performance that each party in a business deal or contract expects from the other party. For example, in a sale of goods one party provides the goods and the other provides money as the two forms of consideration.

consolidation. Joining the financial statements of two or more companies in a holding company structure so that a single financial position is presented.

CROSS–REFERENCE:

holding company, p. 427

consolidation, in merger. A combination of two or more businesses into a third, entirely new, corporation. The new corporation absorbs the assets and, possibly, liabilities of both original corporations, which cease to exist. The legal and financial characteristics of a consolidation are basically the same as those for a merger.

When is a consolidation preferable to a merger? Possible situations are the following:

1. *For Firms of Equal Size.* When a large and small firm combine, normally

the small firm is merged into the large firm. For firms of equal size, however, it may be difficult to get either of the boards of directors to agree that their company should terminate by being merged into the other company. In these cases, a new company is the better choice.

2. *When a New Charter Is Desired.* Companies receive their corporate charters at the beginning of their existence from an individual state. In many cases, the charters contain undesirable features that restrict the firm as it reaches maturity. A consolidation represents an opportunity to obtain a new corporate charter with more favorable features than in either of the charters of the existing companies.

Because mergers and consolidations involve the combining of two or more firms into a single firm, the term "merger" is commonly used to refer to both forms of external growth.

CROSS-REFERENCE:
mergers, p. 460

constant costs. In break-even or profit-volume analysis, a measure of the change in variable costs. If the firm is producing in a range of constant costs, each incremental unit of production will have the same approximate variable cost; that is, if one unit costs $5, the next unit will cost $5.

CROSS-REFERENCES:
break-even analysis, how to use, p. 32
break-even analysis, p. 325

constant dollar. A unit of currency that is mathematically calculated so that it has the same purchasing power at all times even though price levels may be changing. Stated differently, it is a future dollar that has the same purchasing power as today's dollar.

CROSS-REFERENCES:
profits, how to maintain under inflation, p. 59
currency, p. 369

contingency need. A need for cash that arises because a firm has an unanticipated requirement for cash.

CROSS-REFERENCE:
cash, p. 341

contingent liability. A possible future claim against a business whose effect is not easily measured at the present time. For example, damages that may be due as the result of a lawsuit which may be settled unfavorably to the company would be a contingent liability for the company. Contingent liabilities are not normally incorporated in the liability section of the firm's balance sheet.

CROSS-REFERENCE:
liabilities, p. 452

contingent projects. In capital budgeting, a situation that exists when the utility of one proposal is contingent upon the acceptance of another. For example, a firm that is considering the construction of a new headquarters building will also need to build a new employee parking lot. The building and the parking lot would be contingent projects.

CROSS-REFERENCE:
capital budgeting, p. 329

controller. A key financial officer in a corporation. It is increasingly common for the controller to be responsible for the management of the firm's assets. Included in this responsibility are the areas of profit planning, capital spending, cost measurement, control of inventories, and corporate accounting.

CROSS-REFERENCES:
treasurer, p. 538
vice-president finance, p. 545

controller and treasurer, distinguishing between. The distinction between the functional areas of the controller and treasurer has occurred within the past 20 or so years for most firms. Originally, "treasurer" was the title given to the chief financial officer of the firm. Since World War II, the field of controllership, particularly with respect to developments in budgeting and financial reporting, became recognized as a distinct functional area. Firms began to identify the controller as the chief accounting officer who gathered data, prepared management reports, and monitored the accounting functions of the firm. The treasurer became the chief financial officer with responsibilities in the area of funds management. A logical development was to create a new top financial position to supervise both activities—the vice-president finance.

Many firms still maintain that the controller is the chief accounting officer while the treasurer is the chief financial officer, both working for a member of the top management group called the vice-president finance. In a sense, this is an unfortunate and outdated distinction since both positions are concerned with financial matters. The controller is usually an accountant and is thoroughly familiar with accounting matters. Still, his job demands that he apply the tools of finance to the accounting data to facilitate financial decision making. He moves beyond the accounting area into the activities of finance and participates in such tasks as planning, budgeting, and forecasting. Rather than make the distinction of chief financial and chief accounting officer, it is more accurate to distinguish the two positions as the manager of funds and the manager of assets.

conversion feature. A right that may be included in a bond or preferred stock offering allowing the holder to convert the security into another type of security (usually common stock) at a specified price during a specified period of time.

CROSS-REFERENCES:
bond, p. 323
preferred stock offering, p. 481
conversion premium, p. 358
forcing the conversion, p. 413
long-term financing, how to compare different alternatives, p. 139

conversion premium. The difference between the current market price of common stock and the price at which the stock may be purchased using the conversion feature in a bond or preferred stock offering. For example, if a $1,000 bond is convertible into 25 shares of common stock, the conversion price is $1,000/25, or $40 per share. If the current market price of the common stock is $36, the conversion premium is $4. Expressed as a percent, the conversion premium is $4/$36, or 11 percent.

CROSS-REFERENCES:
conversion feature, p. 358
convertible securities, characteristics of, p. 360
forcing the conversion, p. 413

conversion price and ratio. The conversion feature on a convertible security may be exercised only under the specified terms and conditions contained in the original offering of the security. Both the conversion price and conversion ratio are established at the time the security is sold. These are:
1. *Conversion Ratio.* This gives the number of shares of common stock to be received in the event the holder surrenders the convertible security to the corporation. For example, a $1,-000 bond may be convertible into 25 shares of common at any time prior to December 31, 1984. The conver-

sion ratio would be 25 shares to one bond.

2. *Conversion Price.* This is the effective price paid for the common stock when the conversion takes place. It is calculated by the following formula:

$$\text{conversion price} = \frac{\text{par value}}{\text{shares received}}$$

For the $1,000 bond convertible into 25 shares of common stock, the conversion price would be $1,000/25=$40 per share.

CROSS-REFERENCES:
forcing the conversion, p. 413
**long-term financing, how to
compare different alternatives,** p. 139

conversion value. The value of a bond or preferred stock in terms of the market value of the common stock into which it may be converted. The conversion value is calculated by multiplying the conversion ratio times the current market price of the common stock. For example, if a bond is convertible into 20 shares of common stock at a time when the common stock is selling for $60 per share, the conversion value is 20 times 60 or $1,200.

CROSS-REFERENCES:
value, intrinsic of common stock,
p. 543
forcing the conversion, p. 413

convertible bond. A debt security of a firm that can be converted into common stock or other security at a stated price, under stated conditions, at the option of the holder. When the bond is issued, the conversion price will be higher than the current price. In the future, the market price may rise above the conversion price. This will increase the value of the bond and make it attractive to convert it into stock. In return for this feature, a convertible bond normally requires the firm to pay less interest than would be paid for a comparable nonconvertible bond.

CROSS-REFERENCE:
**long-term financing, how to
compare different alternatives,** p. 139

convertible currency. Currency of a nation that may be freely exchanged or converted into the currency of another nation. A national currency is fully convertible if the government of the country allows the currency to be used freely for the purchase of goods or currencies from other nations.

CROSS-REFERENCES:
international finance, p. 437
monetary reserves, p. 464

convertible security. A bond or share of preferred stock that can be converted, at the option of the holder, into shares of common stock of the same corporation. Once the conversion option is exercised, the common stock cannot be exchanged later back to the bond or preferred stock.

Using Convertibles To Lower the Cost of Financing A primary reason for the use of convertible securities is to lower the cost of financing new investments. A convertible security offers its holder a chance to share in future capital gains if the price of the firm's common stock rises above the conversion price. In the meantime, the security holders can expect to receive regular interest or dividend payments as a fixed income. In return for the capital-gains opportunity, the firm is able to offer the security with a lower interest rate or dividend than would be required for nonconvertible issues. This has the effect of lowering financing costs.

Using Convertibles To Sell Common Stock at Higher Prices   A second major reason for the use of convertible securities is to sell common stock at prices higher than the current market price. When it is seeking long-term financing, the firm may actually prefer to sell common stock rather than add to its debt level. If the price of the common stock is temporarily depressed, an excessive number of common shares would be required to raise the needed funds. By setting the conversion premium 10 to 20 percent higher than the current market price, the firm will give up 10 to 20 percent fewer shares when the security is finally converted than would be required if common stock were sold at the depressed price.

CROSS-REFERENCE:
market premium, p. 457

convertible securities, characteristics of.

A number of characteristics are generally associated with convertible securities:

1. *Inclusion of a Call Feature.* Most convertible securities are callable at the option of the company and at a specified price.
2. *Protection Against Dilution.* Most convertible offerings contain a provision that protects the convertible against dilution from stock splits, stock dividends, or the sale of common stock at low prices. In the event of a stock dividend or stock split, the conversion ratio would automatically be adjusted to prevent dilution. For example, suppose that a $100 par preferred stock was convertible into 4 shares of common stock and the company declared a 2-for-1 stock split. After the split, the preferred stock would be convertible into 8 shares of common stock.
3. *Conversion Premium.* The conversion price is normally set 10 to 20 percent

above the prevailing market price of the common stock at the time the convertible security is sold. This conversion premium may be expressed in dollars or as a percent:

$$\text{conversion premium} = \text{(conversion price)} - \text{(prevailing market price)}$$
(dollars)

$$\text{conversion premium} = \text{(conversion price} - \text{market price)}/\text{market price}$$
(percent)

Using our example of the $1,000 bond convertible into 25 shares of common stock, let us assume a prevailing market price of $35 per share. The conversion price is $40, so the premium may be expressed as

$$\text{premium} = \$40 - \$35 = \$5$$

$$\text{premium} = \frac{\$40 - \$35}{\$35} = 14.3\%$$

CROSS-REFERENCES:
call feature, p. 328
dilution, p. 381
conversion premium, p. 358

convertible security, determining the coupon.

The firm establishes the interest or dividend yield on a convertible security in conjunction with its investment bankers. As a first step, the firm determines the interest yield or dividend that would be demanded by investors on a straight debt or nonconvertible preferred stock offering. Then, an attempt is made to analyze the impact of differing conversion premiums on the interest rate or dividend yield. The larger the conversion premium—that is, the more the stock has to rise in value before it becomes profitable to convert the security—the higher the yield that will be required.

The Figure illustrates the relationship between the yield demanded by

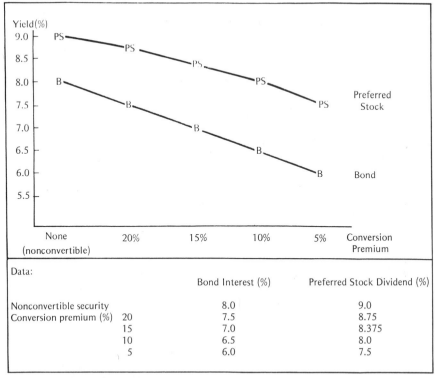

Data:		Bond Interest (%)	Preferred Stock Dividend (%)
Nonconvertible security		8.0	9.0
Conversion premium (%)	20	7.5	8.75
	15	7.0	8.375
	10	6.5	8.0
	5	6.0	7.5

Relationship Between Required Yield and Conversion Premiums for Convertible Securities.

investors and the conversion premiums for bonds and preferred stock. In this example, the firm and its investment banker have analyzed existing market conditions at a time when the firm is considering long-term financing through either debt or preferred stock financing. They have developed the tabular data in the Figure.

These data can be used by the firm to determine whether it wants to issue convertible securities and, if it does, what conversion premium it should attach to the offering.

CROSS-REFERENCE:
coupon rate, p. 368

corporate bonds, characteristics of. A security representing a long-term promise to pay a certain sum of money at a certain time with a fixed rate of interest payable to the holder of the bond. The specific promises and details of the issue are written in the bond indenture, the agreement between the corporation and the bondholders. Corporate bonds are normally issued in denominations of $1,000, and interest may be paid annually or semiannually.

The following are some of the classifications used to identify the differing characteristics of corporate bonds:
1. *Secured Versus Unsecured Bonds.* A debenture is a bond backed or secured only by the general credit of the corporation. It is the most widely used debt security of American corpora-

tions. Although a debenture is not secured by specific assets, its holders have a claim to the corporation's assets if the interest and principal payments are not made. In some cases, the bond debenture will specify that the claim to assets is secondary to the claims of other bondholders. Such a bond is called a subordinated debenture. Some bonds will be secured by specific assets. A mortgage bond is secured by a mortgage lien on a piece of property or on a building. A collateral trust bond is secured by collateral, such as stocks or bonds held by a trustee. An equipment trust bond is secured by a piece of machinery or equipment, such as a locomotive, whose title is deposited with a trustee.

2. *Bond Maturity.* Bonds have a fixed maturity specified in the bond indenture. A serial bond issue has portions that mature in small amounts at periodic intervals. As an example, bonds numbered 1 to 100 may mature in 1977, 101 to 200 may mature in 1978, and so on. A sinking fund bond issue requires the corporation to set aside money at regular intervals, usually payable to a trustee, so that sufficient funds will accrue to repay the principal at maturity. This technique increases the chances that the firm will have sufficient funds set aside to redeem the issue when the time arrives. The setting aside of money at intervals for the gradual payment of a debt is called amortization.

3. *Ownership.* Bearer bonds or coupon bonds are owned by the person who has physical possession of them, just as a dollar bill is owned by its bearer. These bonds are said to be highly negotiable in that they are easily transferred or sold to other parties. These bonds have coupons attached to them, which represent the interest payments on specified dates. To re-

ceive interest, the bearer presents the coupon to the agent of the corporation, normally a bank. Registered bonds require that the owner's name be listed on the books of the corporation or its agent. When such a bond is sold, the agent must be notified. Interest payments are mailed by check to the registered owner. A registered bond, although somewhat less negotiable than a bearer bond, offers the owner a high degree of safety from theft.

4. *Special Features.* Bonds may be classified by the special features associated with them, such as the following:
   a. Interest on income bonds does not have to be paid unless the firm earns sufficient income to cover the interest payment. Income bonds are usually issued in connection with the reorganization of a financially troubled firm.
   b. Convertible bonds can be converted into common stock or another security at a stated price, under stated conditions, at the option of the holder. When the bond is issued, the conversion price will be higher than the current price. In the future, the market price may rise above the conversion price. This will increase the value of the bond and make it attractive to convert it into stock. In return for this attractive feature, a convertible bond normally requires the firm to pay less interest than would be paid for a comparable nonconvertible bond.
   c. Attached warrants used to increase the attractiveness of a bond issue permit the bondholder to buy shares of common stock during a stated time period and at a given price. If the warrants are detachable, they may be separated from the bonds and sold as separate securities. Such warrants are

often listed for trading on the major exchanges.

d. Callable bonds contain a provision in the bond indenture that allows the corporation to retire the issue at a fixed price prior to maturity. The call price is normally slightly above par. Most bonds have a call feature, and usually the bondholders are given the option of converting the bond into common stock during the period between the call and the retirement date.

CROSS-REFERENCE:

bonds, p. 323

corporate bonds, examples involving.

EXAMPLE: A bond indenture requires a firm to set aside sufficient funds to retire 12.5 percent of the principal each year so that a bond may be retired at maturity. The bond offer was for $1,000,000 and was issued in 1976. What type of bond is this? When will it mature?
ANSWER: It is a sinking fund bond, maturing in 8 years (100/12.5 percent = 8).
EXAMPLE: A firm issues a bond that is not secured by specific assets. The bond has a provision in the indenture that other bonds have a first priority on the firm's assets in the event of liquidation of the firm. What kind of bond is this?
ANSWER: A subordinated debenture.
EXAMPLE: A $1,000 bond can be converted into 30 shares of common stock at any time prior to 1979. Stock is currently selling for $28 per share. If the bond were converted and the stock were immediately sold, how much would the bondholder gain or lose (assume a $20 cost for the transactions)?
ANSWER: The bondholder would receive 30 shares of stock worth $28 each or $840 worth of stock. When the stock is sold, he would receive $840 − $20 or $820, a loss of $180 from the $1,000 value of the bond.
EXAMPLE: In the previous problem, at what selling price of the stock would the bondholder neither gain nor lose?

ANSWER: When the value of 30 shares is $1,020, he neither gains nor loses. $1,020/30 = $34 per share selling price.
EXAMPLE: A bondholder has a $1,000 bond convertible into 50 shares of a firm's stock. The stock is currently selling for $25. The bond has been called at $1,050. If he converts the bond and sells the stock, he will have a $25 commission to pay. Allowing the bond to be called has no transaction cost. Which alternative yields the most money?
ANSWER: Allowing the call brings in $1,050. Converting yields 50 shares times $25 = $1,250 − $25 transaction costs = $1,225. Converting the bond yields $175 more than allowing the call.
EXAMPLE: A bond has 20 detachable warrants that allow a person to buy 20 total shares of common stock at $10 per share. The stock is currently selling for $15. It costs $20 to cash in the warrants. Approximately what value would the warrants have if they were detached and sold?
ANSWER: With the warrants, an investor can save $5 per share for 20 shares or $100. $100 minus the $20 transaction costs means the warrants should be worth approximately $80.

corporate form, advantages of.

The corporate form of business enterprise is employed by most large firms because it offers three major advantages over sole proprietorship or partnership:

1. *Limited Liability.* Sole proprietors and general partners are both personally liable for the debts of their businesses. If the business fails and cannot pay its debts, the creditors can force the owners to sell their homes or other assets to fulfill the business obligations. This is not true under the corporate form. Once an owner has fully paid for whatever shares he is purchasing, the owner has no further liability to the firm or to the creditors of the firm. This protection against unlimited liability allows strangers to invest in the common stock of a corporation without fear of losing their personal assets.

2. *Perpetual Existence.* Corporations may be granted a perpetual charter or a 20-or-more-year charter, which can be easily renewed. This allows the corporation to conduct its business indefinitely as long as it is sufficiently profitable to avoid bankruptcy. This is an advantage over sole proprietorships, which cease at the death or retirement of the owner, and partnerships, which are legally dissolved upon the withdrawal, death, or bankruptcy of one of the partners.
3. *Ease of Transferring Ownership.* Because the ownership of a corporation is represented by shares of stock, a portion or all of the ownership can be easily transferred by the sale of stock. In noting this advantage, we must distinguish between two types of corporations:
   a. *Closed corporation* is the term used to describe a small, family-owned corporation in which most of the owners are tied together along either family or friendship lines. These account for approximately 99 percent of all corporations, and the owners of a closed corporation will experience difficulties in finding buyers for their shares of stock.
   b. *Publicly traded corporations* represent the largest corporations and account for the great bulk of all corporate assets. The shares of over 5,000 such companies are listed on the different stock exchanges or are quoted in the over-the-counter market. Shares of stock in these large companies have an extremely high degree of transferability, and incorporation represents a significant advantage over other business forms for these firms.

CROSS-REFERENCE:
limited liability, p. 453

corporation. A legal entity created under the law and empowered to own assets, to incur liabilities, and to engage in business operations. The classic definition of the corporation was written by Chief Justice Marshall in 1819:

A corporation is an artificial being, invisible, intangible, and existing only in contemplation of the law. Being a mere creature of law, it possesses only those properties which the charter of its creation confers upon it, either expressly, or as incidental to its very existence. [Dartmouth College vs. Woodward, 4 Wheaton (1819)].

Several characteristics of the corporate form are important:
1. *It Is Formed Under the Laws of a Specific State.* The incorporators must select a state and then file a certificate of incorporation with the appropriate state agency. This includes such information as the name of the corporation, its purposes, the amount of stock authorized, and the location of the main office. After the certificate and any required fees are accepted by the state, a charter is issued. The incorporators take the charter, which spells out the relationship between the corporation and the state, and then adopt a set of bylaws to regulate the internal management of the firm. Once this is done, the corporation is ready to begin business operation.
2. *It Exists Apart from Its Owners.* A corporation is not group of people who have formed a business; it is a separate business entity. Ownership is represented by equity securities. If an individual holding an ownership interest should die, the shares of stock will pass on to his heirs or estate in accordance with the law. The operations of the corporation will probably not be affected.
3. *It Is Advantageous for Large Business Operations.* The corporate form is especially

suited for large, complex business activities.

correlation coefficient. A numerical value ranging from -1.0 to $+1.0$ that measures the degree to which two variables are related. A correlation coefficient of 1.0 indicates a direct positive correlation where, if one variable increases, the second variable will increase by a like amount. A -1.0 coefficient indicates a high degree of reverse or negative correlation where a rise in one variable will be accompanied by a like drop in a second variable. A zero coefficient indicates no correlation between two variables.

cost of capital. The rate of return the firm requires from an investment in order to increase the value of the firm in the marketplace. With this in mind, three aspects of cost of capital should be noted:
1. *It Is Not a Cost as Such.* A firm's cost of capital is really a rate of return that will be required on new projects available to the company. Although it may be calculated on a cost basis, it is in fact a hurdle rate.
2. *It Represents a Minimum Rate of Return.* If a firm's capital-budgeting proposals do not offer a rate of return equal to or greater than the cost of capital, the firm can be expected to suffer a decline in the market value of its common stock. The cost of capital is thus a minimum rate of return that will cause the market value of the firm to

remain constant or to increase when it is required of new projects.

cost of capital, factors affecting. In analyzing either the firm's capital structure or its cost of capital, three factors are particularly important:
1. *Degree of Favorable or Unfavorable Financial Leverage.* If a firm is unable to achieve favorable financial leverage, it is difficult to discuss either the cost of capital or optimal capital structure. Unfavorable financial leverage indicates a low level of profitability, which makes borrowing more costly than return. On the one hand, the firm would lose by borrowing. On the other hand, the firm would be unable to issue additional stock in a low-profit company. A firm in this situation must first raise profits; then it can begin to analyze how favorable financial leverage affects cost of capital and capital structure. For a profitable firm with favorable financial leverage, the degree of leverage will be an important element in determining the cost of capital and optimal structure.
2. *Effects on the Market Price of Common Stock.* The firm must be concerned with how investors perceive its actions with respect to changes in the mix of debt and equity securities. If addi-

Three Important Factors in Analyzing Cost of Capital and Capital Structure.

Financial Leverage		Common-Stock Prices	Corporate Taxes
Favorable?	Lowers cost of capital.	If market perceives risky capital structure, prices will decline.	High corporate taxes encourage debt in capital structure.
Unfavorable?	Hurts ability to change capital structure.	If required rate of return (K_0) is too low, prices will decline.	Corporate taxes lower cost of debt and hence lower overall cost of capital.

tional debt is viewed as greatly increasing the degree of risk for the common shareholders, the price of the common stock will decline. On the other hand, the debt may be viewed favorably as the proper use of favorable financial leverage, thus causing the stock price to rise. Similarly, the cost of capital can influence stock prices. If the cost of capital is too low, shareholders may feel that the firm accepts low-profit proposals; this would lower stock prices. If the cost of capital is too high, the firm may be perceived as missing good profit opportunities; this too could have its effect on stock prices.

3. *Level of Corporate Taxes.* With corporate taxes near a 50 percent rate, a firm must consider the tax effects of differing capital structures. Since debt involves interest charges that are deductible before taxes, the use of debt securities can provide lower-cost financing than preferred stock or other equity securities. The level of taxes also affects the cost of capital, since lower-cost debt tends to reduce the overall cost of capital.

These three factors, with some of their effects on cost of capital and capital structure, are shown in the Table.

CROSS-REFERENCES:

Miller and Modigliani on cost of

cost of capital, importance of. The cost of the funds available for investment by the firm are closely linked to the firm's capital structure. Most companies have a variety of financing sources, including short-term debt, long-term debt, preferred stock, common stock, and earnings retained in the firm. Measuring the cost of this capital becomes a part of the theory of capital structure, since each type of financing will affect the other types. For example, a firm can borrow debt funds at relatively low rates of interest up to a certain point. Until this point is reached, the use of debt financing will lower the overall cost of capital. This is shown in the Figure. When the debt-equity ratio becomes too high, the firm may have to pay high rates of interest to borrow. This will raise the cost of capital. At a high debt-equity ratio, the firm may not be able to borrow at all. In this situation, the firm may float stock to bring the debt-equity ratio back into line with expectations. Even though the stock may be offered at relatively low market prices, the additional equity will reduce the amount of risk faced by the firm's creditors.

Without a knowledge of the firm's approximate cost of capital, the firm will have difficulties in two areas:

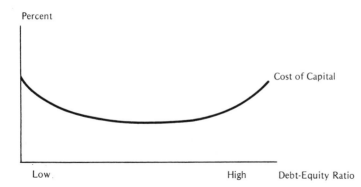

A View of Cost of Capital and Its Relationship to Capital Structure.

1. *What Securities Should Be Used to Raise Additional Funds?* To answer this question, the firm must know its existing capital structure, the cost of the different components, and the effect of issuing debt or equity securities on the overall cost of capital. Knowing the existing cost of capital and the cost of raising additional funds can help the financial manager in selecting financing.
2. *What Cutoff Point Should Be Selected for Capital-Budgeting Proposals?* The cost of capital separates those proposals which maintain or increase the firm's net present value from those which may decrease it. Since this decision is essential in capital budgeting, a knowledge of the cost of capital is important.

CROSS-REFERENCE:
capital structure, p. 335

cost of equity capital. A cost that is imputed to the equity funds provided by the owners of a business in the weighted average approach to calculating cost of capital. The cost of equity capital becomes, in effect, a required return on the ownership funds invested in a business.

CROSS-REFERENCES:

weighted average cost of capital, how to calculate, p. 158
capital asset pricing model, p. 279

cost of goods sold. A category of expenses on a firm's income statement that represents an accounting allocation of the cost of raw materials, labor, overhead, and other expenses that can be matched against the goods sold by the firm. It contains a mixture of fixed and variable costs.

CROSS-REFERENCE:
receivables management, how to evaluate differing credit policies, p. 108

cost of living. A general term that is used as an estimate of price levels in an economy. In the United States, the cost of living is monitored by the Department of Commerce and is based upon changing prices for a "basket" of items commonly purchased by consumers. Rises in the prices of items in the basket cause rises in the Consumer Price Index which is the term given to the measurement of the cost of living.

cost-plus pricing. A form of establishing the selling price for goods or services so that the purchaser pays the full cost of the product or service plus an agreed upon profit margin to the company selling the goods or performing the services.

cost-push inflation. A rise in price levels which occurs as a result of rises in the cost of the raw materials or labor which are needed to produce goods and services.

CROSS-REFERENCE:
inflation, p. 431

coupon rate. The stated rate of interest on a bond.

CROSS-REFERENCES:
bonds, how to calculate value of, p. 124
convertible security, determining the coupon, p. 360

covariance. A statistical value that measures the risk between two variables. It is calculated from a formula with two elements:

1. *Correlation Coefficient(r).* This is a measurement of the degree of relationship between two variables. It is calculated by a formula that measures goodness of fit of data to the regression line and is symbolized by the letter r. If the r is close to zero, the fit is poor and the relationship is said to be weak or nonexistent. If r is close to plus or minus one, a strong correlation or linear relationship exists. In calculating a covariance for two securities, the forecasted return for each security is the variable that is correlated.

2. *Standard Deviations(σ's).* The standard deviation, a measure of the expected dispersion of the return, is needed for each variable.

The covariance is calculated by multiplying the correlation coefficient by the standard deviation of each variable as follows:

$$Cov_{XY} = (r_{XY})(\sigma_X)(\sigma_Y)$$

where

Cov_{XY} = covariance of security x to security Y

r_{XY} = correlation coefficient of security x to security Y

σ_X = standard deviation of security x

EXAMPLE: A security has a correlation coefficient of $-.3$ to the overall market and a standard deviation of expected return of 1.2 percent. The market standard deviation is .6 percent. What is the covariance of the security to the market? ANSWER: Minus .0022, as follows:

$$Cov_{sec,mkt} = (-.3)(.012)(.006) = -.0022$$

CROSS-REFERENCE:
capital asset pricing model, p. 279

credit terms. The conditions of payment offered by a firm to its customers who do not immediately pay for goods or services. Credit terms will include the amount of the cash discount in the discount period, if any, and the period of time during which the payment must be received.

CROSS-REFERENCES:
revolving credit agreement, p. 511
risk classes, p. 515
risk-class approach, p. 515

cumulative preferred stock. All dividends in arrears on this kind of preferred stock must be paid prior to distributing any dividends to common stockholders. It differs from noncumulative preferred stock which does not entitle the holder to the eventual receipt of dividends which were skipped by the board of directors. Most preferred stock is cumulative.

CROSS-REFERENCE:

preferred stock, p. 481

cumulative voting. A system of casting ballots for the directors of a corporation under which each shareholder is entitled to a total number of votes equal to the number of shares owned multiplied by the number of directors to be elected. All of the votes may be cast for a single candidate or they may be distributed among the candidates at the discretion of the shareholder. Cumulative voting allows minority stockholders to elect one or more of the directors of a corporation.

CROSS-REFERENCE:

corporation, p. 364

currency. The coins and paper money used in business and personal transactions that are part of a nation's money supply. Currency is normally distinguished from demand deposits which comprise the bulk of most nations' money supply.

CROSS-REFERENCES:

current assets. A subsection that contains all assets which will be converted into cash within the current accounting period or within the next year (see Figure). It includes the following:

1. *Cash.* The money held in checking accounts or savings accounts, cash registers, and petty cash.
2. *Marketable Securities.* Stocks or bonds of other firms or government agencies that the firm has purchased. Rather than allow cash to be idle in a checking account, firms may purchase securities issued by other organizations. These securities will pay a return either in the form of interest or dividends. In addition, they are highly liquid and can be quickly converted to cash if the firm needs money.
3. *Accounts Receivable.* When a firm makes a sale on credit, it gains the right to collect money from the purchaser. This is shown on the balance sheet as an account receivable. If the firm has a credit policy that goods must be paid for in 30 days from date of purchase—a policy of *net 30,* the bulk of the receivables will be converted to cash in the next 30 days. If the firm is experiencing liquidity problems, the receivables can be used as collateral (security) for a bank loan. Because the receivables will usually become cash in a relatively short time (few firms have credit terms longer than 30 to 60 days), they are considered to be highly liquid.
4. *Inventories.* These are goods held by the firm for eventual resale. Portions of the inventories may be raw materials, goods tied up in the production process, or finished goods ready to be sold. Inventories are carried at their cost on the balance sheet. They are considered the least liquid of the current assets because they are two steps away from cash. First, they must be sold (which creates a receivable) and, second, the receivable must be collected.

Marketable Securities	Accounts Receivable	Inventories
The securities of another firm. Pay a return. Quickly convertible to cash.	Highly liquid. Converted to cash in less than 60 days. May be used as collateral for short-term borrowing.	Goods held for resale Least liquid of current assets. Two steps away from cash.

Characteristics of Current Assets.

CROSS-REFERENCES:

working capital, how to balance sources of funds, p. 121
marketable securities, p. 457
accounts receivable, p. 306
inventories, p. 441

current dollar. A unit of currency that is not adjusted during a period of inflation. Therefore, its purchasing power will fluctuate over a period of time.

CROSS-REFERENCES:

profits, how to maintain under inflation, p. 59
currency, p. 369

current liabilities. Balance sheet accounts representing debts of the firm that must be paid during the current accounting period, normally 1 year. Examples are the following:
1. *Accounts Payable.* When a firm makes purchases on credit, it incurs an obligation to pay for the goods according to the terms given by the seller. Until the cash is paid for the goods, the obligation to pay is recorded in an accounts-payable account.
2. *Wages Payable.* If, at the end of the accounting period, the firm owes wages to any of its employees, the amount is shown in this account.
3. *Notes Payable.* If the firm owes money against promissory notes that mature during the next year, the debt should be shown in this account. If a note is due in the future, but not in the next

year, it will be recorded in a long-term account.
4. *Tax Liabilities.* At the end of the accounting period, the firm may owe taxes to the federal, state, or local government. In these cases, the obligations are shown as tax liabilities.

CROSS-REFERENCE:

balance-sheet accounts, titles and arrangement, p. 318

current market value approach to common stock. A major technique of common stock valuation considers the price of individual stocks compared to other indicators in the marketplace. If the analyst believes that a stock is worth more in terms of market value than the asking price, he recommends purchasing the stock. In a sense, this is a matter of hunting for bargains among fundamentally sound stocks.

Three techniques are within the scope of the current-market-value approach to stock valuation:
1. *Overall Market Is Depressed.* An investor can make purchases only when the market appears to be at a low for most stocks. This would occur after a broad-based decline in the level of stock prices as measured by the Dow Jones average or some other indicator. The rationale for this technique is that the current market value of almost all stocks is below a *normal* current market value and hence prices will soon rise. This approach

has appeal to mutual funds and other investing organizations who can sell a number of stocks at apparent cyclical highs and reinvest in a number of stocks at apparent lows.

2. *Industry Comparison.* With this approach, a firm or investor will seek purchases that seem to be bargains compared to other firms in the industry. This might occur when similar stocks have risen in price while the stock of one firm has lagged behind for no apparent reason. If the lagging firm can be acquired during a period of rising stock prices, the acquisition may call attention to the low price and the stock may gain in value. This is a case of a single firm's current market value being below the expected or normal value.

3. *Cyclical Lows.* A number of common stocks have market prices that follow a cyclical pattern. As an example, for a number of years Comsat traded in

a range from approximately $40 to $60. As soon as the price neared $60, it began to drop until it neared $40; then it would begin to rise. For this kind of stock, an analyst can check the historical data and determine the likely cyclical low. The firm would purchase the stock, anticipating that it would recover to its former price level in a cyclical upswing. In this situation, the cyclical low is below the expected current market value in the near future.

The intrinsic-value and current-market-value approaches overlap in situations where the current market value seems low compared to the intrinsic value. Both methods are concerned with locating undervalued and overvalued stocks and seeking stocks that offer high value for the price paid for the security.

EXAMPLE: An investor has plotted the annual high and low stock prices for a specialty steel processing firm as follows:

	1969	1970	1971	1972	1973	1974
High	38	37	43	49	55	60
Low	19	17	21	27	36	40

The current price of the stock in early 1975 is $44. Can a current-market-value approach be used with this stock?

ANSWER: Yes. This appears to be a cyclical stock with 20 or so points difference between the annual highs and lows. At $44, the stock may be at a cyclical low.

CROSS-REFERENCES:
intrinsic-value analysis, p. 439
Graham and Dodd approaches to common stock value, p. 246
common stock valuation, five approaches, p. 354

current ratio and acid test. The current

ratio is a ratio of the firm's total current assets to its total current liabilities. A low ratio is an indicator that a firm may not be able to pay its future bills on time, particularly if conditions change causing a slowdown in cash collections. A high ratio may indicate an excessive amount of current assets and may indicate a failure to properly utilize the firm's resources. To determine whether this ratio is high, low, or just right, the analyst should consider such factors as the firm's past history, goals, and the current ratios of similar companies. As a general rule, a 2/1 ratio is considered acceptable for most firms.

The quick ratio or acid test is a more precise measure of liquidity than the current ratio because inventories, which are the least liquid of current assets, are excluded from the ratio. The quick ratio may be calculated two ways:

$$\frac{\text{cash} + \text{marketable securities} + \text{accounts receivable}}{\text{current liabilities}}$$

or

$$\frac{\text{current assets} - \text{inventories}}{\text{current liabilities}}$$

Inventories require a two-step process to convert them to cash. They must be sold, converted into receivables (with the markup), and collected. The acid test is so named because it shows the ability of a firm to pay its obligations without relying on the sale and collection of its inventories.

As a guideline, a 1/1 quick ratio is deemed adequate for most firms. A higher ratio may have several meanings. It could indicate that the firm has excessive cash or receivables, both signs of lax management. Or it could indicate that the firm is cautiously ensuring sufficient liquidity. A low ratio is usually an indication of possible difficulties in the prompt payment of future bills.

CROSS-REFERENCES:
liquidity, how to analyze with ratio, p. 49
working capital, how to balance source of funds, p. 121
quick ratio, p. 500
acid-test ratio, p. 307

cutoff point. In capital budgeting, the deciding line between whether a proposal will be accepted or rejected. Proposals will be ranked from the highest to the lowest priority and then a cutoff point will be selected after carefully considering the number of projects, the goals of the firm, and the availability of capital to finance the capital budget.

CROSS-REFERENCE:
capital budgeting, p. 329

D

date of record. The date on which dividends or stock rights accrue to the owners of the stock (holders of record) as recorded in the firm's stock ledger. Owing to a lag in bookkeeping procedures, the critical date is four business days prior to the date of record. The holder of record on the fifth business day before the date of record is entitled to the dividends or rights and the stock sells cum dividends or cum rights (with dividends or with rights) up to that point. On the fourth business day prior to the date of record, the stock goes ex dividends or ex rights (without dividends or without rights) and purchasers of stock from this point on are not entitled to receive the dividends or rights.

CROSS-REFERENCE:
stock dividends, p. 527

dealer. A person or firm who trades securities in the role of a principal who buys for his own account and sells securities from his own inventory.

CROSS-REFERENCE:
secondary markets, p. 519

debenture. An unsecured bond issued on the basis of the general credit of the corporation. Holders of debentures have a claim on the firm's assets after the claims of all secured creditors have been satisfied.

CROSS-REFERENCES:
bond, p. 323
long-term financing, how to compare alternatives, p. 139

debt. Money owed by one person or firm to another person or firm. A debt security is written evidence of the existence of a debt obligation, commonly the certificate issued along with bonds or notes.

debt-asset ratio. The ratio of total debt to total assets of the firm, useful in an analysis of the firm's capital structure. A high ratio may indicate that an excessive portion of the firm's assets are financed by debt. A low ratio may indicate that the firm is failing to take advantage of favorable financial leverage.

CROSS-REFERENCES:
pooling and purchase methods, how to use in merger accounting, p. 91
long-term financing, how to compare different alternatives, p. 139
ownership factors, how to analyze with ratios, p. 51
capital structure ratios, p. 338

debt-equity ratio. A ratio of the firm's total debt to its total equity that is used in the analysis of the firm's capital structure. If the ratio is high, it may indicate that the firm has excessive debt and will experience difficulty in locating further debt financing. If the ratio is low, it may indicate a failure to use cheap borrowed funds to raise the return earned on the common stock.

CROSS-REFERENCES:
pooling and purchase methods, how to use in merger accounting, p. 91
ownership factors, how to analyze with ratios, p. 51
Miller and Modigliani on cost of capital, p. 213
Schwartz on capital structure theory, p. 230
capital structure ratios, p. 338

debt, cost of. The cost of debt is generally considered to be the most reliable cost to calculate because interest charges are known and fixed by agreement between the firm and its creditors. A two-step process is used to calculate the after-tax cost of debt:

1. *Calculate the Effective Cost.* The *effective cost* of debt is the actual cost and may differ slightly from the coupon rate because the net proceeds (amount of money actually received by the firm) differ from the par value. Normally, effective cost is calculated using a bond table. In the absence of such a table, a simple formula has been developed to consider all the factors involved with effective cost:

effective cost = K_i

$$= \frac{interest + [(P - NP)/n]}{(P + NP)/2}$$

where

interest = annual interest payment in dollars

NP = net proceeds of bond or note

P = par value of bond or note

n = number of years to maturity

As an example of the use of this formula, a firm has debt of $100,000 in the form of a bond. The firm realized only $98,000 when it sold the bond last month because the bond dealer received a 2 percent commission. The bond has a 5 percent coupon and will mature in 10 years. The effective cost is

$$K_i = \frac{5,000 + [(100,000 - 98,000)/10]}{(100,000 + 98,000)/2}$$

$$= \frac{5,200}{99,000} = 5.25\%$$

For outstanding bonds, the analyst can simplify this calculation, since the net proceeds represents historical data and the weighted-average method is concerned with current data. If the net proceeds were treated as being the same as the par value, the formula for the problem would be

$$K_i = \frac{5,000 + [(100,000 - 100,000/10]}{(100,000 + 100,000)/2}$$

$$= \frac{5,000}{100,000} = 5\%$$

The 5,000/100,000 is the same as interest/par value. Thus, for outstanding debt the formula can be expressed as

$$\text{effective cost} = K_i = \frac{interest}{D_{mkt}}$$

2. *Convert the Effective Cost to an After-Tax Basis.* To convert the debt cost to an after-tax figure, the following formula is used:

$$K_{i(AT)} = K_{i(BT)}(1-TR)$$

where $K_{i(AT)}$ = after-tax cost of debt

$K_{i(BT)}$ = before-tax cost of debt

TR = corporate tax rate

As an example, if the before-tax cost of debt equals 7 percent, the after-tax cost will equal 7 percent times $1 - .50$ = 3.5 percent.

EXAMPLE: A firm has $3,000,000 in accounts payable, bonds, and mortgage at a 7 percent average cost. The net proceeds for the offering was $2,700,000. The offering has a 5-year maturity. If it is a new offering, what is the after-tax effective cost? If it is an outstanding debt, what is the after-tax cost?

ANSWER: For a new offering:

Before-tax K_i

$$\frac{210,000 + [($3,000,000 - 2,700,000)/5]}{(3,000,000 + 2,700,000)/2}$$

$$= \frac{\$270,000}{2,850,000} = 9.5\%$$

After-tax K_i

$$= 9.5\%(1 - .50) = 4.75\%$$

For existing debt:

Before-tax K_i

$$= \frac{210,000}{3,000,000} = 7\%$$

After-tax K_i
$= 7\%(1 - .50) = 3.5\%$

CROSS–REFERENCE:
weighted-average cost of capital, how to calculate, p. 158

decision point. In the development of a decision tree, a decision point is shown whenever the firm must choose between alternative courses of action.

CROSS–REFERENCES:
risk in capital budget, how to measure, p. 25
decision tree, how to build one, p. 185
decision tree, p. 375

decision rule. In capital budgeting, a hurdle rate that must be achieved by new proposals. Because of the difficulty in calculating cost of capital, a firm may designate an acceptable rate of return as a hurdle rate for new proposals. Such a designation would be a decision rule.

CROSS–REFERENCE:
net present value, how to compare proposals, p. 17

decision tree. A graphic display of the relationship between a present decision and possible future event, future decisions, and their consequences. The sequence of events is mapped out over time in a format resembling branches of a tree. Because the events are linked chronologically with forecasted probabilities where appropriate, the decision tree allows a systematic look at decisions and their forecasted outcomes.

CROSS–REFERENCES:
risk in capital budget, how to measure, p. 25
decision tree, how to build one, p. 185

decision point, p. 375

declining-balance method. An accelerated method of depreciation that may be used to depreciate assets more rapidly than would be allowed by the straight-line method. Also, known as double-declining balance method.

CROSS–REFERENCES:
residual values, how to forecast, p. 66
depreciation, how to calculate, p. 188
depreciation, p. 379

default. The failure to pay interest or principal payments on a firm's fixed obligations that may result in liquidation of the firm or legal action by the firm's creditors.

CROSS–REFERENCE:
cash safety level, p. 346

deferred charges. On a firm's balance sheet, an asset account reflecting money given for expenses or costs incurred for benefits which will be realized in a later accounting period.

CROSS–REFERENCE:
balance sheet, uses of, p. 319

deficit in balance of payments. A deficit occurs when a nation's receipts and credits from other countries are smaller than the nation's payments and obligations to other countries, measured over a period of time. When receipts and credits exceed payments and obligations, a surplus occurs.

In order to better understand the use of the word deficit in discussions on a nation's balance of payments, several distinctions should be noted:

1. *Fundamental versus Financing Accounts.* Some accounts are considered fundamental to a nation's economic activities with the rest of the world. As an

---

Example of Measuring Deficit or Surplus Above or Below the Line.

SITUATION: A nation experienced inflows of 700,000,000 krona and outflows of 650,000,000 krona of goods and services during a recent year. The nation financed a portion of its imports by reducing its gold stocks by 35,000,000 krona of gold and it increased its liability to foreigners by 15,000,000 krona. What is the deficit or surplus?

SOLUTION:	ABOVE THE LINE	BELOW THE LINE
A deficit of 50,000,000 krona.	Imports . . . . 700 Exports . . . . 650 deficit 50	Decrease in gold . . . . . 35 Increase in liabilities . . . . 15 deficit 50

Example of Measuring Deficit or Surplus Above or Below the Line.

example, the export of goods is an economic activity that will bring foreign exchange into the hands of a nation's citizens or banking system. The import of goods has the reverse effect. Both imports and exports are fundamental transactions affecting economic activity. On the other hand, the exchange of gold to redeem a nation's currency is a financing transaction. The nation does not sell sufficient goods to earn foreign exchange to redeem its currency so it must give up a portion of its monetary reserves. This financing transaction is basically different from the fundamental transaction involving goods to be imported or exported.

2. *Above or Below the Line.* Economists draw a line to separate the fundamental accounts from the financing accounts. The economic accounts that contribute to a deficit or surplus are placed above the line. The financing accounts that help pay for a deficit or that are increased by a surplus are placed below the line. A deficit or surplus can be measured either above or below the line, as is shown in the simplified example in the Figure.

3. *Different Economists Draw Line at Different Places.* A major difficulty in dealing with the concept of deficits is that economists do not fully agree on

which accounts are fundamental and which are financing in nature. As a result, deficits or surpluses must be reported in terms of the approach used in dividing the fundamental from the financing accounts.

PROBLEM: A nation imports goods worth 100,000,000 marks and exports goods worth 120,000,000 marks. Its liabilities to foreigners increase by 10,000,000 marks and its gold reserves increase by 30,000,000 marks. What is the nation's balance of payments deficit or surplus?

ANSWER: A surplus of 20,000,000 marks. Above the line, exports exceed imports by this amount (120 − 100). Below the line, gold increased by a greater amount than liabilities increased (30 − 10).

deficit in the 1960s, United States. In August 1971, President Nixon formally recognized that the dollar was overvalued compared to other major currencies and he announced that the dollar would no longer be supported at its official or par exchange rate. This amounted to a *de facto* devaluation which was followed by a formal devaluation in December 1971.

The devaluation of the dollar was the final step in a series of U.S. actions to deal with deficits throughout the 1960s. Some of these actions were:

1. *Interest Equalization Tax (1963).* In July, 1963, President Kennedy proposed a tax on foreign securities purchased by U.S. investors. Prior to this tax, foreign securities offered a higher yield than comparable American securities. The interest equalization tax reduced the yield on foreign securities purchased by American investors to the same approximate yield as offered by American securities. With the net returns at approximately the same levels, the better-known, lower-risk U.S. securities were more attractive to investors. Foreign institutions and companies were thus excluded from Wall Street and it was hoped that U.S. long-term capital would not go abroad. Most observers agree that the interest equalization tax had only a limited effect, if any, on the U.S. balance of payments deficits.

2. *Restraints on Foreign Direct Investment (1965).* In February, 1965, President Johnson announced a program of voluntary restraints on foreign direct investment. American business firms were asked to minimize capital outflows from the United States in support of their foreign operations. They were also asked to reduce deposits in foreign banks. Although the program was well received and supported, it had limited effect on the deficits. The program was tightened and, in January 1968, it was replaced by a mandatory program of restraints. This much-stricter program did not correct the U.S. balance of payments deficits.

3. *Controls on Lending by U.S. Commercial Banks (1968).* The Federal Reserve established restrictions on foreign lending by the large U.S. commercial banks. Loans to borrowers in Western Europe and other industrialized countries were to be reduced according to the Federal Reserve guidelines.

This program also appears to have had minor effects on deficits.

CROSS-REFERENCES:
currency, p. 369
dollar, alternatives for support in 1971, p. 388
fiscal policy, effect on balance of payments p. 406

deficit of parent country, actions by multinational firms. A parent country may be defined as the country where the multinational firm has its headquarters, board of directors, and the bulk of its shareholders. The firm conducts its domestic operations in the parent country and its foreign operations in other countries. As a general rule, the officers and managers of the firm feel their strongest allegiance to and have their closest ties with the government of the parent country.

A multinational firm can help its parent country reduce deficits by a variety of means including:

1. *Borrow Abroad to Support Foreign Operations.* When a firm uses the currency of its parent country to invest abroad, the parent country experiences capital outflows. Borrowing foreign currencies eliminates these outflows and contributes to reducing a deficit.

2. *Borrow Abroad to Support Domestic Operations.* A multinational firm may be able to borrow money in the capital markets of nations with balance of payments surpluses. These funds can be transferred to the parent country and be invested in domestic operations. This would provide a capital inflow to the parent country.

3. *Remit Funds Held Abroad.* A multinational firm may be holding cash balances in a number of banks throughout the world. If all excess funds are returned to banks in the

parent country, the funds help reduce deficits.

4. *Increase Exports and Decrease Imports.* A large firm can sell more of its domestic production overseas to earn foreign exchange for the parent country. At the same time, it can reduce any imports to the parent country reducing the need for foreign exchange. Both actions will help the parent country reduce its deficit.

CROSS-REFERENCE:
deficit in balance of payments,
p. 375

deficit situation, dilemma of multinational firm. In many cases, the multinational firm will be holding extremely large cash balances of a currency. If the firm attempted to convert the currency, the resulting pressure might force a devaluation. On the other hand, holding the currency helps support its value and may help the nation avoid a devaluation.

The decision to hold the currency and suffer a loss should it be devalued versus converting the currency and forcing the devaluation may be complex and difficult to make. The firm must be concerned with the political ramifications of its action and the possibility that the local government will impose controls in the future. It must also consider its responsibilities to assist the government and people of the country in developing and stabilizing the economy. On the other hand, a large loss from a devaluation (when it finally comes) can cause serious operating problems for a firm.

This type of decision complicates the role of the multinational firm in a deficit situation.

deficits in local country, actions by multinational firms. A local operation country is a foreign nation where the multinational firm has a manufacturing facility or sales outlet. From the point of the view of the parent firm, the operation is that of a foreign subsidiary and the foreign nation's currency is a local currency.

A multinational firm can help the local operation country reduce its deficits by a number of actions including:

1. *Purchase Materials Locally.* Raw materials for a local production operation can be purchased in many countries. By purchasing them locally, the firm minimizes imports to the local operation country.

2. *Export to Other Markets.* The production from the local operation can be exported to neighboring countries, an action which will bring in foreign exchange.

3. *Minimize Remittances to Parent Company.* The subsidiary can be required to remit only minimal fees, royalties, interest payments, and profits to the parent firm. In most situations this is not realistic and will only happen if the local government places restrictions on remittances.

deflation. A persistent decline in the general price level in a nation's economy. The opposite of inflation.

CROSS-REFERENCE:
inflation, p. 431

delist. The removal of a security from the list of those traded at a major exchange, generally because the security or the issuing company no longer meets the standards or requirements of the exchange.

demand deposit. Money held in a checking account at a commercial bank that may be withdrawn at any time, normally by the writing of a check.

demand-pull inflation. A rise in price levels which results from a demand for goods and services that exceeds the available supply.

CROSS-REFERENCES:

inflation, p. 431
cost-push inflation, p. 368

depletion. In the tax law, a reduction in the quantity of a fixed asset, normally a natural resource such as oil or gas, which may be charged against the firm's revenues to reduce the firm's federal income taxes. This is a noncash expense similar to depreciation.

CROSS-REFERENCE:

depreciation, p. 379

depreciation. A reduction in the value of a fixed asset because of wear and tear, accidental damage, or obsolescence. This reduction in value is taken as a noncash, operating expense by the firm and is used to reduce the firm's revenues when reported for tax purposes. Depreciation has the effect of reducing the firm's reported income, its federal income taxes, and shields money which can be retained by the firm to replace its fixed asset at the end of its service life.

CROSS-REFERENCES:

inflation in the capital budget, how to analyze, p. 11

flow-of-funds statement, how to develop from balance sheet and income statement, p. 38
profits, how to maintain under inflation, p. 59
tax factors affecting return, how to evaluate, p. 72
depreciation, how to calculate, p. 188
depletion, p. 379
double-declining balance method, p. 391
noncash charges, p. 468
salvage value, p. 517

depreciation schedule. A formal record on a fixed asset that shows the asset's book value each year, annual depreciation, and other items of information.

CROSS-REFERENCE:

depreciation, p. 379

detachable warrant. A warrant is a security attached to another security that gives the holder the right to buy shares of stock during a stated period of time and at a given price. A detachable warrant may be separated from the bond and sold as a separate security. Such warrants are often listed for trading on the major exchanges.

CROSS-REFERENCE:

warrant, p. 547

Simplified Depreciation Schedule.

Stone Crusher, Serial No. 224715, Purchased June 23, 1976
Cost: $115,000 + 17,000 installation
Book salvage value: $25,000, June 1981

Year	Book Value	−	Annual Depreciation	=	Ending Book Value
0	132,000	−	0	=	132,000
1	132,000	−	35,667	=	96,333
2	96,333	−	28,533	=	67,800
3	67,800	−	21,400	=	46,400
4	46,400	−	14,267	=	32,133
5	32,133	−	7,133	=	25,000

devaluation. A reduction in the value of a national currency in terms of another national currency. A devaluation may be expressed by lowering the gold or silver content of the currency.

CROSS-REFERENCE:
currency, p. 369

devaluation, effects of. As a nation tries to deal with its balance of payments deficits through monetary and fiscal policies and capital controls, it may finally decide that its currency is overvalued compared to other national currencies. In this situation, devaluation is the final effort to eliminate the deficits. A devaluation has two effects which help eliminate deficits:

1. *Makes Foreign Goods More Expensive.* The local currency is worth less compared to other currencies after a devaluation. More local currency is needed to buy foreign goods. This causes the prices of foreign goods to rise and discourages their purchase.

2. *Makes Domestic Goods More Attractive to Foreigners.* Foreign currencies can purchase greater amounts of domestic goods per foreign unit of currency. This encourages foreigners to buy domestic goods.

devaluation of the dollar, august 1971. Through the summer of 1971, the United States attempted to deal with the pressures on the dollar using the short-term alternatives. As it became apparent that 1971 would bring the largest balance of payments deficit in U.S. history, President Nixon finally decided to allow the devaluation of the dollar. On Sunday evening, August 15, the president announced:

1. *Suspension of Convertibility.* Foreign central banks could no longer convert their dollars into gold at the official rate of $35 per ounce. In effect, this was a de facto devaluation of the dol-

lar since the dollar was already pegged against floating currencies at a lower rate than $35 per ounce of gold.

2. *Import Surcharge.* A 10 percent additional tariff was placed on most imports into the United States. This increased the prices of imports and was designed to reduce the volume of foreign goods sold in the United States.

3. *Price Freeze.* Prices of domestic goods and services were frozen. This was designed to make U.S. goods more attractive both domestically and in foreign markets.

The suspension of convertibility into gold was, in effect, an announcement that the dollar could no longer be used as the basis for a gold exchange standard. The dollar had occupied such a prominent role in international finance since 1946 on the basis of its strength. Domestic inflation and balance of payments difficulties had eroded this strength and a new system would be needed.

development bank. A term used to describe any of the banking organizations that make medium- to long-term loans to assist in the economic development of underdeveloped areas of the world. Among the major activities of development banks are:

1. *Encourage Direct Investment.* The banks provide funds and assistance for direct private investments in underdeveloped countries. These investments can be designed to develop basic industries, such as petroleum or steel, to encourage industrialization as would be the case with manufacturing of textiles or metal products, or develop or diversify the agricultural base of the nation. A development bank could participate in these activities as a part owner with an equity position or as a creditor by extending a loan.

2. *Finance Economic Development.* Development banks use their funds for infrastructure activities similar to those undertaken by the World Bank group.
3. *Provide Business Credit.* Funds can be loaned to local businessmen to finance working capital requirements, particularly when such additional working capital will allow the company to export its products. This can provide badly needed foreign exchange for the national economy.
4. *Assist in the Formation of Capital Markets.* Some development banks become involved in the creation and operation of national stock exchanges to develop a market for equity securities. The development bank can also assist in bringing together investors who can pool their funds for the purchase of debt securities.

CROSS-REFERENCE:
nacional financiera, p. 466

differential after-tax cash-flow stream. In capital budgeting, the kind of cash flows that make up the cash-flow stream. This essentially reflects an incremental approach to decision making in the capital-budgeting process.

CROSS-REFERENCES:
cash-flow stream, how to calculate, p. 3
refunding a bond issue, how to make the decision, p. 152

dilution. A decrease in the proportional share of ownership of a firm. When new common stock is issued by a firm, the existing shareholders suffer a dilution of ownership unless they exercise a preemptive right to purchase a portion of the new shares.

CROSS-REFERENCE:
convertible securities, characteristics of, p. 360

dilution of earnings. The use of common stock to finance less profitable projects than currently financed, with a consequent decline in earnings per share.

CROSS-REFERENCES:
acquisitions, how to analyze, p. 78
Solomon on future earnings per share, p. 240

direct inventory costs. In inventory management, the expenditures immediately connected to buying and holding goods. Examples are materials cost, order costs, and carrying costs.

CROSS-REFERENCES:
inventory management, how to set up system for, p. 103
inventory, management of important items, p. 444
inventory, costs of, p. 442

direct placement. A bond or other security issue that is sold directly to one or more purchasers, generally financial institutions such as banks, life insurance companies, or pension funds. Since a direct placement is not available to the general public, the issue does not have to be registered with the Securities and Exchange Commission.

CROSS-REFERENCES:
security, financial, p. 519
primary issue, p. 488

discount. A price reduction, normally 1 to 2 percent, granted in return for rapid payment on a credit sale.

CROSS-REFERENCES:
present value of money, how to calculate, p. 19
forward market, how to calculate bid and ask quotes, p. 171
premiums and discounts, causes of, p. 484
premiums and discounts in forward market, p. 485

present value factor, p. 486
terms of the trade, p. 536

discount. In international finance, a situation that exists when a currency is worth less in the forward market than in the spot market. EXAMPLE: The exchange rate between francs and sterling is 9.5fr/1£ spot and 9.7fr/1£ 90 days. Which currency is at a discount? ANSWER: The franc because more francs are needed in the forward market to purchase sterling than are needed in the spot market.

CROSS-REFERENCES:

premium, p. 484
premiums and discounts, causes of, p. 484
premiums and discounts in forward market, p. 485

discounted cash flow. A present-value method of calculating the rate of return for a capital budgeting proposal. Also called internal rate of return.

CROSS-REFERENCES:

net present value, how to compare proposals, p. 17
internal rate of return, p. 436
present-value techniques, how to avoid being manipulated by, p. 23

discount factor. In capital budgeting, the value in a present-value table that can be applied against future receipts of cash to bring them back to a present value.

CROSS-REFERENCES:

bonds, how to calculate value of, p. 124
present value, p. 486
internal rate of return, how to calculate, p. 15

disequilibrium. In international finance, a situation that exists when the supply-and-demand schedules for a currency are not in balance. An excessive demand for a currency will exist when foreigners or speculators want to purchase the currency to use its high purchasing power to buy goods or to make a speculative profit when its value is raised. An excessive supply of the currency will exist when the currency is overvalued in terms of other currencies and will not purchase the same amount of goods as other currencies. Both excessive demand and excessive supply are said to be disequilibrium states for the currency.

diversification. A technique for limiting the risks of investment by spreading the money to be invested among a number of securities or companies, rather than investing all available funds in one security or company.

CROSS-REFERENCE:

growth, reasons for seeking, p. 423
capital asset pricing model, p. 279

dividend. A dividend is a payment to stockholders of a particular class of stock by the corporation as a distribution of earnings. Basically, there are three types of dividends:
1. *Cash Dividends.* These are the most common form and are expressed in terms of dollars per share. Thus, if a firm declares a dividend of $4 per share and a shareholder has 100 shares, he will receive a check for $400 as his share of the cash dividends.
2. *Stock Dividends.* These occur when the board votes to give each shareholder additional stock on a percentage basis. A 5 percent stock dividend will give 5 shares of the company's stock to an investor holding 100 shares when the dividend is declared. Stock dividends are less desirable than cash but may be more desirable than no dividend at all, particularly if the market does not drop the price of the

common stock in response to the dividend.

3. *Property Dividends.* These are very rare, but may result in the distribution of bonds, preferred stock, stock of other companies, other securities, or merchandise. An example of a merchandise dividend might be the distribution of small bottles of perfume by the company manufacturing the perfume.

CROSS-REFERENCES:

dividend decisions, nature of. A firm's dividend policies have the effect of dividing the firm's after-tax profit into two categories:

1. *Funds to Finance Long-Term Growth.* These are represented on the balance sheet by the retained earnings account. Earnings retained by the firm have traditionally accounted for approximately two-thirds of the firm's long-term financing. The remaining one-third has been provided by debt and by new issues of preferred and common stock.

2. *Funds to Be Distributed to Shareholders.* These are represented by the cash dividends declared by the board of directors and paid to the common shareholders.

Two Possible Approaches to Dividend Decisions

Because dividend policies affect both long-term financing and the return distributed to shareholders, the firm may adopt two possible viewpoints on the decision to pay dividends. These are:

1. *As a Long-Term Financing Decision.* With this approach, all the firm's after-tax profits can be viewed as a source of long-term financing. The declaration of cash dividends reduces the amount of funds available to finance growth and either restricts growth or forces the firm to find other financing sources. Thus, the firm might accept a guideline to retain earnings as long as either of two conditions exist:

   a. *Sufficient profitable projects are available.* The acceptance of highly profitable projects represents a worthwhile growth goal for most firms. As long as such projects are available, the firm can retain earnings to finance them.

   b. *Capital structure needs equity funds.* To avoid the high risk associated with excessive debt, the firm must have a balance of debt and equity financing. Because of the costs of floating common stock, retaining earnings is preferable as equity financing. Thus, earnings may be retained as part of a long-term financing decision related to the management of capital structure.

   With either of these guidelines, cash dividends are viewed as a remainder. Dividends represent a distribution of earnings that cannot be profitably reinvested by the firm.

2. *As a Maximization of Wealth Decision.* With this approach, the firm recognizes that the payment of dividends has a strong influence on the market price of the common stock. Higher dividends increase the value of the stock to many investors. Similarly, low dividends decrease the value. The firm must, in a maximization of wealth sense, declare sufficient divi-

dends to meet the expectations of investors and shareholders.

Most firms treat the declaration of dividends as a maximization of wealth decision. The validity of this approach depends on whether dividend policies really affect the market price of common stock. Theoretical arguments have been developed that dividends do not affect market price. On the other hand, the preponderance of evidence suggests that dividend policies have profound effects on a firm's position in the stock market. We may therefore conclude that a maximization-of-wealth approach correctly deals with the dividend decision.

dividend growth model. An approach to the valuation of common stock developed by Myron J. Gordon that assumes that future dividends per share are the sole determinant of the intrinsic value of a common stock.

CROSS-REFERENCES:
Gordon on common stock value, p. 255
Walter and Gordon on dividend decisions, p. 260

dividend informational content. A concept identified with Miller and Modigliani that dividend changes provide the *occasion* for price changes of the firm's common stock, not the *cause* of the price changes, because the dividend announcement reflects management's expectations of future earnings and growth opportunities. The informational content of dividend announcements is identified with the theorists who believe that dividends do not affect the value of common stock in perfect markets.

CROSS-REFERENCES:
Miller and Modigliani on dividend policy, p. 264

Gordon on common stock value, p. 255
Walter and Gordon on dividend decisions, p. 260

dividend payout. The ratio of dividends per share to earnings per share used to compare the level of a firm's dividends with the level of its earnings.

CROSS-REFERENCES:
ownership factors, how to analyze with ratios, p. 51
long-term financing, how to compare different alternatives, p. 139
normal dividend payment, p. 469

dividend ratios. The common stockholder is very concerned about the position taken by the firm with respect to the payment of cash dividends. If the firm is paying insufficient dividends, the stock will not be attractive to investors desiring some current income from their investment. If it pays excessive dividends, it may not be retaining adequate funds to finance future growth.

To pay consistent and adequate dividends, the firm must be liquid and profitable. Without liquidity, the firm will be unable to locate the cash needed to pay the dividends. Without profits, the firm will not have sufficient retained earnings to make dividend declarations. Firms cannot declare dividends if the balance in their retained-earnings accounts is not at least as large as the amount of the dividend. A more important factor is that, without profits, the firm will not have the resources to pay the dividends.

Two dividend ratios are particularly important:
1. *Dividend Payout* (DPS/EPS). This is a ratio of dividends per share to earnings per share. It tells what percentage of the firm's earnings is being paid to the common shareholder in the form of dividends. The percent-

age not paid out is retained for the firm's future needs.

2. *Dividend Yield* (DPS/MP). This is a ratio of dividends per share to the market price per share. It gives the current return to the investor as a percentage of his investment. It is of interest to potential shareholders who are considering purchasing the firm's stock and who desire dividends as a source of income.

Guidelines for these two ratios vary widely. Firms often attempt to pay approximately 50 percent of their earnings as dividends. If the firm is experiencing a need for funds to support its operations, it might allow the dividends to decline in relation to earnings. If the firm lacks opportunities to utilize funds generated by retained earnings, it might allow the dividends to increase in relation to earnings. In either case, consistency of dividend payment would be important to investors, so changes would be gradual.

The dividend yield to a stockholder ranges from zero to 6 or 7 percent. No dividend yield exists for a firm that does not declare dividends. High-growth firms may declare dividends, but the yield may only be 1 or 2 percent. For mature industrial firms, the yield may be 3 or 4 percent. When stock prices are depressed or for utilities or similar firms, the yield may reach 6 or 7 percent.

CROSS-REFERENCES:
ownership factors, how to analyze with ratios, p. 51
dividend payout, p. 384
ownership ratios, p. 475

dividend stability, importance of. The overwhelming majority of mature corporations have dividend policies that emphasize regular and steady dividend declarations. Although earnings may fluctuate from year to year, the dividend will not. The relationship between dividends and earnings is shown in the Figure. Note that the dividends rise with the long-term earnings trend but do not fluctuate on a year-to-year basis.

A number of arguments may be advanced to underline the importance of steady dividend payments including:

1. *Perception of Stability.* When a firm declares a regular dividend, investors accept the declaration as a sign of

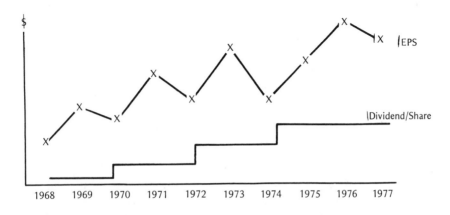

Relationship Between Dividends and Earnings.

continued normal operations. At the same time, a reduction in the declared dividend will draw immediate attention and will be taken by many as a sign of potential or expected trouble in the future. Many investors will immediately sell their stock without checking further and this selling pressure will cause a decline in the market price of the stock. Stable dividend declarations avoid this reaction on the part of investors.

2. *Preference of Investors.* The common shareholders of mature corporations generally prefer to receive steady dividends. They expect to receive an approximate amount of cash each quarter and they may make advance commitments to invest or spend the money. If a firm fails to declare a dividend, these investors will seek to invest in firms that provide a steady cash payment each quarter.

3. *Routinizing of Dividend Decisions.* By establishing a stable dividend policy, the board of directors avoids a lengthy quarterly discussion on dividend levels. Unless circumstances warrant a possible change, the regular dividend can be declared. This policy avoids wasting the time of the board and allows its members to concentrate on more important matters facing the firm.

4. *Flexibility of the Extra Dividend.* With a steady dividend policy, the firm can flexibly handle a period of temporarily high earnings. This is accomplished by declaring an extra dividend for the quarter. This allows a larger distribution of earnings without raising the expectations of investors.

dividend yield. The ratio of dividends per share to market price per share used to compare income offered to shareholders as a percent of the market price of their stock.

CROSS-REFERENCE:
ownership factors, how to analyze with ratios, p. 51

dividends, constraints on paying. While most firms recognize the investor demand for dividends, several factors may restrict the firm's ability to declare and pay dividends. These are:

1. *Insufficient Cash.* Although a firm may have adequate income to declare dividends, the firm may not have sufficient cash to pay the dividends. The firm's liquid funds may be tied up in receivables or inventory or the firm may be short on liquid funds due to commitments to fixed assets.

2. *Contractual Restrictions.* If a firm is experiencing liquidity or profitability difficulties, creditors may require restrictions on dividends as part of any new loan arrangements. In this situation, the firm agrees as part of a contract with a creditor to restrict dividend payments. As an example, a loan agreement may prohibit dividends as long as the firm's debt-equity ratio is in excess of 1.2/1. The firm would be forced to retain earnings to increase equity and thus reduce the debt-equity ratio. A second example would be a bond indenture that restricts the dividend payout to 20 percent of earnings during the life of the issue. The low payout requires the firm to retain cash to reduce the risk of default on interest or principal payments on the bond.

3. *Legal Restrictions.* Occasionally a firm will be legally restricted from declaring and paying dividends. The most common example is found in those states where the law requires that all dividends must be paid from current or past income. Firms incorporated in these states must have adequate retained earnings to declare dividends. In the absence of retained earnings, the firms are barred from declaring

dividends even though they may have sufficient cash to make the payments.

dividends, why investors want them. Most investors expect two forms of return from the purchase of common stock. These are:

1. *Capital Gains.* The investor expects an increase in the market value of the common stock over a period of time. If, for example, the stock is purchased at $40 and sold for $60, the investor will realize a capital gain of $20. Capital gain may be defined as the profit resulting from the sale of capital investments, in this case common stock.

2. *Dividends.* The investor expects, at some point, a distribution of the firm's earnings. From mature and stable corporations, most investors expect regular dividends to be declared and paid on the common stock. This expectation takes priority over the desire to retain earnings to finance expansion and growth.

A number of factors may be analyzed to help explain the investor's expectation of dividends over capital gains. Perhaps the three major factors are:

1. *Reduction of Uncertainty.* The promise of future capital gains or a future distribution of earnings involves more uncertainty than a distribution of current earnings. A current dividend represents a present-value cash inflow to the investor that cannot be lost if the firm later experiences operating or financing difficulties. This reduction of uncertainty is one factor explaining investor preference for current dividends.

2. *Indication of Strength.* The declaration and payment of cash dividends carries an information content that the firm is reasonably strong and healthy. The dividend declaration reveals liquidity since cash is needed to make the dividend payment, and this cash must be taken away from the firm's operations. The declaration reveals profitability, and more importantly, the expectation of future profitability since the firm would probably conserve its cash if the management were preparing for future difficulties.

3. *Need for Current Income.* Many shareholders require income from their investments to pay for their current living expenses. These investors may be reluctant to sell their shares in order to gain cash. Cash dividends provide current income to these investors without affecting their principal or capital.

CROSS-REFERENCE:
capital gain, p. 333

diversification approach to common stock value. This approach to common-stock valuation involves selecting a variety of stocks from among the major publicly traded corporations. It also applies to a firm making a number of small, not necessarily related, acquisitions. It is used by large firms and institutional portfolio managers in situations where the investing organization desires to reduce risks by selecting stocks from different industries. With the diversification method of acquiring stock, the desire to diversify becomes a more important goal in forming a corporate pyramid or portfolio than the search for value. Once the primacy of diversification is established, the analyst will use intrinsic value, current market value, or some other means to select the exact stock to be acquired.

EXAMPLE: A mutual fund has concentrated on transportation stocks, including railroads, trucking lines, and airlines. The fund's executive vice-president foresees a decline in the transportation industry and recommends converting some of these shares of stock into manufacturing and lei-

sure-industry securities. Which approach to valuation is being used?
ANSWER: Diversification approach. Purchasing stock in other industries is placed as a first priority; valuation will be second.

CROSS-REFERENCE:
common stock valuation, five approaches, p. 354

dollar, alternatives for support in 1971. The actions of Germany and many other nations in the spring of 1971 were in response to a fundamental weakness of the dollar. The United States could have followed any of several courses of action to support the dollar, thus avoiding the de facto revaluations of other currencies. Some of these possible actions were:

1. *Ask Foreign Central Banks to Hold Dollars.* Other nations could add more dollars to their stock of monetary reserves supporting their currencies. They were becoming increasingly reluctant to do this. In 1971, it was apparent that the dollar was declining in value compared to other major currencies. Nations holding dollars would suffer a decline in the value of their holdings if the dollar continued to weaken (as it did). Thus, other nations did not want to add to their dollar holdings and it was unlikely that foreign central banks would accept this alternative.

2. *Redeem Dollars for Gold.* By 1971, the United States' holdings of gold had dropped to approximately 11 billion dollars worth at the exchange rate of $35 per ounce. This compares to holdings in excess of 25 billion dollars at the end of World War II. The United States had been redeeming dollars for gold throughout the 1960's and this trend could continue. The problem was that foreign individuals and nations held many more dollars than could be redeemed

for gold. In 1971, Morgan Guaranty Trust Company estimated that over 60 billion U.S. dollars were held abroad, either in foreign banks or in foreign branches of U.S. banks. The United States did not hold sufficient gold to consider redemption as a viable solution to the problem of the weakness of the dollar. As a matter of fact, it can be argued that reducing the U.S. holdings of gold would further weaken the dollar since it reduced the reserves supporting the dollar.

3. *Use SDR's and Other IMF Mechanisms.* With the aid of the International Monetary Fund, the United States could have absorbed some of the excess dollars. Once again, the amount of dollars in the hands of foreigners was too large for this to be a viable alternative.

4. *Issue Treasury Bonds to Foreign Governments.* The United States could have offered to exchange treasury bonds for the dollars held by foreign central banks. This would allow foreign governments to collect interest on their dollar holdings. This would solve some problems but not others. For example, it would not remove the excess deutschmarks from the German economy and thus Germany would continue to feel inflationary pressures.

5. *Impose Foreign Exchange Controls.* The United States could have imposed restrictions on the use of the dollar. Some restrictions already existed in the areas of foreign direct investment by U.S. firms and the purchase of foreign securities by U.S. citizens. Additional controls could have been placed on the purchases of foreign currency by U.S. citizens and firms. This action would have destroyed the international monetary system and returned the system to the disastrous period of the 1930's.

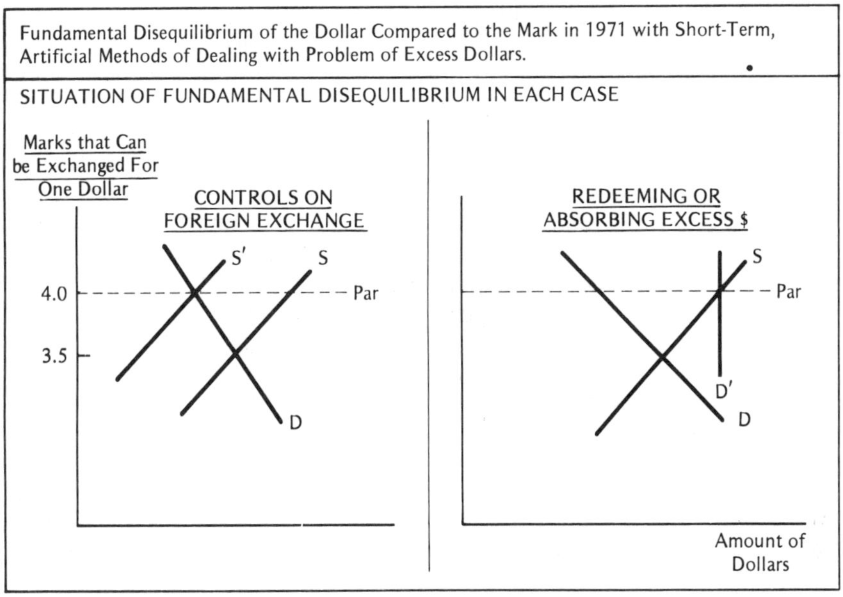

Fundamental Disequilibrium of the Dollar Compared to the Mark in 1971 with Short-Term, Artificial Methods of Dealing with Problem of Excess Dollars.

The above alternatives are basically short-term, artificial methods of dealing with the problem of excess dollars. The Figure diagrams the fundamental disequilibrium situation between dollars and deutschmarks. The par exchange rate was 4 DM/$1 and, at this rate, the supply of dollars exceeded the demand for dollars. At approximately 3.5 DM/$1, the two currencies would be in equilibrium.

The diagrams show how the short-term alternatives would deal with the excess dollars. With controls on foreign exchange, the supply of dollars would be cut back to S′, thus eliminating the excess dollars. With the alternatives to redeem or absorb the excess dollars, the demand would be artificially increased to D′. Both situations offer stop-gap solutions until the fundamental disequilibrium is corrected.

CROSS-REFERENCE:
deficit in the 1960's, United States, p. 376

dollar, correcting fundamental disequilibrium in 1971. The United States had two major alternatives for correcting the fundamental disequilibrium between the dollar and other major currencies in 1971. These were:

1. *Deflate the American Economy.* In 1971, the demand for goods and services in the American economy exceeded the supply. This forced up domestic prices on goods, a situation that made them less attractive to foreign buyers. At the same time, the high prices made foreign products attractive to Americans. Thus, the United States was experiencing a reduction in its exports and increases in its imports. This situation was aggravated by the

fact that military personnel and their dependents who were stationed in foreign countries were purchasing foreign goods and services. These factors contributed to balance of payments difficulties and led to the accumulation of dollars abroad. Deflating the economy means that the government has taken measures to reduce domestic demand for goods and services, reduce domestic price levels, and encourage surpluses of goods to be sold abroad. This would restore the balance of payments to an equilibrium position, an action that would result in equilibrium between the dollar and other currencies.

2. *Devalue the Dollar.* The second alternative is to devalue the dollar. The lower purchasing power of a devalued dollar will result in reduced imports. The higher purchasing power of foreign currencies will increase exports. Equilibrium will be achieved at a new exchange rate.

The Figure shows the effects of these longer-term solutions to the problem of disequilibrium between the dollar and mark. By deflating the U.S. economy, the government reduces the price of U.S. goods and makes them attractive to foreigners. This increases the demand for dollars. At the same time, foreign goods are less attractive, so U.S. citizens reduce purchases of them, thus reducing the supply of dollars in the hands of foreigners. The supply of and demand for dollars shift to S' and D' respectively and equilibrium is achieved at the 4 DM/$1 exchange rate. With a devaluation of the dollar, the exchange rate is adjusted to the actual supply and demand equilibrium, a point near 3.5 DM/$1.

CROSS-REFERENCE:

deficit in the 1960's, United States, p. 376

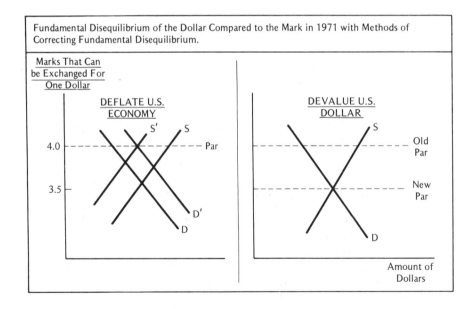

Fundamental Disequilibrium of the Dollar Compared to the Mark in 1971 with Methods of Correcting Fundamental Disequilibrium.

domestic corporation. A corporation that is chartered by the state in which it operates. Many states favor domestic corporations with lower taxes than foreign corporations.

CROSS-REFERENCE:
foreign corporation, p. 414

double-declining balance method. An accelerated method of depreciation that may be used to depreciate assets more rapidly than would be allowed by the straight-line method.

CROSS-REFERENCES:
residual values, how to forecast, p. 66
depreciation, how to calculate, p. 188
depreciation, p. 379

Dow theory. A method of securities market analysis designed to identify major price trends of the market as a whole or of a particular class of securities, without forecasting the extent or duration of the trend.

Dow-Jones averages. Financial statistics on publicly traded common stock and bond offerings compiled by the Dow-Jones Company, and showing the highest, lowest, and closing-price averages for a composite group of stocks and bonds. The Dow-Jones averages are widely used as indicators of market levels. Common stock averages are divided into 30 industrials, 20 transportation companies, and 15 utilities. A 65 stock composite average is also given.

draft. An instrument drawn by one person (drawer) ordering a second person (drawee) to pay a specified sum of money to a third person either on sight (a sight draft) or at some future time (a time draft). Also called a bill of exchange.

CROSS-REFERENCES:
acceptance, p. 304
bank acceptance, p. 320
bill of exchange, p. 322

Du Pont chart. A graphic device popularized by the Du Pont Corporation that focuses on the elements of return on investment. The Du Pont chart correctly points out the roles of asset turnover and profit margin in increasing return on investment.

CROSS-REFERENCES:
return on investment, p. 509
return on investment, how to lever, p. 69

E

earning power. Earning power is calculated by dividing NIAT by total assets. It is a measure of the after-tax return achieved by the company compared to the firm's resources. It links after-tax profits to the book value of the assets. If a firm is utilizing its assets efficiently, it will have a high earning power when compared with similar firms.

Earning power may be viewed as the firm's after-tax return on investment. Many managers use the term return on investment when they are relating NIAT to assets. When others use the term return on investment, the analyst should always ask what the person means.

The three major ratios linking profits to resources are given in the Table.

CROSS-REFERENCES:
profitability, how to analyze with ratios, p. 56
net income after taxes, p. 466

Comparing Three Major Ratios Linking Profits and Resources.

Return on Investment (ROI) EBIT/assets	Return on Equity (ROE) NIAT/equity	Earning Power (EP) NIAT/assets
Measures ability of management to earn a return on resources.	Measures ability of firm to convert operating profits into after-tax return for common shareholders.	Measures efficiency of firm in achieving an after-tax return on resources. Also called after-tax ROI.

earnings available to the common shareholder (EACS). A profit measure calculated by subtracting dividends payable to preferred stockholders from the firm's net income after taxes. This is the correct profit measure to use in the calculation of return on equity for a firm with outstanding preferred stock.

CROSS-REFERENCES:
mergers, how to analyze profitability in a ten-step process, p. 85
return on equity, p. 509

earnings before interest and taxes (EBIT). The firm's income from its operations before allocating any funds to cover interest payments on its debt or corporate income taxes.

CROSS-REFERENCES:
leverage, how to use in profit planning, p. 44

profitability, how to analyze with ratios, p. 56
profits, how to maintain under inflation, p. 59
profit-volume analysis, how to use, p. 64,
long-term financing, how to compare different alternatives, p. 139

earnings before taxes (EBT). A firm's income before the payment of corporate income taxes.

CROSS-REFERENCES:
leverage, how to use in profit planning, p. 44
profit-volume analysis, how to use, p. 64

earnings per share (EPS). Stockholders are concerned about the earnings that will eventually be available to pay them dividends or which are currently used to expand their interest in the firm because the firm retains the earnings. These earnings may be expressed on a per-share basis. Earnings per share is calculated by dividing earnings available to the common shareholder by the number of shares outstanding. Shares authorized but not issued, or authorized, issued, and repurchased (treasury stock), are omitted from the calculation.

A year-by-year comparison of earnings per share can be very informative to the investor. As an example, an investor is considering the purchase of a large bloc of shares of either firm A or B. Each stock will sell for $40 per share. The earnings trend for the two firms is as follows:

	Firm A EPS	Firm B EPS
1970	1.23	2.55
1971	1.42	2.98
1972	1.65	2.06
1973	1.87	2.24
1974	2.15	2.03
1975	2.45	2.45

In the last year the two firms have identical earnings per share. Firm A began at a low EPS, but has steadily progressed and has doubled EPS in 5 years. Firm B has held steady in EPS and has displayed wide fluctuations over the 5 years. The trends of the two earnings streams appear to forecast a brighter future for firm A than firm B.

CROSS-REFERENCES:
acquisitions, how to analyze, p. 78
common stock value, how to compare two or more stocks, p. 83
mergers, how to analyze profitability in a ten-step process, p. 85

Graham and Dodd approaches to common stock value, p. 246
Schwartz on capital structure theory, p. 230
Solomon on future earnings per share, p. 240

earnings ratios. A grouping of financial ratios which provide information on the earnings of the firm and how earnings affect the price of common stock. The common earnings ratios are earnings per share, price earnings multiple, and capitalization rate.

CROSS-REFERENCES:
ownership factors, how to analyze with ratios, p. 51
ratios, p. 501
ownership ratios, p. 475

economic order quantity (EOQ). The size of an order for an item of inventory that will result in the lowest total of order costs and carrying costs. A number of mathematical models are available to calculate the economic order quantity.

CROSS-REFERENCES:
inventory management, how to set up system for, p. 103
inventory management system, p. 445

effective cost of debt. The actual cost to the firm of a debt offering. This may differ slightly from the coupon rate because the net proceeds (amount of money actually received by the firm) differ from the par value. In most cases, the effective cost is calculated using a bond table.

CROSS-REFERENCE:
coupon rate, p. 368

efficient frontier. The outer edge of a set of portfolios where each portfolio on the frontier provides the highest possible expected return for any degree of risk or the lowest possible degree of risk for any expected return. In the Figure, the boundary ABCD defines the efficient set of portfolios or efficient frontier. The shaded area shows all portfolios and portfolios A through F are specifically identified. Of the six shown, only A through D are efficient portfolios.

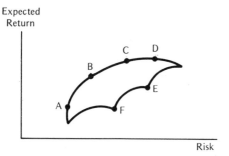

Expected Return / Risk

CROSS-REFERENCE:
capital asset pricing model, p. 279

efficient portfolio. A selection of securities from those available in the general market that provides a maximum return for a given level of risk or a minimum risk for a given level of return.

CROSS-REFERENCE:
capital asset pricing model, p. 279

encumbrance. A claim, such as a lien, on a fixed asset or item of value, such as a security, that prevents the asset from being sold or pledged with a free and clear title.

CROSS-REFERENCE:
lien, p. 452

equilibrium under a gold standard. When the supply of a nation's currency approximates the demand for it, a situation of equilibrium exists. This means two things:
1. *Sufficient Money Available.* The nation's economy and banking system have sufficient funds to finance trade, carry on domestic business transactions, and provide capital needed for investment and development.
2. *Excess Money not in Economy.* When an economy has more money than goods and services to be purchased, inflationary pressures result. Prices tend to rise to absorb the excess money and this changes the value of the currency compared to other currencies. This does not happen when supply approximates demand.

Internationally, equilibrium results when exchange rates are set to reflect price and interest levels. Figure 1 shows the differing situations, as follows:
1. *The Equilibrium Situation.* The supply-and-demand schedules for the currencies cross at the exchange rate between the currency and gold.
2. *Excessive Demand for the Currency.* In this situation, the exchange rate is too low. The currency is undervalued in terms of gold and thus will purchase more goods or services than other currencies. Foreigners and speculators want to purchase the currency and use its higher purchasing power to buy goods or to make a speculative profit when its value is raised.
3. *Excessive Supply of the Currency.* In this case, the exchange rate is too high. The currency is overvalued and will not purchase the same amount of goods as other currencies. People want to get rid of the currency and purchase other currencies at the official exchange rate. Since the high exchange rate means they get excessive amounts of other currencies, they will have more purchasing power in the other currencies.

As an example of the effects of disequilibrium on a currency, let us consider a person who has one ounce of gold and $10. The individual wants to purchase potatoes with the gold and dollars. Potatoes are priced so that 100 pounds can be purchased for either one ounce of gold or $10. In terms of price levels, the equilibrium exchange rate would be $10 per ounce of gold. This rate is shown in the equilibrium situation in Figure 1. The disequilibrium situations are $10 for .9 ounce and $10 for 1.1 ounces of gold.

Figure 2 shows that more potatoes can be purchased by converting the currency or gold in the disequilibrium situations. This is not true in the equi-librium situation.

Disequilibrium of purchasing power causes pressure on currencies. Individuals will purchase and hold the currency that purchases the most goods; that is to say, the currency with the highest purchasing power. As a result of the excessive supply or demand of a currency, the exchange rates will begin to shift (if the governments allow this). The result will be a movement toward an equilibrium situation.

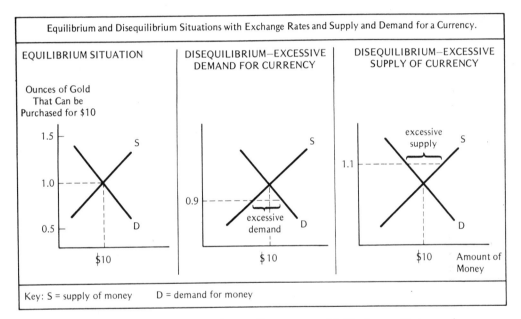

Equilibrium and Disequilibrium Situations with Exchange Rates and Supply and Demand for a Currency.

An Example of the Effects of Disequilibrium.		
Exchange Rate 1 oz. = $10 Equilibrium	Exchange Rate 0.9 oz. = $10 Excess Demand for $	Exchange Rate 1.1 oz. = $10 Excess Supply of $
1 oz. buys 100 lbs or $10 buys 100 lbs	1 oz. buys $11.10 $11.10 buys 111 lbs. (dollars buy more than gold so people want dollars)	$10 buys 1.1 oz. 1.1 oz. buys 110 lbs (gold buys more than dollars so people want gold)

An Example of the Effects of Disequilibrium.

equipment trust bond. A bond that is secured by a piece of machinery or equipment, such as a locomotive, whose title is deposited with a trustee.

equity. The ownership rights in a company. It arises from several sources. Owners purchase the preferred or common stock either through an initial offering or through later sales by the firm. Or the firm retains a portion of its profits and reinvests them in the firm. In these cases, equity does not represent money held by the firm. It does show the sources of assets and approximately what portion of the assets is financed by the owners and retention of earnings.

1. *Preferred Stock.* This account reflects the amount of preferred stock outstanding, if any. The dollar amount of the account is usually equal to the number of shares outstanding times the par value of the stock. If a firm has 100,000 shares of $100 par preferred stock outstanding, the account will show $10,000,000 as a balance.
2. *Common Stock.* This account shows the capital contributed by the owners of the firm to purchase the stock of the firm. The dollar amount of this account is usually equal to the number of outstanding shares of stock times the par or stated value of the stock. Thus, if a firm has 1,000,000 outstanding shares of $50 par stock, the common stock account will show $50,000,000 as a balance.
3. *Contributed Capital in Excess of Par* (also called premium or surplus). This account records money given to the

firm by its owners for stock purchased in excess of the par or stated value of the stock. If the shareholders purchase 1,000,000 shares of $50 par stock for $75 per share, the firm would record $50,000,000 in the common stock account and the remaining $25,000,000 in this account.
4. *Retained Earnings.* This account shows the dollar value of ownership rights that result from the firm's retention of past income. Each year, if the firm makes a profit, it might wish to pay cash dividends (payments from profits) to its owners. If it does not declare dividends equal to its entire net income after taxes, the firm is retaining a portion of the after-tax profits to finance future growth. By keeping some of the profits, the firm is able to purchase new assets without having to borrow or sell additional stock.

equity securities, examples involving.
EXAMPLE: An investor holds 300 shares of $100 par preferred stock with a 5 percent dividend. The investor paid $80 per share for the stock. How much does he receive in dividends?
ANSWER: $1,500 annually ($5 dividend times 300 shares). The dividend is calculated on the par value of the stock, not on the price paid by the holder.
EXAMPLE: A 6 percent cumulative preferred stock has not paid dividends in 2 years. In the third year, the firm declared dividends on both preferred and common stock. An investor has 100 shares of the preferred stock. How much did he receive in dividends ($100 par)?
ANSWER: $1,800. The cumulative stock was in arrears by $12 per share. The current preferred dividend of $6 is also due before the com-

mon shareholders can receive dividends. The firm has to declare an $18 dividend per share of preferred and the holder of 100 shares would receive $1,800.

EXAMPLE: A firm has been liquidated and the assets sold. After paying off the creditors, the firm has $7,000,000 to distribute among the preferred and common shareholders. The firm has outstanding 50,000 shares of 4 percent, $100 par preferred stock and 100,000 shares of $1 par common stock. How much will each shareholder receive?

ANSWER: Since the preferred stock has preference to assets, the preferred shareholders receive full payment before the common shareholders receive any money. At $100 per share, it takes $5,000,000 to pay off the preferred stock ($100 × 50,000 shares). The remaining $2,000,000 is divided among the 100,000 common shares at $20 per share ($2,000,000/100,000 = $20). Each preferred shareholder receives $100 and each common shareholder receives $20.

EXAMPLE: A firm has declared a 10 percent stock dividend. The firm's stock sells for $20 per share. If the market price does not change in response to the stock dividend, how much additional value would be gained by a shareholder who originally had 200 shares?

ANSWER: He would now have 20 additional shares (200 × 10 percent) worth $20 per share, or $400 more market value.

EXAMPLE: A firm has declared a 20 percent stock dividend. The firm's stock sold for $50 before the dividend but dropped to $45 after the dividend. If an investor had 100 shares, how much would he gain or lose in market value?

ANSWER: The old value was 100 shares times $50, or $5,000. The new value is 120 shares times $45, or $5,400. He gains $400.

EXAMPLE: A shareholder owns 500 of the 6,000 outstanding shares of a small company. The company has decided to issue 2,000 new shares. How many of these shares does the shareholder have the right to purchase?

ANSWER: The shareholder's preemptive right allows him to maintain his proportionate share of ownership in the firm. Before the new issue, he had 500/6,000 or 8.33 percent of the firm; 8.33% times 2,000 shares is 167 shares. He has the right to purchase a minimum of 167

shares (he could probably purchase more if he wanted to, the firm agreed, and some shares were left after all shareholders exercised their preemptive rights).

European Investment Bank (EIB). Established in 1958 under the auspices of the European Economic Community, the bank assists in the economic integration of the nations associated with the Common Market. It also makes contributions to underdeveloped regions within the European Economic Community and its associated overseas countries and territories.

ex dividend or ex right. Terms that indicate that a stock is selling without a recently declared dividend or right. The ex dividend or ex right date is four business days prior to the date of record. In order to receive the dividend or right, the stock must be purchased five days prior to the date of record when it is selling cum dividends or cum rights.

CROSS-REFERENCES:
dividend, p. 382
common stock, p. 351

excess profits tax. When the Internal Revenue Service believes that a firm is retaining earnings that are not needed in the business solely to avoid paying taxes on the dividends, this tax will be levied. This situation occurs primarily in family-owned businesses where only a few owners are the major shareholders.

exchange rates. A major difference between domestic and international business is that economic transactions are conducted in more than one currency. For example, when an American firm sells goods to a German firm, the American firm desires payment in dollars while the German firm desires to make payment in Deutschmarks. It is possible for a buyer to pay in one currency while a seller receives payment in another currency because of the existence of exchange rates and the foreign exchange market. These may be defined as:

1. *Exchange Rate.* The price of one currency in terms of another. For example, it may be possible to exchange 6 pesos for one dollar. The exchange rate would be 6/1.
2. *Foreign Exchange Market.* This is the institutional structure that facilitates the exchange of currencies. It consists primarily of banks and foreign exchange dealers who are linked internationally by a telephone and teletype network.

CROSS-REFERENCES:
capital budgeting international, how to calculate capital cost, p. 163
equilibrium exchange rates, how to calculate, p. 169
foreign exchange market, p. 414

exchange rates, flexibility in. From World War II to 1976, the International Monetary Fund has governed a system of fixed exchange rates. The benefit of such a system is stability when currencies maintain approximately the same value. In recent years, it has become apparent that inflation, governmental policies, and other factors have caused currency values to change markedly from year to year. Under a fixed exchange rate system, this produces frequent devaluations. To overcome the unsettling nature of constant devaluations, a number of reforms had been proposed, including:

1. *Widening the Bands.* The Smithsonian Agreement implemented this reform by broadening the range of fluctuation from 2 percent to 4 1/2 percent. In 1972, the European Economic Community (EEC) or Common Market countries modified this approach by agreeing to allow their own cur-

rencies to fluctuate against each other in a range of 2 1/4 percent but against outside currencies in a range of 4 1/2 percent. This is the so-called snake in the tunnel, with the 2 1/4 percent being the "snake" fluctuating in the 4 1/2 percent "tunnel." This seems to be a suitable compromise for a group of economically integrated countries seeking a narrow band for their own currencies but a broader band against other currencies. The advantage to widening the bands is that currencies can have greater fluctuations before a devaluation is necessary. This may allow more time to correct disequilibrium and may result in fewer devaluations.

2. *Crawling Peg.* This approach would replace the occasional large devaluation with a series of mini-devaluations (or revaluations). When a currency moved, say, one percent from its par or peg rate, a new par would be established. Each change in exchange rate would be relatively small and the risk of large losses through large devaluations would be eliminated.

Floating exchange rates is the approach that was basically adopted in 1976 after several years of allowing selected currencies to float. This reform allows currencies to float in response to long-term fundamental factors. In the short-term, central banks can intervene in the market to minimize wide fluctuations caused by temporary pressures.

CROSS-REFERENCE
exchange rates, p. 395
Smithsonian Agreement, p. 522

exchange ratio. In mergers or acquisitions, the ratio by which two firms exchange common stock. The exchange ratio is the factor that determines how much common stock is issued or sold in making an acquisition.

exchanges, regional and local. Less than 10 percent of the securities traded on organized exchanges are traded at a variety of regional and local exchanges. The exchanges are located in cities in different parts of the country and include the Midwest Stock Exchange in Chicago and the Pacific Coast Stock Exchange in California. The importance of these exchanges has diminished owing to two factors:

1. *Nationwide Communications.* The availability of rapid communications between the New York and American Exchanges and the rest of the country has resulted in ease of trading on the major exchanges.
2. *Organization of Over-the-Counter Market.* The NASD's successful efforts to organize the over-the-counter market have diminished the need for local exchanges to trade strictly local securities.

expected return. In portfolio theory, the likely return from investing in a portfolio of securities or capital assets. The expected return is the sum of the individual returns from each security or asset weighted by the percent of each security in the total portfolio. The formula is:

$$E(Rtn) = \sum_{j=1}^{n} [Rtn_{(j)}][\%_{(j)}]$$

where

$\sum_{j=1}^{n}$ = sum of the values for a portfolio with "n" securities beginning with security "j" (which is the first security) and ending with security "n".

$Rtn_{(j)}$ = expected return or likely return on security "j".

$\%_{(j)}$ = dollars invested in security "j" as a percent of the dollars invested in the total portfolio.

expected value. Using a weighted-average approach to the calculation of risk and return in a project, the expected value is a mathematical value that expresses the likelihood of different risks and their effect on the return from a proposal. It is synonymous with a weighted average. Normally, a project with the highest expected value is most attractive to a firm.

exposed foreign exchange position. In international finance, a situation that exists when a bank or corporation has greater obligations in one currency with respect to borrowing or holding than it has balancing obligations. For example, suppose a business holds $4,500,000 and owes $2,500,000. The firm has a holding exposure of the difference between the two figures, or $2,000,000. If the dollar were devalued, the firm would lose more value in its cash than in its debt obligations and the exposure would produce a loss in terms of purchasing power in other currencies.

CROSS-REFERENCE:

hedging foreign exchange transactions, how to evaluate alternatives, p. 173

exposure. In international finance, a situation that exists whenever a firm, bank, or individual can suffer a loss as a result of holding or owing foreign exchange. International cash and debt management has a number of techniques designed to minimize exposure.

CROSS-REFERENCE:

hedging foreign exchange transactions, how to evaluate alternatives, p. 173

extension. In voluntary settlements or bankruptcy situations, an arrangement whereby creditors receive payment in full on debts owed to them but with the payments occurring on a delayed basis. Extensions are commonly granted to increase the likelihood of payment by allowing the firm to overcome its immediate difficulties and resume successful opérations. When an extension occurs in a voluntary settlement, frequently all creditors agree to accept a slowing of payments. When an exten-

sion occurs in a formal bankruptcy situation, the court may request all creditors to agree to the extension.

CROSS-REFERENCES:

act of bankruptcy, p. 308
bankruptcy, p. 320
Chandler Act, p. 347
Chapter X reorganization, p. 348
Chapter XI reorganization, p. 348
composition, p. 355
voluntary settlement, p. 545

external analysis. The process of determining the significant operating and financial characteristics of a firm from accounting data when performed by outsiders to the firm. External analysis is generally performed by creditors, stockholders, or investment analysts. It makes use of existing financial statements and involves limited access to confidential information on a firm.

CROSS-REFERENCES:

liquidity, how to analyze with ratios, p. 49
profitability, how to analyze with ratios, p. 56
ownership factors, how to analyze with ratios, p. 51

F

factor. A specialized type of finance company that provides a source of short-term funds for a firm by purchasing its accounts receivable for immediate cash and then collecting the receivables at a later time. Factoring companies tend to specialize in a single industry and provide services in the area of credit, bookkeeping, and financial consulting.

CROSS-REFERENCE:
accounts receivable, p. 306

factoring. The action a financial institution takes when it purchases accounts receivable from a business firm in order to provide the firm with immediate cash. The financial institution, called a factor, usually accepts the credit risks associated with the receivables it purchases. A written agreement is normally used to spell out the exact conditions, costs, and procedures for the factoring arrangement. The factor discounts the face value of the receivables in order to cover administrative costs and provide for the risk of bad debts.

CROSS-REFERENCE:
pledging of accounts receivable, p. 481

fair trade act. A state law dealing with resale price maintenance which allows a manufacturer of branded merchandise to sign a contract with a distributor whereby the distributor must sell the product at a fixed price and which forbids the sale of the merchandise at lower prices.

favorable financial leverage. A situation that exists when a firm is financing a portion of its assets with limited-return securities and the firm's before-tax return on investment is greater than the percentage of interest or dividend being paid on such securities. For example, a firm earning 8 percent on assets financed with 5 percent bonds has favorable financial leverage. Also called trading on the equity.

CROSS-REFERENCES:
financial leverage, how to analyze, p. 34
trading on the equity, p. 538
unfavorable financial leverage, p. 541

federal reserve banks. Twelve banks established as a part of the Federal Reserve System that act as depositories for the reserves of the member banks in their respective districts, act as creditors for their member banks, act as dealers in government securities, and as a fiscal agent for the Treasury, and aid in the management of the nation's money supply.

CROSS-REFERENCE:
regulation q, p. 508

FIFO. The first-in, first-out method of inventory valuation and reporting of cost of goods sold that assumes that the oldest inventory is used up first. In a period of rising price levels, this technique tends to show current values of inventory on the firm's balance sheet but undervalues the cost of goods sold on the income statement.

CROSS-REFERENCE:
inventories, p. 441

finance. A specialized, functional field found under the general classification of business administration. The term finance can be defined as the management of the flows of money through an organization, whether it be a corporation, school, bank, or government agency. Finance concerns itself with the actual flows of money, as well as any claims against money.

Finance, or financial management, is an applied field of business administration. Principles developed by financial managers or borrowed from accounting, economics, or other fields are applied to the problems of managing money. Finance has its own theories and principles, but is fundamentally concerned with applications.

CROSS-REFERENCE:
fields of finance, how to distinguish, p. 196

finance differentiated from accounting.

Accounting is concerned with the recording, reporting, and measuring of business transactions. Using a widely accepted double-entry bookkeeping system, accounting provides data on an organization's activities. The data may be historical, as in the case of last year's balance sheet, or they may be a forecast of future operations, as in the case of next year's operating budget. Finance makes use of the information provided by the accounting system to make decisions to help organizations achieve their objectives. Stated briefly, accounting is a data-collection process dealing with accurate recording and reporting; finance is a managerial or decision-making process.

Although accountants and financial managers perform different tasks, careers in the two areas frequently overlap. It is not unusual, for example, for a young man or woman to study accounting and then take a position as an accountant. This may be in a corporate setting or with a firm of certified public accountants. As the accountant masters his discipline, he will become aware of the financial problems facing his firm or clients. Increasingly, he will advise with respect to courses of action being contemplated by the firm. After a number of years, he may discover that he has become a financial analyst or manager and is no longer doing any accounting on a day-to-day basis.

finance differentiated from economics.

Economics is concerned with analyzing the distribution of resources in a society. It studies transactions among people involving goods and services with or without the exchange of money. It is interested in supply and demand, costs and profits, and production and consumption. The broad and highly developed field of economics is closely related to other social sciences, such as sociology, political science, and psychology. Economics may be conveniently divided into two major categories:

1. *Microeconomics,* which is basically a body of theory that studies the way businesses make decisions about pricing and production in different kinds of markets and under differing assumptions. Also called price theory or theory of the firm, microeconomics tries to explain how rational persons make business decisions.

2. *Macroeconomics,* which is the study of the overall economic situation of a nation or group of nations; it attempts to relate such factors as production and consumption into a meaningful view of national economies. It uses definitions such as gross national product (GNP) to measure the level of economic activity and has developed fairly sophisticated means for forecasting the future.

The field of finance rests heavily on the work of economists and makes use of many economic tools. It begins with the theories and assumptions developed in microeconomics and attempts to apply them to explain the workings of a modern business firm. It borrows forecasting and other models from macroeconomics and tests them against current situations to predict the results from varying courses of action being considered by the firm. Finance is less concerned with theory than is economics. Finance forecasts for the individual firm; economics forecasts for the industry and the overall level of economic activity.

finance paper. Short-term, unsecured promissory notes of large finance companies issued for periods of 30 days to one year in order to raise short-term funds. Finance paper has been growing in importance in recent years as a marketable security because it offers a high degree of safety and yields in excess of the yields on Treasury securities.

CROSS-REFERENCES:
security, financial, p. 519
commercial paper, p. 351

financial analysis. The process of determining the significant operating and financial characteristics of a firm from accounting data. It makes extensive use of the financial statements as well as a variety of the financial ratios.

It is important to distinguish between techniques of internal and external analysis:
1. *External Analysis.* This is performed by outsiders to the firm, such as creditors, stockholders, or investment analysts. It makes use of existing financial statements and involves limited access to confidential information on a firm.
2. *Internal Analysis.* This is performed by the corporate finance and accounting departments and is more detailed than external analysis. These departments have available more detailed and current information than is

available to outsiders. They are able to prepare *pro forma,* or future, statements and are able to produce a more accurate and timely analysis of the firm's strengths and weaknesses.

Separating Causes and Symptons of Problems
Financial analysis is used primarily to gain insights into operating and financial problems confronting the firm. With respect to these problems, we must be careful to distinguish between the cause of the problem and a symptom of it. A *cause* is a situation that produces a result or effect; in our case the result is a problem. A *symptom* is a visible indicator that a problem exists. The firm may observe symptoms, such as a low level of profits, but it must deal with causes of problems, such as high costs. If it does not deal with the problem cause, the firm will probably not be able to correct the problem.

Financial ratios are used to locate symptoms of problems. Once the symptoms have been located, the financial analyst must determine the cause of any problem. Then, he must find a solution for it. Examples of symptoms, causes, and solutions of problems are given in the table on page 404.

CROSS-REFERENCES:
ratios, p. 501
ratios, kinds of, p. 501

financial assets. The common stock, preferred stock, and bonds issued by corporations or governments. These assets are easily identified with specific returns, are easily purchased and sold in capital markets, and are available from a wide variety of sources with different risk and return characteristics.

CROSS-REFERENCES;
capital assets, p. 328
intangible assets, p. 436

Symptoms, Causes, and Solutions for Problems Revealed by Financial Ratios.

Symptom	Problem	Solution
Abnormal liquidity ratio	Inadequate cash	Raise additional funds.
	Excessive receivables	Restrict terms of trade; institute a more aggressive collection policy.
	Excessive inventory	Improve inventory management.
	Excessive current liabilities	Obtain additional long-term financing.
Abnormal profitability ratio	High production costs	Institute cost cutting measures.
	Idle assets	Sell excess or obsolete assets.
	Inadequate sales	Increase size and quality of sales force; improve advertising.
	Inadequate selling price.	Raise it.
	High administrative expenses	Reduce them.
	Excessive interest payments	Seek lower-cost debt financing; seek equity financing.

financial leases. Financial leases have assumed a major role in the financing of buildings and equipment for American industry. Some characteristics of financial leases are the following:

1. *Fixed Obligation.* A financial lease imposes a fixed obligation on the firm. The obligation is not cancelable and is similar to the requirement to pay interest on outstanding debt.
2. *Long Time Period.* Financial leases are written to cover a period of at least 1 year and frequently 5, 10, 15, or 20 years. During this period of time, the firm must fulfill the requirements of the lease, even though the asset may become obsolete and no longer useful for business operations.
3. *Fully Amortizing Lease.* The agreement is written so that the lease will cover the service life of the asset. If a firm leases a piece of equipment with an expected life of 12 years, the lease period will be approximately 12 years. If an asset has an indefinite life, as in the case of an office building, the lease will be written as though the service life were, say, 20 years. In this case, the building would be fully amortized, even though it may have a residual value at the end of the lease period.
4. *Profit During the Lease Period.* The lease payments will total more than the original cost of the asset, which allows the lessor to make a profit on the lease arrangement during the lease period. If the asset has any residual value, this will be an additional profit to the lessor.

Enforcement of Financial Leases Leasing offers the firm an alternative to long-term debt financing. The firm borrows an asset, rather than cash, and incurs a fixed obligation to make payments over an extended period of time. This obligation must be met, just as the firm must meet its interest and principal payments on debt. In the event a firm defaults on its lease, the firm may not return the assets to the lessor and end the obligation. The lessor may bring the lessee to court and request the court to force continued payments on the unpaid portion of the lease. Courts do not usually enforce the lease, but damages may be awarded to the lessor for breach of the lease contract. The very act of bringing the suit to court will frequently have detrimental effects on the lessee's credit rating and ability to borrow or lease in the future.

CROSS-REFERENCES:

leasing, p. 449
leasing, higher cost of, p. 450

financial leverage. The most widely accepted definition refers to a situation in which a firm has issued limited-return securities and has a before-tax return on investment which, as a percent, differs from the interest rate or dividend being paid on the limited-return securities. If the return on investment exceeds the interest rate, the firm is making money as a result of its limited-return securities and is said to have favorable financial leverage. This is sometimes called trading on the equity. If the return on investment is less than the interest rate, the firm is said to have unfavorable financial leverage.

A second definition refers to the degree to which changes in operating income or earnings before interest and taxes (EBIT) will affect earnings before taxes (EBT). Financial leverage is expressed as a ratio of EBIT to EBT. This is also called fixed-charges leverage.

CROSS-REFERENCES:

financial leverage, how to analyze, p. 34
Durand on cost of capital, p. 203
Miller and Modigliani on cost of capital, p. 213

Schwartz on capital structure theory, p. 230
capital structure management, goals of, p. 337

financial norms, determining. One of the most difficult aspects of financial analysis involves the determination of the appropriate norms against which an individual firm may be judged. At least five guidelines may be used:

1. *Industry Norms.* A firm may be compared against the financial ratios of other firms in the same industry. This will be only partially satisfactory in most cases because industry norms vary widely from the strongest to the weakest firm in the grouping. Frequently, an average for the industry will offer little utility because the spread is so wide. The analyst can use industry norms to see how the firm compares to other individual firms. For example, if the firm is second highest in profit in a 10-firm industry, it is relatively profitable.

2. *Similar Firms.* If we compare the firm with similar firms in other industries, we often gain a better insight into the financial condition. For example, if we are examining a growth firm in a nongrowth industry, it makes sense to compare it with other growth firms in other industries.

3. *Historical Trends.* We can compare a firm with itself—or rather with its own performance over a period of time. It is a good sign if the firm is maintaining or increasing its profits, and a bad sign if its liquidity is dropping.

4. *Future Expectations.* Economists and analysts make efforts to forecast conditions in the future. These expectations can be used as norms to compare firms today. For example, in 3 years an analyst may expect a surge of investor confidence and hence an

increase in the normal price-earnings ratios. How will this affect the individual firm being evaluated?

5. *Common Sense.* This is the catch-all guideline that is so frequently ignored. If all else fails, the analyst can use subjective judgment and reason. For example, a 2 percent return on investment can never be a norm because it is too low for rational investors. At the same time, a 60 percent ROI is too high. Common sense tells us that 20 percent is more reasonable as a norm.

CROSS-REFERENCES:

normal dividend payout, p. 469
normal price-earnings multiple,
p. 470

financial risk. The likelihood that a firm will not be sufficiently profitable either to cover interest payments on its debt or to pay dividends to shareholders. If the firm falls short of its profit goals, it may be able to cover operating expenses but not the financing costs of its original investment.

CROSS-REFERENCE:

lease-buy decision, how to make it,
p. 132

financial statement. An organized collection of data formated according to logical and consistent accounting procedures. Its purpose is to convey an understanding of some financial aspects of a business firm. It may show a position at a moment in time, as in the case of a balance sheet, or may reveal a series of activities over a given period of time, as in the case of an income statement. Financial statements are the major means employed by firms to present their financial situation to stockholders, creditors, and the general public. The majority of firms include extensive financial statements in their annual reports, which receive wide distribution.

CROSS-REFERENCES:

balance sheet, p. 317
flow-of-funds statement, p. 410
income statement, p. 429

financial statements, uses of. Financial statements are major tools in understanding what happens to the firm's money as the firm pursues its business activities. When used together, the balance sheet, income statement, and flow-of-funds statement offer valuable insights into the firm's efforts to achieve liquidity and profitability.

Financial statements have two major uses in financial analysis. First, they are used to present a historical record of the firm's financial development. When compiled over a number of years, a trained analyst can determine important financial factors that have influenced the growth and current status of the firm. Second, they are used to forecast a future course of action for the firm. A *pro forma* financial statement is prepared for a future period of time. It is the financial manager's estimate of the firm's future performance.

first-in, first-out (FIFO). A method of inventory valuation and the reporting of cost of goods sold that assumes that the oldest inventory is used up first. In a period of rising price levels, this technique tends to show current values of inventory on the firm's balance sheet but undervalues the cost of goods sold on the income statement.

CROSS-REFERENCES:

inventories, p. 441
inflation, effect on balance sheet,
p. 432

fiscal policy, effect on balance of payments. A means of reducing balance of payments deficits through the tax and spending programs of the government.

Some of the governmental fiscal actions are:

1. *Tax Breaks for Exporters.* The government can use tax breaks or even direct subsidies to encourage private enterprise to export their production. This will result in higher profits from foreign sales than domestic sales and will bring in foreign exchange to reduce a deficit.

2. *Higher Tariffs on Imports.* To discourage foreign goods and to make them less competitive than domestic goods, the government can raise tariffs. Closely related, the government can place controls on the volume of goods that can be imported.

3. *Programs to Attract Investment Capital.* The government can take many steps to encourage foreigners to transfer long-term capital to the country. By building highways or rail facilities in isolated areas of the country, investors may be attracted to develop raw materials. Tax incentives can be offered to make it more profitable to invest in one country than in others. Other programs can also be used.

4. *Encourage Economic Diversification.* Many times the bulk of a nation's foreign exchange will be earned by one or two products or a few industries. Examples include the Central American countries with their heavy reliance on bananas, coffee, and cacao, the Middle East nations who are petroleum exporters, and Chile with its heavy exporting of copper and iron ore. By using government spending for diversification of the economic base, the nation earns additional foreign exchange while reducing its reliance on market conditions for a single product as the primary determinant of its balance of payments situation.

5. *Reduce Government Spending Abroad.* In many cases, government programs require the spending of large sums of money on foreign products or in support of the nation's international goals. It may be possible to reduce the size of these programs with significant savings of foreign exchange.

CROSS-REFERENCES:
deficit in the 1960's, United States, p. 376
monetary policy, effect on balance of payments, p. 463

fiscal year. A period of twelve consecutive months designated by an organization for the reporting of its financial activity or budgeting. When the designated period is January through December, the fiscal year and the calendar year coincide. As a general rule, a firm will use the calendar year as its fiscal year in the absence of other considerations. In determining its fiscal year, a firm considers its level of business activity and attempts to close its books during a lull that is not likely to disrupt its activities.

fixed asset. A subsection of the balance sheet that contains the assets used by the firm to generate revenues. These assets will not be converted into cash in the current accounting period unless they are damaged, become obsolete, or are otherwise replaced. Two representative accounts are plant and equipment, and land:

1. *Plant and Equipment.* This account includes the physical assets owned by the firm. Buildings, machinery, and other equipment are recorded at cost and are adjusted by the depreciation recorded each year.

2. *Land.* This account would list the property owned by the firm. Since land does not wear out with use (as does machinery), this account is not accompanied by an accumulated depreciation account.

a.	b.
Machinery $150,000 Less accumulated depreciation ($30,000)	Machinery (at cost less accumulated depreciation) $120,000

Two Methods of Showing Plant and Equipment of a Balance Sheet.

Plant and equipment may be shown on a balance sheet using either of two conventional formats. One method shows both the total cost of the plant and equipment and the total of the accumulated depreciation charged against the account. For a machine costing $150,000 with 3-year depreciation of $10,000 per year, the balance sheet would show the entry on the left-hand side of the Figure. The second method shows only the net value of the machinery on the right-hand side of the Figure. In both cases, the net or book value of the machinery is $120,000.

The first method by separating cost and total depreciation provides more information to the analyst. The net book value alone may conceal outdated plant and equipment. As an example, consider two firms with a book value for machinery of $750,000. Firms A and B show the machinery on their respective balance sheets as follows:

Machinery (cost - accumulated depreciation)*

$750,000

If a person did not notice the asterisk (which probably indicates that the amount of accumulated depreciation is listed in a footnote), it would appear that the firms have the same kind of fixed assets. But suppose the firms showed the machinery as follows:

From this information, we see that Firm A has a great deal more machinery, but it is probably quite old since it has been depreciated to 25 percent of its original cost. Firm B has less machinery, but it is apparently much newer since it has been depreciated to only 75 percent of its original cost. Knowing the relative age and amount of machinery might be very useful to a financial analyst studying a balance sheet.

CROSS-REFERENCES:
inflation in the capital budget, how to analyze, p. 11
flow-of-funds statement, how to develop from balance sheet and income statement, p. 38
protecting local assets in high-inflation country, how to, p. 177
depreciation, how to calculate, p. 188

fixed-asset financing. In a lease-buy situation, the company is faced with the financing of fixed assets. The purchase alternatives will involve secured financing methods. Each of these will share the following characteristics found in fixed-asset financing.
1. *Down Payment Is Required.* The banks, finance companies, or other institutions require the borrower to pay some portion of the purchase price in advance. This is commonly called a down payment.

	Firm A	Firm B
Machinery (at cost)	$3,000,000	$1,000,000
Less accumulated depreciation	($2,250,000)	($250,000)

2. *Assets Are Collateral.* The specific assets financed by the loan are pledged to secure the debt. In the event of liquidation, the creditor may take the assets and sell them to compensate for a failure to pay the loan. The creditor will have first claim on the proceeds from the sale of the assets compared to the claims of bondholders or other creditors.

3. *Installment Payments Are Made.* The schedule for the repayment of the loan is established so that interest and a portion of the principal are paid in a series of payments.

4. *Assets and Debt Recognized on Firm's Books.* Unlike leasing alternatives, the total cost of the assets is included in the fixed assets reported on the firm's balance sheet. The debt created by the financing is shown in the liabilities section as part of the firm's capital structure.

5. *Assets Possessed by Owner.* During the financing period, the borrower has possession, though not necessarily title, to the assets. Once the final payment is made, the borrower gains the title if it was not transferred at some earlier time.

CROSS-REFERENCE:
asset, p. 313

fixed-charges leverage. In profit planning, a leverage factor that compares operating income (EBIT) to earnings before taxes (EBT). The difference between EBIT and EBT is the interest on the firm's debt and this fixed financial charge produces the leverage. Fixed-charges leverage reflects the firm's ability to use financial charges to magnify the effect of changes in EBIT to changes in EBT and earnings per share.

CROSS-REFERENCES:
leverage, how to use in profit planning, p. 44

financial leverage, how to analyze, p. 34
EBIT, p. 392
EBT, p. 392

fixed costs. Constant charges or expenses that do not vary with the level of production or sales. Most general and administrative expenses are fixed costs. The concept of fixed costs is an integral part of break-even analysis.

CROSS-REFERENCES:
break-even analysis, how to use, p. 32
leverage, how to use in profit planning, p. 44
profit-volume analysis, how to use, p. 64
varying sales levels or costs, how to analyze effect of, p. 74
break-even analysis, p. 325
income statement, marginal analysis format, p. 430

fixed rate financing. A situation that exists when an individual or firm borrows money at an interest rate that does not change over the life of the loan. It differs from variable rate financing where the interest charges will fluctuate according to activities in the money markets.

CROSS-REFERENCE:
variable rate financing, p. 544

float. As a noun, this is the amount of money tied up in checks which have been written but have not yet been collected. Float exists because of the time required for a check to be mailed, processed in the firm's accounting department, and processed through the banking system's check-clearing procedures. As a verb, float refers to the selling of a new security issue, as to float a bond offering.

CROSS-REFERENCES:

bond, p. 323
kiting, p. 448

flotation costs. The expenses involved with preparing, underwriting, and selling new security issues. Flotation costs will be amortized over the life of a bond offering.

CROSS-REFERENCES:
refunding a bond issue, how to make the decision, p. 152

flow of funds, schematic. Perhaps the most valuable use of financial statements is to gain an understanding of how funds flow through the organization. The schematic is a representation of the internal and external flow of funds. In analyzing this figure, note that the flows are continuous. In a complex business organization, funds are in constant use and movement throughout the firm.

CROSS-REFERENCE:

flow-of-funds statement, how to develop from balance sheet and income statement, p. 38

flow-of-funds statement. The flow-of-funds or Sources-and-Uses-of-Funds statement shows the movement of funds into the firm's current-asset accounts from external sources such as stockholders, creditors, and customers. It also shows the movement of funds to meet the firm's obligations, retire stock, or pay dividends. The movements are shown for a specific period of time, normally the same time period as the firm's income statement.

Sample Flow-of-Funds Statement The flow-of-funds statement for the King Trucking Company shows the sources and application of funds for 1973 and 1974. The difference between sources and uses is shown as an increase or decrease in net working capital. If the firm has

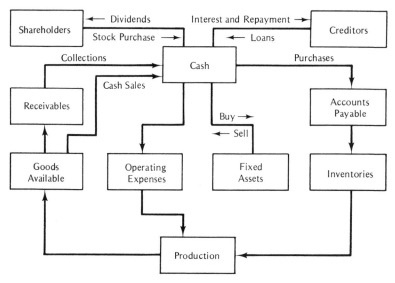

Flow of Funds Through a Firm.

KING TRUCKING COMPANY Flow-of-Funds Statement (year ending December 31, 1974)

	1974	1973
Sources of funds		
Net income from operations	$148,262	$127,065
Noncash expenses, including depreciation	107,296	92,297
Total funds from operations	255,558	219,362
Proceeds from long-term borrowing	92,621	41,832
Sale of property	6,101	1,499
Sale of common stock	2,112	1,804
Total Sources of Funds	$356,392	$264,497
Application of funds		
Expenditures for property and equipment	$234,511	$174,408
Miscellaneous investments	4,728	3,215
Payment of cash dividends	50,924	48,107
Funds held by trustee for plant construction	975	45,378
Total Application of Funds	$291,138	$271,108
Increase (Decrease) in Net Working Capital	$ 65,254	$ (6,611)

more funds coming in than going out, net working capital increases, because current assets increase more quickly or decrease less quickly than current liabilities. When uses are greater than sources, the reverse is true.

Most corporations print a flow-of-funds statement as part of their annual reports. In the event this is not the case, the analyst can develop one from the balance sheet, income statement, and accompanying notes to the annual report. Because of the variety of styles of financial statements and the differing accounting procedures used by corporations, the development of a flow-of-funds statement requires a thorough grasp of the relationship among accounts.

CROSS-REFERENCES:

sources and uses of funds, p. 523
flow-of-funds statement, how to develop from balance sheet and income statement, p. 38

flow-of-funds statements, three formats. The flow of cash and funds through an organization is commonly measured using three basic formats:

1. *Measuring Changes in Net Working Capital.* This format has three major categories: sources, uses, and changes in net working capital.

2. *Balancing Sources and Uses.* A second format contains only two categories: sources and uses. The sources must equal the uses. In this format, the changes in the current accounts are considered to be either sources or uses. The rules are the following:

   a. *Sources* are decreases in current assets and increases in current liabilities. When the firm reduces a current-asset account, it is viewed as a source of funds. An increase in a current-liability account is treated in the same manner as a long-term liability increase.

b. *Uses* are increases in current assets and decreases in current liabilities. This format is less useful to the financial manager than one that measures changes in net working capital. For accounting purposes, sources may be viewed as balancing uses. For financial purposes, this is not true. When a firm increases its cash account, for example, it is not using funds. Rather, it is holding funds to make them available when needed. Changes in net working capital reflect liquidity, an important use of fund statements. The balancing of sources and uses makes it more difficult to measure changes in liquidity.

3. *Measuring Changes in Cash.* This format has three categories: sources, uses, and changes in the cash balance. This format considers the current accounts to be part of the sources and uses profile, but cash is excluded. It treats changes in current accounts in the same manner as the format balancing sources and uses. This statement, usually called a cash-flow statement, is useful for focusing on the most liquid of current assets—the cash account. It is more restricted in scope than the statement that measures changes in net working capital.

Of the three common formats, the most useful for financial purposes is the format illustrated in column **a** of the Table. With some exceptions, the best measure of liquidity is given by measuring changes in net working capital. The cash-flow format in column **c** of the Table is also useful. Column **b** of the Table is an accounting format and requires the analyst to prepare calculations to measure changes in the firm's liquidity.

CROSS-REFERENCES:

net working capital, p. 467
sources and uses of funds, p. 523

Examples of Three Formats for Flow Statements.

(a) Net Working Capital Format (does not itemize current accounts)		(b) Sources Equal Uses Format (itemizes current accounts)		(c) Cash-Flow Format (separates changes in cash)	
Sources		**Sources**		**Sources**	
NIAT	$ 50,000	NIAT	$ 50,000	NIAT	$ 50,000
Depreciation	30,000	Depreciation	30,000	Depreciation	30,000
Funds fr. opera.	80,000	Funds fr. opera.	80,000	Funds fr. opera.	80,000
Sale of bonds	60,000	Sale of bonds	60,000	Sale of bonds	60,000
Sale of machinery	40,000	Sale of machinery	40,000	Sale of machinery	40,000
		Inc. wages pay.	10,000	Inc. wages pay.	10,000
		Dec. accts. rec.	15,000	Dec. accts rec.	15,000
Total Sources	$180,000	Total Sources	$205,000	Total Sources	$205,000
Uses		**Uses**		**Uses**	
Dividends	$ 30,000	Dividends	$ 30,000	Dividends	$ 30,000
Retire bonds	65,000	Retire bonds	65,000	Retire bonds	65,000
		Dec. accts. pay.	50,000	Dec. accts. pay.	50,000
		Inc. cash	60,000		
Total Uses	$ 95,000	Total Uses	$205,000	Total Uses	$145,000
Inc. Net Work Cap.	$ 85,000			Incr. Cash	$ 60,000

Year	Market Value	Gain (Loss) in Market Value	+ Cash Dividends	= Total Return	Return Divided by Beginning Market Value	Actual Market Rate of Return = MKT (Rtn)
0	550	—	—			
1	600	50	40	90	90/550	.164
2	740	140	50	190	190/600	.317
3	710	(30)	40	10	10/740	.014
4	820	110	60	170	170/710	.239
5	900	80	65	145	145/820	.177
					TOTAL	.911/5 yrs.
					Average MKT (Rtn) =	18.2 percent

(1) Hundreds of millions of dollars

forecasting expected rate of return. In developing the expected rate of return E(Rtn) or market rate of return, E(Rtn)mkt, two approaches are commonly used:

1. *Use Past Market Returns.* This method assumes that investors will require future returns which are similar to past returns. Therefore, to solve the expected rate of return, we simply calculate prior market returns and use them as an estimate of E(Rtn). As an example, suppose we had five years of data as above:

Over the 5-year period, the market had differing returns each year with an average annual market rate of return of 15.8 percent. This could be used as an estimate of expected rate of return.

2. *Forecast Next Period's E(Rtn).* The second, and conceptually more sound, method of determining the expected rate of return is to prepare a forecast of likely future returns. Historical data is only valid to the extent that current and future conditions reflect past conditions. If, for example, a nation is experiencing an economic recovery following a period of stagnation or recession, past returns will not provide valid estimates of future expected returns. A better approach to estimating E(Rtn) would be to forecast interest rate levels, money supply, corporate profits, government spending, and similar variables that affect the expected rate of return. By incorporating these variables in a simulation model along with current security price levels, price-earnings multiples, and dividend policies, an analyst can forecast the expected rate of return for an investment in a portfolio of financial or capital assets.

CROSS-REFERENCE:
capital asset pricing model, p. 279

forcing the conversion. If the price of the common stock rises above the conversion price, the firm will be able to force the security holders to convert into common stock. For example, suppose that the price of common stock has risen to $50 for a company whose $1,000 bonds can be converted into 25 shares of common stock. Also assume that the bond is callable at $1,050. If the bond is called, the bondholder must either surrender the bond for $1,050 or convert it into 25 shares of common stock worth $50, a total value of $1,250. Naturally, most bondholders would convert the bond even if they planned to immediately sell the common stock and buy another bond of a different firm. The action of calling a convertible security when the conversion value significantly exceeds the call value is called forcing the conversion.

CROSS-REFERENCES:
conversion feature, p. 358
conversion premium, p. 358
conversion price and ratio, p. 358
conversion value, p. 359

foreign corporation. A corporation chartered outside the state in which it operates, from the point of view of the operating state.

CROSS-REFERENCE:
domestic corporation, p. 391

foreign exchange. This term is used commonly with two distinct meanings, as follows:
1. *Currency of Foreign Nation.* When businessmen refer to the currencies of other nations, they commonly refer to their need for foreign exchange.
2. *Converting of Currencies.* Exchanging one national currency for a different national currency at some given or agreed upon exchange rate is a foreign exchange transaction.

Sources of Foreign Exchange The need for foreign exchange arises from the needs of a number of customers, from transactions such as:
1. *Exports and Imports.* While domestic business is carried out in a single currency, foreign trade involves two or more currencies. The importer frequently wishes to pay in his own national currency; the exporter desires payment in his national currency. The foreign exchange market facilitates the exchange.
2. *Sale of Securities.* When common stock or bonds are purchased by foreign investors, foreign exchange is needed to complete the transaction.

3. *Business Remittances.* The subsidiaries of multinational firms remit funds in various forms to the parent company or, at the parent's direction, to other subsidiaries. Foreign exchange is needed for these transactions.
4. *Tourist Expenditures.* When persons travel abroad, they need foreign currencies to purchase foreign goods and services. These transactions are accomplished through the foreign exchange market.

CROSS-REFERENCES:
forward market, how to calculate bid and ask quotes, p. 171
black market, p. 322
blocked currency, p. 322
currency, p. 369
hedging, p. 425

foreign exchange market. A communications network linking a number of participants including the following:
1. *Commercial Banks.* Many of the leading commercial banks in the United States and abroad provide facilities and services related to foreign exchange. The banks serve individuals and firms seeking to convert currencies or transfer monies from one nation to another.
2. *Brokers and Dealers.* A foreign exchange broker brings together buyers and sellers of national currencies. For this service, he will receive a commission that varies according to the size of the exchange, the currencies involved, and the terms of the contract. A foreign exchange dealer purchases and sells currencies for his own account. The dealer makes his profit from the spread between what he pays for a currency and what he receives for it.
3. *Businesses and Individuals.* The largest group of participants in the foreign exchange market are the many businesses and individuals requiring the currencies of other nations.

Foreign Exchange Transactions Transactions occur through the use of a communications network linking commercial banks, brokers, and dealers. The network consists of:

1. *Telephones.* Most brokers and dealers work out of small quarters with crowded desks and numerous telephones. Their offices are connected by direct telephonic lines to other brokers and to the foreign exchange departments of commercial banks and other institutions. Information is exchanged and deals are actually consummated over the phone.

2. *Cables.* The most common method of conducting foreign exchange transactions is through the use of electronic cablegrams. An individual or business will contact a bank and request the delivery of foreign exchange. The bank will send a cable to a foreign bank ordering the transaction to occur. As an example, suppose a French importer wants to send dollars to a United States exporter in return for goods to be shipped. The importer will ask his Paris bank to cable the funds to a New York bank, as of a given date and under stipulated conditions, so the dollars can be credited to the exporter's account. Simultaneously, the French bank will withdraw francs from the French importer's account.

3. *Airmail Transfers.* Transactions can be conducted by mail in the same way that cable transactions occur. Airmail is cheaper but slower than cable transfers.

4. *Drafts.* A draft is a written order to a bank that can be used to complete a foreign exchange transaction. Suppose in the above example, the French importer had funds with the Paris office of First National City Bank. The importer could send a written order directly to the New York First National City Bank office authorizing dollars to be paid to the U.S. exporter. Upon making the payment, the bank would remove the equivalent amount of funds from the account of the French importer in the Paris branch.

Levels of Transactions Foreign exchange transactions occur at three different levels:

1. *Commercial Level.* Individuals and firms seeking to convert currencies conduct transactions with commercial banks. The foreign exchange section of a bank's international department buys and sells differing national currencies. This section maintains balances of the paper currency of other nations for the use of tourists and business travelers.

2. *Wholesale Level.* Larger transactions occur when banks exchange currencies with other banks or with dealers or brokers. Wholesale transactions frequently surpass the equivalent of a hundred million U.S. dollars.

3. *Central Bank Level.* When a national bank accumulates an excessive amount of the nation's currency and such currency cannot be exchanged with other banks or with dealers, the nation's central bank will intervene to remove the excess currency from the market. Prior to this intervention, exchange rates will fluctuate to reflect supply and demand factors for the different currencies. Central banks also deal with each other to correct imbalances in the foreign currencies available in each nation.

Forms of business organization compared.

Sole Proprietorship — Most common form of organization. Easy to establish.

Partnership — General. Limited.

Corporation — A legal entity. Exists separately from owners.

preferred by large organizations because
- Liability Is Limited.
- Existence Is Indefinite.
- Ownership Is Easily Transferred

more so with publicly traded than with closed corporations.

CROSS-REFERENCES:

sole proprietorship, p. 523
partnership, p. 477
corporation, p. 364

forward contract. In international finance, an agreement between two parties to exchange a stipulated amount of one currency for a stipulated amount of another currency at a specified exchange rate at a specified future date. No money is exchanged when the agreement is reached so no money is tied up during the life of the contract. At delivery, both parties provide the agreed-upon amounts of each currency.

CROSS-REFERENCES:

forward market, how to calculate bid and ask quotes, p. 171
hedging foreign exchange transactions, how to evaluate alternatives, p. 173

forward market. In international finance, the commercial banks, brokers, and dealers who facilitate foreign-exchange transactions where delivery occurs at a stipulated future date. Two parties agree to exchange a specified amount of one currency for a specified amount of another currency at a given exchange rate. No money is exchanged when the agreement is reached so no money is tied up during the life of the forward contract. At delivery in 30, 60, 90, or the days stipulated, both parties provide the agreed-upon amounts of each currency.

CROSS-REFERENCES:

forward market, how to calculate bid and ask quotes, p. 171
hedging foreign exchange transactions, how to evaluate alternatives, p. 173

franchise. A contractual arrangement that allows one party to use the name, trademark, or goodwill of another party in a business venture. A typical franchise might involve a retail fast-food operation where the franchisor has a nationally known and advertised operation and the franchisee operates the business as an independent business after paying a franchise fee.

fully amortizing. In leasing or loan agreements, a situation where the asset is completely written off during the period of the financing. If a leased asset is not fully amortized during the lease period, the residual value at the end of the lease must exceed the scrap or salvage value in order for the lessor to earn a profit.

CROSS-REFERENCE:

amortization, p. 310

fundamental factors. In intrinsic value analysis, the major elements of common stock value, namely:
1. Value of the firm's assets
2. Likely future earnings
3. Likely future dividends
4. Likely future growth rate

CROSS-REFERENCE:
intrinsic value analysis, p. 439

funds. This term is commonly used with a number of meanings, ranging from the broad to the very restricted. Some managers use the term funds to refer to all financial resources held by a firm. In this usage, all the firm's assets—both fixed and current—would be forms of funds. A more specific definition limits funds to current assets, those assets which are usually converted into cash within the next 12 months. With this definition, funds would include cash, marketable securities, accounts receivable, and inventories. Fixed assets, such as property, plant, and equipment, would be omitted. Still another definition identifies funds as the difference between current assets and current liabilities. A firm's current liabilities are those debts which must be paid during the next year. With this usage, only the excess of current assets over current liabilities is considered as funds. The most restricted usage of the term equates funds with the firm's cash.

CROSS-REFERENCE:
assets, p. 313

funds from operations. The firm may gain funds from a number of sources. Over a long period of time the most important source is funds from operations. Essentially, these funds come from the everyday business of the firm. To calculate the amount of funds from operations, we can use two different calculations:

1. *NIAT Plus Noncash Expenses.* Funds from operations may be calculated by adding back any noncash expenses (primarily depreciation) to the reported net income after taxes. This is a mechanical operation that correctly reflects the fact that depreciation and other noncash expenses shield a portion of the firm's sales. They appear on the income statement as expenses and thus reduce net income. In fact, no funds were needed for the noncash expenses. Funds are used when a piece of equipment is purchased, not when it is depreciated. The purchase would be treated as a use of funds; the depreciation is added back to net income to get the inflow of funds from operations.

2. *Sales Minus Cash Expenses.* The second method begins with sales and deducts all cash expenses or changes in funds. Only operating expenses, interest, and taxes are deducted in the calculation of funds from operations. Two methods of calculating the funds from operations are:

	Cash Basis	Accounting Basis
Sales	$100,000	$100,000
Less cash expenses	−60,000	−60,000
Less noncash expenses (depreciation)		− 8,000
Earnings before interest and taxes		32,000
Cash remaining	40,000	
Less interest payments	−10,000	−10,000
Less taxes	−11,000	−11,000
Net income after taxes		11,000
Cash remaining	19,000	
Add back noncash expenses		+8,000
Funds from Operations	$ 19,000	$ 19,000

CROSS-REFERENCES:
flow-of-funds statement, how to develop from balance sheet and income statement, p. 38
net income after taxes, p. 466

funds, managing. Funds may be viewed as the liquid assets of the firm. The term funds includes cash held by the firm, money borrowed by the firm, and money gained from purchasers of common and preferred stock.

In the management of funds, the financial manager acts as a specialized staff officer to the president of the company. He is responsible for having sufficient funds for the firm to conduct its business and to pay its bills. He must locate money to finance receivables and inventories, make arrangements for the purchase of assets, and identify sources of long-term financing. Cash must be available to pay dividends declared by the board of directors.

The management of funds has both liquidity and profitability aspects. If the firm's funds are not adequate, the firm may default on the payment of bills, interest on its debt, or on the repayment of the principal at the time a loan is due. If the firm does not carefully choose its financing methods, it may pay excessive interest costs with a subsequent decline in future profits.

Goals of the Firm An overview of how the goals of the firm are achieved through goals and functions of finance is presented at foot of page.

future earnings per share. In the planning process, a projection of future earnings to focus on future results of today's decisions.

CROSS-REFERENCES:
lease-buy decision, how to make it, p. 132
Solomon on future earnings per share, p. 240
mergers, how to analyze profitability in a ten-step process, p. 85

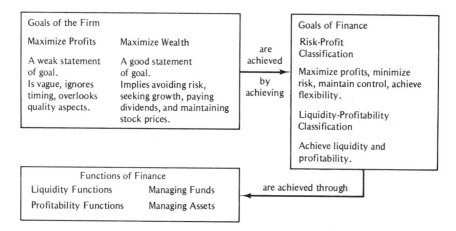

Relationship Between Goals of the Firm and Goals and Functions of Finance.

G

GNP implicit price deflator. An index number issued every month by the U.S. Department of Commerce that represents a reasonable approximation of the price changes that occurred in previous periods. It is widely accepted by the accounting profession as a measure of the impact of inflation in the general economy and has been approved by the Accounting Principles Board as the appropriate inflation measure to use in reporting price-level changes on financial statements. It has a broader base than the Consumer Price Index which is occasionally used as an inflation factor.

CROSS-REFERENCE:
profits, how to maintain under inflation, p. 59

going-concern value. The value of the securities of a profitable firm that has prospects for indefinite future business. The value of such a firm would be expressed in terms of the future profits, dividends, or growth-rate.

CROSS-REFERENCES:
value, differing concepts of, p. 543
Graham and Dodd approaches to common stock value, p. 246

gold standard—1870s to World War I. The first formal system for handling foreign exchange transactions started in the 1870s when the major nations declared a par value for their currencies in terms of gold. This began the period of the International Gold Standard which was characterized by the following:

1. *National Currencies were Defined in Terms of Gold.* To achieve this, gold was given a fixed value in terms of the nation's currency. For example, one ounce of gold might be worth 35 dollars. Or, it might be worth 210 pesos.

Since both currencies are defined in terms of gold, they can be converted at the rate of 210 pesos to 35 dollars, a 6 P/$1 exchange rate.

2. *Nations Agreed to Convert Their Currencies into Gold.* Each nation adhering to the gold standard not only defined its currency in terms of gold, it also agreed to exchange gold for the currency, if demanded. This allowed people to hold or spend the currency while having confidence in it. If any question arose as to the value of a nation's currency, it could be resolved by converting the currency into gold at the stipulated rate.

3. *Gold Prices Were Tied to Domestic Price and Interest Levels.* Stability of international transactions occurs when a nation's currency is fairly valued in terms of its purchasing power and ability to earn a return if invested. A properly valued currency eliminates any incentive to convert the currency into gold and to export the gold for profit. Under the gold standard, the nations worked together to achieve a world-wide price system for goods, an equilibrium in the supply and demand for currencies, and stable exchange rates.

CROSS-REFERENCES:
currency, p. 369
gold standard, revised, p. 419

gold standard, revised. The advent of World War I caused a breakdown of the international gold standard. The heavy financing requirements of the war and the disruptions of normal trading patterns brought monetary disorder to the major industrial nations. Massive amounts of paper money were printed and distributed to provide financing for the war and reconstruction of national economies after the war. After the war, nations agreed on a revised gold standard with the following characteristics:

1. *Gold No Longer Disciplined the Money Supply.* The money supply had grown far more rapidly than the mining of gold added new gold to the national reserves. Thus, for many nations, the size of the money supply was no longer tied to the nation's holding of gold. Most nations also reduced the number of gold coins in circulation replacing them with paper money.

2. *Foreign Exchange Supplemented Gold as Reserves.* Monetary reserves are the gold or other stores of value which a nation uses to support the value of its national currency. Over the centuries, gold has been used as a reserve to back up currency. Other precious metals were also used, notably silver. After World War I, international reserves of gold and silver were not sufficient to support the value of national currencies. For this reason, many nations began to accumulate foreign exchange as a supplement to gold in their monetary reserves. The British pound sterling, and later the U.S. dollar, were held by nations as stores of value to support their currencies.

At the beginning, the revised gold standard worked reasonably well. National economies recovered and world trade revived. The worldwide depression of the late 1920s destroyed the system, largely because of:

1. *Unilateral Devaluations.* A devaluation is a lessening of the value of a currency in terms of gold or other currencies. When a nation's currency is worth less in terms of other currencies, the nation's citizens cannot buy foreign products easily. Thus, they must spend their money at home. To increase economic activity, nations did not want to import foreign products when they could produce their own. This led many nations to devalue their currencies unilaterally. This destroyed any international attempts to find the supply and demand equilibrium for a currency.

2. *Tight Foreign Exchange Controls.* A foreign exchange control is a restriction placed by a nation on the converting of its currency into other currencies. Many nations placed tight controls on the exchange of their currencies for the currencies of other nations.

It may be argued that the destruction of the international monetary system during the 1930s increased the severity of and prolonged the worldwide depression. Whatever the merit of this argument, the revised gold standard was destroyed and a new system did not emerge until the end of the second world war.

CROSS–REFERENCES:
currency, p. 369
Gold Standard,—1870's to World War I, p. 418

gold tranche of IMF. The gold tranche is a term used to describe the 25 percent of the IMF quota paid in gold. A nation may exercise its drawing rights on a virtually automatic basis as long as the total drawings do not exceed the gold tranche. The gold tranche is decreased any time a nation purchases foreign currency. On the other hand, it is possible for the gold tranche to increase beyond the original 25 percent paid in gold. The gold tranche increases when other nations purchase a nation's currency.

PROBLEM: A nation joins the IMF and is assigned a 100,000,000 peso quota. The nation pays 25 percent in gold and 75 percent in pesos. The exchange rate is 6 P/$1. The nation purchases $3,000,000 from the Fund under its drawing rights. How large is the nation's gold tranche?

ANSWER: 7,000,000 pesos. It was 25,000,-000 pesos before the drawing of 18,000,000 *pesos ($3,000,000 × 6 P/$1 = 18,000,000 pesos). The new gold tranche is 25,000,000 − 18,000,000 = 7,000,000 pesos.*

PROBLEM: After the nation borrowed the $3,000,000 from the IMF, another nation purchased 27,000,000 pesos. What happens to the gold tranche?

ANSWER: It rises from 7,000,000 to 34,000,000 pesos since the gold tranche increases when other nations purchase a nation's currency.

Once a nation has exercised drawing rights reducing the gold tranche to zero, the IMF becomes increasingly watchful on future drawings. In order to continue drawing currencies, the nation must be taking steps to eliminate the deficits in its balance of payments. Once the nation has reached 200 percent of its quota, no further borrowings are allowed.

A final note might be useful on drawing rights. The exercise of such rights may be viewed as either a borrowing or a purchase of foreign currency. If the borrowing is within the gold tranche, the nation may be viewed as purchasing the currency with the gold on deposit at the IMF. Above the gold tranche, the nation assigns its own currency to the IMF but is, in effect, borrowing the currency of other nations. The terms "borrow" and "purchase" are frequently used synonomously when discussing drawing rights.

CROSS-REFERENCE:
International Monetary Fund, p. 438

goodwill. Under the purchase method of accounting for acquisitions, an intangible asset account on the balance sheet of the acquiring firm that represents the difference between the fair market value of the acquired firm and the book value of that firm. The creation of a goodwill account is not viewed favorably in most acquisitions or mergers. The goodwill must be amortized or written off by the consolidated firm. In this context, it becomes a noncash expense that reduces the firm's reported earnings. At the same time, it cannot be deducted for tax purposes and does not provide a tax shield to the firm.

CROSS-REFERENCE:
pooling and purchase methods, how to use in merger accounting, p. 91

Gordon model. A mathematical model developed by Myron J. Gordon to calculate the intrinsic value of common stock by measuring the present value of future dividends. The model may be written:

Intrinsic Value =

$$\frac{Div_{curr}}{CR_{norm} - (CR_{act})(\% RE)}$$

where

Div_{curr} = current dividend in dollars (annual basis)

CR_{norm} = capitalization rate demanded by the market for a stock of this type

CR_{act} = actual capitalization rate based on the firm's current earnings (provided they are relatively normal) and current market price

% RE = percentage of future earnings the corporation is likely to retain

CROSS-REFERENCES:
Gordon on common stock value, p. 255
Walter and Gordon on dividend decisions, p. 260

gross margin. The income statement item that is calculated by subtracting the firm's cost of goods sold from its sales.

CROSS-REFERENCES:

liquidity, how to analyze with ratios, p. 49
income statement, management format, p. 430

gross profit margin. A ratio that links sales and profits is the gross profit margin, which is calculated by dividing the gross margin by sales. This ratio shows the profits relative to sales after the direct production costs are deducted. It may be used as an indicator of the efficiency of the production operation and the relation between production costs and selling price.

$$\begin{array}{l}\text{Gross} \\ \text{Profit} \\ \text{Margin}\end{array} = \frac{\text{sales - cost of goods sold}}{\text{sales}}$$

The difference between profit margin and gross profit margin lies in the general and administrative expenses. These are included in the profit margin; thus profit margin presents a total operations picture. They are excluded from the more narrow profit measure of gross profit margin.

CROSS-REFERENCES:

profitability, how to analyze with ratios, p. 56
profit margin, p. 491

growth approach to common stock value. The growth approach seeks stocks of firms with outstanding prospects of long-term increases in sales and profits. The real value of these firms is dependent upon a high degree of sustained growth of revenues accompanied by similar growth of earnings. Purchases of growth stocks frequently result in large returns on the initial investment over a number of years. These purchases may also result in con-

siderable losses should the growth cease, a situation that normally causes large declines in the market price of the growth stock.

CROSS-REFERENCES:

common stock value, how to compare two or more stocks, p. 83
Graham and Dodd approaches to common stock value, p. 246
Gordon on common stock value, p. 255

growth, internal versus external. A firm is said to be growing internally when it increases sales and profits by expanding its own operations. It may purchase new machinery to increase its capacity to produce existing products, or it may purchase machinery and train its sales force to produce and sell a new product. In either case, management is committing itself to an expansion of existing activities. In one case, the firm seeks a larger volume of sales with current products. In the other, the firm begins to expand into new product areas and markets.

Internal growth may be funded from sources inside or outside the firm. Internal sources include retained earnings and the funds shielded by depreciation and other noncash expenses. If outside funds are sought, the firm may offer debt or equity securities to raise money. Even though the firm receives funds from external sources, the firm is experiencing internal growth, since the money is used to expand existing operations.

External Growth External growth occurs when a firm takes over the operations of another firm. The acquiring firm may purchase the assets or stock, or may combine with the second firm. Since the second company has sales and assets of its own, the first company does not have to generate the new business from scratch. The term acquisition is generally used to refer to the taking over of assets in the process of external growth.

External growth offers a number of advantages over internal growth:

1. *Rapid Expansion.* Taking over the operations of another firm is the quickest path to growth. The acquiring firm eliminates the lead time for ordering and installing machinery, producing the product, and achieving sales in the marketplace.

2. *Immediate Cash Inflows.* Since the firm is taking over an operating business, it will realize almost immediate inflows as customers receive their goods and pay for them. These inflows would not be received if the firm had to begin new construction of facilities and then the production of goods.

3. *Reduction of Risk.* Whenever a firm enters a new market, it takes a calculated risk. Will the new products sell in sufficient volume to be profitable? Will the firm's managers be able to make the proper decisions in the new operating environment? The acquired firm will be operating, perhaps successfully, in an environment that is familiar to its managers. By entering a field through an established and experienced management, we reduce the chances for failure.

4. *Economies.* Entering a new market involves a number of start-up costs. A start-up cost is an initial expense occurred when a firm begins a new operation. It may be the cost of training a new sales force or paying the legal fees required for the new activity. Frequently, these costs can be held to a minimum by purchasing an operating firm. For example, it would be less expensive to take over a firm with a strong marketing force than to have to compete with the marketing force by building one's own marketing department. The reduction of start-up costs offers economies from external growth.

CROSS-REFERENCE:

acquisitions, three approaches, p. 307

growth, measurement of. Financial managers use the term growth to mean increases in the size and activities of a firm over the long run. Three measures of corporate growth are commonly used:

1. *Increases in Sales.* This widely accepted measure gives an indication that a firm is able to maintain its competitive position, increase either the size or number of its primary markets for goods and services, and achieve the stability that usually accompanies a large volume of sales. Increase in sales is a direct indicator of growth in a firm's operating areas.

2. *Increases in Profits.* This measure is frequently used by the financial community and stockholders of a firm. It shows the firm's ability to convert growth in sales and operations into increasing returns to shareholders. The growth in profits is normally measured through increases in the firm's earnings per share.

3. *Increases in Assets.* Steady increases in a firm's operating resources may also be viewed as an indication of growth. This is the least desirable method of measuring growth. Although most firms must increase their assets to increase capacity for production and sales, a firm's assets may increase without a corresponding increase in sales or earnings per share, an indication of inefficiencies rather than growth. Because of this possibility, increases in assets should not be used by itself as an indicator of growth.

CROSS-REFERENCE:

Durand on cost of capital, p. 203

growth, reasons for seeking. A number of reasons may be offered as to why firm's seek to grow. Among the more important ones are the following:

1. *Diversification.* Most firms recognize that diversifying their operations reduces the risk of failure. If a firm produces a single product, it is subject to the market pressures on the product. If demand diminishes rapidly, the firm will experience an unsettling cutback in its production. If a competitor introduces an improved version of the product or a substitute for it, the firm may no longer be able to compete in the marketplace. Since demand and competitive factors are difficult to predict, the only certain safeguard against a market disaster is diversification. If the firm is operating in a variety of markets with many products, it can better cope with a cutback in a single product or market.

2. *Stability.* When a firm is able to achieve a large volume of sales, it becomes more stable than firms with smaller volumes of sales. The high level of revenues allows production economies and other cost-saving techniques, which allow a high margin of profit on sales. Also, the high sales level allows a deep penetration of most of the firm's markets. If a firm dominates a market, it is better able to withstand pressures and problems in the market.

3. *Operating Economies.* Large firms are able to achieve economies not available to small firms. As an example, Proctor and Gamble is a large producer and seller of nondurable consumer products such as soaps, paper products, and food items. Because of its size, the firm is able to purchase large blocs of television advertising time at lower rates than firms purchasing fewer blocs of time. The reduced advertising rates are an economy that would not have been available if Proctor and Gamble had not grown to its present size.

4. *Profits from Turn-Around Situations.* When a firm is operating below its potential profit levels, a new management could remove inefficiencies and solve problems, resulting in a dramatic rise in profits. Such a firm offers a turn-around situation. When a firm is doing poorly but has strong potential for improvement, the firm will become the target of acquiring firms. The stock of the poorly managed firm will be depressed or selling at a low price in the market. It will offer a bargain to an acquiring firm because, if profits can be restored to higher levels, the stock price will rise correspondingly.

CROSS-REFERENCES:

diversification, p. 382
turn-around situations. p. 539

H

hard currency. In international finance, a national currency that is likely to maintain its current value or gain in value compared to other currencies because the nation has a strong economy and sound balance of payments position. A hard currency is also said to be a strong currency.

CROSS-REFERENCES:
currency, p 369
dollar, alternatives for support in 1971, p 388
foreign exchange, p 414

hedging. Defined as the purchase or sale of foreign exchange for the sole purpose of avoiding losses which can occur from changes in exchange rates. It is the opposite of speculation, which involves the purchase or sale of a currency, usually on a forward basis, with the goal of making a profit on changes in rates of exchange.

The most common method of hedging is to execute a forward contract to buy or sell a currency. This "locks in" the rate of exchange and eliminates any risk from changes in the spot market exchange rate between the two currencies. This is relatively easy to accomplish with a call to the international department of a firm's bank. Or a contract can be executed directly through the facilities of the International Monetary Market of the Chicago Mercantile Exchange.

A second hedging method avoids the forward market completely. Under the borrowing alternatives, the individual or firm makes an immediate conversion of currencies in the spot market and then holds a currency until the delivery date of the business transaction. The details of this more-complicated hedging method are discussed under "Hedging Foreign Exchange Transactions, How to Evaluate Alternatives."

The term cover is used synonomously with the term hedge. When an individual hedges a foreign exchange position, we say he has covered his exposure or that he has a covered position.

CROSS-REFERENCES:
hedging foreign exchange transactions, how to evaluate alternatives, p. 173
foreign exchange, p. 414

hedging alternatives. When an individual or business is due to receive a foreign currency at some future date, three choices are available for dealing with foreign exchange risk:
1. *Full Exposure.* The individual can decide to do nothing until the foreign currency is delivered. At that time, the spot market will determine the value of the foreign currency in terms of the national currency. The individual will benefit if the foreign currency has increased in value since it will purchase more of his national currency. He will lose if the reverse has occurred.
2. *Forward Market Alternative.* The individual can execute a forward contract to sell the foreign currency on the date it is due to be delivered. The forward rate will be fixed and the position is fully covered.
3. *Borrowing Alternative.* The individual can borrow foreign currency today and convert it. The due date on the loan will be the same as the delivery date of the currency he is due to receive. When he receives the currency in the future, he pays off the loan. If the amounts are calculated correctly, no exposure results since he converted from the foreign currency in today's spot market.

Alternatives for Dealing with Foreign Exchange Risk.	
WHEN RECEIVING A FOREIGN CURRENCY	**WHEN A FOREIGN CURRENCY IS OWED**
1. <u>Accept full exposure</u>. When currency is actually received, convert it.	1. <u>Accept full exposure</u>. When currency is actually due, purchase it in spot market.
2. <u>Forward market alternative</u>. Execute contract to sell foreign currency for future delivery.	2. <u>Forward market alternative</u>. Execute contract to buy foreign currency at future date.
3. <u>Borrowing alternative</u>. Borrow foreigh currency and convert it today. When foreign currency is received, use it to repay foreign loan.	3. <u>Borrowing alternative</u>. Borrow national currency today and convert it to foreign currency. When payment due, deliver foreign currency.

Alternatives for Dealing with Foreign Exchange Risk.

If an individual owes a foreign currency to be delivered at some future date, three similar choices are available to him. All six alternatives are outlined in the Figure.

CROSS–REFERENCE:

hedging foreign exchange transactions, how to evaluate alternatives, p. 173

hedging guidelines. As the firm considers whether to hedge a foreign currency transaction, a number of guidelines may prove useful:

1. *Knowledge of Market.* The firm should have a solid knowledge of the market for its products, but it may not understand the market for foreign exchange. Unless it has excellent knowledge of capital markets, or unless its bank provides such knowledge, the firm generally would seek to hedge its transactions.

2. *Frequency of Hedging the Specific Currency.* Major currencies are involved in frequent hedging and speculating transactions and the cost of hedging may be nominal. Weak currencies, however, may not participate in such hedging because high risk results in few speculators willing to offer forward contracts. The cost of hedging these currencies may be so high as to offset any risks from currency fluctuations. Unless a currency has an active forward market, it will be difficult and costly to hedge it.

3. *Risk Preference.* Every business firm has its own policies towards accepting risk. Some firms are willing to accept foreign exchange risks while others are not. If a firm is willing to accept this kind of risk, it may profit from doing so. At the same time, it must be prepared to lose if the currencies move the wrong way.

4. *Size of Transactions.* A firm may be willing to remain exposed on relatively small transactions where the risk of loss will not cause a serious drain on the firm's resources. Large transactions, on the other hand, may be hedged because a mistake in judgment could prove disasterous.

5. *Number of Transactions.* If a firm has many small transactions involving a variety of currencies, it may be willing to ignore hedging techniques. Gains in one currency will be offset by losses in another so the firm is diversifying and thus reducing its risk. If all of a firm's transactions involve the same foreign currency, hedging may be attractive.

CROSS-REFERENCE:
hedging foreign exchange transactions, how to evaluate alternatives, p. 173

holder of record. The individual who owns stock according to the records of a firm and who is designated as the recipient of dividends or stock rights.

CROSS-REFERENCE:
ex dividend or ex right, p. 397

holding company. A corporation that owns a controlling interest in the voting stock of one or more other corporations called subsidiaries. In some cases, as little as 10 to 15 percent of a firm's stock may be sufficient ownership to control the firm. In this kind of business combination, both firms continue to exist even if the holding company has 100 percent of the voting stock of the subsidiary. If the holding company actively engages itself in the management of the subsidiary, the holding company is also called a parent company.

The holding company form of business combination is desirable to firms for a number of reasons:

1. *Ease of Ownership.* The holding company can purchase the common stock of publicly traded firms without difficulty. No formal approval is required by either firm's stockholders.
2. *Lower Cost.* If the common stock is purchased in small installments over a period of time, the price of the stock may not be affected. If the shareholders of the soon-to-be subsidiary knew that another firm was seeking control, the price of the stock would probably rise.
3. *Leverage and Control.* Because a firm can be controlled with only 10 percent of

the voting stock (assuming the rest is widely held), a holding company allows the control of a large amount of assets with a small investment.

4. *Diversification.* Since control is possible with a small investment, the holding company can purchase the stock of different firms, thus diversifying its investments.
5. *Avoiding Foreign Corporation Status.* A domestic corporation is chartered by the state in which it operates. A foreign corporation is chartered outside the state. Since many states favor domestic corporations with lower taxes and other privileges, a large corporation may establish a domestic holding company to conduct its operations in these states. If the parent operated directly in the state, it would lose the benefits of the domestic status.

CROSS-REFERENCES:
consolidation, p. 356
mergers, p. 460
acquisition, p. 307

horizontal integration. A combination of firms in the same line of business, as when two manufacturers of shoes merge.

CROSS-REFERENCE:
vertical integration, p. 544

hurdle rate. The level of return a proposal must reach before it is acceptable to a firm.

CROSS-REFERENCES:
net present value, how to compare proposals, p. 17
weighted average cost of capital, how to calculate, p. 158

income. Like profits, income is a measure of the difference between sales and costs. Unlike profits, income indicates that a precise accounting process has been used in its calculation. Thus, we may define income as an accounting measure of profits.

There are three terms commonly used to record income:

1. *Earnings Before Interest and Taxes (EBIT).* This is the difference between the firm's operating revenues and operating expenses. Because it is a measure of income from operations, it is also called operating income.

2. *Earnings Before Taxes (EBT).* This is the difference between the firm's revenues and two kinds of expenses: operating expenses and expenses of paying interest on the firm's debt. When a firm borrows money to finance its assets, it incurs mandatory interest payments each year. These may be viewed as financial expenses (related to the financing of the firm) rather than operating expenses. Earnings before taxes is a measure of operating and financial profit.

3. *Net Income After Taxes (NIAT).* This is the difference between revenues and all expenses and taxes paid by the firm. This measure of income is also called *earnings after taxes.*

EXAMPLE: *A firm has $3,000,000 in revenues, $1,800,000 in operating expenses, $600,000 in annual interest payments, and pays a 50 percent corporate income tax. What are the firm's earnings before interest and taxes? earnings before taxes? net income after taxes?*
ANSWER: *(000's)EBIT = $3,000-1,800 = $1,200; EBT = $3,000-1,800-600 = $600; NIAT = $3,000-1,800-600-300 = $300.*

CROSS-REFERENCES:
earnings before interest and taxes, p. 392
earnings before taxes, p. 392
net income after taxes, p. 466

income and working capital distinguished. The distinction between income and working capital or funds is quite important. The firm cannot pay its bills with income or profit. Bills must be paid in cash. A high level of income is important as an indicator that the firm will be able to generate sufficient working capital for its liquidity needs. But if the firm were to invest its cash in new machinery or land, it might lack the funds to meet its current obligations. A reverse situation may be true with a low level of income. Although the firm is not profitable, it may be able to acquire funds through borrowing, floating stock, or selling fixed assets. Because income and funds have different meanings and implications for the firm, the financial manager must monitor both profits and liquidity as measured by the firm's income from operations, and the level and changes of working capital.

Funds or Working Capital and Income

Terms Defined	*Relationship between Income and Funds*
Cash = cash	Firms cannot pay bills with income.
Current assets = liquid assets = funds = working capital	Funds may be generated by income.
Net working capital = current assets—current liabilities	Funds may be generated by other means.
Assets = total resources	Funds are liquidity matter.
	Income is profit matter

CROSS-REFERENCE:
working capital, p. 551

income bonds. A bond that pays interest only when earnings are available to pay the interest. Income bonds are commonly used during the reorganization of a failing or bankrupt business firm.

CROSS-REFERENCES:
bond, p. 323
bankruptcy, p. 320

income statement. A report of the firm's activities during a given fiscal period, normally 1 year. It shows the revenues and expenses of the firm, the effect of interest and taxes, and the net income for the period. It may be called by other titles, such as the profit-and-loss statement or the statement of earnings.

Whereas the balance sheet offers a view of the firm at a moment in time, the income statement summarizes the profitability of operations over a period of time. It is an accounting device designed to show stockholders and creditors whether the firm is making money. It can also be used as a tool to identify the factors that affect the degree of profitability.

The income statement is prepared in accordance with generally accepted accounting procedures. The various accounts on the books of the firm are carefully defined and then placed in a specified format on the statement. Most large firms hire a certified public accountant at the end of the fiscal period to certify the accuracy of the firm's financial statements. When this is done, we can usually rely on the accuracy of the profit picture presented on the income statement.

Sample Income Statement   The income statement for the Donaldson Company illustrates a format suitable for presentation to the stockholders in a firm's annual report. It begins with the firm's revenues, deducts expenses and taxes, and shows the income or loss. From this statement we can discover certain items of interest to potential creditors or owners of the company. For example, we see that the firm had a profit after taxes in 1973, but it had a loss in 1974. This indicates that the firm is experiencing difficulty. If we check the net sales, we see that sales dropped by approximately 50 percent between 1973 and 1974. This appears to be the major factor affecting the reversal from a profit to a loss.

CROSS-REFERENCES:
audit, p. 314
balance sheet, p. 317
flow-of-funds statement, p. 410

DONALDSON COMPANY Income Statement (year ending December 31, 1974)

	1974	1973
Net Sales	$9,570	$14,740
Cost of sales and operating expenses		
Cost of products sold including delivery expenses	8,670	10,790
General and administrative expenses	940	1,000
Interest charges	260	200
Total Cost of Sales	9,870	11,990
Earnings (losses) before taxes	(300)	2,750
Federal taxes on income	0	1,375
Net Income (Loss) After Taxes	$ (300)	$ 1,375

DONALDSON AND COMPANY Income Statement—Management Format

		1974	1973	
	Total revenues	$9,570	$14,740	Operating
	Cost of goods sold	8,670	10,790	effects
	Gross margin	900	3,950	
Four	Administrative expenses	940	1,000	
profit	Operating income (EBIT)	(40)	2,950	
measures	Interest charges	260	200	Financing effects
	Earnings before taxes (EBT)	(300)	2,750	
	Federal income taxes	0	1,375	Tax effects
	Net income after taxes	$ (300)	$ 1,375	

income statement, management format. For management purposes, the analyst should modify the income statement to separate each major type of cost and taxes. When this is done, two new items will appear that are not part of the Donaldson Company statement:

1. *Gross Margin.* The amount of profit the firm realizes as a result of the difference between the cost of goods sold (direct production costs) and the receipts from sales.
2. *Operating Income (EBIT).* The before-tax income after all operating expenses have been deducted from total revenues. This is also alled earnings before interest and taxes.

With the format shown in the income statement, the analyst is able to focus on four distinct measures of profit. Gross profit margin is a direct measure of the profit from sales. Operating income is the profit from operations. Earnings before taxes contains both operating factors and the cost of financing the firm's debt. Net income after taxes is the final profit after all expenses and taxes have been paid.

CROSS-REFERENCES:

gross margin, p. 421
earnings before interest and taxes, p. 392

income statement, marginal analysis format. Another approach to preparing the income statement breaks out operating expenses into fixed and variable costs. These costs replace the cost of goods sold and operating expenses on the income statement. Three new items appear on the statement:

1. *Variable Costs.* These are those costs that vary in direct proportion to changes in the volume of production. This category will contain the bulk of the expenses found in cost of goods sold, but will also contain some general and administrative expenses.
2. *Fixed Costs.* These are constant charges that do not vary with the level of production. Most general and administrative expenses are fixed costs, as are some charges in cost of goods sold.
3. *Marginal Contribution.* This is the profit measure calculated as the difference between total sales and total variable costs. This is the profit available to the firm to cover fixed costs, interest, and taxes, and to provide a net income after taxes. Marginal contribution may be calculated in total, as is the case on the income statement, or on a per unit basis, in which case it is the difference between the selling price per unit and the variable cost per unit.

DONALDSON AND COMPANY Income Statement—Marginal-Analysis Format

		1974	1973	
	Total revenues	$9,570	$14,740	Two different
A new	Variable costs	6,590	8,530	categories of
profit	Marginal contribution	2,980	6,210	operating
measure	Fixed costs	3,020	3,260	expenses
	Operating income (EBIT)	(40)	2,950	
	Interest charges	260	200	
	Earnings before taxes (EBT)	(300)	2,750	
	Federal income taxes	0	1,375	
	NIAT	$ (300)	$ 1,375	

When the expenses on the income statement are divided into variable and fixed costs, we are using a technique called marginal analysis. This format allows the analyst to develop relationships between the level of sales and the expenses incurred to make the sales. By definition, the fixed costs will not change with differing levels of output. If the level of fixed costs is high, the firm must generate a large volume of sales to cover them. If the level is low, the firm will have less difficulty covering them. In either case, the firm must cover fixed costs with its marginal contribution. Marginal analysis helps the analyst to focus on marginal contribution—a key measure of profit that must first cover fixed costs, then interest and taxes, and finally provide a profit to shareholders.

CROSS-REFERENCES:
variable cost, p. 544
fixed costs, p. 409
marginal contribution, p. 456

indenture. A legal document accompanying a bond issue that states the conditions under which the bonds have been issued, the duties of the issuing firm, and the rights of the bondholders. In addition to providing information, such as stipulating the coupon rate and maturity date, the indenture may contain provisions for the firm to provide specific collateral, establish a sinking fund to retire the issue, or provide other restrictive covenants.

CROSS-REFERENCE:
bond, p. 323

indirect inventory costs. In inventory management, the losses of revenues as a result of management decisions. Examples of indirect costs are the cost of funds tied up in inventory and the cost of running out of goods to sell.

CROSS-REFERENCES:
inventory management, how to set up system for, p. 103
inventories, p. 441
inventory, costs of, p. 442

inflation. The sharp drop in the value of a nation's currency that causes rapid rises in general price levels. Two types of inflation are of the most interest:
1. *Demand-Pull Inflation.* When the demand for goods and services exceeds the available supply, potential customers bid up the prices. In effect, there is an excess of currency, and price levels must rise to absorb the currency.
2. *Cost-Push Inflation.* Price levels are generally set to allow a profit above the costs associated with producing

goods and services. If costs are rising rapidly, they will have an inflationary effect on prices.

By the mid-1970s, the United States had entered into an economic period where most economists were predicting long-term inflation. Between 1925 and 1970, the United States had price-level changes averaging 2 percent annually. Between 1975 and the year 2000, economists are forecasting inflation in excess of 6 percent annually. This higher level of inflation will have impacts on economic activity and financial managers must be prepared to deal with it.

CROSS-REFERENCES:

inflation in the capital budget, how to analyze, p. 11
residual values, how to forecast, p. 66
capital budgeting international, how to calculate capital cost, p. 163
protecting local assets in high inflation country, how to, p. 177
demand-pull inflation, p. 378
cost-push inflation, p. 368

inflation, effect on balance sheet. High levels of inflation cause distortions in the value of balance-sheet items. Over a long period of time, the distortions can become quite significant. The different effects are discussed for each balance-sheet area.

Cash Account   With respect to cash and marketable securities, two important effects can be noted:
1. *Additional Cash Must Be Held Over Time.* As price levels rise, the firm must keep more cash on hand to meet its obligations. Thus, in an inflationary setting, the firm must plan to gradually increase its cash balance.
2. *Purchasing Power of Cash Declines Over Time.* When a firm is holding a steady level of cash over time, it will experience a loss in the purchasing power of the money.

Accounts Receivable   With respect to the firm's accounts receivable, two similar effects will result from inflation:
1. *Additional Receivables Must Be Financed Over Time.* Rising prices for the firm's goods will result in larger receivables' balances. This additional working capital must be financed at some cost to the firm.
2. *Receivables' Purchasing Power Declines While Outstanding.* Until the receivables are collected, they are fixed in dollar value. When the dollars arrive, they will have a lower purchasing power than when the goods were sold which created the receivables.

Inventories   In any discussion on inflation, three approaches to inventory valuation should be noted:
1. *First-in, First-out (FIFO).* This method assumes that the oldest inventory is used up first. In fact, this approximates the physical movement of the inventory.
2. *Last-in, First-out (LIFO).* This method assumes that the most recent inventory is used up first. The LIFO method does not approximate the physical movement of the inventory, but it may be argued that it does match the economic movement of the inventory. This reasoning points out that the firm's profits are the difference between selling price and current costs, not the difference between selling price and historical costs that existed when the inventory was purchased.
3. *Next-in, First-out (NIFO).* This method assumes that the next item of inventory to be purchased is the correct cost basis for the last item sold. It is based on the argument that the correct current cost will be reflected the next time the firm purchases inventory. At the present time, this method is not permitted under the regulations of the Internal Revenue Service.

In an inflationary setting, the three methods of valuation for inventories have markedly different effects on inventory value:

1. *Effect of FIFO.* This inventory technique tends to show current values of inventory on the balance sheet but undervalues the cost of goods sold on the income statement.
2. *Effect of LIFO.* This technique gives a more accurate reflection of current costs on the income statement but undervalues the inventory account. Over a period of time with high inflation, the dollar value of inventory may become almost insignificant as a balance-sheet item.
3. *Effect of NIFO.* Even though it cannot presently be used, this technique would be fairly accurate in estimating cost of goods sold but would significantly undervalue inventory in periods of high inflation.

Whatever the accounting method, inflation will cause rises in the cost of a firm's raw materials and finished goods. Like cash and receivables, the additional cost of the inventory must be financed by the firm. Unlike cash and receivables, the inventory need not lose in terms of purchasing power. Since it has not yet been sold, the firm has the option of raising prices to offset the effects of inflation.

Fixed Assets In recording fixed assets, accountants have traditionally used the original cost of the asset. In an inflationary economy, the cost principle does not reflect the replacement cost of existing assets. Two important effects result from this situation:

1. *Fixed Assets Are Grossly Undervalued.* As the firm depreciates the asset from its original cost, the resulting book value will usually be considerably below the actual market value of the assets.
2. *Firm Not Preparing To Replace the Asset.* Depreciation allows a firm to shield a portion of its revenues to reflect the

cost of purchasing the fixed asset. When the asset is no longer serviceable, the firm is supposed to have shielded sufficient cash to purchase a new asset. Under inflation, this does not happen. The firm has only shielded sufficient cash to purchase a machine at the historical price, not the much higher current price. Thus, inflation causes the firm to suffer a capital depletion on its fixed assets that must be covered from profits or from new external financing.

Liabilities With respect to liabilities, the firm gains from the effects of inflation. When the firm finally repays its debts, it will do so in dollars that have less purchasing power than when the money was borrowed. If the cost of debt reflects the expected loss due to inflation, the effect is not significant. If the cost of debt does not reflect expected inflation, the firm is taking advantage of relatively cheap money as a result of the inflation.

Equity With respect to equity, inflation has no real effect on the common stock, premium, or retained earnings accounts. These are historical accounts and will be understated to the extent that assets are undervalued as a result of inflation. Still, it is almost meaningless to say that inflation has any effect on these accounts.

CROSS-REFERENCES:
cash accounting, p. 342
accounts receivable, p. 306
inventories, p. 441

inflation, effect on profits. High levels of inflation result in an overstatement of the actual profits received by a firm and reported on the firm's income statement. Two factors account for most of the overstatement:

1. *Understatement of Cost of Goods Sold.* A majority of American firms have tra-

ditionally used the first-in first-out (FIFO) method of accounting for inventory. The oldest goods, and lowest-cost goods under inflation, are shown on the income statement in cost of goods sold. The lower reported cost of goods sold will result in higher taxes to be paid on the higher reported profits. This will be incorrect if the firm is not generating sufficient funds to replace any depleted inventory items that have risen in cost during the period. That is, a portion of the firm's profits may have to be used to restock inventory and return the firm to its original inventory position. When this happens, the understatement of cost of goods sold results in an overstatement of profits.

2. *Capital Depletion on the Firm's Fixed Assets.* It has already been noted that depreciation is not sufficient to replace the firm's fixed assets when they wear out. In effect, the firm is suffering a capital depletion or a decline in its fixed assets. To return to its original asset position, the firm must use a portion of its reported profits or must seek outside financing. The need to use profits to replace depleted capital means the firm overstated profits.

Measuring Inflation's Effect on Profits We can measure the effect of inflation on profits by comparing FIFO, LIFO, and NIFO methods of accounting for inventory and by allowing for an inflation factor in depreciation calculations. The Table makes such a comparison. Data are given for a firm with $1,000,000 in sales, $440,000 in cash expenses for the purchase of inventory, $300,000 in cash administrative expenses, and $100,000 in interest payments. The columns are set up as follows:

1. *FIFO Column.* The depreciation is charged according to the original depreciation schedule and the ending

inventory rises with inflation and the techniques employed in FIFO accounting.

2. *LIFO Column.* Original depreciation is used and the inventory value does not rise in accordance with the LIFO accounting. Cost of goods sold does rise (reflecting the inflation) as compared to the FIFO method.

3. *NIFO Column.* Although not currently allowed, the NIFO column in our example actually results in a lower inventory than at the start of the period (in dollars, not units of inventory). It also results in a larger cost of goods sold than the other columns. Depreciation is not adjusted.

4. *NIFO Plus Adjusted Depreciation Column.* This is similar to the NIFO column, but the depreciation has been adjusted by 25 percent to reflect higher replacement costs for fixed assets.

Even though all the columns reflect identical sales and identical physical inventories, the profits drop as the accounting method attempts to mirror inflation. With each drop in profits, the cash flow rises because of the noncash charges to cost of goods sold and depreciation. In a period of high inflation, the NIFO plus adjusted depreciation column is the most accurate indicator of profits (relatively low) and cash flow (higher to overcome inflation's effects on invested capital).

Conclusions on Inflation's Effect on Profits
From the above discussion and from the data in the Table, we might conclude the following:

1. *LIFO Decreases Profits But Increases Cash Flow.* As compared to FIFO, the LIFO method of valuing inventory provides an additional expense and tax shield to the firm. In periods of inflation, this results in a lower reported income, but the tax shield allows the firm to retain more cash from its operations.

2. *LIFO Is More Accurate and Useful Than*

Effect of Different Accounting Methods on Profits in a Period of Inflation.

(000s) BOOK PROFITS	FIFO	LIFO	NIFO	NIFO Plus Depreciation Adjustment
Sales	$1,000	$1,000	$1,000	$1,000
Cost of goods sold:				
Beginning inventory	160	160	160	160
+ Cash purchases and expenses	+440	+440	+440	+440
+ Depreciation	+40	+40	+40	+50
− Ending inventory	−300	−160	−140	−140
= Cost of goods sold	340	480	500	510
Gross margin	660	520	500	490
General and administrative	300	300	300	300
EBIT	360	220	200	190
Interest	100	100	100	100
EBT	260	120	100	90
Taxes	130	60	50	45
NIAT	130	60	50	45
CASH FLOW				
Sales	$1,000	$1,000	$1,000	$1,000
− Cash purchases and expenses	−440	−440	−440	−440
− General and administrative	−300	−300	−300	−300
− Interest	−100	−100	−100	−100
− Taxes	−130	−60	− 50	− −45
Cash flow to firm	+30	+100	+110	+115

FIFO. Although LIFO results in a dramatic understatement of inventory value, it provides a more accurate measure of the actual profits to the firm. It recognizes the higher costs of replacing inventory under inflation and allows the firm to retain cash. This cash can be used to meet the higher expenses of purchasing goods.

3. *NIFO Plus Adjusted Depreciation May Have Planning Value.* The NIFO plus adjusted depreciation technique cannot be used for tax purposes but it may have a role in profit planning. Since it gives the most accurate indication of profits, the firm may be able to use it in establishing selling price or some other aspect of profit planning.

CROSS-REFERENCES:
profit planning, how to price the use of a capital asset, p. 53
profits, how to maintain under inflation, p. 59
inflation factor, p. 435

inflation factor. In profit planning, the annual percentage rate of inflation that will apply to a firm's costs and capital needs during the next operating period. A firm usually selects an inflation factor from one of three sources: the GNP implicit price deflator, an industry index, or a specific factor developed for the firm.

CROSS-REFERENCES:
profits, how to maintain under

inflation, p. 59
inflation, effects on profits, p. 433
inflation in the capital budget, how to analyze, p. 11

informational content of dividends. A concept forwarded by Miller and Modigliani that states that dividends convey information on management's estimates of future earnings and growth. Because of the informational content of dividends, dividend changes provide the occasion for price changes but they are not the cause of the changes.

CROSS-REFERENCE:
Miller and Modigliani on dividend policy, p. 264

institutional finance. A specialized field that examines savings and capital formation and the roles played by banks, insurance companies, and pension funds.

intangible asset. Resources listed on a firm's balance sheet that have value but do not represent physical property or securities. Intangible assets include such items as goodwill, patents, trademarks, franchises, and licenses.

CROSS-REFERENCES:
capital asset pricing model, p. 279
financial asset, p. 403
capital asset, p. 328

Interamerican Development Bank (IDB). This bank was established in 1959 by the United States and 19 Latin-American countries. It makes both "hard" and "soft" loans to assist in economic development of its Latin-American members. The United States provides a considerable portion of the capital with other funds coming from contributions from member countries or from the sale of bonds.

interest. A payment made by a borrower of money to a lender of money as compensation for the use of the money. Interest will be in addition to a repayment of the principal at the conclusion of the loan period.

CROSS-REFERENCES:
profits, how to maintain under inflation, p. 59
tax factors affecting return, how to evaluate, p. 72
compound interest, p. 355

interest-rate risk. The possibility of a loss of principal of a fixed-return security, because of increases in the general level of interest rates.

CROSS-REFERENCE:
bond values, how to measure interest rate risks on, p. 182

intermediation. A process by which savings are accumulated by financial institutions from businesses and households with excess funds and then lent out or invested so as to provide capital for an economic system. The banks, insurance companies, and pension funds which perform this function are called financial intermediaries.

internal analysis. The process of determining the significant operating and financial characteristics of a firm from accounting data when performed by the firm's own finance or accounting department. Internal analysis uses detailed and current information that is not available to outsiders and is generally more accurate than external analysis.

CROSS-REFERENCE:
external analysis, p. 400

internal rate of return. In capital budgeting, a calculation of the actual rate of return provided by a specific stream of net cash benefits as compared to a specific net cash outlay. It uses a trial-and-error approach to find the discount factor that equates the original investment to the net cash benefits. Once found, this discount factor is the rate of return on the stream. Also called discounted cash flow.

CROSS-REFERENCES:
internal rate of return, how to calculate, p. 15
present value techniques, how to select correct one, p. 22
discounted cash flow, p. 382

International Development Association (IDA). The International Development Association was created in 1960 as an affiliate of the World Bank. Although its activities are similar to those of the bank, it differs as follows:
1. *Purpose.* The IDA is the "soft loan" window of the World Bank Group. It advances funds to the poorest of the developing countries on low interest or interest-free terms; the maturity period may be as long as 50 years; and repayment schedules can begin with a 10-year grace period. Although the IDA makes loans only to member governments or organizations guaranteed by those governments, its activities are designed to help those nations that could not borrow on conventional terms.
2. *Resources.* Unlike the World Bank, the International Development Association does not issue bonds for a major portion of its funds. Rather, most of its capital comes from the subscription of member countries. A second source of capital is contributions made by the World Bank from its own income.

CROSS-REFERENCE:
World Bank, p. 556

international finance. A specialized field that examines economic transactions between nations.

CROSS-REFERENCE:
part 6, international finance in the "how to" section, p. 161

International Finance Corporation (IFC). A member of the World Bank Group is the International Finance Corporation established in 1956. Its important characteristics are:
1. *Purpose.* The IFC attempts to further economic growth in its developing member nations by investing in private enterprises. Local government guarantees are not required for the loans to be made.
2. *Criteria for Investment.* The IFC makes investments in private business ventures that:
   a. Offer a reasonable prospect of earning sufficient profits so that the venture has long-term prospects for success.
   b. Offer economic benefits to the host country. Basically this means that the activity has the potential to contribute to the national economy through the earning of foreign exchange, increasing employment, or exploiting the nation's natural resources so as to benefit the local economy.
   c. Need local equity capital. The IFC is willing to take a noncontrolling equity position in its business ventures. When the business is established, the IFC frequently sells its participation to private investors, thus freeing capital for more investments.
3. *Resources.* The IFC capital is provided by subscriptions from member nations and from funds borrowed from the World Bank. In addition, funds are provided by the repayment of loans and by selling its equity par-

ticipations in local ventures once the ventures are established and profitable.

CROSS–REFERENCE:
World Bank, p. 556

International Monetary Fund (IMF). The International Monetary Fund was established under the terms of the Bretton Woods Agreement and began operations in 1946 with 39 member nations. Since its creation, the IMF has been the dominant institution for dealing with international transactions among the nations of the free world.

Goals of the International Monetary Fund
The International Monetary Fund was designed to deal with a broad range of programs and problems that had previously hampered the financial dealings among nations. Among the goals of the fund were:

1. *Promote Exchange Rate Stability.* Member nations agreed to establish fixed exchange rates which would not fluctuate in response to short-term supply and demand pressures. A nation would fix the value of its currency in terms of gold but would not be required to convert the currency into gold upon demand. The U.S. dollar alone remained convertible into gold at the rate of $35 per ounce. Once a nation had fixed its exchange rate in terms of both gold and dollars, the nation would take steps to maintain the value of its currency within one percent of the fixed, or par, value. This would be accomplished largely through the buying or selling of foreign exchange or gold, with the assistance of the IMF as needed.

2. *Eliminate Exchange Restrictions.* The nations of the free world wanted to encourage the resumption of world trade and the free movement of capital, particularly capital designated to help rebuild war-damaged economies. Exchange restrictions are an obstacle to trade and capital flows. The IMF monitored a system of multilateral payments and encouraged the unrestricted conversion of currencies. Under such a system, a balance of payments deficit with one nation could be offset by a surplus with other nations. Deficits in trading with a nation could be offset by surpluses in the movement of capital. The elimination of exchange restrictions was an important element in the postwar system of international finance.

3. *Avoid Disequilibrium in Dealings Among Nations.* In the 1930s, balance-of-payments difficulties caused nations to take actions that were damaging to both national and international prosperity. Once a disequilibrium situation arose, nations took steps that aggravated it. The IMF was empowered to use its bag of currencies to provide funds to temporarily meet deficits. At the same time, the facilities and expertise of the fund could be used to develop solutions to the imbalances. These actions could not always eliminate disequilibrium among currencies, but they could shorten the duration and minimize the impact of disequilibrium.

While these are the most important goals of the International Monetary Fund, the fund pursued related goals, including those of economic development. A statement of the purposes of the fund is taken from Article I of the Bretton Woods Agreement as follows:

1. To promote international monetary cooperation through a permanent institution which provides the machinery for consultation and collaboration on international monetary problems.

2. To facilitate the expansion and balanced growth of international trade,

and to contribute thereby to the promotion and maintenance of high levels of employment and real income and to the development of the productive resources of all members as primary objectives of economic policy.

3. To promote exchange stability, to maintain orderly exchange arrangements among members, and to avoid competitive exchange depreciation.
4. To assist in the establishment of a multilateral system of payments in respect to current transactions between members and in the elimination of foreign exchange restrictions which hamper the growth of world trade.
5. To give confidence to members by making the fund's resources available to them under adequate safeguards, thus providing them with opportunity to correct maladjustments in their balances of payments without resorting to measures destructive of national or international prosperity.
6. In accordance with the above, to shorten the duration and lessen the degree of disequilibrium in the international balances of payments of members.

Governance of the International Monetary Fund
The International Monetary Fund is governed by a board of governors that includes representatives from all member nations. Voting on matters is weighted on the basis of IMF quotas assigned to each nation. As a general rule, the larger nations with the most international activities cast the most votes. For example, at one point the United States was authorized to cast approximately 25 percent of all votes. The United Kingdom and other nations of western Europe cast a total of 27 percent of the votes. The nations generally discuss matters at considerable length prior

to voting. Some matters are determined by a majority vote, some by four-fifths, and some require a unanimous vote.

CROSS-REFERENCES:
gold tranche of IMF, p. 420
quota of IMF, p. 500
Bretton Woods, p. 326

international monetary system. The group of institutions and mechanisms that allows nations and citizens of nations to carry on business with each other. Within the framework of this system, trade is conducted, capital flows are accommodated, exchange rates are established, and payments between nations are balanced.

CROSS-REFERENCES:
International Monetary Fund, p. 438
World Bank, p. 556

intrinsic-value analysis. The primary goal of intrinsic-value analysis is to allow a comparison of the intrinsic or real worth with the current market price or with the proposed purchase price of common stock. The fundamental factors affecting the value of a firm usually change less rapidly than the market factors that influence the price of the stock in the marketplace. When the financial manager locates a wide variance between intrinsic value and the asking price of a proposed acquisition, the firm may be able to greatly benefit from the acquisition.

The two major uses of intrinsic-value analysis are to locate clearly undervalued and clearly overvalued firms or stocks. In the case of a clearly undervalued stock, the market has not discovered that fundamental factors justify a higher market price for the stock. That is, the stock is worth more than its selling price. As soon as the investing public discovers this situation, such as when

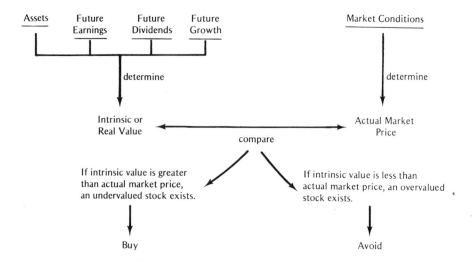

Comparison of Intrinsic Value and Actual Market Price.

management announces higher earnings per share than previously expected, investors will buy the stock and force a rise in its price. The persons or firms that purchased the stock when it was undervalued would profit. For overvalued stock, the reverse situation is true. When investors holding the stock discover that it is overvalued, they will sell their shares, causing a drop in market price. It is thus wise to avoid purchasing overvalued stocks.

An overview of intrinsic value and its uses is presented in the Figure above.

The intrinsic-value approach will not work in all cases because of three major limitations:

1. *Marketplace May be Slow to Recognize Real Value.* If the investing public does not discover the intrinsic value of the common stock, the firm's stock may remain undervalued or overvalued for a long period of time.
2. *Stocks of Highly Speculative Firms.* Firms whose activities are highly speculative in nature are not readily analyzed using intrinsic-value analysis. Stock in oil-exploration companies, gold-mining companies, or firms at-

tempting to profitably develop new inventions has a value that depends on future uncertainties rather than on fundamental financial factors. In these situations, the real value may hinge on a single event, such as the discovery of oil. Intrinsic-value analysis has no technique to evaluate this kind of situation.
3. *High-Growth Stocks.* Firms with records of extremely rapid growth will command high prices in the marketplace because investors are optimistic with respect to continuing future growth. When a stock has unusually high prospects for future growth in sales and profits, such as IBM and Xerox in the 1960s, its intrinsic value is a function of whether growth can be sustained. Because of future uncertainties concerning continuous growth, the intrinsic-value approach cannot adequately be used with high-growth situations.

EXAMPLE: An analyst has reviewed the possible acquisition of a privately owned manufacturer of costume jewelry. The analyst has determined that the firm is in a growing industry, and has high-quality products; and a solid margin of prof-

its. Its sales force is well trained and highly effective. The real value of this firm based on its projected future earnings is $3,000,000. Which approach is being used by this analyst?

ANSWER: Intrinsic-value approach. The analysis concentrates on fundamental factors affecting the future of the business.

EXAMPLE: An insurance company is considering the acquisition of a small manufacturing firm. The firm has had a steady volume of sales and somewhat outdated fixed assets. Its main potential for the future lies in a patented process it holds for plastic coating of specialty papers used for certain types of printing. The firm can expect booming sales if the expected demand for the process materializes. Can intrinsic-value analysis be applied to this situation?

ANSWER: Intrinsic value is of limited use. This is a highly speculative situation that cannot be properly handled by fundamental financial factors.

CROSS-REFERENCES:

inventory. The goods held for eventual resale by the firm. As such, inventories are a vital element in the efforts of the firm to achieve desired sales levels. Depending upon the nature of the industry and firm, inventories may be durable or nondurable, perishable or nonperishable, valuable or inexpensive. Whatever the nature of the inventories, the accounting process is careful to distinguish goods held for resale from other current assets, such as office supplies or furniture, which are not sold but are used to help the firm conduct its business.

CROSS-REFERENCES:

inventory, benefits of holding. By holding inventories, the firm is able to separate the processes of purchasing, producing, and selling. If firms were not willing to hold adequate raw materials and finished goods, purchasing would take place only when immediate production and sales were anticipated. When a customer signed a purchase agreement, the firm would not be able to offer rapid delivery. When the firm scheduled production runs, it would achieve none of the economies that longer runs provide. Inventories are used to provide cushions so that the purchasing, production, and sales functions can proceed at their own optimum paces.

In achieving the separation of these functions, the firm realizes a number of specific benefits:

1. *Avoiding Losses of Sales.* If the firm does not have goods available for sale, it will lose sales. Customers requiring immediate delivery will purchase their goods from the firm's competitors, and others will decide that they do not need the goods after all, if they have to wait for delivery. The ability of the firm to give quick service and to provide prompt delivery is closely tied to the proper management of inventory.

2. *Gaining Quantity Discounts.* If a firm is willing to maintain large inventories in selected product lines, it may be able to make bulk purchases of goods at large discounts. Suppliers will frequently offer a greatly reduced price if the firm will order double or triple its normal requirement. By paying less for its goods, the firm will be able to increase profits, as long as the costs of maintaining the inventories

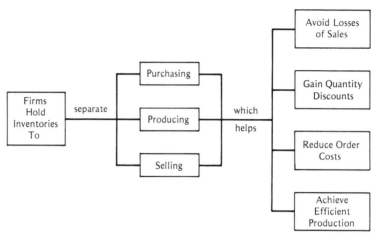

Why Firms Hold Inventories.

are less than the amount of the discount. For example, if the cost of storing an item for the extra time is estimated at $1 and the discount is $3, the firm will benefit by $2 per unit from the quantity discount.

3. *Reducing Order Costs.* Every time a firm places an order, it incurs certain costs. Forms must be typed, checked, approved, and mailed. When goods arrive, they must be accepted, inspected, and counted. The invoice must be checked with the goods and then sent to the accounting department so that the supplier can be paid. The variable costs associated with individual orders can be reduced if the firm places a few large rather than numerous small orders.

4. *Achieving Efficient Production Runs.* Once an assembly line or piece of machinery is prepared to receive certain raw materials and perform selected production operations, a setup cost has been incurred. This cost must be absorbed in the subsequent production run. If the setup cost is $200 and the run produces 200 units, the cost is $1 per unit. A longer run of 2,000 units would reduce the setup cost to $.10 per unit. Inventories assist the firm in

making sufficiently long runs to achieve efficient production. If the firm had to change setups frequently, it would experience high unit costs of production.

Adequate inventories also protect against shortages that would delay or halt production. If the firm has scheduled a long run and begins production, only to discover a shortage of a vital raw material, the production may be halted at considerable cost to the firm.

inventory, costs of. When a firm holds goods for future sale, it exposes itself to a number of risks and costs. The effective management of inventory involves a trade-off between having too little and too much inventory. In achieving this trade-off, the financial manager should realize that risks and costs may be closely related. Some costs, such as the purchase price of the goods, involve little risk and may be calculated in advance with some accuracy. Other costs, such as damage to the goods in the warehouse, are incurred only when a risk materializes. Because risks may be viewed as possible future costs, we shall include them as cost items in the following discussion.

The benefits of holding inventory have already been discussed; basically it helps to reduce risks, hold down costs, and increase revenues. To examine inventory from the cost side, we shall identify five categories of costs. The first three are direct costs, the costs immediately connected to buying and holding goods. The last two are indirect costs, the losses of revenues that will vary with differing inventory management decisions.

The five costs of holding inventories are the following:

1. *Materials Costs.* These are the cost of purchasing the goods plus transportation and handling. This may be calculated by adding the purchase price (less any discounts), the delivery charges, and the sales tax (if any).

2. *Order Costs.* These are the variable costs of placing an order for the goods. Each separate shipment involves certain expenses connected with requesting and receiving materials. Examples of these costs are the typing of the order and the inspection of the goods after they arrive. The fewer the orders, the lower the order cost will be for the firm.

3. *Carrying Costs.* These are the expenses of storing goods. Once the goods have been accepted, they become part of the firm's inventories. The following are examples of different kinds of carrying costs:

   a. *Storage Costs.* The firm must provide for storage space, usually through the operation of a warehouse or supply room. The firm must employ workers to move, clean, count, record, and protect the goods. All of these activities dealing with the physical holding of the goods are considered storage costs.

   b. *Insurance.* In spite of the best precautions, firms must protect themselves against such hazards as fire or accidents in the warehouse. Larger amounts of inventory require larger amounts of insurance. The insurance premiums represent a carrying cost on inventory.

   c. *Obsolescence and Spoilage.* When firms hold goods, they expose themselves to the possibility that the goods will not be salable when the time arrives. Obsolescence is the cost of being unable to sell goods because of current market factors deriving from changes in styles, tastes, or other factors. If a product is no longer wanted, the firm will have to sell it at a fraction of its value or destroy it. Spoilage occurs when a product is not salable because of deterioration during storage, such as foods that rot, plants that die, garments that are attacked by moths, candles that discolor, or chemicals that decompose.

   d. *Damage or Theft.* Although a firm will make every effort to protect goods against damage and safeguard items against pilferage, goods will be damaged and stolen. A portion of these expenses will not be covered by insurance and will be losses to the firm. In some businesses, particularly retail stores and firms producing luxury products such as alcoholic beverages, damage and theft may constitute major carrying costs.

4. *Cost of Funds Tied up in Inventory.* Whenever a firm commits its resources to inventory, it is using funds that otherwise might be available for other purposes. A portion of the inventory will be financed by trade credit from suppliers and will involve no cost. If the firm buys clothing on terms of net 30, the clothing may be sold before the firm has to pay its supplier. The balance of the inventory must be financed from the firm's general funds and will involve a cost.

If the firm is considering an expansion of inventory and plans to borrow to obtain funds, the firm will have to pay interest on the additional debt. If the firm finances additional inventory through the sale of common stock, an opportunity cost is involved. The firm has lost the use of funds for other, profit-making purposes. Whatever the source of funds, inventory has a cost in terms of financial resources, and excess inventory represents an unneeded cost.

5. *Cost of Running Out of Goods.* Whenever a firm incurs shortages of products, it incurs costs. If the firm is unable to fill an order, it risks losing a sale. If the firm runs out of raw materials, it may force a costly shutdown of the production process. Adequate inventory helps reduce additional costs and lost revenues caused by shortages.

CROSS-REFERENCES:
direct inventory costs, p. 381
indirect inventory costs, p. 431

inventory, kinds of. Three types of inventories may be identified:

1. *Raw Materials.* These are goods that have not yet been committed to production in a manufacturing firm. Raw materials range from iron ore awaiting processing into steel to electronic components to be incorporated into stereo amplifiers.

2. *Goods In Process.* This category includes those materials that have been committed to the production process but have not been completed. Goods in process include such items as components and subassemblies that are not yet ready to be sold.

3. *Finished Goods.* These are completed products awaiting sale. In a manufacturing firm, they are the final output of the production process. For retail firms and wholesalers, they are usually referred to as the merchandise inventory.

Many firms tie up considerable financial resources in each of the three types of inventories. Income-tax data from the Internal Revenue Service show that inventories average approximately 20 percent of a manufacturing firm's total assets. For retail firms, the figure is closer to 30 percent. These percentages indicate that, for most product-oriented firms, investment in inventory is an important commitment of funds.

inventory, management of important items. In using the computer to minimize the costs of holding inventories, the major emphasis is on items that are considered to be important to the firm's operations. Not all inventory items deserve careful management. If a firm can run out of an item without losing a sale or disappointing a customer, it may waste money to spend time and effort keeping a close watch on the item. Or if the item accounts for relatively few sales in terms of dollars, the firm may spend more managing it than it returns in profits. The types of inventory items that might be considered important to a firm include the following:

1. *High-Cost Items.* If a firm is holding relatively expensive and valuable inventory, such as a jeweler or a firm making certain kinds of electronic components, the loss of a single item can be very costly. These items must be closely managed to prevent theft, breakage, or other loss.

2. *High-Volume or High-Profit Items.* If inventory is important because it accounts for a high volume of sales, it should be managed carefully. The same is true if the item has a high profit margin and a shortage would be costly in terms of lost profits.

3. *Bottleneck Items.* In a production process, certain items are needed for many of the firm's finished goods. If

these items are not available, production may be forced to shut down. As an example, an electronics firm may use the same transistor in a number of its components. If this single transistor were not available, most of the firm's production would be stopped. This bottleneck at a certain point in the production process could prove to be very costly.

CROSS-REFERENCES:
direct inventory costs, p. 381
bottleneck item, p. 325

inventory management, minimizing costs. The goal of effective inventory management is to minimize the direct and indirect costs associated with holding inventories. The inventory specialist estimates the differing expenses with varying inventory levels and chooses the level with the lowest total cost.

The Figure illustrates total inventory costs at five possible levels:

Note that the direct inventory rises with the size of the average inventory.

The cost of funds tied up also rises. Estimated lost sales and production delays decline with increased holdings until they level off at some low level (but never reach zero, since the firm would always expect some shortages). The goal, then, is to find the point at which total costs are lowest, in this example, 30,000 units.

In the Figure we compared only five levels of inventory. With the aid of a computer, we could quickly examine all levels of inventory and determine the optimum holding. The computer is invaluable in managing complex inventories that require us to set levels for a number of items.

CROSS-REFERENCES:
inventory management, how to set up system for, p. 103
order costs, p. 475

inventory management system. A single model that incorporates all of the factors that a firm must consider in order to

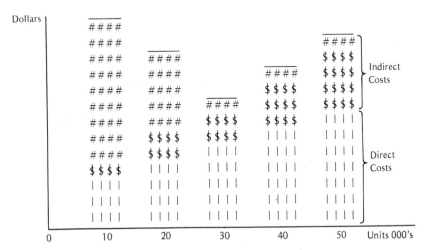

Total Inventory Costs by Direct and Indirect Costs.

minimize the overall costs of carrying inventories. An effective inventory management system involves 3 subsystems: economic order quantity, reorder point, and stock level. The computer brings these subsystems together in the process of managing the firm's inventory.

CROSS-REFERENCES:

inventory turnover. The liquidity of a firm's inventory may be calculated by dividing cost of goods sold by the firm's inventory.

$$\text{inventory turnover} = \frac{\text{cost of goods sold}}{\text{inventory}}$$

The cost of goods sold is for the period being studied, normally 1 year. Two factors are important in calculating this ratio:
1. *Cost of Goods Sold Is More Accurate Than Sales.* The sales figure includes a markup for profit. Thus, a $50 sale may turn over only $30 of inventory. Cost of goods sold in this case would be $30 and would measure actual movement of inventory.
2. *Average Inventory May Be Used.* The inventory may be calculated using an average figure in a manner similar to averaging accounts receivable in calculating the accounts receivable turnover.

The significance of inventory turnover is that it helps the analyst measure the adequacy of goods available to sell compared to the actual sales. In this context, the carrying of inventory involves two risks:
1. *Running Out Of Goods To Sell.* In some industries, customers place orders and are willing to wait for production and delivery of the goods. In most

industries, running out of stock means a loss of sales. When a customer needs an item immediately that the firm does not stock, he will purchase it elsewhere with a consequent loss of profit for the firm. If this happens repeatedly, it can be very costly.
2. *Excessive Carrying Charges Caused by Excessive Inventory.* Maintaining inventory requires the firm to make expenditures for storing the goods, protecting them from theft or breakage, and handling them. If the firm maintains unneeded inventory, it is paying for unnecessary warehouse space, insuring goods that it does not have to hold, and incurring other costs that can be a financial burden on the firm.

Because the manager must compromise between running out of goods to sell and investing in excessive inventory, either a high or low ratio may be an indication of poor management, as follows:
1. *High Turnover May Indicate Future Shortages.* A high inventory turnover will result from the firm maintaining extremely low stocks of goods or raw materials. The low level of finished goods may indicate that the firm will suffer future loss of sales due to an inability to deliver goods promptly. The low level of raw materials could cause future shutdowns of the firm's production line, resulting in higher costs.
2. *Low Turnover May Indicate Overstocking of Inventory.* A low inventory turnover will result from excessive inventory being carried by the firm. The firm may be incurring high costs from overstocking finished goods or raw materials. At the same time, the firm may be carrying obsolete goods in its inventory.

It should be noted that different firms will turn over their inventories at markedly different rates. A firm that has many items at varying stages of production might be expected to have a relatively low turnover. If the inventory contains only a few fast-moving items, a high turnover would be expected. The analyst should remember that high and low turnovers are relative terms. The current turnover must be compared to previous periods or to some industry norms before it is designated as high, low, or normal. The nature of the business should also be considered in analyzing the appropriateness of the size and turnover of the inventory.

Alternative Calculation of Inventory Turnover
An alternative calculation of inventory turnover divides the firm's sales by its inventory. This is less accurate as a measure of turnover since the sales figure includes a mark-up for profit. Because of the profit, the alternative calculation will give a higher turnover than the calculation using cost of goods sold.

$$\text{inventory turnover} = \frac{\text{sales}}{\text{inventory}}$$

Why is an alternative calculation of inventory turnover needed? The answer is that a number of companies who publish financial statistics use the ratio of sales to inventory when they calculate inventory turnover. Dun and Bradstreet, for example, regularly publishes industry norms for industry turnover using sales to inventory. In order to have a figure that can be compared with figures developed by Dun and Bradstreet and others, the analyst must use this alternative calculation of inventory turnover.

CROSS-REFERENCES:
liquidity, how to analyze with ratios, p. 49
liquidity, p. 453

investment banking. The underwriting or sale of securities by financial specialists whose primary function is to facilitate the formation of new capital for businesses and governments. This function is performed by a person, partnership, or corporation called an investment banker.

CROSS-REFERENCE:
commercial bank, p. 351

investment opportunities approach. In the determination of dividend policy, an analytical evaluation that is concerned with the opportunities shareholders have to invest dividends if declared by the firm. If the shareholders can earn a higher return by investing dividends than the firm can earn by retaining earnings, dividends should be declared. If the firm has more profitable opportunities than the shareholders, earnings should be retained.

CROSS-REFERENCES:
Gordon on common stock value, p. 255
Walter and Gordon on dividend decisions, p. 260
Miller and Modigliani on dividend policy, p. 264

investment tax credit. A credit that may be used to reduce the taxes of a firm that has purchased either new or used capital equipment with which to conduct its business. The amount of the deduction will vary with current laws but frequently is in the range of 7 to 10 percent. If the credit cannot be used in a single year, it may be carried back or forward in accordance with IRS regulations. Investment tax credits are approved by the Congress in order to stimulate capital expenditures by business firms.

CROSS-REFERENCE:
lease-buy decision, how to make it, p. 132

K

kiting. The writing of checks against money that has not yet been deposited in the firm's checking account. Kiting is made possible by the float in the banking system (the time required for a check to clear). Since it is illegal to write checks in excess of the balance in the checking account, kiting may be viewed as an illegal practice. Normally, a firm will not be prosecuted if sufficient money has been deposited in the account by the time the check clears. To protect against a "bounced" check, the firm may arrange with the bank for overdraft rights that guarantee that the bank will pay on the check even though the firm may have insufficient funds in the account.

It is not uncommon for firms to use check kiting to slow down their dis-bursements and thus reduce their requirements for cash. A common technique is the payment of funds from a geographically distant bank. One firm makes all its disbursements from a bank located in Montana so as to increase the time a check is in transit. A second technique of kiting is to write checks at some stipulated percent above the cash balance in the checking account. From historical data, the firm may be able to determine that only 80 percent of its checks are cashed within three days. Using this information, the firm will overdraft its checking account knowing that the funds will be deposited before the checks are presented for payment.

CROSS-REFERENCE:

float, p. 409

L

lag. The time between an action and the cash flow resulting from that action.

CROSS-REFERENCE:
cash flow forecast, how to prepare a, p. 97

last-in, first-out (LIFO). A method of valuing inventory and reporting cost of goods sold that assumes that the most recent inventory is used up first. During a period of inflation, this technique undervalues the inventory on the balance sheet but is more accurate than FIFO in reflecting current costs on the income statement.

CROSS-REFERENCES:
first-in, first-out (FIFO), p. 406
inflation, effect on balance sheet, p. 432
inflation, effect on profits, p. 433
inventory, costs of, p. 442

lead time. The period of time between placing an order for inventory and receiving the goods.

CROSS-REFERENCE:
inventory management, how to set up system for, p. 103

leasing. In addition to debt and equity financing, firms have a third source of long-term funds that can be used as a source of assets. Leasing is an arrangement that provides a firm with the use and control over assets without receiving title to them. A lease is the written agreement allowing the use of the assets for a specified period of time. The lease is signed by both the owner of the assets, called the lessor, and the user, called the lessee.

Basic Types of Leases There are three basic types of leases:

1. *Operating Lease.* The operating lease does not impose any long-term obligation on either the lessor or lessee and may usually be canceled by either the owner or user of the assets after giving a certain stipulated notice. An example of an operating lease would be the rental of office space on a 2-year lease cancelable on 60-day notice. This is a familiar kind of lease to most people but is of limited importance to the financial manager.
2. *Service Lease.* Under this arrangement, the lessor provides both financing and servicing of the asset during the lease period. The computer industry, notably International Business Machines (IBM), leases large computer systems under service agreements. Truck and automobile leasing firms also offer service leases.
3. *Financial Lease.* This is a long-term lease on fixed assets that may not be canceled by either party. As a source of funds, the financial lease is basically the same kind of alternative as long-term debt financing. This kind of lease is of primary concern to the financial manager.

CROSS-REFERENCES:
profit planning, how to price the use of a capital asset, p. 53
residual values, how to forecast, p. 66
lease-buy decision, how to make it, p. 132
financial leases, p. 404
operating lease, p. 471
option to purchase, p. 473
option to terminate, p. 474

lease cost, shorthand calculation. Although financial managers should correctly use a present value cash comparison of leasing versus borrowing, in some cases a measure of the relative cost is desired without detailed calculations. One such measure is the before-tax effective cost.

The before-tax effective cost of leasing may be calculated by the following formula:

$$\frac{\text{asset cost}}{\text{lease payment}} = \text{annuity factor}$$

Once we have the annuity factor, we use the annuity table to get the effective cost. Suppose, for example, that for a 10-year lease we get an annuity factor of 5.72. We go to the 10-year line in the annuity table and find the value closest to 5.72. At 12 percent the value is 5.650. Since this is closest to 5.72, we conclude that the lease cost is approximately 12 percent.

EXAMPLE: A firm can lease a $3,000,000 fixed asset for 15 years for $350,000 a year. What is the effective cost of the lease?
ANSWER: $3,000,000/350,000 = 8.57. In the 15-year line, this is closest to 8.559 in the 8 percent column. The effective cost is approximately 8 percent.

Although this technique can be useful as a quick estimate of effective cost, note its major shortcomings:

1. *Before-Tax Comparison.* Since this method omits the tax factors in leasing versus buying, it is really very difficult to compare the effective lease cost with any effective buying cost.

2. *It Only Works with Small Residual Values.* If the cash salvage value of the asset is likely to be sizable, this method ignores it. The effective cost of leasing is much higher when the firm loses the residual value on a valuable asset, such as real estate.

CROSS-REFERENCE:

lease-buy decision, how to make it, p. 132

lease funds, sources of. A number of financial institutions and special leasing companies provide funds for leasing. A firm seeking funds for this purpose will find a variety of institutions competing for its business.

1. *Banks.* Large commercial banks have become increasingly interested in lease financing. Either directly or through the use of a holding company, a bank will make arrangements to purchase equipment and lease it to a customer. This allows the bank to provide an additional service, which helps it to attract the customer for other business and financial services.

2. *Life Insurance Companies.* These firms have become prominent in the long-term leasing of real estate. A life insurance company has large cash inflows that must be invested until needed to make payments on policies. These monies are frequently invested in office buildings or warehouses, which are leased to the occupants under either a financial, service, or operating lease.

3. *Finance Companies.* Commercial finance companies and leasing companies are important sources of funds for specialized equipment and machinery. These companies usually employ a staff of experts who are thoroughly familiar with the resale market for specialized equipment and who can therefore develop the terms of the lease agreement.

leasing, higher cost of. As a cost of financing, leasing will generally be more costly than borrowing for several reasons:

1. *Profit for the Lessor.* The leasing company must pay for its money at rates comparable to other market rates and then must charge a premium to the lessee. This premium represents the profit to the lessor for arranging the financing.

2. *Payment for Expertise.* The leasing company must have employees who are thoroughly knowledgeable on all aspects of the equipment or real estate

Overview of Issues Related to Leasing.

Topic	Issue	Comment
Cash outlay	Does leasing eliminate the need for a down payment?	In some cases. In others, the firm is able to borrow 100% of the asset cost.
Cost	Is leasing more costly than borrowing?	Usually. In some cases, the expertise of the leasing firm allows economies that reduce the cost of leasing below borrowing.
Piecemeal financing	Does leasing help avoid a series of increasingly costly small debt issues?	Not usually since the firm will have other alternatives, including short-term financing or a larger long-term offering than needed.
Borrowing capacity	Does leasing increase the firm's borrowing capacity?	Yes, in most cases. Analysts and the investing public are less conscious of leases than of debt.
Obsolescence	Does leasing shift the risk of obsolescence from the lessee to the lessor?	No. In most cases the risk of obsolescence is considered in the lease contract and the lessee is charged accordingly.
Release from investment	Does leasing allow a firm to gain a release from a bad investment?	Rarely. If the lease is written so that the lessor does not recover his full investment during the lease period, yes. If not, as is usually the case, the asset is fully paid for during the lease period.
Freeing funds	Does leasing free a firm's funds for investment in high-profit current assets?	No. All assets are needed. The leasing may be a way to gain additional assets but it does not free funds for more profitable investments.
Cash salvage value	Is the loss of cash salvage value a cost to leasing?	Yes. The loss of the cash salvage value increases the cost of leasing compared to buying.

being leased. The cost of expert advice to help draw up the lease agreement must be included in the lease payments.

3. *Related Services.* Frequently, a lease agreement includes services related to the equipment. The lessee must bear the cost of such services in the lease payments.

In spite of the general statement that leasing is more costly, the real cost of leasing versus debt financing can only be determined by an analysis of cash flows, using present-value techniques or some other measurement of cost. In some cases, the specialized knowledge of the leasing company allows a lower lease cost. For example, if the leasing company makes volume purchases of equipment, the company may be able to buy equipment at a lower price than the firm. This would allow the leasing firm to calculate its charges on a lower base than debt calculations and result in a lower cost for leasing.

CROSS-REFERENCE:
financial leases, p. 404

leasing, overview. The different issues related to leasing versus buying should be considered in the light of the individual situation being faced by the firm. The various issues and some characteristics are illustrated in the Table.

CROSS-REFERENCES:
piecemeal financing, p. 478
sale and leaseback, p. 517

level-rental plan lease. A straight lease that obligates a firm to make a series of identical payments over the service life of the asset. As an example of this form of lease, consider a lease agreement on a machine costing $100,000. The leasing firm will finance the asset under a level-rental plan to yield 10 percent over a 5-year lease period. The amount of the annual payment would be determined with the aid of a present-value table. The formula is

$$\frac{\text{annual payment}}{} = \frac{\text{asset cost}}{\text{present-value factor (annuity table)}}$$

Using the annuity table, the present-value factor for 5 years at 10 percent is 3.791. The calculation of the annual payment is

$$\text{annual payment} = \frac{\$100,000}{3.791} = \$26,378$$

Under this lease agreement, the lessee would have use of the asset for 5 years for an annual payment of $26,378.

CROSS-REFERENCE:
lease-buy decision, how to make it, p. 132

leverage. A general, dictionary definition of the term leverage would refer to an increased means of accomplishing some purpose. In some cases, as with lifting heavy objects, leverage allows us to accomplish things not otherwise possible.
    In the area of finance, we can identify many different types of leverage.

All types deal with some means of increasing or accelerating profits. In most cases, the effects are reversible, so the leverage may be favorable or unfavorable.
    We distinguish several different types of leverage. Each will link a profit measure, such as return on investment or earnings before taxes, with another area of a firm's operating or financial situation. Each type of leverage may be used as a tool of financial planning, because each provides insights into specific areas of the firm's anticipated profits.

CROSS-REFERENCES:
leverage, how to use in profit planning, p. 44
unfavorable financial leverage, p. 541
financial leverage, how to analyze, p. 34
favorable financial leverage, p. 401

liabilities. The debts of a firm. These are normally divided into current liabilities and long-term liabilities.

CROSS-REFERENCES:
accounts payable, p. 305
contingent liability, p. 357
long-term liabilities, p. 455

lien. A legal claim against the physical property, such as a lien on a building, which is obtained as collateral for the payment of the mortgage or other legal debt.

CROSS-REFERENCE:
encumbrance, p. 394

LIFO. The Last-In, First-Out method of valuing inventory and reporting cost of goods sold that assumes that the most recent inventory is used up first. During a period of inflation, this technique undervalues the inventory on the balance sheet but is more accurate than FIFO in reflecting current costs on the income statement.

CROSS-REFERENCES:
FIFO, p. 401
inflation, effect on balance sheet, p. 432
inflation, effect on profits, p. 433
inventories, p. 441

limited liability. A feature of the corporate form of organization that provides legal protection for the owners of a business firm against losing more than their initial investment in the business. A disadvantage to sole proprietorship and partnerships is that they generally do not afford limited liability to the owners.

CROSS-REFERENCE:
corporate form, advantages of, p. 363

limited-return securities. The preferred stock or bonds issued by a firm which offer a stated or fixed return to the holder, as opposed to common stock which offers unlimited return.

CROSS-REFERENCE:
financial leverage, how to analyze, p. 34

line of credit. The maximum amount of money or merchandise that a lender or supplier will extend to a firm without further credit analysis or collateral. The firm can borrow or purchase on credit against the line as long as all payments are current and the total borrowing does not exceed the amount of the line of credit.

CROSS-REFERENCE:
annual cleanup, p. 310

liquidation value. The value of the securities of a firm if it is assumed that the firm were to go out of business. In effect, the liquidation value is calculated by assuming that the firm sells its assets, pays off its creditors, and divides the remainder among its shareholders.

CROSS-REFERENCES:
liquidity, p. 453
value, differing concepts of, p. 543

liquidity. The firm's ability to pay its bills as they come due, normally measured by comparing the amount of the firm's current liabilities with its liquid assets.

CROSS-REFERENCES:
liquidity, how to analyze with ratios, p. 49
receivables management, how to evaluate differing credit policies, p. 108
acid-test ratio, p. 307
current ratio, p. 371
cash, needs for, p. 345
liquidation value, p. 453
net working capital, p. 467

liquidity functions. In seeking sufficient liquidity to carry out the firm's activities, the financial manager performs tasks such as the following:

1. *Forecasting Cash Flows.* Successful day-to-day operations require the firm to be able to promptly pay its bills. This is largely a matter of matching cash inflows against outflows. The firm must be able to forecast the sources and timing of inflows from customers and use them to pay its creditors and suppliers.
2. *Raising Funds.* The firm receives its financing from a variety of sources. At different times some sources will be more desirable than others. A possible source of funds may not, at a given time, have sufficient funds available to meet the firm's needs. Or the funds may be prohibitively expensive. The financial manager must

identify the amount of funds available from each source and the periods of time during which the funds will be needed; then he must take steps to ensure that the funds will actually be available and committed to his firm. As an example, he may decide to sell additional shares of the firm's stock to raise money. When a firm issues new common stock, it generally uses the services of an investment banker. The banker helps the firm to find sufficient purchasers to buy all the new shares at a fair price to the firm. If the issue is not properly timed, it may fail to raise the money needed by the firm.

3. *Managing the Flow of Internal Funds.* A large firm will have a number of different bank accounts for varying operating divisions or for special purposes. The money that flows among these internal accounts should be carefully monitored. Frequently, a firm will have excess cash in one bank account when it has a need for cash elsewhere in the firm. By continuously checking on the cash levels in the headquarter's and each operating division's accounts, the manager will be able to achieve a high degree of liquidity with minimum external borrowing. Shortages and the costs associated with short-term borrowing are reasons to aggressively control the use and distribution of the firm's money.

CROSS-REFERENCE:
profitability functions, p. 493

liquidity-profitability approach to financial goals. This classification states that the financial manager has two goals to achieve:

1. *Liquidity.* By liquidity we mean that the firm has adequate cash on hand to meet its obligations at all times. Stated another way, the firm will be able to pay all its bills when due and have sufficient cash to take any unanticipated discounts for large cash purchases. In addition, the firm must have a certain level above its expected needs to act as a reserve to meet emergencies.

2. *Profitability.* This goal requires the firm's operations to yield a long-term profit for the stockholders as part of the overall goal of maximizing the present value of the common stock.

CROSS-REFERENCE:
profits, how to maintain under inflation, p. 59

lock-box. A post office box used to speed up cash collections. A customer mails the payment of a bill to a firm at a designated post office box. The firm's bank will empty the box on at least a daily basis, deposit the checks directly in the firm's account, and send the firm a listing of the collections along with any enclosures sent in by the customers. Lock-boxes will generally be regionally disbursed and funds, when received, will be wired to the firm's primary bank. In setting up a lock-box system, a firm must weigh the benefits of more rapid cash collections against the costs of setting up the system.

long-range planning. The process of establishing goals for a period in excess of one year and developing ways to reach them. To be effective in a corporate setting, long-range planning must coordinate inputs from marketing, production, finance, and the other operating areas of the firm and bring them together in a single course of action consistent with the objectives of the firm.

CROSS-REFERENCE:
planning, p. 479

long-term capital gain. A profit made on the sale of a capital asset when the asset is held for a predetermined period of time, normally 6 months to a year, so that the gain receives a special tax treatment by the Internal Revenue Service.

CROSS-REFERENCES:

tax factors affecting return, how to evaluate, p. 72
capital gain, p. 333

long-term liabilities. Balance sheet accounts representing debts of the firm which will not be paid off during the next year. Examples are the following:

1. *Notes Payable.* These are promissory notes with maturities in excess of 1 year. When the note enters its final year, it will be transferred to a current-liabilities account.

2. *Bonds.* The major source of long-term financing for most firms is through the issuance of bonds. Bonds are usually sold (floated) to the general public in the form of debentures. A debenture is a general obligation of the firm and is not secured by specific physical assets. Frequently, the balance sheet will list all major bond offerings currently outstanding and the interest owed on the bonds on an annual basis.

3. *Mortgages.* When a firm borrows money for the long term with land or a building pledged as specific collateral, the debt is shown on the balance sheet as a mortgage.

CROSS-REFERENCES:

flow-of-funds statement, how to develop from balance sheet and income statement, p. 38
long-term financing, how to compare different alternatives, p. 139
liabilities, p. 452

margin purchases. The buying of securities when a portion of the purchase price has been borrowed.

CROSS-REFERENCE:
margin requirement, p. 456

margin requirement. A regulation of the Federal Reserve System that stipulates the minimum percentage of a purchase price that may be borrowed in a margin purchase of securities.

CROSS-REFERENCE:
margin purchases, p. 456

marginal analysis. An approach to profit planning which breaks down an income statement into fixed and variable costs. Break-even analysis is an extension of marginal analysis.

CROSS-REFERENCE:
varying sales levels or costs, how to analyze effect of, p. 74
break-even analysis, p. 325

marginal contribution. A profit measure calculated by subtracting total variable costs from total sales. It may be calculated on a unit basis by subtracting the variable cost per unit from the selling price per unit. It may also be expressed as a percent when the marginal contribution in dollars is divided by the revenues in dollars. Marginal contribution is an important concept in break-even analysis.

CROSS-REFERENCES:
leverage, how to use in profit planning, p. 44
profit-volume analysis, how to use, p. 64
income statement, marginal analysis format, p. 430
break-even analysis, p. 325

marginal cost of capital. The cost that new financing has on the firm's weighted-average cost of capital. If a firm raises more than a given amount of debt or equity, it will raise the specific cost of that kind of financing. This will raise the weighted-average cost of capital for the firm. For example, if a firm raises considerable funds through debt financing, the interest costs will rise. This will raise the weighted-average cost of capital. Similarly, a large equity offering

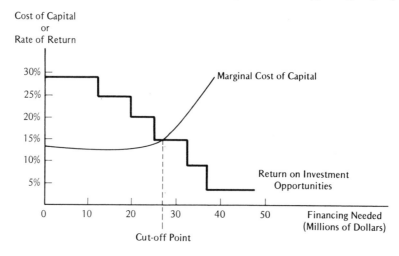

can only be successful at a lower price for the common stock. The lower issue price will raise the firm's cost of capital.

CROSS-REFERENCES:
weighted-average cost of capital, p. 548

market for corporate securities, overview (see Figure below).

CROSS-REFERENCES:
primary issue, p. 488
secondary markets, p. 519
over-the-counter market, p. 475

market rate of return[E(Rtn)Mkt]. The expected return on the market portfolio; that is, on a portfolio consisting of all securities weighted at their respective market values. For example, assume that the market is defined as all common stocks listed on a regional stock exchange. Further assume that these stocks were worth 900 million dollars today, that they rose from 850 million dollars one year ago, and that they declared and paid cash dividends of 60 million dollars in the past year. The market rate of return could be calculated by the formula:

$$E(Rtn)Mkt = \frac{V_1 - V_0 + Div}{V_0}$$

where
$E(Rtn)Mkt$ = market rate of return

V_1 = value of securities at market at end of year one

V_0 = value of securities at market at year zero

Div = dividends paid during period

In our example, the market rate of return would be (000's):

$$E(Rtn)Mkt = \frac{900,000 - 850,000 + 60,000}{850,000}$$

$$= \frac{110,000}{850,000}$$

$$= 12.9 \text{ percent}$$

CROSS-REFERENCE:
capital asset pricing model, p. 279

market premium. The amount by which the market price of a convertible security exceeds the value of an equal-risk security lacking a conversion feature.

CROSS-REFERENCE:
convertible security, p. 359

market price. The expected value of a security if it is sold to persons or institutions normally purchasing such a security.

CROSS-REFERENCE:
common stock value, how to compare two or more stocks, p. 83

market value. The value of the securities of a firm as reflected in the bond or stock market's perception of the firm.

marketable securities. Short-term debt securities that can readily be converted into cash to provide a firm with liquidity, while still earning a return on its funds. Marketable securities include Treasury bills and notes, certificates of deposit, and commercial paper.

materials cost. In inventory management, the purchase price plus transportation and handling of the items of inventory.

maximization of profits. A frequently stated goal of the firm is to maximize profits. Many businessmen believe that as long as they are earning as much as possible while holding down costs, they are achieving this goal. Profit maximization has the benefit of being a simple and straightforward statement of purpose. It is easily understood as a rational goal for a business and it focuses the firm's efforts toward making money.

Profit maximization is widely professed, but in fact the concept has several weaknesses:

1. *It Is Vague.* The problem here lies in a definition of the term profits. Profits in the short run may be quite different from profits in the long run. If a firm continues to operate a piece of machinery without proper maintenance, it may be able to lower this year's operating expenditures. This will increase profits. But the firm will pay for the short-run saving in future years when the machine is no longer capable of operating because of prior neglect. Clearly, maximizing profits does not mean neglecting the long-term picture in favor of short-term considerations.

2. *It Ignores Timing.* Because money received today has a higher value than money received next year, a profit-seeking organization must consider the timing of cash flows and profits. If a firm is maximizing profits, does it select a 3-year project with a 20 percent return or a 5-year project with a 17 percent return? The 17 percent project may result in greater total profits if the firm could not immediately reinvest its profits when they were received from the 3-year project.

3. *It Overlooks Quality Aspects of Future Activities.* Businesses do not carry on their activities solely with an eye to achieving the highest possible profits. Some businesses have placed a higher value on growth of sales, and are willing to accept lower profits to gain the stability provided by a large volume of sales. Other businesses recognize that diversifying their activities into different products or markets strengthens the firm, even though it may result in short-term declines in profits. Other firms use a portion of their profits to achieve social goals or to make contributions to society. It is widely observed that nonprofit factors influence the determination of corporate goals, even in firms professing to maximize profits.

CROSS-REFERENCE:

profits, p. 490

maximization of wealth. Another frequently encountered objective of a firm is to maximize the value of the firm over the long run. This goal may also be stated as the maximization of wealth, when wealth is defined as the net present worth of the firm. Rather than focusing directly on profits, this goal emphasizes the impact of profits on the current market value of the firm's securities, notably its common stock. Naturally, there is a correlation between the present worth of a firm and its value over the long run. If the firm will be highly valuable for the foreseeable future, it will have a high current value. The reverse would be true for a firm with poor future prospets.

The maximization-of-wealth objective is linked to the long-term profits of the firm. A simple calculation that links current value with long-term profits is given below at foot of page.

As an example, if a firm expects a profit of $100,000 a year for many years into the future, the firm would have a present worth of $1,000,000 to a person who was considering purchasing the firm and who desires a 10 percent return on the money invested ($100,000/.10 = $1,000,000). If the firm expected $150,-000 profit each year, we would expect the firm to have a higher present value. By applying the formula, we can see that the firm's present worth would increase to $1,500,000 ($150,000/.10).

Maximization of wealth implies other factors in addition to profits. Long-run value is affected by the firm's growth, the amount of risk it offers to investors, the price of its stock, and the dividends it pays. As a general guideline, a firm that is maximizing wealth must do the following:

1. *Avoid High Levels of Risk.* If a firm is taking a long-term perspective on its business operations, it must avoid unnecessary or high levels of risk. Projects that promise exceptionally high profits with relatively high degrees of risk are not accepted. Accepting these projects over the long-run means that a single major failure might jeopardize the firm's continued operation.

2. *Pay Dividends.* Dividends are payments from the firm to the stockholders who own the firm. Dividends must be consistent with the firm's and stockholders' needs. During the firm's early, high-growth years, dividends may be small or may take the form of stock to allow the firm to conserve its cash. As the firm reaches maturity and needs to retain less cash to finance its expansion, it will be able to pay out a larger share of profits as dividends. By paying consistent, reasonable dividends, the firm helps attract investors seeking dividends, which maintains the value of the stock in the market and keeps up its present worth.

3. *Seek Growth.* As a firm increases sales and develops new markets for its products, it protects itself against a business setback that might drive it

Formula	Definition of Terms
$Val_{curr} = \dfrac{earn.}{des.\ ret.}$	where Val_{curr} = current market value in dollars earn. = forecasted annual earnings des. ret. = return on the investment desired by the investor

Current Value Expressed as a Function of Future Earnings.

from the marketplace. A large, stable, and diversified volume of sales provides a cushion for the firm against economic recessions, changes in consumer preferences, or other reductions in demand for the firm's products. For this reason, firms taking a maximization-of-wealth approach are continually seeking growth in sales and earnings.

4. *Maintain Market Price of Stock.* The value of the firm's common stock in the marketplace is a matter of primary concern to a management pursuing a goal of wealth maximization. It is the price of the common stock that is, in effect, being maximized. A company's management can take a number of positive steps to maintain the market price of the stock at reasonable levels. By taking time to explain company actions, the managers can encourage individuals to invest in the firm's stock, thus creating a demand for the stock. By seeking sound investments, the firm will appear to be a wise investment choice over the long term. These and other actions can help to draw attention to the firm and keep the present worth of its stock at high levels.

Maximization of wealth is more useful than maximization of profits as a statement of the objective of most business firms. It properly points out that the profit factor should be considered from a long-term point of view. At the same time, it balances this single factor with related goals such as growth, stability, risk avoidance, and the market price of the firm's stock.

CROSS-REFERENCE:
wealth, p. 548

merger. A combination of two or more businesses in which only one of the corporations survives. The other corporation goes out of existence and its assets and, possibly, debts are taken over by the surviving corporation. In a merger of companies X and Y, company X may continue while Y ceases to exist.

The merger may occur four ways:
1. *Purchase of Assets.* The assets of company Y may be sold to company X. Once this is done, company Y is a corporate shell with a capital structure but no resources. The company will then be legally terminated and company X survives in the asset merger.
2. *Purchase of Common Stock.* The common stock of company Y may be purchased. When company X holds the stock of company Y, company Y will be dissolved.
3. *Exchange of Stock for Assets.* Company X may give shares of X common stock to the shareholders of Y for the assets of Y. Then Y is terminated by a vote of its shareholders, who now hold X stock.
4. *Exchange of Stock for Stock.* Company X gives its shares to the shareholders of Y. Then Y is terminated.

State laws govern the merger of firms into a single economic unit. In most cases, the merger must be recommended by the boards of directors of both firms and must be approved by a majority to three fourths of the shareholders in accordance with the applicable state laws.

Kinds of Mergers Three major types of mergers have been important in the development of large American corporations:
1. *Horizontal Merger.* This is the joining of two firms in the same area of business. Examples would be the combining of two book publishers or two manufacturers of toys.
2. *Vertical Merger.* This is the joining of two firms involved in different stages of the production or distribution of the same product. Examples would be the combining of a coal company and a railroad that carries the coal or the joining of a typewriter manufac-

turer and a chain of office supply stores.

3. *Conglomerate Merger.* A conglomerate is a firm that has external growth through a number of mergers of companies whose businesses were not related either vertically or horizontally. A typical conglomerate might have operating areas in manufacturing, electronics, insurance, and other unrelated businesses.

CROSS-REFERENCES:
statutory merger, p. 525
acquisitions, how to analyze, p. 78
mergers, how to analyze profitability in a ten-step process, p. 85
conglomerate, p. 356
consolidation in merger, p. 356
takeover strategies in mergers, p. 535

mergers, overview of.

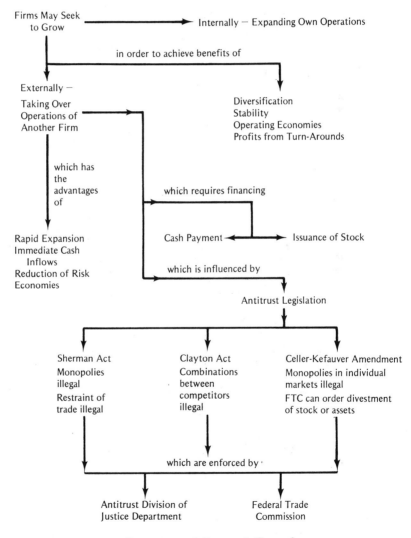

Overview of External Growth.

mergers, tax factors affecting. An important factor affecting external growth is the level of taxation and the tax regulations. A number of studies have been conducted since World War II; these indicate that tax considerations have played a major role in mergers and acquisitions. Two kinds of tax effects are particularly important as factors in business combinations:

1. *Tax-Loss Credits.* When a corporation sustains an ordinary operating loss, the loss may be averaged over an 8-year period. This is designed to allow a firm with widely fluctuating income to gain the full tax benefits from its losses. The law requires the firm to carry a loss back 3 years and forward 5 years. The loss is first carried back to the earliest year. If the loss exceeds the earnings before taxes, it is used to reduce EBT to zero; the balance is used to reduce earnings in the next year; and so on. If the loss carry-back exceeds the earnings for the 3 prior years, a loss carry-forward allows the firm to gain a tax credit in the future years up to 5 years ahead.

EXAMPLE: A firm has a loss of $4,000,000 in 1974. It had an EBT of $500,000 in 1971, $1,200,000 in 1972, $300,000 in 1973, $1,500,000 in 1975, $3,000,000 in 1976, and $2,000,000 in 1977. How is the loss applied to reduce the firm's taxes?

ANSWER: The loss is applied as follows (figures are in millions of dollars):

When two corporations merge, the privilege of applying the tax carry-back or carry-forward can be gained by the new corporation. Thus, a profitable firm can benefit from tax breaks that cannot be used by an unprofitable firm. A corporation can acquire a firm with a tax loss, operate it as a subsidiary, and combine the tax returns to gain the tax refund or savings. A combination would be especially attractive if the acquiring firm can turn around the unprofitable firm at the same time it is benefiting from the tax shelter.

Normally, a tax loss carry-back or carry-forward can be gained by a combination if the following apply:

a. The acquisition was made for a sound business purpose, not solely to gain the tax break.

b. The tax-loss firm is held at least 2 years by the acquiring firm.

c. The business operations of the tax-loss firm are continued by the acquiring firm.

2. *Converting Ordinary Income to Capital Gains.* Shareholders receive dividends as their primary income from common-stock investments. The first $100 of dividends ($200 if jointly owned by husband and wife) is excluded from taxable income. All dividend income above $100 is taxed as ordinary income.

When a shareholder sells common stock for more than the purchase price, the profit is taxed by either of two methods. If the stock was held for less than one year, the gain is taxed as ordinary income. If the stock was held for a period in excess of

Year	Old EBT	Loss Carry-Back	Carry-Forward	New EBT	Tax Saving or Tax Refund
1971	.5	.5		0	.25
1972	1.2	1.2		0	.6
1973	.3	.3		0	.15
1975	1.5		1.5	0	.75
1976	3.0		.5	2.5	.25
		2.0	2.0		

12 months, the profit is taxed as a capital gain. The tax rate for the long-term gain is the same as for ordinary income, but only one-half the gain is included in the tax calculation. This has the effect of cutting the tax on the capital gain to a maximum of 25 percent (for stockholders in the 50 percent bracket).

Rather than continue to pay 50 percent tax on dividends, a shareholder might decide to sell out and accept the capital gain with its 25 percent tax rate. Evidence indicates that this is a motive in many business combinations.

monetary policy, effect on balance of payments. A means of reducing balance-of-payments deficits is through a governmental program that restricts the amount of money in circulation. This works for several reasons including:
1. *Helps Hold Down Prices.* By restricting the growth of the money supply, a nation encourages reductions in the rate of inflation.
2. *Makes Exporting More Attractive.* Since the nation does not have sufficient money supply to purchase all the products of the national industries, companies are encouraged to export to gain additional sales and higher prices for their goods.
3. *Makes Importing Less Attractive.* The lower prices and lack of excess money tends to discourage foreigners from bringing goods into the country.
4. *Attracts Investment.* If a policy of tight money results in economic stability and steady price levels, foreigners

may be attracted to invest in the stable economic environment.

Monetary policy, though possibly effective, is not a popular way for governments to deal with balance-of-payments deficits. The drawbacks include:
1. *Hurts Economic Growth.* An expanding money supply provides funds for economic activity and growth in the gross national product. It also encourages higher levels of employment than does a program of tight money. Most nations consider economic growth and full employment to be higher goals than elimination of deficits and thus decline to employ monetary policy to correct deficits.
2. *Difficult to Use Effectively.* An economy may have many pressures that cause inflation and balance of payments deficits. Restricting the size of the money supply cannot always be used effectively to deal with deficits. Highly developed countries, such as the United States and United Kingdom, with broad capital markets and large financial institutions can effectively use monetary policy, if they are willing to pay the price. Lesser-developed countries with limited resources and capital cannot easily use monetary policy to reduce the size of deficits.
3. *Has Time Lag Between Action and Results.* Controls on credit and the money supply must be gradually applied. Thus, considerable time is required before they have any effect on balance of payments deficits. This time lag means that monetary policy offers a longer-term approach to dealing with deficits, but it is not effective within a time period of a few months or a year.

monetary reserves. The stores of value supporting a national currency. The monetary reserves must be of unquestionable value in a stable monetary system. In addition, the growing need for currencies to finance world trade and other international transactions means that monetary reserves must be capable of expansion. Using this dual yardstick, three major monetary reserves have been:

1. *Gold.* Throughout history, gold has been accepted as a store of value. Recent developments have reinforced the fact that individuals and nations desire to hold gold. But gold has a flaw as a monetary reserve because the world's supply of gold is limited and new sources of gold are relatively few compared to the industrial and monetary needs for gold. If a new monetary system relies heavily on monetary gold to support its currencies, we might expect problems with expanding currencies to meet international needs.

2. *Convertible Currencies.* The U.S. dollar and British pound sterling are the convertible currencies that have traditionally been held as monetary reserves. Both currencies have experienced difficulties in recent years and have declined in value. They do not meet the standard of unquestioned value. Another problem arises when the currencies expand internationally to meet the needs of other nations. The only way for foreigners to get dollars or sterling to hold as reserves is for the United States and United Kingdom to run balance-of-payments deficits. It is difficult to have balance-of-payments deficits and remain as a strong and stable currency. The dollar achieved this goal for many years through the 1950s and 1960s, but finally the deficits destroyed international confidence in the currency.

3. *Special Drawing Rights (SDR's).* The International Monetary Fund has artificially created SDR's and many observers hope this unit will become the monetary reserve of the future, replacing both gold and convertible currencies. SDR's are created by a bookkeeping entry and hence can be increased steadily to meet needs. The value of SDR's can be held stable as long as the IMF nations support them and accept them. Although it is too early to draw conclusions on the success of the SDR's, they offer a hope for a future reserve asset that is both strong and capable of expanding to meet the world's liquidity needs.

CROSS-REFERENCES:

money market. Financial intermediaries, such as banks and insurance companies, that form the link between suppliers and demanders of short-term funds. As is shown in the diagram, the money market differs from the capital market where long-term funds are handled. The key participants in both money and capital markets are the financial intermediaries who handle the funds, and the private individuals, businesses, and state and federal governments who act as suppliers or users of funds. The money market is an intangible linkage of financial institutions with no central location, although a large number of the transactions take place in New York City. The capital market has a similar informal linkage as well as formal organizations such as the New York Stock Exchange, the New York Bond Exchange, and the over-the-counter market.

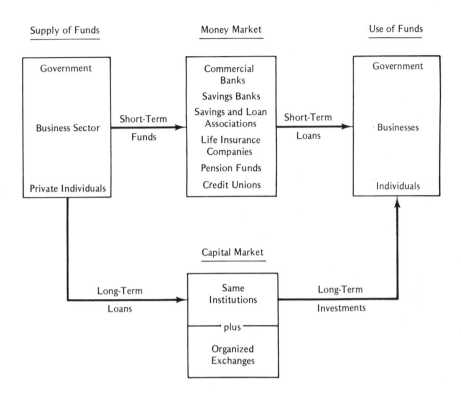

Supply of Funds   Money Market   Use of Funds

Government	Commercial Banks	Government
Business Sector	Savings Banks / Savings and Loan Associations / Life Insurance Companies / Pension Funds / Credit Unions	Businesses
Private Individuals		Individuals

Short-Term Funds →

Short-Term Loans →

Capital Market

Long-Term Loans →

Same Institutions

— plus —

Organized Exchanges

Long-Term Investments →

mortgage bond. A bond secured by a lien on real property or buildings. A first mortgage bond gives the holder a priority claim on the assets. A second mortgage bond gives a secondary claim, following the claim of a first mortgage holder.

municipal bonds. Debt securities used by governmental bodies at the state and local levels to raise money to finance governmental activities. The distinguishing characteristic of municipal bonds in the investment community is that the interest is exempt from federal income taxes and may also be exempt from state income taxes in the state in which the bonds are issued. The tax exempt status of municipal bonds makes them particularly attractive to wealthy individuals in high tax brackets.

mutually exclusive project. Two or more capital-budgeting proposals that provide alternative solutions to a single problem so that the acceptance of one eliminates the others from further consideration. An example would be a conveyor belt competing with a forklift to move boxes in a warehouse.

N

Nacional Financiera. In addition to regional development banks, many individual nations have established their own national banks. An example of a national development bank is the *Nacional Financiera* in Mexico. This bank was founded in the 1930s with an original goal of assisting the Mexican bank system. Since the 1940s, the bank has primarily been concerned with Mexican industrial development. Generally it is viewed as an example of what can be accomplished by a successful national development bank.

CROSS-REFERENCE:
Development Bank, p. 380

national association of security dealers (NASD). An association of brokers and dealers who trade securities in the over-the-counter market. The NASD regulates the over-the-counter market and has rules and regulations designed to promote fair dealings between dealers, brokers, and customers. Violation of the regulations of the NASD may result in disciplinary action or loss of membership for member firms and individuals.

CROSS-REFERENCE:
over-the-counter market, p. 475

negotiable. A term describing checks, drafts, or securities that may be transferred from one person to another by means of an endorsement or delivery.

negotiable certificate of deposit. The receipt for a time deposit in a bank that can be traded from one individual to another. A strong secondary market exists for negotiable certificates of deposit with yields above those on Treasury bills.

CROSS-REFERENCES:
certificates of deposit, p. 346
treasury bills, p. 538

net cash benefits. In capital budgeting, the differential after-tax cash flow which will result from a proposal.

CROSS-REFERENCES:
cash-flow stream, how to calculate, p. 3
internal rate of return, how to calculate, p. 15
risk in capital budget, how to measure, p. 25

net cash outlay. In capital budgeting, the differential after-tax cash needed to finance a capital-budgeting proposal.

CROSS-REFERENCES:
cash-flow stream, how to calculate, p. 3
internal rate of return, how to calculate, p. 15

net income after taxes (NIAT). A firm's after tax earnings, as reported to its shareholders.

CROSS-REFERENCES:
flow-of-funds statement, how to develop from balance sheet and income statement, p. 38
profitability, how to analyze with ratios, p. 56
profit-volume analysis, how to use, p. 64
Miller and Modigliani on cost of capital, p. 213
funds from operations, p. 417

net present value. In capital budgeting, a calculation of the return provided by a specific stream of net cash benefits as compared to a specific net cash outlay using the firm's cost of capital. If the value of the benefits exceeds the value of the outlay, the stream has a higher return than the cost of capital and therefore the proposal is acceptable. If the present value of the benefits are less than the outlay, the project does not achieve a rate of return equal to the firm's cost of capital and therefore it is not acceptable. To compare projects with differing dollar amounts, the present value of the net cash benefits may be divided by the present value of the net cash outlay to get a profitability index.

net proceeds. The amount of money actually received by the firm as the result of a securities offering.

net working capital. The difference between a firm's current assets and current liabilities. Net working capital is useful as a measure of the firm's liquidity.

net worth. The value of the ownership rights in a business, also called equity.

net write off. In accounting, the removal of a fixed asset from the books of the company when both the asset at its original cost and the associated accumulated depreciation are removed. A net write off is viewed as a source of funds when an analyst is preparing a flow-of-funds statement using a balance sheet and income statement for a firm.

New York Stock Exchange. In addition to the over-the-counter market, corporate securities can be traded on the various stock exchanges. A stock exchange is a central location where members may buy or sell securities. Stocks and bonds may be listed by companies seeking greater marketability of the stock and greater liquidity for shareholders, who may, through their brokers, bring the stocks to the exchange to be traded.

The New York Stock Exchange is the largest in the country and accounts for the majority of dollar value and number of shares of stock traded on all U.S. exchanges. Historically, the exchange is traced back to a group of businessmen who began trading securities on Wall Street in the 1790s. Stocks and bonds can be traded on the floor of the New York Stock Exchange only by members. There are over 1,300 members, each of whom must own a seat, which is identical to membership. Only individuals may own seats but the individual may be associated with others in a corporation or partnership.

next-in, first-out (NIFO). A method of inventory valuation and reporting cost of goods sold that assumes that the next item of inventory to be purchased is the correct cost basis for the last item sold. It is based on the argument that the correct current cost will be reflected the next time the firm purchases inventory. During a period of rising prices, this technique would undervalue inventory on the balance sheet but would be fairly accurate in estimating cost of goods sold on the income statement. NIFO is a planning tool only since, at the present time, it is not permitted under the regulations of the Internal Revenue Service.

CROSS-REFERENCES:
inflation, effect on balance sheet, p. 432
inflation, effect on profits, p. 433

noncash charges or expenses. Expenses that are deducted for tax purposes on the firm's income statement but which require no cash outlay. Depreciation is the most common noncash charge.

CROSS-REFERENCE:
depreciation, p. 379

nontaxable reorganization. Tax considerations will affect the form of external growth. In an acquisition of stock for cash, the seller will be required to pay taxes on any gain in value he receives as a result of the sale. For example, suppose a stockholder paid $100,000 for 5,000 shares of stock and now he is selling the stock for $500,000. The seller will be required to pay capital gains taxes on the $400,000 difference between what he originally paid for the stock and the selling price today. The requirement to pay taxes on the gain may affect his willingness to sell the common stock.

To avoid the payment of these taxes immediately, a business combination must qualify as a nontaxable reorganization under the terms of the Internal Revenue Service code. A reorganization is defined as a readjustment of corporate structure or ownership and may occur either when one corporation acquires the stock of another or when an existing corporation changes its capital structure or name, place, or form of organization. The following conditions generally apply to all nontaxable reorganizations:

1. The reorganization must be a sound business purpose, as opposed to being a scheme to avoid taxes.
2. There must be a continuity of ownership interest by the former stockholders of the acquired corporation.
3. The combination must comply with both the technical form and the intention of the law and Internal Revenue regulations.

To qualify as a nontaxable reorganization, a business combination may assume one of three forms, called types A, B, and C reorganizations because they are discussed in paragraphs (A), (B), and (C) in a section of the Internal Revenue code. The types and their characteristics are as follows:

1. *Type A: Statutory Merger or Consolidation.* This merger takes place in strict compliance with a state statute and is frequently called a statutory merger. The key features of this type of merger are the following:
   a. It is the only form of nontaxable reorganization in which the acquiring corporation may give considerable amounts of cash, bonds, or nonvoting stock.
   b. The continuity-of-interest requirement may be met if the selling shareholders retain voting stock equivalent to as little as 50 percent of their premerger voting interest.

c. Many state statutes are not acceptable to all parties and may not be usable for a merger. The statute may have restrictions, burdensome requirements for completing the merger, or other objectionable features.

d. The surviving corporation under most state laws must assume the liabilities of the acquired corporations.

2. *Type B: Exchange of Stock for Stock.* This occurs when a firm acquires the stock of another corporation solely in exchange for voting stock of the acquiring corporations. Key features are the following:

a. The acquiring firm must receive at least 80 percent of the common (voting and nonvoting) stock of another firm in a single transaction or in a series of transactions taking place in a short period of time. This allows the acquiring firm to gain the 80 percent of the stock through exchanges with a number of shareholders.

b. No cash, property, securities, or nonvoting stock may be issued by the acquiring corporation in the deal.

c. The acquired corporation may be continued as a subsidiary of the acquiring corporation, or at the option of the acquiring corporation, a merger or consolidation may take place.

d. If the acquiring firm retains the acquired firm as a subsidiary, the liabilities of the subsidiary firm do not become obligations of the parent firm.

3. *Type C: Exchange of Stock for Assets.* This occurs when a firm transfers substantially all its assets to the acquiring corporation mostly in exchange for voting stock in the acquiring corporation. Key features are the following:

a. The acquired firm must transfer at least 90 percent of the fair market value of its net assets (an amount equal to the firm's equity) in the transaction.

b. Some or all of the liabilities of the acquired corporation may be assumed by the acquiring company. In this case, the assets transferred must equal at least 70 percent of the acquired firm's total assets.

c. Cash, not to exceed 20 percent of the gross assets, may be issued as part of the transaction.

d. The acquiring firm may refuse to assume the liabilities of the acquired firm, thus reducing dangers from unknown or contingent obligations.

CROSS-REFERENCES:

reorganization, p. 508
statutory merger, p. 525

normal dividend payout. The ratio of dividends to earnings that is expected by the stockholders and investing public so that they will continue to purchase and hold the stock. If the actual payout is higher than the normal, the stock will rise in value because income-conscious investors will purchase it for the dividends. If the actual payout is lower than the normal, the same investors will seek other stocks.

CROSS-REFERENCES:

dividend payout, p. 384
Graham and Dodd approaches to common stock value, p. 246
Gordon on common stock value, p. 255
Walter and Gordon on dividend decisions, p. 260
Miller and Modigliani on dividend policy, p. 264
financial norms, determining, p. 405

normal price-earnings multiple. A ratio of market price to earnings per share that is expected when a firm is realizing a satisfactory return on its capital and the stock market is not disturbed by unusual psychological or economic factors.

CROSS-REFERENCES:
price-earnings ratio, p. 486

financial norms, determining, p. 405

normal probability distribution. A bell-shaped curve with a distribution of likely events equally and symmetrically on both sides of the most likely or mean value.

CROSS-REFERENCE:
probability, p. 488

O

open account. A credit sale that occurs when no formal note is signed to acknowledge the debt. The only documents evidencing the sale will be a purchase order, shipping invoice, and perhaps a billing statement. The open account facilitates the transaction of business and reduces the paperwork required for a credit sale.

Two major exceptions to the open account should be noted:

1. *Revolving Charge Plan.* The charge card phenomenon has become very popular for financing purchases of a variety of consumer items. BankAmericard, Mastercharge, and similar plans require an individual to provide detailed background information and a signed request for credit on demand. If the application is approved, a card is issued that allows the individual to make credit purchases by showing the card and signing a draft. In a sense, the draft becomes a formal note acknowledging the debt.

   Firms who use the revolving charge plans are able to rapidly collect the cash for their credit sales from the bank that provides the plan. The bank accepts the risk of nonpayment in most cases. In return for the rapid payment and transfer of risk of nonpayment, the firm pays a service charge to the bank of 2 to 6 percent.

2. *Financing of Consumer Durables.* Consumer durables are major items such as automobiles and appliances sold to individuals for their personal use. Since these items involve large sums of money compared to other individual purchases, the purchaser normally signs a formal note to finance them. By signing the note, the purchaser is allowed to pay for the items over a period of months or years. The note spells out the terms of payment, the interest charges, and the right of the holder of the note to reclaim the asset if payments are interrupted or halted. Normally, the note is not carried as a receivable but is discounted to a bank. The bank holds the note and gives the firm cash for the sale of the item.

CROSS-REFERENCE:
revolving charge plan, p. 511

operating budget. A financial plan prepared for the short-term, normally one year, that is concerned with the revenues and expenses related to the firm's daily operations. It differs from the capital budget which is prepared for the long-term and which deals exclusively with major investment proposals.

CROSS-REFERENCES:
capital budget, p. 329
capital budget cash inflow, two sides, p. 329

operating income. The firm's profit from its operations before any interest payments are made or corporate income taxes are paid. Also called earnings before interest and taxes (EBIT).

CROSS-REFERENCES:
leverage, how to use in profit planning, p. 44
earnings before interest and taxes, p. 392

operating lease. An agreement that does not impose any long-term obligation on either the lessor or lessee and may usually be cancelled by either the owner or user of the assets after giving a certain stipulated notice. An example would be the rental of office space on a 2-year lease cancellable on 60-day notice.

CROSS-REFERENCE:
leasing, p. 449

operating leverage. A measure of how fixed costs magnify the effects of changes in a firm's revenues as compared to its earnings before interest and taxes (EBIT). If a firm has large fixed costs compared to its sales, it will have a high degree of operating leverage.

CROSS-REFERENCE:
leverage, how to use in profit planning, p. 44

opportunity cost. From economics, the return a firm could have earned on its funds had it not made an investment. For example, if a firm invests in a proposal offering an 8 percent return while passing up a similar-risk proposal offering 6 percent, the opportunity cost of the 8 percent proposal is 6 percent.

opportunity need. A need for cash that arises because a firm has a chance to profit from having cash available.

optimal capital structure. The cost of capital plays an important role in managing the firm's capital structure. We seek the cost of capital to know the rate of return on projects above which the firm will increase in value. Similarly, the decision to employ debt or equity financing must be made in light of its effect on the value of the firm.

In studying the firm's cost of capital and capital structure, it is useful to express the value of the firm in the following formula:

$$V_{mkt} = D_{mkt} + PS_{mkt} + CS_{mkt}$$

where

V_{mkt} = overall market value of the firm

D_{mkt} = value of the firm's debt; except for new issues, this value is the face or redemption value of the debt

PS_{mkt} = value of the firm's preferred stock; except in situations where the preferred stock may soon be retired at some premium above par, this value is the par value of the stock

CS_{mkt} = value of the firm's common stock; this is always a market rather than a book value

Note that this formula expresses a firm's value as the sum of the values of the different components of the firm's capital structure.

The optimal capital structure for a firm may be defined as that relationship of debt and equity securities which maximizes the value of the firm's common stock in the marketplace. If a firm borrows and this action helps increase the common-stock value, the borrowing has moved the firm toward its optimum capital structure. If the borrowing helps cause a decline in the market value of the common stock, the debt offering has moved the firm away from its optimum capital structure.

Three points are important with respect to a firm's optimal capital structure, as follows:

1. *It Occurs at Both $V_{mkt(max)}$ and $CS_{mkt(max)}$.* When a firm's common stock is at its maximum value, the total value of the firm is also maximized, because, from the firm's point of view, the debt and preferred stock are valued at the face or par value. Although the creditors and preferred-stock shareholders are concerned about fluctuations in market value, the firm's obligation to these securities is limited by the securities' face values. Neither type of security is expected to fluctuate in the marketplace in line with the firm's success. Both securities offer a fixed

return and, in normal times, will have a value that fluctuates with the level of interest rates and preferred stock yields, not with corporate profits. (An exception to this statement occurs when the securities have the right to share at some point in profits, as is the case of participating preferred stock.)

2. *Common-Stock Value Is Maximized on a Per-Share Basis.* In discussing the optimal capital structure, the maximum value of the common stock is viewed on a per-share basis. A firm can always increase the total value of the common stock by issuing additional shares. If this action helps cause a decline in the per-share value of the common stock, the firm has moved away from its optimal capital structure. Although many cost-of-capital formulas deal with the total value of the firm and the total value of common stock, we should be aware that the stock value must be maximized on a per-share basis for the firm to be at its optimal capital structure.

3. *A Link May Exist Between Cost of Capital and Optimal Capital Structure.* Much controversy exists in the financial literature as to the link between a firm's cost of capital and its optimal capital structure. Some analysts contend that the optimal capital structure occurs when the firm's cost of capital is at its lowest point. Others have contended that the cost of capital is fixed and is not affected by capital structure. The linkage between cost of capital and capital structure is a matter of concern to financial analysts.

The optimum capital structure of a firm may be stated in a formula as follows:

$$V_{mkt(max)} = D_{mkt} + PS_{mkt} + CS_{mkt(max)}$$

CROSS-REFERENCES:

Schwartz on capital structure theory, p. 230
optimal capital structure, how to determine, p. 147

option to purchase. This plan gives the lessee the right to purchase the asset at a declining price after each year of the lease period. It is frequently offered as a joint feature with the level-rental or option-to-terminate forms. In most cases, the rental payments are neither increased nor accelerated. Instead, the option's cost is realized when the lessee exercises it. The longer the lessee waits before exercising the option, the greater the total cash outlay for the asset, because the optional purchase price decreases at a slower rate than the rentals accumulate. An example of an option-to-purchase plan is given in the Table.

Option-to-Purchase Lease Form.

	$100,000, 5-year, 10% Level-Rental Agreement with Option to Purchase			Total Capital
Year	Purchase Price as % of Original Cost	Puchase Price ($)	Cumulative Level-rental Payments ($)	if Option Is exercised ($)
1	85	85,000	26,378	111,378
2	68	68,000	52,756	120,756
3	52	52,000	79,134	131,134
4	36	36,000	105,512	141,512
5	20	20,000	131,890	151,890

option to terminate. This plan allows the lessee to gain a release from the lease agreement prior to its expiration date. In return for this option, the rental payments may be affected in either or both of the following ways:

1. *Increase in Total Rental.* The total amount of renting the asset may be increased as a cost of providing an option to terminate. The extra income from a number of leases will help the lessor make up losses when a percentage of the lessees exercise the option to terminate.

2. *Acceleration of Payments.* The lease agreement may provide for larger payments in the early years of the lease, which represents an acceleration of cash inflows for the lessor. Receiving more money earlier provides extra income for reinvestment by the lessor. The larger early receipts also help to compensate the lessor for the rapid decrease in market value of the assets during the first years of service life, in the event the asset is returned under the termination option.

As an example of an option-to-terminate lease using the 5 year, 10 percent, $100,000 asset of the level-rental plan, the annual payments might be raised from $26,378 to $30,000. Some minimum time period would probably be required, so the contract might allow an option to terminate with 60-day notice at any time after the first 36 months of the contract.

A second variation of this lease agreement might provide for an acceleration of payments. The $26,378 payment for 5 years represents a total of approximately $132,000. Retaining this same total payment, a lease with an option to terminate after 2 years could be written with a ayment stream as shown in the Table at the bottom of this page. With the accelerated-payments option, the total payments are approximately the same as with the level-rental plan, but $102,000, or 77 percent of the rental is paid by the end of the second year. After this time, when the option can be exercised, the rental payments are much lower than for the first 2 years. To terminate would be costly to the firm because it would be losing the use of relatively inexpensive assets. Still, to continue making payments would be

Payment Streams Under Level-Rental and Option-to-Terminate Lease Plans.

$100,000 Asset Under a 5-year, 10% Lease Agreement

Year	Level Rental	Option to Terminate[a] Higher Rental Payments	Option to Terminate[b] Accelerated Payments
1	$ 26,378	$ 30,000	$ 51,000
2	26,378	30,000	51,000
3	26,378	30,000	10,000
4	26,378	30,000	10,000
5	26,378	30,000	10,000
	$131,890	$150,000	$132,000

[a] With 60-day notice after 36 months of lease period.
[b] With 60-day notice after 24 months of lease period.

more costly if the firm is not profitably able to utilize the assets.

CROSS-REFERENCE:
leasing, p. 449

order costs. In inventory management, the variable costs of placing an order for an item of inventory.

CROSS-REFERENCES:
inventory management, how to set up system for, p. 103
inventory management, minimizing costs, p. 445

overdraft. A form of borrowing that occurs when a bank honors a check that is written in excess of the balance in a depositor's account. Many banks offer overdraft privileges on checking accounts as a means of making it easier for a customer to borrow money.

CROSS-REFERENCE:
demand deposit, p. 378

over-the-counter market. An informally organized grouping of brokers and dealers all over the country. It handles both primary issues and secondary transactions, and is the largest securities market, both in terms of the number and dollar volume of securities traded. It handles all corporate securities and a large volume of government bonds.

The over-the-counter market is a negotiated market, because prices are established by individual bargaining between customers and sellers. Normally, a customer works through a broker to locate a dealer who is always prepared either to buy or sell a certain stock or bond. These dealers make a market for the specific security. As an example, let us consider the dealer who makes a market for the common stock of Hardwicke Company. This dealer will always carry an inventory of Hard-

wicke stock and will quote prices at which he will buy or sell the stock. He may quote a bid price of 8 and an ask price of 8¼. This means he is willing to buy Hardwicke shares at $8 in lots of 100 shares, or he is willing to sell shares at $8.25 in lots of 100 shares. The customer's broker may call the dealer making the market and bargain or negotiate in an attempt to get a better price.

Most brokers and dealers in the over-the-counter market are members of the National Association of Securities Dealers (NASD), which numbers approximately 4,000 members. The NASD attempts to regulate the over-the-counter market and promote fair dealing between dealers or brokers and customers. It encourages its members to limit the spread between the bid and ask prices to less than 5 percent. Members may not split commissions with nonmembers, thus greatly limiting nonmembers from acting as brokers in the market. Violations of regulations of the NASD may result in disciplinary action or loss of membership.

Price quotations in the over-the-counter market are available on a daily basis from NASD members. Some 10,-000 stocks and 2,000 bonds are quoted. The NASD also compiles a daily quote listing of bid and ask prices for publication in periodicals such as the *Wall Street Journal.*

CROSS-REFERENCES:
bid, p. 322
ask, p. 313
national association of security dealers, p. 466

ownership ratios. Ownership ratios assist the stockholder in analyzing his present and future investment in a company. A stockholder is interested in the way certain variables affect the value of his holdings. The ratios compare the value of the investment with factors such as debt, dividends, earnings, and the market price of the stock. By understanding the profitability and liquidity ratios, the owner gains insights into the soundness of the firm's business activities. By investigating ownership ratios, the stockholder is able to analyze the likely future market value of the stock.

Three major groupings of ownership ratios are:

1. *Earnings Ratios.* These provide information on the earnings of the firm and how earnings affect the price of common stock. The earnings ratios are earnings per share, price-earnings ratio, and capitalization rate.
2. *Capital-Structure Ratios.* A firm's capital structure is the relation of debt to equity as sources of the firm's assets. The two ratios that reflect capital structure are the debt-equity ratio and the debt-asset ratio.
3. *Dividend Ratios.* These provide measures of the adequacy of dividend payments. The two ratios are dividend payout and dividend yield.

CROSS-REFERENCES:

ownership factors, how to analyze with ratios, p. 51
earnings ratios, p. 393
capital-structure ratios, p. 338
dividend ratios, p. 384
ratios, kinds of, p. 501

P

par value. The stated or face value of stocks or bonds.

CROSS-REFERENCES:
flow-of-funds statement, how to develop from balance sheet and income statement, p. 38
authorized capital, p. 315

parent company. A holding company that actively engages in the management of a subsidiary, from the point of view of the subsidiary.

CROSS-REFERENCES:
subsidiary, p. 533
pyramiding, p. 496
pyramids, risk and leverage in, p. 498

participating preferred stock. Preferred stock that offers its holders the right to participate with common shareholders in dividend distributions beyond a certain level. The preferred stockholders receive their stated dividends first, then the common shareholders receive a certain dividend. If further dividends are declared, both preferred and common shareholders participate to the degree stated in the preferred stock certificate. Most preferred stock does not offer this opportunity and is called nonparticipating.

CROSS-REFERENCES:
preferred stock, p. 481
common stock, p. 351

partnership. A business activity carried on by two or more persons who intend to share the resulting profits or losses. Although a partnership can be formed almost as easily as a sole proprietorship, it is wise to draw up a written agreement to avoid future conflicts over such matters as the responsibilities of individual partners or the means for sharing profits. Two types of partnerships should be noted:
1. *General Partnership.* Under this agreement all partners are liable for the debts of the business. This is the most common form of partnership agreement.
2. *Limited Partnership.* Under this agreement, a partnership will have one or more general partners. Other individuals may be designated as limited partners whose liability is limited to the amount stipulated in the agreement. The limited partner normally does not share in the management of the business but will share in the profits to the extent specified in the agreement.

Although partnerships involve written agreements in most cases, the agreement is not treated as a financial security. The partnership agreement is viewed as a legal contract rather than as a security evidencing ownership of a business.

payback. The easiest and least precise of the cash-flow methods for capital budgeting and has been widely used for a long period of time. The payback period is the length of time needed to regain the original net cash outlay. The calculations are in dollars and are not adjusted for the time value of money. For the two cash-flow streams in the Table, the payback periods are 3 years for project A and 3 ⅓ years for project B.

The payback method is useful as a supplemental tool in the capital-budgeting process. Although it should not be used alone, it highlights the liquidity aspects of projects. It shows how quickly cash will return to the firm. This may be valuable in high-risk situations or when the firm is short on cash.

Payback Periods on Two Cash-Flow Streams.

Year	Project A					Project B
0	−18,000					−26,000
1	+ 6,000 ⎤					⎡+ 7,500
2	+ 6,000 ⎬ —3 years		Payback	3-1/3 years —		+ 7,500
3	+ 6,000 ⎦		Period			+ 7,500
4	+10,000					+18,000

Weaknesses of Payback Method Although it has some utility, the payback method suffers from weaknesses as follows:

1. *Too Much Emphasis on Liquidity.* If payback is the main criterion for project selection, liquidity would receive priority over profitability. This would not be correct for long-term investments.

2. *No Recognition of Cash-Flow Variation.* One project may have cash inflows of $3,000 the first year, $4,000 the second year, and $5,000 the third year. A second project may have $5,000, $4,000, and $3,000 for years 1 to 3, respectively. If both projects involved net cash outlays of $12,000, the payback would be 3 years for each. But the second project would give more cash earlier and would be more valuable. This kind of situation cannot be adequately handled by payback.

3. *Cannot Handle Projects of Differing Economic Lives.* If two projects cost $250,000 and have $50,000 a year annual cash inflows after taxes, the payback period would be 5 years for each. If one project had an estimated life of 7 years and the other a 10-year life, the additional revenues in years 8 to 10 would not be reflected in the payback criterion. But these revenues make the longer project more valuable.

CROSS-REFERENCE:
capital-budget cash inflow, two sides, p. 329

p/e factor or multiple. Alternate terms for the price-earnings ratio which is the ratio of market price of one share of common stock to the earnings per share of the stock.

CROSS-REFERENCE:
price earnings ratio, p. 486

permanent working capital. The cash, receivables, and inventory required on a continuing basis over the entire year for a firm to carry on its operations.

CROSS-REFERENCES:
working capital, how to balance sources of funds, p. 121
working capital, nature of, p. 554

petty cash. A cash fund in many businesses whereby money is kept on hand for disbursements that are too small to justify the use of checks.

piecemeal financing. One argument offered in favor of leasing is that it helps the firm avoid the high costs of piecemeal financing. If a firm is expanding by adding relatively small amounts of fixed assets at regular intervals, the firm will have to locate a series of funds to finance the growth. If the firm chose a succession of small bond issues, the financing may become very costly, because each successive issue would have a higher cost than previous issues, a factor that considers the added risk of each new offering. The process of financing by offering an increasingly expensive series of debt offerings is called piece-meal financing.

The validity of this argument depends upon whether a firm has alternatives to a series of small offerings. In most cases, suitable alternatives are available, such as the following:

1. *First Short-Term, Then Long-Term Financing.* A firm could finance each small acquisition with short-term debt. At some point, the firm would convert the short-term debt to long-term debt with a single bond issue large enough to cover all the earlier financings.

2. *Larger Long-Term Offering than Needed.* When the firm is facing a small need for funds, the firm has the option of making a large bond offering. A portion of the proceeds could be used for the initial requirement while the balance is invested in marketable securities. As later needs arise, the firm would take a portion of the funds invested in the marketable securities and use the money to finance the assets. Once the large long-term issue is exhausted, the firm could consider floating another large offering for future needs.

CROSS-REFERENCE:
leasing, overview, p. 451

planning. The specific process of setting goals and developing ways to reach them. Stated another way, planning represents the firm's efforts to predict future events and be prepared to deal with them.

Planning Process As a general rule, a firm's formal planning process will involve the efforts of a number of departments. It may be supervised by a department of one or more persons called long-range planning. This department will coordinate inputs from marketing, production, finance, and other operating areas of the firm. The different departments work together to ensure that they are working toward the same goals and taking actions consistent with the objectives of the firm.

Once plans are agreed upon by the operating units, they are usually presented to the management committee or chief operating officer of the firm. At this level they will be challenged and either approved with possible modifications or returned to the operating units for further analysis. The final plans, whether short or long term, will become the blueprint for the firm's future operations.

Planning basically involves two major areas for analysis:

1. *External Factors.* The starting point in the planning process is the operating environment of the firm. The planner evaluates the outlook for the economy as a whole. Will the firm be operating during a period of economic growth and expansion? Or will the next 1 to 3 years be a period of recession and stagnation? As part of the total environment, the firm considers the expected level of activity in its industry and possible changes in the market for its products. Is the industry anticipating growth or decline? Does the firm have a stable market for its products? Is the firm's competition gaining or losing strength? Thus, the analysis of external factors considers both the overall economy and the individual industry as a framework for the next operating periods.

2. *Internal Factors.* A number of factors are internal in the sense that they are under the control of the firm. For example, such items as cash levels, kind and amount of inventories, and the nature of the fixed assets are operating elements that can be varied by the firm. This is not true for the external factors, such as a national recession or an industry decline.

CROSS-REFERENCE:
long-range planning, p. 454

planning, benefits of. As a result of engaging in the planning process, the firm realizes a number of benefits:

1. *Anticipation of Future Problems and Opportunities.* Planning involves people at different levels in the organization and forces them to think ahead. This has the effect of encouraging managers on varying levels to anticipate possible problems and to attempt to identify potential opportunities.

2. *Coordination of Actions.* Because they are involved in planning discussions with others in management positions, managers begin to coordinate future courses of action. Frequently, early coordination facilitates the achievement of company goals by increasing communication and reducing potential conflicts. The very process of setting goals and subgoals gives the different operating areas a common focus and encourages everyone to pursue compatible courses of action.

3. *Assistance in Control.* Plans may be used as tools to help managers control their areas of operation. A detailed plan gives departments and divisions specific goals to pursue and means to achieve the goals. As the firm conducts its operations, managers can watch for variations from the plan that indicate a need for tighter supervision and control.

4. *Providing Standards of Performance.* A comparison of the plan with actual performance during the planning period can be used to provide a standard of achievement. Did the company reach the goals outlined in the plan? If not, why not? Did certain areas do exceptionally well? Answers to questions such as these will help the firm evaluate its own performance during a recent operating period.

CROSS-REFERENCE:
part 2, profit planning, in "how to" section, p. 32

planning, controllable factors. The most developed portion of the firm's short- and long-term plans deals with internal factors and stresses:

1. *Market Demand for the Product Line or Services.* The firm can decide, after a careful evaluation of the external factors, what mix of products or services it will offer in the marketplace. If the firm produces its existing product line, what sales are likely? If it changes or modifies its products, will sales increase or decrease? These kinds of questions are analyzed in this part of the plan.

2. *Future Costs.* A firm may have a number of opportunities to reduce the costs involved with its products in future periods. The purchase of new and more modern equipment may increase fixed costs while reducing variable costs. Should the equipment be purchased? Better scheduling or planning may help minimize production or administrative expenses. High cost areas in the firm may be examined to see how economies could be achieved.

3. *Sources of Funds.* As the firm makes its plans for future expenditures, it will analyze the funds available to finance its activities. If sufficient funds are not predicted, steps will be taken to locate money as needed at reasonable costs.

These factors are internal only in the sense that the firm has the ability to influence them to a greater or lesser degree. The firm cannot have very much impact on the overall level of economic activity for the entire nation, but it can affect the demand for its product by more aggressive advertising or changes in product pricing or design. It cannot control inflation, but it can take actions to reduce costs. It cannot make money available in the economy, but it can find institutions and individuals who will make funds available for its needs.

pledging of accounts receivable. A pledge or an assignment of accounts receivable may be provided as collateral for a short-term loan. The highly liquid nature of receivables make them an attractive short-term loan collateral. A lender may advance a loan with a value of 50 to 90 percent of the value of an assignment of selected accounts. When the receivable is collected, a portion of it is forwarded to the lender, thus reducing the amount of the outstanding loan. Frequently, the pledging of receivables is used as a continuous source of financing. As accounts are collected, new accounts which are acceptable to the lender are substituted, allowing the firm to maintain a relatively constant loan balance.

CROSS-REFERENCES:
accounts receivable, p. 306
factoring, p. 401

pooling of interests. A method of accounting for a business combination that assumes a continuity of both the asset values and the ownership of the combined firms. In effect, the balance sheets of the merged firms will be reported as though it were a single firm. This method is generally preferred by corporations seeking a merger.

CROSS-REFERENCES:
pooling and purchase methods, how to use in merger accounting, p. 91
mergers, p. 460

portfolio. The combination of investments held by an individual, mutual fund, or other entity, consisting of securities or fixed assets or a combination of both.

portfolio risk. The degree of risk inherent in the investment in a portfolio of financial or capital assets. This is an important concept in the capital asset pricing model which seeks a reduction of portfolio risk through diversification. Portfolio risk is generally viewed in two components:
1. *Systematic Risk.* Also known as market-related risk, this is the part of portfolio risk that cannot be eliminated by diversification.
2. *Unsystematic Risk.* Also known as diversifiable risk, this is the part of portfolio risk that can be eliminated through diversification.

CROSS-REFERENCE:
capital asset pricing model, p. 279

portfolio theory. A body of knowledge that deals with the relationships between risk and return in portfolios. The goal of portfolio theory is to select optimal combinations of financial or capital assets in terms of achieving the highest possible expected return for any degree of risk or the lowest possible degree of risk for any expected return.

CROSS-REFERENCE:
capital asset pricing model, p. 279

preemptive right. A right that allows the common shareholder to purchase shares of newly issued common stock in order to maintain his proportionate ownership in the firm. When exercised, this right allows the existing owners to avoid a dilution of their interest in the corporation.

CROSS-REFERENCE:
common stock, p. 351

preferred stock. An equity security that is given a preference over other stock of the corporation. Although preferred stock is a form of equity security, it combines features of both debt and common stock. Some of the most important features are the following:

1. *Preference to Dividends.* Dividends may be declared on preferred stock after the firm has paid its operating expenses, covered its interest charges, and paid the applicable taxes. The preferred stock has preference over common stock when dividends are distributed. The actual payment of the dividend is discretionary and must be declared by the board of directors. If the board declines to declare a dividend, it is declining to *share the profits of the firm with the shareholders.* Thus, the omission of a dividend is not the same as the default on a debt, since the dividend is not a fixed obligation of the firm. Whenever dividends are declared, the preferred stockholders must receive their dividend before a dividend can be paid to common stockholders.

2. *Preference to Assets.* In the event of liquidation of the firm, the preferred shareholders occupy a middle ground between creditors and common shareholders. A bond is a senior security in the sense that its claims to assets are senior to the claims of the preferred and common stockholders. After the assets are liquidated, the bondholders are paid off first. If any money is left over, the preferred shareholders are paid second. If money is still remaining, it is shared by the holders of the junior security, the common shareholders. Just as the bondholders can only receive assets equal to the face value of the debt, so the preferred shareholders can only receive assets equal to the par value of the stock. For $100 par preferred stock the maximum settlement in a liquidation is $100 per share.

3. *Basically a Fixed Return.* The maximum return on preferred stock is usually limited to the stated dividend. Thus, a 5 percent $100 par issue will return no more than $5 per share per year. In some cases the preferred stock will contain a participating feature that allows the holder to share in earnings above some specific point. As an example, a participating feature may state that, if the common stock dividend is greater than $2 per share, the preferred stockholders will share equally in the additional dividends. Although preferred stock may have this feature, the great majority of issues are nonparticipating and result basically in a fixed return for the preferred shareholder.

4. *Indefinite Life.* Most preferred stock issues have no stated maturity. At the same time, most issues have a call feature in a manner similar to corporate bonds. This allows the firm to retire an issue should the firm decide that the preferred stock has become too expensive or has otherwise outlived its usefulness.

5. *Usually Nonvoting.* Most preferred stock does not contain provisions to allow its holders to vote or have other voices in the management of the firm. Sometimes an exception is stated in the stock certificate. For example, the preferred shareholders may become entitled to vote should the firm miss a specified number of consecutive dividends. Other provisions for voting are also occasionally found, but for the most part, preferred stock is nonvoting.

6. *Cumulative Dividends.* Most preferred stocks have a cumulative feature which requires that unpaid dividends in any one year must be carried forward to the next. When this happens, the preferred dividends are said to be in arrears. The dividends accumulated in arrears must be paid before the corporation can pay any dividends on common stock. If this feature is not present, the stock is noncumulative.

7. *Miscellaneous Features.* Preferred stock can have other features similar to

bonds. The stock certificate can provide that the preferred stock be convertible into common stock at the option of the holder. Or the issue may provide for a sinking fund to allow the orderly retirement of the stock over a period of time or at the end of a certain time period. The number and type of other features that can be incorporated into a preferred stock issue are limited only by the market situation and needs of the firm.

CROSS-REFERENCES:
financial leverage, how to analyze, p. 34
weighted-average cost of capital, how to calculate, p. 158
Durand on cost of capital, p. 203
call feature, p. 328
call premium, p. 328
conversion feature, p. 358
participating preferred stock, p. 477

preferred stock, cost of. The cost of preferred stock is calculated by the formula:

$$K_{ps} = \frac{\text{dividend}}{\text{PS}_{mkt}}$$

where
dividend = expected dividend per share
PS_{mkt} = par or face value of the preferred stock on a per share basis

As an example, a $100 par preferred stock with a 6 percent coupon will have a cost of $6/$100, or 6 percent. Since dividends for preferred stock are paid after taxes, this is the after-tax cost of preferred stock.

A new issue of preferred stock requires the same kind of adjustment for net proceeds as is used for a new debt offering. In the formula, the net pro-

ceeds replaces the par value. Thus, if a 6 percent, $100 par preferred stock were actually sold with a $90 net proceeds, the effective cost would be $6/$90, or 6.67 percent.

EXAMPLE: A firm sells $500 par preferred stock with a 7 percent coupon. What is the effective cost?
ANSWER: $35/$500 = 7%.

CROSS-REFERENCE:
weighted-average cost of capital, how to calculate, p. 158

preferred stock, value of. Preferred stock may also be valued using a capitalization technique. This differs from the capitalization technique for bonds because preferred stock normally has no specified maturity. Most preferred stock has a call feature that allows the issuing firm to retire or convert it to common stock at the firm's option. Since the call date is usually unknown, we view the value of preferred stock as being the stream of future dividends discounted to the present value. The formula is

$$\text{present value} = \frac{\text{preferred dividend}}{\text{capitalization rate}}$$

where
preferred dividend = annual dividend in dollars
capitalization rate = current yield on preferred stock of firms offering similar safety and record of declaration of dividends

As an example of the use of this formula, a firm may have a 5 percent $100 par preferred stock at a time when similar stocks yield 3.70 percent. The value of the stock is

$$\text{value} = \frac{\$5}{.037} = \$135.10$$

If the preferred stock has a specified maturity date, it is valued using the same technique as for bonds. We discount the stream of expected future dividends and the call or maturity value to determine the current value.

EXAMPLE: GAC Corporation preferred stock pays a $1 dividend. Preferred stock of this quality is currently yielding 5½ percent. What is the value of this stock?
ANSWER: $18.18. $1.00/.055 = $18.18.

CROSS–REFERENCE:
call feature, p. 328

premium. In merger or acquisition negotiations, an additional amount of money or value of stock above the market value of the stock of the firm to be acquired. A premium is offered to encourage the shareholders of the to-be-acquired firm to surrender their stock.

CROSS–REFERENCES:
flow-of-funds statement, how to develop from balance sheet and income statement, p. 38
acquisitions, how to analyze, p. 78
mergers, how to analyze profitability in a ten-step process, p. 85
refunding a bond issue, how to make the decision, p. 152
recapture, p. 502

premium. In international finance, a situation that exists when a currency is worth more in the forward market than in the spot market.
EXAMPLE: The exchange rate between francs and krona is 4.2fr/1Kr spot and 4.5fr/1Kr 60 days. Which currency is at a premium?
ANSWER: The krona because one krona will buy more francs in the forward market than in the spot market.

CROSS–REFERENCES:
discount, p. 382
forward market, p. 416

spot market, p. 524
premium or discount on foreign exchange, how to calculate, p. 176

premiums and discounts, causes of. The premium or discount for a currency in the forward market is owed to primarily two factors:

1. *Interest Rate Differentials.* When two national capital markets have differing levels of domestic interest rates, the differences will be reflected in the forward market for the two currencies. Suppose, for example, the United States' and Canadian dollars are equally strong at the existing exchange rate. Suppose, further, that Canadian one-year interest rate on high-grade securities is 8 percent and U.S. rates are 10 percent. Canadian investors would be attracted to purchase U.S. dollar securities, hold them for one year, and then guarantee their conversion back into Canadian dollars at a rate fixed under a forward contract. Without premiums or discounts, the investor would make a 2 percent profit by investing in U.S. dollar securities over comparable securities in Canadian markets. This process of guaranteeing a higher profit at no risk is a form of arbitrage. To keep large amounts of Canadian dollars from flowing to the United States, the forward market will have the Canadian dollar at approximately a 2 percent premium against the U.S. dollar. The additional profits from the higher U.S. interest rates would be lost when the money was converted back at the forward market's discount rate for the U.S. dollar.

2. *Relative Strengths of Currencies.* The second factor reflected by a premium or discount is the relative strength of the two currencies. Investors, including multinational corporations and banks, prefer to hold strong currencies. If they are forced to hold bal-

ances of weak currencies, they may execute forward contracts to allow them to get back into strong currencies at the end of a period of time. In return for guaranteeing an individual or firm the right to get out of a weak currency at the end of a period of time, forward contracts will be quoted at exchange rates that put the weak currency at a discount against the strong currency. Similarly, strong currencies will be quoted at a premium against weak currencies.

Both of the above effects are present in any quoting of forward market exchange rates. The effects may be complementary or may be offsetting. Sophisticated international money managers spend considerable amounts of time analyzing interest levels and relative strengths of currencies as they move money between capital markets and as they take steps to protect the value of their cash holdings.

CROSS-REFERENCES:

forward market, how to calculate bid and ask quotes, p. 171
premium or discount on foreign exchange, how to calculate, p. 176
discount, p. 382

premiums and discounts in forward market. The exchange rates between currencies will generally differ in the spot and forward markets. A currency trades at a premium when it is worth more in terms of another currency in the forward market than in the spot market. For example, suppose the exchange rate between dollars and francs is $1/4 fr spot and $1/4.1 fr one-year. The same dollar can purchase more francs in the forward market than it can in the spot market and thus is said to be trading at a premium against the franc.

Similarly, a currency trades at a discount against another currency when it is worth less in the forward market than is the spot market. In our example with francs and dollars, the franc trades at a discount against the dollar. The spot exchange rate is 4 fr/$1 while the forward rate is 4 fr/$.9756. In terms of the two currencies, one currency's premium is the other currency's discount.

EXAMPLE: The exchange rate between francs and pound sterling is 9.5 fr/1 £ spot and 9.7 fr/1£ 90 days. Which currency is at a premium and which is at a discount?

ANSWER: The pound sterling will purchase more francs in the forward market and therefore it is at a premium. The franc is at a discount against the pound sterling.

Two general principles can be identified with respect to premiums or discounts in forward markets:

1. *High Yields Produce Discounts in Forward Markets.* If a currency can be invested at a high yield compared to other currencies, the high yield will push the currency toward a discount in forward markets. The high interest rates will attract foreign investors who will seek forward contracts to ensure that they will be able to return to their own national currency. In order to have the currencies in equilibrium, the high yield available from one currency must be offset by a discount on that currency in the forward market. For currencies of equal strength, a high yield will mean a discount in the forward market.

2. *Currency Weakness Produces Discount in Forward Market.* An expected decline in the purchasing power of a currency will push that currency towards a discount in forward markets. If interest rates are equal in two national capital markets, the forward market will reflect discount for the weak currency and a premium for the strong currency.

CROSS-REFERENCES:

forward market, how to calculate bid and ask quotes, p. 171

premium or discount on foreign exchange, how to calculate, p. 176
discount, p. 382

present value. Today's worth of a future sum or stream of dollars discounted at a specified rate.

present-value factor. In the process of discounting cash flows, as occurs in capital budgeting and leasing, the present-value factor is the figure found in a present value table that can be applied against a cash inflow or outflow to determine its value in year zero. It is also called the discount factor.

price-dividends ratio. The ratio of the price-earnings ratio to the dividend payout for a firm. The price-dividends ratio is used in the Capitalization of Dividends approach to the valuation of the firm's common stock.

price-earnings ratio (P/E). Calculated by dividing earnings per share into the market price of the stock (MP/EPS), it is the most important measure of value used by investors in the marketplace. Many investors consider no other factor prior to making purchases.

The P/E ratio is used as a going-concern method of valuing stock. As long as the firm is a viable business entity, its real (or going-concern) value is reflected in its profits. The P/E ratio considers after-tax profits and market price, and links earnings per share to activity in the market. If a stock has a low P/E multiple, for example 8/1, it may be viewed as an undervalued stock. If the ratio is 40/1, it may be considered overvalued.

The P/E ratio may be used several ways:

1. *To Determine Expected Market Value of a Stock.* Within any given industry, there is usually a wide variation in the P/E multiples for the firms. One firm may trade at 10/1 while another trades at 25/1. If the firms are somewhat similar, the P/E ratio may help to identify the undervalued and overvalued stocks. For example, if we expect a firm to have a 15/1 multiple because other firms have this multiple, and if the firm has an EPS of $3, we can say the stock has a value of (15/1) ($3) or $45. This is an example of using a normal P/E multiple to calculate an expected market value. Note that the actual market price may be higher or lower than $45. If it is lower, we may be buying an undervalued stock. If it is higher, we may be avoiding an overvalued stock.

2. *To Determine Future Market Value of a Stock.* If the stock is purchased today for $45 and has $3 EPS, what will it be worth in 5 years when EPS are $7? If the P/E ratio stays approximately

Price-Earnings Ratios Expressed as Capitalization Rates.

Price-earnings ratio	5/1	8/1	10/1	12.5/1	15/1	20/1	25/1	30/1	35/1	40/1
Capitalization rate	20%	12.5%	10%	8%	6.67%	5%	4%	3.33%	2.9%	2.5%

15/1, the stock will be worth (15/1) ($7) or $105. If EPS only go to $4, it will be worth (15/1)($4) = $60.

3. *To Determine Capitalization Rate of a Stock.* The P/E ratio may be used to measure the rate of return investors demand before they will purchase a stock. The reciprocal of the P/E ratio is EPS/MP and gives this return. If the stock has $3 EPS and sells for $45, the marketplace demands that the stock return 3/45 or 6.67 percent. This is the stock's capitalization rate. A 6.67 percent capitalization rate means the firm earns 6.67 percent on the value of the common stock. If investors did not require this return, they would pay more for the stock and the rate of return or capitalization rate would drop.

CROSS-REFERENCES:

acquisitions, how to analyze, p. 78
common stock value, how to compare two or more stocks, p. 83
Graham and Dodd approaches to common stock value, p. 246
Schwartz on capital structure theory, p. 230
ownership factors, how to analyze with ratios, p. 51

price-specie-flow mechanism. Under the gold standard, the price-specie-flow mechanism was the process that forced currencies toward an equilibrium in terms of their relative purchasing power. This mechanism may be defined as a process whereby paper money is converted into gold and the gold flows between nations to restore equilibrium between currencies. Two concepts are critical to an understanding of this mechanism.

1. *Quantity Theory of Money (MV = PT).* This fundamental economic theory states that the money supply (M) times the velocity of circulation or turnover (V) is equal to the price levels or price index (P) times the volume of transactions (T). The MV represents the available money while the PT represents the demand for money or the amount of economic activity.

Prior to World War I, economists thought that V and T were relatively constant over time, an assumption that was basically correct. Thus, the M and P had to vary directly and proportionally. This means that any increase in the money supply would have a resultant increase in price levels. Decreases in money would result in lower prices.

Following this reasoning, money flowing from one country to another would affect the purchasing power of both currencies. The money flow could be used to bring currencies into equilibrium with each other.

2. *Specie = Gold and Gold Coins.* Under the gold standard, nations agreed to convert their currencies into gold. As part of this pledge, nations minted gold coins (specie). If currencies came into disequilibrium, gold would flow from one country to another. This would lower one country's money supply and raise the other. In a short period of time, the exchange rates would be back in equilibrium.

The mechanism did not work perfectly and there were some complications. For example, the physical movement of gold would involve costs such as shipping and insuring. Also, costs would be incurred melting down one nation's coins and minting the gold into the coins of another nation. Another problem occurred when nations experienced difficulty in converting their currencies into gold and had to suspend redemptions for short periods of time. In spite of these costs and problems, the price-specie-flow mechanism and the pledge of major nations to convert their currencies into gold brought stability to international transactions during the period of the gold standard.

CROSS-REFERENCE:
currency, p. 369

primary issue. The offering of stocks or bonds that have never been previously issued. The offering may be made two ways:
1. *Direct Placement.* A bond or stock issue may be placed directly with the individuals or company who will own the securities. A firm may agree, for example, to place $10,000,000 with four life insurance companies, who will hold the bonds and collect the interest as it comes due. The agreement can be worked out directly between the corporation and a representative of the insurance companies.
2. *Underwritten Placement.* An offering may be made by a corporation through an investment banker, a principal who acts as the middleman between the issuer and the public. In this role, the investment banker is an underwriter of the offering, who brings together a group of other investment bankers to underwrite or purchase the entire offering. Once

the underwriting syndicate has made the purchase, it will resell the securities to a variety of individuals and institutions through the mechanisms of the over-the-counter market.

CROSS-REFERENCES:
direct placement, p. 381
underwriter, p. 541

prime rate. The level of interest charged by the nation's leading banks on business loans to its best customers. The prime rate is widely used as a reference point for other lending rates and may fluctuate in response to money market conditions.

CROSS-REFERENCE:
variable rate financing, p. 544

principal. The face value of a loan or security upon which interest is earned or paid.

pro forma financial statement. A balance sheet, income statement, flow-of-funds statement, or other financial statement that projects a financial condition at some future time or in some future period. Pro forma statements are important in budgeting and financial planning.

probability. The likelihood of a certain event, normally expressed as a percentage. If an outcome is expected 4 out of 10 times, the probability is said to be 40 percent.

CROSS-REFERENCES:
risk in capital budget, how to measure, p. 25
standard deviation, how to measure risk with, p. 195
weighted-average approach to risk and return, how to use, p. 197
normal probability distribution, p. 470

probability distribution. In statistics, a range of estimates of the likelihood of the occurrence of differing future outcomes. As an example, consider an investment with a 50 percent chance of returning $100,000, a 25 percent chance of returning $50,000, and a 25 percent chance of returning $150,000. The following probability distribution can be drawn to reflect these likelihoods of occurrence.

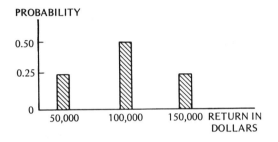

Since a limited number of values are identified, this is a discrete probability distribution. If all possible values could be achieved between the highest and lowest value, a continuous probability distribution would exist, as follows:

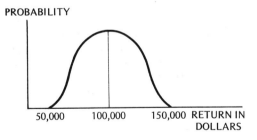

CROSS-REFERENCES:
capital asset pricing model, p. 279
normal probability distribution,
p. 470

problem-solving process. Financial tools should be applied in a logical, overall problem-solving process. It is the manager's job to find a systematic manner of developing valid information from available data. A common six-step process may be outlined as follows:

1. *Gather Relevant Data.* Knowledge of a firm's activities can be obtained from many sources. Production workers, engineers, salesmen, analysts, managers, and secretaries can provide valuable data. Company reports from the marketing, personnel, accounting, and other departments can contain material that is already prepared for computer processing, if this is desirable. The financial manager should make every effort to determine the location of useful data and the methods to rapidly and accurately collect them.

2. *Select Appropriate Tools.* Finance has developed an array of tools that can be applied to the processing of data. The financial manager must have a knowledge of the available techniques and must be able to choose the correct tool for the problems at hand.

3. *Process the Data.* Depending on the amount and complexity of the data, the processing may be done by hand, calculator, or computer. Care must be taken throughout the processing to ensure that the tools properly accept and accurately handle the supplied data.

4. *Examine the Information.* The final phase of processing produces information to be used by the manager. It should be formatted to allow a grasp of the pertinent aspects of the problem. The information should be carefully evaluated. Is it useful? Can it be applied to the problem at hand?

5. *Identify Alternative Courses of Action.* With accurate and timely information, the manager will be able to distinguish different courses of action that will solve the problem facing the firm. Each alternative must be identified, its strengths and weaknesses determined, and its likely success

evaluated in terms of achieving the goal or solving the problem.

6. *Select One Alternative.* The final step in financial problem solving is to select a single course of action and begin its implementation.

profit. There is no general agreement as to a specific definition for the term profit. Some of the more common meanings of profit are as follows:

1. *Margin Between Selling Price and Costs.* Profit may be viewed simply as the difference between the selling price for a product and the costs associated with producing and marketing the product. If the product costs $10 and is sold for $15, the profit would be $5.

2. *Bottom Line on a Profit-and-Loss Statement.* Some analysts use the term profit to refer to the difference between revenues and expenses as reported by the firm's accountants. The firm's profit is a specific figure that is determined according to strict accounting procedures and reported on the bottom line of a profit-and-loss statement.

3. *Economic Surplus.* To an economist, the term profit may have several possible meanings, all tied to the allocation of resources and the surplus revenues from operations. Profits may be discussed in relation to such concepts as total revenues and total costs and marginal revenues and marginal costs.

profit center. The management of subsidiaries in a pyramid poses many problems for parent firms. A commonly used technique is to designate the subsidiary as a profit center. A profit center is any operating unit of a firm or any subsidiary which is given a profit goal and is held accountable for achieving that goal. The following are important characteristics of a profit center:

1. *Profit Goal Defined in Advance.* The parent organization and the profit-center manager work out a profit goal in advance of the operating period. The goal may be stated in dollars (for example, $50,000), as a ratio (for example, a 30 percent ROE), or in some other manner. But both the parent and subsidiary know the goal in advance.

2. *Control over Revenues and Costs.* In the decentralized structure of profit centers, each one must have control over its own costs and ability to earn revenues. The parent should not place restrictions on the size of the sales force or the use of the company plane. As long as the profit center is charged for all expenses, the profit-center manager should have authority to incur the costs he thinks are needed. The subsidiary must also be allowed to set its own prices and take steps needed to bring in revenues without interference.

profit center, problems with. Although the profit-center structure frequently results in a high level of profits, it poses several problems for the parent company:

1. *Allocating Headquarters Services.* A subsidiary will occasionally require the services of the parent or headquarters staff. A lawyer may be needed for a patent search for a new product. Specialized tax expertise and advice may

be helpful to the subsidiary's accounting department. The structure must make arrangements to account for the costs of these and similar services. A problem arises when the subsidiary does not want the services and does not want to be charged for them. As an example, how does the parent allocate the cost of printing the annual report if a profit center objects to paying part of it?

2. *Interdivisional Pricing.* When one profit center sells a product to another, a price must be established. Should the selling unit make its regular profit? Should the buying unit get the product at cost or near cost?

3. *Research and Development.* The parent may have a department that is working on technology for future products. Since the profit centers will eventually benefit, should they not pay a part of the cost? But how much? Which center will benefit the most?

4. *Inherited Costs.* Management will frequently commit itself to projects that involve continuing costs over a long period of time, or that involve mistakes which will be costly in the future. If the management changes, will the new manager of a profit center have to be accountable for long-term costs that resulted from the decisions of the old manager?

5. *Performance Measurement.* One of the most difficult jobs is determining which profit centers are doing good jobs. Different operations face different conditions, market factors, and cost factors. A factory in an urban area will have high labor costs; a rural factory will have lower costs. The parent company must set goals that are realistic in light of existing conditions and measure performance against the goals, not against other profit centers.

CROSS-REFERENCE:

subsidiary, p. 533

profit margin. The firm's profit margin is calculated by dividing operating income by sales. Both figures are normally taken from the income statement. The significance of this ratio is that it helps measure the relationship between sales and operating profits. If the profit margin is inadequate, the firm will not be able to achieve satisfactory returns for its investors.

$$\text{profit margin} = \frac{\text{operating income}}{\text{sales}}$$

The profit margin is an indicator of the ability of the firm to withstand adverse conditions, which may arise from several sources, such as the following:

1. *Falling Prices.* If the general price level in the marketplace experiences a decline, does the firm have a sufficient margin to drop its price and still show a profit on individual sales?

2. *Rising Costs.* If the firm is caught in a period of rising costs when it cannot raise its prices, will the firm continue to be profitable?

3. *Declining Sales.* Can the firm withstand unexpected drops in sales and still show a profit?

Similarly, the profit margin may be used as an indicator of possible success under favorable conditions, such as the following:

1. *Rising Prices.* If the firm is able to raise its prices, how quickly will profits rise?

2. *Lowered Costs.* If supplies and materials decline in price, what profits can be expected?

3. *Increasing Sales.* If the firm is able to gain large increases in sales without adverse price or cost effects, what would be the profit forecast?

CROSS-REFERENCES:
profitability, how to analyze with ratios, p. 56

profit planning, weaknesses of. Profit planning using accounting data and different leverage concepts are highly useful to firms with stock outstanding in the hands of public investors or institutions. External analysts are very concerned with reported profits and capital structure, and this influences the market price of the firm's stock.

In spite of the value of these techniques, they have weaknesses, as follows:

Short-Term Outlook Because of the many factors involved, future earnings are usually projected only a year or two in advance. It is assumed that the situation will remain the same after this period. In fact, it might be better to use a technique that projects the entire life of a new investment, as is done with capital budgeting.

Improperly Handled Depreciation Depreciation and the other noncash expenses serve to reduce the net income and future earnings per share. Actually, these expenses shield a portion of the revenues from sales and provide a cash inflow to the firm. The larger the depreciation, the more desirable the project on a cash-flow basis, but not on an accounting basis.

This problem is partly handled by the firm's accountants who prepare the annual reports. Although the firm takes advantage of accelerated depreciation to maximize cash flow, straight-line depreciation is reported in the stockholders' literature so as not to understate profits.

Assets at Book, Not Market, Value In profit-planning techniques, for consistency, the firm's assets are recorded at book value rather than at actual market value. Since all firms use the same general depreciation schedules and record assets at cost, comparisons can be made. If every firm made an estimate of the current market value of its assets, wide discrepancies would exist between firms with similar assets.

The effect of listing assets at book value in most cases is to overstate ROI and the turnover on the use of the assets. Completely depreciated machinery shows a return on zero assets, whereas no asset can exceed its actual cost. This is not a serious problem, but should be noted.

CROSS-REFERENCES:
leverage, how to use in profit planning, p. 44
profits, how to maintain under inflation, p. 59

profitability analysis, schematic. Many factors influence a firm's profitability. Each factor in turn will affect the profitability ratios. In analyzing a firm's profitability from ratio analysis, we must recognize the interrelationships of factors. The schematic identifies factors that affect each of the different profit ratios and shows which ratios help explain other ratios.

Note the cumulative effect of the individual factors. Every factor affects earning power, even though none leads to it directly. For example, high production costs, which affect gross profit margin, have an effect through profit margin, return on investment, return on equity, and finally earning power. The reason one ratio explains another is that the factors that affect it also affect the other.

CROSS-REFERENCE:

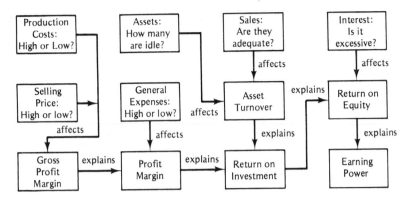

Factors Affecting Profit and the Interrelation of Profitability Ratios.

leverage, how to use in profit planning, p. 44

profitability functions. In seeking profits for the firm, the financial manager can perform specific functions such as the following:

1. *Cost Control.* Most large corporations have detailed cost accounting systems to monitor expenditures in the operational areas of the firm. Data are fed into the system on a daily basis and computer processed; reports are printed containing important information on activities. Because he supervises the accounting and reporting functions, the financial manager is in a position to monitor and measure the amounts of money spent or committed by the company. He may be the first person to recognize rising costs for supplies or production processes, and he can then make recommendations to bring costs back under control.

2. *Pricing.* Some of the most important decisions made by the firm will involve the prices established for its products, product lines, and services. The philosophy and approach to the pricing policy are critical elements in the company's marketing effort, image, and sales level. Determination of the appropriate price should be a joint decision of the marketing and finance managers. The marketing manager provides information on how differing prices will affect demand in the market and the firm's competitive position. The financial manager can supply important information about costs, changes in costs at varying levels of production, and the profit margins needed to successfully carry on the business. In effect, finance provides tools to analyze profit requirements in pricing decisions and contributes to the formulation of pricing policies.

3. *Forecasting Future Profits.* The financial manager is usually responsible for gathering and analyzing the relevant data and making forecasts of profit levels. To estimate profits from future sales, the firm must be aware of current costs, likely increases in costs, and likely changes in the ability of the firm to sell its products at established or planned selling prices. Many variables affect these items, and finance must receive cost inputs from purchasing and production and sales inputs from marketing. Once costs and sales are forecasted, the data must be arranged in a financial format to calculate the expected

profit. In the same way, before funds are committed to new projects, the expected profits must be determined and evaluated. Will the profits justify the initial expenditure?

4. *Measuring Cost of Capital.* Most firms receive capital from creditors and owners, that is, from both debt and equity sources. Each different source of funds is likely to involve a different cost of capital. The short-term debt may be expensive compared to the long-term debt. Preferred or common stock may bring substantially different returns to the holders of each, a factor that influences the cost of funds from each source. The financial manager studies the costs associated with each source and determines the profits required from operations to pay for borrowed funds and to provide a satisfactory return for the owners. This process is called determining the firm's cost of capital.

profitability index. A ratio of the present value of cash inflows from a project divided by the present value of the cash outlay. The ratio is used in the net present value approach to measuring return from a capital-budgeting project. All cash flows are brought back to the present value using the firm's cost of capital as a discount factor. The index is then calculated. If the profitability index is greater than one, a project is acceptable. If less than one, it should be rejected. This is sometimes called the benefit-cost ratio.

profitability ratios. There are two major categories of profitability ratios:

1. *Profits in Relation to Sales.* It is important from a profit standpoint that the firm be able to generate adequate profit on each unit of sales. If sales lack a sufficient margin of profit, it is difficult for the firm to cover its fixed costs, fixed charges on debt, and to earn a profit for shareholders.

2. *Profits in Relation to Assets.* It is similarly important that profit be compared to the capital invested by owners and creditors. If the firm cannot produce a satisfactory profit on its asset base, it may be misusing the assets.

In addition to these two categories, the analyst links the profit ratios through a ratio of sales to assets. An important factor in the firm's ability to produce profits is the relationship between the level of sales and the level of assets required to attain the sales.

profit-risk approach to financial goals. This classification scheme recognizes that finance deals with creating the proper framework to maximize profits while minimizing risk. In pursuing this balance, the firm must develop controls over flows of funds while allowing sufficient flexibility to respond to changes in the operating environment. This classification method identifies four goals:

1. *Maximize Profits.* Finance should strive for a high level of primarily long-

term and secondarily short-term corporate profits.

2. *Minimize Risk.* Finance should always seek courses of action that avoid unnecessary risks and anticipate problem areas and ways of overcoming difficulties.

3. *Maintain Control.* Funds flowing in and out of the firm must be constantly monitored to assure that they are safeguarded and properly utilized. The financial reporting system must be designed to provide timely and accurate pictures of the firm's activities. Errors or weaknesses should be located and corrected without undue delay.

4. *Achieve Flexibility.* The firm should always be prepared to deal with an uncertain future. Flexibility is gained by careful management of funds and activities. If the firm has located sufficient sources of funds in advance of needs, it will be flexible when money is required. If it identifies and analyzes a variety of potential projects, it will have flexibility in determining its future courses of action. Finance attempts to be as flexible as possible in providing the funds or data needed to support the production and marketing areas of the firm.

CROSS-REFERENCE:
risk and return, major decision areas, p. 513

profit-volume analysis. A modification of break-even analysis that results in a tool relating profits to sales at different operating levels.

CROSS-REFERENCES:
break-even analysis, how to use, p. 32
profit–volume analysis, how to use, p. 64
break-even analysis, p. 325

prospectus. A document that may be issued to potential buyers of a new security that describes the major characteristics of the offering. For public offerings, the prospectus is reviewed for fraudulent or misleading statements by the Securities Exchange Commission (SEC).

CROSS-REFERENCE:
red herring, p. 507

proxy. A certificate by which the holder of common stock transfers his voting rights to another party, normally an officer or manager in the company.

CROSS-REFERENCE:
acquisitions, three approaches, p. 307

proxy fight. A situation that occurs when more than one group attempts to gain control of the voting stock for the purpose of making major changes in the firm's activities or management.

CROSS-REFERENCE:
acquisitions, three approaches, p. 307

public finance. A specialized discipline that deals with governmental financial matters, particularly the pursuit of nonprofit goals.

CROSS-REFERENCE:
fields of finance, how to distinguish, p. 190

public offering. A bond or stock issue that is sold to the general public, generally with the assistance of investment bankers. In many cases, the investment banker will form a syndicate to underwrite the security issue. The underwriters purchase the security issue and resell it to other investors.

CROSS-REFERENCES:
money market, p. 464

registration statement, p. 508

publicly traded security. A bond or stock that may be purchased through an organized exchange or through the over-the-counter market. Publicly traded securities are handled by dealers who make a market for the specific security and are owned by investors who have no management interest in the issuing firm.

CROSS-REFERENCES:

common stock value, how to compare two or more stocks, p. 83
mergers, how to analyze profitability in a ten-step process, p. 85

purchase method. A method of accounting for a business combination that assumes a new ownership and a need to reappraise the assets of the acquired firm in light of current market value. The balance sheet is restated to reflect the current values as the combination is completed. If a firm is acquired for a price in excess of its book value, the excess is recorded either as an increase in value on specific depreciable assets or in an account titled "goodwill".

CROSS-REFERENCE:

pooling and purchase methods, how to use in merger accounting, p. 91

pyramiding. Through the use of a technique called pyramiding, parent-subsidiary relationships may be used to allow one firm to control a number of other firms. Pyramiding may be defined as controlling several or many firms with a relatively small investment in each. As little as 10 percent of a firm's stock may be sufficient to control the firm. This fact facilitates pyramiding.

Actual pyramids in American business are highly complicated structures that are put together and managed through complex legal, financial, and

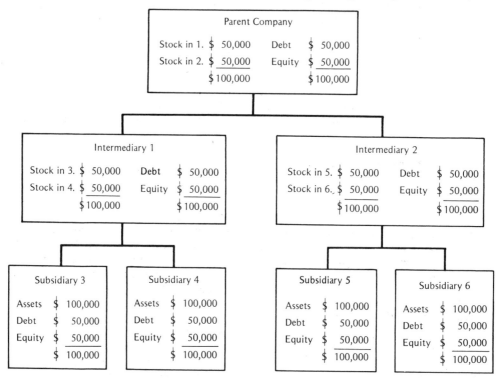

Corporate Structure Using Pyramiding.

communications arrangements. For our purposes, we shall examine a model of a pyramid rather than an actual operating structure.

Sample Pyramid As an example of the pyramid structure, consider a firm that has $50,000 in cash and is able to borrow another $50,000. It may use its $100,000 cash to buy all the stock in two intermediary companies, 1 and 2. Once it owns these companies, they may be instructed to borrow $50,000 each. This will give the original firm, now a parent company, control of assets valued at $200,000. Each intermediary firm uses its cash to buy the equity in subsidiary firms 3, 4, 5, and 6. If these firms borrow

$50,000 each, the parent will be controlling firms with $400,000 in assets as a result of its initial $50,000 in equity investment. The pyramid structure is shown in the figure.

In the pyramid in the figure the subsidiaries are operating companies that own assets and produce revenues. The intermediaries are holding companies with no assets other than the stock in other companies. The revenues earned by the operating companies are passed on to the holding companies and then on to the parent company.

CROSS-REFERENCES:

parent company, p. 477
subsidiary, p. 533

TABLE 1

Comparing Profits with Favorable and Unfavorable Financial Leverage in Corporate Pyramid Shown in Figure

	Favorable Financial Leverage					Unfavorable Financial Leverage			
	No Consolidated Return					No Consolidated Return			
	15% ROI and 10% Interest					8% ROI and 10% Interest			
	Subsidiaries					*Subsidiaries*			
	3	4	5	6		3	4	5	6
EBIT	15	15	15	15	EBIT	8	8	8	8
Interest	5	5	5	5	Interest	5	5	5	5
EBT	10	10	10	10	EBT	3	3	3	3
NIAT	5	5	5	5	NIAT	1.5	1.5	1.5	1.5

	Intermediaries				*Intermediaries*	
	1	2			1	2
100% Dividends to inter-mediaries	10	10	100% Dividends to inter-mediaries		3	3
Interest	5	5	Interest		5	5
After-tax-income	5	5	Lost		(2)	(2)

100% Dividends to parent:	10		No Dividend to parent:	
Interest	5		interest=	
After-tax-income	5		loss	(5)

Return on Equity = 5/50 = 10%

No return on equity. Intermediaries lose $2,000 each; parent loses $5,000.

NOTE: Figures based on pyramid in the previous figure. All figures in thousands except final statement in second column.

pyramids, risk and leverage in. Significant financial leverage may be achieved through the use of a pyramid structure. In the pyramid in the previous figure, a $50,000 equity is used to borrow $350,000 and thus finance $400,000 in assets. This will work fine as long as the firm's return on investment exceeds its interest rate. In Table 1, for example, the pyramid is shown with a 10 percent interest rate on $350,000. The first structure has a 15 percent ROI in the operating subsidiaries. The profit is sufficient to cover the interest payments of the intermediaries and the parent leaving a $5,000 parent after-tax income. The second structure shows an 8 percent ROI, which is not sufficient to cover the interest payments. The result is a loss of $9,000, $2,000 in each intermediary and $5,000 in the parent.

The data in Table 1 are compiled without the use of a consolidated income tax return at the parent level. In these examples, the intermediary and parent companies have interest payments but no operating income. Thus, these companies are unable to gain a tax credit for the interest payments. If the parent were eligible to file a consolidated return, as it actually is since it owns 100 percent of the subsidiaries and intermediaries, the interest payments at the parent and intermediary levels could be used to shield a portion of the operating revenues from the subsidiaries. The effect, which is shown in Table 2, is to increase the net income after taxes in the example with favorable financial leverage and reduce the loss in the example with unfavorable financial leverage.

TABLE 2

How Consolidated Returns Improve Profits or Reduce Losses.

Favorable Financial Leverage Consolidated Return 15% ROI and 10% Interest			Unfavorable Financial Leverage Consolidated Return 8% ROI and 10% Interest		
EBIT	60	(15% × 400)	EBIT	32	(8% × 400)
Interest	35	(10% × 350)	Interest	35	(10% × 350)
EBT	25		EBT	(3)	
NIAT	12.5				
ROE = 12.5/50 = 25%					

With a consolidated return, ROE increases from 10% to 25% due to tax shield on interest of intermediaries & parent.

With a consolidated return, the loss decreases from a total of $9,000 to $3,000.

NOTE: Figures based on pyramid in the previous figure. No consolidated return shown in Table 1.

As these examples illustrate, the opportunities for leverage are high in pyramids, but so are the risks. Slight improvements in profit margins or asset turnover can be converted into large rises in the earnings per share of the parent company. Similarly, small decreases in the operating profits can create a situation where the parent or intermediary cannot meet its interest payments. Since the pyramid is already highly levered, it is unlikely that the firm would be able to borrow to meet its fixed charges. The result may be a collapse of the pyramid and possible bankruptcy.

CROSS-REFERENCES:

parent company, p. 477
subsidiary, p. 533

pyramids, taxation in. The U.S. corporate tax regulations are a critical element in pyramiding. The tax rate applied to dividends paid by one corporation to another will vary with the degree of ownership by the parent or holding company. Two situations are possible:

1. *Less Than 80 Percent Owned.* To minimize corporate taxes on dividends, the subsidiary must be 80 percent or more owned by the parent company. If the subsidiary is not 80 percent owned, 15 percent of the subsidiary's dividends to the parent are treated as ordinary income and are subject to taxation at the parent's corporate income tax rate. The computation is

(dividends)(15%)(corporate tax rate)

2. *At Least 80 Percent Owned.* When the parent company owns at least 80 percent of the subsidiary's common stock, two possible savings occur:
   a. *No part of the dividends is taxed.* The entire amount of the dividends from the subsidiary is considered to be additional net income after taxes.
   b. *A consolidated return may be filed.* A consolidated return is a single tax return that combines the parent's and subsidiary's revenues and expenses. It will save the parent money in a situation where the parent has a loss while the subsidiary has a profit. Through the use of a consolidated return, the parent's loss can be used as a tax shield for a portion or all of the subsidiary's profit. This has the effect of reducing the taxes paid in the pyramid.

EXAMPLE: A company receives $80,000 in dividends from a subsidiary that is 60 percent owned. How much additional tax must the company pay on the dividends?

ANSWER: $6,000. The calculation for dividends from subsidiaries that are less than 80 percent owned is (dividends) (15%) (corporate tax rate) = ($80,000) (15%) (50%) = $6,000.

EXAMPLE: A company declares $100,000 in dividends. Eighty-five percent of the dividends are paid to its parent company; the remaining 15 percent are distributed to other shareholders. How much of the dividends are received by the parent and how much taxes are paid on the dividends?

ANSWER: $85,000 is received and none of it is subject to additional tax since the parent owns more than 80 percent of the subsidiary.

CROSS-REFERENCES:

parent company, p. 477
subsidiary, p. 533

Q

quota of IMF. The resources of the International Monetary Fund originated from a pool of gold and national currencies contributed by member nations. Each nation was assigned a quota based on its national income, monetary reserves, foreign trade and payments patterns, and general level of economic activity. Three aspects of the quota are significant.

1. *Measures Contribution to IMF.* The size of the quota is, in effect, a measure of the nation's contribution to the IMF. Twenty-five percent of the quota was paid in gold and 75 percent was paid in the national currency. These contributions provided the bag of currencies for the fund.
2. *Defines Size of Drawing Rights.* A drawing right is the privilege of each IMF nation to purchase needed currencies to finance international transactions. A nation may exchange its own currency for foreign currency up to 25

percent of its quota annually, subject to certain provisions.
3. *Determines Voting Power.* Each member nation's voting power is tied directly to the size of its quota.

CROSS-REFERENCE:
International Monetary Fund, p. 438

quick ratio. Also called acid test, is a ratio of current assets minus inventories to current liabilities. The quick ratio is a more precise measure of liquidity than the current ratio because inventories, the least liquid of current assets, are excluded from the ratio.

CROSS-REFERENCES:
liquidity, how to analyze with ratios, p. 49
working capital, how to balance source of funds, p. 121
current ratio and acid test, p. 371
acid-test ratio, p. 307

R

ratios. A ratio is a fixed relationship in degree or number between two numbers. In finance, ratios are used to point out relationships that are not obvious from the raw data. Some uses of ratios are the following:

1. *To Compare Different Companies in the Same Industry.* Ratios can highlight the factors associated with successful and unsuccessful firms. They can reveal strong firms and weak firms, overvalued and undervalued firms.
2. *To Compare Different Industries.* Every industry has its own unique set of operating and financial characteristics. These can be identified with the aid of ratios.
3. *To Compare Performance in Different Time Periods.* Over a period of years, a firm or an industry will develop certain norms that may indicate future success or failure. If relationships change in a firm's data over different time periods, the ratios may provide clues on trends and future problems.

From all the financial accounts on the balance sheet, income statement, and flow-of-funds statement, it is possible to formulate countless ratios. To be successful in financial analysis, the analyst must select only those ratios that provide significant information about a firm's situation.

CROSS-REFERENCES:
cash safety level, how to calculate, p. 101
earnings ratios, p. 393

ratios, kinds of. Financial ratios may be classified a number of ways. One classification scheme uses three major categories:

1. *Liquidity Ratios.* These examine the adequacy of funds, the solvency of the firm, the firm's ability to pay its obligations when due.
2. *Profitability Ratios.* These measure the efficiency of the firm's activities and its ability to generate profits.
3. *Ownership Ratios.* These are generally linked directly or indirectly to profits and liquidity. They assist the stockholder in evaluating the activities and policies of the firm that affect the market price of the common stock.

CROSS-REFERENCES:
financial analysis, p. 403
profitability ratios, p. 494
ownership ratios, p. 475

ratios, use for comparisons. As an example of the use of ratios, compare two firms with the same earnings before interest and taxes—$300,000. To reach this level, firm A invested $1,000,000; firm B invested $1,500,000. Even though both firms have the same return in dollar amounts, as a return on the investment we have

$$\text{firm A} = \frac{\$300,000}{\$1,000,000} = 30\%$$

$$\text{firm B} = \frac{\$300,000}{\$1,500,000} = 20\%$$

Through the use of a ratio, we see that firm A has a higher return because it achieves its $300,000 EBIT on a smaller investment than firm B. Ratios allow this kind of comparison, which provides additional information concerning the significance of financial data.

A second ratio allows us to compare the return on a given volume of sales. If firm A has $3,000,000 in sales and firm B has $2,000,000 in sales, a margin of profit for each firm would be

$$\text{firm A} = \frac{\$300,000}{\$3,000,000} = 10\%$$

$$\text{firm B} = \frac{\$300,000}{\$2,000,000} = 15\%$$

These ratios show that firm B is able to generate the same EBIT on a smaller volume of sales than firm A. From the two sets of ratios, we may conclude that firm A is using its assets more efficiently to generate income but that firm B generates more income from each dollar of sales. Other ratios could be used to make further comparisons.

CROSS-REFERENCES:

liquidity, how to analyze with ratios, p. 49
ownership factors, how to analyze with ratios, p. 51
profitability, how to analyze with ratios, p. 56

ratios, users of. Different analysts will desire different kinds of ratios, depending largely on who the analyst is and why he is evaluating the firm. Some users of ratios are the following:

1. *Short-Term Creditors.* These persons hold obligations that will soon mature, and they are concerned with the firm's ability to pay its bills promptly. In the short run, the amount of liquid assets determines the ability to pay off current liabilities. These persons will be interested in liquidity.

2. *Long-Term Creditors.* These persons hold bonds or mortgages against the firm and are interested in current payments of interest and eventual repayment of principal. The firm must be sufficiently liquid in the short term and have adequate profits for the long term. These persons examine liquidity and profitability.

3. *Stockholders.* In addition to liquidity and profitability, the owners of the firm are concerned about the policies of the firm that affect the market price of the firm's stock. Without liquidity, the firm could not pay cash dividends. Without profits, the firm would not be able to declare divi-

dends. With poor policies, the common stock would be poorly priced in the market.

recapitalization. A voluntary rearrangement of the capital structure so as to change the preferred or common stock accounts in terms of the number of shares outstanding, the par value of the shares, the market price of the shares, or other change. Common recapitalizations occur to bring higher-priced stock into a more affordable trading range or to rearrange the capital structure so as to facilitate a merger or acquisition.

CROSS-REFERENCE:
reorganization, p. 508

recapture. A premium that occurs when a depreciable asset is sold for an amount greater than its book value but less than its original purchase price. This premium or "recapture" is taxable at the firm's normal tax rate.

receivables. Asset accounts representing amounts owed to the firm as a result of the sale of goods or services in the ordinary course of business. The value of these claims will be carried on the balance sheet under titles such as accounts receivable, trade receivables, or customer receivables.

Accounts receivables play a major role in the conduct of business for most firms. The great majority of companies do not demand immediate payment in cash when they sell goods to their regular, creditworthy customers. This is true both for firms engaging in retail trade and firms whose primary business involves sales to other businesses. Because of this practice, most sales require the firm to carry a receivable for a customer for a period of from 10 to 60 days.

Receivables represent a significant current asset that must be financed on a continuing basis. Data from the Internal

Revenue Service indicate that notes and accounts receivable make up 40 to 50 percent of the average firm's current assets. Thus, receivables rival inventories as the largest single current asset.

CROSS-REFERENCES:

liquidity, how to analyze with ratios, p. 49
receivables management, how to evaluate differing credit policies, p. 108
receivables management, how to use a risk-class approach, p. 113

receivables, financing costs of. If a firm is considering adopting a credit policy that will change the size of its accounts receivable, it must consider the cost of additional funds or the savings from freeing funds. Three costs are commonly used:

1. *Cost of New Long-Term Debt.* When the firm expands its assets, it may consider increasing its long-term debt. If the new borrowing would cost 6 percent, this could be used as a simple method for calculating the cost of funds tied up in receivables. The advantage of this method is its ease of calculation. The disadvantage is that it probably understates the real cost of funds. The firm's cost of capital would be more accurate.

2. *Cost of Existing Long-Term Debt.* When the firm is reducing its assets, it may be able to decrease its existing long-term debt. If the firm could pay off a 6 percent note by reducing receivables, this could be used as a savings from the new credit policy.

3. *Cost of Capital.* This considers the overall cost of all the firm's sources of funds, and is the best measure of the financing costs for receivables. If it is not known, the firm will generally use the cost of long-term debt. Whatever the method, the cost of financing receivables should always be

included in decisions on changing a firm's terms of trade.

CROSS-REFERENCE:
cost of capital, p. 365

receivables, changing collection costs and bad-debt losses. Collection costs and bad-debt losses are the two components of administrative expenses that are most affected by changes in the level of receivables. Techniques for estimating likely changes in administrative expenses are as follows:

1. *Changes in Collection Costs.* The costs of collecting delinquent accounts will usually be a fairly constant percentage of the total receivables. If receivables change by a fixed percent, collection costs will change by a similar percent. For example, a firm may have collection costs of $5,000 when its receivables are $80,000. This is a ratio of 5/80, or 6.25 percent. If the firm adopts a policy that increases receivables to $120,000, the collection costs would be expected to be (.0625)($120,000), or $7,500.

It should be pointed out that the relationship between collection costs and receivables usually holds even though firms may be making sales to riskier customers when they change the terms of trade to attract more customers. It might be argued that collection costs should be higher with sales to customers with lower credit ratings. Two factors oppose this argument: (1) the higher costs are offset to some degree by economies that accrue with the larger collection activities; (2) the firm will make some efforts to hold collection costs in line with previous expenditures.

2. *Changes in Bad-Debt Losses.* If a firm increases credit sales by a fixed percentage, bad-debt losses will increase by a larger percentage in most cases. The amount of increase must be es-

timated by the marketing and finance managers most familiar with the firm's situation. For example, a firm may estimate $3,000 bad-debt losses on credit sales of $500,000. If its sales double as the result of a change in the terms of trade, bad-debt losses should increase by more than double, perhaps to $7,000.

Note that this technique compares the bad-debt losses to the credit sales, not to the balance of the receivables. A ratio of bad debts to receivables is more difficult to use, since bad-debt losses are more closely related to the level of sales.

3. *Changes in Miscellaneous Administrative Expenses.* The remaining administrative expenses will change only slightly compared to the changes in sales and receivables. Additional bookkeeping is required for increases in sales, but to a smaller degree. As a guideline, changes in miscellaneous expenses will be 5 to 10 percent of the percentage of change in receivables.

CROSS-REFERENCES:
average collection period, p. 315
collection costs, p. 351

receivables, costs of. As with all assets and operations, the willingness to allow credit sales involves certain costs. With respect to receivables, we can identify four major costs to the firm:

1. *Financing the Receivables.* Carrying accounts receivable ties up a portion of the firm's financial resources. These resources must be financed from one of three sources: (1) past profits retained in the business; (2) contributed capital from the owners; or (3) debt provided by creditors. In any of these cases, the firm incurs a cost for the use of the funds.
2. *Administrative Expenses.* To keep records on credit sales and payments,

the firm accepts additional expenses. For example, it may hire a receivables bookkeeper, provide an adding machine and supplies, and allocate office space for a working area and files. In addition, most firms conduct investigations of potential credit customers to determine their creditworthiness. These and other expenses, such as telephone charges and postage, comprise the administrative costs of maintaining receivables.

3. *Collection Costs.* When an individual or company does not pay its bill on time, the firm must take additional steps to increase the chances for eventual payment. Such actions require the firm to incur collection costs. Money will initially be spent to prepare and mail reminders that the payment is overdue. If these are not successful, the firm may hire personnel or collection agencies to visit the delinquent customer and demand payment.

4. *Bad-Debt Losses.* After making serious efforts to collect on overdue accounts, the firm may be forced to give up. If a customer declares bankruptcy, no payment will be forthcoming. If the customer leaves the city or state, it may be too costly to trace him and demand payment. In these cases, the firm is forced to accept a bad-debt loss on the account. Most firms anticipate that bad-debt losses will be incurred in the normal course of business. High-risk customers may be the major source of these losses, but occasionally a sound firm will unexpectedly run into liquidity problems and eventually enter bankruptcy. These losses are properly viewed as a cost of administering a credit policy.

CROSS-REFERENCES:
liquidity, how to analyze with ratios, p. 49
collection costs, p. 351

receivables policies. The firm should establish its receivables policies after carefully considering both the benefits and costs of different policies. Three major factors should be analyzed:

1. *Profits.* The firm should investigate different possibilities and forecast the effect of each on its future profits. The cost of funds tied up in receivables, collection costs, bad-debt losses, and money lost with discounts for early payment should be compared with additional sales or losses of sales as a result of each proposed policy.

2. *Growth in Sales.* Sometimes firms are willing to accept short-term setbacks with respect to profits if a new policy enables the firm to significantly increase its sales. Or a firm may adopt a certain policy to gain a foothold in a previously closed market. Because growth is so important aside from profits, it should be viewed as a separate factor in determining receivables policies.

3. *Possible Problems.* In spite of increased sales and profits, some policies may be accompanied by obvious and annoying problems. For example, by relaxing its credit terms, the firm may gain new customers. But if the firm's management must be concerned with collection policies and bad debts on a continuing basis, the firm might not be able to focus on its goals of increasing sales and reducing costs through other means. In such a case, the firm may choose to maintain tight credit with the intention of building sales without changing its terms of trade.

In any case, the final decision should be made after forecasting profits, considering the impact of the new policies on growth of sales, and evaluating the difficulties that will accompany the new policies. If a firm feels that the disadvantages of a liberal credit policy outweigh increased profits and sales, the policy should be rejected. If growth is important, policies that encourage expansion into new markets will be sought. If profits are the main concern, policies will be found to promote the chances for long-term profits.

CROSS-REFERENCE:
liquidity, how to analyze with ratios, p. 49

receivables, purpose of. Every commitment of financial resources in a firm is expected to contribute to the goal of maximizing the present value of the firm in the marketplace. The commitment of funds to accounts receivable is no exception. In support of this objective, we can identify three goals of maintaining receivables.

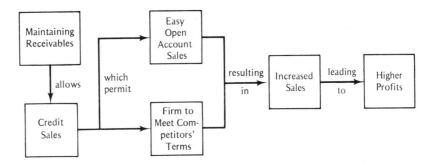

Flowchart Showing the Purpose of Maintaining Receivables.

1. *To Achieve Growth in Sales.* If a firm permits sales on credit, it will usually be able to sell more goods than if it insisted on immediate cash payment. Many customers are not prepared to pay cash when they purchase. They prefer to write a check at a later time rather than carry a checkbook with them. Or they may want the bill to be sent to their accounting department where it will be processed. In other cases, the purchase order may be transmitted over the telephone with instructions to send the goods and bill for later payment. Finally, many firms do not have the available cash to make immediate payment upon the receipt of goods. They must wait until they resell the goods before they will have money to pay for them. Because of these and other factors, fewer sales could be expected if a firm eliminated its credit policies.

2. *To Increase Profits.* If the direct result of maintaining receivables is to increase sales, an indirect result is that the additional sales will normally result in higher profits for the firm. This is the case when the marginal contribution or gross margin is greater than the additional costs associated with administering the credit policy. If the firm does not realize higher profits from its credit policy and maintaining receivables, it should consider an all-cash sales program.

3. *To Meet Competition.* As a defensive measure, most firms establish credit policies similar to the policies of competitors. It is a common practice in American business for the terms of trade to be identical throughout an industry, with wide variances in practices from one industry to another. In the same area, textiles may be purchased on terms of 2/10 EOM (a 2 percent discount if payment is made by the tenth day of the next month), whereas stationery supplies carry terms of net 30. By adapting its terms of trade to the industry norms, a firm will avoid the loss of sales from customers who would buy elsewhere if they did not receive the expected credit.

All three goals have a single purpose —to generate a larger flow of operating revenue, and hence profit, than would be achieved in the absence of a commitment of funds to accounts receivables.

CROSS-REFERENCE:
liquidity, how to analyze with ratios, p. 49

receivables ratios. Two ratios are used to measure the liquidity of a firm's accounts receivable:

$$\text{accounts receivable turnover} = \frac{\text{sales}}{\text{accounts receivable}}$$

$$\text{average collection period} = \frac{\text{accounts receivable}}{\text{daily sales}}$$

The accounts receivable turnover is a comparison of the size of the firm's sales and the size of its uncollected bills from customers. If the firm is having difficulty collecting its money, it will have a large receivables balance and a low ratio. If it has a strict credit policy and aggressive collection procedures, it will have a low receivables balance and a high ratio. The average collection period compares the receivables balance with the daily sales required to produce the balance. If the firm has $1,000 of sales each day and a receivables balance of $50,000, it took 50 days to accumulate the receivables (highly simplified statement). More important, if neither sales nor receivables change, it will take the firm 50 days to collect the $50,000 currently held as receivables. This is why the ratio reflects the average collection period.

Several techniques are available to help the manager analyze the significance of the receivables turnover and average collection period:

1. *Make Comparisons with Other Firms in the Industry.* Since conditions concerning the terms of trade and selling practices are usually standardized throughout an industry, this comparison can indicate whether the firm is lax or strict in its collection and sales policies.

2. *Compare Ratios with the Terms of Trade.* The terms of trade are a very important factor in analyzing receivables. To illustrate, let us compare two firms with average collection periods of 44 days. Firm A has terms of 2/10 net 30 (indicating that the firm gives a 2 percent discount for payment on its receivables within 10 days and expects full payment in 30 days). For this firm, a collection period of 44 days means that a number of receivables are still uncollected on the final due date of the 30 days. Firm B has terms of 2/10 net 60. For this firm, a period of 44 days means that collections are probably well within the 60-day time period. Without further information, we could conclude that firm B is doing a better job of collecting its receivables than is firm A.

3. *Use Only Net Credit Sales.* Sales figures may include both cash and credit sales. Since only credit sales become receivables, a more accurate turnover is given if only credit sales are used in the ratio. The same is true for the average collection period.

4. *Use Average Receivables Figures.* If the analyst takes the beginning and ending receivables balance and divides by 2, the average receivables balance may give a more accurate picture of turnover and collections than a single ending figure. A monthly view (add all the ending monthly balances and divide by 12) might be even more accurate. The averaging technique makes sense for firms whose ending receivables balance is not a normal figure.

5. *Avoid Cyclical Figures.* The analyst must always beware of applying ratio analysis to firms operating in industries with cyclical sales. The busy season will distort the ratios in one direction; the quiet season, in the other. Even the average of the busy and quiet periods may not be useful. It would be better to develop two sets of ratios: the turnover and collection period during (1) the busy period, and (2) during the quiet period.

CROSS-REFERENCES:
liquidity, how to analyze with ratios, p. 49
accounts receivable turnover, p. 307
average collection period, p. 315

receiver. An individual appointed by a judge or referee in bankruptcy proceedings to take responsibility for the property of a bankrupt firm and protect the interests of creditors during the period between filing for bankruptcy and the appointment of a permanent trustee or the dismissal of the petition.

CROSS-REFERENCE:
bankruptcy, p. 320

red herring. A prospectus for a security offering that has been filed with the Securities Exchange Commission (SEC), but has not yet been approved for sale. The name is derived from the fact that a statement indicating the tentative nature of the offer is stamped in red on the face of the prospectus.

CROSS-REFERENCE:
prospectus, p. 495

refunding. The process of issuing a new security in order to retire an existing security, often done to lower financial costs or to change the firm's capital structure.

CROSS-REFERENCE:
refunding a bond issue, how to make the decision, p. 152

registered bond. A bond issued by a government or corporation that requires that the owner's name be listed on the books of the corporation or its agent. A registered bond is less negotiable than a bearer bond but offers a higher degree of safety from theft.

CROSS-REFERENCE:
bearer bond, p. 321

registration statement. A document that must be prepared by a corporation under the Securities Act of 1933 before stock or bond offerings will be registered, so that they may be sold to the general public.

CROSS-REFERENCE:
public offering, p. 495

regulation Q. A Federal Reserve System regulation specifying the amount of interest that banks may pay on various types of accounts.

CROSS-REFERENCE:
federal reserve banks, p. 401

reorder point. In inventory management, the level of inventory at which the firm places an order for more goods. The reorder point is generally expressed in terms of units of inventory.

CROSS-REFERENCES:
inventory management, how to set up system for, p. 103
inventory management system, p. 445

inventories, p. 441

reorganization. In voluntary settlements or bankruptcy situations, a changing of the assets and financial structure to reflect true values of assets and to provide an equitable settlement of claims. A reorganization allows the firm to continue in existence, frequently with new owners who were the original creditors. Chapter X of the Chandler Act of 1938 describes legal procedures to be followed in the reorganization of a bankrupt corporation.

CROSS-REFERENCES:
arrangement, p. 312
bankruptcy, p. 320
Chandler Act of 1938, p. 347
Chapter X reorganization, p. 348
Chapter XI reorganization, p. 348

reorganization. A readjustment of corporate structure or ownership that may occur when one corporation acquires the stock of another or when an existing corporation changes its capital structure or name, place, or form of organization. To qualify as a nontaxable reorganization under the terms of the Internal Revenue Service code, the following conditions must apply:
1. The reorganization must be a sound business purpose, as opposed to being a scheme to avoid taxes.
2. There must be continuity of ownership interest by the former stockholders of the acquired corporation.
3. The combination must comply with both the technical form and the intention of the law and Internal Revenue regulations.

CROSS-REFERENCES:
nontaxable reorganization, p. 468
corporation, p. 364

required return. In the capital asset pricing model, the minimum expected return needed from an investment so that investors will purchase and hold the securities or assets involved.

CROSS-REFERENCE:
capital asset pricing model, p. 279

residual value. The expected or actual value of a fixed asset at the end of its service life.

CROSS-REFERENCES:
profit planning, how to price the use of a capital asset, p. 53
residual values, how to forecast, p. 66
salvage value, p. 517

restrictive covenants. Requirements in a loan agreement that place constraints on the borrowing firm. Examples are restrictions on the level of working capital, sale of fixed assets, future borrowing, salaries of officers, the use of proceeds from borrowings, and the declaration of dividends.

retained earnings. The portion of net income after taxes (NIAT) which is not paid out as dividends to common shareholders. An account on the balance sheet in the equity section which shows the total earnings retained through the date of the balance sheet.

CROSS-REFERENCES:
flow-of-funds statement, how to develop from balance sheet and income statement, p. 38
long-term financing, how to

compare different alternatives p. 139

return on equity. The return on equity may be calculated two ways:
1. *Earnings Available to the Common Shareholder Divided by Total Equity.* The earnings available to the common shareholder (EACS) is calculated by taking NIAT and subtracting dividends payable to preferred stockholders. The total equity is taken from the balance sheet.
2. *NIAT Divided by Total Equity.* This calculation is used for firms with no preferred stock outstanding.

Return on equity is used to measure the after-tax profits that accrue to the common shareholders. It is useful in analyzing the ability of the firm's management to realize an adequate return on the capital invested by the owners of the firm.

CROSS-REFERENCES:
profitability, how to analyze with ratios, p. 56
pooling and purchase methods, how to use in merger accounting, p. 91
earnings available to the common shareholder (EACS), p. 392

return on investment (ROI). The key indicator of profitability for a firm. It matches operating profits with the assets available to earn a return. Firms that are efficiently using their assets will have a relatively high return. Less efficient firms will have a lower return.

Comparing Three Major Ratios Linking Profits and Resources.

Return on Investment (ROI) EBIT/assets	Return on Equity (ROE) NIAT/equity	Earning Power (EP) NIAT/assets
Measures ability of management to earn a return on resources.	Measures ability of firm to convert operating profits into after-tax return for common shareholders.	Measures efficiency of firm in achieving an after-tax return on resources. Also called after-tax ROI.

Return on investment may be calculated two ways:

1. *EBIT Divided by Assets.* The firm's return on investment is a ratio of its operating income to the assets used to produce the income.
2. *Asset Turnover Times Profit Margin.* The size of a firm's return on investment is a function of the margin of profit on sales and the amount of sales generated on the asset base. A formula for return on investment is:

$$\frac{\text{profit}}{\text{margin}} \times \text{asset turnover} = \frac{\text{return on}}{\text{investment}}$$

$$\frac{\text{EBIT}}{\text{sales}} \times \frac{\text{sales}}{\text{assets}} = \frac{\text{EBIT}}{\text{assets}} = \frac{\text{return on}}{\text{investment}}$$

As is illustrated in the formula, when the multiplication is performed, the sales in the denominator of the profit margin and the sales in the numerator of the asset turnover cancel out, leaving EBIT/assets. The DuPont chart, so called because it was first used by the DuPont company, shows the factors producing return on investment

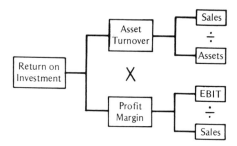

DuPont Chart.

Return on investment may be calculated on an after-tax basis. When this is done, the firm's net income after taxes (NIAT) is divided by total assets. This ratio is often called return on total assets.

CROSS-REFERENCES:

return required, formula. The rate of return required by a firm from its investments may be viewed by using a formula with three components:

$$\text{rate of return} = R_o + r_{bus} = r_{fin}$$

where R_o =   rate of return at zero risk level. If the firm operated in a totally risk-free environment, it would still demand some return as compensation for the time and effort expended in its operations.

r_{bus} =   business risk, whick is a premium added to the required return because of the risk that the firm will not have the ability to successfully operate in the business community. The firm's products may not sell, its machinery may not operate properly, or other business or operating factors may cause failure.

r_{fin} =   financial risk, which is the chance that the firm will not be sufficiently profitable either to cover interest payments on its debt or to pay dividends to shareholders. If the firm falls short of its profit goals, it may be able to cover operating expenses but not the financing costs of its original investment.

CROSS-REFERENCE:
risk and return, major decision areas, p. 513

revenue. The revenue from the firm's operations and investments will be the first item to appear on the income statement. As a general rule, this revenue will be reported using one of four approaches:

1. *Sales.* This term is used interchangeably with revenues for most companies and refers to a firm's net sales for the period.
2. *Net Sales.* This term refers to the difference between the firm's gross sales and any returns or discounts. Every time an item is sold, the firm's books will record a sale. If the item is later returned, the value of the item must be deducted from the gross sales for the period. Similarly, on credit sales the firm may offer a lower price for prompt payment. If the customer takes the discount, the dollar value of the discount must be deducted from gross sales.

EXAMPLE: A firm has $200,000 of sales in June. Items sold for $3,000 are returned and prompt payments give customers $1,500 in discounts. What is the net sales figure for the firm in June?

ANSWER: $195,500. The calculation is: $200,000 gross sales minus $3,000 returns minus $1,500 discounts equals $195,500.

3. *Revenues.* Although many firms use this term synonomously with sales, a firm may have revenues from other sources. For example, a firm may own securities and may receive interest or dividends from them. A firm may wish to identify this revenue separately from sales in an account such as revenue from investments or other income.
4. *Cash and Credit Sales.* Many firms, particularly retail operations such as department stores, have significant cash sales. These firms may identify cash and credit sales separately. If this is not done, analysts generally assume that all or virtually all sales are made on credit.

CROSS-REFERENCES:
inflation in the capital budget, p. 11
break-even analysis, how to use, p. 32

reverse split. A reduction of the outstanding shares of common stock of a firm, accomplished by exchanging new shares of stock for existing shares in some predetermined proportion. This is the opposite of a stock split. As an example, a firm may have 200,000 outstanding shares of $1 par common stock. It declares a 1-for-2 reverse split. After the split, it will have 100,000 shares of $2 par stock. A reverse split is normally used to keep the price of the stock from falling below a certain level, frequently around $10 per share. The fact that the stock is falling below $10 and the need of the company to declare a reverse split to keep the price up are both indicators of financial difficulty.

CROSS-REFERENCE:
stock split, p. 530

revolving charge plan. A credit card arrangement, such as BankAmericard or Master Charge, where an individual is granted credit upon demand after providing a detailed background statement, applying for a credit card, and signing a draft at the time of each purchase.

CROSS-REFERENCE:
open account, p. 471

revolving credit agreement. A form of a line of credit whereby the bank guarantees that the amount of the line will be available at any time during the term of the agreement regardless of economic conditions. A revolving credit agreement is generally more expensive than a simple line of credit because the funds are guaranteed even during periods of tight money. These agreements are frequently written for more than one year and thus can represent a form of intermediate-term financing. This differs from a line of credit which is normally less than a year and is considered short-term financing.

CROSS-REFERENCE:
credit terms, p. 368

right. A privilege given to existing shareholders when new shares are being issued by a corporation to purchase a specified number of the new shares in order to maintain their percentage share of ownership. Rights are usually offered at a price below the existing market for the stock and hence they have value and may be sold to another party before their expiration date. The value of a right may be calculated by the following formula:

$$\frac{\text{Mkt Pr} - \text{Sub Pr}}{\text{Stk Ratio} + 1} = \text{Value of Right}$$

Where

Mkt Pr	=Market value of one share of outstanding stock
Sub Pr	=Subscription price on one share of new stock
Stk Ratio	=Ratio of the number of shares of outstanding stock to the number of new shares to be issued.

EXAMPLE: A company has 1,000,000 shares of outstanding common stock selling at $22 per share. It plans to offer an additional 200,000 shares to existing stockholders at $18 per share. What is the theoretical value of one right? ANSWER: 67 cents, as follows:

Mkt Pr	=	$22
Sub Pr	=	$18

$$\text{Stk Ratio} = \quad 1,000,000/200,000 = 5 =$$

$$\frac{\$22 - \$18}{5 + 1} = \frac{4}{6} = \$.67$$

Each right gives a shareholder a claim on one-fifth of a share of common stock. For a full share, the price is 5 times $.67 or $3.33 + $18 for a total of $21.33 per share for a nonshareholder to purchase 5 rights at their theoretical value and exercise them.

CROSS-REFERENCE:
common stock, p. 351

risk. In a statistical sense, a future situation which can be quantified by assigning probabilities to the varying outcomes. This differs from uncertainty which cannot be quantified. In a non-statistical sense, risk and uncertainty are used interchangeably to refer to the variability of returns associated with the capital-budgeting project.

CROSS-REFERENCES:
risk in capital budget, how to measure, p. 25
long-term financing, how to compare different alternatives, p. 139
Durand on cost of capital, p. 203
classics in financial theory, p. 203
capital asset pricing model, p. 279

risk and return, general pattern. When firms are evaluating investment proposals, they will find that higher-return projects are usually accompanied by higher levels of risk. Conversely, low-return proposals involve minimal risk. These relationships are illustrated on page 513 by the general pattern line as well as by the specific proposals.
Of the five proposals, only project D breaks the pattern. With an 18 percent expected return, project D would normally be expected to have a medium-high degree of risk.

Project	A	B	C	D	E
Return	10%	14%	16%	18%	20%
Degree of Risk	Low	Medium-low	Medium	Medium-low	High

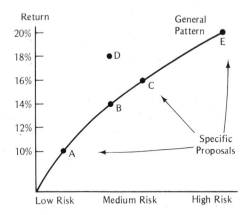

risk and return, major decision areas. The study of finance may be approached through an examination of the major decision areas linked to risk and return. In an overview of financial decision-making, eight important areas can be identified:

1. *Financial Analysis and Control.* This area makes extensive use of financial statements, such as the balance sheet and income statement, and financial ratios, such as return on investment and earnings per share. From the statements and ratios, the financial manager extracts important operating and financial information, and evaluates the data with respect to li-

quidity, profitability, and potential or actual problem areas. He seeks measures of the firm's return and degree of risk.

2. *Profit Planning and Budgeting.* In this area, the manager is attempting to forecast next year's operating and financial performance. He makes plans to conduct certain activities, and estimates the likely return from the activities. In this plan, he anticipates dangers and avoids unnecessary risks.

3. *Working-Capital Management.* In this area is the safeguarding and controlling of the firm's current assets and the planning for sufficient funds to pay current bills. Excessive, idle cash is identified and invested to earn a return while care is taken to avoid the risk of inadequate cash to pay bills on time.

4. *Capital Budgeting.* This area is concerned with the cash flows from newly invested capital. If the firm is planning on spending money (an outflow), what is the return from the investment (the inflows)? How much risk is involved in the project?

5. *Cost of Capital.* The firm must decide the degree of risk and level of return required on investments. The return must be sufficiently high so as to increase the value of the firm's stock. Cost of capital is the area concerned with the cutoff point or rate of return demanded on new investments.

6. *Sources of Funds.* If the firm has attractive possibilities for the investment of money, where will it get the funds to invest? Money may be available

from creditors, owners, or from retained profits. The sources of money
and the cost of funds from each
source are included in the scope of
this area.

7. *Valuation Theory.* Given current and
potential operating characteristics,
how much should a firm's stock be
worth? What can be done to increase
its value? These and similar issues are
taken up in this area.

8. *Acquisitions.* When a firm wishes to
acquire another firm, it must consider all the financial and operating
impacts. It must determine a fair
price to pay for the other firm's stock.
These are issues related to acquisitions.

CROSS-REFERENCES:

return required, a formula, p. 510
**risk-return analysis, how to use a
systems approach,** p. 192
**capital structure, internal factors
affecting,** p. 336
**profit-risk approach to financial
goals,** p. 494

**risk and uncertainty, distinguishing be-
tween.** In dealing with an unknown future, it is useful for the financial
manager to make the distinction between uncertainty and risk. Uncertainty
may be defined as the unforeseen
chance of future losses or dangers. Since
the loss is not foreseen, the firm cannot
deal with uncertainties directly in its
planning process. As an example of uncertainty, a firm investing in a foreign
country may not foresee a revolution
and takeover by an unfriendly group.
This was the case in Cuba in the late
1950s. Firms investing in Cuba, for the
most part, did not anticipate a successful revolution and did not assess its
likely impact on their operations. A second example would be an electrical fire
that destroys the firm's warehouse for
finished goods. Because of the low sta-

tistical frequency of major fires, most
firms would not be prepared to continue
operations without interruption after
such an event.

Risk, on the other hand, may be defined as the chance of future loss that is
foreseen. An example would be a firm
estimating the likelihood of total loss of
its sugarcane crop in Cuba due to poor
weather or other factors. In this case,
the danger can be identified—poor
weather. If we know the likelihood of
disastrous weather, we can forecast
possible losses. A useful technique is to
assign probabilities to risk and say, for
example, that there is a 40 percent
chance of failure due to foreseen factors.

As an example of the assigning of
probabilities, we shall use a firm's estimate of the prospects of a failure of an
important crop that is used as a raw
material in the firm's production process. The analyst has researched agricul-
ture records between 1913 and 1972 and
determined that the crop was good to
excellent in each year with the following exceptions:

1918—midsummer drought; 40
percent of crop ruined.
1933—heavy rains during harvest-
ing; 90 percent loss.
1937—floods; major loss.
1946—late-summer drought; 50
percent loss.
1952—floods; serious damage.
1967—excessive heat; 30 percent
of crop ruined.

These data show that in 6 of the 60
years, or 10 percent of the time, the crop
was damaged as a result of adverse
weather conditions. The damage ranged
from "serious damage" to 90 percent
loss, with an average near or below 50
percent. In the language of probabilities
he would conclude that "there is a 10
percent chance of an average loss of 50
percent of the crop."

EXAMPLE: A firm has submitted bids on 215

projects in the past 12 years, and been awarded the contract on 43 of these jobs. The chief engineer is currently preparing the 216th bid. What are the chances that he will win the contract? ANSWER: 20 percent. If the overall situation has not changed, the firm has a history of winning 43/215 of its bids, or 20 percent.

CROSS-REFERENCE:
uncertainty, p. 541

risk classes. Categories of customer credit when a firm establishes different credit terms for customers based on the soundness of the customers.

CROSS-REFERENCE:
credit terms, p. 368

risk-class approach. In receivables management, a method of approving credit sales so that decisions to extend credit may be made routinely. The firm establishes a certain number of risk classes ranging from the strongest and most established customers to the weakest firms. A separate credit policy is developed for each class. When a customer first applies for credit, the customer will be investigated and placed into one of the classes. This will eliminate the need to make separate decisions on extending credit each time the customer wants to make a purchase.

CROSS-REFERENCES:
receivables management, how to use a risk-class approach, p. 113
credit terms, p. 368

risk in capital budgets. When preparing capital budgets, firms face three choices for dealing with risk:
1. *Ignore It.* Many firms approach capital budgeting without referring to the risk elements of proposals. A number of firms use this approach and appear to be satisfied with the results. In essence, these firms are assuming that all projects have similar risk factors and that the future is too uncertain to allow a rational risk analysis. There is some logic to this point of view.
2. *Apply Rigorous Mathematics.* A second approach involves the application of statistics and mathematical techniques to the issue of risk. Rigorous mathematical models may be developed, data gathered, and the computer used in identifying relationships and risk factors. This method is useful as a supplemental technique, but should not be used alone for several reasons:
   a. Important data may not be available or may not be timely.
   b. Unknown to the manager, the assumptions underlying available data may be changing.
   c. Statistical theory is not yet fully developed to allow complete reliability on mathematical techniques and assumptions.
3. *Blend Mathematics with Intuition.* Many financial managers utilize a mixture of risk factors and empirical knowledge to deal with risk in capital budgeting. They know that risk is present in all projects and that mathematical techniques can help focus on it. Models can be used to confirm judgments or to highlight errors, omissions, or other weaknesses of proposals. The material in this Handbook will be useful to managers with this orientation.

Three Sources of Risk The firm is basically confronted with risk from three sources:
1. *Size of the Investment.* A large project involves greater risk than a small project solely in terms of the importance of success versus failure. If a large project collapses, it may destroy the firm, forcing it into bankruptcy. A smaller investment is less risky because it is less significant to the firm's efforts to survive.

2. *Reinvestment of Cash Flows.* Should a firm accept a project that offers a 20 percent return for 2 years or one that offers a 16 percent return for 3 years? The answer depends upon the rate of return available for reinvesting the proceeds from the 20 percent, 2-year project. The danger that the firm will not be able to reinvest funds as they become available is a continuing risk in managing capital budgets and cash flows.

3. *Variability of Cash Flows.* Will the project bring in the expected return? Forecasting accurately the likely returns is the most difficult area of risk management for capital budgeting.

CROSS-REFERENCE:

risk in capital budget, how to measure, p. 25

risk, time effects on. Capital budgets involve projections of risk over extended periods of time. Since subjective probabilities consider future risk factors, we can expect more accuracy for next year's projection than for longer projections. Stated another way, the dispersion of likely returns is greater over time. This dispersion is shown in the figure.

Because of the greater dispersion over time, we can also say that project riskiness increases over time. In the figure the first year will bring returns between $60,000 and $200,000. By year 5, the return may be as little as −$20,000 or as much as $280,000. The expected return, or most likely return, is still $130,000, but the range of possible returns (or risk of not receiving the expected return) is much greater.

There are two major reasons why project riskiness increases as we estimate further into the future:

1. *Risks Are Harder to Identify.* It is difficult enought to identify the dangers to the success of a proposal in its early

stages. But some trends are recognizable. For example, inflation may be increasing or slowing down. A recession may be beginning or ending. The government may be expanding or contracting its budget. Five or 10 years into the future, these items are less predictable and risks associated with them are more difficult to identify.

2. *Probabilities Are Harder to Estimate.* The assigning of the likelihood of high, most likely, and low sales or profit estimates becomes increasingly difficult as we forecast 2, 5, or 10 years into the future.

First Year

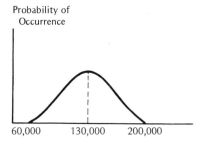

Fifth Year

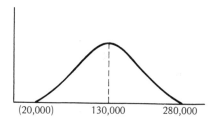

Project Riskiness Increases over Time.

round lot. A quantity of stocks, usually 100 shares, which are used as a basic trading unit in the sale and purchase of securities.

CROSS-REFERENCE:

secondary markets, p. 519

S

safety level. The minimum amount of cash needed by a firm to avoid or minimize the possibility of cash shortages.

CROSS-REFERENCES:

cash flow forecast, how to prepare, p. 97
inventory management, how to set up system for, p. 103
cash safety level, p. 346

safety stock level. In inventory management, the minimum level of inventory that a firm wants to hold as a protection against shortages.

CROSS-REFERENCE:

inventory management, how to set up system for, p. 103

sale and leaseback. One of the most common forms of financing real property involves the use of sale and leaseback. Retail stores, office buildings, multipurpose industrial buildings, and even complete shopping centers are frequently financed with this method.

Under a sale and leaseback arrangement, the firm seeking long-term financing will purchase or build the desired building. The firm will then sell the building at or near cost to a financial institution, usually a life insurance company or pension fund. Then the firm will lease back the building on a long-term basis. Thus, the firm has use of the building it constructed and designed, but does not have to tie up its capital in owning the building.

Most leasebacks are on a net-net basis, which means that the lessee pays all maintenance expenses, property taxes, insurance, and a lease payment.

In some cases, the lease arrangement will allow the lessee to repurchase the property at the termination of the lease. Firms must be careful when providing this option, because the tax shield provided by lease payments may be endangered by an adverse tax ruling from the Internal Revenue Service.

CROSS-REFERENCE:

leasing, overview, p. 451

salvage value. The expected value of a depreciable fixed asset at the end of the asset's service life. Also called residual value. A cash salvage value is the actual cash received or expected; the book salvage value is the estimate of salvage value contained on the depreciation schedule prepared for the fixed asset. Tax consequences arise when the cash salvage value and book salvage value differ.

CROSS-REFERENCES:

depreciation, how to calculate, p. 188
residual value, p. 509
depreciation, p. 379

salvage value, effects in capital budgeting. When a firm purchases a fixed asset, it records the value at cost and prepares a depreciation schedule. In this schedule, the machine is depreciated using an accelerated method to a value of $25,000. This is the book salvage value, which is defined as the estimated value of the machine at the completion of its service life. The machine may actually be worth more or less than this amount in 5 years, but the accounting records will record it at book salvage value. The stone crusher will be fully depreciated at the end of 1981.

The cash salvage value is defined as the amount of money received by the firm when the machine is finally sold. If the machine is sold for $40,000 in June 1981 and the firm must pay $5,000 to remove it from the plant and transport it to the purchaser, the firm receives a net of $40,000 minus $5,000, or $35,000 cash salvage value.

Simplified Depreciation Schedule.

Stone Crusher, Serial No. 224715, Purchased June 23, 1976
Cost: $115,000 + 17,000 installation
Book salvage value: $25,000, June 1981

Year	Book Value	−	Annual Depreciation	=	Ending Book Value
0	132,000	−	0	=	132,000
1	132,000	−	35,667	=	96,333
2	96,333	−	28,533	=	67,800
3	67,800	−	21,400	=	46,400
4	46,400	−	14,267	=	32,133
5	32,133	−	7,133	=	25,000

A problem arises when the book and cash salvage values are compared. Three situations are possible:

1. *Cash Exceeds Book Salvage Value.* If the firm receives $35,000 from the sale of a machine carried at $25,000 book value, the firm has a $10,000 gain and must pay taxes on the gain. In effect, this means that the depreciation schedule was wrong and allowed too much in tax credits for the wearing out of the machine. When the machine is sold, the firm must show the gain, normally as ordinary income, which is taxable at the corporate rate.

2. *Book Exceeds Cash Salvage Value.* If the firm only received $12,000 from the sale of the $25,000 book value machine, it has a loss of $13,000. The depreciation schedule underestimated the wearing out of the machine. The loss is normally treated as a tax credit against ordinary income.

3. *Book Equals Cash Salvage Value.* If this occurs or if the machine is traded in on a new machine, no tax effects normally need to be considered.

Differing Book and Cash Salvage Values Because of the difficulties of forecasting value into the distant future, the firm expects to have differing book and cash salvage values at the end of a machine's service life. In many cases, a difference is expected before the machine is even purchased. This is true because of two characteristics of the book salvage value:

1. *Firm Seeks the Smallest Possible Book Salvage Value.* Normally, the firm is interested in gaining maximum depreciation and a minimum book salvage value so that it may gain greater tax shields and cash inflows. Thus, the firm may wish to set up a depreciation schedule with a book salvage value that is substantially below the expected cash salvage value of an asset.

2. *Book Salvage Value Must Comply with IRS Guidelines.* The book salvage value is determined in accordance with guidelines from the Internal Revenue Service. This may result in a higher or lower book value than would actually be expected.

Because of these two characteristics of book salvage value, the decision to acquire a fixed asset must consider any difference in the book and cash salvage values. The capital budgeting process covered in this Handbook allows the analyst to handle this difference.

CROSS-REFERENCES:
cash salvage value, p. 346
book salvage value, p. 323

scarce currency clause. Under the rules of the International Monetary Fund, a provision that allows a nation to declare the currency of a creditor nation to be a scarce currency, thus allowing the debtor nation to restrict transactions with that creditor nation until the imbalance in the balance of payments was corrected.

CROSS-REFERENCE:
International Monetary Fund, p. 438

secondary markets. Securities that have been previously issued are traded in the different secondary markets, which include the organized exchanges and the over-the-counter market. The trading is aided by dealers and brokers:
1. *Dealers.* A dealer acts as a principal and buys for his own account and sells securities from his own inventory.
2. *Brokers.* A broker does not buy or sell from his own inventory of securities. He acts as an agent for others and receives a commission for assisting in a transaction.

The same firm or individual may act as either a broker or a dealer at different times and in different transactions in the secondary markets, as long as he discloses his capacity to the customer.

CROSS-REFERENCES:
dealer, p. 373
broker, p. 327
round lot, p. 516

Securities and Exchange Commission (SEC). A governmental agency responsible for administering securities acts and regulations. Its primary goals are to prohibit fraud in connection with securities offerings and to make financial data available to the investing public. All new securities issued by corporations must be registered with the SEC before they can be made availa-ble to the general public. Offerings that do not meet the requirements of the applicable laws may not be issued.

CROSS-REFERENCES:
pooling and purchase methods, how to use in merger accounting, p. 91
security markets, regulation of, p. 520

securities and investment analysis. A specialized field focusing on the measurement of risk and return in the purchases of stocks, bonds, and other securities.

CROSS-REFERENCE:
risk and return, general pattern, p. 512

security, financial. A legal instrument that represents either an ownership or a creditor claim on a company. Two basic kinds of securities are of concern to the financial manager:
1. *Debt Securities.* A debt security arises when a firm borrows money. The firm incurs a liability to repay the amount of money borrowed at some future maturity date. In addition, the firm must pay interest—usually in periodic payments—in return for the right to use the creditor's money.
2. *Equity Securities.* An equity security represents ownership in the firm. Persons who purchase equity securities are entitled to different rights and conditions than the firm's creditors. The exact ownership rights are usually agreed to in advance and may be written in the organizational agreement.

CROSS-REFERENCES:
bull market, p. 327
bid, p. 322
blue sky laws, p. 322
direct placement, p. 381

security market line (SML). The security market line is used in the capital asset pricing model to measure the relationship between risk and return. It differs from the capital market line in two respects:

1. *Covariance Is Risk Measure.* In computing the capital market line (CML), risk is measured using the standard deviation. In computing the SML, risk is measured using the covariance of the individual security with the overall portfolio. This is a key difference because, by using the covariance, the SML recognizes the risk of a single security in terms of its effect on the risk of the portfolio as a whole.

2. *Variance (σ^2) Replaces Standard Deviation (σ).* The second difference is that the market variance (σ^2_{mkt}) replaces the market standard deviation (σ_{mkt}) in the formula, thus changing the position of the SML as compared to the CML.

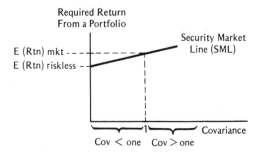

Required Return
From a Portfolio

Security Market Line (SML)

E (Rtn) mkt

E (Rtn) riskless

Covariance

Cov < one   Cov > one

CROSS-REFERENCE:
capital asset pricing model, p. 279

security markets, regulation of. The securities markets in the United States are carefully regulated to ensure that individual investors will be treated honestly and fairly. The 1929 crash of the stock market had been preceded by widespread manipulation of stock prices and misrepresentation of financial data. Following the crash, the federal government took steps to correct the situation. An investigation was conducted that led to the passage of a number of federal security acts and the creation of the Securities and Exchange Commission (SEC) in 1934.

The SEC administers the Securities Act of 1933. This act has two objectives:

1. *To Make Financial Data Public.* The act requires firms to provide investors with financial and other information concerning the securities offered for public sale. If a firm will not disclose the required information, the bonds, preferred stock, or common stock cannot be sold publicly.

2. *To Prohibit Fraud.* The act prohibits misrepresentation, dishonesty, or fraud connected with any offering of stocks or bonds.

The SEC is also responsible for administering a variety of other securities acts and regulations. All new issues by corporations must be registered with the SEC. Those offerings which fail to meet the requirements of the applicable laws will not receive an effective registration statement and may not be issued to the public.

A number of states have laws regulating the sale of securities. Some states, such as New York, Illinois, and California, have relatively strict laws; other states are more lenient. These laws generally apply to securities that are either too small in volume to be included under federal regulations or to securities that are exempted from registration under the rules of the SEC.

The organized exchanges have regulations for listed stocks. The New York Stock Exchange has adopted extensive regulations for its stocks and bonds. The other exchanges have less severe rules.

The NASD has a set of rules and regulations governing behavior in the over-the-counter market. Failure to comply with these rules can bring penalties such as censure, fines, suspension, or expulsion from the organization.

CROSS-REFERENCES:
National Association of Security Dealers, p. 466
Securities and Exchange Commission, p. 519

security risk. The degree of risk inherent in the investment in a single financial asset such as common stock or bonds. This is an important concept in the capital asset pricing model which reduces the risk from investment in individual securities through diversification in a portfolio.

CROSS-REFERENCE:
capital asset pricing model, p. 279

sensitivity analysis. A technique for measuring the effect of one variable on another, used to make an assessment of the risk associated with a proposal or situation. For example, the sensitivity of changes in the selling price of a product may be evaluated in terms of its effect on the firm's profits.

CROSS-REFERENCE:
sensitivity analysis, how to use, p. 193

serial bond. A bond offering in which a certain number of bonds mature each year, thus allowing the issuer to gradually retire the debt.

CROSS-REFERENCE:
bond, p. 323

service lease. Because modern machinery frequently requires specialized maintenance and support, service leases have been growing in importance. Major characteristics of these leases are the following:

1. *Maintenance Included in Lease Cost.* The lessor is responsible for maintaining the equipment and performing all routine servicing and repairs. This feature is considered in the cost of the lease and protects the lessee from having to correct major breakdowns. It also allows the lessor to employ a staff of skilled mechanics who can maintain a large number of leased vehicles, computers, or other equipment.
2. *Equipment May Not Be Fully Amortized.* When a firm amortizes an asset, it completely writes it off during a certain period. In service leases, the lease payments may not be sufficient to allow the lessor to recover the original cost of the asset. This means that the lease period is less than the service life of the asset and the lease is not fully amortizing.
3. *Lease May Be Canceled.* In most cases, the service lease may be canceled by the lessee. In return for this option, the lease may contain provisions for the payment of a penalty if the lease is canceled prior to its expiration. In most cases, a stipulated notice for cancelation is required.
4. *Miscellaneous Services May Be Available.* In addition to the equipment and servicing, the service lease may provide for additional services on the part of the lessor. For example, substitute equipment may be provided during breakdowns, and insurance forms may be processed by the lessor as part of the lease agreement.

CROSS-REFERENCE:
lease-buy decision, how to make it, p. 132

Sharpe Model. In portfolio theory, a method of separating the systematic (market-related) and unsystematic (random-fluctuation) risk components of overall portfolio risk. The model is widely used to calculate expected return from an investment as it requires fewer calculations and less computer capacity than other formulas. It is given in the formula:

$$\text{EXPECTED RETURN} = \text{Alpha} + \text{Beta[Market Return]} + \text{E(Random)}$$

where

Alpha = an expected return in the absence of market factors.

Beta = a regression coefficient that correlates the movements between securities and the overall market.

E(Random) = a random error variable

CROSS-REFERENCE:

capital asset pricing model, p. 279

Sherman Act (1890). A federal statute designed to protect trade and commerce against unlawful restraints or monopolies.

CROSS-REFERENCE:

antitrust factors affecting mergers, p. 311

short sale. A stock transaction where an individual sells a stock that he does not own. The sale is made in the anticipation of a drop in the stock's market price, thus allowing the seller to repurchase the stock and make a profit when the stock is declining in price. In effect, the short seller is selling a stock held by a broker but belonging to another person. At the end of a stipulated period of time, the short seller must repurchase the stock thus covering the transaction.

sinking fund. An investment account under the supervision of a trustee into which borrowers are required to make periodic payments to provide funds for the retirement of a bond offering. Interest is earned on the deposits in the sinking fund and the total payments plus interest are equal to the face value of the bonds at maturity.

Smithsonian Agreement. On December 18, 1971, The Smithsonian Agreement (so named because the IMF met at the Smithsonian Institution in Washington, D.C.) formalized the devaluation of the dollar and laid the groundwork for major changes in the international monetary system. The major points of the Agreement were:

1. *Devaluation of Dollar.* The United States agreed to devalue the dollar from $35 to $38 per ounce, approximately an 8 percent devaluation.

2. *Broadening of Exchange Rate Bands.* The IMF articles of agreement provided for fixed exchange rates with fluctuations of no more than one percent on either side of the fixed rate. This allowed a 2 percent exchange rate fluctuation, or band. The Smithsonian Agreement provided that the band be widened to 4½ percent, 2¼ percent on each side of the fixed par.

3. *Prompt Discussions.* The Smithsonian Meeting involved the world's leading trading nations, the so-called Group of Ten. These nations agreed to conduct prompt discussions to find long-term answers to the problems of the international monetary system.

CROSS-REFERENCES:

currency, p. 369
International Monetary Fund, p. 438

soft currency. In international finance, the currency of a nation that is experiencing fundamental economic weaknesses such as inflation or balance of payments deficits that will cause the currency to decline in value compared to other national currencies in the foreseeable future. A soft currency is also said to be a weak currency.

CROSS-REFERENCE:
hard currency, p. 425

sole proprietorship. A firm owned by a single person who holds the ownership rights to all the assets and who is responsible for all the firm's debts. The single owner will receive all the profits from the firm or will have to suffer any losses. Two aspects of sole proprietorships are noteworthy:

1. *It Is the Easiest Business Form to Establish.* In most cases, an individual begins a sole proprietorship by simply starting up operations. No financial security is required as proof of ownership. The only securities arising from a sole proprietorship are debt securities in the event that the owner borrows money.

2. *It Is the Most Common Form of Business Organization.* Sole proprietorships account for well over half the businesses in the country. Most sole proprietorships are small operations; thus, this form is less important than the corporation in terms of business activity. The corporate form is much more prominent in terms of sales, assets, profits, and contributions to the national economy.

CROSS-REFERENCES:
partnership, p. 477
corporation, p. 364

sources and uses of funds. The figure shows the sources supplying funds to the firm's working-capital pool and the uses removing funds from the pool. The working-capital pool consists of all the current accounts of the firm. In a sense, the pool is a measure of net working capital. Only transactions that affect noncurrent accounts may be classified as sources or uses of funds.

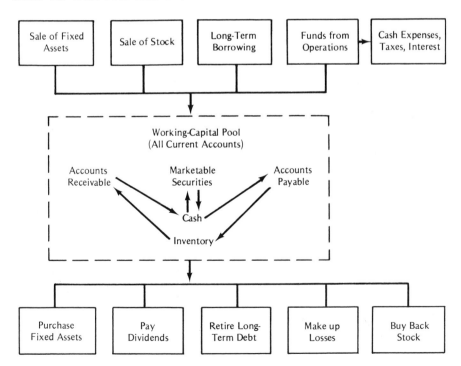

Sources and Uses of Funds and the Working-Capital Pool.

EXAMPLE: A firm takes out a 6-month note and uses the money to increase inventory. Will this transaction affect the size of the working-capital pool? Will it be shown on the flow-of-funds statement?

ANSWER: Since the working-capital pool is a measure of net working capital, increasing a current liability to finance the increase of a current asset does not affect the overall size of the pool. It will not be shown on the flow-of-funds statement because only transactions that affect noncurrent accounts may be classified as sources or uses of funds.

CROSS-REFERENCES:

flow-of-funds statement, how to develop from balance sheet and income statement, p. 38
working capital, how to balance sources of funds, p. 121
flow-of-funds statement, p. 410
flow-of-funds statements, three formats, p. 411

sources of funds, nonoperational. Three nonoperational sources of funds are important to most firms:

1. *Sale of Stock.* Whenever the firm issues additional shares of stock, it receives funds. The receipts are recorded in the cash account, and the source is shown in equity accounts under contributed capital.
2. *Long-Term Borrowing.* Whenever a firm borrows through the use of bonds, mortgages, or other long-term means, the sources are reflected in the long-term liabilities accounts.
3. *Sale of Fixed Assets.* If the firm sells a portion of its fixed assets, the funds are treated separately from funds from operations.

CROSS-REFERENCES:

flow-of-funds statement, how to develop from balance sheet and income statement, p. 38

special drawing rights (SDR's). With in-creasing world trade and limited monetary reserves, the International Monetary Fund approved, at a meeting in Rio de Janeiro in 1967, the creation of special drawing rights. SDR's were created through a bookkeeping entry in 1970 and additional SDR's have been issued since then. An SDR may be defined as an artificially created international monetary reserve which may be exchanged only among central banks. SDR's are initially allocated to member nations of the IMF but may be assigned to creditor nations so that convertible currencies can be made available to debtor nations. SDR's have the full impact of gold in some ways; for example, they are a monetary reserve, do not have to be repaid, and may allow a nation to exercise drawing rights in excess of 200 percent of its quota. They do not, however, increase the size of a nation's gold tranche.

CROSS-REFERENCES:

monetary reserves, p. 464
International Monetary Fund, p. 438

spot market. In international finance, the commercial banks, brokers, and dealers who facilitate the immediate purchase of and payment for the exchange of national currencies. A spot transaction can be made by telephone or by cable with the delivery and payment to be accomplished in a day or two.

CROSS-REFERENCE:

forward market, p. 416

spot and forward exchange markets. A spot transaction involves the immediate purchase of and payment for foreign exchange. The arrangement can be made telephonically or by cable with the delivery and payment to be accomplished in a day or two. These transactions are said to occur in the spot market.

The forward market involves foreign exchange transactions where delivery occurs at a stipulated future date. Two parties agree to exchange a stipulated amount of one currency for a stipulated amount of another currency at a specified exchange rate. No money is exchanged when the agreement is reached so no money is tied up during the life of the forward contract. At delivery in 30, 60, 90, or the days stipulated, both parties provide the agreed-upon amounts of each currency.

EXAMPLE: An importer in France needs 300,-000 krona to pay for a purchase. The current date is March 1st but the krona will not be needed until June 1st. If the importer signs a forward exchange contract with Chase Manhattan Bank, how many francs will he have to deliver at maturity?

> *Chase Manhattan Quotes*
> *Paris Office*
> *Franc/Krona*
>
> *Spot .... .3898kr/1fr*
> *30 day .... .3906*
> *90 day .... .3925*
> *180 day .... .3954*

ANSWER: 764,331 francs must be delivered. Since the period is 90 days, the calculation is 300,000/.3925 = 764,331 francs.
EXAMPLE: An exporter in France will receive 500,000 krona in payment for goods shipped on March 1st. The payment is due to arrive April 1st. If the exporter signs a forward exchange contract with Chase Manhattan Bank, how many francs will he receive at delivery.
ANSWER: 1,280,082 francs. Using the 30 day rate, 500,000/.3906 = 1,280,082 fr.
EXAMPLE: A Swedish exporter is due to receive 120,000 francs in 180 days. If he signs a forward contract with Chase Manhattan, how many krona will he receive at maturity?
ANSWER: 47,448 krona. Using the 180 day rate, 120,000 × .3954 = 47,448 kr.

CROSS-REFERENCES:
arbitrage in foreign exchange markets, how to analyze, p. 161

forward market, how to calculate bid and ask quotes, p. 171
hedging foreign exchange transactions, how to evaluate alternatives, p. 173
premium or discount on foreign exchange, how to calculate, p. 176

standard deviation. A statistical measure of the variability of possible outcomes, generally used as a measure of risk.

CROSS-REFERENCES:
risk in capital budget, how to measure, p. 25
standard deviation, how to estimate in capital budgeting, p. 30
standard deviation, how to measure risk with, p. 195
capital asset pricing model, p. 279

start-up cost. The initial expense occurred when a firm begins a new operation.

statutory merger. A joining of two corporations that takes place in strict compliance with a state statute.

CROSS-REFERENCES:
nontaxable reorganization, p. 468
mergers, p. 460

steady payment loan. A form of long-term, fixed-asset financing involves a steady-payment method of paying principal and interest. The amount of the annual payment is determined with the aid of a present-value table in a manner that is almost identical to the formula for calculating the lease payment under a level-rental plan. The difference is that the down payment is deducted from the asset cost before performing the calculation. The formula is

$$\text{annual payment} = \frac{\text{amount borrowed}}{\substack{\text{present-value factor} \\ \text{(Annuity Table)}}}$$

Steady-Payment Schedule.

$125,000 Asset with $25,000 Down Payment, 5-Year Steady-Payment Loan at 8%

$$annual\ payment = \frac{\$100,000}{8\%\ 5\text{-}year\ annuity\ factor} = \frac{\$100,000}{3.993} = \$25,044$$

Payment Stream

Year	Interest at 8%	Principal Repayment	Total Payment
0		$ 25,000	$ 25,000
1	$ 8,000	17,044	25,044
2	6,636	18,408	25,044
3	5,162	19,882	25,044
4	3,571	21,473	25,044
5	1,851	23,193	25,044
	$25,220 +	$125,000 =	$150,220

An example of the use of this formula is given in the table.

CROSS–REFERENCES:
lease-buy decision, how to make it, p. 132
steady principal reduction loan, p. 526

steady-principal-reduction loan. The steady-principal-reduction method of repaying the loan is one form of long-term financing available to the borrower. With this method, the installment payments will decrease each year, as is shown in the table. The interest is calculated for each period on the outstanding balance. The payment stream is written so that the principal is reduced in equal amounts during each period. The table gives an example of steady principal reduction on a $125,000 asset with a $25,000 down payment.

CROSS–REFERENCES:
lease-buy decision, how to make it, p. 132
steady payment loan, p. 525

stock. An equity security representing ownership of a corporation. The term stock may be used to refer to preferred or common stock.

Repayment Schedule for a $125,000 Asset with $25,000 Down Payment, 8 Percent Interest Factor, and 5-Year Steady-Principal-Reduction Stream.

Year	Interest at 8%	Principal Repayment	Total Payment
0		$ 25,000	$ 25,000
1	$ 8,000	20,000	28,000
2	6,400	20,000	26,400
3	4,800	20,000	24,800
4	3,200	20,000	23,200
5	1,600	20,000	21,600
	$24,000 +	$125,000 =	$149,000

CROSS-REFERENCES:

common stock, p. 351
preferred stock, p. 481

stock dividend. A stock dividend occurs when the board of directors authorizes a distribution of common stock to existing shareholders.[1] This has the effect of increasing the number of outstanding shares of the firm's stock. For example, if a shareholder owns 100 shares of common stock at a time when the firm distributes a 5% stock dividend, the shareholder will receive 5 additional shares.

There are several favorable aspects of a stock dividend:

1. *Conserves Cash.* The stock dividend allows the firm to declare a dividend without using up cash that may be needed for operations or expansion. Rather than seek additional external financing, the firm can retain its funds that would otherwise be distributed to shareholders.
2. *Indicates Higher Future Profits.* Normally a stock dividend is an indication of higher future profits. If the profits do not rise, the firm would experience a dilution of earnings as a result of the additional shares outstanding. Since a dilution of earnings is not desirable, stock dividends are usually declared only by boards of directors who expect rises in earnings to offset the additional outstanding shares.
3. *Raises Future Dividends for Investors.* If the regular cash dividend is continued after an extra stock dividend is declared, the shareholders will receive an increase in cash dividends in the future. For example, a firm may declare a $1 regular dividend and a 5 percent extra stock dividend. A shareholder with 100 shares will receive $100 and 5 additional shares. If the firm continues its $1 dividend, this investor would receive $105, an increase of $5, in the next period.
4. *Has High Psychological Value.* Because of the positive aspects of stock dividends, the dividend declaration is usually received positively by the market. This tends to encourage investment in the stock thus supporting or raising its market price. Instead of experiencing a drop in value after a stock dividend, the price may actually rise.

stock dividend, effect on firm's equity. The stock dividend differs from an issue of new common stock. If the existing shareholders do not have the funds to purchase new stock, their proportion of the ownership in the firm will decline as new investors purchase shares. This is avoided by a stock dividend which is, in effect, nothing more than a recapitalization of the firm. The table shows a firm's equity before and after a 10 percent stock dividend.

Effect of a Stock Dividend on a Firm's Equity.

Assumes a 10% Stock Dividend When the Fair Market Value is $20 per Share

	Before the Dividend	After the Dividend	
Common stock ($1 par)	$ 200,000	$ 220,000	($1 × 20,000 shares)
Premium	600,000	980,000	($19 × 20,000 shares)
Retained earnings	2,000,000	1,600,000	($20 × 20,000 shares)
Total equity	$2,800,000	$2,800,000	

[1] This discussion does not cover preferred stock dividends, although they represent another form of stock dividend.

In this example, the firm has 200,000 shares of stock outstanding when a 10 percent stock dividend is declared. With a fair market value of $20 per share, the total dividend is worth $20 times 20,000 shares, or $400,000. This amount is removed from retained earnings and distributed between the common stock and premium accounts. The original owners still are credited with the same equity, but the capital structure has been modified slightly with a reduction in retained earnings and an increase in contributed capital. The ownership positions of the existing shareholders are not changed at all.

EXAMPLE: A firm has 200,000 outstanding shares of $2 par common stock, a premium account of $3,200,000, and retained earnings of $16,000,000, all before the declaration of dividends. The board of directors declared a $1.50 per-share cash dividend and a 25 percent stock dividend. What are the balances in the equity accounts if the fair market value of the stock is $25 per share?

ANSWER: The cash dividend reduces retained earnings by 200,000 shares $\times$ $1.50 = $300,000.

The stock dividend of 50,000 shares increases common stock by $100,000 (50,000 $\times$ $2 par); premium increases by $1,150,000 (50,-000 $\times$ $23); retained earnings decreases by $1,250,000 (50,000 $\times$ $25). The changes in equity accounts are:

	Before	
Common stock ($2 par)	$ 400,000	to
Premium	3,200,000	to
Retained earnings	16,000,000	to
Total equity	$19,600,000	

After
$ 500,000
4,350,000
14,450,000
$19,300,000

stock-level subsystem. In an inventory management system, the stock-level subsystem keeps track of the goods held by the firm, the issuing of goods, and the arrival of orders. It includes all the records accounting for the goods in stock and allows the calculation of the current level of inventory items.

CROSS-REFERENCES:
inventory management, how to set up system for, p. 103
inventory management system, p. 445

stock option. The right to purchase a specified number of shares of common stock during a stated time period and at a stipulated price. Stock options are frequently given to senior officers of the company as an incentive to work to raise the value of the firm. For example, the firm's common stock may be selling for $20 a share when the president is given an option to purchase 1,000 shares for $22 at any time in the next 3 years. If the stock rises to $40, the president can exercise the option, purchase the stock for $22,000 (1,000 $\times$ $22), and sell it for $40,000 immediately. The capital gain on the sale will be a profit for the president as a direct result of the success of the firm.

CROSS-REFERENCE:
stock repurchase, p. 528

stock repurchase. A repurchase of stock occurs when a firm buys back outstanding shares of its own common stock. Firms repurchase stock for three major reasons:

1. *For Stock Options.* A stock option is the right to purchase a specified number of shares of common stock during a stated time period and at a stipulated price. Stock options are frequently given to senior officers of a company as an incentive to work to raise the value of the firm. When a firm

agrees to such stock options, the firm must have stock available to sell to the officers. Repurchase of stock allows the firm to fulfill options without increasing the total number of shares outstanding.

2. *To Have Shares for Acquisitions.* When a firm is seeking control of another firm, it may be willing to offer its own common stock for the stock of the other firm. In this exchange of stock situation, the firm can repurchase stock to make the acquisition. This allows the takeover without increasing the number of outstanding shares and avoids a dilution of earnings.

3. *To Retire the Stock, Thus Increasing Earnings per Share.* When a firm retires a portion of its stock, the retirement increases the firm's earnings per share. The repurchase of stock for the purpose of retiring it is treated as a form of cash dividend by the Internal Revenue Service. The firm could have distributed dividends with the excess cash. Instead, it chose to reduce the number of shares outstanding so that future dividends could be increased. With this motive, the repurchase decision can be treated similarly to a dividend decision.

CROSS-REFERENCE:
stock option, p. 528

stock repurchase, as alternative to dividends. The Internal Revenue Service does not allow the repurchase of stock to be a regular alternative to the declaration of dividends. Many shareholders would desire such an alternative if it were allowed. This is true because stock repurchases may convert ordinary income from dividends to the capital gains from stock which has risen in value. The table shows the situation of an investor who owns $1,000 of a firm's common stock at the beginning of a 5-year period. In one example, the firm declares a $50 annual dividend and he pays taxes at a 40 percent personal tax rate to have total stock and dividends valued at $1,150 at the end of 5 years. In the second example, the firm uses the dividend money to repurchase stock and the value of the stock increases by the amount of the dividends. The investor has a tax obligation of only half the 40 percent personal tax rate and finishes the 5 years with stock valued at $1,200. The repurchase of stock has resulted in more value to the investor due to the difference in tax treatment between dividends and capital gains.

Benefit to Shareholder from Repurchase of Stock Rather Than Declaration of Dividend.

Investor Holds $1,000 of Common Stock at Beginning of 5-Year Period		
	Firm Declares $50 Annual Dividend Payable to Investor	*Firm Repurchases Stock Increasing Value of Stock*
Value of stock, beginning of period	$1,000	$1,000
Total dividends declared, 5 years	250	0
Increase in value due to repurchase	0	250
Total Value to Shareholder	$1,250	$1,250
Tax implied or actually paid on dividends at 40% personal tax rate	100	
Tax implied or actually paid on capital gains at half 40% rate		50
Net After-Tax Value to Investor	$1,150	$1,200

Effect of a 2-for-1 Stock Split on a Firm's Equity.

		Before the Stock Split	After the Stock Split
Common stock	($1 par, 200,000 shares)	$ 200,000	
	($.50 par, 400,000 shares)		$ 200,000
Premium		600,000	600,000
Retained earnings		2,000,000	2,000,000
Total Equity		$2,800,000	$2,800,000

stock split. A change in the number of outstanding shares of stock achieved through a proportional reduction or increase in the par value of the stock. Only the par value and number of outstanding shares are affected. The amounts in the common stock, premium, and retained earnings accounts do not change. This is illustrated in the table with a 2-for-1 stock split.

Just as the accounting values in the equity accounts do not change, the market price of the stock will normally adjust immediately to reflect a stock split. As an example, a firm may have 2,000,-000 outstanding shares selling for $20 per share. The firm declares a 2-for-1 stock split. After the split, 4,000,000 shares will be outstanding and will sell for approximately $10 per share. A shareholder with 100 shares worth $2,-000 before the split will hold 200 shares worth $2,000 after the split.

Why Firms Declare Stock Splits Several reasons may be offered for the splitting of a firm's common stock, as follows:
1. *Reduction of Market Price of Stock.* The major goal of most stock splits is to reduce the per-share price of a firm's common stock. A lower price per share makes the stock more affordable in round lots (100 shares) to more investors. It requires $10,000 to buy 100 shares of a stock selling for $100 per share. A 4-for-1 stock split would lower the cost of 100 shares to $2,-

500. The investor with $10,000 could still buy the stock and would receive 400 shares. The investor with only $2,500 could also afford to buy a round lot of the stock. By reducing the price, the firm encourages more investors to purchase the stock thus increasing demand and the market price of the stock.
2. *Indication of Future Growth.* The firm's management may use the stock split to inform the market that continued high growth is forecast for the future. The stock of high-growth companies would soon sell for several hundred dollars per share if it were not split periodically. The split thus might have informational value that the firm wants to avoid future high per-share prices for its stock which will occur due to growth.
3. *Reverse Split—An Indication of Trouble.* Instead of increasing the number of outstanding shares of stock, the firm may want to reduce the number. This can be accomplished through a reverse split, which is a reduction of outstanding shares. As an example, a firm may have 200,000 outstanding shares of $1 par common stock. It declares a 1-for-2 reverse split. After the split, it will have 100,000 shares of $2 par stock. The reverse split is normally used to keep the price of the stock from falling below a certain level, frequently around $10 per share. The fact that the stock is fall-

ing below $10 and the need of the company to declare a reverse split to keep the price up are both indicators of financial difficulty. If the firm is not in difficulty, it will expect the market price to rise above $10 due to future earnings, dividends, or growth. With these prospects, it will not declare the reverse split. The declaration of a reverse split is an indication that the firm does not have such prospects.

CROSS-REFERENCE:
reverse split, p. 511

straight-line depreciation. A method of depreciation that reduces the economic value of an asset by equal amounts over equal periods of time. It is calculated by dividing the cost of the fixed asset by its depreciable life. As an example, a $1,-000,000 asset with a $40,000 scrap value at the end of a 20 year service life would have an annual straight-line depreciation of $48,000, as follows:

$$\frac{1,000,000 - 40,000}{20 \text{ years}} = \frac{960,000}{20} = \$48,000$$

CROSS-REFERENCE:
cash-flow stream, how to calculate, p. 3

strong currency. A national currency that is likely to maintain its value or gain in value compared to other currencies in the near future. The strength of the currency can result from artificially imposed exchange rates or it can be due to strong fundamental economic conditions in the country issuing the currency. In the latter case, the strong currency is also said to be a hard currency.

CROSS-REFERENCE
weak currency, p. 547

structure, financial. Large corporations differ widely in the organization of their finance activities, for which there are several reasons:

1. *Varying Needs.* Depending on the nature of the business, size of the firm, and the kinds of financing of operations, firms will have different financial needs. Manufacturing firms require large amounts of capital to purchase the fixed assets needed for production. These firms require detailed accounting of raw materials, processing of goods, and final inventories. Companies whose major outputs are services will have limited concern with the financing of production activities. They may be interested instead in developing a financial system to account for individuals' time spent with each customer and services provided. These different needs help determine the financial organization.

2. *Capabilities of Financial Officers.* The training, skills, and natural abilities of the personnel working on financial problems has an important influence on the structure of the finance functions. If a firm has several highly capable financial managers, they may work in a structure that utilizes their talents to the fullest extent possible. If the managers are less capable, the firm may choose an organization that places less stress on individual personalities and instead emphasizes routine accounting and financial reporting.

3. *Financial Philosophy of the Firm.* Firms vary on a range from the very traditional to the very modern in their approaches to financial management. Some firms make extensive use of computers; other firms employ mechanical systems of record keeping. Some firms do limited planning; others make extensive use of financial data to forecast future conditions. These considerations will affect the organization of the finance area.

CROSS-REFERENCE:
corporation, p. 364

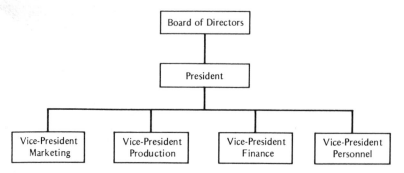

Sample Organizational Structure of a Firm.

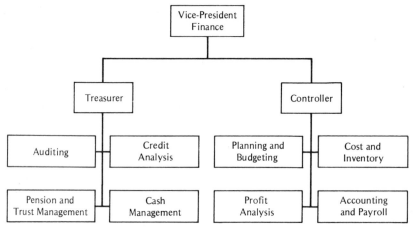

Sample Organizational Structure of a Finance Department.

sub-chapter S corporations. Sub-chapter S of the Internal Revenue Code permits corporations with 10 or fewer individual stockholders to be taxed as a partnership. Instead of paying a separate corporate tax, the firm's earnings are taxed as direct income of the shareholders, regardless of whether the earnings are actually distributed. None of the stockholders may be trusts or other corporations. Sub-chapter S corporation gives shareholders the limited liability benefit of the corporate form while avoiding the double taxation normally associated with the distribution of corporate earnings.

subjective probabilities, increasing accuracy of. To increase the accuracy of subjective probabilities, a number of techniques are used. Some of the important ones are the following:

1. *Build on Past Data.* The financial manager will have past data available, frequently in a form suitable for computer processing. By evaluating the relationships among variables in previous periods, the analyst can forecast similar relationships in future periods. If, for example, an event occurred approximately 40 percent of the time in past periods, it may occur the same percentage of times in the future.

2. *Compare Known Variables to Project Variables.* In forecasting, some future events are more likely than others. For example, social security payments to retired persons are a virtual certainty. We can also rely on the continued operation of city and state governments and the continuation of salary payments to school teachers and other government employees. If we have a proposal that is linked to purchases by retired persons or government employees, we can compare our project variables with these highly likely conditions. That is, we could say that there is an excellent chance that our product will sell because there is an excellent chance that our potential market (retired persons, for example) will be able to purchase the product.

3. *Secure Expert Estimates.* A number of persons and organizations specialize in predicting future events. Economists predict the level of economic activity, psychologists forecast individual attitudes, and research firms predict buyer behavior. These forecasters can perform research and provide estimates that increase the accuracy of Bayesian statistics.

CROSS-REFERENCE:

risk in capital budget, how to measure, p. 25

subordinated debentures. Unsecured bonds issued by a firm with a secondary claim to a firm's assets after the claim of other holders of debentures.

CROSS-REFERENCES:

bond, p. 323
debenture, p. 373

subsidiary. A corporation that is owned or controlled by another corporation called a holding company.

CROSS-REFERENCES:

acquisitions, how to analyze, p. 78
third-country invoicing, how to use to avoid currency controls, p. 179
transfer pricing, how to use to avoid currency controls, p. 180
parent company, p. 477
profit center, p. 490
pyramiding, p. 496

sum-of-the-years' digits method. An accelerated method of depreciation that may be used to depreciate assets more rapidly than would be allowed by the straight-line method.

CROSS-REFERENCES:

depreciation, how to calculate, p. 188
depreciation, p. 379

superpremium. Under Durand's approach to valuation of the firm, a superpremium is the difference between the interest rate demanded by creditors of the firm and the actual interest that must be paid on the bonds if they are issued during a period of relatively low interest rates. The superpremium, according to Durand, will increase the total value of the firm.

CROSS REFERENCE:

Durand on the cost of capital, p. 203

systematic irrationality. The Miller-Modigliani concept used to explain why the investing public would pay more or less for common stock based on differing dividend policies. Miller and Modigliani believe that no conceptual basis exists for dividends to affect stock value and therefore observed differences in value due to dividend policies must be irrational.

CROSS-REFERENCE:

Miller and Modigliani on dividend policy, p. 264

systematic risk. In portfolio theory, the market-related component of risk inherent in an investment in a portfolio of financial or capital assets. Systematic risk is commonly measured by the regression coefficient b, or the beta coefficient. Systematic risk cannot be eliminated through diversification. As an example, consider a portfolio with a beta coefficient of 0.60. At a time when investments in the market overall should yield a 10 percent return and investment in the portfolio should yield 12 percent. Now assume that the market return drops to 5 percent, a 50 percent decline. The portfolio will drop by 60 percent of the market decline or 50% × 60% = 30 percent. A 30 percent drop from 12 percent would produce a return of 8.4 percent on the portfolio. The drop in return from 12 percent to 8.4 percent represents the portfolio's systematic risk which was not eliminated through diversification. Thus, the larger the beta coefficient for a portfolio, the greater is the portfolio's systematic or nondiversifiable risk.

CROSS-REFERENCE:
capital asset pricing model, p. 279

T

takeover strategies in mergers. The successful identification and takeover of another corporation involve complex legal and financial actions on the part of the acquiring firm. In this section some strategic considerations in mergers and acquisitions

Finding a Suitable Acquisition When a firm decides to seek external growth, it begins to search for suitable candidates for acquisition. This will usually involve a team approach, since it will be conducted by the firm's top management, legal staff, bankers, and even outside consultants who specialize in recommending workable corporate unions. When a consultant's recommendation is accepted and the merger is completed, the new firm will pay a finder's fee to the consultant. This may be very sizable, up to 5 percent of the assets of the acquired firm.

The search process may focus on a number of key characteristics, including the following:

1. *Candidates with Net Operating Losses.* To be in a position to make acquisitions, a firm will normally be highly profitable. If the acquired firm has a recent history of operating at a loss, the loss may be applied as a tax carry-back or carry-forward to reduce the taxes of the acquiring firm. This can be a key factor in the desirability of a combination.

2. *Candidates That Must Avoid Improper Profit Accumulation.* Corporations are not allowed to retain earnings that are in excess of the reasonable needs of the business. The Internal Revenue code provides for stiff penalties for firms that retain earnings for the purpose of allowing stockholders to avoid paying personal income tax on the distributed dividends. A firm that is accumulating cash that represents improper retained earnings may be a takeover target. The cash would be useful to the acquiring firm since it can help finance additional growth. The takeover might be desirable to the shareholders of the firm with excess profits since they can avoid paying ordinary income taxes on dividends by paying capital-gains taxes on the sale of the company (at the lower capital-gains rate).

3. *Candidates That Offer Synergistic Prospects.* Synergism is the concept that some combinations have a total that is greater than the sum of the parts; that is, $2 + 2 = 5$. If we combine two firms with the proper operating characteristics, it may be possible to realize synergistic effects. One firm may have a strong research and development capability while the other has a strong marketing force. Together they would be able to develop new products and bring them forcefully to the customer, resulting in profits that neither could achieve alone. This would be an example of synergism.

4. *Candidates with Low Price-Earnings Multiples.* External growth can be particularly beneficial in the short run if the acquired firm is selling at bargain prices in the market. In most cases, the price-earnings ratio is used as the indicator of value in a business combination. A low price-earnings ratio indicates good value.

5. *Candidates with Turn-Around Prospects.* A prime takeover candidate is the firm with low operating profits due to poor management or other controllable factors.

CROSS-REFERENCE:
mergers, p. 460

tariff. A duty levied on goods being imported into a country. An *ad valorem* tariff is a duty levied on goods according to the value shown on the accompanying invoice. Transfer pricing is commonly used to establish low invoice prices and thus reduce the tariff to be paid.

CROSS-REFERENCES:
transfer pricing, how to use to avoid currency controls, p. 180
transfer pricing, p. 538

tender. An offer to sell a definite number of shares at a specific price, normally made when a shareholder is offering shares of stock for sale in response to a request for tenders. Soliciting tenders is common during corporate takeovers.

CROSS-REFERENCES:
acquisitions, how to resist being acquired, p. 81
acquisitions, three approaches, p. 307

terms of the trade. The credit practice of a given industry, normally expressed in symbolic language that reflects the amount of a discount given on sales if the purchaser pays quickly in the time period in which full payment must be made. For example, a term of 2/10 net 30 indicates that the firm gives a 2 percent discount for payments received within 10 days and the firm expects full payment in 30 days. Similarly, net 30 means that no discount is given but full payment is required in 30 days.

CROSS-REFERENCE:

discount, p. 381

third country invoicing. In international finance, a specific method of using transfer pricing to avoid controls on foreign exchange. The following diagram shows how it works. A subsidiary in Country A ships goods worth $100 or 600 pesos to a customer in Country B. A bill for 300 pesos or $50 is sent to a second subsidiary in Country C. The subsidiary in Country C invoices the customer in Country B for the full $100. The customer pays $100 and the subsidiary in Country C pays $50, a situation that results in a $50 overage in Country C. Since Country C was selected because it has no controls on foreign exchange, the $50 overage can be used anywhere in the world at the parent company's discretion and the exchange controls of Country A have been avoided.

CROSS-REFERENCES:
third-country invoicing, how to use to avoid currency controls, p. 179
transfer pricing, p. 538

times interest earned. A useful measure of profit is the times interest earned ratio. It is calculated by dividing the firm's operating income (EBIT) by the interest it must pay on its debt:

$$\text{Times Interest Earned} = \frac{\text{Operating Income}}{\text{Interest}}$$

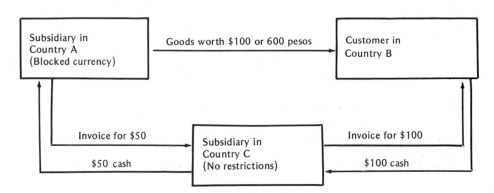

It relates operating profits to the fixed charges created by the firm's borrowing.

The times interest earned ratio provides an indication of the margin of safety between financial obligations and profits. A firm may have an operating profit, but may face difficulty in making excessive interest payments. Or, if it is confronted by a drop in operating profits, it may be unable to meet its debt obligations. In either case, its net income will decline or vanish. A satisfactory guideline for this ratio is that EBIT should be five to seven times interest charges. Thus, a firm could experience an 80 to 86 percent drop in EBIT and still cover interest payments.

EXAMPLE: A firm has a times interest earned ratio of 3/1. What percentage drop can it sustain in operating income and still meet its interest payments?

ANSWER: 67 percent drop. The operating income can decrease to one-third its current level.

CROSS-REFERENCE:

profitability, how to analyze with ratios, p. 56

time value of money. A concept in capital budgeting, profit planning, and asset financing that recognizes that money has a different value depending upon when it is received. That is, a dollar today is worth more than a dollar in the future. A number of sophisticated financial techniques have been developed to handle the time value of money.

CROSS-REFERENCE:

present value of money, how to calculate, p. 19

titles of financial managers. A variety of titles are used in American business to identify the key financial managers. Although there is not complete agreement, many firms designate three major financial positions in their corporate structure. One position is reserved for the top financial officer with respon-

sibilities over all financial activities. Reporting to him are two other financial officers with their main responsibilities separated along the lines of functional areas: asset management and funds management.

A classification system that is currently emerging in large corporations makes use of three titles to identify these three managers:

1. *Vice-President Finance.* This title is reserved for the main financial officer who reports directly to the president of the company. In many cases, a firm will have a finance committee formed from top management and members of the board of directors. In these cases, the vice-president finance normally serves as a member of the committee and may report directly to it.

   The vice-president finance has both line and staff responsibilities. He is accountable for all the firm's financial activities, including control of funds, decision making, management, and planning. He works closely with other members of the top-management team in formulating policies, making decisions, and advising the board of directors. He supervises the members of his own staff, including the treasurer and controller, who work closely with him to monitor the financial impact of operations of other departments.

2. *Treasurer.* The functions related to the management of funds come under the scope of the treasurer. His principal responsibilities include managing the firm's cash flow, forecasting financial needs, maintaining relations with financial institutions, and such operational duties as borrowing, spending, transferring, and safeguarding funds.

3. *Controller.* The functions related to the management and control of assets come under the scope of the controller. He is responsible for such areas as

profit planning, capital spending, measuring costs, controlling inventories, financial studies, and the operational duties involved with corporate accounting and payroll functions.

trading on the equity. A situation that exists when a firm is financing a portion of its assets using limited-return securities and the firm's before tax return on investment is greater than the percentage of the interest rate or dividend being paid on the limited-return securities. This is also called favorable financial leverage. As an example, if a firm is borrowing at 5 percent and earning 8 percent on the money, it is said to be trading on the equity.

CROSS-REFERENCES:
financial leverage, how to analyze, p. 34
favorable financial leverage, p. 401

transactions need. A need for cash that arises from the firm's day-to-day functions of the business. Adequate cash to cover its transactions needs allows a firm to pay its bills on time.

transfer pricing. In international finance, the method of establishing a price for goods or services exchanged between divisions or subsidiaries of the firm located in different countries. As a general rule, market factors are not the dominant element in transfer prices. Instead, the parent will encourage pricing that achieves corporate goals such as avoiding taxes, avoiding controls on foreign exchange, and reducing tariffs.

CROSS-REFERENCES:
third-country invoicing, how to use to avoid currency controls, p. 179
transfer pricing, how to use to avoid currency controls, p. 180

tariff, p. 535

treasurer. A key financial officer in a corporation. It is increasingly common for the treasurer to be responsible for the management of funds. Included in this responsibility are the areas of managing cash flow, forecasting financial needs, bank and financial institution relations, and the safeguarding of funds.

CROSS-REFERENCES:
controller, p. 357
vice-president finance, p. 545

treasury bill. A security representing an unconditional promise by the U.S. Treasury to pay to the holder of the bill a specified amount at maturity. Treasury bills are issued for short periods of time, normally 3, 6, or 12 months. Maturities on these bills are spaced 1 week apart, so the financial manager can purchase the bills that will mature at approximately the same time as his forecasted need for cash.

Two characteristics of treasury bills should be noted:
1. *Non-Interest-Bearing.* Treasury bills are sold at a discount on a bid basis, mainly to securities dealers and large commercial banks, who resell them to individuals and firms. For example, a bank may purchase a $10,000 face-value bill for $9,625 and immediately resell it to a firm for $9,675. If the firm holds the bill for a full 12 months, the treasury will redeem the bill for $10,000. The difference between the $10,000 face value and the $9,675 discount price is the profit to the firm for holding the security.
2. *Most Secure and Liquid Marketable Security.* Treasury bills are the most secure and liquid kind of marketable security. With respect to security, the U.S. government guarantees their re-

demption. With respect to liquidity, there is a large, active market for the bills; they can be quickly and easily sold prior to maturity if the firm runs short on cash.

Closely related to treasury bills are treasury notes and bonds. These are issued for a longer period of time than bills and are interest-bearing. As notes and bonds near their maturities, they are similar to bills in the yield they offer to the investor. They are frequently purchased in lieu of treasury bills.

CROSS-REFERENCE:

negotiable certificate of deposit, p. 466

turn-around situation. Acquisition of a poorly managed firm that offers the prospects of installing new management and quickly raising the firm's earnings.

CROSS-REFERENCES:

turn-around candidate, how to determine purchase price of, p. 95
growth, reasons for seeking, p. 423
mergers, tax factors affecting, p. 462

turn-around situation, spotting one. Firms seeking acquisition candidates will usually pay particular attention to possible turn-around situations. A number of guidelines may be offered to help a firm identify a company with low profits but high prospects for future improvement if acquired:

1. *Recent Drop in Profits for Individual Firm But Not Industry.* If a firm is experiencing internal problems, it may suffer a drop in operating profits. When the firm's overall industry does not suffer such a drop, it is a good sign that the profit decline results from an internal, and thus possibly controllable, factor. A check of industry

profits will frequently reveal this kind of situation, which can be investigated further.

2. *Industries to Be Affected Favorably by Forecasted Economic Changes.* At any time, but particularly in the fall of the year, the nation's economists are predicting future levels of economic activity. Included in these forecasts will be shifts in demand and changes in production for major industries. One year will bring forecasts of reduced production in some industries and increases in others. By analyzing these forecasts, a firm can identify industries with growth prospects in the short- to medium-term and can seek turn-around candidates in these industries. In recent years, economists have made favorable predictions for leisure-oriented industries, transportation industries, and many service industries.

3. *Break in Management Ranks.* Normally, a firm's top management will work together and present a united front to the outside world. Occasionally, some members of the management team will break away and not want to participate in moving the firm on its current course. This may indicate that these managers see a better way to run the firm but are blocked by the controlling managers. If the firm is not profitable, the new ideas of the minority managers may be able to greatly increase profits. These situations call for further investigation.

4. *Laggard Firm in the Industry.* Most industries have a range of firms from the most successful to the relatively unsuccessful. If the less profitable firms have the same machinery and as much experience as the more profitable firms, their problems may result from weak management. Taking over a laggard firm and replacing its

management may bring a rapid increase in profits.

5. *Poorly Performing Firm with Complementary Strength to One's Own Strength.* The acquiring firm may have great strength in marketing consumer products through its sales force and excellent advertising and research departments. This firm may begin to review other firms in the consumer products market looking for low profits and a solid production capability. By merging with these firms, the combined firm would have both the production and marketing expertise and might be able to achieve solid increases in profits in a short period of time.

CROSS-REFERENCE:

part 3, mergers and acquisitions, in "how to" section, p. 78

U

uncertainty. A future state which is not foreseen and therefore cannot be quantified using probabilistic techniques. Differs from risk which can be quantified.

CROSS-REFERENCE:
risk and uncertainty, distinguishing between, p. 514

underwriters. A group of investment bankers and financial institutions that purchase a security issue for resale to other investors. The underwriters generally accept all risks of being able to resell the offering. In some cases, the offering will be handled on a best-efforts basis, whereby the underwriter will sell as many bonds or shares of stocks as can be sold at the agreed-upon price. In this situation, unsold securities are not the responsibility of the underwriters.

CROSS-REFERENCES:
best-efforts basis, p. 321
primary issue, p. 488

unfavorable financial leverage. A situation that exists when a firm has assets financed by limited-return securities and the firm is earning less on the assets than the financing costs. For example, if a firm was earning 6 percent on assets financed with 8 percent debt, it would have unfavorable financial leverage.

CROSS-REFERENCES:
financial leverage, how to analyze, p. 34
leverage, p. 452
favorable financial leverage, p. 401

unsystematic risk. In portfolio theory, the component of risk inherent in an investment in a portfolio of financial or capital assets that can be eliminated through diversification. Unsystematic risk differs from systematic or market-related risk which cannot be eliminated through diversification. As an example, consider a portfolio with a beta coefficient of 0.55. This means that a decline of "x" percent in the return of the overall market will be accompanied by a .55 x decline in the return on the portfolio. The $1 - .55$ or 45 percent that the portfolio's return will not decline represents the unsystematic risk that has been eliminated through diversification. In effect, diversification is eliminating the random movements in the return of individual securities. The random pluses for some securities are offset by random minuses for others and, with a sufficiently large portfolio, the net effect of random movements will approach zero.

CROSS-REFERENCE:
capital asset pricing model, p. 279

usage rate. The rate per day at which an item of inventory is consumed in production or sold to customers.

CROSS-REFERENCE:
inventory management, how to set up system for, p. 103

uses of funds, nonoperational. A firm may apply its funds in a number of areas. A portion of the funds are expended for operations. This is included in the calculation of funds from operations and not identified here. Other uses are the following:

1. *Purchase Fixed Assets.* It is a use of funds when plant, equipment, or land is purchased, not when they are depreciated.
2. *Pay Off Liabilities or Retire Stock.* When long-term debt reaches maturity, the firm must pay it off with available funds. If the firm wishes to reduce

the amount of outstanding stock, it uses funds to repurchase the stock.

3. *Declare Cash Dividends.* If the firm is profitable and pays dividends to its stockholders, the declaration of cash dividends is a use of funds.

4. *Make Up Losses.* If the firm is not profitable, it must apply funds to make up its losses until it does become profitable.

CROSS-REFERENCE:

flow-of-funds statement, how to develop from balance sheet to income statement, p. 38

V

value, differing concepts of. An important role of the financial manager is to make recommendations concerning the value of different securities. When a firm is considering the purchase of marketable securities—debt, preferred stock, and common stock—it must have some knowledge of investment values. If the firm is evaluating an acquisition, it must have techniques to determine how much to pay for the stock to be acquired. Future earnings per share is an important concept linked to the value of common stock in a proposed merger. Aside from mergers, any firm that is considering a public offering of its own stock to raise equity capital is faced with the need to establish a price for the issue. These are all issues related to the valuation of the firm and its securities.

The value of a security may be defined as its worth in money or other securities at a given moment in time. The value is expressed either in terms of a market for the security or in terms of the laws or accounting procedures applicable to the security. A number of differing concepts of value may be identified:

1. *Going-Concern Value.* The value of the securities of a profitable, operating firm with prospects for indefinite future business might be expressed as a going-concern value. The worth of the firm would be expressed in terms of the future profits, dividends, or growth expected of the business.

2. *Liquidation Value.* If the analyst is dealing with the securities of a firm that is about to go out of business, the net value of its assets, or liquidation value, would be of primary concern. After selling the firm's assets and paying off its liabilities, how much would be left for the stockholders to divide? Or if the firm would be una-

ble to pay all its debts after the sale of assets, how much can each bondholder or other creditor expect to receive?

3. *Market Value.* If we are examining a firm whose stock or debt is traded in a securities market, we can determine the market value of the security. This is the value of the debt or equity securities as reflected in the bond or stock market's perception of the firm.

4. *Book Value.* This is determined by the use of standardized accounting techniques and is calculated from the financial reports, particularly the balance sheet, prepared by the firm. The book value of debt is usually fairly close to its par or face value. The book value of the stock is calculated by dividing the firm's equity by the number of shares outstanding.

EXAMPLE: An analyst forecasts an earnings per share for Firestone Corporation of $1.60 and says the stock is worth 15 times this much, or $24. What kind of value is the analyst determining?

ANSWER: Going concern, a value related to future profits.

CROSS-REFERENCES:
going-concern value, p. 419
liquidation value, p. 453
market value, p. 458
book value, p. 323

value, intrinsic of common stock. The price that is justified for a share when the primary factors of value are considered. In other words, it is the real worth of the stock as distinguished from the current market price of the stock. It is a subjective value in the sense that the analyst must apply his own individual background and skills to determine it, and estimates of intrinsic value will vary from one analyst to the next.

The financial manager estimates intrinsic value by carefully appraising the following fundamental factors that affect common-stock values:

1. *Value of the Firm's Assets.* The physical assets held by the firm have some market value. In liquidation approaches to valuation, assets can be quite important. In techniques of going-concern valuation, assets are usually omitted.

2. *Likely Future Earnings.* The expected future earnings of the firm are the most important single factor affecting the common stock's intrinsic value.

3. *Likely Future Dividends.* The firm may pay out its future earnings as dividends or may retain them to finance growth and expansion. The firm's policies with respect to dividends will affect the intrinsic value of its stock.

4. *Likely Future Growth Rate.* A firm's prospects for future growth are carefully evaluated by investors and are a factor influencing intrinsic value.

CROSS-REFERENCES:

Graham and Dodd approaches to common stock value, p. 246
conversion value, p. 359
intrinsic value analysis, p. 439

variable costs. Expenses that vary in direct proportion to changes in the volume of production or sales. Labor and raw materials are examples of variable costs in the production process. Variable cost is an important concept in break-even analysis.

CROSS-REFERENCES:

break-even analysis, how to use, p. 32
leverage, how to use in profit planning, p. 44
profit volume analysis, how to use, p. 64

varying sales levels or costs, how to analyze effect of, p. 74
income statement, marginal analysis format, p. 430

variable rate financing. A situation that exists when an individual or firm borrows money at an interest rate that fluctuates according to the general level of interest rates or some other indicator. For example, a commercial bank may be willing to make a 5-year loan at a rate that is two percent higher than the prime rate, with a new prime rate to be established every month or quarter. As the prime rate fluctuates over the life of the loan, the interest charged will also fluctuate.

CROSS REFERENCES:

fixed rate financing, p. 409
prime rate, p. 488

variable working capital. Additional current assets required at different times during the operating year to support peak periods for sales or production.

CROSS-REFERENCE:

working capital, how to balance sources of funds, p. 121

variance. A statistical measure of dispersion that is calculated by squaring the standard deviation.

CROSS-REFERENCE:

standard deviation, p. 525

vertical integration. The combination of firms in the same line of business but at different stages in the process. An example would be an acquisition of a chain of retail shoe stores by a manufacturer of shoes.

CROSS-REFERENCE:

horizontal integration, p. 427

vice-president finance. Generally, the title reserved for the main financial officer of a corporation. This position involves line responsibility for the firm's financial activities. It also involves staff responsibility advising the chief executive officer and the board of directors.

CROSS-REFERENCES:
controller, p. 357
treasurer, p. 538

voluntary settlement. In situations of insolvency or bankruptcy, an arrangement initiated by a firm with its creditors that allows the firm to continue operations. This is an "out-of-court" agreement that avoids the costs required for legal bankruptcy proceedings. The voluntary settlement may result in liquidation of the firm or may allow the firm to eventually continue operations on a normal basis.

CROSS-REFERENCES:
arrangement, p. 312
bankruptcy, p. 320
Chandler Act of 1938, p. 347
composition, p. 355
extension, p. 400

W

Walter Formula. A mathematical model developed by James Walter to calculate the intrinsic value of common stock by dividing the earnings per share into dividends and retained earnings. The model can be used to decide whether a firm should retain earnings for financing future growth or whether it should pay dividends to allow its shareholders to use the cash for other investments. The Walter formula may be written:

$$\text{Intrinsic Value} = \frac{\text{Div}_{curr} + \dfrac{CR_{act}}{CR_{norm}}(\$RE)}{CR_{norm}}$$

where

CR_{act} & CR_{norm}	= the actual and normal capitalization rates
Div_{curr}	= current dividend in dollars per share
$\$RE$	= retained earnings in dollars per share

CROSS-REFERENCE:
Walter and Gordon on dividend decisions, p. 260

warehouse receipt loan. An agreement under which a bank or finance company takes physical control of a pledged collateral, normally inventory, in return for providing a loan. Once the collateral has been selected, two types of warehousing arrangements are possible. A terminal warehouse is a public facility that is used to store the merchandise for inventory pledged under warehouse receipt loans. The collateral is physically moved to the terminal warehouse. A field warehouse occurs when the lender hires a field warehousing company to separate the collateral from the borrower's other assets on the borrower's premises. A guard is placed with the collateral and may not release the goods without authorization from the lender.

warrant. A security that permits the holder to buy shares of common stock during a stated time period and at a given price. When the option is exercised, the holder must surrender the warrant and pay the firm for the common stock purchased at the option price. For many years, warrants were considered to be speculative instruments rather than investment securities, since the warrant has no value other than as a right to purchase other securities. In 1970, American Telephone and Telegraph raised over $1,000,000,000 through a bond issue with warrants attached. This large financing by a respected corporation led the New York Stock Exchange to reverse its prohibition against listing warrants and may encourage increased future uses of the warrant.

Why Warrants Are Used A firm will attach warrants to bond or preferred stock financing as a "sweetener" in an attempt to achieve one or more of the following:
1. *To Lower the Cost of the Issue.* A firm can offer a lower yield on a fixed-income security if warrants are attached. The warrants offer a promise of sharing in the firm's growth, a favorable feature to the bondholders or preferred shareholders. If the firm's stock rises in value in the period before the warrant-expiration date, the warrants can be exercised and the common stock can immediately be sold at a gain. In return for this possibility, investors will accept a lower coupon rate on the fixed-income security.
2. *To Offset Relatively High Risk.* Some firms represent considerable risk to a creditor and such a firm may not be able to borrow without a promise of some equity participation in the event the firm is extremely success-

ful. In this situation, warrants may be used as an equity "kicker" to make a bond issue more attractive.

3. *To Increase Equity in Future.* Just as a convertible bond can be viewed as a means of increasing common stock at a future higher price, warrants can accomplish the same effect. The option price is generally set 10 to 20 percent above the market price of the stock at the time of the bond issue. If the common stock rises in price, the warrants will be surrendered before the expiration date and the holders of the warrants will buy additional shares of common stock at the option price. The purchase of additional shares will, of course, increase the shares outstanding.

CROSS-REFERENCES:
long-term financing, how to compare different alternatives, p. 139
detachable warrant, p. 379

warrant, effect on capital structure. The use of warrants in long-term financing will have different effects on capital structure than will the use of convertible securities. If a firm issues a convertible bond and forces conversion, the debt will be replaced with equity on the balance sheet. This is not the case with a bond offering with warrants. When the warrants are exercised, the firm's bonds are not retired. Instead, the holder of the warrant pays additional money to the firm in return for the common stock. Thus, the exercise of the warrants will increase the funds available to the firm while not affecting the fixed-income securities outstanding.

CROSS-REFERENCE:
warrant, p. 547

warrant, value of. Warrants have an intrinsic value that may be calculated by the following formula:

$$\text{intrinsic value} = \left(\begin{array}{c} \text{market price of} \\ \text{common stock} \end{array} - \begin{array}{c} \text{option price of} \\ \text{common stock} \end{array} \right)$$
$$\left(\begin{array}{c} \text{number of shares} \\ \text{per warrant} \end{array} \right)$$

As an example of the use of this formula, consider a firm with a bond offering with attached warrants. Each $1,000 bond has 5 warrants attached and each warrant allows the holder to purchase 4 shares of common stock at $30 per share. The common stock is presently selling for $50. The value of the warrant is:

$$\text{intrinsic value} = (\$50 - \$30)(4)$$
$$= \$80 \text{ per warrant}$$

The total value of the 5 warrants attached to each bond would be $80 times 5, or $400.

Note that the formula would give a negative value if the market price is less than the option price. In this situation, the value of the warrant is based on future expectations and the formula cannot be used to calculate intrinsic value.

CROSS-REFERENCE:
warrant, p. 547

weak currency. A national currency that is likely to decline in value compared to other currencies in the near future, normally the next year or so. The weakness can result from artificially imposed exchange rates or it can be caused by fundamental economic conditions such as high inflation or balance of payments deficits in the country issuing the currency. In the latter case, the weak currency is also said to be a soft currency.

CROSS-REFERENCE:
strong currency, p. 531

wealth. The net present worth of a firm.

weighted average. A mathematical value that expresses the likelihood of different risks and their effect on the return from a proposal.

weighted-average cost of capital. The weighted-average cost of capital may be expressed in a single formula that shows cost of capital as the sum of the weighted individual costs of each component of the capital structure. The formula is

$$K_o = \%D_{mkt}(K_i) + \%PS_{mkt}(K_{ps}) + \%CS_{mkt}(K_e)$$

where

K_o	= overall cost of capital
K_i	= cost of debt
K_e	= cost of equity
K_{ps}	= cost of preferred stock
$\%D_{mkt}$	= percentage of debt in the capital structure (maturity or face value)
$\%PS_{mkt}$	= percentage of preferred stock in the capital structure
$\%CS_{mkt}$	= percentage of common stock in the capital structure

As an example of the use of this formula, consider a firm that has $1,500,000 debt at 8 percent, $1,000,000 in preferred stock at 6 percent, and 450,000 shares of common stock at $10 per share. The cost of the common stock has been estimated at 10 percent. Before setting up the formula, we must make several calculations. The preferred- and common-stock costs are already stated on an after-tax basis, since taxes are taken out before dividends can be paid or before earnings per share can be reported. The interest on the debt is stated on a before-tax basis and must be converted. We multiply the interest rate by 1 minus the corporate tax rate. With 50 percent taxes, the after-tax cost of the debt is 8 percent $(1 - 50$ percent$) = 4$ percent. We must also calculate the percentage of each component in the capital structure. The total structure is $1,500,000 debt + $1,000,000 preferred stock + $4,500,000 common stock (450,000 shares times $10) = $7,000,000 at market value. The debt is $1,500,000/7,000,000 or 22 percent; the preferred stock is $1,000,000/7,000,000 or 14 percent; the common stock is $4,500,000/7,000,000 or 64 percent. The formula can be expressed as:

$$K_o = \%D_{mkt}(K_i) + \%PS_{mkt}(K_{ps}) + \%CS_{mkt}(K_e)$$
$$= 22\%(4\%) + 14\%(6\%) + 64\%(10\%)$$
$$= .009 + .008 + .064 = 8.1\%$$

weighted-average cost of capital, assumptions of. The most widely used approach to measuring a firm's cost of capital employs the weighted-average cost of capital. With this technique, the cost of capital is defined as a weighted average of the after-tax costs of the individual components of the firm's capital structure. That is, the after-tax cost

Three Important Assumptions of the Weighted-Average Cost of Capital.		
Component Costs Interrelated	*Current, Not Historical Costs*	*Existing Capital Structure Assumed Optimal*
Low-cost financing may involve higher future costs.	Firm is interested in today's values only.	Method uses existing, not optimal, capital structure.
Only K_o can be used as cutoff point.	Current interest payments, earnings, and stock prices are used.	Valid for profitable firm with traditional mixture of debt and equity.

of each debt and equity securities is calculated separately, given a weighted value in the capital structure, and then added together to get a single overall cost of capital.

The weighted-average cost of capital builds upon three important assumptions:

1. *All Component Costs Are Related.* A firm may be considering a proposal that offers a 10 percent return. The proposal can be financed with debt costing 6 percent. Does it make sense to accept the proposal? The answer is that it depends on the overall cost of capital rather than the cost of debt. If the firm issues the debt at 6 percent, it restricts future courses of action. Since the firm cannot issue debt indefinitely, at some point it will have to utilize equity financing. If the debt issue at 6 percent is perceived as increasing the risk to the common shareholder, the price of the firm's stock may decline. The loss in market value would offset the advantage of the favorable financial leverage on the proposal. Also, the lower stock price would be costly if the firm had to issue new shares of common stock. More shares would have to be issued to raise a fixed amount of needed financing. To avoid this kind of error, weighted-average cost of capital correctly assumes that the different

component costs are related, and only the overall cost of capital can be used as a required rate of return for a new proposal.

2. *Current Costs Are More Accurate Than Historical Costs.* The cost of each component of the capital structure can be analyzed in two ways: the cost at the present time or the cost when the securities were issued. The weighted average method utilizes current costs. Common stock may have been issued at $10 a share 10 years ago, but today it is selling for $100. If the firm used the $10 figure for calculating cost of equity capital, it would not be recognizing that the shareholder is seeking to protect a $100 value of the stock. It would be foolish to make decisions that resulted in a decline from the $100 value toward the $10 value. Thus, current costs are considered to be more accurate than historical costs for calculating cost of capital. With respect to debt securities, the current interest costs and face value of the principal are used. With respect to equity securities, the current earnings, dividends, and market prices are used.

3. *Existing Capital Structure Is Used.* The weighted-average method is not capable of handling issues related to the optimal capital structure for a firm. It is only useful when the exist-

ing capital structure is widely accepted as being satisfactory for the firm in question. Stated another way, the existing capital structure is assumed to be approximating an optimal capital structure. For a reasonably profitable firm with a traditional mixture of debt and equity securities, this assumption is reasonable and does not pose a severe restriction on the calculation of cost of capital.

weighted-average cost of capital, strengths and weaknesses of. There are a number of advantages in the use of weighted-average cost of capital by the firm:

1. *It Is Straightforward and Logical.* Weighted-average cost of capital defines the overall cost of capital as the sum of the costs of the individual components of the capital structure. It employs a direct and reasonable methodology and is easily calculated, either manually or with the assistance of a computer.
2. *It Builds on Individual Debt and Equity Components.* Because it is comprised of the cost of each debt and equity security, the weighted-average technique in fact reflects each element of the capital structure. Small changes in the structure will be reflected as small changes in the firm's overall cost of capital.
3. *It Is Accurate in Periods of Normal Profits.* When the firm is realizing a reasonable level of profits, the weighted-average cost of capital is a fairly accurate cutoff point for the selection of new capital-budgeting proposals, since it takes into consideration the relatively low costs of debt securities and the need to continue to achieve the higher returns required to increase the value of the common stock.

4. *It Is Accurate When the Debt Level Is Reasonable.* The use of debt and the accompanying favorable financial leverage will actually lower the cutoff point needed to maintain or increase the value of the firm. If the debt level is not excessive, the weighted-average method will properly handle the lower-cost debt as a component in the firm's overall cost of capital.

Weaknesses of Weighted-Average Cost of Capital The weighted-average cost of capital has two weaknesses, which are major constraints on its effectiveness in certain situations:

1. *Inability to Handle Excessive Low-Cost Debt.* Short-term debt can represent an important source of funds for firms experiencing financial difficulties. If the short-term debt is in the form of payables, it will usually involve no financing charges. If a firm relies heavily on zero-cost or low-cost short-term debt, the inclusion of the short-term debt in the cost-of-capital calculations will result in a low overall cost of capital. If the firm makes use of this low figure, it will be making an error. A firm with high levels of short-term debt needs a high level of profits. With high profits, the firm can eventually secure long-term financing to eliminate the high-risk, short-term debt. If the firm accepts low-return projects on the basis of a low weighted-average cost of capital, it will be compounding its problems and continuing its exposure to high financing risks.
2. *Inability to Handle Low Profits.* If the firm is experiencing a period of low profitability, the weighted-average calculation of cost of capital will be inaccurate. Just because a firm is realizing only a 2 percent return does not mean that it can accept projects with

a 3 percent return. The minimum acceptable return must be sufficiently high so as to assure a long-term interest on the part of shareholders. If the firm sets low profit goals, the common shareholders will seek higher returns elsewhere. Thus, if a firm is not achieving profits comparable to other firms in its industry, the weighted-average cost of capital will be of limited value.

Correcting Weaknesses of Weighted-Average Method   The weighted-average method of calculating cost of capital is strengthened by mathematically correcting the preceding weaknesses. The two corrections are:
1. *Omit Excessive Short-Term Debt.* If the firm has large payables or other low-cost, short-term debt, the analyst may calculate weighted-average cost of capital without including these items. The omission of this debt will raise the cost of capital and require the firm to earn more on the projects it is willing to accept.
2. *Use Expected Normal Profits.* The analyst can decide the level of profits that the firm should be achieving and, hopefully, that it will be achieving in the near future. These earnings can be used in the calculation of cost of equity capital. This will raise the cost of capital and encourage the firm to seek projects with suitable profits to serve the long-term interests of creditors and shareholders.

working capital. The term working capital is closely related to the term funds and has two common meanings. It is used to mean current assets or current assets minus current liabilities.

To avoid confusion arising from misunderstandings in the usage of terms, financial managers should always question the meaning of a term.

When a colleague uses the term funds, the manager should ask what is meant by the term. In this handbook, the terms are precisely defined as follows:
1. *Cash.* For cash or money deposited in checking or savings accounts, the term cash is used.
2. *Funds or Working Capital.* These two terms are used synonomously to refer to a firm's current assets.
3. *Current Assets Minus Current Liabilities.* The difference between liquid assets and short-term debts is defined as net working capital. This reflects an important measure of a firm's liquidity. Net working capital is the excess cash, receivables, and inventory held by the firm above the level of short-term obligations.
4. *All Financial Resources.* The term assets is reserved for discussions of the firm's total financial resources.

CROSS–REFERENCES:
cash-flow forecast, how to prepare a, p. 97
inflation on the capital budget, how to analyze, p. 11
profit, how to maintain under inflation, p. 59
working capital, how to balance sources of funds, p. 121
income and working capital, distinguished, p. 428
part 4, working capital, in "how to" section, p. 97

working capital, factors affecting. A firm's requirements for working capital are primarily affected by four factors
1. *Volume of Sales.* This is the most important factor affecting the size and components of working capital. A firm maintains current assets because they are needed to support the operational activities that culminate in sales. Over time, a firm will keep a fairly steady ratio of current assets to

annual sales. Normally, this ratio will be between 20 and 40 percent (current assets/sales). This means that a firm realizing constant levels of sales will operate with a fairly constant level of cash, receivables, and inventory, if properly managed. Firms experiencing growth in sales will require additional permanent working capital. If sales are declining, a reduction in permanent working capital would be expected.

2. *Seasonal and Cyclical Factors.* Most firms experience seasonal fluctuations in the demand for their products and services. These variations in sales will affect the level of variable working capital. Similarly, the overall economy will undergo a series of business cycles with varying levels of economic activity. If the economy enters a recession, a firm's sales will temporarily decline because customers will be more cautious in purchasing goods and services. This will decrease the need for variable working capital. A boom period in the economy will have the opposite effect.

3. *Changes in Technology.* Technological developments, particularly related to the production process, can have sharp impacts on the need for working capital. If the firm purchases new equipment that processes raw materials at a faster rate than previously, the permanent need for inventory will be changed. If the faster processing requires more raw materials for efficient production runs, the permanent inventory will increase. If the machine can utilize less expensive raw materials, the inventory needs may be reduced.

4. *Firm Policies.* Many of the firm's policies will affect the levels of permanent and variable working capital. If the firm changes its credit policy from net 30 to net 60, additional funds will be permanently tied up in receivables. If it changes production policies, inventory requirements may be permanently or temporarily affected. If it changes its safety level of cash on hand, permanent working capital may increase or decrease. If the level of cash is linked to the level of sales, variable working capital may be affected.

working capital, identifying excess. To avoid lax management of working capital, the manager should make regular checks to identify excess current assets. Ratio analysis offers a quick and reasonably accurate method for doing this. By comparing ratios with previous periods and industry norms, the manager can locate deviations. The Rock Haven data compares the current accounts us-

---

Sources of Changes in Working-Capital Needs.

Source of Change	Working Capital Affected	Reason
Sales volume	Permanent	Different levels of cash, receivables, and inventory needed at new sales level.
Seasonal and cyclical factors	Variable	Receivables and inventory must be available on temporary basis.
Technology	Permanent	Level of inventory must support the new production capability.
Policies of firm	Both	Some policies tie up working capital; others free it.

Rock Haven Company Working-Capital Ratios Compared to Prior Periods and Industry Norms.

Ratio	1975	1974	1973	1972	Industry
Current assets/total assets	.40	.35	.31	.28	.32
Current assets/current liabilities	3.2/1	2.7/1	2.3/1	2.0/1	2.2/1
(Current assets – inventory)/current liabilities	1.6/1	1.4/1	1.2/1	1.0/1	1.1/1
(Cash + marketable securities)/current assets	.20	.18	.19	.21	.20

ing ratios with prior figures and the norm for the industry. The data indicate that current assets are becoming excessive compared to total assets and current liabilities. Based on these data, the manager should investigate further.

The investigation of Rock Haven Company may determine that current assets have grown out of proportion to total assets. But something is missing.

Current assets are not compared to sales. If the firm has been able to increase sales on the same approximate asset base of buildings and land, we would expect the current assets to increase. Checking this, the manager discovers that the ratio of current assets to sales has remained relatively constant at a range of .18/1 to .20/1 for the past 4 years. This compares to an industry norm of .21/1. To correctly measure whether current assets are excessive, they must be compared with both assets and sales.

working capital, managing. The management of current assets basically involves two processes:

1. *Forecasting Needed Funds.* Changes in the firm's operations can have almost immediate effects on the working capital needed. For example, if suppliers increase the price of raw materials, more money will be tied up in inventories than previously. Even if the firm can increase the price for its final product, it will need additional working capital to support its

sales efforts. An alert manager will observe operating activities and estimate the level of working capital required for future periods.

2. *Acquiring Funds.* Once the needs have been estimated, the manager must acquire the necessary funds from the best source, for the lowest cost, and for the time period involved.

The effective management of working capital is the primary means of achieving the firm's goal of adequate liquidity. It is, after all, the working capital—cash, marketable securities, receivables, and inventory—that will be available to pay bills and meet obligations. It is the net working capital—excess of current assets over current liabilities—that helps measure the degree of protection against problems that might cause a shortage of funds.

Managing working capital requires a number of actions, including the following:

1. *Monitoring Levels of Cash, Receivables, and Inventory.* On a daily or weekly basis, the manager should know how much funds are tied up in each of the current-asset accounts. Questions should be asked. Are the amounts in each account appropriate? How do the balances compare to previous balances? to the firm's standards? to industry norms? Any deviations from expectations should be investigated.

2. *Knowing Percentage of Funds in Current Accounts.* Working capital represents a large investment for most firms.

Some 30 to 60 percent of a firm's total assets will be tied up in current accounts. The manager should be aware of the relationship between current and fixed assets and any changes in the percentage of funds in current accounts.

3. *Recording Time Spent Managing Current Accounts.* Although estimates vary, somewhere between one third and two thirds of the financial manager's time is spent managing the working capital. A knowledge of how much time each member of the finance department spends with current accounts can offer an insight into the effectiveness of working-capital management.

working capital, nature of. The terms funds and working capital refer to the firm's current or circulating assets. Current assets have been defined as assets that are usually converted into cash within the current accounting cycle, or 1 year. Thus, they are cash or near-cash resources. The value represented by these assets circulates among several balance-sheet accounts. Cash is used to purchase raw materials and pay the labor and other manufacturing costs to produce products, which are then carried as inventories. When the inventories are sold, accounts receivables are created. The collection of the receivables brings cash into the firm and the process starts over again.

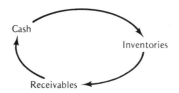

Circulating Nature of Current Assets.

The firm's working capital may be viewed as being comprised of two components:

1. *Permanent Working Capital.* These funds represent the current assets required on a continuing basis over the entire year. It represents the amount of cash, receivables, and inventory maintained as a minimum to carry on operations at any time.

2. *Variable Working Capital.* These funds represent additional assets required at different times during the operating year. Added inventory must be maintained to support the peak selling periods. Receivables increase and must be financed following periods of high sales. Extra cash may be needed to pay for increased supplies preceding high activity.

The diagram graphically displays permanent and variable working-capital needs for different firms. The first firm experiences stable sales; the second firm is in a period of growth. Note that the growth firm has increasing needs for permanent working capital.

Steady Sales Situation

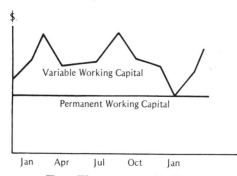

Growth Situation

Two Theories on the Relationship Between Working Capital and Return.

CROSS-REFERENCE:
permanent working capital, p. 478

working-capital pool. All the current accounts of the firm. Since it reflects the overage of current assets over current liabilities, the pool is a measure of net working capital.

working capital, theories on the correct level. To determine the amount of working capital needed by the firm, a number of factors may be included in the analysis, such as the following:

1. *Size of Firm.* It may be argued that a firm's size, either in assets or sales, will affect its need for working capital. A small firm may use extra current assets as a cushion against cash-flow interruptions. Small firms have cash inflows from fewer sources than larger firms and hence are more affected by the failures of a few customers to pay on time. Larger firms with many sources of funds may need less working capital as compared to total assets or sales.

2. *Activities of Firm.* If a firm must stock a heavy volume of inventory or sell on relatively easy credit terms (net 75, for example), it will have greater needs for working capital than firms providing services or making cash sales.

3. *Availability of Credit.* A firm with readily available credit from banks will be able to get by with less working capital than a firm without such credit.

4. *Attitude Toward Profits.* Since all funds have a cost, a relatively large amount of current assets tends to reduce a firm's profit. Some firms want extra working capital and are willing to suffer small costs. Other firms will maintain an absolute minimum of working capital at all times to gain the full profits from operations.

5. *Attitude Toward Risk.* The greater the amount of working capital, particularly cash and marketable securities, the lower the risk of liquidity problems. Firms that do not wish to incur even slight risks of liquidity deficiencies may keep extra cash. Other firms will accept the risks to earn profits and may not even keep adequate cash to always pay bills on time.

Working Capital, Risk, and Return It would seem that the really profitable and successful firms maintain the necessary amount of working capital to meet their needs. In fact, studies indicate that the most successful firms generally keep more than enough working capital available. The theory is that these firms do not want to waste their time worrying about liquidity problems. By maintaining more-than-sufficient funds, they can concentrate their managers' efforts on making money. Thus, we have two theories on the effect of keeping excessive working capital:

1. *Theory 1: High Levels of Working Capital Decrease Risk and Decrease Return.* Proponents of this theory argue that it is logical that extra (and thus unneeded) current assets cost money. If they are kept, the firm must pay for them, and the additional costs lower the after-tax profits and return to shareholders.

2. *Theory 2: High Levels of Working Capital Decrease Risk and Increase Return.* Proponents of this theory have observed the large and successful firms. They argue that the concentration on profits, rather than liquidity, overcomes the extra cost of the excessive working capital and results both in decreased risk and higher return. However, they point out that the working capital cannot be excessive.

Each theory has merit and is worthy of further investigation. No effort will be made here to resolve them. Both agree that inadequate working capital causes high risk and low return. As the figure shows, the theories differ on where the peak profits are reached.

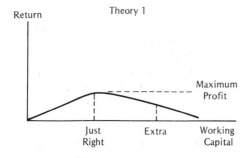

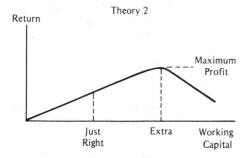

Permanent and Variable Working Capital.

CROSS-REFERENCE:
profits, how to maintain under inflation, p. 59

World Bank. The International Bank for Reconstruction and Development, commonly called the World Bank, was created at The Bretton Wood's Conference in 1944. Important characteristics are:
1. *Conventional Term Loans.* The World Bank follows policies similar to those of commercial banks. It makes loans at interest rates and maturities which are profitable for the bank. To reduce risks, the World Bank makes loans only to governments or to agencies or private firms having a governmental guarantee. As a general rule, loans are only made when other sources of private financing cannot be obtained.
2. *Involvement with Economic Planning.* The

World Bank emphasizes the economic development of developing nations and provides loans for this purpose. The bank provides detailed technical assistance and is closely involved with the economic planning for any projects that it supports. The bank will only participate in soundly conceived economic development projects which are likely to generate sufficient income to repay the loan. The bank requires efficient utilization of the funds on the project including provisions for competitive bidding on major purchases of equipment and materials.
3. *Economic Infrastructure Activities.* A nation's economic infrastructure consists primarily of its transportation facilities, utilities, and capital markets which are necessary for economic development. The World Bank finances many infrastructure projects including electric generating plants and telephone lines, highways, railways, waterways, and airports, irrigation and drainage systems, and local development finance companies. These projects are designed to build the basic industries of a nation and to allow it to attract private investment for further development.
4. *Sources of World Bank Funds.* The World Bank receives its funds from several sources. Approximately one-fifth of the funds are contributed by the members of the bank. Two-fifths of the bank's capital is received from bonds which are denominated in differing currencies and are sold to governments, banks, insurance companies, and other investors throughout the world. The balance of the bank's funds are received from directly placing its loans with investors, the repayment of principle on outstanding loans, and income from its operations.

CROSS-REFERENCE:
Asian Development Bank, p. 313

World Bank Group. The World Bank Group consists of three international financial institutions headquartered in Washington, D.C. The goal of the World Bank is to aid the economic development of its member countries. It provides considerable planning and financial support for international development projects, particularly in developing nations. The group is primarily concerned with improving economic intrastructures, thereby creating an environment that can attract further investment. The three institutions comprising the World Bank Group are the International Bank for Reconstruction and Development, the International Development Association, and the International Finance Corporation.

CROSS-REFERENCES:
International Development Association, p. 437
International Finance Corporation, p. 437

write-off. The accounting transaction whereby a fixed asset is removed from the accounting records of the firm. When a firm sells a fixed asset, the money it receives is a source of funds. To reflect this source, the firm has a write-off of the asset and its accumulated depreciation.

CROSS-REFERENCES:

pooling and purchase methods, how to use in merger accounting, p. 91
flow-of-statement, how to develop from balance sheet and income statement, p. 38
net write off, p. 467

APPENDICES

APPENDIX A: Present Value of Single Dollar.

Year	2%	4%	6%	8%	10%	12%	14%	16%	18%	20%	22%	24%	25%	30%	40%
1	0.980	0.962	0.943	0.926	0.909	0.893	0.877	0.862	0.847	0.833	0.820	0.806	0.800	0.769	0.714
2	0.961	0.925	0.890	0.857	0.826	0.797	0.769	0.743	0.718	0.694	0.672	0.650	0.640	0.592	0.510
3	0.942	0.889	0.840	0.794	0.751	0.712	0.675	0.641	0.609	0.579	0.551	0.524	0.512	0.455	0.364
4	0.924	0.855	0.792	0.735	0.683	0.636	0.592	0.552	0.516	0.482	0.451	0.423	0.410	0.350	0.260
5	0.906	0.822	0.747	0.681	0.621	0.567	0.519	0.476	0.437	0.402	0.370	0.341	0.328	0.269	0.186
6	0.888	0.790	0.705	0.630	0.564	0.507	0.456	0.410	0.370	0.335	0.303	0.275	0.262	0.207	0.133
7	0.871	0.760	0.665	0.583	0.513	0.452	0.400	0.354	0.314	0.279	0.249	0.222	0.210	0.159	0.095
8	0.853	0.731	0.627	0.540	0.467	0.404	0.351	0.305	0.266	0.233	0.204	0.179	0.168	0.123	0.068
9	0.837	0.703	0.592	0.500	0.424	0.361	0.308	0.263	0.225	0.194	0.167	0.144	0.134	0.094	0.048
10	0.820	0.676	0.558	0.463	0.386	0.322	0.270	0.227	0.191	0.162	0.137	0.116	0.107	0.073	0.035
11	0.804	0.650	0.527	0.429	0.350	0.287	0.237	0.195	0.162	0.135	0.112	0.094	0.086	0.056	0.025
12	0.788	0.625	0.497	0.397	0.319	0.257	0.208	0.168	0.137	0.112	0.092	0.076	0.069	0.043	0.018
13	0.773	0.601	0.469	0.368	0.290	0.229	0.182	0.145	0.116	0.093	0.075	0.061	0.055	0.033	0.013
14	0.758	0.577	0.442	0.340	0.263	0.205	0.160	0.125	0.099	0.078	0.062	0.049	0.044	0.025	0.009
15	0.743	0.555	0.417	0.315	0.239	0.183	0.140	0.108	0.084	0.065	0.051	0.040	0.035	0.020	0.006
16	0.728	0.534	0.394	0.292	0.218	0.163	0.123	0.093	0.071	0.054	0.042	0.032	0.028	0.015	0.005
17	0.714	0.513	0.371	0.270	0.198	0.146	0.108	0.080	0.060	0.045	0.034	0.026	0.023	0.012	0.003
18	0.700	0.494	0.350	0.250	0.180	0.130	0.095	0.069	0.051	0.038	0.028	0.021	0.018	0.009	0.002
19	0.686	0.475	0.331	0.232	0.164	0.116	0.083	0.060	0.043	0.031	0.023	0.017	0.014	0.007	0.002
20	0.673	0.456	0.312	0.215	0.149	0.104	0.073	0.051	0.037	0.026	0.019	0.014	0.012	0.005	0.001
25	0.610	0.375	0.233	0.146	0.092	0.059	0.038	0.024	0.016	0.010	0.007	0.005	0.004	0.001	
30	0.552	0.308	0.174	0.099	0.057	0.033	0.020	0.012	0.007	0.004	0.003	0.002	0.001		
40	0.453	0.208	0.097	0.046	0.022	0.011	0.005	0.003	0.001	0.001					
50	0.372	0.141	0.054	0.021	0.009	0.003	0.001	0.001							

APPENDIX B: Present Value of Annuity of $1.

Year	2%	4%	6%	8%	10%	12%	14%	16%	18%	20%	22%	24%	25%	30%	40%
1	0.980	0.962	0.943	0.926	0.909	0.893	0.877	0.862	0.847	0.833	0.820	0.806	0.800	0.769	0.714
2	1.942	1.886	1.833	1.783	1.736	1.690	1.647	1.605	1.566	1.528	1.492	1.457	1.440	1.361	1.224
3	2.884	2.775	2.673	2.577	2.487	2.402	2.322	2.246	2.174	2.106	2.042	1.981	1.952	1.816	1.589
4	3.808	3.630	3.645	3.312	3.170	3.037	2.914	2.798	2.690	2.589	2.494	2.404	2.362	2.166	1.849
5	4.713	4.452	4.212	3.993	3.791	3.605	3.433	3.274	3.127	2.991	2.864	2.745	2.689	2.436	2.035
6	5.601	5.242	4.917	4.623	4.355	4.111	3.889	3.685	3.498	3.326	3.167	3.020	2.951	2.643	2.168
7	6.472	6.002	5.582	5.206	4.868	4.564	4.288	4.039	3.812	3.605	3.416	3.242	3.161	2.802	2.263
8	7.325	6.733	6.210	5.747	5.335	4.968	4.639	4.344	4.078	3.837	3.619	3.421	3.329	2.925	2.331
9	8.162	7.435	6.802	6.247	5.759	5.328	4.946	4.607	4.303	4.031	3.786	3.566	3.463	3.019	2.379
10	8.983	8.111	7.360	6.710	6.145	5.650	5.216	4.833	4.494	4.192	3.923	3.682	3.571	3.092	2.414
11	9.787	8.760	7.887	7.139	6.495	5.937	5.453	5.029	4.656	4.327	4.035	3.776	3.656	3.147	2.438
12	10.58	9.385	8.384	7.536	6.814	6.194	5.660	5.197	4.793	4.439	4.127	3.851	3.725	3.190	2.456
13	11.34	9.986	8.853	7.904	7.103	6.424	5.842	5.342	4.910	4.533	4.203	3.912	3.780	3.223	2.468
14	12.11	10.56	9.295	8.244	7.367	6.628	6.002	5.468	5.008	4.611	4.265	3.962	3.824	3.249	2.477
15	12.85	11.12	9.712	8.559	7.606	6.811	6.142	5.575	5.092	4.675	4.315	4.001	3.859	3.268	2.484
16	13.58	11.65	10.11	8.851	7.824	6.974	6.265	5.669	5.162	4.730	4.357	4.033	3.887	3.283	2.489
17	14.29	12.17	10.48	9.122	8.022	7.120	6.373	5.749	5.222	4.775	4.391	4.059	3.910	3.295	2.492
18.	14.99	12.66	10.83	9.372	8.201	7.250	6.467	5.818	5.273	4.812	4.419	4.080	3.928	3.304	2.494
19	15.68	13.13	11.16	9.604	8.365	7.366	6.550	5.877	5.316	4.844	4.442	4.097	3.942	3.311	2.496
20	16.35	13.59	11.47	9.818	8.514	7.469	6.623	5.929	5.353	4.870	4.460	4.110	3.954	3.316	2.497
25	19.52	15.62	12.78	10.68	9.077	7.843	6.873	6.097	5.467	4.948	4.514	4.147	3.985	3.329	2.499
30	22.40	17.29	13.77	11.26	9.427	8.055	7.003	6.177	5.517	4.979	4.534	4.160	3.995	3.332	2.500
40	27.36	19.79	15.05	11.93	9.779	8.244	7.105	6.234	5.548	4.997	4.544	4.166	3.999	3.333	2.500
50	31.42	21.48	15.76	12.23	9.915	8.304	7.133	6.246	5.554	4.999	4.545	4.167	4.000	3.333	2.500

APPENDIX C: Compound Sum of Single Dollar.

Year	2%	4%	6%	8%	10%	12%	14%	16%	18%	20%	22%	25%	30%	40%
1	1.020	1.040	1.060	1.080	1.100	1.120	1.140	1.160	1.180	1.200	1.220	1.250	1.300	1.400
2	1.040	1.082	1.124	1.166	1.210	1.254	1.300	1.346	1.392	1.440	1.488	1.563	1.690	1.960
3	1.061	1.125	1.191	1.260	1.331	1.405	1.482	1.561	1.643	1.728	1.816	1.953	2.197	2.744
4	1.082	1.170	1.262	1.360	1.464	1.574	1.689	1.811	1.939	2.074	2.215	2.441	2.856	3.842
5	1.104	1.217	1.338	1.469	1.611	1.762	1.925	2.100	2.288	2.488	2.703	3.052	3.713	5.378
6	1.126	1.265	1.419	1.587	1.772	1.974	2.195	2.436	2.700	2.986	3.297	3.851	4.827	7.530
7	1.149	1.316	1.504	1.714	1.949	2.211	2.502	2.826	3.185	3.583	4.023	4.768	6.275	10.541
8	1.172	1.369	1.594	1.851	2.144	2.476	2.853	3.278	3.759	4.300	4.908	5.960	8.157	14.758
9	1.195	1.423	1.689	1.999	2.358	2.773	3.252	3.803	4.435	5.160	5.987	7.451	10.604	20.661
10	1.219	1.480	1.791	2.159	2.594	3.106	3.707	4.411	5.234	6.192	7.305	9.313	13.786	28.925
11	1.243	1.539	1.898	2.332	2.853	3.479	4.226	5.117	6.176	7.430	8.912	11.642	17.921	40.496
12	1.268	1.601	2.012	2.518	3.138	3.896	4.818	5.936	7.288	8.916	10.872	14.552	23.298	56.694
13	1.294	1.665	2.133	2.720	3.452	4.363	5.492	6.886	8.599	10.699	13.264	18.190	30.287	79.371
14	1.319	1.732	2.261	2.937	3.797	4.887	6.261	7.988	10.147	12.839	16.182	22.737	39.373	
15	1.346	1.801	2.397	3.172	4.177	5.474	7.138	9.266	11.974	15.407	19.742	28.422	51.185	
16	1.373	1.873	2.540	3.426	4.595	6.130	8.137	10.748	14.129	18.488	24.085	35.527	66.541	
17	1.400	1.948	2.693	3.700	5.054	6.866	9.276	12.468	16.672	22.186	29.384	44.409	86.503	
18	1.428	2.026	2.854	3.996	5.560	7.690	10.575	14.462	19.673	26.623	35.849	55.511		
19	1.457	2.107	3.026	4.316	6.116	8.613	12.056	16.776	23.214	31.948	43.735	69.389		
20	1.486	2.191	3.207	4.661	6.727	9.646	13.743	19.461	27.393	38.337	53.357	86.736		
21	1.516	2.279	3.400	5.034	7.400	10.804	15.667	22.574	32.323	46.005	65.096			
22	1.546	2.370	3.603	5.437	8.140	12.100	17.861	26.186	38.142	55.206	79.417			
23	1.577	2.465	3.820	5.871	8.954	13.552	20.361	30.376	45.007	66.247	96.888			
24	1.608	2.563	4.049	6.341	9.850	15.179	23.212	35.236	53.108	79.497				
25	1.641	2.666	4.292	6.848	10.835	17.000	26.462	40.874	62.668	95.396				

APPENDIX D: Compound Sum of Annuity of $1.

Year	2%	4%	6%	8%	10%	12%	14%	16%	18%	20%	22%	25%	30%	40%
1	1.000	1.000	1.000	1.000	1.000	1.000	1.000	1.000	1.000	1.000	1.000	1.000	1.000	1.000
2	2.020	2.040	2.060	2.080	2.100	2.120	2.140	2.160	2.180	2.200	2.220	2.250	2.300	2.400
3	3.060	3.122	3.184	3.246	3.310	3.374	3.440	3.506	3.572	3.640	3.708	3.813	3.990	4.360
4	4.121	4.246	4.375	4.506	4.641	4.779	4.921	5.066	5.215	5.368	5.524	5.766	6.187	7.104
5	5.204	5.416	5.637	5.867	6.105	6.353	6.610	6.877	7.154	7.442	7.740	8.207	9.043	10.846
6	6.308	6.633	6.975	7.336	7.716	8.115	8.535	8.977	9.442	9.930	10.442	11.259	12.756	16.324
7	7.434	7.898	8.394	8.923	9.487	10.089	10.730	11.414	12.141	12.916	13.740	15.073	17.583	23.853
8	8.583	9.214	9.897	10.637	11.436	12.300	13.233	14.240	15.327	16.499	17.762	19.842	23.858	34.395
9	9.754	10.583	11.491	12.488	13.579	14.776	16.085	17.518	19.086	20.799	22.670	25.802	32.015	49.153
10	10.949	12.006	13.181	14.487	15.937	17.549	19.337	21.321	23.521	25.959	28.657	33.253	42.619	69.814
11	12.168	13.486	14.971	16.645	18.531	20.655	23.044	25.733	28.755	32.150	35.962	42.566	56.405	98.739
12	13.412	15.026	16.870	18.977	21.384	24.133	27.271	30.850	34.931	39.580	44.873	54.208	74.326	
13	14.680	16.627	18.882	21.495	24.522	28.029	32.088	36.786	42.218	48.496	55.745	68.760	97.624	
14	15.973	18.292	21.015	24.215	27.975	32.393	37.581	43.672	50.818	59.196	69.009	86.949		
15	17.293	20.024	23.276	27.152	31.772	37.280	43.842	51.659	60.965	72.035	85.191			
16	18.639	21.824	25.672	30.324	35.949	42.753	50.980	60.925	72.938	87.442				
17	20.011	23.697	28.212	33.750	40.544	48.884	59.117	71.673	87.067					
18	21.412	25.645	30.905	37.450	45.599	55.750	68.393	84.141						
19	22.840	27.671	33.759	41.446	51.158	63.440	78.968	98.603						
20	24.297	29.778	36.785	45.762	57.274	72.052	91.024							
21	25.783	31.969	39.992	50.423	64.002	81.699								
22	27.298	34.248	43.392	55.457	71.402	92.502								
23	28.844	36.618	46.995	60.893	79.542									
24	30.421	39.083	50.815	66.765	88.496									
25	32.029	41.646	54.864	73.106	98.346									

APPENDIX E: Standard Normal Distribution.

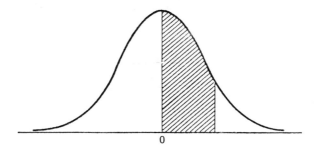

z	.00	.01	.02	.03	.04	.05	.06	.07	.08	.09
0.0	.0000	.0040	.0080	.0120	.0160	.0199	.0239	.0279	.0319	0.359
0.1	.0398	.0438	.0478	.0517	.0557	.0596	.0636	.0675	.0714	0.753
0.2	.0793	.0832	.0871	.0910	.0948	.0987	.1026	.1064	.1103	.1141
0.3	.1179	.1217	.1255	.1293	.1331	.1368	.1406	.1443	.1480	.1517
0.4	.1554	.1591	.1628	.1664	.1700	.1736	.1772	.1808	.1844	.1879
0.5	.1915	.1950	.1985	.2019	.2054	.2088	.2123	.2157	.2190	.2224
0.6	.2257	.2291	.2324	.2357	.2389	.2422	.2454	.2486	.2517	.2549
0.7	.2580	.2611	.2642	.2673	.2704	.2734	.2764	.2794	.2823	.2852
0.8	.2881	.2910	.2939	.2967	.2995	.3023	.3051	.3078	.3106	.3133
0.9	.3159	.3186	.3212	.3238	.3264	.3289	.3315	.3340	.3365	.3389
1.0	.3413	.3438	.3461	.3485	.3508	.3531	.3554	.3577	.3599	.3621
1.1	.3643	.3665	.3686	.3708	.3729	.3749	.3770	.3790	.3810	.3830
1.2	.3849	.3869	.3888	.3907	.3925	.3944	.3962	.3980	.3997	.4015
1.3	.4032	.4049	.4066	.4082	.4099	.4115	.4131	.4147	.4162	.4177
1.4	.4192	.4207	.4222	.4236	.4251	.4265	.4279	.4292	.4306	.4319
1.5	.4332	.4345	.4357	.4370	.4382	.4394	.4406	.4418	.4429	.4441
1.6	.4452	.4463	.4474	.4484	.4495	.4505	.4515	.4525	.4535	.4545
1.7	.4554	.4564	.4573	.4582	.4591	.4599	.4608	.4616	.4625	.4633
1.8	.4641	.4649	.4656	.4664	.4671	.4678	.4686	.4693	.4699	.4706
1.9	.4713	.4719	.4726	.4732	.4738	.4744	.4750	.4756	.4761	.4767
2.0	.4772	.4778	.4783	.4788	.4793	.4798	.4803	.4808	.4812	.4817
2.1	.4821	.4826	.4830	.4834	.4838	.4842	.4846	.4850	.4854	.4857
2.2	.4861	.4864	.4868	.4871	.4875	.4878	.4881	.4884	.4887	.4890
2.3	.4893	.4896	.4898	.4901	.4904	.4906	.4909	.4911	.4913	.4916
2.4	.4918	.4920	.4922	.4925	.4927	.4929	.4931	.4932	.4934	.4936
2.5	.4938	.4940	.4941	.4943	.4945	.4946	.4948	.4949	.4951	.4952
2.6	.4953	.4955	.4956	.4957	.4959	.4960	.4961	.4962	.4963	.4964
2.7	.4965	.4966	.4967	.4968	.4969	.4970	.4971	.4972	.4973	.4974
2.8	.4974	.4975	.4976	.4977	.4977	.4978	.4979	.4979	.4980	.4981
2.9	.4981	.4982	.4982	.4983	.4984	.4984	.4985	.4985	.4986	.4986
3.0	.4987	.4987	.4987	.4988	.4988	.4989	.4989	.4989	.4990	.4990